'Perhaps no subject excites as much attention in Ch
Vickers and Zeng have crafted a comprehensive, tl
analysis of how – and why – China's education syste
attention to issues of ideology, finance, and the
emerging middle-class society, their book will surely become a standard account for years to come.'

Rana Mitter, Director, University of Oxford China Centre

'We have long been in need of a well-researched and up-to-date overview of how the world's largest education system has evolved over time, what it looks like today, and the implications of this transformation. Now such a book is finally available! Vickers and Zeng's study is a pleasure to read, and will be an essential reference for courses on comparative and East Asian education, and for all scholars researching contemporary Chinese society.'

Mette Halskov Hansen, University of Oslo, Author of *Educating the Chinese Individual: Life in a Rural Boarding School*

'Vickers and Zeng provide a thorough and well-researched overview of the post-Mao education system and its relationship with Chinese society and politics, analyzing the changes of the past four decades. With its impressive breadth and depth, this book will be invaluable for anyone who wants to understand how education works in China.'

Vanessa Fong, Amherst College, Author of *Paradise Redefined: Transnational Chinese Students and the Quest for Flexible Citizenship in the Developed World*

Education and Society in Post-Mao China

The post-Mao period has witnessed rapid social and economic transformation in all walks of Chinese life – much of it fuelled by, or reflected in, changes to the country's education system. This book analyses the development of that system since the abandonment of radical Maoism and the inauguration of 'Reform and Opening' in the late 1970s.

The principal focus is on formal education in schools and conventional institutions of tertiary education, but there is also some discussion of preschools, vocational training, and learning in non-formal contexts. The book begins with a discussion of the historical and comparative context for evaluating China's educational 'achievements', followed by an extensive discussion of the key transitions in education policymaking during the 'Reform and Opening' period. This informs the subsequent examination of changes affecting the different phases of education from preschool to tertiary level. There are also chapters dealing specifically with the financing and administration of schooling, curriculum development, the public examinations system, the teaching profession, the phenomenon of marketisation, and the 'international dimension' of Chinese education. The book concludes with an assessment of the social consequences of educational change in the post-Mao era and a critical discussion of the recent fashion in certain Western countries for hailing China as an educational model. The analysis is supported by a wealth of sources – primary and secondary, textual and statistical – and is informed by both authors' wide-ranging experience of Chinese education.

As the first monograph on China's educational development during the forty years of the post-Mao era, this book will be essential reading for all those seeking to understand the world's largest education system. It will also be a crucial reference for educational comparativists, and for scholars from various disciplinary backgrounds researching contemporary Chinese society.

Edward Vickers is Professor of Comparative Education at Kyushu University and co-editor of *Imagining Japan in Post-war East Asia: Identity Politics, Schooling and Popular Culture* (with Paul Morris and Naoko Shimazu, Routledge 2013).

Zeng Xiaodong is a Professor at Beijing Normal University and author of *A Historical Analysis on Education Development in 1978–2008: Key Indicators and International Comparisons* (2008).

Routledge Studies in Education and Society in Asia
Edited by Edward Vickers
Department of Education, Kyushu University, Japan

This series focuses on analyses of educational practices and structures in Asia in their broader social, cultural, political and economic context. The volumes further our understanding of why education systems have developed in particular ways and examine to what extent and why education in Asia is distinctive.

1 **Designing History in East Asian Textbooks**
Identity Politics and Transnational Aspirations
Edited by Gotelind Müller

2 **Globalisation, Employment and Education in Sri Lanka**
Opportunity and Division
Angela Little and Siri Hettige

3 **Re-Evaluating Education in Japan and Korea**
De-mystifying Stereotypes
Hyunjoon Park

4 **Imagining Japan in Postwar East Asia**
Identity Politics, Schooling and Popular Culture
Edited by Paul Morris, Edward Vickers and Naoko Shimazu

5 **Constructing Modern Asian Citizenship**
Edited by Edward Vickers and Krishna Kumar

6 **The Sino-Japanese War and Youth Literature**
Friends and Foes on the Battlefield
Minjie Chen

7 **Education and Society in Post-Mao China**
Edward Vickers and Zeng Xiaodong

Education and Society in Post-Mao China

Edward Vickers
and Zeng Xiaodong

Routledge
Taylor & Francis Group
LONDON AND NEW YORK

First published 2017 by Routledge

2 Park Square, Milton Park, Abingdon, Oxfordshire OX14 4RN
711 Third Avenue, New York, NY 10017

Routledge is an imprint of the Taylor & Francis Group, an informa business

First issued in paperback 2018

British Library Cataloguing-in-Publication Data
A catalogue record for this book is available from the British Library

Library of Congress Cataloging-in-Publication Data
Names: Vickers, Edward, 1971– author.
Title: Education and society in post-Mao China / Edward Vickers and Zeng Xiaodong.
Description: Abingdon, Oxon ; New York, NY : Routledge, 2017. | Series: Routledge studies in education and society in Asia ; 7 | Includes bibliographical references and index.
Identifiers: LCCN 2016054608| ISBN 9780415597395 (hardback) | ISBN 9781315180571 (e-book)
Subjects: LCSH: Education—Social aspects—China. | Educational change—China.
Classification: LCC LC191.8.C5 V53 2017 | DDC 306.430951—dc23
LC record available at https://lccn.loc.gov/2016054608

ISBN: 978-0-415-59739-5 (hbk)
ISBN: 978-1-138-36453-0 (pbk)

Typeset in Times New Roman
by Book Now Ltd, London

Contents

Illustrations

Figures

Tables

Preface and acknowledgements

The idea of writing this book originally arose in 2008, when China was commemorating 30 years of 'Reform and Opening'. We aspired to provide an account of the country's recent educational development that was both reasonably comprehensive, and somewhat more historically informed and critical than much of commentary prompted by that anniversary. We were also acutely conscious of the rather shallow and uncritical nature of much recent Western debate over Chinese education, and concerned about the implications of this for policymaking in societies such as Britain and America.

Having embarked on this enterprise, we soon came to appreciate its enormity; it is easy to understand why most attempts to provide any sort of overview of China's education system take the form of edited collections rather than sole- or jointly authored monographs. Nonetheless, we believe that our approach makes for a more coherent analysis than that offered by most edited collections. Whatever its flaws or oversights – indeed, perhaps because of them – we hope that our interpretation of post-Mao China's educational trajectory will provoke lively debate.

We are very grateful to many colleagues for their support and encouragement while we have been working on this book. Paul Morris and Christine Han made it possible for Vickers to take a one-term sabbatical from the IOE in 2010, when he was kindly hosted by Prof. Yoshida Aya at Waseda University in Tokyo. In early 2011, a visiting scholarship from the EU-funded Erasmus Mundus MALLL consortium enabled Zeng to visit London for two months. Following Vickers' move from London to Kyushu University in Japan, Nonomura Toshiko and Fujita Yuhi helped arrange for Zeng to visit Kyushu University for a term in late 2015. Takekuma Hisao (also of Kyushu University) has been unfailingly supportive. Jeremy Rappleye provided extensive and invaluable feedback on several of the earlier chapters. Xu Jing kindly supplied us with many useful sources for the chapter on vocational education.

Thanks are also due to the editors at Routledge, Stephanie Rogers and Rebecca Lawrence, for their patience with our repeated postponements, and their support in the preparation of the final manuscript. We hope that they and our readers will find that the wait has been worthwhile.

Edward Vickers and Zeng Xiaodong

Abbreviations and terms

BNU	Beijing Normal University
CCP	Chinese Communist Party
CPPCC	Chinese People's Political Consultative Conference
ECEC	Early childhood education and care
ECNU	East China Normal University
Gaokao	College entrance examination
KMT	Kuomintang (Guomindang)
MOE	Ministry of Education
MOF	Ministry of Finance
NPC	National People's Congress
OECD	Organisation for Economic Co-operation and Development
PEP	People's Education Press
PISA	Programme for International Student Assessment
PRC	People's Republic of China
S&T	Science and technology
SEC	State Education Commission*
SEZ	Special Economic Zone
SOE	State-owned enterprise
STEM	Science, Technology, Engineering and Medicine
Zhongkao	Senior high-school entrance examination
TVE	Technical and vocational education
WTO	World Trade Organization

*Between 1985 and 1998, the SEC took the place of the MOE. The MOE was reconstituted in 1998, once again replacing the SEC.

Note on terminology

Throughout the book, we generally use 'junior secondary' to refer to the first three years of secondary schooling (roughly ages 12–15), and 'senior high' to refer to the final three years (from about age 16–18). The Chinese term *zhong xuexiao* (which is used for both) literally translates as 'middle school', so we could have referred to 'junior/senior middle school', a usage found in much of the English-language literature. However, since in some societies 'middle school' is used only to refer to junior secondary level, we have preferred to translate *gaozhong* or *gaoji zhongxue* (literally 'high-level middle school') as 'senior high school'. We hope that this minimises any potential confusion.

Note on names

Throughout the text and in the bibliography, all Chinese names are rendered as in Chinese: surname first, given names afterwards (i.e. Mao Zedong, *not* Zedong Mao). Names, like other Chinese words, are written using *pinyin,* the system for phonetically transcribing Chinese characters that is standard on the mainland.

1 Introduction

Education, development and social change in post-Mao China – framing the debate

> Thirty years ago, … a difficult decision had to be made over whether to press for educational progress rapidly or more gradually. The pursuit of [economic] development has been our iron rule (*ying daoli*): without development, the achievement of a flourishing education system, or a strong and prosperous country, would have been impossible.
>
> Chen Zhili (former Education Minister),
> *The Rising of a Country through Education* (Chen 2008, iv)

> Over the past few years, the issue of equity in education has become the focus of widespread public attention ….[1] The obsession with 'development'[2] has not only led to a dilution of reform, but has also to a certain extent obscured the situation regarding equity. Today, we can already clearly perceive that modernization without equity is soulless modernization, and development without equity is deformed development.
>
> Yang Dongping (2006, 3)

Since the 1980s, East Asia has played host to a long succession of Western educational pilgrims. In the 1980s and 1990s, they headed for Japan, Taiwan, Korea or the other 'tiger' economies, to return as prophets preaching a gospel of 'interactive whole-class teaching', didactic moral or civic education, regular and rigorous testing, an overwhelming curricular focus on Maths, Science and literacy, or various combinations of these (Morris 1998). Underlying the allure of the East were twin assumptions: first, that a clear causal link could be traced between education and economic growth in these societies; and second, that the educational practices relevant to economic success could be isolated, extracted and transplanted into other social and cultural contexts to produce similar results.

In the early twenty-first century, seekers of oriental wisdom have tended to bypass Japan and her neighbours, bound instead for China (while Japanese policymakers – the boot now on the other foot – agonise over the supposed educational roots of their economic stagnation). The same twin assumptions underpin much foreign debate on China's education system, as well as Chinese attempts to borrow educational ideas from overseas. Thus the British Schools Minister returned from a trip to China in early 2009 proclaiming that the wisdom of Confucius would prove invaluable in raising school standards in England (Oakeshott 2009).[3] In 2007, a group of prize-winning school principals were taken East 'to partner up with a Chinese school, see the rapid changes being made to the Chinese education system, and drool' (Shepherd 2007). A massive surge of Chinese investment in 'elite' higher education has meanwhile elicited either admiration or nervousness (or both) from foreign observers (e.g. Jacques 2009, 401–3; Levin 2010). For the transient spectator of the country's developmental progress, often 'China presents no analytical challenges: excellent economic performance must be the result of excellent economic policies' (Huang 2008, 26) – and of excellent educational policies, too.[4]

However, as our opening quotations illustrate, domestic perceptions of China's recent educational record are decidedly mixed. Triumphalism certainly colours many official statements, both reflecting and stoking popular excitement at China's seemingly inexorable rise. Nevertheless, there is broad acknowledgement of the tensions and problems that have emerged during the period of rapid economic growth – not least with respect to inequality and its implications for social and political stability. A relatively open and sometimes passionate public debate ranges across a wide range of educational issues.[5] Moreover, this is not confined within Chinese borders, but engages both China-based scholars and those working overseas.

Our aim in this book is to contribute to that debate by constructing a coherent narrative of China's educational development since the death of Chairman Mao in 1976. While wary of the simplistic assumptions underlying much policy-oriented educational comparison, we by no means deny that there are lessons that those abroad can learn from China's developmental record. However, any attempt to derive such lessons must be founded on an understanding of the educational system in the round, of its relations with the broader social and political context, and of how and why it has changed over time. The existing literature on education and society in China offers invaluable insights into many aspects of educational development, but there is currently no monograph in English that attempts a comprehensive analysis of the entire system over the post-Mao period. This is the gap we aim to fill.

The present volume focuses mainly on the formal education system as conventionally understood, treating this sequentially from the early childhood phase (Chapter 4), through schooling in the compulsory (primary and junior secondary) and post-compulsory years (Chapters 5–10), to tertiary level (Chapters 11–12). At each level of the system, we examine how government policies have affected educational provision; how social, economic and demographic change has created new pressures; and how officials, educators and institutions have tried to adapt to these – and with what effects. The main body of the book is divided into sections dealing in turn with the different phases of education from preschool to college level. Within the largest section, on schooling, are chapters dealing with key issues such as the implications of changes to financial and administrative arrangements, curriculum development, assessment, teacher training, marketisation, and attempts to promote vocationalisation. Following the section on higher education,

Chapter 13 examines the increasingly salient 'international dimension', discussing how various forms of educational internationalisation have influenced society and culture both within China and elsewhere. This theme is pursued further in the final chapter, which critiques the use of the Chinese case in international education policy debate, and proposes an alternative interpretation of its significance for policymakers and researchers.

The analysis of these hugely varied aspects of the system is scaffolded by a narrative of the political and social changes affecting China during the 'Reform and Opening' period, particularly of the shifts in the regime's developmental strategy and the role it has accorded to education. Supplying that narrative is the task of our long Chapter 3, divided into four sections (cited as Chapters 3.1–3.4). This necessarily involves examination both of choices made and of roads not taken or abandoned. In historical analysis – perhaps especially of recent events, where key figures linger on to defend their legacy – there is always the danger of being seduced by assertions of inevitability proffered by actors seeking retrospective legitimacy. This risk is particularly acute when the object of enquiry is as large and complex as China, and when critical analysis is often deflected by claims of Chinese uniqueness or exceptionalism.

In order to establish a perspective from which to critique such claims, in this and the following chapter we attempt to locate China's educational development in comparative and historical context. In Chapter 2, we discuss education's role in post-war East Asian development, querying the frequent characterisation of China as a variant of some 'East Asian model'. The validity of such a characterisation is explored especially through comparisons with Taiwan (a Chinese society that has followed a different developmental path) and India (China's major developing-world competitor and the only other population 'billionaire'), drawing on recent work in economics as well as education. We then look back at the educational legacy of the Mao era, discussing whether this might have prepared the country for pursuit of a more East Asian-style developmental path. The choice of an alternative road, and its subsequent twists and turns, form the central subject of the remainder of this book.

Education and development in contemporary China – four perspectives

First, however, we briefly review the current scholarly debate on Chinese education. At the risk of gross oversimplification, it is possible to see much work in this area as strongly influenced by four broad perspectives or orientations. The first, involving adherence to officially sanctioned orthodoxy, involves endorsement of the policy choices of the past forty years, typically allied to claims that these have been necessitated by China's 'special characteristics' (*tese*) and the unique challenges of her 'national situation' (*guoqing*). The second, labelled here the 'anti-globalist' position, recognises a more mixed picture as far as the record of the post-Mao period is concerned, but tends to attribute negative aspects of this primarily to the malign influence of external forces – 'global capitalism', 'neoliberalism', and so forth – confronting 'developing' China. The third position, which we dub 'practice-oriented', focuses on specific educational problems or issues with a view to identifying practical 'solutions'. Agnosticism regarding the political or historical context for such problems has rendered many followers of this approach complicit in post-Mao efforts to move discussions of education 'from the political to the technical sphere' (Thøgersen 1991, 40). Finally, we identify a cross-disciplinary 'critical' perspective defined by a concern with exploring education's relationships with social, political and ideological tensions. The best examples of this not only eschew a reductionist approach to causal explanation, but also encompass criticism of the very frameworks that structure mainstream educational debate in China, and elsewhere.

As with any such crude attempt at pigeon-holing, it will be found that these four categories overlap considerably, that individual scholars at different times adopt different positions, and that some work combines elements of various perspectives. Nonetheless, they help in mapping the contours of the debate over the recent history of China's education system in a way that transcends any 'Chinese–foreign' divide.[6]

The official or orthodox perspective

The quintessential exposition of the orthodox perspective is naturally found in official publications such as *The Rising of a Country through Education* (quoted above). The current orthodoxy holds that the post-Mao era has witnessed steady educational progress guided by enlightened pragmatists. Policymakers are portrayed as wisely flexible in their adherence to predetermined blueprints, eschewing overweening central planning in favour of the tactic of 'crossing the river by touching the stones' (*mozhe shitou guo he*), as Deng Xiaoping once put it. On the opposite side of that river lies a vision of a strong, technologically advanced China commanding awe and respect abroad, but hazily defined in social or political terms. Defenders of orthodoxy typically insist on China's unique size and complexity, the manifold risks the country faces, and hence the need for continued Communist Party tutelage. Since the 1990s, Confucian tradition has increasingly been invoked to argue the virtues of developmental autocracy (Economist 2010) – or, in the more sophisticated and nuanced formulation of Daniel Bell (2015), of 'political meritocracy'. Other scholars based outside the mainland have invoked culture to differentiate China both from a decadent 'West' and more 'backward' developing countries. Rao *et al.* (2003) thus attribute to 'Confucianism' China's superior record to India's in universalising basic schooling. Meanwhile, Hayhoe juxtaposes an idealised vision of a harmonious, communitarian Chinese order with a dysfunctional 'Western world … where the individual's satisfaction and fulfilment has tended to be given priority over family solidarity and community benefit' (Hayhoe 2006, 361).[7]

Unsurprisingly, though, the principal exponents of this approach are to be found on the mainland itself. Reviewing the state of education policy research there, Yang describes 'a mix of traditional Confucian ethical sermon, Chinese interpretation of Marxism, and policy explanation and/or justification in line with Governments [*sic.*]' (2006, 215). Most scholars, he writes, 'accept the discourses of policy as the governing structures for research' (216). Uncritical acceptance of Talcott Parsons-vintage modernisation theory remains widespread, reflecting a preoccupation with 'catching up' with the West. Theoretical concepts derived from Western scholarship are frequently deployed, but often ill-digested and detached from empirical data. Meanwhile, in educational research in general, and policy-related scholarship in particular, 'personal reflections' tend to dominate published output. The pervasive rhetoric of 'science' (seen as accomplished through Marxism) clashes with the extremely unscientific nature of much social science research. However, as some of the research cited in this volume demonstrates, this damning verdict, while broadly valid when Yang was writing a decade ago, is rather less so today.

The anti-globalist perspective

Orthodox narratives sometimes illustrate China's success by invoking comparisons with 'the West', but disillusionment with the latter defines the 'anti-globalist' position, which blames Western influence for social problems. Official apologists often admit the existence of such problems, but retain faith in the capacity of the Party to overcome them. Anti-globalists are less sanguine – they see China as confronted with a 'world system' operated along 'neoliberal' or 'market' principles that restrict the policy choices available to the regime. Thus Postiglione accurately notes that the 'socialist market economy' has both expanded the range of educational choices available to China's people, and rendered the capacity to exercise choice more than ever 'a function of poverty, gender and ethnicity' (2006, 5). However, stressing the 'astonishing' nature of China's educational accomplishments 'compared with other developing countries' (3), he argues that 'it is the experience with market forces within an expanding global economy that continues to confound efforts to reduce the educational gap between rich and poor' (5). What is at question is therefore not the determination of the government to tackle this gap, but its capacity to do so given the 'global' forces ranged against it. In a similar vein, the historian Prasenjit Duara, acknowledging his debt to World Systems theory, portrays all East Asian states as victims of global forces:

> Over the past 40 years or so, the nation-state in [Japan, Korea, Taiwan and China] has adapted to competitive global capitalism by gradually changing its role from protectionism and redistribution to producing and securing the conditions of competitiveness. In the PRC, this transformation since 1979 has been telescoped and radical.
>
> (2009, 36–7)

While some see 'Western hegemony' as a continuing threat, others greet China's rise as an opportunity finally to overthrow it: a viewpoint expounded by the former editor of the defunct British journal, *Marxism Today*, in his treatise,

When China Rules the World: the rise of the Middle Kingdom and the End of the Western World (Jacques 2009).[8] A rather different perspective is adopted by one of the most prominent of China's 'New Left' intellectuals, Wang Hui (2009). He argues that 'the hegemonic position of neoliberalism in China was established precisely from within a domestic process during which the state's crisis of legitimacy [after 1989] was overcome through economic reform itself' (20). In other words, the regime adopted a 'neoliberal' agenda not under external compulsion, but because domestic political circumstances rendered it attractive. The global discourse promoting market-oriented reforms helped legitimise choices taken for primarily domestic reasons. Moreover, far from seeming to revel, like Jacques, in China's apparent bettering of the West at its own capitalist game, Wang emphasises the social distortions and tensions to which this course has given rise, and identifies the only fundamental solution as 'a transformation of the dependent status of wage labourers … so that they possess the right to participate in society and politics' (Wang 2009, 102).

The practice-oriented perspective

While Wang's arguments place him firmly in the ranks of our 'critical' scholars (see below), many educational researchers have tended to eschew critical reflection for a concentration on technical issues. This approach has undoubtedly been encouraged by the frequent linking of fieldwork opportunities to aid projects funded by international development agencies (see Chapter 13). Such funding typically dictates a focus on identifying technical solutions to specific problems, while avoiding political controversy. The superficiality of any engagement with the social and political context is exacerbated by the need to collaborate with governmental agencies wary of foreign 'interference'. It is not coincidental that some of the most interesting and bold writing on China, both within the country and abroad, has come from historians, anthropologists and other social scientists who tend not to involve themselves in educational aid projects or government-funded, policy-oriented research.[9]

Nevertheless, research conducted from this 'practice-oriented' perspective has yielded invaluable empirical data. Taking just the area of schooling, among the issues that have recently formed the focus of much research are the rural–urban divide, as this relates both to educational access and quality (Bray *et al.* 2004; Li *et al.* 2007); education for the children of migrants from rural areas to the cities (Kwong 2006); gender and educational opportunity (Hannum *et al.* 2009); schooling for 'minorities' (Postiglione 2007); and an emergent class divide in educational opportunity in urban areas (Lin 2006). As this brief list suggests, concerns with inequality have come to dominate scholarly debate (as well as public discourse) on Chinese education, with research highlighting the multi-dimensional and extremely complex nature of this problem – for example with respect to the links between health (physical/nutritional and psychological) and educational achievement in poor communities (Yu and Hannum 2006). Surveying the contemporary educational landscape, Hannum *et al.* (2007) conclude that policymakers are confronted with three particular 'quandaries': persistent inequalities in access to education; inequalities in quality, demanding consideration of 'how to balance the important benefits of … diversification and flexibility … against the cost of a system in which educational qualifications increasingly reflect family origin' (19); and the requirement 'to serve the needs of an increasingly diverse population' (19).

The focus in much 'practice-oriented' research (and increasingly in 'orthodox' literature too) on educational inequality has spawned many quantitative studies. These are typically informed by a 'human capital' paradigm and an interest in the 'rates of return' to different levels or types of education, reflecting the essentially economistic concerns of the researchers involved, or the bodies that fund them. The World Bank has heaped praise on China's achievements in poverty reduction (as measured in GDP statistics) during the 'Reform and Opening' period, although more recent reports express alarm at the extent of inequality (World Bank 2009). Bank studies have hailed increasing income differentials between those with different levels of education as indicating a welcome rise in 'meritocracy' associated with 'deepening' market reforms since the 1990s (Murphy and Johnson 2009, 448). Research has demonstrated that a high-school education 'virtually' guarantees 'an escape from poverty', underlining the economic rationality for underprivileged groups of 'choosing' education – but often overlooking the obstacles to the exercise of this apparently rational choice. The 'phantom' of the 'rational economic actor' stalks the pages of much research on rates of return to education in China, as elsewhere (Marquand 2015, 83).

The critical perspective

Quantitative studies of educational inequality and its economic implications often tacitly assume that policymakers face a range of discrete problems susceptible to targeted solutions, largely ignoring the nexus of social, cultural, political and economic factors in which such problems are embedded. By the same token, they tend to assume a consensus over the ends of education policy, largely restricting debate to technical considerations of 'what works'. Key among the issues overlooked in such practice-oriented work is the role accorded to education in political socialisation, and how this may reflect priorities and discourses that obstruct and undermine the pursuit of equitable and sustainable development.

Pepper's *Radicalism and Education Reform in Twentieth-Century China* (1996) is perhaps the classic attempt to address such issues in the context of modern China. She argues that debates over education's role in modern Chinese state formation have been shaped by tensions between discourses emphasising 'quality' and 'quantity'. On the one hand, educated urban elites have overwhelmingly focused on 'quality' – the use of schooling to nurture and select 'talent' for state service; educating peasants beyond a very basic level was, from this perspective, wasteful and potentially destabilising. Opposing this was a radical critique, espoused in violent form by the Maoists, envisioning a more egalitarian and inclusive model of development that would destroy the ancient barrier between urban elites and rural masses. The persistence into the twenty-first century of this tension between cities and countryside – at a discursive as well as an economic level – is underlined in studies by Yu (2004), who applies the 'reproduction theory' of Bourdieu to an analysis of the urban–rural gap, and Murphy (2004, 2007), who shows how the *suzhi* discourse pervading contemporary educational debate serves to rationalise this continuing divide.

Murphy's work illustrates how understandings of inequality, and strategies for addressing it, reflect complex and often contradictory political priorities, ideological positions and social prejudices. Discussion of *suzhi* (loosely translatable as 'quality') reflects elite concerns over schooling's capacity to equip students for work and citizenship in a 'knowledge economy', while assigning responsibility to individuals and families for their educational performance. This helps to reinforce a sense amongst urban elites that the backwardness of the countryside is somehow the peasants' own 'fault' – and even to convince some villagers themselves that this is so (Murphy 2007). Shue and Wong (2007) also highlight the 'discursive elements' at play in contemporary China 'that have been heavily implicated in concealing, even condoning, certain forms of suffering and social inequality that might otherwise have been eliminated' (11). These include an aggressive culture of 'competition' and public discourses on poverty and individual responsibility reminiscent of mid-Victorian England. Also related to such discourses is a resurgent nationalism, tying CCP legitimacy to an often defiantly belligerent international posture, especially on matters of sovereignty (Vickers 2009a, b). By keeping the spectre of foreign threats, past and present, constantly before the public, nationalism helps – as it has often done in other societies – to distract attention from intractable social problems.

Focus on individual or collective moral failings (of parents, communities or corrupt officials) as the root cause of social problems also distracts attention from more fundamental institutional failings. While differing on many details, the political scientists Pei (2006) and Yao (2010), the economist Huang (2008), and the philosopher Wang Hui (2009) all reject a 'Beijing consensus' on the benefits of marrying political autocracy to market liberalism. On the contrary, they argue that the pursuit of this course explains why problems such as the patchy provision of public goods have proven particularly intractable. Issues of governance loom large in their analysis, particularly in relation to patterns of accountability that have encouraged local officials to prioritise fulfilling centrally mandated targets for economic growth over providing the public goods that local people demand (Shue and Wong 2007).

But governance is not simply a top-down process. Even in 'authoritarian' China, securing popular consent or acquiescence involves appealing to the interests and beliefs of key constituencies. In *Governing Educational Desire* (2011), Kipnis stresses that such acquiescence largely depends on the regime's capacity to expand educational access and demonstrate commitment to meritocracy; Thøgersen, writing twenty years earlier (1991), also noted the centrality of education to Party legitimacy in the post-Mao period. Here culture and politics intersect, though not in the deterministic fashion claimed by apologists for official orthodoxy. A deeply entrenched ideology of meritocracy (not to be confused with actual meritocracy) both shapes popular expectations and supplies a cultural resource that the Party can manipulate. Meanwhile, examinations, curricular content and pedagogy all reflect culturally rooted assumptions of the 'exemplary' function of schooling; and the association of moral exemplariness with social or political authority (Bakken 2000). But with respect both to ideas of meritocracy and of exemplariness, the dialogue between popular expectations and their manipulation by officialdom also contributes to complex and unpredictable cultural change. This is perhaps nowhere better illustrated than in the evolution of the concept of *suzhi* and its association with the critique of 'traditional' educational practices. Growing discontent with the latter among urban elites has stoked demand for overseas education, with profound and unsettling implications – as we discuss in our final two chapters.

The aim of this volume

Our analysis draws on research conducted within each of the four paradigms identified above, but addresses concerns most closely associated with the last. Praising China's educational 'achievements', identifying Chinese 'best practice' for deployment overseas, or using Chinese experience as a mirror in which to view the failings of other systems, are all valid enterprises – up to a point. However, their validity and usefulness depend on the accuracy with which they portray the education system, and their capacity to explain its most salient characteristics in relation to the social and political context. This in turn requires acknowledging how and why that context has changed.

Much existing research deals with contextual factors, especially those relating to politics or ideology, only in rather general terms. Typical is Postiglione's declaration that the range of 'educational choices' produced by 'market forces' must be made 'more widely and fairly accessible to underserved groups' if Chinese education 'is to stay in line with the socialist values that underlay the system' (2006, 19). The sentiment is unobjectionable. But by the time this was written, the irrelevance of 'socialist values' to explaining the drift of education policy was already clear; if socialism means egalitarianism, then contemporary Japan is more socialist than China. Moreover, the attribution of causation to vague and impersonal 'market forces' sidesteps the crucial role of politics and ideology; 'educational choices' have been available not just to disparate social 'groups', but to the political actors shaping the system. Interrogating their shifting ethical and ideological premises is a crucial and neglected part of the story of educational development in post-Mao China.

More fundamentally, though, that story itself remains largely untold. Innumerable edited volumes, journal special issues and book-length monographs offer invaluable insights into various aspects of Chinese education, but these present discrete snapshots rather than a coherent narrative. Exemplary coherence is offered by Pepper (1996) and Thøgersen (2002), but their focus is on the twentieth century, extending no further than the first one or two post-Mao decades. Others have brought impressive theoretical sophistication to the comparative analysis of Chinese education (e.g. Tobin *et al.* 2009; Kipnis 2011). However, Rappleye, commenting on what he sees as a fruitful 'theoretical turn' in comparative education over recent years, observes that this now 'finds the field careening towards the cul-de-sac of theory without history' (2015, 374). This perhaps helps account for the strange neglect of history in so much analysis of education in contemporary China.[10]

It is that neglect that this volume sets out to correct. The subject is so vast that we cannot pretend to a fully comprehensive account. We have deliberately confined ourselves primarily to formal rather than informal educational settings, omitting, for example, any systematic discussion of adult education (for reasons of space as well as our lack of expertise) or of the education of minorities (a vital but fraught and complex subject that deserves a monograph of its own). Although we draw on studies that adopt an ethnographic or case study approach, in attempting to construct a macroscopic narrative, we have been unable to do justice to the diversity of local or grassroots experiences of education. Other deficiencies in both the scope of our treatment, and the nature of our arguments, will suggest themselves to those with greater expertise in specific aspects of the system. But in attempting to provide a coherent narrative, however incomplete and contentious, of post-Mao China's educational development, we hope to provide a starting point for renewed debate over how and why the system has evolved in the way it has over the past four decades.

This involves engaging with the enormous and increasing diversity and complexity of contemporary Chinese society, but also putting this into perspective through the use of comparison. Both in the following chapter and throughout this volume, we make comparative allusion to the educational histories of other societies, particularly those of China's Asian neighbours. Japan provides a particular point of reference, not least because of the powerful influence of Japanese precedents and ideas in modern China. Perhaps in no respect is Japanese comparison more apposite than with regard to the scale and unsettling speed of contemporary change. Writing in 1890, Basil Hall Chamberlain observed, in a much-quoted passage, that:

> To have lived through the transition stage of modern Japan makes a man feel preternaturally old; for here he is in modern times, with the air full of talk about bicycles and bacilli and 'spheres of influence', and yet he can himself distinctly remember the Middle Ages. ... The Japanese boast that they have done in thirty or forty years what it took Europe half as many centuries to accomplish. Some even go further, and twit us Westerners with falling behind in the race …
>
> (1–2)[11]

The similarities between Meiji Japan and twenty-first-century China extend beyond entrenched notions of modernisation as a 'race' to related emphases on education's role in nurturing elite talent, controlling the masses and propagating a nationalist legitimating narrative. Education has contributed to technological advance, growing material prosperity and social mobility for millions, but has also been used to reinforce an authoritarian and exploitative socio-political model.

That story ended badly for Japan. Learning from history – our own and that of others – is crucial to ensuring a similar end does not await either China or its international 'competitors'.

Notes

1 Here Yang continues: 'For a long time, the key terms of educational discourse have been "universalization", "rapid development", "key-point construction", "strive to become world-class", as well as "expanding recruitment to higher education", "mergers", "university cities" and so on'.

2 Literally, 'the bright halo surrounding development' (*fazhan de guanghuan*).

3 The Minister, Jim Knight, was quoted as saying,

> Confucius said that, alongside knowledge, you should have time to think. It is not just about acquisition of knowledge, but about respect for the importance of education and the family, and that is something I would love to see engendered in our culture as well as it is in China.
>
> ('Minister turns to Confucius to raise school standards', *The Times*, 22 February 2009)

4 Suzanne Pepper (1996, Chapter 1) notes the close correlation between overseas perceptions of China's education system and the fortunes of China's economy (with the partial exception of the Mao period – when China became a poster-boy for the Western radical left). She also discusses the presentism and determinism of much writing on China's development in general, and education system in particular. However, it also needs to be borne in mind that the comments that various educational tourists make about Chinese education are often delivered with a domestic agenda in mind. Thus a Western university head returning from a tour of Chinese universities may choose to emphasise the competitive 'threat' posed by elite Chinese institutions largely in order to intensify pressure on his own government to increase funding for his institution.

5 Though constraint remains greater with respect to certain sensitive issues, such as education in Tibet and Xinjiang.

6 Anyone involved in the study of China will be familiar with the common habit of referring to 'the Chinese view' or 'the Western view' on whatever topic is being discussed – a form of stereotyping or essentialising that does nothing to advance the cause of academic exchange and scholarly debate.

7 The other side of this coin being the way in which, throughout the post-Mao period, Chinese scholars have invoked aspects of overseas (especially American) policy and practice to critique aspects of the Chinese educational system.

8 See especially Chapter 12: 'The Eight Differences that Define China'. This view appears to be rooted in a conviction that China enjoys a moral superiority over the West by virtue of its former 'semi-colonial' victimhood. Thus Duara (2009) hails the creation of the Republic of China in 1911, encompassing the entire territory of the Qing Empire, as an unprecedented exercise in enlightened multi-culturalism; others paint a different picture of relations between the Han and other peoples of the empire (for a review of various studies in this vein, see Vickers 2015). Meanwhile, in his analysis of policy on 'minorities' education, Postiglione (2009) is at pains to draw favourable comparisons with Western 'colonialist' practices. For a critique of analyses of education informed by 'world culture theory' (and associated discourses concerning a global 'core' and 'periphery'), see Carney *et al.* (2012).

9 Examples cited throughout this book include Pepper, Thøgersen, Murphy, Hansen and Kipnis (see the later section of this chapter). On 'critical' China-based economists and social scientists respectively, see Huang (2008, 276) and Pei (2006,14).

10 Exceptions include the eulogistic accounts published in Chinese around the 30th anniversary of 'Reform and Opening' in 2008.

11 Characterising Mao's China, or indeed Tokugawa Japan, as 'the Middle Ages' is problematic for many reasons, but this phrase reflects the sweeping nature of the social, cultural and political transformation that both experienced – and the profoundly disorienting consequences for many who lived through it.

2 Comparative and historical perspectives on education and development in contemporary China

Much writing on education and development in China involves comparisons with other developing countries – often fairly cursory, and usually in China's favour. At the same time, the Chinese case is often assumed by Western politicians and media commentators to constitute some variant of the 'East Asian developmental state' – albeit more complex and immeasurably larger than Korea, Taiwan or even Japan. Thus China's advantages are seen as largely attributable to features shared with other East Asian societies, and lacked by other developing nations. However, as we noted in the previous chapter, post-Mao China has been characterised by an intensely competitive social ethos, rising inequality and an ideological emphasis on state-centred nationalism. While suggestive of comparisons with pre-war Japan, these characteristics (or at least the first two) indicate significant differences between contemporary China and post-war East Asia.

References to 'pre-war' and 'post-war' reflect the need for careful attention to periodisation when making comparisons. This applies equally to the history of post-Mao China itself, which is often discussed as a single periodic unit with 1978 as 'Year Zero'. Whereas orthodox scholarship generally depicts the pre-Reform era, especially the Cultural Revolution, as an educational Dark Age, others emphasise the extent to which the developmental achievements of the post-Mao period rest on earlier advances in the provision of public goods, particularly health care and basic education (Bardhan 2010, 8–9). Issues of periodisation relating to education policy are dealt with at length in our next chapter; here we provide a comparative context for analysing the distinctiveness of Chinese development, and the role of education within it.

For this purpose we also look beyond education to the field of economics. Here, headline figures for *per capita* GDP growth show remarkably consistent – and high – rates of increase since 1978, accelerating from the 1990s onwards. However, these belie a significant shift since 1989–91 (Huang 2008). Huang argues that the 1980s witnessed 'bottom-up' growth fuelled primarily by small-scale, rural private enterprise – originating with the 'township and village enterprises' of the 1970s. This was superseded during the 1990s by urban-focused growth, with far closer state supervision.[1] One result was a sharp reduction in the ratio of household income to GDP, so that less of the growth in national wealth reached the pockets of ordinary consumers (42). At the same time, an urban investment boom was financed by a squeeze on rural communities, involving both taxation and reallocation of resources – including land – that might otherwise have been used to support rural public services. Rural primary schools and medical facilities declined, and some localities began charging for immunisation shots. Huang claims that the running down of rural public schooling during the 1990s led to 30 million people entering adulthood as illiterates between 2000 and 2005.

This turn to 'directional illiberalism' was, Huang argues, due less to institutional or legal changes than to leadership messages signalling greater or lesser respect for security of person and property. He also suggests that the shift from a rural to an urban bias in part reflected the backgrounds of key leaders – Zhao Ziyang and Hu Yaobang (key reforming leaders of the 1980s) had their roots in rural provinces, while President Jiang Zemin and Zhu Rongji (the main economic policymaker from the 1990s to early 2000s) were from Shanghai. But the shift to an urban-oriented developmental focus undoubtedly also reflected concerns to pacify the urban population in the aftermath of the risings of 1989.

From around 2005, the Hu Jintao–Wen Jiabao administration attempted to rebalance development in favour of rural areas and underprivileged groups, with some success (Murphy and Johnson 2009, 449). However, vested interests and associated institutional weaknesses had by this point become deeply entrenched, obstructing the governance reforms required to counter kleptocracy and return to a 'welfare-improving growth trajectory' (Huang 2008, 45).[2] Indeed, Huang argues that China today displays a version of 'the state-led [crony] capitalism that ... characterized Latin America', rather than a variant of the East Asian developmental state.[3] Extreme societal inequality and rampant bureaucratic corruption hamper the delivery of public goods. Drawing comparisons with 1970s Mexico, Huang portrays a labour-repressive, investment-heavy pattern of development, featuring huge state-fuelled construction booms in Shanghai (World Expo), Beijing (the Olympics) and elsewhere (280).

However, the trajectory of education policy during the post-Mao period does not precisely mirror that traced by Huang for economic policy. For example, while decentralisation in the 1980s generally boosted the rural economy, in many regions it undermined rural educational provision. In making his case for seeing the early 1990s as a 'Latin American'-style wrong turn, Huang argues that the 1980s witnessed a development strategy more in line with South Korean and Taiwanese precedents – favouring broad-based, small-scale entrepreneurial capitalism. But did a similar pattern hold with respect to education? In order to assess the relevance of the so-called 'East Asian model' to China's educational development, we first need to examine what it actually denotes.

Education and the East Asian developmental state

The influence of East Asian models on Chinese modernisation goes back a long way, with Japan's impact especially early and profound (Fogel 2004, 2009; Duara 2009). In 1977, Deng Xiaoping invoked Meiji-era Japan to emphasise the urgency of catching up 'with the most advanced countries in the world' (Pepper 1996, 479), and the centrality of education to this task. For Deng, this implied concentrating investment on an elite vanguard to lead the nation into the global first division 'within twenty years'. Deng's biographer enthuses that his reintroduction of meritocratic university entrance exams has had 'a cascade of positive results for China', claiming that 'as in Japan, South Korea, Taiwan and Singapore,' these have 'raised the quality of both university applicants and recruits entering the workforce' (Vogel 2011, 207). However, this focus on the system's commanding heights, allied to a prioritisation of military and diplomatic self-strengthening, appears far closer to the thinking of the Meiji statesmen (or the later Stalin) than to the policies of Japan, Korea and Taiwan during the post-war era. Indeed, Gray argues that it was Mao, during his last years, rather than Deng, who was closer to pursuing a variant of the post-war East Asian model of rapid but equitable growth (Gray 2006).

One basis for seeing similarities between China's development and that of the East Asian 'tigers' relates to the alleged importance to both of export-led growth fuelled by foreign direct investment (FDI) (World Bank 2002). However, the post-war development of South Korea and Taiwan relied heavily on the promotion of import-substitution, with minimal FDI. According to Bardhan, post-Mao China's growth has also 'not been primarily export-driven' (2010, 5). As for FDI, the benefits to the host country, or their distribution, depend on the terms it negotiates with investors (Green 2007, 19), once again underlining the importance of governance. Huang attributes the inequities of recent Chinese growth partly to a disproportionate reliance on FDI (Huang 2008).

Education's role in boosting 'human capital' is often seen as crucial to enabling a country to compete for FDI, and then use it to transfer technology and build up local industry (Carnoy 1993). It is also widely assumed that the initial phase of growth, when investment is attracted and industrialisation begins, will witness growing inequality, gradually correcting itself as the entire society is drawn into the modern economy – as postulated by the 'Kuznets curve'. However, the pattern of growth in post-war East Asia was very different, featuring rapid economic development combined with increasing *equality*. This was attributable in part to 'increasing aggregate levels of education' alongside its 'equal distribution' (McMahon 1999, cited in Green 2007, 22). East Asian experience also supports Sen's arguments regarding education's wider importance in promoting individual health, community cohesion and the fostering of other 'capabilities' (1999).[4]

What factors account for this East Asian achievement of growth with equity? A widely shared 'Confucian' culture emphasising educational endeavour, thrift, discipline, hard work and 'utilitarian familism' is often credited (Lau 1981), a view endorsed by authoritarian regional leaders such as Singapore's Lee Kuan Yew (Lee 2000). Vogel notes the very cordial relationship between Lee and Deng Xiaoping, and the latter's admiration for the Singapore model (2011).[5] Since the 1990s, the cult of Confucius has experienced an officially sponsored revival in China. However, this same cultural heritage was previously blamed by Marx, Weber and many Chinese observers, from Lu Xun to Bo Yang (1992), for China's 'backwardness' or 'crisis'. The significance of culture cannot be dismissed, but cultural traditions are always porous, diverse and contested – and 'Confucianism' has been no exception.

Geography and geopolitics also contributed to East Asia's post-war growth, facilitating access to global markets, and attracting large disbursements of American aid. The buoyancy of the global economy during this period assisted economic take-off in Japan and the tigers. However, similar advantages were available to the Philippines and Sri Lanka, both of which stagnated economically (Green 2007). Hence the significance attached by many analysts to economic policies specific to East Asia – such as post-war land reforms (Walder 2015, 333) – and to the 'developmental' role of the state more broadly.

Opinions vary regarding the significance of state intervention,[6] but if these states were particularly 'developmentally oriented', what made them so? Johnson attributes this to the situational nationalism of 'late developing economies' not only in contemporary East Asia, but also – and prototypically – in imperial Germany and Meiji Japan – where perceptions of a collective existential crisis supply both motivation and popular legitimacy for economic activism (1995, Chapter 2). Darwinian 'eat-or-be-eaten' visions of the world order have been strongly influential ever since the Victorian thinker Herbert Spencer was invited to advise the Japanese government (Duara 2009, 24).[7] The Japanese example has in turn influenced many subsequent East Asian regimes, for whom the global Cold War and regional 'Cold Civil Wars' contributed to a strong consciousness of crisis or external threat after 1945 (Mitter and Major 2004).

In political terms, situational nationalism and a Darwinian worldview have been associated with profound instrumentalism and authoritarianism. Perceptions of a national existential crisis are fostered to legitimise subordination of individual aspiration to state-defined notions of the 'greater good'. The priority of boosting national defence and state power dictate a relentless focus on those aspects of education, especially science and technology, deemed most likely to yield competitive advantage for the state. They also imply a minimalist approach to public welfare guarantees, helpfully legitimised by Confucian 'utilitarian familism'; the relative weakness of public welfare provision remains a feature even of East Asia's wealthiest societies, compelling strong reliance on support from family and employer (Economist, 2016). At the individual level, therefore, consciousness of both patriotic duty and personal necessity have tended to fuel 'educational desire' (Kipnis 2011), while channelling it towards those areas deemed most useful by the authorities.

Far from being the exclusive province of authoritarian nationalists, however, instrumentalism is also implicit in the human capital paradigm favoured by 'practice-oriented' researchers. Education's importance to economic prosperity seems clear; less so is what kind of education is most important, and for whom. Economists debate the social (as distinct from individual) 'rates of return' to secondary and higher education, but there is broad consensus regarding the importance of basic schooling. The World Bank's *East Asian Miracle* report highlighted 'variations in primary school enrolment rates' as crucial to explaining the region's relative success (World Bank 1993, 54; cited in Green

2007, 36). The sequential expansion of primary, secondary and tertiary education, with public investment focused on the earlier phases, has been credited with reducing the tendency for inequalities to rise in post-war Korea, Taiwan and Japan (McMahon 1999; Tilak 2002; Green *et al.* 2006). Educationally more unequal societies such as Singapore and Hong Kong have exhibited greater income inequality.[8] But across northeast Asia at least, relatively uniform and apparently effective systems of schooling were maintained at minimal cost, with average public spending on education lower (as a proportion of GDP) than in most developed countries. Irrespective of their impact on 'skills', in distributional terms these systems reflected, and helped to underpin, relatively high levels of social equality.

Relative equality of educational outcomes in Japan, Korea and Taiwan was promoted by systems of comprehensive, neighbourhood-based primary and junior secondary schooling, with automatic grade promotion and a large proportion of mixed group work and group assessment. Equality of resources was promoted through measures such as the rotation of teaching staff between schools. Education systems were highly centralised and standardised, with schools enjoying little managerial autonomy. This framework of strong, centralised bureaucratic control 'facilitated the regulation of student flows through different tracks and subject areas' (often related to manpower planning), and fostered 'the strong normative standards and expectations for all students' widely credited with the region's high average attainment levels (Green 2007, 43).[9] However, these same achievements are also associated with the authoritarianism and instrumentalism noted above.

So too are a strong emphasis on didactic moral instruction, and on rituals and practices calculated to reinforce collectivism and uniformity (Green 2007, 44). Meiji Japan in this respect also provided a highly influential template for its neighbours (Harrison 2001). In pre-war Japan, the emphasis on uniformity and blind loyalty was most intense at primary level (Ienaga 2001); in a highly elitist system, the small number who entered tertiary education were, to borrow Bertrand Russell's ironic phrase, 'licensed to think' (1932, 12). But in post-war Japan, Korea and Taiwan, uniformity and collectivism implied a favouring of comprehensive schooling over vocational/academic 'tracking' or early specialisation, even at senior secondary level. This orientation has come under increasing strain in recent years amidst perceptions that 'creativity' and critical thinking skills are now needed for success in the 'global knowledge economy' (Kariya and Rappleye 2010). Reforms aimed at encouraging such skills have been blamed for undermining some of the structural and ethical features responsible for these systems' relatively uniform outcomes (Kariya 2011). The instrumental focus on economic ends that informs such reforms is meanwhile reflected in attempts to direct 'critical thinking' to the problems of robotics rather than politics. China's post-Mao leaders have similarly attempted to adhere to Meiji precedent, deploying Western technology for 'practical use', while inculcating a conservative version of traditional ethics to maintain civic discipline.

In its 'situational nationalism', political socialisation strategies and focus on 'human capital' development, there are thus parallels to be drawn between contemporary China and post-war Japan, Korea or Taiwan – but in other respects the contrasts are stark. Whereas, in the latter, collectivism to varying degrees implied relative equality of opportunity and horizontal solidarity (within communities, classrooms and workplaces), in post-Mao China it has been associated with suspension of distributional concerns and a pervasive ethos of competition. And while Leninist 'democratic centralism' also characterised Taiwan and Korea when they were fast-developing one-party states, educational egalitarianism and uniformity helped create the basis there for a common civic consciousness that has since underpinned democratisation. In post-Mao China, by contrast, education has reinforced deep social divisions between urban and rural residents, and the middle classes and the rest, fostering the entrenchment of contradictory vested interests. In the short term, this may facilitate the pursuit of control through divide-and-rule (Wright 2010); but in the longer term it makes a smooth, Taiwan-style transition from authoritarianism harder to envisage.

The case of Taiwan – and comparisons with the mainland

In alluding to possible links between China's 'developmental state' and Taiwan's, Green observes that 'it remains for historians to trace fully their common and variant inheritances from the … legacies of the Chinese nationalism of Sun Yat-sen and Chiang Kai-shek' (2007, 47). This task was subsequently tackled by a different scholar named Greene (2008). Focusing on efforts to coordinate science and technology (S&T) policy with the needs of industry (epitomised by Hsinchu Science Park), she argues that the KMT first adopted 'developmental statism' on the mainland during wartime, abandoned it following the retreat to Taiwan, then rediscovered it during the late 1960s and 1970s. That rediscovery is portrayed as a response to American advice, domestic pressure and various crises (the oil shocks, loss of the ROC's UN seat, the death of Chiang Kai-shek) that imperilled KMT legitimacy.

This strategy led to increasing proportions of graduates working in the applied sciences, more state spending on research and development (largely related to the needs of high-tech industry), and measures to reduce, then reverse, an earlier brain-drain. K.T. Li, one of the policymakers involved, later claimed that a pragmatic, 'problem-oriented approach to policy formation' explained its timing, arguing that only in the late-1970s did the need to upgrade the technological and industrial infrastructure become obvious (Greene 2008, 143). But in fact, the KMT had earlier had other priorities, prompting it to concentrate on primary and secondary rather than higher education. Not least amongst these was the drive to promote the standard national language (Mandarin) and to socialise politically restive 'native Taiwanese' as patriotic Chinese.

The KMT's failures in the realm of political socialisation (Vickers 2007b) contrast with the relative success of its S&T and industrial policies. Greene views this record as 'a model of how a Leninist Party-State can merge political authority and the modernizing impulses of its technocrats to build institutions and coordinate educational and economic plans to promote economic modernization and development' (150). She also sees post-Mao China as having adopted elements of KMT developmental statism, including an ideological fusion of scientism and patriotic traditionalism (158–9).[10] The extent to which early post-Mao S&T policy in China was influenced by the Taiwanese example is unclear,[11] but there is evidence of active mainland interest since at least 1986, when Nankai University (in Shanghai) established an Institute of Taiwan Economics (153). The mainland links of elderly ROC technocrats were also important in facilitating cross-straits exchanges in this field.[12]

S&T development in the contemporary People's Republic of China (PRC) has shared many features with the Taiwanese case, reflected in its prominence in successive five-year plans, the establishment of university-affiliated science parks, and a pervasive scientistic rhetoric, epitomised by President Hu Jintao's (2002–12) 'scientific development concept' (*kexuefazhanguan*). The CCP's top leadership also became increasingly technocratic as a result of reforms to internal party promotion practices instituted during the 1980s.[13] By 2002, 22 of 25 Politburo members had university-level education (compared with none in 1982), and by 2003, 98 per cent of provincial leaders had gone to college (compared with 20 per cent in 1982), and nearly 20 per cent held PhDs (Greene 2008, 155).

Absent from Greene's comparison of the KMT and CCP 'developmental states' is much account of social or political context. Her perspective, like those of the technocrats she studies, seems essentially top-down and economistic. Ironically, she criticises the 'top-down' nature of S&T policymaking in the PRC, but with reference to official 'intolerance' of 'others' in the scientific community or industry.[14] Highlighting how, in Taiwan, 'technocrats were able to harness state power while simultaneously listening and responding to the advice of outsiders' (163), she expresses the hope that the PRC leadership can emulate the ROC in this respect. However, the basis for a civil society space 'outside' the Party-State is far more fragile on the contemporary mainland than in the Taiwan of the 1980s. And China's Communist rulers have shown little sign of willingness to emulate aspects of the ROC system that contributed to eroding the KMT's status as a dominant Leninist party.

Greene's own essentially technocratic perspective is reflected in the implication that governance issues represent a technical hitch to be overcome in the interests of greater efficiency. Scholars associated with the 'critical' perspective we outlined in the previous chapter tend to be less sanguine in this regard. Huang, for example, cites Sen's distinction between two types of high-growth economies, exemplified by Taiwan and Brazil, and argues that China, at least since the 1990s, conforms more to the latter than the former (2008, 242). Contrasting China with Taiwan in terms of the relative strength of private sector investment, he emphasises that East Asian 'developmental states' were not command economies.[15] In Taiwan, entrepreneurs were genuinely consulted and involved in policymaking, whereas in China enterprises remain excluded from government policymaking (280). Moreover, in pre-1980s Taiwan the conditions already existed for broad-based 'bottom up' growth fuelled by small-scale private entrepreneurship, thanks in large part to relatively high *per capita* levels of spending on public goods, including education.[16]

Huang contends that conditions similar to those of 1960s–70s Taiwan existed in mainland China during the 1980s, when the 'first generation of Chinese entrepreneurs', many from rural backgrounds, was 'quite well-educated' (242). Health and education '"prepare" a population for economic participation' (Drèze and Sen, cited in Huang 2008, 242), and, in this respect, as Sen observes elsewhere, 'the extent to which post-reform China [has drawn] on the results achieved in pre-reform China needs greater recognition' (1999, 260). Despite suggestions in much educational literature, especially of the orthodox or practice-oriented persuasion, of steady improvements since the advent of the Reform era, the picture is rather more complex and confused. Hannum *et al.* claim that evidence 'indicates that the early years of market transition saw slight contractions in educational access, but that subsequently, the reform period has seen a steady expansion' (2007, 9), before acknowledging that broader 'socio-economic inequalities may actually be intensifying' (10).[17] Some indicators suggest that social inequality peaked in the late 1990s, while others show subsequently declining income inequality *within* both urban and rural economies, but increasing inequality *between* urban and rural areas (Shue and Wong 2007). Writing in 2007, Shue and Wong saw the latter outcome primarily as a consequence of 'the important role played by government policy in shaping distributional outcomes' (4), involving reforms to social security provision 'focused overwhelmingly on the urban population' (7).[18]

The fact that both the post-Mao mainland and late Martial Law-era Taiwan witnessed the adoption of a growth-oriented S&T policy by a Leninist Party-State should therefore not distract us from important differences in context and consequences. In Taiwan, the earlier prioritisation of investment in primary and secondary schooling helped ensure that the benefits of growth – including the employment and further education opportunities associated with S&T policy – were relatively widely shared. Social inequality, as measured by the Gini coefficient, declined from the already-low figure of 0.321 in 1964 to 0.287 in 1984, rising to 0.326 by 2000 (Directorate-General of Budget, Accounting and Statistics, 2000). (In the 1970s, Taiwanese society was actually more equal than famously 'egalitarian' Maoist China: Walder 2015, 331.) Rising prosperity and levels of education, along with this relatively even distribution of income, facilitated Taiwan's remarkably smooth transition to political democracy during the 1990s. The PRC regime may have sought to boost economic growth by borrowing features of the KMT's S&T policy, but public policy priorities, and financial and governance arrangements, helped ensure that the nature of growth and its social consequences would be very different on the other side of the Taiwan Strait.

A different perspective – comparisons with India

If comparisons between the contemporary PRC and the post-war experience of its East Asian neighbours highlight some of the more problematic aspects of China's developmental and educational record, then comparisons with other 'developing' countries often cast it in a rather more favourable light. Studies of an orthodox bent have often emphasised China's 'developing' status, since this supports a narrative underlining the country's relative success in 'catching up' with the West and Japan. Not just in GDP terms but across the range of 'human development indicators', China has outperformed most of its 'Third World' peers. Moreover, the narrative of Chinese success has been trumpeted by development practitioners associated with the market-liberalising, state-minimalist 'Washington Consensus'. For the World Bank in particular, China has exemplified policies such as decentralisation, the introduction of user fees, and wider use of market mechanisms in public service provision, that it has been keen to 'sell' elsewhere. China's economic success has made it a useful stick with which to beat countries such as India (Drake 2001). The nature and extent of China's embrace of markets and neoliberalism, and their educational and social effects, are issues to which we return in later chapters.

Nevertheless, evidence from comparative studies of educational outcomes demonstrates incontrovertibly China's superiority *vis-à-vis* India. Data from the UN *World Development Reports* cited by Drèze and Sen show adult literacy rates of 65 per cent and 41 per cent respectively in 1980, rising to 94 per cent and 63 per cent in 2010, indicating a widening lead for China (2013, 113). Despite China experiencing severe problems of its own with marketisation (to be discussed in Chapter 9), advocacy of private provision of basic services has made far greater inroads in India. China has more or less universalised basic education on a publicly funded basis, while avoiding the runaway inflation of public sector salaries seen in India, and consequent strains on school funding and distortion of teacher recruitment (132–3). While the male–female literacy gap amongst 18-24-year-olds in China had effectively disappeared as of 2010 (99 per cent literacy for both genders), in India it remained significant (88 per cent male to 74 per cent female) (66). And in healthcare and child nourishment too, available statistics show China outperforming India by significant margins.

Statistics may not tell the whole story. Huang (2008, 242–4) and Postiglione (2006, 4–5) note the unreliability of Chinese government figures, and it is on these that the UN surveys rely. Moreover, authoritarian regimes such as China's tend to be better at image management than a shambolic but relatively open democracy like India. Indian squalor and misery are highly visible, but poverty in China is more quarantined – not least through a household registration system designed to limit rural–urban migration. Residency-related restrictions on access to public services mean that, as of 2016, an estimated 60 million Chinese children (one in five of the total) are 'left-behind' in villages, living without their migrant parents, though mostly attending school (Sudworth 2016). In India, for all the discrimination, degradation and neglect, state regulations do not impose such psychological or emotional trauma on children. Nor – except briefly during Indira Gandhi's 'Emergency' – has the Indian state attempted coercive population planning. Through education and improvements to women's social opportunities, by the 1990s, Kerala had achieved reductions in fertility greater, and more sustainable (because rooted in women's agency and changed popular attitudes), than China achieved through its coercive 'One Child Policy' (Sen 1999, 199; 220).[19] This coercion, symptomatic of a fundamentally instrumentalist conception of state–citizen relations, has imposed costs both statistically visible (e.g. in skewed gender ratios),[20] and invisible (i.e. psychological or emotional). Amongst the latter may be counted (at least in part) the peculiarly intense competitive ethos that permeates the education system and society more broadly (see Fong 2004 and subsequent chapters in this volume).

GDP *per capita* is of course a standard statistical measure of economic performance, if an unreliable indicator of overall welfare (Sen 1999). However, in so far as such figures provide a useful benchmark, Huang insists that they overstate China's superiority over India. He claims that a measure including 'intangible wealth' (encompassing factors such as educational achievements and the rule of law) gives a ratio of only 1.13 in China's favour, as opposed to 1.6–1.8 on more conventional measures (Huang 2008, 271). 'A state-led economic model,' he states, 'can build up output capacity very quickly,' boosting raw GDP figures, 'but it does not lead to wealth creation' (271). Financing constraints on private firms in early twenty-first-century India appeared substantially lower than in China; the former on a level with Southeast Asia, the latter with countries of the former Soviet bloc (Russia and Romania) (273). This, Huang argues, helps to explain why more of India's growth has been associated with small-scale private entrepreneurship, contributing to actual increases in household income. The greater strength of India's 'soft' infrastructure – including access to finance, security of property and the rule of law – makes it easier for genuinely private entrepreneurship to flourish there; in China, business success relies far more on cultivating and securing state backing.

This state of affairs in China is attributed by Huang largely to a shift away from the more broad-based pattern of growth pursued in the 1980s. While a few provinces, most notably Zhejiang (the richest), have since broadly maintained that approach, others, epitomised by Shanghai and Jiangsu, have switched to a more state-led, urban-centred model. While many economists have argued that China surpassed India due to its policies in the 1990s, Huang contends that China was far richer than India long before then. And like Amartya Sen (1999), he attributes this partly to the legacy of improvements in public health and basic education under Mao; in the words of another Indian economist, Pranab Bardhan, to the extent that the Chinese are 'better capitalists now,' it 'may be because they were better socialists then' (2010, 9). By contrast, whether under the neo-socialist Nehru or subsequently, Indian education policy and spending priorities have consistently favoured established elites, though with significant state-to-state variations (Kamat 2007; Drèze and Sen 2013). Indeed, in emphasising the need to correct such imbalances, the Indian Prime Minister in 2005 spoke of adopting the 'Chinese model', particularly as regards the widespread provision of primary education and basic healthcare (Economist 2005).

Ironically, by that point rural services in China had suffered from two decades of neglect and underfunding; the 'Chinese model' Manmohan Singh was praising appeared defunct (Drèze and Sen 2013, 15, 67 and 343, n. 18). Meanwhile, China's central government pumped 94 per cent of its own education budget into the tertiary sector, effectively resigning any role in balancing inter-regional inequalities (Huang 2008, 246). Despite an increase from 1998/9 in resource transfers to poorer provinces, partly associated with the much-heralded *Western Development Initiative* (*Xibu Da Kaifa*) (see Chapter 3.3), as of 2004 the central government was allocating only 30 per cent of all budgetary expenditures (for education and overall), with the rest falling to local governments (Shue and Wong 2007, 3). Moreover, Shue and Wong suggest that most central government disbursements were 'bailing out under-funded local social security schemes, filling other funding gaps, and paying for the mandated wage increases of civil servants at local levels'; budgetary spending on public services remained 'just too low', at 2–2.5 per cent for education, and 2 per cent for health (3).[21] By contrast, according to Kamat, total budget allocations for education spending in India were around 3.5 per cent in the 1990s, rising to 4 per cent as of 2007, with a rising proportion earmarked for elementary education (2007, 99). Drèze and Sen provide a rather lower figure of 3.3 per cent for 2010 (2013, 66). Nonetheless, in the mid-2000s it looked as if India might be poised to adopt a more egalitarian approach, leaving China to pursue a Nehruvian focus on tertiary education and scientific research (see Chapters 11 and 12).

In fact, that new dawn for Indian education is yet to arrive. Although Parliament in 2010 took the significant step of legislating a fundamental 'right to education', the capacity to enforce this – or of those denied it to claim it – remains highly doubtful (Kumar 2010). Meanwhile, difficulties in monitoring and enforcement, as well as strong discourses amongst Indian elites favouring privatisation and market mechanisms, continue to weaken the state's capacity as an educational provider, with detrimental consequences for equitable access (Kumar 2007; Jeffery *et al.* 2007; Drèze and Sen 2013). Taken as a whole, China continues to outperform India by some margin in the scope and quality of its provision of public services, including education – and indeed has stretched its lead further since the early 2000s, as the central government has increased subsidies to poorer regions, and reinstated a 'socialised' system of basic healthcare (Drèze and Sen 2013, 66; see Chapter 5 in this volume). However, neither country has come close to matching the uniformly high level of provision exemplified by post-war Japan or the East Asian 'tigers', nor their combination of high growth and declining inequality.

The extent to which the earlier experiences of Japan and its smaller neighbours can offer developmental templates for sub-continental giants like China and India is certainly debatable. Drawing comparisons at the level of Indian states or Chinese provinces is perhaps more appropriate. The likes of Kerala or Tamil Nadu exhibit a relatively broad-based model of private entrepreneurship, allied to strong universal public provision of basic education, that somewhat resembles Korean or Taiwanese precedents; but the stifling of local economic growth (partly due to regulatory dysfunction) has made both reliant on migrant labourer remittances in a manner more reminiscent of the Philippines. China's

Zhejiang Province has achieved both broad-based economic growth and relatively well-funded, universal educational provision, but without the emphasis on egalitarianism and uniformity found in the post-war 'tigers'. By the late 1970s, however, China as a whole had in fact already attained relatively high levels of basic education along with relative income equality (albeit uniformly low), and seemed set to follow a developmental trajectory quite similar to those of its East Asian neighbours. But in the event, it took a rather different course. The reasons for this are to be found not only in the history of the post-1978 'Reform and Opening' era itself – our principal focus here – but also in what preceded it.

The Maoist legacy

China has served, since the 1980s, as the poster-child for a market-friendly approach to development, emphasising 'privatization, cities, free markets and industry' (Pepper 1996, 517), with increasing social stratification portrayed as an inevitable consequence of modernisation (518). However, in the 1970s it was widely seen as the model for a very different developmental vision – underpinned by a radical attempt to deploy schooling as a tool of egalitarian social reform. The country seemed to offer hope to those in the international development community who had been puzzling over how to construct modern education systems in developing countries without exacerbating the urban–rural divide. By the late 1970s, universal elementary schooling was basically achieved for rural as well as urban populations (except for ethnic minorities), with state financing in cities, and collective support with minimal state assistance in rural areas.[22] Outside observers were also impressed by the way that the education system effectively unified schools, whether state- or community-financed, within a single, uniform model – effectively delivering comprehensive education on a continental scale.[23] The reasons for the subsequent abandonment of this model, and pursuit of a more stratified, elitist approach, stem fundamentally from internal politics rather than shifts in foreign trends – which China arguably led rather than followed.

Pepper argues that the way in which the model of an egalitarian, unified system of basic education had been achieved 'contained the seeds of its own destruction', ensuring 'a mighty backlash' from the educational establishment and from those targeted as 'class enemies' (Pepper 1996, 518). The educational politics of the Cultural Revolution were the culmination of 'an evolving critique almost as old as China's modern school system itself.' On the one hand was an established vision, inherited from the imperial era, of education as the vehicle for high culture and the route to elite membership and political power (519); on the other, a 'radical' challenge that envisaged schools contributing to an egalitarian remodelling of society. Both the critics (often associated with the May 4 Movement of 1919),[24] and their opponents, acted from a mixture of traditional and Western-inspired principles and assumptions. Thus the 'radicals' included the Confucian revivalist Liang Shu-ming, leader of the 'Rural Reconstruction Movement' (Alitto 1979), as well as iconoclastic Communists.

Educational reformers of rival camps meanwhile traded charges of 'mechanical copying,' accusing their opponents of superficially attempting to borrow whatever seemed to be the latest world trend.

While educational traditionalists generally insisted on fostering 'quality' through 'regular', state-funded, academically oriented schools, the 'radical' reformers favoured rapidly expanding 'quantity', through 'irregular' (local, community-funded) ventures if necessary. Late Qing and Republican era reforms generally reflected the 'priorities of professional educators' wedded to the 'quality' agenda. Thus state funding was concentrated on 'key schools', some adapted from old imperial academies, and on institutions of higher learning. China's early modernisers, Pepper argues, 'essentially ignored [Meiji] Japan's mass-level achievement together with the leadership, funding and administrative arrangements necessary to accomplish it' (523). She blames this for pre-1949 China's 'poor record in eradicating illiteracy', though Dikotter (citing VanderVen) suggests that the educational achievements of the Republican era should be seen in a rather more positive light (2009, 66).

Meanwhile, in the Communists' 'base area' of Yan'an from the late 1930s, precedents emerged for two approaches to educational reform. First was a radical village- or community-based scheme for extending basic education through 'irregular' (*minban*) initiatives and adaptations of the old *sishu* (the rudimentary multi-grade, single-room, single-teacher schools found in many Chinese villages) (for more on *minban* schooling, see Chapter 9). This was then challenged from 1938 by newly arrived urban leftists who advocated closing schools and curtailing enrolments to improve standards. By the mid-1940s, the Yan'an leadership appeared to have concluded that creating a system of mass education in a rural setting required: determined leadership from the top; adequate enforcement mechanisms; concerted efforts to elicit local support (and funding); and, essential to maintaining the latter, a degree of uniformity in standards between rural and urban areas. Given the resistance amongst educated elites (including many teachers) to the rapid universalisation of rural schooling, 'enforced political and ideological obedience' ultimately came to be seen as a prerequisite for radical reform (Pepper 1996, 524).

Rather than pursuing this agenda after 1949, the Chinese Communists (CCP) deferred to their Soviet 'big brothers', who by this time had institutionalised a regular and structurally elitist system. However, borrowing from the USSR was not wholesale or uncritical. Soviet precedents adopted included a restructuring of higher education to focus on science and technology, and a greater geographical dispersal of tertiary-level institutions; amongst those rejected were the egalitarian assumptions of Soviet pedagogy and 'various irregular remnants' from the more radical period of the Soviet Union's own past (525). Meanwhile, the introduction of nationwide college-entrance examinations amounted to a re-establishment of the system of imperial examinations abolished in 1905. The construction of a conventional college-preparatory schooling system centred in urban areas was considered essential to train the personnel needed to build up Soviet-style heavy industry, and this created an opportunity for Chinese educators 'to reassert inherited assumptions about how to produce a quality product' (526). With 'irregular' initiatives now abandoned or discouraged, the new education system continued to rest on 'a base of mass illiteracy', while also producing increasing numbers of primary and secondary school graduates for whom there was no place at a higher level of education, or 'insufficient jobs commensurate with their level of training'. These were amongst the 'typical developmental dilemmas' to which the 1950s Soviet model, Pepper argues, provided 'no solution' (526).

However, CCP ideals also committed the Party to overturning the established class structure. To some within the Party, apparently including Mao himself, the emphasis during the 1950s on the need for highly trained personnel seemed to imply that the existing educated elite would 'perpetuate itself into the indefinite future' (527). By the late 1950s, Mao and some of his colleagues were thus searching for alternatives to the Soviet model – spurred on by a growing ideological and strategic rift with the USSR, with which Mao increasingly sought to compete for leadership of the Communist world. This rift inclined Chinese leaders to emphasise the indigenous origins of the Cultural Revolution, and the Great Leap Forward that preceded it, but Pepper suggests that the main features of both movements, at least as regards education, were actually inspired by the Soviet cultural revolution of the 1920s. 'The earlier Stalin,' she remarks, 'had everything in common with Mao as of 1958' (528). By contrast, Mao offered a 'comprehensive and trenchant critique' of 1950s-vintage Stalinism, on the 'pragmatic' as well as ideological grounds that this stifled popular participation in development (Gray 2006, 662). In Gray's view, Mao's interest in transforming peasant 'consciousness' (to which education was crucial) reflected his perception that entrepreneurial rural development would require – as Gunnar Myrdal (1968) was observing at the same time – 'psychological as well as economic changes' amongst the rural masses (Gray 2006, 661).

Plans to expand rural educational access that coincided with the Great Leap (1958–61) were undermined not only by that movement's disastrous economic consequences, but by internal contradictions. The establishment of quality-oriented urban key schools was authorised in the midst of a drive to promote largely vocationalised provision for the masses. The result of this was that 'in city and countryside alike, ... the targeted clientele [rejected] agricultural and "*minban*" alternatives as inferior versions of "real" regular state-run schools' (Pepper 1996, 528). The 1958 key point hierarchies also attempted to 'adapt for regional and nationwide use principles of regional representation and educational achievement inherited from the imperial past, when [in the *keju* or civil service examinations] carefully controlled proportions of candidates were maintained at every level and in every region' (530). An emphasis on class or family background (peasant or proletarian = 'good') in key school entrance criteria meanwhile had the effect of inclining headmasters to favour the children of Party cadres, in part because, amongst those from 'good class backgrounds', these would likely prove most academically competitive.[25] The effect, as Pepper puts it, was to restore 'another time-honoured function of the imperial bureaucratic tradition by inducting the children of a newly empowered "outsider" political establishment into the rarefied world of China's intellectual elite' (530).

In education, the Cultural Revolution took radicalism much further, abandoning a hierarchical, stratified system of schooling altogether, and turning urban youth into Red Guards, before rusticating them along with 'intellectuals'. Teaching and research in universities were decimated, though enrolments recovered, quantitatively at least, by the mid-1970s (416); but basic education in rural areas received a very significant boost (Han 2008; Thøgersen 1991, 2002). By 1976, elementary school enrolment rates were 96 per cent, up from 84.7 per cent in 1965, with promotion rates to junior and senior secondary school at 92 per cent and 63.7 per cent of graduates from the previous level (up from 44.9 per cent and 26.4 per cent respectively) (Pepper 1996, 417). However, the strategy was undermined in part by the way in which earlier initiatives (adoption of the Soviet emphasis on nurturing 'talent', and the key school system) had strengthened professional educators' assumptions concerning the selective, elitist purpose of schooling. Once these assumptions were tied to the ideological 'two-line struggle' in 1966, and 'the lives and careers of all China's top leaders were simultaneously jeopardized', the ultimate result was, in Pepper's words, 'a foregone conclusion' (531).

Pepper portrays China's educated urban elite as a pseudo-Brahminical caste deeply suspicious of educational egalitarianism. She implies that Mao was right in perceiving that the success of an egalitarian model of development depended on challenging the economic, institutional and ideological foundations of urban, elite dominance. In the event, even though most educators remained committed to the 'principles of regularity', associating radical egalitarianism with abysmal quality, Pepper's interviews revealed that many saw their own schools as the high-'quality' exceptions that proved the rule. Many were shocked by the manner in which these were systematically dismantled from 1978, when thousands of rural primary schools were closed or shorn of their junior secondary extensions, key point schools re-established, enrolments strictly capped, and rigid stratification reimposed. This supports her suggestion that Mao and the 'radicals' could perhaps have avoided or moderated the eventual backlash if they had pursued their goals consistently from 1949. As it was, the political and intellectual elite so savagely persecuted during the Cultural Revolution returned quite literally with a vengeance after 1976, more than ever convinced of the folly of egalitarian educational experimentation.

Chinese education and the 'East Asian model'

The years between the end of the Cultural Revolution in 1976 and the formal onset of 'Reform and Opening' in 1978 are widely seen as marking a new educational dawn for China. Destructive Maoist radicalism was rejected, and a sensible, pragmatic rebuilding begun, as the People's Republic came in from the cold and joined the East Asian 'miracle'. In the economic and political spheres, there are strong grounds for such a view. Walder notes how the post-Mao leadership, desperate to revive growth, found 'enviable ... models' on 'China's doorstep' (2015, 342), though Gray actually locates the origins of China's economic take-off (rooted in rural commune- and brigade-based 'Township and Village Enterprises') in the early rather than the late 1970s (2006). Mao, he argues, was convinced that 'growth with equity would be faster' (662), and Korean and Taiwanese experience appeared to bear this out. Either way, Chinese attraction to the East Asian growth model was strengthening in the 1970s, as the economic limitations of the Soviet template became more apparent. In politics, no East Asian society, even Japan, was a functioning multi-party democracy in the late 1970s – indicating the potential for accelerating growth through market mechanisms and opening to the world, while maintaining one-party dictatorship (Walder 2015, 342). In the educational sphere, however, there seems little room for doubt: if 'growth with equity' defined the post-war East Asian developmental model, and if schooling was crucial to this achievement, then Chinese policy from the late 1970s marked a move not towards this model, but away from it.

Rising inequality, in education and more broadly, thus emerges as a central theme in the story of post-Mao China. Comparisons with India still make the overall Chinese achievement in delivering public goods appear impressive, and impressively equitable, though the picture is complicated by large inter-state or inter-provincial variations. Comparisons with post-war Korea, Taiwan or (to a lesser extent) Japan, on the other hand, suggest that there was nothing necessary or inevitable in the abandonment of egalitarianism. Anti-globalists may explain this move as a consequence of China's entrapment in the tentacles of Western-dominated capitalist globalisation, whose guiles a poor, developing country was ill-equipped to resist. But Pepper's analysis suggests that the reasons are to be found much closer to home, in the domestic political dynamic produced by the association of egalitarianism with Maoist terror, and in deep-rooted assumptions concerning the selective and elitist purposes of schooling.

Associated with this dramatic turn away from egalitarianism has been a fundamentally instrumentalist vision of state–citizen relations, illustrated most starkly in 'population planning' policy (whereby the state decides who can have children, and how many) and the rigid household registration system (determining, from birth, each citizen's entitlements and social role). In itself, this instrumentalism marked no break with the Mao era: what changed was the conception of the ends in the service of which the masses were to be instrumentalised. Whereas under Mao they were pressed into the service of a totalitarian (if also egalitarian) political vision, under Deng they were to be utilised above all for pursuit of the 'four modernisations'. For both, the grip of the Party-State over the levers of power was non-negotiable, though while Mao sought to bypass the party apparatus, concentrating authority in his own hands and establishing a direct rapport with the masses, under Deng and his successors the party was to evolve into a more conventional, Soviet-style oligarchy. Ironically, however, it did so while steadily jettisoning its socialist ideological baggage, compelling it to take on board a new legitimating narrative. This has increasingly come to be centred on the twin themes of competition and nationalism.

The combination of an instrumentalist conception of state–citizen relations with an ethos of competition and nationalism has pervaded modern East Asia; indeed, it is this that defines Johnson's 'situational nationalism of the late industrialisers'. What distinguishes post-Mao China from post-war Japan, Korea or Taiwan is the social pervasiveness of the competitive ethos, and its dissociation from discourses of equal opportunity and uniform citizenship. In those societies, the sense that common citizenship implies common entitlements became deeply entrenched in the post-war period, constraining political elites and contributing to democratisation. In China, the fragmentation of citizenship and entitlements (to education and other public goods), especially along urban–rural lines, has been associated with a 'divide-and-rule' strategy (Wright 2010). Meanwhile, in seeking to maintain and legitimise their control over the separate and irreconcilable vested interests thus fostered, the authorities have resorted to xenophobic nationalism. The resultant tensions form another key theme of our analysis.

Despite the focus in this chapter on the relationship between education and economic development, these ethical or ideological issues remind us that education's social role, for better or worse, involves far more than supplying 'human capital' to fuel economic growth. The example of the East Asian 'tigers' shows that, beyond producing a literate and numerate labour force, and supplying a leaven of elite 'talent', education's economic importance may lie less in boosting growth than in distributing the benefits it can confer. Concerns with economic and distributional issues are central to 'practice-oriented' research, with its tendency to assume that 'effectiveness' in these respects is susceptible to technocratic fixes. However, such approaches tend to overlook or ignore the political role of education, and its association with the enhancement or restriction of 'capabilities' in the broadest sense (Sen 1999). By the same token, technocrats typically display a fundamental incuriosity concerning curriculum and pedagogy, or *what* is taught or learnt, and *how*. When the spotlight is trained on such issues, the educational achievements of East Asian societies lose some of their gloss. Curriculum as a tool of deadening conformity, the inculcation of homogenous and totalising visions of national identity, rigid and narrowly focused systems of public assessment, and intense credentialism as a mass pathology are interlinked phenomena found to varying degrees across the region. These involve social and psychological costs unreflected in GDP figures or PISA test results. In China, these costs have been especially acute.

How typically 'East Asian' post-Mao China seems thus depends very much on our focus and perspective. Seen in the light of the economic record of its post-war neighbours, to whose 'growth with equity' education contributed, contemporary China appears divergent. However, shift the focus to politics and culture, and extend the perspective to the late nineteenth century, and significant similarities with those neighbours emerge. Though Pepper hails the 'mass-level achievement' of Meiji Japanese education, contrasting it with the performance of Republican and Communist China, this was definitely not associated with equitable distribution of the fruits of growth; pre-war Japanese society was class-ridden and profoundly hierarchical, and its economic model deeply exploitative (Dower 1975).

Curricula for morality, history and other subjects sought to render the masses unthinkingly loyal to the imperial state, with bureaucratic control even extending to attempts at regulating teachers' reading matter (455). And when Tokyo Imperial University was founded in 1886, its mission was defined as teaching and investigating 'those mysteries of science and learning, arts and crafts *which are of practical service to state necessity*' (454; Dower's emphasis). In the following chapter, as we discuss the development of education policy in China from the late 1970s, the relevance of these Meiji precedents will become readily apparent.

Notes

1 The extent of state involvement is often disguised by convoluted ownership arrangements, but Huang shows that corporations such as Lenovo and Haier, often touted as standard-bearers of capitalist modernisation, are essentially state-controlled entities bankrolled by investment channelled through Hong Kong: 'McKinsey's exhortation that China has "the best possible" business model is equivalent to urging other poor countries to acquire their own Hong Kong' (6).

2 This conclusion is also echoed by Yao Yang of Peking University's China Center for Economic Research (2010), who argues that 'ultimately, there is no alternative to greater democratisation if the CCP wishes to encourage economic growth and maintain social stability'.

3 A conclusion echoed by Shue and Wong (2007, 1).

4 Though it is doubtful whether Sen would regard the East Asian states as exemplary models of 'development as freedom' in other respects, e.g. the position of women and minorities, or the use of schooling to inculcate homogenous and totalising national identities.

5 Deng's early meetings with Lee coincided with the Singaporean leader's launch of a *Learn from Japan* campaign (Avenell 2013).

6 Green (2007) summarises this debate by noting how Wolf (2004) sees state attempts to manage markets as peripheral, whereas the World Bank (1993) saw them as more significant, and Stiglitz (1996) argued that East Asian states actually helped to make markets by playing an 'entrepreneurial role'. Japan and Korea in particular protected domestic markets and promoted exporters.

7 Duara also describes the role that Japan played in transmitting Darwinist ideas to leading Chinese modernisers such as Liang Qichao.

8 Though of course causation in such cases can, and does, run in both directions.

9 Here Green cites Reynolds and Farrell (1996) and Green and Steedman (1993).

10 Earlier, Greene notes how the KMT's 'New Life' movement of the 1930s attempted to combine 'scientism' with Confucian traditionalism (Greene 2008, 31).

11 Coincidentally, the PRC held its own National Science Conference in 1978 (Greene 2008, 152), the same year as Taiwan held an important S&T conference of its own.

12 Nankai was the *alma mater* of Wu Dayou, one of the leaders of S&T policy in Taiwan. In 1993, K.T. Li was invited to a conference in Dalian on China's economic reforms, and then travelled on to Nanjing where his *alma mater* (Dongnan University) 'inaugurated a reading room in his name' (Greene 2008, 153).

13 The acquisition of academic credentials by party functionaries was specifically required by a 1983 directive, stipulating that by 1990 all cadres from county level up would be expected to have a college-level education (Pepper 1996, 489).

14 She alludes here to the way in which the Ministry of Science and Technology in 2004 banned circulation within the PRC of the 2004 Chinese supplement of *Nature* that was critical of state S&T policy (Greene 2008, 164).

15 Here Huang cites K.T. Li's exhortation to Taiwan's government in the 1980s to look at things 'from the entrepreneur's point of view' (280).

16 Zhang *et al.* (2007) note that despite increasing investment in 'public goods' (basic infrastructure, including schools) in rural areas during the period 1998–2003, so that levels in China are now higher than in many developing countries, compared with other East Asian nations at the time of their 'take off', China doesn't look so good. It now invests between $40 and $50 per person in rural areas – but Japan in the 1950s–60s spent about $400 per capita, and in South Korea in the 1970s–80s the comparable figure was over $200 (Shue and Wong, 8).

17 Here they cite the findings of Connelly and Zheng (2007) regarding the persistence of the urban–rural gap in incomes, and a widening gap in the take-up of post-compulsory education, based on analysis of census data through 2000.

18 The government has sought to replace the 'three pillars' of the old socialist social security system (the planned economy allocation of 'iron rice bowl'-style employment, *danwei* support for schools, health care, etc., and lifelong *danwei* membership). The state's new 'Social Insurance' scheme (relatively generous by the standards of developing countries) in 2007 covered 43 per cent of the urban labour force, but excluded the rural population and migrant workers in cities. The situation for rural residents has since improved somewhat.

19 Kerala's fertility rate by the mid-1990s was 1.7, compared with China's 1.9 – both having had similarly high rates in the 1970s (Sen 1999, 220).

20 Though of course it must be noted that gender ratios in the Indian population as a whole are also massively skewed – though due to popular prejudice and state neglect, rather than as a by-product of state action. In Kerala and Tamil Nadu, however, this skewing of gender ratios has not occurred (Sen 1999, 220).

21 Shue and Wong attribute this to 'anxiety about being unable to meet the wage bill for county-level personnel (and the political instability that might cause)', arguing that the transfer system has created 'perverse incentives for local officials to pad their staffs rather than to pursue more efficient uses of available resources'. A 2001 survey (cited by Murphy 2007) showed that in Jiangxi Province only 2 per cent of public spending on education was coming from the centre – while the 'fees-for-tax' reform of 2004 'appears only to have worsened the situation in poor regions' by removing a reliable local source of income, and increasing reliance on the centre (Shue and Wong 2007, 9).

22 Although Pepper notes that this distinction in financing perpetuated the urban–rural divide, just as the rhetoric surrounding transfer of urbanites 'downwards' to the countryside perpetuated the negative associations surrounding rural work.

23 Han Dongping (2008) and Stig Thøgersen (2002) essentially support Pepper's account of education in rural areas during the Cultural Revolution, with two studies focusing on different counties in Shandong Province.

24 Though Dikotter (2009) questions the significance often attached to this 'movement'.

25 The compulsion to ingratiate themselves with the politically powerful was of course another significant motive.

3 The politics of education in post-Mao China

An overview

> America has 1.2 million scientific researchers, the Soviet Union has 900,000, and we have only 200,000. ... From the Meiji Restoration, Japan began to emphasize technology, to emphasize education, and expended great effort on [developing these fields]. … [Since] ours is a proletarian [modernization], we should be able to perform better than them …
>
> In education we must walk on two legs (*liangtui zoulu*) – we must emphasize universalization (*puji*), along with the raising [of standards] (*tigao*). We must set up key primary schools, key middle schools, and key universities. Through a system of strict examinations, we must gather the most outstanding people in key middle schools and key universities.
>
> (Deng Xiaoping, 24 May 1977 – 'Respect knowledge, respect talent' (*zunzhong zhishi, zunzhong rencai*), IED 1573)

Deng's statement epitomises the competitive logic – the urge to 'catch up' – that has animated official policy throughout the Reform era. Much 'practice-oriented' research highlights how education has contributed to real – if very uneven – improvements to the livelihoods of Chinese people, but as we emphasised in Chapter 1, this often overlooks the political dimension: education's role in 'justifying the ways of the state to the people and the duties of the people to the state' (Green 1990, 80). Thøgersen writes that ordinary 'parents did not send their children to school primarily in order to save the nation or build socialism but because they expected the education system to make a positive difference at the personal level' (2002, 6). However, for their political masters that nation-building function has been of supreme importance. From this perspective, Deng differed from Mao perhaps more over means than ultimate ends. Both aspired to build a strong, technologically advanced Chinese state, with a citizenry unquestioningly loyal to the Communist authorities. While their differences were far more than tactical, their divergent socio-economic visions were both intimately related to concerns to maintain Party legitimacy and control. Egalitarian or not, both viewed the world through a neo-Darwinian lens, whereby cut-throat international competition required an instrumentalist conception of state–citizen relations, subordinating the individual to pursuit of national self-strengthening.

Mao sought legitimacy directly from the 'peasants and workers' – over the heads of, and in opposition to, his Party colleagues and 'intellectual' urban elites – in the process attempting to homogenise society in the name of equality. His successors have tolerated or cultivated more diverse constituencies, not least the very elites Mao attempted to destroy. The increasing complexity of educational politics reflects the divergent interests of various groups – semi-skilled rural migrants, college-educated urbanites and so forth – whose strengthening or emergence owes much to earlier Reform-era policy shifts. Amidst rapid and often unpredictable (or unpredicted) social change, the post-Mao Party has struggled to articulate a clear vision of the kind of society it aspires to create, often defaulting to crisis-response mode, while insisting on the need for 'stability' or 'harmony'. At the same time, shifting priorities in education policy reflect calculations of the relative importance of different constituencies, and decisions over whose interests to privilege, that imply a social vision of sorts.

The four main sections in this chapter (3.1–3.4) analyse the national politics of education since the mid-1970s. The first reviews developments between the launch of 'Reform' in 1977/8, when higher education was prioritised, and 1985, when the Central Government signalled a renewed focus on basic schooling. The second covers the years 1985–93, marked by the political turbulence surrounding the Student Movement of 1989. The period from 1992 to 1993 (dealt with in the third section) witnessed the relaunch of marketisation and significant reforms affecting education: first radical fiscal decentralisation, and later a major expansion of higher education. Disquiet over burgeoning inequality – one consequence of the 1990s reforms – prompted attempts at redress after 2002 (especially from 2004 to 2005), discussed in our fourth section. Finally, in a fifth section, we briefly assess developments since the accession of President Xi Jinping.

This rather conventional periodisation should not obscure the complexity of continuity and change across the Reform era as a whole. As Baum notes (1996), political, ideological and economic currents were often cross-cutting – *fang* (relaxation of official control) in one area could be accompanied by *shou* (the tightening of control) in another. This has certainly been true of education, where administrative and budgetary decentralisation have been accompanied by attempts to reinforce political control and ideological conformity – even as the content of official ideology has itself evolved.

Nor should our periodisation obscure important continuities with the pre-Reform period. Urban elites have continued to agonise over how to unchain the nation's destiny from the perceived deadweight of a vast, backward rural hinterland (Pepper 1996; Thøgersen 2002). Meanwhile, educational debate is shaped by ingrained and widely shared cultural assumptions concerning schooling's role in inculcating a 'correct' understanding of morality and human relationships, familial or political (Bakken 2000). Perceptions of this moralising function merge with projects of state legitimation, but also answer parental expectations especially salient across 'Confucian' East Asia, where modernising elites have often adopted an explicitly 'pedagogic' political posture (Fitzgerald 1996).

Also traceable to longstanding tradition are expectations of education's selective function. Examinations originated as a tool for the recruitment of talented administrators, and retain this role. But maintaining a mythology of meritocracy also became crucial to regime legitimation. Schooling inculcated morality, and examinations ensured that future rulers were selected from those whose mastery of this moralising curriculum reflected superiority not just in academic attainment, but also in character. The meritocratic ideal also reinforced a faith in education as a route away from a lifetime shovelling night-soil in the village towards a more fragrant and lucrative career behind a desk. But the bureaucracy or the modern economy cannot provide unlimited employment for graduates schooled in an aversion to manual labour. Hence educational reformers have long sought to promote vocational learning, with the aim of diverting most students away from aspirations to elite status, and into economically 'useful' occupations (Curran 2005). In this respect, too – as we shall see in Chapter 10 – post-Mao reformers have picked up where their pre-Mao forebears left off.

Finally, whatever model of schooling has been favoured at different times, ways have had to be devised to pay for it. Though theoretically unitary, a state the size of China could never hope to both fund and administer mass education primarily from the centre. Policy on the funding and management of basic education thus revolves around how to construct a necessarily devolved system, balancing local responsibility with an element of redistribution sufficient to secure national cohesion. In this respect, as we shall see, governmental actions tend to speak louder than official words. Movements to reform a household registration system that effectively enforces rural–urban apartheid have been tentative and patchy – reflecting both urban vested interests and concerns over 'stability'. Exhortations to local officials to 'correctly' implement centrally mandated policies have not been matched by concerted efforts to ensure a uniform national standard of educational provision. The authorities in Beijing face a dilemma – wanting or needing to devolve responsibility, but fearful of the consequences of instituting systems of local accountability that might ensure effective delivery. Meanwhile, corruption has burgeoned as officials have sought extra-legal means both of boosting dire local finances and lining their own pockets (see Chapter 5).

As society has become more diverse and unequal, but also more educated and prosperous, the Party has adopted more sophisticated techniques of control and accommodation (Gries and Rosen 2010). Both the 'One Child Policy' and the effective demise of the cradle-to-grave world of the old state-owned enterprise (SOE) have intensified a competitive social ethos. Competition for credentials, and for jobs, fuelled by concentrated familial investment in the prospects of 'little emperors' or 'empresses' (Fong 2004), helps focus attention on the private sphere of personal ambition, rather than the public realm of political action – at least while the economic bandwagon keeps rolling. As responsibilities previously borne by a tangled web of institutions – ministries, SOEs and communes – have been transferred to local governments, the latter have found themselves central to the struggle to satisfy 'educational desire' (Kipnis 2011). The central leadership, for its part, represents most problems as ones of implementation rather than policy – deflecting any criticism from the benevolent autocrats in Beijing towards their corrupt and ineffective local agents. Meanwhile, the Party nationally has increasingly trumpeted the fulfilment of patriotic aspirations – reflected in and encouraged by the content of schooling – for asserting China's status as a global power.

The recurrent themes of this analysis of education policy since the 1970s are thus those we outlined in the conclusion to the previous chapter: rising inequality, and with it the entrenchment of powerful vested interests; an increasingly pervasive ethos of competition which, given the association of qualifications with status, has fed rampant credentialism; the persistence of fragmented citizenship, underpinning inequality in access to education, but implicated in a 'divide-and-rule' governance strategy; and, deployed to justify the subordination of individual to nation, and citizen to state, a legitimating narrative no longer socialist (in any meaningful sense), but increasingly nationalist. Mao was gone, but politics remained very much 'in command'.

3.1 NURTURING TALENT AND PROMOTING SCIENCE (1977–85)

At the outset of the 'Reform and Opening' era, education, in Pepper's words, 'set the pace' for more general efforts to reverse the radical Maoist tide. The quotation from Deng Xiaoping that begins the present chapter illustrates this. Science and education fell within Deng's remit as deputy premier, and – deploying a military metaphor – he described his role as 'chief of the rear area; my work consists of searching out talent, supporting scholars and teachers, and supplying money and equipment' (quoted in Pantsov 2015, 330). One of the earliest reformist initiatives was the convening of a National Education Conference in April 1977, followed by a series of related meetings in 1978 (Baum 1996, 56–8). Indeed, Pepper argues that the pre-Cultural Revolution educational establishment was already 'poised for a comeback victory' as early as 1975, when the Education Ministry, abolished in the early stages of the Cultural Revolution, was re-established and began issuing 'quality-enhancing' instructions (1996). Only Mao's death was necessary to enable the establishment to clinch this triumph. Thus 1977 witnessed an internal Party decision to restore the *gaokao*, or national college entrance examinations (in July), and instructions to the People's Education Press to begin editing new, nationally unified teaching materials for primary and secondary schools.

Amidst the intra-Party struggles following the Chairman's death, the decision to roll back his educational measures enjoyed particularly broad support. While economic and political reform presented thornier dilemmas, education reform was an easier sell. Finally resolving the 'red versus expert' conundrum, almost all could agree that 'expertise' was urgently needed, a consensus reflected in the early restoration of the *gaokao*. This signified a decisive reintegration of the political and intellectual establishments – precisely what the

Cultural Revolution had been designed to abolish. Leading reformers such as Hu Yaobang forged close relations with a 'brains trust' of advisers in institutions such as the newly established Chinese Academy of Social Sciences (CASS) (Baum 1996). Calls to raise the 'quality' of the cadre force later led, in 1983, to a decree making a college degree a requirement for senior cadres down to county level from 1990 onwards. As Pepper puts it, 'the categoric Confucian association between knowledge and bureaucratic office had been formally re-established' (Pepper 1996, 489).

One question that has arisen amongst scholars relates to the nature and extent of foreign influence over these post-Mao education policy shifts (an issue to which we return in Chapter 13). Lewin *et al.* characterise a 1985 statement by Deng on the fostering of technical and scientific talent as the 'key' to modernisation as 'redolent of the "modernization theory" promulgated by Western academics in the 1960s' (1994, 17); others have pointed to the very active involvement of the World Bank in China during this period (Yang R. 2010). However, Pepper's work demonstrates both the strong 'indigenous' roots of opposition to Maoism, as well as the extent of references to Chinese experience in Western debates (if there was cross-national influence, it was not all one-way). Seemingly contradictory appeals to (Confucian) tradition on the one hand and Western precedents for 'modernisation' on the other should be seen as aspects of an eclectic strategy for building a reformist coalition.

'Key schools' and the rebuilding of higher education

Higher education was the sector that, as a result of the Cultural Revolution, the reformers saw as having fallen most catastrophically behind the West, the Soviet Union and Japan. Hence early initiatives aimed to restore the flow of 'talent' into China's universities, while raising instructional quality, to ensure the supply of a technocratic and scientific vanguard needed to spearhead modernisation. The distributional concerns of radical Maoism were not just accorded a lower priority, but comprehensively rejected. The reinstatement of urban 'key point' schools, the closure of many rural junior middle and high schools, moves to vocationalise much of the secondary sector, and the restoration of the *gaokao* were all part of a strategy for concentrating educational investment on the nurturing of a modernising elite.

The re-establishment of the 'key point' system had begun in 1976, and for two years proceeded alongside the continued quantitative expansion of schooling. However, reformers chafed at the 'waste' of resources on 'low quality' education for rural youth who, it was widely held, did not need to attend middle school (Pepper 1996, 485). The priority was seen as repairing a decimated tertiary sector. As early as 1977, a secret memorandum was circulated calling for the reduction of rural promotion rates, and between 1978 and 1982 thousands of rural junior secondary and high schools were closed in the name of 'quality'. Promotion rates from elementary to junior secondary school fell from 94 to 66 per cent; and thereon to high school from 71 to 32 per cent. Nationwide, over 60 per cent of all high schools were closed, with a corresponding reduction in enrolments (481). A central aim here appears have been what Pepper terms a 'dual adjustment', reducing the number of graduates from the college-preparatory stream of key point schools while increasing the places available at tertiary level. By the early 1980s, there was rough equilibrium – with about 600,000 graduates of key point high schools competing for about the same number of places in higher education (483). The blatant elitism of the 'key point' concept attracted some public complaint, prompting a superficial 'weakening' of the system and renaming of 'key' institutions later in the decade. However, in fact if not in name, key point schools survived and flourished; a school's reputation, once established, tended to ensure that it attracted both greater funds (public and private) and the best qualified teachers (Thøgersen 1991, 82).

When the educational targets of the Sixth Five Year Plan were announced in the spring of 1981, the overwhelming focus was on development of higher education (IED 1981, 1921). In May of the same year, China's first long-term loan agreement with the World Bank saw just over half of the 1.3 billion dollar total for 1981–96 earmarked for higher education, especially 'key point' programmes in the sciences (IED 1981, 1935). Speeches on education by key reforming leaders reflected a similar pattern of priorities. A November 1982 speech by Zhao Ziyang detailed numerous targets for higher education – an increase of 42 per cent in student numbers between 1980 and 1985, and annual recruitment of 20,000 postgraduate students by 1985 – while mentioning no plans to increase primary or secondary enrolments (IED 1982, 2051).

The overwhelming priority accorded to higher education was further illustrated by Deng's leading ally (at least in the early Reform years) amongst the more senior Party leaders, Chen Yun, who in July 1982 spoke of the need to 'improve the living conditions of middle-aged intellectuals' (those between 35 and 50). These people were, Chen proclaimed, amongst the most crucial to the success of development work now and in the coming years, so it was in the state's interests to make sure that they were well looked after. 'One of the main reasons why Japan and West Germany were able to recover so fast after the war', he declared, 'was that they preserved these key workers and fully deployed their abilities' (IED 1982, 2021).

However, 'preservation' and 'deployment' of existing intellectual manpower was considered insufficient to achieve rapid scientific and technological advance; active engagement with the West would also be necessary. Thus in 1978, Deng Xiaoping ordered the Education Ministry to send 10,000 students to the USA as quickly as possible, and ordered all leading cadres to make at least one trip overseas. 'Deng's aim', writes Pepper, 'was to graft the ways and means of capitalism onto China's socialist system in the hope of making it work more effectively' (Pepper 1996, 490). Universities were encouraged to forge ties with their Western counterparts – although, even amidst the liberalising excitement of the early post-Mao years, the potential political risks attached to such a strategy occasioned significant concern amongst leading reformers (Zhao 2009).

Basic schooling, vocationalisation and education for the masses

Although the 1990s are often seen as a time of particularly acute crisis for rural education, as fiscal reforms severely dented local revenues (see below), the 1980s were in many ways as bad, or worse. Decollectivisation and the rapid expansion of rural industry, by rendering families more dependent on their own production, increased the 'opportunity costs' of education, or the advantages of school nonattendance or early dropout (Lewin *et al.* 1994). At the same time, the weakening of collective arrangements for school funding hit many local education budgets. As the *minban* sector was sidelined, Maoist work-study experiments wound down, and many commune senior middle schools closed, rural education experienced a significant setback. The percentage of children entering school registered a slight but notable decline after 1976 (Pepper 1996, 483), while the proportion completing primary schooling and progressing to the next level fell dramatically (see above).

If it is therefore correct, as Huang and others have argued, to see the 1980s as a golden age for the rural economy, the same was not true for rural education. Concentration on the key point system and the nurturing of 'talent' at tertiary level implied a marked bias towards urban China. The rationale for this was rehearsed by Zhao Ziyang during a Politburo discussion on 27 May 1980:

> China has one billion people, and its economy is not developed or balanced, so we can't raise the level of education at the same rate everywhere. … [T]hose areas with better conditions must raise the level of their education, while we should not place such great expectations on more backward areas. We must focus on the key points (*yao ba zhongdian zhuahao*). Investment in education and teaching resources must be concentrated, so that advanced areas can be raised up first. With uniform expectations (*pingjun yaoqiu*), we can't achieve anything … [W]herever there is an area with better foundations, we should quickly send talented people, and concentrate our efforts on establishing good universities and key high schools there.
>
> (IED 1980, 1813)

As in economics, where the early 1980s witnessed the establishment of the first 'Special Economic Zones' (SEZs), calls to allow different regions to proceed 'at different speeds' and 'in line with local conditions' became mantras of education policy at this time. A March 1981 Ministry 'Opinion' calling for a six-year system of primary schooling thus noted that only Beijing, Tianjin and Shanghai were currently equipped to adopt this model (IED 1981, 1915). Other areas were warned to proceed cautiously, moving from a five- to six-year system only when availability of trained teachers and suitable facilities allowed this without compromising 'quality'. Such statements disguised the extent to which official policy actually involved dismantling or scaling back educational provision in many areas.

Determining the 'quality' of education provided in the village schools of the 1970s is hard, given the anecdotal nature of much of the evidence, and the hostility of most Chinese sources, official or unofficial (including the memoirs of formerly rusticated intellectuals). The sort of Spartan conditions depicted in Ah Cheng's novella, *Haizi Wang* (*King of the Children* – filmed by Chen Kaige in 1987), in which a 'sent-down' high-school student assigned to teach at a village school in 1976 finds that his students have no textbooks, were no doubt commonplace. However, as was noted in the previous chapter, the view that Mao-era village schools were generally useless or worse is not borne out by local case studies (Pepper 1996; Thøgersen 2002; Han 2008), nor by measures of general literacy in 1970s China compared with India (Sen 1999) (see previous chapter).

Senior political figures were nonetheless insistent that the Cultural Revolution era had been an unmitigated disaster for education, rendering a restoration of 'quality' imperative. In February 1981, Yang Xiufeng (Minister of Education in the pre-Cultural Revolution years) spoke of the urgent need to 'increase education spending as a proportion of our GDP' in order to improve a 'backward situation' (IED 1981, 1908) – a call often repeated by educationalists over the next thirty years. But in lamenting a fall in 'spending per student' at secondary level of 55 per cent between 1965 and 1978, he failed to note that this had happened in the context of a huge rise in student numbers. Instead, he highlighted the 'shameful' statistic that, as of 1975, China ranked 141st out of 150 states in per-student spending. School facilities were often very poor 'even in Beijing'. This, he concluded, underlined the pressing need to raise educational 'quality' (*zhiliang*), and ensure thorough training of morals, mind and body (*de, zhi, ti*).

Yang did acknowledge, however, that the relatively low cost to the state of educational provision was largely down to the widespread use of *minban* teachers (see Chapters 5, 7 and 9). These teachers, generally lacking formal qualifications, were employed by communes or villages, rather than by the state, at very low salaries paid from funds raised within local communities themselves (and thus not factored into figures for public spending per student). According to Yang, these constituted 60 per cent of the total teaching workforce as of 1981, and 72 per cent in rural areas. He emphasised that their pay and conditions had to be improved – though with a focus on primary rather than junior secondary schooling. 'Some middle school teachers, and the majority of primary school teachers', he urged, 'should gradually be made employees of the state', provided they were 'qualified'. The rate of progress would 'naturally' depend on local circumstances, and it was 'unrealistic' for the state to bear all the costs: provision and maintenance of premises and facilities should be largely left to the local community. Yang nonetheless stressed the 'new contradictions' resulting from rural decollectivisation, as the institutions that had previously paid *minban* salaries were abolished or weakened, and the value of those salaries relative to average incomes plummeted. He concluded:

> I must therefore say a little more about the problems affecting teachers in the hope of bringing this issue to general notice. If the teaching force is unstable and ill at ease, this will not just have a serious impact on the quality of education, but will also increase social instability in many other respects.

Concerns to maintain 'stability' – political and social – were at the heart of much official thinking on education but, for some, dictated restricting rather than expanding rural access to schooling. It was feared that overproduction of junior secondary or senior high graduates risked nurturing a population of under-employed, semi-educated ex-peasants schooled in an aversion to manual labour. As it was, mass closures, particularly of junior middle schools, in the late 1970s and early 1980s, sparked protests in many areas (Pepper 1996, Chapter 17). However, these proved manageable in the context of growing opportunities for gainful employment within a rapidly expanding rural economy. In effect, the Party's technocrats were engineering a situation in which the economically liberated peasants would be incentivised to divert their energies away from 'excessive' or inappropriate schooling – with its tendency to encourage potentially destabilising aspirations to urban employment – and towards the raising of agricultural and rural industrial productivity.

This in turn would ease the task of feeding and otherwise funding the still largely state-socialist urban economy, including the (invariably urban-based) key point high schools and universities. Indeed, in the cities the restoration of the pre-Cultural Revolution *status quo* meant, amongst other things, a revival of the *danwei zhi* (or 'work unit system'), with educational institutions at every level run by and for government bodies and state enterprises (see Chapters 4 and 5). The household registration or *hukou* system meanwhile ensured that rural residents were denied access to the urban services that their taxes and labour supported. If economic liberalisation was the carrot encouraging peasants to stay in their villages, the *hukou* system was the stick deterring them from migrating to the cities – where the largely unreformed urban economy remained incapable of providing them with gainful employment.

The high priority accorded to security and stability in official calculations is further illustrated by the main exception to the underfunding of rural education – arrangements for basic schooling in 'border areas', largely populated by 'minority nationalities'. An October 1979 directive stipulated that *minban* teachers in such areas should be fast-tracked to state-employed (*gongban*) status. 'Strengthening inter-ethnic solidarity' (*minzu tuanjie*), 'stabilizing border regions' and promoting their 'socialist modernization' were cited as overriding goals (IED 1979, 1748). The same document stressed that teachers elsewhere would have to 'carry on eating however much they are eating now'. This contrasts tellingly with official solicitude for teachers of 'experimental' classes in regular (invariably urban) primary and junior secondary schools, who the following month were awarded extra payments and subsidies (IED 1979, 1757).

Moves to vocationalise much senior secondary schooling were also intimately linked to concerns over social stability. Vocationalisation was seen as a means of curbing applications to the 'quality' stream of regular higher education, and instead equipping more students with economically useful skills (Thøgersen 1991). The closure of rural junior secondary schools was accompanied by calls to promote technical education, with the aim of promoting agricultural productivity (e.g. a State Council notice of May 1983; IED 2087). However, the initial focus of plans to extend junior secondary education (regular or vocational) was urban, not rural. In 1982, the Sixth Five-Year Plan envisaged the universalisation of junior secondary education in urban areas by 1985 (IED 1982, 2055). But for senior high schools, 'reform' was to be prioritised over expansion. 'Regular' senior high schools were assigned a recruitment target of 2.8 million students by 1985 – a reduction of one million from 1980 levels. By contrast, vocational middle schools (*zhiye zhongxue*) were mandated to increase recruitment by 1.16 million to 1.4 million (a rise by a factor of 5.5). Little wonder that, as Lewin *et al.* note (1994), the supply of qualified vocational teachers could not keep up with the pace of expansion in this sector, though this was just one of many problems (see Chapter 10).

The combination of rural-focused economic reform with quite draconian new restrictions on educational access for rural residents make 'liberalisation' a misleading characterisation of developments during the early Reform years. While economic policy harnessed rural energies to the cause of promoting growth, education policy was effectively tasked with reinforcing stability, which meant keeping the peasants in their place. Endorsement of the concept that some would 'get rich first' implied expanded social opportunity for all, and many farmers did indeed profit. But educational reforms from the late 1970s, by privileging the key point sector at the expense of rural schooling, ensured that access to qualifications, status and, ultimately, power would flow disproportionately to urban elites. The resultant tensions were not just social and economic, but ideological: this was clearly not what Mao, or for that matter Marx, had advocated. The Party would need to adapt its legitimating narrative, and here education, once again, had a central role to play. But while intra-Party consensus over the restoration of educational elitism came relatively easily, the revision of socialist messages proved far more contentious.

Redefining political correctness for the post-Mao era

Enduring divisions within the Party ensured that ideological change was effectively fudged throughout the 1980s. The 'Four Cardinal Principles' – Marxism, dictatorship of the proletariat, Communist Party leadership and 'the socialist road' – were promulgated by Deng in 1979, and reaffirmed in the PRC Constitution of 1982, but interpretations of them differed widely. Perhaps more than anything else, what underpinned the broad reformist coalition was shared experience of Cultural Revolutionary victimhood and determination to forestall a repeat performance by preventing a return to one-man autocracy. In June 1981, the Central Committee's 'Resolution on certain questions in the history of our Party' publicly acknowledged Mao's 'mistakes', assessing his legacy as 'seven parts good and three parts bad' (IED 1981, 1941). While he was thus largely spared the posthumous loss of face suffered by Stalin, Mao's successors, like those of the Soviet dictator, vowed to abjure personality cults forever after. However, divisions soon emerged between those who felt that a measure of political liberalisation would be needed to enforce official accountability and guard against abuses of power, and others who feared that any relaxation of 'democratic centralism' would threaten Party authority. Liberalism on economic and political matters often, but by no means always, went together, as exemplified by Hu Yaobang, Zhao Ziyang, and some younger officials in their entourages. But the reverse was also often true. For many, talk of encouraging greater 'bottom-up' participation in decision-making evoked raw memories of humiliation at the hands of Mao's Red Guards.

Unlike the relatively liberal advocates of political reform as the solution to corruption and poor governance, conservative, often older, voices stressed 'the moral and spiritual sources of behavioural malfeasance' (Baum 1996, 194). Spiritual malaise demanded spiritual solutions. Thus calls for 'thought reform' followed the 'Democracy Wall' episode of 1978–9 and the *Gengshen* reforms of 1980 (in some ways the high tide of political liberalisation). They increased again from mid-1982, as concerns over rising corruption and 'decadent' Western influences prompted exhortations to promote 'socialist spiritual civilisation'. In short, every time a loosening of constraints on freedom of expression led, as it inevitably did, to public criticism troubling to senior leaders, such episodes of *fang* were followed swiftly by periods of *shou*, or reassertions of ideological orthodoxy. By the same token, when reaction spawned challenges to the case for economic reform and 'openness' to the West, and threatened prospects for trade expansion and technology transfer, a halt would be called and the pendulum would swing back in a liberal direction. Such shifts were generally signalled through public pronouncements by Deng himself.

For example, on 2 July 1983, at the height of the 'Anti-Spiritual Pollution Campaign', the Propaganda Ministry issued an 'Opinion on Strengthening Propaganda and Education in Patriotism', urging revisions to curricula for subjects such as History and Geography. However, three months later, Deng effectively called a halt to the whole campaign, with a speech that coined the 'three towards' (*san ge mianxiang*). 'Education', he declared, 'must face towards modernization, face towards the world, and face towards the future' (IED 1983, 2134). This reflected fears that over-emphasising the hostility or corrupting influence of the outside world threatened to undermine the wider case for reform. Nevertheless, the most senior leaders, such as Deng and Chen Yun, seemed to retain faith in the power of education to transform both public and personal morality. By early 1985, rising concerns over corruption on the part of the 'sons of high officials' (*gaogan zidi*) contributed to another swing of the pendulum. Looking to shore up his support on the right flank, on 6 May Deng fulminated against 'bourgeois liberalization', equating it with 'taking the capitalist road'. He decried the rise in thinking that 'worships the "democracy" and "freedom" of Western capitalist countries', insisting that 'China must modernize, but absolutely not liberalize, and absolutely not take the road of Western capitalism' (IED 1985, 2274). The first half of 1986 saw a toning down of such rhetoric and renewed discussion of institutional reform, but continuing internal Party tensions led Deng later that year to sacrifice his top reformist protégée, Hu Yaobang, in an attempt to appease the conservatives.

Like Mao and many an earlier Confucian emperor, Deng thus revealed a propensity to resort to *jiaohua*, or 'transformation through education', to curb official misconduct or public discontent – even if his programmes of 'thought reform' differed in content from his predecessor's. At the very least, invoking the power of education to inoculate against any moral or cultural contagion consequent on economic liberalisation or opening to the West was key to reassuring conservative elements within the Party. Reaffirming the Marxist faith through curricula and textbooks, even while contravening it in economic and commercial policy, was part of a tacit bargain struck with the state-socialist old guard as Deng sought to maintain the momentum of reform through the mid-1980s. It was a fragile compact that was soon to be tested to breaking point.

3.2 BACK TO BASICS? (1985–93)

The year 1985 is widely seen as a watershed in Chinese education policymaking, since it witnessed the promulgation of the first comprehensive post-Mao blueprint for educational development. To symbolise the importance attached to education, a new State Education Commission (SEC) was also created, ostensibly giving education more institutional clout within government. The 1985 reforms were otherwise largely an attempt to lend coherence to various initiatives already underway, bringing greater efficiency and focus to projects such as senior secondary vocationalisation. They also publicly affirmed the central government's commitment to universalising basic education, even while an ever-greater portion of the burden of delivery was shifted to local governments. The emphasis in 1985 on basic education, and the promulgation in April 1986 of the Compulsory Education Law, mandating the universalisation of nine years of compulsory education by 2000, signalled the beginning of a new phase in the development of the system. Urgent repairs to higher education, and the demolition of 'Leftist' excrescences at lower levels, prioritised after 1976, were seen as essentially complete by the mid-1980s. It was time to look afresh at the entire structure, and plan for new construction.

Compulsory education, vocationalisation, and financial and administrative reform

'The basic aims', began the document officially launching the 1985 reforms, 'are to raise the quality (*suzhi*) of the nation, to produce more talented personnel (*rencai*), and to produce good talented personnel' (IED 1985, 2285). It was thus made clear from the start that a renewed focus on the expansion of basic education would involve no compromise over quality. Officials were reminded, in a series of subsequent pronouncements from Beijing, of the need to ensure quality and restrain enrolments in areas with 'unsuitable' economic conditions. In September 1986, this was spelt out by the Party's Central Committee in comments that disapprovingly noted the 'reappearance' in some areas of the tendency to expand junior secondary places through the practice of primary schools 'wearing hats' (*dai mao*) (IED 1986, 2496). It was stressed that the rate of progress towards full implementation of compulsory education would vary from province to province depending on levels of development, and that 'practical' decisions would have to be taken at provincial or local (township or county) level.

No decisions were more practical than those relating to school funding. Financial constraints constituted both the most severe challenge to extending educational access, and the most powerful factor restraining local authorities in poorer regions from expanding 'unsuitable', 'low-quality' provision. Writing in 1994 on 'the impact of the 1985 reforms' (and implicitly discounting the impact of earlier Maoist initiatives), Lewin *et al.* observed that

> China has been able to achieve high enrolment rates despite devoting a relatively small percentage of GNP and of its national budget to education. For much of the 1980s less than 3% of GNP and about 6% of government expenditure were allocated to education.
>
> (1994, 214)

These figures, as they acknowledge, do not account for the extent of communal or extra-budgetary 'contributions' to the financing of basic education. Lewin *et al.* also attribute China's ability to achieve so much with so little to the low level of salary costs, held down in part by the fact that, as of 1987, 'as many as 45 percent' of teachers were still 'publicly supported' (*minban*) (214) (see previous section). In 1988, the average spending on education per Chinese child was about 5 per cent of *per capita* GDP, compared with a mean for low-income countries of about 13.5 per cent (214). In 1993, the SEC committed to raising the proportion of GDP spent by the state on education to 4 per cent, although this ambition would remain unrealised until 2012 (Zhou *et al.* 2016, 111; see Chapter 5).

Meanwhile, financial decentralisation served as a highly effective brake on inappropriately rushed expansion. In 1985, 'transferring responsibility for developing basic education to local level' was explicitly linked to 'systematically implementing nine years of compulsory education' (IED 1985, 2285). A 'systematic' approach involved giving freer rein to 'local initiative', in recognition of the fact that local authorities, aware of local economic conditions, would be best able to adapt educational provision to suit them. By the same token, however, reliance on 'local initiative' in financial matters ensured that wealthier areas, better able not just to fund high schools but also to provide employment for their graduates, would produce more of them. The *hukou* (household registration) system, by deterring mobility from rural to urban or from poorer to richer regions, constituted an additional restraint on over-rapid educational expansion in 'backward' areas.

By the late 1980s, Party leaders had reasons to worry about any development that might boost the flow into China's cities of over-educated peasants with aspirations beyond their station. In the cities, still largely unreformed economically, problems of inflation, discontent at the distribution of the benefits of reform, and growing outrage at official corruption, all worsened during the late 1980s – especially affecting those on fixed incomes (including students) (Baum 1996, 191). 'The comprehensive reform of urban education' was a key focus of policy during these years, with moves from five- to six-year primary schooling and towards universal junior secondary education proceeding most rapidly in urban areas. The return of 'sent-down' intellectuals, the revival of higher education and the re-establishment of key point schools also meant that the cities were increasingly populated by 'talented personnel' demanding suitable outlets for their talents. Notwithstanding the establishment of the first SEZs during this decade, the continuing dominance of SOEs, staffed through centralised manpower planning, restricted the capacity of the urban economy to accommodate such aspirations.

The rural economy during the late 1980s continued to grow at a healthy pace, albeit with significant regional variations; but official pronouncements emphasised that variation was to be embraced. In October 1986, a widely circulated editorial in *People's Education* (*Renmin Jiaoyu*) discussed 'What we can learn from Pingdu', a rural county near Qingdao (Shandong Province). Though very poor and under-developed until 1980, with threadbare educational facilities, Pingdu now boasted a high-quality schooling system with a stable teaching force. The latter achievement was particularly noteworthy, given low salaries and problems with teacher retention during these years (problems that would worsen in many areas during the 1990s). Average rural incomes in the county had increased from 98 yuan per person in 1979 to 624 in 1985, but the editorial stressed that educational improvements were not just the 'natural' result of rising prosperity, pointing to examples of more prosperous areas elsewhere with sub-standard provision. Pingdu's experience therefore illustrated the potential of 'local initiative'. In a country as large and varied as China, national policies could not be expected adequately to address local circumstances; local authorities should creatively develop their own strategies within the broad guidelines set in Beijing, feeding back to the centre the results of their experience (IED 1986, 2526). The following year, the SEC similarly publicised the exemplary record of Hebei Province, where the Governor, Gao Yang, had encouraged early experiments in diversifying educational funding (IED 1987, 2606–7). Despite the upbeat tone in which such 'models' were celebrated, the subtext was clear: local authorities could not expect subsidies from the centre. In education, every province or county must fend for itself.

At the same time, the SEC never missed an opportunity to stress that educational development should proceed alongside and serve economic development, chiefly through regulating the supply of 'talent' (*rencai*). This was intimately related to the goal of 'adapting the structure of secondary education, and energetically promoting vocational education' (IED 1985, 2285). In 1987, He Dongchang (Minister of Education from 1982 to 1985, then Vice-director of the SEC from 1985 to 1992) reiterated the urgent need for a change of 'direction' in rural education (IED 1987, 2656). Invoking comparisons with West Germany, Japan and America in terms of workforce 'quality' and productivity (particularly in the field of technology), he related this to the need to promote high-quality and comprehensive basic education in rural areas. The following year, citing the example of France (which he had just visited), He attributed the 'advanced' state of French agriculture to its highly developed system of agricultural and vocational education (IED 1988, 2789). In the same year, the journal *Renmin Jiaoyu* lamented the tendency of rural schools to foster aspirations to leave the countryside and pursue further (academic) education. It blamed over-reliance on rote learning for a failure to develop generic skills of independent learning or problem solving. Rural school graduates were portrayed as lacking 'knowledge of the technology of production' and being 'unable to adapt themselves to the needs of the [rural] market economy'. Passing 'examinations in chemistry and physics' implied no knowledge of 'the nature and uses of pesticide and agricultural machinery' (Lewin *et al.* 1994, 25).

The vocationalisation drive was broadly endorsed by observers associated with the international development community, even if problems were noted. The latter included difficulties with teacher recruitment resulting, in part, from the rapidity of the expansion. In Pan'an county, Zhejiang, Lewin *et al.* found that 'the percentage of teachers reaching the qualification "requirement" in different types of schools was 30% in [regular] senior secondary schools, 14% in vocational and technical schools, 30% in junior secondary schools, and 68% in primary schools' (1994, 29–30). Nonetheless, they adjudged vocational education to have been relatively successful in addressing skills shortages resulting from rapid economic growth and the educational failures of the Cultural Revolution. In other developing countries, vocational training had been expanded in attempts to solve existing unemployment problems (an approach perhaps best summarised as 'if we train them, jobs will come'). China, on the other hand, was credited with pursuing economic policies that rendered the rural labour market capable of absorbing vocational graduates, thus preventing mass migration to the cities, and rising urban unemployment. Lewin *et al.* also saw the barring of vocational students from sitting the *gaokao* as important in limiting credentialism (1994, 220).

However, as we discuss further in Chapter 10, vocationalisation was a strategy beset with contradictions, and inconsistently pursued. When given an option, parents and students almost invariably chose the 'regular' route; Cultural Revolutionary efforts to erase the stigma of 'education through labour' had spectacularly backfired. The One Child Policy also threatened to undermine popular acceptance of vocationalisation. Families with multiple children might resign one child to the vocational track – but when all hopes were invested in a single offspring, this was far less likely (Lewin *et al.* 1994, 220). Lewin *et al.* do not remark on the particular prevalence of one-child families in China's cities (population planning being more laxly enforced in the countryside), which during the 1990s witnessed the rise of an educated, increasingly affluent, middle class. Such social and economic changes were to have significant implications for educational development.

It was thus ironic that Lewin *et al.*'s approving comments on China's rural-focused 'strategies for industrialization' (220) were published at precisely the point (1993–4) when the focus of economic policy was shifting in favour of the cities (Huang 2008; see previous chapter). The decisive nature of that shift, and its significance, would only become apparent in retrospect, but in 1993 Lewin *et al.* could already see that 'trends to increase the proportion of educational expenditure derived from local sources' risked exacerbating 'differences between the amount of resource available per child in relatively rich and relatively poor areas' (1994, 217). The fact that most of the fieldwork for their study was conducted in Zhejiang, perhaps the wealthiest and most 'developed' province, may have inclined them to take a relatively rosy view of China's educational achievements and prospects. Even there, however, they noted that 'the levy of additional taxes, raised officially by the State Council in 1990 from 1 to 2 per cent, places a heavy burden on some communities' (29).

The year 1990 also saw the Jomtien Conference, and UNESCO's 'Education for All' declaration. China's record in expanding access to basic education and raising literacy meant that it was already widely hailed as a developing country model, even if, in the era of the 'Washington Consensus' (Mundy 2002), many observers preferred to forget the pre-Reform foundations for these achievements. In 1990 itself, international praise for post-Mao China's educational record was nonetheless relatively muted. This was due less to awareness of its complex and problematic nature than to the opprobrium China attracted following the 1989 Tiananmen Incident. The crushing of the Student Movement would have immediate implications for higher education, but the related political turmoil also crucially influenced the calculations that would shape China's subsequent economic and educational development.

Higher education and the Student Movement of 1989

The last major aim of the 1985 reforms related to tertiary education. By the mid-1980s, reformers were increasingly voicing doubts over the use of centralised manpower planning for allocating students to courses and graduates to jobs. The 1985 plan envisaged greater institutional autonomy in such areas, by the same token introducing a degree of competition in the hope that this might induce a greater focus on economically 'relevant' skills (IED 1985, 2285). However, policymakers proceeded cautiously, and not just because of conservative opposition within the Party. As Lewin *et al.* noted in the early 1990s (1994), while some graduates might embrace a more open labour market, others would fear the withdrawal of the 'iron rice bowl' of a guaranteed position after graduation. As the urban economy experienced a downturn in the late 1980s, fear and suspicion of reform in this area became just one ingredient in a cocktail of grievances that sparked campus demonstrations across the country.

Policymakers continued to hail science as the key to modernisation, but talked less of the further expansion of higher education than they had in the first flush of reformist enthusiasm. Vice-Premier Li Peng, whose portfolio included the directorship of the SEC, declared in his 1988 'Work Report' that 'Science and technology are the key, education is the foundation', but called for 'more science and technology workers to directly serve economic development', so as to more rapidly 'transform the results of scientific and technological work into productive force'. He emphasised the vital importance of basic education to 'raising the educational level and the *suzhi* [quality] of the entire nation', and stressed that this should become a 'key point' (*zhongdian*) of educational work. In higher education, meanwhile, the priority was to nurture a more competitive spirit in order to raise 'quality' (IED 1988, 2735).

The cooling ardour of some senior leaders for further university expansion was related to the limited capacity of the still mostly state-run urban economy to absorb 'high-level talent'. However, it also reflected the failure of many intellectuals to requite the regime's passionate embrace of higher learning with loyal endorsements of the Party line. Disenchantment was fuelled from the mid-1980s by several related phenomena, including a new wave of free expression in the arts and literature, increasing socioeconomic discontent in the cities, and a sharply increasing urban crime rate (Baum 1996, 189). Rising urban inflation later in the decade, especially serious for those on fixed incomes, helped intensify discontent on university campuses. A sense of relative impoverishment amongst students and professors heightened their fury at the corrupt behaviour of unaccountable university administrators, accused of skimping on catering and facilities while lining their own pockets (see Chapter 11).[1] Resentment derived additional intensity from intellectuals' traditional sense of themselves as an elite charged with guiding China's destiny. The legacy of twentieth-century 'patriotic' student activism, dating back to the post-World War I May Fourth Movement, further reinforced a sense of obligation to speak out on issues affecting national interests or dignity, ranging from Japanese historical revisionism to domestic corruption.

As leaders realised that universities were not just nurseries of scientific 'talent', but also potential hotbeds of 'bourgeois liberalization', their response alternated between threats and blandishments. A notable liberal was the physicist Fang Lizhi, whose Chinese University of Science and Technology in Hefei became one of the early centres of student protest. In November 1986, Fang embarked on a speaking tour of Chinese universities, calling for political democratisation. The following month, Deng Xiaoping raised the 'banner of opposition to bourgeois liberalisation', demanding a resolute response to 'student disturbances'. The compilers of the official compendium of education policy documents explain that this was a response to protests in Hefei, Beijing and elsewhere, where 'a very small number' of students had challenged the leadership of the Party and the principles of socialism, had obstructed traffic, and generally disrupted public order (IED 1986, 2561). However, late 1988 found Deng in more emollient mood, 'considering educational issues from the perspective of grand strategy' (IED 1988, 2796). Alluding to complaints he had recently heard from an old Peking University professor, he stressed the need to ensure proper pay and conditions for teachers, 'however difficult this may be'. 'Solving educational problems', he opined, should be a priority, 'even if it means sacrificing a little speed' in terms of economic development. Otherwise, he warned, there would be cause for regret 'in 20 years time'.

But trouble would arrive far sooner than that. As student protests escalated in March 1989, Deng confided in the visiting President Museveni of Uganda: 'Our greatest error of the past ten years has been in the field of education' (IED 1989, 2851). He pinpointed in particular the weakness of 'thought and politics work'. While the economy had grown, and living standards improved, 'we have not told the people, including Party members, that they ought to hold fast to our traditions of struggling to overcome hardship'. Alluding to corruption amongst the children of senior officials, a major complaint of the protesters, he argued that 'with these traditions, we can combat the phenomenon of corruption, and old cadres can control their children'. Looked at 'dispassionately', he claimed, this moral 'error' was a more serious concern than problems such as inflation.

This targeting of 'thought and politics work' reflected once again the tendency of Party elders to see 'thought reform' as the stock solution to social problems or political discontent. Calls for the strengthening of instruction in 'thought and politics' punctuated the late 1980s, returning with renewed force after 4 June 1989. Less than three weeks after that fateful date, the *China Education Newspaper* (*Zhongguo Jiaoyu Bao*), alluding to Deng's earlier comments, published an editorial entitled 'Reflecting on the Greatest Error, Strengthening Thought Education' (IED 1989, 2869). The following month, Jiang Zemin, newly installed as Party General Secretary, stressed the crucial role of moral education (IED 1989, 2872). 'Forget the great ideals of Communism', he raged, 'some young people nowadays don't even have basic national self-respect or ... patriotism!'. In a move to inculcate future university students with such sentiments, the SEC in late July mandated activities for primary schools taking the theme 'Fervently love the CCP, fervently love the socialist motherland, fervently love the Chinese People's Liberation Army' (IED 1989, 2873).

A hiatus in economic reform also ensued, as Zhao Ziyang's fall seemed to mark the victory of those, such as Li Peng, who had argued for a more measured pace of change. Li applied the brakes to educational reform, too. Speaking in late November, he emphasised China's status as a 'developing country', massive population and relative poverty, warning that it would take 'thirty to fifty years to reach the standard of middle-level developed countries' (IED 1989, 2902). Recycling earlier Deng slogans, he called for education to 'face modernization, face the world, and face the future', and to 'serve socialist construction'. With regard to higher education, he stated that:

> The number of higher education institutions in our country is already sufficient for our current level of economic development, and the important thing now is to raise the quality of teaching. The content and methods of teaching must be reformed, to ensure that graduates can meet the needs of society.

Adult and continuing education received far more attention in Li's speech, perhaps reflecting a perception that mature students would be more focused on acquiring work-related skills, and less politically excitable. These priorities were reiterated in the 1991 outline for the Eighth Five-Year Plan. Progress in universalising basic education and expanding 'secondary-level vocational and technical education' were emphasised, and substantial attention was devoted to adult education. However, in the sphere of higher education, it was stated that 'postgraduate and undergraduate education should basically remain at the current scale' (IED 1991, 3138).

Meanwhile, the student activists, prodigal children of Reform, were subjected to a sweeping crackdown. Those student leaders who did not escape into exile were detained, with ringleaders subjected to long sentences of 'reeducation through labour'. Meanwhile, intensive programmes of military training for all college students were introduced, targeted especially at those universities most central to the protests, such as Peking and Fudan (IED 1990, 3024). New regulations relating to the 'management of order on campuses' were introduced in late 1990 (IED 1990, 3029), and ideological education work was stepped up. A set of behavioural 'rules' for higher education institutions listed as the first rule:

> Protect the interests of the Motherland. Do not engage in any activity that harms the honour or glory of the Motherland, breaches the four basic principles, or endangers social order. Oppose any activity that destroys social peace and unity'.[2]
>
> (IED 1990, 3029)

The halting of university expansion, combined with this more disciplinarian regime, seemed to indicate harder times ahead for China's gilded urban youth. However, it would not be long before another dramatic policy shift brought the distribution of educational and economic privilege into closer alignment, to the signal benefit of the nascent urban middle class.

Political and ideological shifts, and the renewal of reform

Perhaps even more traumatic for Party leaders than the events of June 1989 was the subsequent spectacle of Communist collapse in Eastern Europe and the Soviet Union. As Americans celebrated the 'End of History' and the dawn of a 'unipolar' world, many Chinese – not just within the Party – perceived the fulfilment of fears spawned in earlier twentieth-century conflicts, and nurtured through decades of propaganda and schooling. The dismemberment of the Soviet Union, the vision of a triumphant, 'hegemonic' America, China's post-Tiananmen ostracism, and widespread Western speculation that the Beijing regime would also fall, perhaps heralding a breakup of the Chinese state, all contributed to achieving what programmes of 'thought reform' could never have done alone. They lent credence to depictions of a hostile and dangerous world, in which foreign forces would take advantage of Chinese weakness to undermine the stability and integrity of the state. After all, what foreigners had apparently just done to the Soviet Union, they had – as every Chinese schoolboy knew – tried to do to China a century earlier. This was crucial to explaining why, as Marxist orthodoxy crumbled in the 1990s, faith in that other 'enlightenment' creed, liberalism, seemed to evaporate with it (see Barmé 2000).

The liberal beliefs that had animated many 1980s intellectuals were reflected in the documentary series *He Shang* (River Elegy), broadcast in the summer of 1988. Baum summarises the message of the series:

> Painting a grim picture of the enervating long-term effects of China's insular traditions and atavistic values, the authors of "River Elegy" were openly and severely critical of the dogmatic chauvinism inherent in classical Confucianism and revolutionary Maoism alike; by the same token, they were lavish in their praise of modern Western technology, institutions and values.
>
> (Baum 1996, 231–2)[3]

But in the early 1990s, triumphalist, Western-led 'globalisation' seemed to many a predatory and menacing force – an impression reinforced by NATO involvement in the agonising dissolution of Yugoslavia. Despite fresh memories of the 1989 crackdown, 'many intellectuals [during the 1990s] were more supportive of their own government and more critical of the West than at any time since the May Fourth Movement of 1919' (Fewsmith 2008, 7).

Party ideologues in the early 1990s were quick to tap strains of xenophobic patriotism amongst students and intellectuals. Although the Mao-era Stakhanovite exemplar, Lei Feng, featured in a 1990 campaign aimed at primary students (IED 1990, 2952), propagandists increasingly emphasised patriotic rather than revolutionary heroism. Educators were instructed to use 1990's 150th anniversary of the Opium War for this purpose (IED 1990, 2956). In June that year, the 'National Flag Law of the People's Republic of China' was enacted, followed by 'strict' regulations governing school flag-raising ceremonies (IED 1990, 2998). Jiang Zemin, catapulted to the top of the Party in 1989, made promotion of patriotic education a central theme of his leadership. In May 1990, he marked the anniversary of the Fourth of May Movement with a speech on 'Patriotism and the Mission of our nation's intellectuals' (IED 1990, 2972). The following year, he instructed the education ministers, Li Tieying and He Dongchang, to enhance the use of 'modern Chinese history' in '*guoqing* ['national situation'] education for young people' (IED 1991, 3126). Noting that the recently reopened 'Museum of the Chinese Revolution' had published, at his suggestion, a book entitled *Overwhelming Righteousness* on outstanding heroes from modern Chinese history, he urged Li and He to use this in instructing both the masses and Party cadres, and especially young people.

The concept of the 'national situation' to which Jiang referred was central to the Party's post-Tiananmen efforts to bolster its legitimacy. China's 'situation' was portrayed as precarious, with the fruits of economic reform and hard-won national unity and stability threatened by both internal and external forces. Internal threats included the strains of over-population, growth of which was only beginning to be curbed by the One Child Policy; the menace of corruption; fissiparous tendencies in the provinces; and separatism in Xinjiang and Tibet (which also witnessed disturbances in 1989). External threats included Western plots for China's 'peaceful evolution', code for the dismantling of the socialist regime and possible USSR-style dismemberment of its territory. Above all, the stability and security necessary for continued growth and increased prosperity could only be guaranteed, so *guoqing* propaganda maintained, by keeping the Party's steady hand on the national tiller.

However, it was only in early 1992 that the economic direction in which the Party intended to steer finally became clear. The venerable Deng, in his final major political intervention, visited the SEZs of Shenzhen and Zhuhai, and the cities of Shanghai and Wuchang, in a 'Southern Tour'. His itinerary was as significant as his speeches, since the SEZs on which he lavished praise were regarded with intense suspicion by conservatives. Calling for 'more courage in the pursuit of reform and opening', he urged, 'we must dare to experiment, not be like women with bound feet' (IED 1992, 3266). While alluding to 'rightist' and 'leftist' deviations from Party orthodoxy, he attacked 'leftism' as the major danger, since it was scaring people away from the path of reform. He scorned the idea that 'the further left' one was, 'the more revolutionary', but defiantly reaffirmed his faith in Marxism: 'I believe that the number of people in the world who admire Marxism will increase, because Marxism is science (*makesizhuyi shi kexue*)'. However, he emphasised that the achievement of true socialism would only come 'after a long period'.

The Marxist fulminations of the mid-1980s against 'bourgeois liberalization' had thus been succeeded, after many twists and turns, by a decisive shift in favour of the urban bourgeoisie. For while economic reform once again gathered impetus from 1992, its direction and focus were very different. Henceforth the urban economy was to be the chief object of policymakers' concern. Since the cities had remained largely unreformed economically during the 1980s, this might be presumed to involve an enlargement in the scope of a broadly consistent reformist strategy. However, as Huang has argued (2008; see Chapter 2), new patterns of taxation and the corporatism of urban capitalism meant that, during the 1990s, China's cities grew at the expense of the countryside.[4] The Party had seemingly concluded that any organised challenge to its authority would emanate from urban workers and professionals, not from the peasant masses, who had remained largely quiescent in 1989. It was therefore the urban population, and the nascent middle class in particular, that emerged as the regime's crucial political constituency, and the chief beneficiary of economic and educational policies. Seen from the perspective of 'class struggle' – a term rapidly losing favour in Party circles – perhaps the student protests had not been such a failure after all.

3.3 MARKETISATION TRIUMPHANT (1993–2002)

The shift in the Party's 'class' alignment would eventually be codified in Jiang Zemin's 'Three Represents' (*san ge daibiao*), promulgated in 2000 (IED 2000, 534), and the 2002 decision to allow 'capitalists' to become card-carrying Communists. In another symbolic move, the new millennium saw the pictures of workers, peasants, and minority nationalities that had hitherto adorned the PRC currency replaced by the portrait of Chairman Mao – now representing the supreme authority of a Party essentially purged of socialist ideology. As Jiang explained in his February 2000 speech, in the 'new historical situation' the overriding objective was to generate the wealth that would enable the Chinese state to strengthen itself and weather the myriad challenges ahead.

These changes in rhetoric and symbolism did not so much prefigure further policy shifts, as signify how far China had already come. Communists were parlaying influence into entrepreneurial success long before Party membership was opened to 'capitalists' (see Chapter 5). Indeed, as early as 1992, Deng Xiaoping himself – when relaunching the marketisation drive – had formally announced the end of class struggle, declaring that 'to get rich is glorious' (Woronov 2016, 10). The 1990s set the seal on the transition to 'Capitalism with Chinese Characteristics' (Huang 2008), with the dismantling of most urban remnants of state socialism. However, the same decade witnessed fiscal reforms, in 1994, designed to strengthen the central state's revenue-raising capacity, and by the same token its ability to guide and stimulate urban growth. This fiscal recentralisation took place alongside continued decentralisation of responsibility for providing public goods, including health and education. The overall effect was to further boost the development of the country's already most developed regions, while leaving many of the poorest to stagnate. By the early 2000s 'the highest provincial primary expenditures per student, in Shanghai, were more than ten times greater than the lowest', with this ratio having roughly doubled during the 1990s (Hannum *et al.* 2007, 6).

Beijing's pronouncements on education nonetheless proclaimed the overriding priority of achieving the 'two basics': 'basic' universalisation of compulsory education, and the 'basic' eradication of illiteracy. These were given top billing in a 1993 *Gangyao* ('Framework') setting out the main aims of education policy for the next decade, which also called for the continued expansion of vocational education and adult education. This formally espoused calls made (informally) as early as 1984 for the allocation of 4 per cent of GDP to public spending on education. However, with most education spending raised and disbursed at local level, the 4 per cent target remained a dead letter. Central government programmes for rural areas, often involving agriculturally focused technical training, targeted selected 'model' counties, and did little to balance fiscal inequalities. Meanwhile, local authorities were still exhorted to attend to the links between education and the economy, and develop educational provision 'on the basis of the real situation' (IED 1993, 3447).

Alongside the 'two basics', the 1993 *Gangyao* also identified the 'two comprehensives' and the 'two key points'. The former entailed 'comprehensively' adhering to the Party 'line' in education, and raising 'quality'; the latter, constructing 'key point' higher education institutions and developing 'key' disciplines. Since 'key point' universities were the only ones for which central government had direct responsibility, they received the bulk of its education budget. The 1993 *Gangyao* heralded the launch of the '211 Project' for Chinese higher education, with the aim of creating 100 'high standard' (*gao shuiping*) universities for the twenty-first century. In the spirit of recognising the increasingly varied 'real situation' in different parts of the country, diversification of school curricula and teaching materials was also recommended.

Despite this renewed emphasis on the development of 'high-level talent' (almost invariably to be found in the cities), increasing urban–rural inequalities prompted central officials to voice concern at the failure of local authorities to prioritise spending on basic schooling. Thus Vice-minister of Education Liu Bin declared in 1996 that achievement of the 'two basics' must be the 'priority of priorities' (*zhong zhong zhi zhong*) (IED 1996, 3936). The central authorities moved to strengthen educational governance by instituting stricter laws – guaranteeing levels of educational investment, for example – and by introducing enhancements to enforcement and inspection procedures (IED 1997, 4209). However, the effectiveness of such measures was limited by the weakness of the rule of law and, crucially, by the fact that in the system for evaluating the performance of local cadres, maximising economic growth still trumped all other considerations (Shue and Wong 2007).

The decade closed amidst intense public debate over problems with educational 'quality' and growing urban–rural or inter-regional imbalances in access. One response was the adoption of 'quality education' (*suzhi jiaoyu*) as a new rallying cry. Calls for education to 'take the raising of citizens' *suzhi* as the basic objective' referred to reorienting teaching and learning away from exam-focused rote memorisation, and towards fostering skills of analysis and 'critical thinking' (*suzhi jiaoyu* was the main theme of the Third National Education Work Conference in 1999 – IED 1999, 292). However, the deficient *suzhi* – defined as moral as well as intellectual 'quality' – of lower-ranking officials and the general populace was also represented as a principal barrier to the achievement of official educational goals. If only peasants, minorities and other under-privileged groups could be brought to fully appreciate the importance of education, then half the battle would be won. As Murphy has argued (2004, 2007), '*suzhi* discourse' thus served both to legitimise and reinforce the established focus on 'quality', and to place much of the blame for problems such as high dropout rates amongst rural students on the supposed fecklessness of the peasants themselves.

The State Education Commission was meanwhile reconstituted, in March 1998, as a normal Ministry – ostensibly as part of broader administrative reforms aimed at downsizing the bureaucracy.[5] This measure may also have been intended to manage expectations: re-establishing the Education Ministry signified the overcoming of the educational 'emergency' that had prompted the SEC's creation. Nevertheless, even as the Party predictably trumpeted success in achieving the 'two basics' on time, there was growing recognition that education was exacerbating rather than ameliorating socio-economic inequalities. Funding arrangements, curricular diversification, continued focus on 'key point' institutions and talk of *suzhi* – all against the backdrop of the urban economic boom – were leaving the countryside ever further behind. Significant attempts by Beijing to address the central challenge of inequality would come only after 2002.

Chinese universities take a great leap

The embrace of diversification during the 1990s reflected the growing disparities in outlook and aspiration that educational and economic reforms were fostering. Central government pronouncements acknowledged this phenomenon in a number of ways. In an April 1997 address on 'hot topics related to education', Zhu Kaixuan (SEC Vice-director 1993–98; Minister of Education 1998–2003), attempting to boost evidently flagging confidence in the achievability of the 'two basics', reassuringly noted that 'basic' would be defined as 'in districts accounting for 85 per cent of the national population', and not 100 per cent (a definition promulgated by the State Council in 1994; IED 1994, 3661). Furthermore, citing an official categorisation of China's regions into three 'levels', he observed that 90 per cent of the wealthiest 'level one' (*yi pian*) districts (metropolitan or coastal), with 370 million people, had already universalised nine years of compulsory education. By contrast, only 40 per cent of 'level two' districts (630 million people) and 22 per cent of 'level three' districts (190 million people) had achieved this goal (IED 1997, 4209).

Zhu concluded that the remaining task was not as daunting as some might think. However, his figures illustrated the educational gulf between different regions. Universalisation of primary and junior secondary education in urban areas brought increased demand for senior high-school places. Official statistics show overall urban senior high enrolment rising from 56.6 per cent in 1990 to just over 80 per cent in 2000, while the rural figure barely climbed from just over 18 per cent to around 22 per cent (though rural junior secondary enrolments rose faster) (Connelly and Zheng 2007a, 72; 2007b, 87). This upset the equilibrium between regular senior high-school places and university admission quotas that the government had striven to achieve during the 1980s. Even while some rural areas struggled to achieve the 'two basics', middle-class urbanites were increasingly pressing for expanded provision of tertiary education.

But satisfying this demand was virtually impossible within the established system of state-subsidised higher education, with state-mandated job placements for graduates. The early-to-mid-1990s saw officials struggling to square their focus on the 'two key points' with accommodation of urban aspirations and market demand. The result was a growing bifurcation of higher education. Generous public funding was maintained for 'key' institutions, subsidising their 'talented' students, but off-quota enrolments funded through user fees were increasingly permitted. Meanwhile, the state-socialist system of job allocation was dismantled (with some exceptions), and the graduate labour market liberalised. The regime thus maintained the elitist focus of public investment, while catering to mass demand for tertiary education at little or no expense to the central state. In this respect, it was essentially following the model of Japan and the East Asian tigers during their high-growth period. But in addition to the other problems with this model, inequality of access in China was institutionalised through a college entrance examination system that hugely favoured residents of the largest cities (see Chapters 8, 11 and 12).

The path to higher education massification nonetheless did not run smooth, as the controlling instincts of senior officials and fresh memories of student unrest prompted nervousness over untrammelled expansion. 'Provisional' rules on the establishment of '*minban* [effectively private] higher education institutions' were announced in 1993 (see Chapters 9, 11 and 12) (IED 1993, 3548) (though private provision had in fact already made significant inroads during the 1980s, especially in adult and vocational further education; see Mok 1997). However, in the 'regular' higher education sector, outright private providers remained rare – more common (especially after 1998) was the franchising of branch campuses by established institutions. By the middle of the decade, concerns over corruption and lax regulation were mounting. In June 1994, Vice-premier Li Lanqing, speaking at a National Higher Education Conference, warned against the unregulated proliferation of institutions and expansion of enrolments (IED 1994, 3654). The State Council called for a focus on 'internal development' rather than expansion, reaffirming the emphasis on improving quality (IED 1994, 3661).

Marketisation received more unequivocal endorsement when sweeping reforms to higher education administration were unveiled later in 1994. Explaining the changes, Zhu Kaixuan decried the 'relatively large [negative] influence' that inconsistent policies had had on higher education development during the 1980s (IED 1994, 3724). He also noted that, of 1,080 tertiary education institutions, 35 were under the authority of the SEC and another 325 under 63 different central ministries (the remainder were administered at provincial level). Reforms 'by the Year 2000' would render top-down regulation, over matters such as recruitment quotas, significantly less intrusive. This would not simply be a case of 'switching mothers-in-law' (*huan popo*), but would mean clearer regulation and more autonomy. Freed from bureaucratic micro-management, universities would be compelled to 'face towards the socialist market economy'. Rationalisation, Zhu enthusiastically noted, would also involve institutional mergers. As we discuss in Chapters 9 and 11–13, such proposals clearly echoed ideas associated with neoliberal 'new public management', but this implied no slavish adherence to foreign models.

The definitive leap to massification came in 1998, transforming college education into a middle-class rite of passage for most urban youth by the early years of the new century. As early as 1996, the SEC had countenanced a 50 per cent increase in enrolments over 1990 levels, to 6.5 per cent of the national 18–21 age cohort (IED 1996, 3970),[6] but the post-1998 expansion went much further. Higher education continued to play a central role in the Party's plans for 'creating a prosperous nation through science and education' (*ke jiao xing guo*), as Jiang Zemin put it in a seminal speech at Peking University in May 1998 (IED 1998, 90). However, universities were no longer seen simply as generators of elite 'talent', but also as instruments of social policy.

Expanding higher education enrolments involved doubling down on the commitment to urban-focused development, since only economically thriving cities could provide the masses of new graduates with appropriate employment. Graduate employment was to prove increasingly problematic, as we note in

Chapter 12. But fee-based expansion of college places and intensified labour market competition had the advantage, for the regime, of diverting youthful energies away from politics towards more mundane career-oriented concerns. The snatching away of the iron rice bowl, and dilution of college graduates' elite status, eroded students' sense of entitlement, and with it their tradition of political engagement. And as memories of Mao-era hardships and subsequent political upheavals faded, messages trumpeting China's seemingly inexorable 'rise' increasingly resonated amongst the young.

Nurturing selectively critical thinkers

The Patriotic Education Campaign, launched in 1990, was in full swing by the middle of the decade. The extent to which the various vehicles for 'patriotic' messages – from school texts to films to various media and, eventually, the Internet (IED 1999, 395) – transformed popular attitudes, or tapped into already widespread sentiments, remains moot. University students during the 1980s had engaged in relatively spontaneous demonstrations over issues such as Japanese prime ministerial visits to Tokyo's Yasakuni Shrine (Baum 1996). Moreover, as Fewsmith notes (2008), the collapse of the USSR and Yugoslavia lent plausibility to portrayals of malevolent Western 'hegemonism'. Renewed economic growth meanwhile boosted the regime's claims to performance legitimacy. Notwithstanding doubts concerning the effectiveness of patriotic education in shaping popular attitudes (e.g. Fairbrother 2003), many young urbanites during the 1990s and thereafter were thoroughly imbued with nationalistic sentiments, even if these did not conform precisely to the patriotic templates disseminated from Beijing (see Reilly 2012).

The Party certainly placed considerable faith in the utility of patriotic education as an instrument for moulding opinion. In August 1994, disparate initiatives were brought together in a *Gangyao* [Framework] for the Implementation of Patriotic Education (IED 1994, 3680). The document reiterated calls for instruction in modern and contemporary history, stressing China's long struggle against foreign invasion and oppression, eventual liberation, and the crucial role of the Communist Party. Major museums and memorials were designated 'bases for patriotic education', and an initial list of one hundred such 'bases' issued. More sweepingly, the *Gangyao* envisaged the creation of a 'social atmosphere of patriotic education' (*aiguozhuyi jiaoyu de shehui fenwei*). This would not only encompass media, arts and cultural policy, but would also involve permeating festivals and public holidays with patriotic content – the Spring Festival (Chinese New Year), 1 May, 4 May and 1 October (Chinese National Day) holidays were especially singled out. Thus Chinese life, private as well as public, would increasingly be structured around a patriotic calendar.

Punctuating this calendar were anniversaries and other events that invited, or demanded, a patriotic response. In early 1995, the SEC instructed all educational institutions to 'thoroughly implement patriotic education on the theme of the 50th anniversary of victory in the War of Resistance against Japan' (no similar activities had been mandated for the 40th or 30th anniversaries) (IED 1995, 3796). A year later, primary and secondary schools were told to ensure 'thorough implementation' of patriotic education relating to China's recovery of the exercise of sovereignty over Hong Kong (IED 1996, 3929). Meanwhile, current events, such as the 1999 NATO bombing of China's Belgrade Embassy, required a calibrated official reaction: unrestrained outrage risked stoking popular demands for vengeance, but too subdued a response would suggest weakness in the face of foreign 'bullying'. Having mounted the tiger of popular nationalism, the Party could not bank on an easy ride.

As the regime repositioned itself as the trustee of the ancient and glorious legacy of Chinese civilisation, propaganda and textbooks increasingly celebrated the history, legends and heroes of the ethnic Han majority. This shift away from a notionally class-based socialist identity towards a more ethno-cultural vision of nationhood posed particular challenges for relations between Han Chinese and various 'minority nationalities'. The patriotic education programme included 'activities to develop *minzu* [nationalities] general knowledge' (*minzu changshi jiaoyu*), with the aim of promoting consciousness of China as a 'multi-ethnic' country and fostering inter-ethnic solidarity (*minzu tuanjie*). These activities would inculcate sentiments of 'knowing my China and loving my China' (*zhi wo Zhonghua, ai wo Zhonghua*) (IED 1996, 4049). However, in the troubled Western regions of Tibet and Xinjiang, such programmes appeared to have little positive effect on inter-ethnic relations (see Vickers 2009a, b).

Strategies of 'thought reform' were also deployed to fend off another species of internal challenge: that of the Falun Gong (*falun dafa*) movement. This attracted a large following in the mid-1990s, especially amongst groups with whom patriotic messages were perhaps less likely to resonate – middle-aged and elderly people with fixed salaries of declining real value (a category including many teachers), retirees on small fixed stipends, or laid-off SOE workers. Ironically, the *qi gong* practices with which Falun Gong was associated were initially celebrated as aspects of China's glorious indigenous medical traditions. But the organisational scope of the movement and its capacity for mass mobilisation came to be seen as a challenge to Party authority. The 1999 crackdown was justified by the Education Ministry with reference to the 'physical or mental harm' suffered by some students who had engaged in the excessive or unregulated practice of *qi gong* (IED 1999, 321).[7] Falun Gong practices and beliefs were classified as 'superstition or heterodoxy', and were identified as contravening the main surviving plank of Marxist orthodoxy: the commitment to 'science'. In an August 2000 notice on 'professional ethics' amongst schoolteachers, the Ministry highlighted the promulgation of 'scientific knowledge' and the rejection of 'superstition or heterodoxy' (IED, 2000, 676).

The concept of *suzhi* ('quality') was also invoked in this document to refer to the ethical standards exhibited by teachers, students, parents or officials – but the term had wider applications. The pseudo-eugenic formulation of 'population quality' (*renkou suzhi*) enjoyed wide currency, featuring in a 1996 speech by Premier Li Peng on 'implementing population planning and raising the population quality of poor areas', which implicitly linked overbreeding of low-quality offspring to the moral deficiencies of sexually incontinent peasants (IED 1996, 4050). Meanwhile, calls for 'quality education' accompanied preparations for an overhaul of the school curriculum from 2000 (IED 2000, 484), with Minister Chen Zhili calling for a new focus on skills of creativity, critical thinking and problem solving. The *suzhi jiaoyu* rhetoric was inspired in part by contemporary moves in neighbouring countries, such as Japan, where concerns over 'skills' formation, examination stress and excessive homework had sparked similar calls for reform (see Chapter 6; also Rappleye 2007).

Calls for 'quality' in education therefore blended aspirations to reinforce political control through moral and patriotic education with the contradictory desire to nurture critical and creative thinkers for the 'knowledge economy'. Economic concerns also spurred increased interest both in ICT education and in manipulation of the Internet for propaganda purposes (IED 1997, 4204; 1999, 395). However, consequent refinements to pedagogy and improvements to school facilities further widened the gulf between prosperous coastal and metropolitan regions and everywhere else. One key message of the patriotic education campaign was that what benefited the nation would, soon enough, benefit all. But its plausibility in this respect was strained by rapidly mounting inequality.

Growing inequality

By no means all rural areas lost out amidst the fiscal and economic restructuring of the 1990s. As noted in Chapter 2, Zhejiang Province continued to experience relatively broad-based economic growth, endowing rural communities there with a greater capacity for funding basic public goods.[8] But as Zhejiang began in some respects to resemble its renegade neighbour, Taiwan, many inland regions were left further behind. The urban–rural divide overlapped with a growing East–West divide, and as the differential in incomes and opportunities expanded, migration to the cities accelerated – despite continuing restrictions on migrants' access to urban public services.

Awareness of problems with the financing of rural education is evident in many central government pronouncements during these years. In November 1993, the State Council promulgated 'methods for speedily resolving problems with the delayed payment of teachers' salaries' (IED 1993, 3574), and later the same month the SEC banned the levying of various supplementary charges by schools (IED 1993, 3575). However, similar notices or warnings were repeatedly issued throughout the decade, indicating continuing and widespread circumvention. Though corruption was certainly a factor here, more fundamental problems were insufficient revenue and the weakness of local accountability mechanisms (see Chapter 5). While Beijing continued to exhort local authorities to prioritise the 'two basics', it provided little money for this purpose. Although inequality in aggregate expenditures per student in 'regional rural primary schools' compared with those in coastal areas only marginally increased over the decade, evidence suggests that poorer provinces were raising more of their revenue from 'extra-budgetary sources', primarily fees (Li *et al.* 2007, 33). Many poorer families thus faced higher costs. Meanwhile, the government licensed the activities of charitable organisations, notably Project HOPE, which sought donations from prosperous urbanites to fund schools in poorer areas (see Chapter 9).

Beijing's failure to supply balancing payments reflected the Finance Ministry's apparent prioritisation of other areas (e.g. military spending) over education (Vickers 2007a, 66). Willingness to disburse greater funds to local level was also constrained by suspicion that lower-level officials would siphon off resources for private gain. Baulking at governance reforms that might have assured greater local accountability, the central government funded targeted schemes designed to exemplify what was possible if only officials, educators and parents would raise their *suzhi* and strive together for the common good. For example, a 'Prairie Fire Programme', launched in 1988 to spread awareness of science and technology in rural areas, promote agricultural productivity, and help 'create a prosperous nation through science and education', was extended from 1995 (IED 1995, 3905). Invoking the *guoqing* (national situation), leading cadres such as Vice-Premier Li Lanqing harped endlessly on the unique challenges of achieving 'Education for All in a Developing Country with a Large Population', while sternly lecturing local officials on their responsibilities (IED 1994, 3654). 'Taking the responsibility for illiteracy work constitutes genuine governmental behaviour', declared Zhu Kaixuan in February 1995 (IED 1995, 3774).

In late 1999, an ostensibly more ambitious scheme for uplifting 'backward' regions was announced: the 'Great Western Development Strategy' (*Xibu da kaifa*). This followed declarations of the success of a 1995–8 drive to universalise compulsory education in 'poor regions of the country' (the 'level two' regions referred to above) (IED 1999, 224). If official statistics were to be believed, this left only the 'third-level' or 'poorest' regions, mostly in the West, short of full universalisation. Signalling the leadership's determination to rectify this, the 'Steering Group' for the *Xibu da kaifa* was a roll call of influential Party figures (IED 2000, 491). However, much of the planned new investment was to take the form of province-to-province assistance, rather than direct grants from the centre – most central government spending was directed to large infrastructure projects such as the national network of expressways or the new railway to Lhasa. This pattern led some to see the programme as primarily an exercise in boosting the development of the prosperous East through facilitating access to the natural resources of hitherto 'remote' regions (Vickers 2007a, 64).

In education, Li *et al.* note the relatively high spending on infrastructure (i.e. school buildings) relative to other budget items (e.g. salaries) in central and especially western regions through the 1990s (2007, 32–3). The prioritisation of investment in construction was a feature not just of projects associated with the *Xibu da kaifa*, but also of the general pattern of China's development from the 1990s (see Chapter 5). This was related partly to local officials' desire to impress visiting dignitaries with concrete monuments to their diligence, and partly to the opportunities for speculation that construction projects afforded.[9] The result was a large number of new school buildings (often shoddily built),[10] as well as a rash of prestige projects constructed on land requisitioned from farmers. Throughout western China, as elsewhere in the country, vast 'university cities' (*daxue cheng*) sprang out of the wilderness – from Lhasa to Lanzhou, and Chongqing to Urumqi.

Parts of the west also benefited from collaborative programmes involving overseas aid organisations, though the priorities of key actors were not always mutually consonant (Carney 2008), and results were distinctly mixed. While the focus of a 1996–2001 UNDP project in five western provinces was on girls' education, local officials unconvinced of this agenda were simply happy to take the extra funding (Wang X. 2010, 12). The government's decision to concentrate its own, related 'Spring Buds Programme' on poor, remote, border and minority regions derived from security and nation-building concerns which foreign donors did not prioritise (IED 1994, 3642). The relative largesse thus directed at regions such as Tibet has provoked resentment amongst many Han Chinese (Leibold 2014).[11] Meanwhile, the benefits of this investment have been uneven and disputed, with nomadic communities often resisting externally imposed educational practices (Postiglione 2007; Postiglione *et al.* 2014), while inland boarding schools cater to 'minority elites' (Chen 2014). Whether at elite or grassroots level, in the most sensitive border regions the goal of cementing 'minority' loyalty to the Chinese state appears as remote as ever (see Leibold and Chen 2014).

As the rural–urban divide widened, accelerating urban growth was fuelled by the labour of a vast influx of rural migrants. Precise numbers are unclear, since migrants were not officially registered in the areas where they actually lived and worked. One 2007 study put the total figure for migrant children at about 20 million (Chen and Liang 2007). An SEC notice of 1996 stipulated that migrant children must register as temporary residents (almost impossible at this time) and then apply to a local school; if rejected, they could apply to the local authorities – who would then have the responsibility for 'solving' the issue (IED 1996, 3965). In other words, provision of schooling to migrant children was essentially left to the discretion of local governments that had little incentive for generosity. As a result, migrant children generally studied in migrant-run schools, or not at all, with estimated enrolment rates varying widely. In Beijing, where the situation was perhaps worst, estimates ranged from 40.5 per cent down to 12.5 per cent (Chen and Liang 2007, 120; see Chapter 9).

Surveying the educational scene at the turn of the century

Having defied international predictions of their regime's collapse, China's leaders felt entitled to a degree of self-congratulation as they toasted the new century. Meanwhile, the country continued to receive international plaudits for its educational success, compared with other 'developing' countries. Citing this successful record in a 1999 Cambridge speech, Jiang Zemin significantly chose to emphasise the contribution of culture rather than socialism. Quoting Confucius, 'the outstanding educationalist produced by China 2,550 years ago', Jiang credited the fact that his country had 'achieved in a generation what other countries took several centuries to achieve' to the long and glorious cultural traditions that defined the 'essence' of the Chinese nation (IED 1999, 413).

Nevertheless, in their internal counsels senior leaders were far less sanguine. Early in 2000, in a general 'discussion of educational issues', Jiang addressed the Politburo in the wake of two shocking incidents in Zhejiang – one involving a student killing his mother after receiving unsatisfactory grades at school, and another in which two students had murdered a classmate in a dispute over money. Tackling the causes of such incidents, Jiang reflected, would require greater stress on 'moral education'.[12] Observing that the preponderance of one-child families intensified parental pressure on children, he called for the maintenance of curricular space for 'thought and values' instruction and activities promoting 'all-round healthy growth' (IED 2000, 513). Recapitulating themes of the *suzhi jiaoyu* campaign, he opined, 'We must not make young people spend the whole day inside poring over books, we must let them participate in social activities, broaden their horizons and increase their experience of society'. 'Thought and values' education would, meanwhile, help to remind all involved that 'university is not for everyone'; China's development required workers for 'labour-intensive industries' as well as talent for 'knowledge-intensive industries'. Young people must stand ready to serve the needs of national development in whatever way they could, with whatever talents they had. Developing a systematic programme for education must therefore start with 'education in patriotism, collectivism and socialist thought'.

Whereas Jiang focused on the realms of consciousness and 'thought', in 1999 Zhang Baoqing (Vice-minister of Education) had offered a more down-to-earth critique of the state of Chinese education, focusing especially on issues of funding (IED 1999, 472). He began on a positive note, praising the educational achievements of the 'Reform and Opening' period to date. Decentralisation since the 1980s had, he wrote, stimulated a greater degree of 'activism' at local level. The years between 1985 and 1992 had witnessed significant improvements in educational facilities at local level (buildings, classroom furniture and so forth), while the post-1992 period had seen a 'stable increase' in educational investment and greater use of 'law' to govern the system. Steady, incremental progress in educational investment had been accompanied by a diversification of its sources – including user fees and foreign investment at college level.

However, Zhang then homed in on 'problems and contradictions' in the system for financing education. He sharply commented on the 'extremely acute' contradiction between the proclaimed status of education as a 'strategic priority', and the actual level of public spending. In observations that would return to haunt officials in the wake of the 2008 Sichuan earthquake, he claimed that China still had 20 million square metres of 'dangerous school buildings'. The cost of necessary infrastructural improvements, the expensive 211 and 985 Projects, and various teacher training programmes, simply could not be met out of existing budgetary allocations. While recognising that funding was not unlimited, given the realities of China's *guoqing*, he appealed for a more 'far-sighted' approach. 'The greater the poverty', he expostulated, 'the more education is needed; the greater the difficulty, the more education must be supported'. Recent years had 'witnessed a number of countries make startling achievements' in extending educational access to the poor, and China should follow their example. While he does not name these countries, it seems more than likely that he had in mind those on China's East Asian doorstep.

Far from following that example, Zhang went on, China was in fact failing to uphold its own Education Law (enacted in 1995). Not only had the government failed to raise education spending to 4 per cent of GDP; such spending had actually fallen (in proportional terms) from 3.04 per cent of GDP in 1990 to 2.46 per cent in 1996, before rising slightly to 2.5 per cent in 1997. Changes to the taxation system earlier in the decade had involved no guarantees for levels of educational investment, and in practice education was often neglected when allocations were determined at local level. Moreover, he contended, even those resources that were disbursed were often wasted due to the practices of 'emphasizing distribution and neglecting management', or 'emphasizing amount and overlooking effectiveness'. A key problem was that financial authorities were not held accountable for the delivery of educational services, and educational administrators were not held liable for the effectiveness with which they used their funds. Unifying financial and administrative responsibility for education had been repeatedly urged by central government, but little action had been taken. Here Zhang's critique appears to draw on a neoliberal rhetoric of 'accountability', heard throughout the developing world since the 1980s, and often used to justify an offloading of direct government responsibilities for public service funding and provision onto local actors. However, his central focus on the level of public spending suggests that his comments were primarily aimed at the Ministry of Finance for its refusal to honour the 4 per cent commitment.

A question often elided in discussions of 'accountability' relates to the identity of those to whom actors are ultimately to be held accountable. In this respect, at least, there was unity between Zhang and his Finance Ministry antagonists. The key to solving these problems, he argued, was to 'further raise recognition of the importance of leadership [on educational issues] at each level of party and government'. In order to improve funding and administration, arrangements for inspection and oversight by leaders at each level of the Party-State hierarchy had to be strengthened. It was thus evident that Zhang, like other leaders, continued to envisage improved efficiency coming through strengthened oversight from above, rather than greater accountability from below. As Beijing began, from the mid-2000s, to contemplate more concerted attempts to tackle educational inequality and related financial and administrative issues, this question of governance would remain a central 'contradiction'.

3.4 VESTED INTERESTS AND THE LIMITS OF REFORM (2002–16)

China's post-2002 leadership faced none of the sense of imminent crisis that had confronted their predecessors in 1989. Formal accession to the WTO was imminent, Beijing had been anointed as host of the 2008 Olympics, and the economy was experiencing double-digit annual growth. Thanks to the fiscal consolidation of the mid-1990s, central state finances were in rude health and foreign currency reserves accumulating. Moreover, suggesting newfound political 'maturity', Hu Jintao became the first supreme leader to accede to power by a regular, legalistic process, rather than through inter-factional feuding or civic upheaval. China seemed well on the way to achieving the power, international status, prosperity and stability long craved by patriots of all stripes.

However, significant tensions existed beneath this serene political landscape. Since the early 1990s, a state-driven, urban-oriented form of marketisation had exacerbated social inequality and, in certain regions, undercut provision of public services. The commercialisation of huge swathes of the former public sector during the 1990s had transferred enormous wealth and power to networks of cadres and entrepreneurs (see Bian *et al.* 2001). China was not the only (*de facto*) post-socialist state to breed a powerful class of entrepreneurial 'oligarchs', but it differed from the Russian variant. There, Putin ruthlessly purged the overmighty barons of commerce (only to replace them with his own loyalists); in China, the collective post-Deng leadership sought to co-opt the capitalists, formally welcoming them into the Party from 2002. This reflected the already intimate connections between business and Party-State elites, but also ensured that any future attempt to confront oligarchic concentrations of wealth and power would involve intra-Party factional struggles, threatening the regime's cohesion and legitimacy (Overholt 2012).

In any case, Hu's character, the manner of his ascent and the benign economic situation made him loth to engage in confrontation. From a relatively humble background, and lacking familial ties to any major CCP factions, Hu had emerged relatively unscathed from the factional battles of the 1980s; ready to suppress resistance from outside the Party, he preferred to ignore divisions within it.[13] This reluctance to acknowledge contradictions was reflected in the dominant slogans of his tenure: 'the harmonious society' (*hexie shehui*), 'stability' (*weiwen*), 'not wavering' (*bu zhe teng*). Critics accused Hu and Wen of 'beating the drum and passing the flower' (*ji gu chuan hua*) – taking credit for good fortune while leaving tough decisions to their successors. This inaction also helped ensure that those successors themselves would be drawn from amongst the most vested of vested interests.

But prevalent conditions supplied little stimulus for radical reform. The incessant harping on 'harmony' was, in truth, an indicator of its absence; low-level local discontent was endemic. Nonetheless, as Overholt observed in 2012, 'today's leaders govern incrementally because they can, and because dissipation of the sense of national urgency has depleted public support for stressful change' (122). This 'incrementalism' involved distributing state largesse to sooth particular resentments, while eschewing fundamental reforms to state institutions or governance. Though education spending continuing to decline as a percentage of GDP until around 2005, public expenditure on education, health, welfare, infrastructure and the military was thereafter significantly increased. Additional

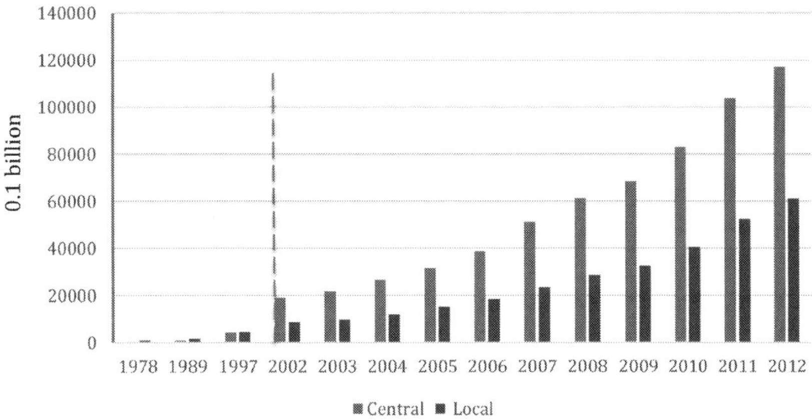

Figure 3.1 Revenues of central and local governments (province and below), 1978–2012 (selected years).

Source: NBS.

funding was also channelled into the projects (discussed in the previous section) aimed at developing 'backward' regions.

Despite mounting inequality – reflected in a 2008 Gini coefficient of 0.491 (Han *et al.* 2016, 22) – the 'social volcano' has so far remained dormant. In addition to extensive and sophisticated state repression, this owes something to the effects of such social spending, increasingly involving transfer payments from the centre to provincial governments. Whereas 'decentralisation' – fiscal and managerial, if not political – was the government's default position during the 1980s, from the mid-1990s a marked recentralisation had begun. At first, this primarily involved squeezing more money out of the provinces for central government coffers but, from the mid-2000s, funding increasingly flowed the other way. An inevitable concomitant was the creation of greater dependency on Beijing, reinforcing, to some extent, the latter's influence over local power centres (Figure 3.1) (see Chapter 5; also Lin 2013). At the same time, the capacity of the Party to cater in different ways to varied constituencies – urban and rural, coastal and hinterland, young and old – meant that 'acceptance of authoritarianism' was real and widespread (Wright 2010). The CCP may not have commanded enthusiastic adoration among the 'broad masses', but there is no evidence that most Chinese actively desired regime change.

While addressing isolated cases of social discontent, the regime's strategy was thus to avoid tackling the deeper structural problems of which these were symptomatic. In examining the implications of this approach for education policy, we first discuss the increasingly significant role of public opinion and the media in shaping debate, highlighting some of the key issues that aroused concern. We then turn to the growing challenges of squaring common national

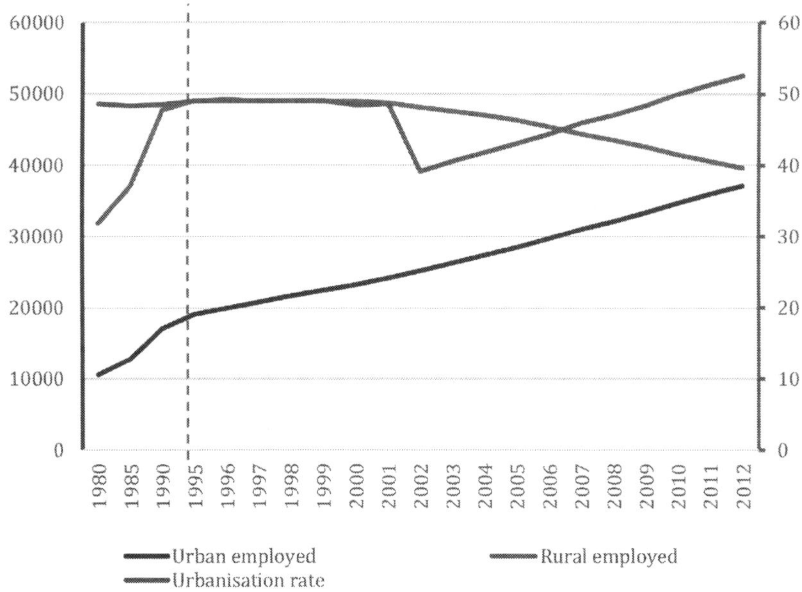

Figure 3.2 The urbanisation rate, 1980–2012 (selected years).

Source: NBS.

priorities for educational development with the increasingly divergent interests and agendas of different provinces and regions. Underlying this divergence has been the continuing acceleration of urbanisation (Figure 3.2), complicated by the continued, if modified, enforcement of the *hukou* (household registration) system. We therefore finish by examining the failure to introduce fundamental reform in this area, its implications for equitable access to education, and what this reveals about the broader politics of the Hu–Wen period.

Public debate and topics of concern

As noted in earlier sections of this chapter, the parameters for critical public debate have repeatedly shifted during the Reform era – at some times loosening (*fang*), at others tightening (*shou*). While some subjects – the authority of the Party, or the status of China's borders – have remained strictly off-limits, at times relatively open debate over other aspects of public policy has been permitted. Critique of the ideological content of education remains taboo (see Vickers 2009a; Vickers and Yang 2013). But in other respects, the Hu–Wen era witnessed a surge of media interest in educational issues, informed by increasingly sophisticated and penetrating academic surveys and investigative reporting. This debate also reflected a growing sophistication in the state's engagement with the media – print, broadcast and online.[14]

For media organisations, this focus on education is fundamentally market-driven: few subjects exercise urban readers more than the educational prospects of their offspring. As discussed in the previous section, official encouragement of educational aspiration, for example through the big expansion of higher education in 1998, was an attempt to channel urban energies into the pursuit of individual or familial betterment, thereby both boosting the economy and dampening political activism. Rhetorical collectivism, exhorting patriotic loyalty to nation and Party-State, was accompanied by a pervasive ethos of intense individualistic competition (Hansen 2013; see Chapter 6). And informing and legitimating this ethos were neoliberal economic arguments and *suzhi* discourse attributing ultimate responsibility for success or failure to the individual (Murphy 2004; Vickers 2009b).

There was more to this than neoliberalism; such arguments also tapped cultural attitudes or beliefs concerning education, credentials and worldly success that remain deeply entrenched across East Asia (see Chapters 2 and 9). But in making educational provision so central to the tacit contract between state and citizen, the Party effectively invited public judgement over this issue. Shanghai's PISA results might seem a triumphant vindication of this strategy. However, as we argue in our concluding chapter, this triumph was far less sweeping than it at first appeared. While Western policymakers and commentators fretted about being 'surpassed' by Shanghai, domestic debate focused on a range of intractable tensions and contradictions, educational and otherwise. As the editors of a 2012 'Blue Book' on the state of Chinese society emphasised, despite a picture of generally rising prosperity, the country faced a range of daunting social problems, from the still-growing urban–rural income gap, to rising graduate unemployment (Ru *et al.* 2012). Such concerns formed the subtext for continuing debate over education and broader social reform.

The 2010 'Gangyao' and China's educational 'challenges'

Westerners aghast at Shanghai's stunning 2009 PISA success would have been profoundly discombobulated to read a document issued the following year by China's Education Ministry. The tone of the 2010 'Outline National Plan for the Long-term Reform and Development of Education (2010–2020)' (hereafter 2010 *Gangyao*) was far from celebratory. To be sure, the *Gangyao* – the first such document since 1993 – hailed a catalogue of 'historic achievements'. However, in sketching out an agenda for further reform, it criticised many aspects of the current system. 'We must clearly recognize', declared the preface, 'that education is still not [adequately] serving national economic and social development or the need to provide a good education to the masses of the people' (MOE 2011b, 5). It cited students' 'poor ability to adapt to the needs of society and the labour market' and lack of 'creativity'; 'inflexible' structures and management practices; 'unbalanced' development in urban and rural areas and across regions; and insufficient overall investment.

In alluding to such problems, the *Gangyao* reflected a widespread sense of heightening 'contradictions' in China's educational development. In early 2009, prior to finalising the *Gangyao*, the Ministry had launched a public consultation. An unprecedented move, this underlined the document's propaganda function – as a gesture towards pluralism and a signal of the regime's concern for education, epitomised by Premier Wen Jiabao.[15] Amongst the issues that emerged from the consequent media debate were: a shortage of affordable kindergarten places (see the next chapter); the cost and quality of higher education (see Chapters 11 and 12); and perceptions of inadequate public investment. In addition to these issues, the *Gangyao* detailed a range of policy challenges, with ten subsections identifying 50 specific 'tasks'. But whereas the previous 1993 *Gangyao* had accompanied Deng's relaunch of marketisation, the 2010 document was a parting statement by an outgoing administration. The extent to which their successors have adhered to this framework is debatable; as of 2016, a 'mid-term review' slated for 2015 has yet to appear.

Concern over public discontent was crucial to the context out of which the *Gangyao* emerged. In late 2009, just as Shanghai's PISA success was announced, in Beijing the Politburo chose to eject the Education Minister, Zhou Ji (in post since 2003). Indeed, the timing, and unprecedented nature, of the *Gangyao*-related public consultation suggest that it may have been partly intended to set Zhou up for a fall. Though reputedly 'clean', Zhou's top-down managerial style and poor communication skills helped to seal his fate, perhaps also contributing to his key perceived failure: an inability to extract from the Finance Ministry funding for achieving the totemic 4 per cent of GDP target for public spending on education (something his successor, Yang Guiren, achieved by 2012 – see below).[16]

But of all the causes of public discontent, at least for urban Chinese, perhaps the most acute related to the consequences of intense credentialism, ranging from the costs of private tuition to the cramping of teaching and learning. This was one major factor in the accelerating exodus of children from wealthier families to schools in the English-speaking West (see Chapter 13). A May 2010 feature article entitled 'Education without Heart' (*wu 'xin' de jiaoyu*), in the weekly newspaper *Southern Weekend* (*Nanfang Zhoumo*), voiced the widespread sense of crisis. The author lamented how preparation for the college entrance exam (*gaokao*) determined learning 'from the moment [children] enter school'. Not only was this intellectually deadening, but the resulting competitiveness was also morally corrupting: 'High scores have become the symbol of the "new socialist person." Whether or not a student has morals, or really believes in socialism, or is a compassionate person – none of this is important. Scores determine everything' (Yu 2010).

The curricular reform of 2001–2 had been meant to tackle just such problems. However, in the absence of significant reform to *gaokao* syllabuses, exhorting schools and teachers to effect a transformation in 'knowledge, attitudes and values' was largely ineffective. This closely paralleled the experience of neighbouring Japan, where attempts from the 1990s to make secondary schooling more 'relaxed' ran up against the brick wall of unreformed university entrance examinations (Bjork 2011). In China, as in Japan, a major consequence of attempts to enforce more 'relaxed' schooling was therefore an enormous upsurge in demand for examination-preparatory supplementary tutoring, as we discuss in Chapter 9.

The tension between reformist rhetoric and the demands of examination preparation also fuelled resistance amongst many teachers. Even if they agreed with the broad aims of curricular change, many found the new official guidelines and textbooks confusing. In addition, as noted in the previous section, the new emphasis on critical thinking and continuing demands for didactic moralising were fundamentally contradictory. But concerns regarding the *moral* impact of rapid social change on China's youth were widely shared (as Yu's *Nanfang Zhoumo* article testifies). On social media, talk of the 'children of the 90s' as *xiao guai shou* ('little monsters') or even *nao can* (mental defectives) was often linked to complaints that schools were failing to nurture morally upstanding individuals. Meanwhile, the curricular stress on *suzhi* and 'skills' was criticized as 'elitist', since only selective 'key schools' could hope to realise such aims; the challenges for teachers and pupils in 'ordinary' schools, especially in the countryside, were of an entirely different order (see Chapter 6).

Charges of 'elitism' related to another key focus of educational debate: inequality. Prominent in shaping public discussion of this issue was the sociologist and public intellectual Yang Dongping, whose career reveals how certain activists were tolerated and co-opted, while helping to shape public opinion and official policy. Formerly a high-flying cadre assigned to the Propaganda Department of the Beijing Institute of Technology (*li gong da xue*),[17] in 1989 Yang had been stripped of his post for supporting the Student Movement. After embarking on an academic career, during the 1990s he moved into television production, working on CCTV's 'Tell it like it is!' (*shi hua shi hua*), and 'The Great Lecture Hall of the Century' (*shiji da jiangtang*) (broadcast by the Hong Kong-based Phoenix channel). His investigative reports gained huge audiences, and requests from groups or individuals desperate to air their grievances. But these documentaries invariably focused on abuses at local level, sedulously avoiding direct criticism of the central government.

In 2002, Yang founded the 'Twenty-First Century Research Institute', and returned to educational research. Focusing on inequality, he bitterly criticised the treatment of migrant children, and attacked the privileged access of urban residents and the wealthy to the best state schools and colleges.[18] In 2004, he was named one of China's 'fifty most influential intellectuals' by the magazine *Nanfang Renwu Zhoukan* – perhaps indicating that Party leaders were preparing to embrace certain aspects of his agenda. In 2010, coinciding with the release of the *Gangyao*, his institute compiled the first 'Blue Book of Education' (*Jiaoyu lan pi shu*), surveying the educational situation across China (Yang D. 2010). In the same year, he was appointed to the State Council's 'National Advisory Committee on Education', along with various establishment luminaries. He subsequently extended his critique to aspects of China's intensely competitive 'educational culture', such as the phenomenon of so-called 'Tiger Mothers' and the fashion for 'Mathematical Olympiads', whose effects on child development he described as more corrupting than 'sex, gambling and drugs' (Yang D. 2011). Educators and parents, he opined, should pay more attention to socialising youngsters as polite, considerate citizens – for example by teaching them to smile and say 'thank you'. As other Chinese commentators have done, in this respect he explicitly cited Japan as a model (see Rappleye 2007).[19]

The continued inadequacy of educational investment was highlighted in the 2010 'Blue Book'. But in this area Hu and Wen were determined to leave a clear legacy. In 2012, it was announced that the 4 per cent benchmark for public spending on education had finally been achieved, and that governments at all levels would be held to this target. However, the top-down approach to ensuring this threatened to result in serious distortions and waste. In some poorer provinces, good uses were found for the extra central funding: Jilin and Heilongjiang, for example, paid off university debts and raised per-student spending. But demands for matching funds from provincial authorities could mean diversion of local revenue from other priorities. Meanwhile, the wealthiest regions such as Beijing and Shanghai already had a surplus of school places, but little desire to fill them with the obvious candidates: children of migrant workers. National rules on teachers' pay also restricted them from raising staff salaries to match the high local cost of living. Seeking for ways to spend the extra money, Beijing poured funds into new facilities of sometimes dubious value, conferences, short-term projects, and a plethora of training programmes. Overworked teachers complained of their transformation into 'training slaves' (*peixun de nuli*) (see Chapter 7).

Disparate conditions bred diverse concerns. Middle-class urbanites might fret over examination pressure, much as some Japanese had done since the 1980s, as prosperity made goals besides the frenetic pursuit of wealth seem newly important. Readers of the highbrow press might 'tut-tut' as a rash of university scandals revealed the extent of corruption, plagiarism and other forms of malpractice. They might ask, with Qian Xue-shen, 'father of the Chinese missile', 'Why can our colleges still not produce outstanding talent?' (Yang D. 2010, 'Abstract'). But outside the major metropolitan centres, the questions asked were likely to be very different, and far more mundane.

Central planning for divergent regions

The pell-mell marketisation of the 1990s and early 2000s left one feature of Stalinist centralism firmly in place: the Five Year Plan. Both central and local governments have continued to prepare these documents, even while depriving themselves of many of the levers of old-style central planning. Nonetheless, as we discuss in Chapters 5 and 9, the selective invocation of *laissez-faire* principles should not disguise Beijing's retention of significant levers of command and control. Stalinist-inspired state socialism may have gone, but the Party still permeates the institutions of an ostensibly decentralised, marketised society, wielding tools such as the cadre evaluation system to ensure that agreed targets are taken seriously (at least on paper). Five Year Plans – part term report, part manifesto – still seek to establish legitimacy in the eyes of the regime's increasing divergent constituencies.

Well before the Hu–Wen decade, the plans of different provinces reflected this divergence. In education, more prosperous regions, primarily in the East, have tended to view attempts to maintain or impose unified national standards as irritating restraints on their pursuit of 'excellence'. The archetypal case is Shanghai, the first municipality permitted (from the early 1990s) to set its own curriculum standards and issue its own textbooks. As noted above (3.1), such departures from socialist uniformity have typically been justified by virtue of the vanguard status of more 'advanced' regions, portrayed as experimental proving grounds for modernisation and inspirational exemplars for less-developed areas. From the advent of the 'Great Western Development Strategy' (*Xibu Da Kaifa*), 'advanced' regions were also expected to make more tangible contributions to modernisation in the hinterland. But this was a relatively small price exacted by the centre for their continued freedom to race ahead of the provincial pack.

For their part, however, Western or poorer regions have, above all, demanded more money from the centre, while complaining that nationally set standards and targets are unrealistic. From 2005, with the launch of the *New Socialist Countryside* scheme (see below), and more especially since 2012, substantial extra funding has been funnelled into education. But this does not appear to have significantly narrowed the gaps between wealthier and poorer regions, not just in funding, but also in access to higher education and the capacity to attract or retain key personnel (see Chapters 5, 7 and 8). Meanwhile, cutting across all regional divides, the *hukou* system and fiscal decentralisation still make rural or urban residency status perhaps the major cleavage in Chinese society.

Before turning to that issue, particularly as it relates to college access, we first illustrate the extent of regional divergence in educational conditions by examining the provincial plans submitted under the Eleventh Five Year Plan (2006–10). A useful comparative analysis of these plans was undertaken by researchers at the Shanghai Academy of Educational Science (Xu *et al.* 2012), who followed standard official practice in grouping the provinces into three categories: 'advanced', 'middle-level' and 'less-developed'.

The 'advanced' group included Beijing, Shanghai and Tianjin, as well as coastal provinces from Guangdong in the south to Liaoning in the north. Here, by 2007, not only was compulsory education 'universalised', but access to high schooling had become near-universal for many. Tianjin, for example, boasted a participation rate of 90 per cent. There too, official figures reported three years of preschooling for 91 per cent of children, and a 50 per cent participation rate in higher education. 'Issues of concern' identified by planners in these regions tended to include: rising popular expectations; the problems posed by rapid urban development for rural–urban 'balance'; the tension between the objectives of *suzhi jiaoyu* and stubbornly high student workloads; shortfalls in the supply of trained technical workers reflecting popular aversion to vocational education; and the need for 'thought reform' to transform such problematic attitudes. The solutions proposed, apart from exhortations to greater 'effort' all round, tended to reflect a strong human capital orientation, unabashed elitism, and a neoliberal faith in the virtue of 'competitiveness'. Raising the 'quality' of higher education, and enhancing its contribution to technological innovation, was generally prioritised. These provinces also expressed a determination to maintain their vanguard status.

Noticeably absent from the plans of 'advanced' regions, and largely invisible in the official statistics on which they drew, were the needs of migrant workers. Migrant numbers – according to the State Council's own figures – grew from 121 million in 2000 to 245 million in 2013, or from 9.6 per cent to 18 per cent of China's total population; most were concentrated in the cities of the eastern seaboard (Feng 2015). As we have seen, the plight of this group attracted growing attention from the media and public intellectuals during these years, and amongst central state officials concerned with preserving social stability. But provincial officials generally had little incentive to highlight such issues. Even where it was theoretically possible for migrant children to access urban schools, bureaucratic hurdles and, crucially, the *gaokao* system (see Chapters 8 and 9), forced many back to schools in their 'home' provinces. Hence, arguably the most acute educational issue involving 'advanced' regions was largely displaced to poorer provinces lower down the human capital supply chain.

Provinces classed as 'middle level' by Xu *et al.* included two giant suppliers of migrant workers (Hunan and Henan), Hebei (surrounding Beijing and Tianjin), the southwestern megalopolis of Chongqing (itself a major migrant magnet), and Heilongjiang in the Northeast. High-school participation rates were in excess of 45 per cent (over 80 per cent in Chongqing), with enrolment in higher education exceeding 15 per cent (only Hunan falling below 20 per cent). Problems highlighted by planners included: large rural–urban inequalities; adaptation to rapid demographic transformation (all but Hunan were facing declining student numbers); persistent funding shortages; the 'quality' of the teaching workforce; and difficulties in implementing *suzhi jiaoyu* curriculum reforms. Plans called for a redoubling of efforts to close the rural–urban gap in basic schooling: rural compulsory education should be 'the priority of priorities'. Enhanced development of technical and vocational education was also urged, as was raising 'the quality of higher education' – though this was not accorded the same priority as in 'advanced' provinces.

For 'middle-level provinces', problems in the compulsory phase were portrayed as primarily qualitative, but in 'less-developed' provinces, the persistence of quantitative challenges was acknowledged. In Guangxi and Guizhou, although planners had hailed a 'breakthrough' in achieving 'the two basics', it was noted that enrolment rates of 90 per cent fell short of fully 'universal' provision. Senior high enrolment stood at 30.5 per cent in Guizhou, and 46 per cent in Guangxi, while college enrolments (11 per cent and 15 per cent respectively) were significantly lower than in 'middle-level provinces'. Here, glaring inter-regional and inter-school inequalities, 'serious' funding shortfalls, inadequate provision of senior high schooling, and a 'very weak' contribution of education to economic and social development were all cited as pressing problems. Moreover, as Xu *et al.* observed, some objectives outlined in the plans from these provinces betrayed the hollowness of much of their 'breakthrough' rhetoric. These included 'reducing drop-out levels' in the compulsory phase, 'standardising' management procedures, and strengthening the monitoring of boarding schools. The plans for 'less-developed' provinces also acknowledged the persistence of a phenomenon supposedly eliminated in the 1990s – the use of *daike* (substitute) teachers at primary and junior secondary level (see Chapters 7 and 9).

Apparently signalling new determination to tackle social inequality and rural under-development, in early 2006 the State Council launched the 'New Socialist Countryside' initiative (*xin shehuizhuyi nongcun jianshe*). The 'agricultural tax' on rural households was scrapped, and by 2008 all fees for compulsory education outlawed under the 'two waivers, one subsidy' (*liangmian yibu*) scheme, which also provided US$5 monthly grants to rural boarding school students. However, as *The Economist* noted (2006), 'despite promised transfers of Y103 billion annually to fill the resulting hole in local finances', it was 'not clear' that this would be sufficient. A quarter of the new funding was supposed to come from local governments, which might well 'have other plans for it'. Regarding rural public spending more generally, a 2012 Ministry of Finance report hailed a decade of progress in increasing central funding for the 'three rural issues' (*san nong*): 'agriculture, rural villages and farmers' (*nongye, nongcun, nongmin*). As a result, it claimed, central government disbursements to rural communities had increased faster than overall government spending (by 21.4 per cent compared with 4.5 per cent) – so that, by 2012, they accounted for 19.2 per cent of spending on the *san nong* (up from 13.7 per cent in 2003) (MOF 2012). But this still left local governments on the hook for the remaining 80 per cent.

The 'New Socialist Countryside' scheme involved constructing new 'super-villages' with larger and better-equipped schools and clinics, designed to serve as local hubs for public service provision. This extended earlier schemes for concentrating schools, from upper primary level onwards, in rural townships, with the aim of raising 'quality'. Such moves were also designed to facilitate greater curricular standardisation, so furthering the project of 'turning peasants into modern Chinese citizens' (Murphy 2004). But the shifting of public service provision into 'super-villages' also fed the already-noted propensity of local officials to pour money and concrete into prestige projects calculated to impress their superiors. While many rural children benefited from such investment, many others in the poorest and most remote districts did not.

A key reason for this was the closure of many small rural primary and junior secondary schools that accompanied the concentration policy (Figures 3.3 and 3.4). Such closures meant longer, potentially more hazardous, commutes for many children, and increased opportunity costs in terms of lost farm labour. The extreme competitiveness of secondary schooling, and the wages available to migrant labourers, also heightened the opportunity costs of remaining in school, especially for low-achieving rural students, leading to increased 'dropping out' by students from the poorest areas (Yi *et al.* 2012). The requisitioning of rural land for the construction of 'new villages' – or the prospect of it – meanwhile occasioned widespread resentment or suspicion. Highlighting such problems, Yang Dongping argued that small village primary schools should be retained and supported. Reports of deaths or injuries involving children travelling long distances to school added to pressure on the authorities (Wang 2011; Jiang 2014).

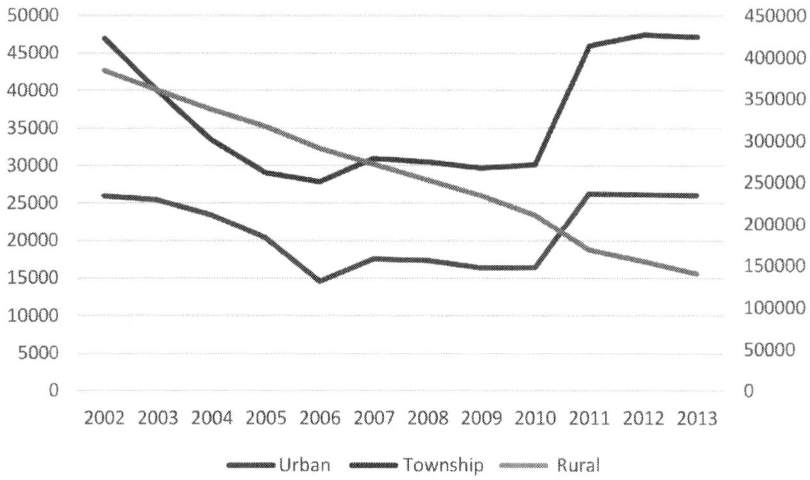

Figure 3.3 The pattern of distribution of rural primary schools, 2002–13.

Note: The *y*-axis on the right is set for rural schools.

Resources: Department of Education Development and Planning, MOE, *Educational Statistics Yearbook of China*, People's Education Press.

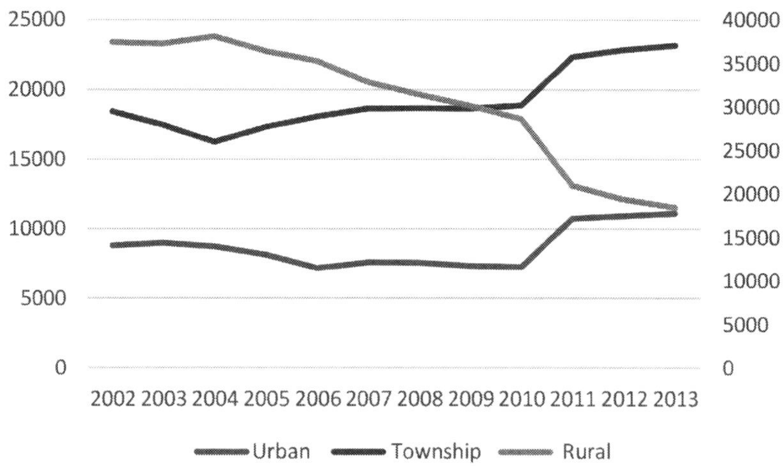

Figure 3.4 The pattern of distribution of rural junior high schools, 2002–13.

Note: The *y*-axis on the right is set for rural schools.

Resources: Department of Education Development and Planning, MOE, *Educational Statistics Yearbook of China*, People's Education Press.

In September 2012, the State Council called for closures of rural primary schools to cease, while raising the possibility that some might be reopened (State Council 2012).

The crucial impasse: Educational equity, residency and college access

But as Yang and others constantly emphasised, of all the barriers to equitable access to public services, the most crucial and intractable remained the residency system itself (Fan 2012).[20] The New Socialist Countryside scheme was at bottom an attempt, through raising the rural quality of life, to stem the migrant tide – a Canute-like enterprise. From around 2008, the government changed tack, at least rhetorically, and began promoting 'integration' of the country and the city (*cheng xiang yitihua*) (as Yang, for one, had been urging). Linked to this were reforms to the *hukou* system designed to facilitate easier access for migrants to urban public services. Since the 1990s, the central authorities had repeatedly exhorted provinces and municipalities to reform practice in this area, but the very fact of repetition indicated the limited impact of exhortation (see Chapter 9). Where education was concerned, allowing migrant children to enrol in metropolitan schools had limited practical significance, so long as their *hukou* disqualified them from taking the college entrance examinations (*gaokao*) outside their 'home' province. Prior to the late 1990s, when higher education was the preserve of an elite minority, this contradiction had less serious implications. But as the massification of tertiary education gathered pace, the entitlement to sit for the *gaokao* in a particular region became a key determinant of life chances for millions. (The *gaokao* system is more fully explained in Chapter 8.)

In 2011, the State Council announced a new solution to this impasse – requiring that, by 2014, out-of-province students be allowed to sit for the *gaokao* in the province where they actually lived. However, the limits of effective central authority were reflected in the strategy for achieving this: rather than legislating a common nationwide procedure, Beijing required all provinces to submit separate 'out-of-area *gaokao*' (*yi di gaokao*) plans by the end of 2012. At the core of the problem lie the fiendishly complex province-by-province quotas governing college entry (see Chapter 8). Amongst the first to comply with the new directive were Shandong, Henan, Anhui and Hunan; their high populations, dearth of top-ranked universities, and high *gaokao* cut-off scores for access to elite institutions meant that no one would choose to sit for college entrance there. A joke had it that allowing migrants to sit for the *gaokao* in Shandong was 'like giving a birth quota to a 90-year-old woman'. At the other extreme, Tibet, Xinjiang and Qinghai missed the submission deadline entirely; with amongst the lowest cut-off scores, opening up the *gaokao* in these provinces might trigger a destabilising flood of educational in-migration by credential-seeking ethnic Han. Shanghai, meanwhile, submitted a plan that envisaged opening up the local *gaokao* only to the children of select categories of migrant, all of them in white-collar employment (see Fu 2013).

The political sensitivity of *gaokao* quota reform in China's most privileged communities was illustrated by a 2015 protest in Beijing. Qualification to sit for the *gaokao* in a particular province or municipality is linked to attendance at a local high school. The affiliated high school of the Minzu University of China (in Beijing) had traditionally educated students recruited from amongst 'minority' ethnicities, dispatched to the capital by provincial governments across the country. Like many key point high schools, it had begun to diversify its admission procedures through 'autonomous recruitment' (*zi zhu zhao sheng* – see Chapters 5 and 9). This was partly a matter of boosting funding, but here a newly appointed principal also felt under pressure to enhance the school's reputation (Wu 2015). Since key point Beijing high schools confer on their students the coveted right to sit for the municipal *gaokao* and thus gain easier admission to elite local universities, applications flooded in. By 2010, more than half of students were not 'minorities' but the offspring of high-scoring, relatively well-heeled Han families from other provinces. In 2014–15, around 50 graduates of this school gained admission to Tsinghua and Peking Universities, accounting for 14 per cent of Beijing's quota for these institutions. After news of this got out, groups of local parents, outraged at the alien threat to their Beijing 'birthright', mounted protests outside the school gates. The municipal Education Commission lent its support, and in September 2015 the State Ethnic Affairs Commission banned the school from recruiting Han students, and prohibited all applications from Zhejiang, Shandong, Fujian or Henan (populous and overwhelmingly Han provinces) (Wu 2015).

The Minzu University affiliated high school, given its exceptional capacity to recruit from across China, represented a loophole in the provincially fragmented college entrance system – and, as such, offered a glimpse of the likely future for other elite urban high schools if *hukou* restrictions were lifted. The rush by out-of-province parents to exploit this opportunity, and the furious protests from those whose privileges were thus threatened, indicated the potentially explosive nature of this issue. For all the apparent willingness of the post-2012 Xi administration to deploy strong-arm tactics, the government's reaction in this instance illustrates limits to its determination to confront vested interests. It is to education policy since the 2012 transition that we now turn.

EDUCATION AND POLITICS SINCE 2012: THE END OF REFORM?

President Hu and Premier Wen had presided over a period of unprecedented plenty, allowing the Party to offer better public services, improved livelihoods, or the plausible prospect of both to most social constituencies – even while inequality increased (Wright 2010). While strong economic growth continued, the leadership could put off systemic reform, deploying palliative measures to alleviate the strains caused by the anachronistic *hukou* regulations. And with Party luminaries jockeying for position in the run-up to the 2012 leadership transition, the premium on stability and 'harmony' was enhanced.

The drama of that year itself highlighted the tensions in China's political and social fabric. Whereas Jiang Zemin and Hu Jintao were both tapped for the leadership by Deng Xiaoping, Xi Jinping enjoyed no such imprimatur. Like many of his colleagues and rivals, he was the 'princeling' son of a first-generation revolutionary. The rise of the princelings seemed to suggest that, in the absence of any robust constitutional process, or the authority of a charismatic leader, networks of nepotism were taking over the Party. It was significant, therefore, that the most threatening challenge to Xi's ascent came from Bo Xilai, the Chongqing Party Secretary. Himself a princeling, Bo was also a charismatic political figure who had positioned himself as a 'Red' campaigner for greater social equality, and a fervent opponent of corruption and crime. His apparent popularity demonstrated the potential appeal of this platform, even though he himself was brought down by a bizarrely convoluted corruption scandal.

The Bo–Xi confrontation of early 2012 dramatised for a rapt public the dynastic nature of intra-Party factionalism (see Garnaut 2012). This was potentially damaging for a Party that, since 1978, had staked its legitimacy not only on its capacity to deliver rapid economic growth, but also on its ability to transform society if not along democratic, then at least along ostensibly meritocratic lines. As we have seen, the early Reform period was marked by campaigns to educate (or re-educate) Party cadres, and to institute stringent educational criteria for recruitment to government positions. Meanwhile, on college campuses around the country, party membership was an honour supposedly bestowed in recognition of intellectual as well as moral and political qualities; entry to the elite was in theory open to all on the basis of merit (see Yan 2014, and Chapter 12). It was certainly the case that, for much of the Party elite during the 'transition from state socialism to market capitalism', education had served 'as a capital-conversion mechanism to help the politically privileged obtain new forms of advantage' (Bian *et al.* 2001, 834). But the meritocratic myth had nonetheless become a cornerstone of CCP legitimacy in the post-Mao era.

The spectacle of the 2012 leadership transition potentially undermined that myth's credibility. Xi Jinping, Wang Qishan, Bo and others may have been intelligent, capable, highly qualified individuals – but it was clearly their connections, rather than their personal merits, that had been crucial to their ascent (and, in Bo's case, arguably his descent too).[21] Talk of the princelings as the 'Red Second Generation' (*hong er dai*) suggested that, after forty years of Reform, 'Redness' – defined by descent more than ideology – might still trump 'Expertise'.

It was no doubt in part awareness of the regime's vulnerability on this score that prompted President Xi to adopt an exceptionally hard line on official corruption. Ironically, he also borrowed certain of the populist tactics deployed by the disgraced Bo, especially his 'Red' rhetoric and selective nostalgia for Maoist egalitarianism. Into this mix was added the further ingredient of a newly assertive nationalism, manifested in a muscular foreign policy. All of this is widely interpreted abroad as evidence of strength on the part of Xi and his regime. However, with uncertain economic prospects threatening the government's capacity to sustain the promise of improved livelihoods, these policy shifts can also be seen as somewhat frantic attempts to shore up regime legitimacy. And perhaps on no issue is public sentiment more febrile, and the potential threat to legitimacy therefore greater, than education.

Signalling left but turning right?

Although throughout this book we refer to 'the Chinese education system', this does not denote a single, unified entity. As subsequent chapters will demonstrate, the concentration of resources, in education as in other sectors, has given rise to a congeries of sub-systems increasingly divergent from province to province or county to county, and across or within administrative boundaries: public, private or some hybrid of both; elite- or 'mass'-oriented; 'regular' or vocational; formal or 'shadow'. While preaching patriotism and national unity, through education and other means the post-Mao authorities have in practice institutionalised a deeply fragmented model of Chinese citizenship.

Drawing together those fragments to form a more unified and more equitable nationwide system for providing education and other public goods is possibly the central challenge confronting China's leadership today. However, considerable confusion and uncertainty pervade both central government policy itself, and its reception or interpretation at local level. For example, a new objective of promoting urbanisation to boost national growth – reversing earlier attempts to encourage farmers to stay put – implies rapid further expansion in demand for urban public services. How, then, are these to be paid for? One problem here arises from the gap between the government's vision for urbanisation and the aspirations of most migrants. The government wants urban growth spread relatively evenly across provinces, and concentrated in second-tier conurbations, but migrants are drawn above all to Beijing, Shanghai, Tianjin and the most prosperous coastal provinces (Zhejiang, Jiangsu and Guangdong). With regard to educational opportunity, the pull of these regions is overwhelming. But if urban growth continues to be concentrated there, Party leaders fear the consequences for political and social stability – and environmental sustainability (Wang and Wang 2015).

Moderating regional imbalances and realising the aspiration for a more even spread of urbanisation would require a much greater redistributive and coordinating role for central government. But here Beijing has continued to send mixed signals. On the one hand, the principle that provinces and municipalities are primarily responsible for raising and distributing school funding remains. On the other, part-funded mandates imposed by the State Council relating to various aspects of educational provision have proliferated over the past decade. One example of this, relating to a new push to expand provision of early childhood education and care, is dealt with in the following chapter. Here as in other cases (e.g. the tightening of rules on school 'zoning' or the use of selective entrance tests; see Chapter 8), the combination of central diktat, top-down cadre evaluations and local unaccountability can make for selective compliance, waste and continued neglect of those most in need.

Meanwhile, calls for an intensification of reform and local 'innovation' have coincided, since 2012, with a heightened insistence on ideological 'correctness' and corruption-avoidance liable to deter risk-taking on the part of subordinate officials. Whether this ultimately contributes to greater responsiveness to local needs remains to be seen. But there is a fundamental tension between the confrontation with entrenched vested interests that would be required to secure this, and the regime's overwhelming concern to shore up political stability and Party supremacy. We return to that tension in our concluding chapter, but it will form a running theme of the remainder of this book.

Notes

1 A major slogan of the 1989 Student Movement, as Zeng recalls, was *Da dao guan dao!*, or 'Down with trafficking by officials!'.

2 This was followed in subsequent years by similar rules for students at secondary and primary levels.

3 Zhao Ziyang seemed to approve, and reportedly gave a copy of the documentary to the visiting Singaporean leader Lee Kuan Yew (Baum 1996, 232).

4 And not for the first time. Dikotter (2013) points out that the introduction of the *hukou* system in 1958 was intended to secure the food supply for urban industry, with crops forcibly requisitioned from the countryside for distribution to the cities during the *Great Leap Forward* and after.

5 The consequent reduction in personnel was partly illusory, since the place of many permanent officials was taken by others 'seconded' – *jie dao* – from colleges, universities or other institutions (including, during this period, Zeng, the present co-author).

6 Entry to postgraduate courses remained strictly regulated, though even at this level a 50 per cent increase was registered between 1990 and 1996 (IED 1996, 3936–41). This would be insufficient to provide qualified staff to cater for expanded student numbers – a shortfall partly made up through overseas study. See Chapter 13.

7 The case for the harmfulness of Falun Gong was buttressed by a widely broadcast video (of dubious authenticity) of a supporter 'self-immolating' on Tiananmen Square.

8 The fact that the major fieldwork for the studies of 'Chinese' education by Lewin *et al.* (1994) and Rao *et al.* (2003) was conducted in Zhejiang raises questions over their representativeness (especially in the latter case, where the claims made are more sweeping).

9 Hence the popular saying, 'Wherever the expressway is built, the head of the transport bureau goes to jail' (*gaosu gonglu diu dao na-er, jiaotongtingzhang dao zai na'er*).

10 As testified by the collapse of so many schools in the Sichuan earthquake of 2008.

11 It was partly to address this perception that relatively impoverished Han regions were being neglected that a new project, the 'Rise of Central China Plan' (*Zhongbu jueqi jihua*), was launched in 2004. This appears to have featured the same focus on construction as the *Xibu da kaifa*.

12 As Rappleye observes (2007), Chinese leaders' predilection for moral education was one reason for their apparent attraction to Japanese precedents during the 1990s.

13 Hu Jintao had been close to former Premier Hu Yaobang (no relation) during the 1980s, before the latter's dismissal. Assigned in 1988 to the post of Party Secretary in Tibet, Hu the younger rose in Deng's estimation following the decisive quelling of March 1989 protests in Lhasa. He was subsequently quick to endorse the crackdown against student protesters in Beijing that June. Wen Jiabao, for his part, was a close aide of Zhao Ziyang, the Party Secretary dismissed for sympathising with the demonstrating students (Lam 2006, 8).

14 *Sina Weibo* – China's answer to Twitter – was launched in August 2009, and Hu and Wen both registered accounts the following year. However, since 2012 the authorities have become far more suspicious of such tools.

15 In 2008, Wen himself had been instrumental in pushing through a tuition-free programme for teacher education for students from Western regions (see Chapter 7) – a popular initiative (especially in the target regions) that nonetheless met with resistance from normal universities simultaneously charged with pursuing enhanced global 'rankings' (see Chapter 12).

16 Zhou's personal reputation was and remained good; he was seen as a relatively 'clean' official. But ironically his very 'cleanliness' may have contributed to his downfall, in so far as it hampered his capacity for behind-the-scenes dealmaking.

17 Cadre positions in higher education institutions have often served as a launch-pad for high-flying Party officials: current premier Li Keqiang occupied a similar position to Yang's in Peking University during the 1980s.

18 In 2012, Yang was involved in a very public spat with Liu Pengzhi, principal of Renmin University's Affiliated High School, over the role of money and influence in securing places in this highly prestigious school for children of the powerful. Yang openly equated practices euphemistically labelled 'school choice' with the issue of corruption (for further discussion of controversy over admission practices at Renmin University, see Chapter 8).

19 Indeed, Yang's comments on these moral failings are reminiscent of Jiang Zemin's remarks a decade earlier, quoted in the previous section.

20 Yang was far from alone in this. Zhang Qian-fan of Peking University's Law School also campaigned for migrant students' college access through the '*yi di gao kao*'. But unlike Yang, he couched his arguments in the language of 'human rights', and was thus largely ostracised.

21 For analysis of the networks of current CCP leaders see Brown (2014).

4 Early childhood education and care

We start our more detailed, thematic analysis of education in post-Mao China at the earliest phase of formal instruction outside the home: early childhood education and care (ECEC). This chapter traces major shifts in ECEC policy and practice, with some reference to the pre-Reform period as well as to the years since 1978. As we saw in Chapter 3, the marketisation of provision, the rising expectations of parents (especially in the cities), and the ambition of the government to groom 'talent', even from infancy, have been major themes in the story of post-Mao China's educational development. These and other factors have combined to gear ECEC towards increasingly sophisticated, but sometimes contradictory, pedagogical goals. The same processes have also given rise to increasingly stratified provision, with 'world-class' kindergartens for the wealthy and privileged, and inferior preschools, or none at all, for those disadvantaged by income or residency. At the same time, the disorienting rapidity of societal change, along with increased exposure to global fashions in educational thought and practice, have prompted concern over the socialising role of kindergartens. In all these respects, changes to ECEC provision have echoed or prefigured shifts in primary and secondary schooling.

A fairly comprehensive system for the provision of early childhood care had developed around the collective institutions of the Maoist era, with the aim of freeing more women to work outside the home. The post-1978 period saw a shift towards greater emphasis on educational goals, as maximising the talent of the infant population was seen as one element of the strategy for achieving the 'four modernisations'. Meanwhile, however, the collective institutions that provided most childcare were undercut by marketising reforms, first in the countryside and then, after 1992, in the cities. During the 1990s, it was therefore ECEC, rather than schooling or higher education, which offered the greatest scope to private providers. The same period witnessed a growing international focus on ECEC, with the OECD's first *Starting Strong* report describing it as 'the first step in lifelong learning and a key component of a successful educational, social, and family policy agenda' (OECD 2001). Since 2011, the ECEC sector has finally found itself in line for accelerated development, receiving substantial injections of public investment. All this has produced a mix of public providers dating back to the days of the command economy; a vibrant but disorderly private sector; and – more recently – a bureaucracy set upon building a more unified and comprehensive system, but whose capacity to do so remains uncertain.

Beginnings: Childcare and women's liberation

> *Nan zun nü bei, fu ci zi xiao* ('Men are to be respected and women regarded as inferior, fathers are to exercise benevolence and sons to practise filial piety').
> (Confucian aphorism)

The more professionalised 'vanguard' of the ECEC field (i.e. the minority of better-equipped urban kindergartens with qualified teaching staff) has arguably proved even more susceptible to shifting trends and influences than the schooling system proper. This is in large part because curricular content, teaching materials and pedagogical approaches have generally been subject to lighter-touch official supervision than those for primary and secondary schools. The first two decades of the twentieth century, which witnessed the real advent of modern educational provision in China, saw significant borrowing from Japan in the field of ECEC (as in schooling) – reflected in the use of games, songs and poems, conversation and craft activities. During this period, Zhang Zhidong, an early proponent of educational modernisation, invited Japanese experts to advise on the establishment of kindergartens (Tang and Zhong, 2000, 326). However, as relations with Japan cooled, and as America became the prime destination for overseas study, the pattern of foreign influence shifted. Key educational reformers of the interwar period, such as Tao Xingzhi and Chen Heqin (both students of John Dewey), advocated 'progressive' education. Catchphrases of this movement included 'Education from Life' (*shenghuo ji jiaoyu*) and 'Nature and Society are both living materials for instruction' (260).

The ancient saying quoted at the head of this section encapsulates the patriarchal assumptions that the Communists sought to overturn after 1949. The Party's keenness to promote social and ethical 'modernisation', in particular by championing the rights of women, was symbolised in its very first legislative act – the passage of the 'Marriage Law'. By outlawing polygamy and concubinage, this went further in challenging traditional attitudes than the Kuomintang on Taiwan, or Hong Kong's colonial authorities, were willing to venture until the 1970s. It served notice of official intent to radically transform society, beginning with its most basic constituent unit: the family. Policy on ECEC reflected this determination to 'liberate' women from their role as carers – if only to conscript them for the task of socialist construction. Women would be unable to 'hold up half the sky', as Mao envisaged, if they were left holding the baby.

After 1949, when China was engaged in wholesale borrowing from the Soviet Union, early childhood education was influenced by the contemporary Soviet insistence on a subject-based curriculum. The Education Ministry's 1952 'Temporary regulations for kindergartens' thus stipulated a curriculum divided into six discrete 'subjects': physical education, language, environmental knowledge, art and craft, music and arithmetic. However, arguably the most fundamental shift in the ECEC system during this period was the large-scale introduction of boarding kindergartens, as a function of the emphasis on facilitating female participation in the workforce.

In the 1952 regulations, the Ministry spelt out the principal goals of ECEC:

> The duties of kindergartens are: to nurture young children according to the principles of new democratic education, and to promote their all-round physical and psychological development in preparation for entering primary school; at the same time, to reduce the burden of childcare borne by mothers, so as to give them time to participate in political activities, productive labour, cultural and educational activities, and so on.
>
> (IED 1952, 144)

This stipulation reflects the high priority accorded in these early post-'liberation' years to the objective of facilitating female participation in the workforce. Elsewhere in the same document (clauses 6 and 20), it was stated that: every locality should 'establish boarding kindergartens, providing care, food and lodging for infants, in order to enable their parents to work'; and that rural regions should 'establish seasonal kindergartens, in order to enable women to engage in productive labour in regions where agriculture, nomadic herding, fishing, etc. [are widespread]'. The children of 'professional, peasant and working women', not those of unproductive housewives, were to have first call on limited preschool places.

The phenomenon of state-run boarding kindergartens persisted well into the post-Reform period; foreign visitors to a Kunming kindergarten in the mid-1980s were shocked to find 60 per cent of children boarding from Monday to Friday (Tobin *et al.* 2009, 23). Staff reportedly rejected the 'bourgeois logic' that it was best for young children to be cared for primarily by their mothers (31). In a period when most households had little disposable income, boarding kindergartens were seen as providing facilities and stimulation for small children that was unlikely to be unavailable at home.

The financing and management of ECEC in the pre-Reform era

The emphasis in state policy on bringing women into the workforce influenced arrangements for financing and staffing kindergartens. In 1956, the Education, Health and Interior Ministries issued a joint statement stating blandly that the primary function of nurseries (*tuo'ersuo*) and kindergartens was to help mothers care for and educate their children, but also stipulating that all necessary 'expenditure, staffing, accommodation and day-to-day administration' was 'the responsibility of the relevant work unit' (IED 1956, 578). There was thus no single, unified, public system of ECEC – instead, work units would separately arrange provision for the children of their own workers. Depending on the nature of the work unit, public subsidies were channelled through three different conduits:

1 payments to local educational authorities by government departments, military units and other official bodies, in return for access for their workers to publicly provided ECEC;
2 provision organised by SOEs for their own workers: in the era of the command economy, every SOE 'work unit' was its own mini-state, with teachers, nurses, childcare workers and other welfare providers employed on the same basis as other SOE workers;
3 street committees (*jiedao zhumin weiyuanhui*) or rural communes (*cunmin dadui*): for those not employed by large enterprises, local collectives could provide nursery care.

ECEC provision was thus theoretically universal, but in reality highly fragmented and variable. Until the 1980s, it fell within the remit of the *danwei* (work unit)-based welfare system, with kindergarten staff treated as employees of the *danwei* rather than of the local Education Bureau (MOF 1973). In the cities, this delivered some form of publicly subsidised childcare to most families, but in the countryside, where the vast majority of the population lived, formal provision was patchy or non-existent. This *danwei*-based approach to public service provision was a legacy of the highly militarised forms of governance developed by the Communist Party during its pre-1949 'guerrilla' phase. After collectivisation in the 1950s, SOEs, urban street committees and rural communes continued to frame the lives of a regimented population. Each form of collective unit provided cradle-to-grave welfare (including ECEC) to its members, but did so according to highly differing standards; the most significant divide was between urban and rural dwellers, as designated by the household registration (*hukou*) system. A high degree of administrative fragmentation, in a context of juridical absolutism and formal unity, is a longstanding feature of Chinese imperial governance.[1] But the *hukou* system was a Communist innovation that lent this fragmentation a new rigidity, and formally consigned the rural population to second-class citizenship. Even as the welfare system, and ECEC provision with it, has undergone wrenching change from the 1980s onwards, this division has been essentially preserved.

Meanwhile, Chinese debates over ECEC have also revolved around another division much more familiar internationally: that between 'care-focused' and 'education-focused' preschooling (Pascal and Bertram 1998). In many developed countries, ECEC has undergone a transition from the former to the latter, while experiencing a corresponding process of professionalisation. As this has happened, there has often been a transfer of administrative responsibility for ECEC – for example from the Welfare Ministry to the Education Ministry.[2] In the case of China, as we shall see, these processes have been greatly accelerated during the post-1978 period – and particularly since the early 1990s.

1978–85: The restoration and extension of the ECEC system

With education high on the agenda of the post-Mao leadership, the 1977 National Education Conference called for the urgent 'restoration and reconstruction' (*huifu he chongjian*) of all levels of schooling, including preschooling (see Chapter 3.1). However, an increasingly enthusiastic embrace of Western ideas and practices in urban intellectual circles was somewhat at odds with the 'restored' Soviet-inspired models for educational provision, from preschool level upwards. Meanwhile, economic reforms – particularly the decollectivisation of the countryside – undermined the old arrangements for funding public goods, including ECEC (with consequences outlined in Chapter 3.2).

A shift in emphasis: From liberating mothers to nurturing 'talent'

Although enthusiasm for 'science' and 'modernisation' in the early Reform period was most obviously signalled at the high school and college level, it was also evident in a reordering of priorities at lower rungs of the educational ladder. If China was to 'catch up' with the West and Japan in terms of scientific and technological prowess, young Chinese would need a head start. In October 1979, the State Council convened a conference of officials from five departments to discuss issues relating to the 'restoration and reconstruction' of ECEC. The resulting directive notably omitted any reference to the objective of keeping mothers in the workforce, instead emphasising investment in 'talent':

> The nurturing of children in the early years ... forms the basis [for the growth of] talented individuals (*rencai*), and is essential in order to significantly raise the scientific and cultural level of the entire Chinese nation. ... To devote effort to [the development of small] children, and to assign to this task the necessary personnel, resources and funding, is an important construction project (*jianshe shiye*), and an investment in the future.
>
> (IED 1979, 1739)

This marked a major shift in official thinking – or at least in official rhetoric. ECEC was henceforth portrayed as important not primarily as an instrument for liberating mothers from the burden of childcare, but for its contribution to improving the nation's stock of human capital. This emphasis on fostering high-quality talent rather than on facilitating women's employment was consistent with the broader reaction against Maoist revolutionary extremism. One facet of the liberalisation of Chinese society in the 1980s was the popular re-emergence of conventional notions of femininity, but the Party itself also increasingly promoted the idea that women's primary role was as 'mothers of development' rather than direct participants in it (see Chapter 6; also Fincher 2014).

The strengthening of danwei*-based provision of ECEC*

Reform to the *danwei*-based system for funding and administering ECEC was not seriously countenanced in the early 1980s (when the urban economy remained largely unreformed), although the transfer of responsibility for ECEC policy (for children over 3) from the Ministry of Health to the Education Ministry signalled the heightened emphasis on its educative role. In the context of the decentralisation of responsibility for administering and financing public services, the state was in no position to mandate uniform, nationwide standards of provision. Instead, *danwei*-run preschools, where these existed, were to form the basis for expanding provision of 'high-quality' ECEC. Bureaux of urban planning and construction were urged to address provision of childcare in their plans, and from about 1983 SOEs were tentatively permitted to open up their childcare facilities to the local community (Wang Y. 2009). This was referred to as 'socialising' (*shehuihua*) *danwei* preschools – a euphemism for marketing their services to fee-paying parents from outside the work unit. Typically, it was stipulated by the State Council that 'socialised' provision of ECEC should be pioneered – in selected urban areas – by provinces or municipalities that possessed the necessary 'conditions' (*tiaojian*).

Meanwhile, changes to the urban economy during the 1980s were already beginning to highlight the anachronism of the *danwei*-based system for public service provision, with access determined by residency. For example, as construction companies in urban areas increasingly struggled to recruit labour, they took on growing numbers of temporary workers from the countryside – the first ripples in what was to become a swelling tide of 'migrant workers' (*nongmin gong*). Since these workers generally did not bring their families with them – their residency status preventing them from accessing welfare benefits (including ECEC) restricted to urban residents – the kindergartens run by such enterprises often failed to recruit sufficient numbers of children. Since these 'closed' *danwei* preschools were unable to divert their welfare budgets to other purposes, this created one spur to 'socialising' SOE preschools, as a means of turning a profit from an under-utilised resource (Xu and Li 1995).

The established *danwei*- or commune-based system for ECEC provision was only sustainable so long as Chinese society was treated as a great 'national syndicate' (*guojia xindijia*). In other words, while the command economy persisted, it mattered little whether ECEC expenditure appeared on the accounts of the local government or those of SOEs. However, the move towards a 'socialist market economy', which gathered speed during the 1990s, compelled different units of this notional national 'syndicate' to operate as independent, profit-making entities, competing for resources and clients. This in turn undermined the willingness or capacity of enterprises to continue providing ancillary services that might be seen as a drain on profits and a drag on competitiveness (Zeng X. 2006).

The impact of Economic Reform on ECEC

The marketisation of provision, the rising expectations of parents (especially middle class urbanites with singleton children), and the ambition of the government to groom 'talent', even from infancy, have combined to gear ECEC towards increasingly sophisticated, but sometimes contradictory, pedagogical goals. The same processes have also created an increasingly stratified system, in which the most wealthy and privileged have access to 'world-class' preschools, while those disadvantaged by income, residency or geography make do with poorer-quality provision or none at all. At the same time, the disorienting rapidity of China's social transformation, along with increased exposure to global fashions in educational thought and practice, have prompted concern over the socialising role of kindergartens – specifically the part that they can or should play in imparting 'Chinese values'. In all these respects, changes to ECEC have been intimately connected to changes affecting primary and secondary schooling, with similar trends in curricula and pedagogy affecting all sectors. But as we shall see, the particularly intense marketisation of the ECEC sector has given it a pivotal role in entrenching social privilege and ossifying China's re-emergent class divide.

Pedagogy – professionalisation and standardisation

The increased emphasis on the educational, as distinct from the childcare, role of preschools was reflected in official efforts to promote a professionalisation and standardisation of ECEC practice. Separate guidelines were issued for urban kindergartens (in 1979) and their rural counterparts (1983) (MOE 1979, 1983). The titles of the relevant documents are significant: urban kindergartens warranted a formal 'ordinance' (*tiaoli*) governing their 'work', but the rustic equivalent was entitled 'Several opinions on the development of rural kindergartens'. This signified an acceptance of the urban–rural divide in preschooling, as in primary and secondary schooling, and a willingness to countenance exacerbating it in pursuit of high quality provision for the cities. The regulations stipulated different curricula, facilities and staff qualifications for urban and rural kindergartens. Hence the raw figures in Table 4.1 do not give an accurate picture of the distribution of access to ECEC: not only did rural preschools constitute a declining proportion of the national total, but the qualitative divide between urban and rural preschools was widening.

However, the financial self-sufficiency of the ECEC sector, in addition to its non-compulsory status, meant that 'opinions', or even ordinances, issued by the

Table 4.1 Number of kindergartens and enrolments (children aged 3–6), 1978–85 by location

Year	*No. of kindergartens*				*No. of children enrolled (10,000)*			
	Total	*Urban*	*County town*	*Rural*	*Total*	*Urban*	*County town*	*Rural*
1978	163,952	16,292	6,651	141,009	787.75	138.45	70.26	579.04
1979	165,629	18,953	7,523	139,153	879.23	168.67	82.68	627.88
1980	170,419	18,357	8,686	143,376	1,150.77	174.64	97.13	879.00
1981	130,296	20,886	8,986	100,424	1,056.22	202.90	105.42	747.90
1982	122,107	19,005	11,293	91,809	1,113.09	231.43	126.12	755.54
1983	136,306	25,049	12,329	98,928	1,140.25	249.96	137.43	752.86
1984	166,526	25,435	18,988	122,103	1,294.74	285.10	176.22	833.42
1985	172,262	26,320	23,998	121,944	1,479.69	332.94	222.77	923.98

Source: NBS.

Ministry in relation to ECEC did not carry the same force as those relating to primary or secondary schooling. For example, although the Education Ministry required that kindergarten teachers should have graduated from Early Childhood Education Normal Schools (*you'er shifan xuexiao*), or possess equivalent qualifications, many *danwei* continued to assign teaching positions to women within the *danwei* who were unable or unwilling to undertake manual labour. And although Ministry documents in the 1980s already talked of 'socialising' *danwei* preschools (i.e. allowing them to offer places to families outside the *danwei* on a fee-paying basis),[3] partly as a means of furthering its regulatory agenda, commercialisation did not truly take off until the 1990s. While the Education Reform decree of 1985 marked the start of a drive to universalise compulsory education (see Chapter 3.2), in the field of ECEC the mid-1990s restructuring of SOEs marked a more significant juncture. Until that point, official calls for greater standardisation continually ran up against the entrenched *danwei*-based structure of provision. Fundamental reform was yet to come.

Inside the kindergarten – a mid-1980s snapshot

The classic comparative study of early childhood education, *Pre-school in Three Cultures* (Tobin *et al.* 1991), presents an account of a single day in a single Chinese kindergarten (Daguan in Kunming, Yunnan Province) in 1985.[4] The authors acknowledge the huge gulf between ECEC provision in urban and rural areas, explicitly confining their attention to the former. Salient features of Chinese preschooling as depicted in this study include a regimented, collectivist ethos, and a highly teacher-centred, didactic approach to instruction. This didacticism is epitomised by an account of a 'block play' activity that involved distributing identical sets of blocks before requiring each child, individually, to follow instructions for constructing models out of them (Tobin *et al.* 2009, 43–4). Teacher–student ratios were high, and some teachers were not professionally trained. Most students were boarders, and this was reflected in an emphasis on teachers' role as 'parent surrogates'. Signs on the walls of boarding classrooms proclaimed 'the *you'eryuan* is my home; my teachers are like my mother' (33). However, a relatively strict disciplinary regime was also maintained. Partly to promote good 'posture', but also for purposes of order and control, children were required to sit with their hands folded behind their backs, as still happens today in many Chinese primary schools. Kindergarten classrooms, with their orderly rows of desks, also looked like primary classrooms – a reflection of continued adherence to the Soviet model, with its subject-based curriculum designed to prepare children for the serious work of primary school.

Determination to maintain discipline was reinforced by concerns related to the likely impact of the One Child Policy. The ECEC system in the mid-1980s was just receiving its first intake of singleton children, amidst much talk of the danger of 'spoiling' to which these 'little emperors' would be exposed (37–8). For some preschool teachers, this placed an added premium on the boarding experience, and on the collectivist ethos that kindergartens had espoused throughout the Communist era. Manifestations of this ethos included daily communal physical exercise; communal visits to the toilet; the singing of patriotic songs; and recounting of stories of revolutionary heroes. A strong sense of community during this period, accentuated by the relatively Spartan conditions that teachers and students then had to endure together, was something that older teachers later recalled with more than a hint of nostalgia (Tobin *et al.* 2009, 24–6).

1986–92: The deepening of conflicts between ECEC and the *danwei*-based welfare system

Promulgated around the time that Tobin and his colleagues were conducting their fieldwork, the 'Compulsory Education Law' of 1986 signified that the universalisation of nine years of compulsory education had officially become the overriding priority for education policy. Official documents reflect the overwhelming focus during this period on issues of funding, teacher training and curricular reform relating to the compulsory phase. In this context, reform of ECEC was very much relegated to the ministerial back burner: of 748 policy documents issued by the SEC between 1986 and 1992, only five related to ECEC (IED). Moreover, these few pronouncements heralded no new initiatives, but reiterated previous calls for greater standardisation and professionalisation of teaching, or dealt with issues of health and safety.

However, even while ministerial attention was diverted elsewhere, existing funding arrangements for ECEC began to unravel. The agricultural boom that followed reform of land-use rights in 1978 prompted leading officials to consider favourably other measures of qualified economic decentralisation, in the belief that granting more managerial autonomy to enterprises would similarly boost productivity. This led to the policy of 'transforming profits into tax' (*li gai shui*), whereby SOEs were required to pay tax (at varying rates depending on the size and profitability of the enterprise), and permitted to retain any remaining profits – thus introducing an element of profit-and-loss accounting into the command economy. This policy, introduced in two stages between 1980 and 1984, had mixed results in terms of improving SOE efficiency (State Council 1984). However, it contributed to a fundamental undermining of the *danwei*-based system of welfare provision.[5]

With the introduction of *li gai shui*, *danwei*-run preschools (along with schools, hospitals and old people's homes) increasingly came to be viewed by management as a drag on profits. Moreover, since most SOEs had been formed in the period between 1954–8, the late 1980s saw many workers reaching retirement, implying rising demands on *danwei* medical services and provision of care for the elderly. The One Child Policy was meanwhile contributing to a declining birth rate, and hence falling demand for preschools. In this context, SOE managers were presented both with a growing mismatch between service provision and demand, and with heightened incentives for cutting welfare costs. Although reforms specifically targeting the *danwei*-based welfare system came only in 1994, many enterprises had thus already begun to cut back on investment in

ECEC well before that – often through measures such as merging preschools or subcontracting their management to private companies (Zeng X. 2006).

1993–2002: Marketisation and the weakening of ECEC funding arrangements

As we noted in Chapter 3.3, the marketisation drive of the mid-1990s brought major change to China's cities, hitherto still dominated by the institutions of the command economy. This involved a radical reduction in the fiscal subsidies that most SOEs could expect to receive from the state. The practice of permitting enterprises to retain profits to pay for employee welfare provision, already weakened by the *li gai shui* reforms, was further undermined, as the state sought to increase revenue and incentivise SOEs to focus on raising profitability. The consequent erosion of the financial basis for SOE welfare provision meant that, as the decade wore on, more and more *danwei*-run kindergartens were either closed or transferred to private management. Between 1993 and 2002, the total number of SOE-run kindergartens declined from almost 28,000 to around 9,500. Although local governments were in theory free to use some of their increased revenue to expand public provision of ECEC, preschooling – unlike universalisation of primary education – was not a major official priority. With quantitative expansion of public preschooling failing to keep pace with demand, the private sector stepped in; by the end of the decade, private ECEC institutions outnumbered public ones (see Table 4.2).

Meanwhile, the urban neighbourhood collectives or 'street committees', many of which had previously provided small, rudimentary, not-for-profit childcare centres or preschools, found it increasingly hard to sustain their operation in the increasingly competitive environment created by marketisation. Collective-based urban provision suffered in the 1990s a fate similar to that of collective

Table 4.2 Number of kindergartens 1993–2002 by type, and total enrolments

Year	*Total*	*Urban*	*Rural*	*Township*	*Collective*	*Private*	*Public*	*SOE, etc.*[a]	*Total children enrolled*
1993	165,197	3,1882	10,4901	28,414	119,437		1,7861	27,899	25,525,380
1994	174,657	35,773	103,073	35,811	112,462	18,284	20,645	23,266	26,302,725
1995	180,438	37,256	106,665	36,517	114,863	20,780	21,561	23,234	27,112,328
1996	187,324	36,037	110,428	40,859	115,736	24,466	25,217	21,905	26,663,270
1997	182,485	35,819	107,348	39,318	106,738	24,643	30,694	20,410	25,189,638
1998	181,368	35,910	104,252	41,206	99,649	30,824	31,741	19,154	24,030,344
1999	181,136	37,301	101,896	41,939	90,979	37,020	35,710	17,427	23,262,588
2000	176,000	36,907	93,495	45,434	80,722	44,317	35,219	15,578	22,441,806
2001	111,706	278,48	53,003	30,855	55,682	44,526		11,498	20,218,371
2002	111,800	293,05	49,133	33,314	53,838	48,365		9,549	20,360,245

Source: NBS.

Note: [a] Including government departments or bureaux.

arrangements in the countryside following the land reforms of the late 1970s and early 1980s; as the urban command economy was reformed, these collectives lost their funding (Zeng X. 2006).

Of the three funding mechanisms for public welfare provision established in the era of the command economy (see above), only the *danwei*-based system as it related to official work units (government departments, bureaux, universities, etc.) entered the new millennium more or less intact. At the same time, marketisation allowed the kindergartens run by these state organs, with their protected funding and privileged status, to open their doors to paying customers from outside the *danwei*. Trading on their long-established reputations for quality, they were typically able to out-compete most purely private providers. In aiming to move the urban economy towards a 'modern enterprise system', the 1994 reforms thus resulted in the withdrawal of state support from all but a privileged few kindergartens in key public *danwei*, leaving the bulk of urban parents unable to secure a place in the limited number of public preschools at the mercy of an increasingly stratified and expensive ECEC market (Zeng X. 2006, 11–16).

The impact on ECEC of the reforms of the mid-1990s was also related to developments in the overall administration of the sector. A 1979 National Work Conference on ECEC had produced regulations stipulating that the Education Ministry should supply curricular and pedagogical guidelines for kindergartens, while promoting standardisation of provision (IED 1979, 1739). Meanwhile, a 'Leading Work Group for Early Childhood Education' (*tuo you gongzuo lingdao xiaozu*) was tasked with coordinating with the Education and Health Ministries, the All-China Federation of Trades Unions and the All-China Women's Federation (*quan guo fu lian*) – all of which claimed a stake in the ECEC sector. However, with ECEC a relatively low priority for these various organisations, this arrangement did not prove effective in securing public resources sufficient to compensate for the erosion of collective provision.

With emphasis on the educative (as opposed to caring) function of ECEC continuing to strengthen, ultimate responsibility for regulating all aspects of ECEC increasingly rested with the SEC/Ministry of Education. But the Ministry's role was restricted to regulation and exhortation: it provided virtually no resources for ECEC, leaving it to different localities to determine the appropriate level of investment in this sector. Nor did it have much authority over the remaining *danwei* kindergartens, which fell under the remit of other state organs. In any case, during the 1993–2002 period the Ministry's attention was concentrated overwhelmingly on the universalisation of basic education and construction of an elite higher education sector. In this context, ECEC in China's burgeoning cities was increasingly left to the vagaries of the market, while state provision was largely sacrificed to the cause of SOE reform (Zeng X. 2006).

2002–9: Private providers transform the ECEC system

By the early years of the twenty-first century, successive waves of economic reform had thus drastically undermined the old system of ECEC. However, this resulted less from direct intervention in the childcare sector than, indirectly, from fiscal reform and the gradual dismantling of the command economy. Between 2002 and 2004, the central government initiated a second round of SOE restructuring which sought to further trim extraneous 'social' functions – with the twin aims of enhancing SOE efficiency and consolidating provision of public services. In order to avoid disruption in the delivery of compulsory education, financial and administrative responsibility for former *danwei*-run primary and secondary schools was transferred to local governments. But the State Council document that dealt with the fate of *danwei* schools and their staff made no provision for *danwei* kindergartens or nursery schools (MDET 2002; State Council 2004).

Ever since moves to reform the command economy began in the 1980s, their implications for ECEC provision had been a blind spot. Under growing pressure to cut costs and enhance profitability, enterprises increasingly came to see the running of kindergartens as a troublesome burden. Local education bureaux, for their part, were not used to regarding ECEC as central to their plans for educational development, given the long practice of regarding childcare as the responsibility of *danwei* and neighbourhood collectives. In the absence of strong pressure from above, budgetary provision for this sector generally remained minimal.

Meanwhile, private providers increasingly stepped into the breach. By 2008, of a total of 33,165 urban kindergartens, 7,514 (22.7 per cent) were publicly run, 2,622 (7.9 per cent) were operated by collectives (i.e. street committees), with the remaining 23,029 (69.4 per cent) private (NBS 2008) (for shifts in ECEC provision from 2002 onwards, see Table 4.3). This represented a dramatic change

Table 4.3 Number of kindergartens 2002–9 by type, and total enrolments

Year	*Of which*								
	Total	*Urban*	*Rural*	*Township*	*Collective*	*Private*	*Gov.*	*Other sectors*[a]	*Total children enrolled*
2003	116,390	31,652	505,61	34,177	51,774	555,36		9,080	2,003,9061
2004	118,000	32,938	54,260	30,701	47,575	62,167		8,157	20,894,002
2005	124,402	33,299	60,221	30,882	24,054	68,835	256,88	5,825	21,790,290
2006	130,495	31,828	64,719	33,948	22,680	75,426	268,77	5,512	22,638,509
2007	129,086	32,946	61,343	34,797	19,710	77,616	266,97	5,063	23,488,300
2008	133,722	33,165	64,303	36,254	18,432	83,119	274,49	4,722	24,749,600
2009	138,209	33,496	66366	38,347	17,542	89,304	269,58	4,405	26,578,141
2010	150,420	35,845	71,588	42,987	15,077	102,289	292,57	3,797	29,766,695
2011	166,750	53,547	58,684	54,519	13,162	115,404	310,44	1,805	34,244,456
2012	181,300					124,638			36,857,600

Source: NBS.

Note: [a] Refers primarily to kindergartens run by traditional 'work units'.

from the situation twenty years previously, when the vast majority of kindergartens were run either by *danwei* or local street committees. By 2008, private provision thus played a far greater role in ECEC than in any other educational sector (on the role of the market at primary and secondary levels, see Chapter 9).

The attractiveness of the preschool sector to commercial operators was enhanced by continuing vagueness regarding their legal status. Since they were not classified as purely educational institutions, preschools were exempted from the legal restrictions (largely honoured in the breach) on profit-taking in the education sector,[6] but profits made from the preschool business were not subject to taxation. Private investment consequently poured into the ECEC sector to take advantage of the 'double benefit' of tax-free profits. The sector also bifurcated, with expensive institutions (offering curricular embellishments such as English classes and piano lessons) on the one hand, and very cheap and rudimentary ones on the other. While many expensive private kindergartens have faced accusations of false or misleading advertising, at the opposite end of the scale a race to cut costs has given rise to concerns over safety and quality.

Another glimpse inside the kindergarten – Tobin's 2002 visits, and reflections on pedagogy and ethos

Returning to China in 2002 to follow up his mid-1980s fieldwork, Tobin observed how the activities of 'public' preschools had been influenced by broader marketisation of the sector (Tobin *et al.* 2009). His original fieldwork site, Daguan kindergarten in Kunming, opened its doors to fee-paying clients during the 1990s, and subsequently upgraded its facilities. New buildings and equipment, along with teachers' salaries, continued to be paid for by the Provincial Government, even though Daguan by the late 1990s was competing for paying clients in the ECEC market. The competitive position of kindergartens is largely determined by 'rankings' conferred through a system of government inspections – with physical resources and teachers' qualifications and (perceived) competence being the key criteria (36).[7] The dual, or 'hybrid' role of state organs – as both poacher and gamekeeper, or entrepreneur and regulator – is glaringly apparent (37). As we discuss in Chapter 9, this is a phenomenon that has also been evident in other sectors of the education system.

The continuing shift from childminding to 'academic' instruction as the central function of preschooling has been reflected in the decline in public boarding preschools – although expensive private boarding kindergartens have emerged cater to children of the new entrepreneurial elite, with their long working hours and frequent business trips (Tobin *et al.* 2009, 33). The concern with 'spoiling' that followed the advent of the One Child Policy in the 1980s meanwhile appeared largely to have evaporated by the early 2000s. Instead, as preschools compete for paying clients, and as the educational level and expectations of middle-class urban parents have risen, teachers increasingly feel caught between parental pressure to focus on academic preparation, and their own beliefs regarding what is 'good for children' (37–40). These beliefs have in turn undergone a shift since the 1980s towards more 'child-centred' ideas. The 'progressivist' turn in ECEC thinking has been closely related to exposure to foreign, especially American, ideas and practice in this field – but also harks back to the early-twentieth-century phase of Deweyan influence on Chinese educational thought (41–2; see also Tang and Zhong 1993).

While 'child-centred' approaches are generally associated in America and elsewhere with an emphasis on small class sizes, in Chinese preschools high teacher–student ratios still predominate. Moreover, it is the more commercially successful preschools, attracting the highest numbers of pupils, that tend to have some of the highest ratios. Tobin *et al.* note that small class sizes have not become associated in China with educational quality (35) – if anything, the opposite is the case, as low pupil numbers may be seen as an indicator of the low popularity of a preschool (or school), and hence of its poor quality (see also Kipnis 2011). More recently, however, it appears that the contrast between typical class sizes in urban and rural kindergartens (the latter about double the size of the former) has aroused some concern amongst Chinese ECEC researchers (see below).

Official support for progressivism and child-centredness has perhaps had less to do with any benefits to the individual child than with the belief that such approaches promote the skills and creativity essential for fostering economically productive 'talent'; the same is true of the wider push, since the 1990s, for 'quality education' (*suzhi jiaoyu*) (see Chapter 6). Shanghai, with its history of openness to the West, has taken a lead in promoting such reforms – publishing its own 'progressive' set of preschool guidelines a year in advance of the publication by the Ministry of Education, in 2001, of *Guidelines for Kindergarten Education – Trial Version.* These called for an emphasis on 'respecting children', 'active learning', 'teaching for individual learning needs', 'play-based teaching and learning' and 'teaching and learning through daily life' (Liu and Feng 2005, cited in Tobin *et al.* 2009, 64). Elite public kindergartens and some expensive private kindergartens have competed to adopt methods and acquire facilities associated with this new progressive paradigm. Nonetheless, there is more to this than a marketing ploy – to varying degrees, preschool curricula have incorporated more free play and provided more opportunities for children to initiate or shape activities themselves (see Tobin *et al.* 43–4 and 60–4).

Both pedagogy and the broader ethos of preschools have reflected China's social transformation, as collective institutions have weakened, the population has become more mobile and urban, and competition and individualism far more salient. Remarking on changes to kindergarten toilets and their use, informed by a concern to enhance children's privacy and 'provide a sense of sex difference' (50), Tobin *et al.* detect a growing 'bourgeoisification' of Chinese society as it strives to 'jump into late modernity and to participate successfully in global capitalism' (51). However, they also note a number of constants in Chinese preschooling, many taken for granted by Chinese teachers themselves, which they attribute to 'implicit cultural logic'. These include an emphasis on 'mastery and performance'; on 'shared bodily routines' such as daily group calisthenics; and the practice of 'critique', whether involving children evaluating a story told by a classmate, or teachers reviewing each other's performance (244).

Another constant that emerges from this account is an emphasis on identity and patriotism. Defending their tolerance of gunplay amongst kindergarten children, many Chinese teachers argued that this reflected 'the general respect for soldiers in our country', and saw it as a form of 'patriotic education' (74). However, the singing of patriotic songs (other than the national anthem) and the telling of stories about revolutionary heroes (such as Lei Feng), common activities in the mid-1980s, seemed to have disappeared from the curriculum by 2002 (74–5). At the same time, many educators and social commentators were voicing concern over the perceived dangers of globalisation or excessive 'Westernisation', seen as threatening a socially disruptive 'values vacuum' (Wang X. 2002). Linked to such fears is growing popular and official interest in indigenous traditions, with the state sponsoring a selective revival of 'Confucian' ideology. At preschool level, moral and patriotic education has been pursued through the celebration of festivals associated with the traditional calendar – in particular Qing Ming and the Mid-Autumn Festival (both involving veneration of ancestors through tomb-sweeping rituals) – seen by most teachers as more appropriate for small children than tales of revolutionary heroism (Tobin *et al.* 2009, 75). This reflects the ideological shifts of the Hu–Wen era discussed in Chapter 3.4, to which we return in our analysis of the school curriculum in Chapter 6.

Growing popular cultural self-confidence as well as official 'patriotic' rhetoric have contributed to an apparent 'abating' in 'the hunger for outside ideas' in the Chinese ECEC sector (235). However, as Tobin *et al.* argue (citing Gita Steiner-Khamsi), a decreasing willingness to acknowledge foreign inspiration for policies does not necessarily denote decreasing interest in overseas ideas or practice. When elites view their own country as 'backward' (as China's certainly did in the first three decades of 'Reform and Opening'), the 'foreignness' of educational ideas may help to legitimate them domestically; but in other periods their foreign origins are deliberately downplayed – especially, in the case of contemporary China, if those origins happen to be Japanese (often the case since the 1990s; see Rappleye 2007) (236). The process of 'indigenising' Chinese education policy discourse, already noticeable in 2009, has been greatly intensified during the presidency of Xi Jinping (see Chapter 3.4).

Plans to expand publicly subsidised provision of ECEC

Much existing research on preschooling in China, including the work of Tobin *et al.* focuses on 'elite urban public preschools' – but as of 2007, 60 per cent of Chinese preschools were private (Zhou 2015) (rising to around 70 per cent by 2010). Tobin *et al.* also posit a 'wave theory of educational change' – with reform beginning in more globalised 'core' areas such as Beijing and Shanghai and radiating outwards to cities such as Kunming, and later to the countryside (246). But in the early 2000s, signs of this 'wave' reaching China's rural hinterland, or inundating the migrant underclass in the cities, were hard to detect; peasant and migrant children overwhelmingly remained 'behind before they begin' (Luo *et al.* 2012). From 2010, however, rural areas in particular have become the focus of a major ECEC reform driven by the central government.

In Chapter 3.4, we noted how the drafting of the 2010 *Gangyao* ('Framework') for educational development to 2020 involved an unprecedentedly wide-ranging consultation process. Submissions to that consultative exercise suggested that problems with the availability and quality of ECEC ranked high on the list of public concerns. Critics pointed out that the gross ECEC enrolment rate – estimated at 50.9 per cent for 3–6-year-olds as of 2009 – was lower than that of certain other 'developing' countries (e.g. in Latin America), and that spending on ECEC had accounted for less than 1.5 per cent of total educational investment in the first decade of the twenty-first century. Attention was drawn to the huge urban–rural divide in the uptake of ECEC: as high as 99 per cent in some 'advanced' urban areas, enrolment was as low as 10 per cent in many rural regions (Zhou 2011). The general level of teacher qualifications and the standard of facilities in rural areas were also generally far inferior to those in the cities. Where ECEC provision existed at all, in many villages it took the form of shared childminding or 'mother-and-baby' socialising. For example, in one Hunan village visited by Japanese sociologist Ako Tomoko, older women had clubbed together to organise a number of social activities in the village hall, which were also attended by mothers seeking companionship and opportunities for their small children to play together (Ako 2009, 194–5).

Zhou (2011) claims that the 2009–10 consultation exercise and increased media coverage partly account for the new priority accorded to ECEC in official policy. In 2010, provincial governments were instructed to produce plans for the development of ECEC, and in 2011 the central authorities promulgated the first of two 'three year action plans' (2011–13 and 2013–16). Up to 2012, at least 5.6 billion yuan had been contributed by the central authorities specifically for rural areas, primarily in the impoverished west, much of which was used for the construction of new kindergartens and the conversion of old primary schools into preschools. Overall, tens of billions more were disbursed in subsequent years; between 2010 and 2012, ECEC spending as a proportion of total spending on education doubled to 3.4 per cent (Hong *et al.* 2015).

Investigation of the initial impact of this project suggests a somewhat mixed picture. The urban–rural gap in gross enrolments, already narrowing prior to 2011, has continued to close. The average qualifications level of rural teachers also rose, though only marginally faster than that in urban areas (and from a considerably lower base). Meanwhile, differences in average class size remained stark, with a teacher–student ratio of 1:21 in urban areas and 1:45 or more in rural regions as of 2012 (Hong *et al.* 2015). Problems with regulation contributed to a preference for concentrating spending more on concrete 'hardware' (i.e. buildings and equipment) than on 'software' (teacher training, curriculum development, etc.) (Zhou 2011), an issue we noted in Chapters 3.3–3.4. As Zhou puts it, 'whether the government in [impoverished western and central] areas really uses the funding for early childhood education, or uses it in the most appropriate ways in early childhood education still remains to be seen' (Zhou 2011, 30). Although the action plans encompassed ambitious targets for teacher training, doubts were voiced as to whether the existing training infrastructure would prove capable of meeting those targets (Zhou 2011). Hong *et al.* (2015) note that no mechanism was established for rewarding kindergarten teachers who undertook training, 'which negatively affected the outcome of the project'. And despite the extra investment, the divide in 'physical conditions' and equipment between rural and urban kindergartens appeared actually to be increasing – according to official data cited by Hong *et al.* (2015).

In addition to problems of coordination between central and local governments, negotiations between central ministries also skewed the focus of the recent ECEC 'action plans'. The MOE has pushed for investment primarily in public preschools, since it lacks the capacity to monitor or regulate those in the private sector. The Finance Ministry, for its part, was particularly concerned to demonstrate that central funding dedicated to ECEC was reaching 'under-privileged' populations. Showing that money spent on urban preschools is reaching a poorer clientele is problematic. Partly as a result, the central government directed its subsidies overwhelmingly to the construction of public kindergartens in rural townships. This ensured improved statistics for ECEC provision in 'poorer areas', but did nothing to address the needs of one of the most under-served demographics – the children of rural–urban migrants. Most regions evidently remain reluctant to open up their public preschools to migrants from other provinces; according to Hong *et al.* (2015), only Liaoning, Zhejiang and Shandong had done so by 2014.

This was just one instance of the wide variance between the plans submitted by different provinces and municipalities – a variance sanctioned by the State Council, which reiterated the familiar expectation that 'developed' areas would move faster than 'developing' areas towards providing free ECEC for all (Zhou 2011). While Beijing committed itself to a significant expansion of public provision, many other provinces did not limit themselves in this way. Shenzhen announced an increase in public subsidies for both public and private preschools, while Chongqing offered support to not-for-profit *minban* (i.e. private) kindergartens, which agreed to regulate their fee levels in return for this subsidy. (The general absence of a system for inspecting private preschools means that controlling fee levels in return for subsidies remains the main means whereby state authorities are able to regulate them.) The substantial inter-provincial differences in funding available for ECEC were illustrated by the declared 'minimum funding standards' – from an annual 400 yuan per child in Henan, to 2,400 yuan in Liaoning (Hong *et al.* 2015). Meanwhile, an indication of the continuing stratification of public preschooling (leaving aside the private sector) is provided by monthly fees for preschools in Shanghai (as of 2016): according to institutional 'rankings', these ranged from 125 yuan per month for a 'grade 3' establishment to 800 yuan for a 'city-level model kindergarten' (*shi ji shifan yuan*), with extra charges for extended childcare (Shanghai Municipality 2016).[8]

Conclusion

As this chapter has shown, the wide variance in the availability of ECEC, and the extreme stratification of preschooling in urban areas, have been exacerbated by the undermining or destruction of older collective arrangements and the emergence of a patchily regulated market. By the early twenty-first century, many urban residents could access ECEC of a relatively high quality in state-run, though fee-charging, preschools, but those on lower incomes, rural residents, and migrants were far less well served. While some Chinese scholars (of a more neoliberal persuasion) criticised the government's approach to public service provision as exemplifying the attitude of 'the parent who wants to manage absolutely everything',[9] others (such as Yang Dongping) were increasingly voicing the opposite criticism (see Chapter 3.4). In the field of ECEC, in stark contrast to later stages of schooling, by the early 2000s a small number of private providers had rapidly achieved a quantitative dominance of the market. The challenge was thus one of establishing a new balance between public and private provision, and a new regulatory framework, in a sphere where until quite recently the state, in various forms, had held total sway. The 'action plans' implemented since 2011 suggest that the MOE, as well as some provincial-level entities (e.g. Beijing), are determined to wrest back substantial control of ECEC from the private sector. But as the example of Shanghai demonstrates, this does not imply any flattening of the hierarchy separating elite state preschools from their more run-of-the-mill counterparts.

It is hard to overestimate the social implications of the highly uneven pattern of access to ECEC, in terms both of quantity and quality, which has emerged since the 1980s. Elite urban kindergartens, some animated by child-centred ideas, but generally offering the enhanced prospects of access to key point primary schools, combine a strong focus on 'Chinese' identity (albeit nowadays conceived in cultural rather than overtly political terms) with an increasingly individualistic, 'child-centred' ethos. Meanwhile, the vast majority of children who are insufficiently wealthy or privileged to secure access to elite ECEC, are not only disadvantaged in access to key point institutions later on, but are also socialised differently from their wealthier urban peers, as comparative urban–rural data on class sizes and facilities indicates. A pattern of individualism for an elite and collectivism for the masses has thus come to be established at the earliest phase of public instruction.

As we shall see in the subsequent section on schooling, this pattern is sustained through primary and secondary level, as key point institutions at every phase both incentivise competition lower down the system, and prime their pupils for future competition. At later stages, the state has attempted to moderate the competitive impulse within the public sector, but resistance from vested interests, and the pervasive operation of the market (not least with respect to 'shadow education' – see Chapter 9) have largely frustrated such efforts. As discussed in the following chapter, a context of continuing fiscal decentralisation and weak bottom-up accountability mean that the central authorities and local officialdom do not always espouse quite the same agenda, even if the latter must signal compliance with mandates handed down from above. But the differential funding of 'ranked' state-run educational institutions, both within and across jurisdictional boundaries, remains a crucial and largely unchallenged feature of the system, from preschool level onwards. To borrow Xiong's metaphor (2015), if the educational career of the Chinese child consists of a frenetic race up a steep 'ladder' of tests and examinations, most children have found the bottom rung of that ladder either 'broken', or entirely missing.

Notes

1 In its Communist form, this was termed 'a high degree of devolution beneath a high degree of centralisation' (*Gaodu jizhong xia de gaodu fenquan*).
2 For example, Tobin *et al.* (2009) discuss calls in Japan, where nursery schools are administered by the Welfare Ministry and kindergartens by the Education Ministry (*Monkasho*), for ECEC to be consolidated under the latter (though such calls have so far been resisted).
3 Fees at this time were quite low – as were urban salaries. SOEs were also not motivated to maximise profits, since the command economy essentially remained in place in urban China.
4 Tobin's method of 'video-cued multi-vocal ethnography' does not assume that one kindergarten can represent the whole of Chinese pre-school education, but uses a film of a day in this single institution as a prompt for discussions with teachers and educationalists from around China (and Japan and the USA).
5 Initially (in 1980), this reform was applied 'experimentally' to 100 enterprises, before being rolled out nationally in 1984.
6 The Minban Education Promotion Law of 2002 (see Chapter 9) restricted private operators of educational businesses to a 'reasonable return' (*he li hui bao*) on their investment – although the failure clearly to define 'reasonableness' in practice allowed considerable leeway for profit-taking. In 2015 the MOE proposed a revision to the 2002 law to tighten up the rules on profit-taking, and prevent private kindergarten investors from 'having their cake and eating it' – but a divided National People's Congress failed to pass this measure.
7 Tobin *et al.* (2009, 36) note that many rudimentary preschools, including the vast bulk of rural ones, do not qualify for a ranking at all. They also observe that private preschools are included in the system of rankings in some cities or counties, but not in others.
8 Hong *et al.* (2015) mention that Shanghai is one region that operates a voucher scheme for preschools, aimed at helping poorer families, but they do not explain how this works, or what the value of the vouchers is.
9 Xiao Gongqin, *Yuanli xuanxiao de minzu zhuyi*, in *Jingji guancha bao* ('Economic Observer'), 23 August 2010.

5 The funding and administration of basic education

For those with long enough memories, post-Reform debates over the funding of education might have aroused a strong sense of *deja vu*. As we noted in Chapters 2 and 3, the rejection of radical Maoist egalitarianism from 1978 involved renewed talk of a 'trade-off between equity and efficiency'; scarce resources, it was insisted, needed to be concentrated on nurturing elite talent to lead the charge towards modernisation. This echoed the priorities and policies of half a century earlier, when a visiting League of Nations mission found that:

> Within the existing system of public education, the central government generally supported the tertiary level, provinces were primarily responsible for secondary schools, and elementary instruction was financed mainly by county or sub-country districts. But public as well as private and foreign funds were drawn to the secondary and tertiary levels. Meanwhile, counties and villages lacked the resources to keep their end of the bargain ...
>
> (Pepper 1996, 39)

In 1931, the foreign experts had strongly criticised this elitist bent, instead emphasising 'efficiency as a precondition for more equitable distribution' (39). They decried the 'enormous abyss' between the circumstances of 'the masses of the Chinese people ... and the intelligentsia educated in luxurious schools and indifferent to the wants of the masses' (League of Nations 1932, cited in Pepper 1996, 38–9). Insisting that the universalisation of basic education should be prioritised, they stressed the need for effective public administration and finance, and the wastefulness and inefficiency of purely local or private initiative. Good governance was key to effective and equitable provision of basic education.

So far, so platitudinous. In the post-Mao era, too, the crucial importance of governance to the delivery of public goods has been a refrain of advice dispensed to Chinese officials by international agencies and numerous researchers. But the tendency of many such experts, typifying the 'practice-oriented' school identified in Chapter 1, has been to represent governance as a technical matter of targeted interventions to enhance 'capacity'. Wary of questioning domestic political arrangements, many have preferred to treat education as a depoliticised arena dominated by questions of 'effectiveness' or 'efficiency' (see Chapter 13).

Sidelining political issues in favour of a resolute focus on human capital generation tended to make for harmonious relations with Chinese officialdom. And World Bank advisors, in particular, warmed to China's 'executive-led' governance model. For them, an attraction of dealing with the People's Republic was senior leaders' decisiveness, which they contrasted with India's frustratingly 'quarrelsome, fractious' and 'short-term' political culture (Drake 2001, 227).

However, the ostensible depoliticisation of education and the sponsorship of international agencies camouflaged the introduction, or reintroduction, of a highly politicised ideology of pseudo-meritocratic competition allied to strong-state nationalism. As we argue in Chapter 9, the Chinese adoption of 'neoliberal' ideas and practices (associated with the 'Washington Consensus'), while superficially radical (especially since 1992), has in fact been provisional and selective. But the resort to market mechanisms and private initiative has been intimately related to perceptions of a 'trade-off between equity and efficiency' rooted in fundamentally elitist and statist assumptions about the purposes of education. In other words, giving selective rein to the market has enabled the state to conserve more of its own resources for nurturing a purportedly meritocratic modernising elite.

In this chapter, we focus on the public funding of basic education (primary and junior secondary) since the 1970s, and on the evolving relationship between financial and administrative arrangements. A key theme here involves the shifting balance between the responsibilities of central, provincial and lower-level governments. We therefore begin by discussing different ways of conceptualising centralisation and decentralisation, and how these relate to an analysis of policy on educational funding and governance. We then outline the formal structure of the system for administering schooling, before analysing how this has related to the pursuit of state goals for the extension of compulsory schooling. The effectiveness with which these goals have been pursued, we argue, has less to do with conventional bureaucratic processes than with the operation of the Party's own systems for disciplining and evaluating its cadres – making it hard to categorise the administrative structure as 'centralised' or 'decentralised'. Such distinctions are more easily drawn with respect to finance, where we show how radical decentralisation of responsibility for school funding in the 1980s and 1990s has given way, since the Hu–Wen administration (2002–12), to a significant degree of recentralisation. In the conclusion to the chapter, we return to the centrality of politics, and examine how, beneath the ebb and flow of Beijing's reach and responsibilities, key political imperatives persist.

Conceptualising 'centralisation' and 'decentralisation' in Communist China

In discussing the nature and extent of 'decentralisation' in post-Mao China, it is important to bear in mind that we are dealing with a system that has remained, in certain essential respects remains, communist – even if it has largely ceased to be socialist. Brown (2009) identifies six defining features of a communist system: the political monopoly of the Communist Party; 'democratic centralism';[1]

non-capitalist ownership of the means of production; a command (as distinct from a market) economy; the declared aim of building communism; and 'the existence of, and sense of belonging to, an international Communist movement' (112). Of these, the last four have all more or less been jettisoned during the post-Mao era, but the first two have been emphatically upheld. What this has meant is that the Party itself, while by no means monolithic, has constituted a highly centralised grid undergirding a much more decentralised administrative and economic structure.

The forms taken by decentralisation in contemporary China have thus not involved meaningful 'devolution', defined by Hawkins as 'transfer of authority to an autonomous unit which can act independently without permission from the centre' (2000, 443). They have more typically involved some combination of 'deconcentration' ('transfer of tasks and work but not authority') and 'delegation', whereby decision-making authority is transferred from higher to lower levels, but 'can be withdrawn by the centre'. As we note in the following chapter, moves to decentralise curriculum development have illustrated this, with the authority of the centre decisively reimposed when suspicions of ideological deviance or fears of political instability are aroused (see also Vickers and Yang 2013). Even in the case of Hong Kong, since 1997 seemingly the one case of true devolution within the People's Republic, the difficulty of reconciling political autonomy with the Leninist logic of the national regime has become increasingly apparent (see Morris and Vickers 2015). And as Hong Kong also shows, the presence of a thriving private sector does not in itself necessarily imply a high degree of decentralisation: there, as elsewhere in China, the nexus of state and business interests has rendered the latter highly dependent on political favour.

Nevertheless, even if decentralising measures were politically circumscribed, responsibility for providing public goods was substantially delegated to local level during the early Reform era. Oi, writing in 1995, used the term 'local state corporatism' to describe the entrepreneurial role of local administrative units and SOEs. With local officials acting as a 'board of directors', and the Communist Party secretary as the chief executive officer, this was crucial to explaining 'the massive upsurge in rural industry on the edges of agriculture and state industry' (1995, 1132). Indeed, as we noted in Chapter 2, some scholars trace the origins of this local entrepreneurialism to the latter years of the Mao era itself (e.g. Gray 2006). But the flipside of that release of entrepreneurial energy was the tendency for decentralisation to become 'self-reinforcing', as local state actors built up power bases 'through control of state assets during the marketization process' (Painter and Mok 2008, 139). To the extent that local officials were transformed into 'businessmen and capitalists', they often came to occupy 'new resource bases to resist the central state', a process that, in the words of Painter and Mok, threatened to undermine 'the accountability, integrity and legitimacy of public service delivery to the point where a vicious cycle of declining state capacity may have been set in train' (140).

The term 'vicious cycle' is apt, since decentralisation in education has been as much as result of weak state capacity as a cause of it. It initially arose not as a considered strategy on the part of the central government but as an *ad hoc* response by local authorities to the administrative upheaval caused by the abolition of the rural communes. Hawkins argues, citing Bray, that the 'motives for decentralisation in education were principally fiscal'; though underlying this was the state's determination to prioritise investment in key point institutions (2000, 445) (see below). Many schools were forced to charge fees to make up for lost funding, while government regulation struggled to catch up with reality on the ground. From 1985, the newly proclaimed goal of universalising nine years of compulsory schooling was accompanied by no commitment from the central authorities to pay for it. Instead, fiscal decentralisation was more clearly codified, with the speed of educational progress to be determined by 'local conditions', and costs borne by 'subordinate units' in a manner to be determined by provincial governments (Lin 2013, 6; see Chapter 3.2). As we saw in Chapter 3.3, a high point of administrative decentralisation was reached in the early 1990s, and even though fiscal recentralisation began from around 1994, this did not initially lead to increased disbursements from central to local governments for education. Instead, the 1993 *da gang* ('framework') for education talked of 'breaking the government monopoly' in provision of schooling, and giving greater scope to individuals and groups to run schools (Painter and Mok 2008, 143). It was only with a raft of measures introduced from the early 2000s onwards that a major drive to recentralise funding for education began, with increased contributions from the central state to the costs of schooling (and other public goods). However, as we shall see, the effectiveness of these measures remains in doubt, due to entrenched resistance to attempts to impose greater standardisation and uniformity on a radically elitist and unequal system.

The administrative structure – an overview

The mainland PRC consists (as of 2016) of 31 provinces, autonomous regions (e.g. Tibet and Xinjiang) or self-governing municipalities (Beijing, Tianjin, Shanghai and Chongqing).[2] These vary massively in terms of size, terrain, climate, population, culture, language and economic conditions. The senior leaders of all (the most senior being the provincial party secretary) are appointed directly by the central government, generally following a 'rule of avoidance' stipulating that top provincial officials do not serve in their home province. In population they range from Henan, with almost 100 million inhabitants, to Ningxia, with just six million. School-age populations also vary widely, though not necessarily in direct correspondence with overall population figures; in that respect, especially since the 1990s, massive rural–urban migration has complicated the picture in ways that are difficult to track.

As discussed in the previous chapter on ECEC, under the command economy, responsibility for welfare provision (including schooling) rested primarily with the local collective (rural commune or 'street committee') or 'work unit' (*danwei*). However, with the abolition of agricultural communes at the outset of the Reform period, most administrative and financial responsibility for provision of education fell to villages (for primary schools) and townships (for secondary schools). Arrangements for urban areas were different, not least because the command economy remained largely unaltered there until the early 1990s; but in the early Reform period, and indeed until the early 2000s, the vast bulk of China's population still lived in the countryside.

As the structures of local administration were reformed, so were the size and the ethos of the bureaucracy that ran them. According to Painter and Mok, bureaucratic employment increased by nearly 80 per cent from 1978 to 1987, as 'local bureaucratic empires' arose 'buttressed by new forms of rent-seeking'; a process associated with what they term a 'cellularisation' of the state (2008, 140). The rampant commercialisation of 'service delivery units' (*shiye danwei*), including schools, accelerated after 1993, but charging of fees – often 'off-budget and of dubious legality' – was widely practised from the early Reform years, as a result of 'both informal, bottom-up stratagems and top-down encouragement' (141). As the remuneration of many public employees was thus 'part-privatised', their identity as public servants was itself transformed. The implications of this for schools and teachers are discussed further in Chapters 7 and 9.

From the 1970s through the 1980s, townships and villages were the entrepreneurial motor of the Chinese economy, even if one consequence of administrative and fiscal decentralisation was to widen inequalities in education, and to stimulate a growth in pseudo-private (or *minban* – i.e. people-managed) provision in many rural areas (see Chapter 9). But in the early 1990s, the introduction of marketising reforms to the urban economy was accompanied by measures to recentralise the taxation system (through the *fen shui zhi*, introduced from 1994), increasing remittances to the centre from township and village level, even while the latter retained responsibility for funding public services (see Chapter 3.3). Intensifying financial pressures contributed to a drastic reduction in the number of township-level entities (from around 70,000 in the 1980s to about half that in 2005), with many merging with or absorbed by the growing cities, to which more and more rural residents now migrated in search of work.

The status of the township in the system for administering and funding education in rural areas was fundamentally altered by 'to the county' (*yi xian wei zhu*) fiscal reforms implemented across China between 2001 and 2004 (Liu *et al.* 2009) (though first adumbrated in a 1994 State Council 'Suggestion' – see Lin 2013, 7). Rather than townships raising funding directly from rural parents in the form of fees, more of the financial burden for basic schooling was now to be borne by county governments, through a combination of their own taxation revenue and transfers from central and provincial governments. Subsequently, the abolition of the land tax in 2006, and the simultaneous scrapping of school fees and various supplementary charges, rendered townships almost entirely dependent on allocations from counties for school funding. In Gansu, township governments paid about 70 per cent of the costs of compulsory education in 2000, but just 10 per cent by 2008 (Liu *et al.* 2009, 465).

The implications of this reform for the management of education at local level were profound. Prior to the early 2000s, many township governments appointed their own school district governors and maintained authority over the appointment of school heads and the deployment of teachers. However, as townships lost much of their fiscal independence of county governments, they also tended to lose their managerial authority; increasingly, county governments appointed school district governors, and often also took a role in decisions over the deployment of school heads and teachers. The junior status of township officials, their lack of electoral accountability to local communities, and the workings of the system for evaluating cadres (see below), in any case spurred them to ingratiate themselves with county superiors; the fiscal reforms reduced many to the role of functionaries carrying out orders from above. However, as Liu *et al.* show for Gansu, the reform spawned various managerial models involving different combinations of the authority of township or county governments, and school district governors. Different models were associated with differing perceptions by teachers of the transparency or fairness of arrangements for their remuneration and promotion. Strong leadership from a locally based (though county-appointed) district governor appeared to make for higher teacher morale and better student performance than direct governance by the more remote county authorities (2009).

In urban areas, meanwhile, reform followed a different trajectory. The maintenance of the command economy until the early 1990s, and the concentration of key point institutions in cities, meant that urbanites were relatively well-served by state-funded schools of one sort or another, even while their cash incomes stagnated. But the fiscal reforms of the 1990s, combined with the contemporaneous restructuring of SOEs (see Chapter 3.3), brought significant changes to the funding and administration of urban schooling. Between the 1990s and early 2000s, most *danwei*-managed schools were transferred to the authority of district governments. Constrained state funding, along with marketisation fever, saw many key point schools capitalise on their prestige, 'transforming' themselves into pseudo-private entrepreneurial entities, and earning huge sums in parental fees or 'contributions'. Meanwhile, outside the remit of the local educational authorities, non-formal schools emerged to cater for a burgeoning population of migrant children. These and other issues relating to the marketisation of urban schooling are dealt with in Chapter 9, where we also note how, since the early 2000s, cities, like rural areas, have witnessed a drive to reassert state authority over schools and impose greater standardisation.

Cadre discipline, competition and the campaign to universalise compulsory education

Once the central government in 1985 mandated the universalisation of 'nine years of compulsory education', it was ultimately up to officials at county or township level to make this happen. Securing their compliance was essentially a matter of imposing discipline from above, rather than rendering them accountable to local residents (though some argue that village elections have injected a real element of democracy at grassroots level – see Bell 2015). The contrasting example of India, where local accountability has been enforced through regular elections, while the capacity of the centre to discipline lower-level state officials has been weak or patchy, might appear to highlight the strengths of the Chinese approach, given how China has outperformed its South Asian neighbour in terms of the delivery of basic public goods (see Chapter 2).

However, at least until the fiscal reforms of the early 2000s, the central government imposed targets on local officials while providing little of the funding required for meeting them. Instead, the party resorted to two stock tactics: propaganda, or 'governing the country through slogans' (*kouhao zhiguo*); and the system of cadre evaluations. Both evoked the militarisation of society that has been a hallmark of communist states (Brown 2009, 111; on China see Strauss 2006). While Mao's mass mobilisation was rejected by his successors, the 'campaigning' mode of public administration survived. The ultimate goal of a socialist utopia receded into the indefinite future, but metaphors of military struggle were deployed in the service of more targeted campaigns, including population planning and the drive to universalise compulsory education.

In discussing questions of governance, and specifically the problem of organising, motivating and monitoring subordinate officials, many Chinese scholars during the 1990s invoked the concept of 'rule of law' (*fa zhi*), contrasting it with the traditional Chinese practice of 'rule *by* law' or 'rule by men' (*ren zhi*).[3] In education as in other fields of public policy, Li and Li argued that reliance on 'rule by men' rendered implementation of official objectives overly dependent on the capacity of superior officials to ginger their subordinates into action (1999). As the saying goes, 'Always huge problems, always huge problems, but when the big leader comes, suddenly they disappear'.[4] The toadying attitudes thus encouraged are exemplified by the typical practice of attributing significant local achievements, such as advances in the provision of education, above all to 'the special attention [given to this area] by the leaders' (*lingdao zhongshi*).

But the ability of the central government to command allegiance, feigned or real, to its objectives has been due less to the charisma of individual leaders than to the system for evaluating and promoting subordinate officials (in which leaders admittedly play a crucial role). In his analysis of the implementation of the 'Tax Sharing System' (*fen shui zhi*) from 1994 onwards, Zhou identifies what he calls the 'promotion tournament model' as a key factor in explaining the behaviour of local cadres (Zhou 2007). This establishes a competition whereby prospects for advancement relate to performance against whatever criteria are prioritised at a particular time by superordinate authorities. In this situation, 'tightly-defined responsibilities and all manner of quotas' constrain subordinate officials (Murphy 2007, 75), involving readily quantifiable targets such as levels of school enrolment in the compulsory years. For most of the Reform era, GDP growth has been seen as the criterion to trump all others, although Lin cites research (focusing on the 1994–2002 period) showing that 'provincial leaders are promoted based on revenue contribution to the centre rather than economic growth, other things being equal' (2013, 16). But whatever the criteria, the system of top-down evaluations ensures that 'provincial leaders, whether in rich or poor areas, are likely to serve their principal in Beijing rather than their grassroots constituency' (Lin 2013, 20), with the same pattern replicated at lower levels of the hierarchy (Murphy 2007, 78–9).

The designation of universalising nine years of compulsory education as a 'strategic priority', re-emphasised by the *gangyao* of 1993, was backed up by the inclusion of school enrolment figures as a 'pass-or-fail' (*yi piao fou jue*) criterion in official work evaluations (*kao he*). Inability to demonstrate compliance with targets for school enrolment could thus result in failure to obtain promotion or desired work assignments, as well as loss of status and reputation. This has been described as 'governance by pressure' (*yalixing zhengfu*) (Rong *et al.* 1998, 28–35).

However, compliance with quantitative targets did not necessarily betoken commitment to qualitative equity: schooling for all did not mean that all would receive the same quality of schooling. Despite repeated exhortations from Beijing since the early 1990s to equalise levels of educational spending at local level, responsibility for determining how to achieve this remained, in practice, primarily with provincial authorities. And as Lin shows (2013), the latter tended not to prioritise this objective, irrespective of their capacity to pay for it. The setting of other objectives, such as minimum levels for teacher qualifications, or the number of school buildings and key facilities, has similarly not meant that inequalities in pedagogical quality or the physical condition of schools have narrowed (on teachers, see Chapter 7).[5] Lin claims that policy on key point schools 'forced' local officials to concentrate spending on these institutions (2013, 16), though he also acknowledges that this practice in fact directly serves officials' own interests, since their children mostly study at these institutions (150, n. 91).

Besides such policy contradictions or conflicts of interest, there have been suggestions that the increasing plethora of targets imposed from above may have contributed to cynicism and target fatigue amongst officials bewildered by 'inspectorial overload' (Zhou and Lian 2011). Officials faced with lengthening checklists of indicators and targets, but ignorant of or unpersuaded by the rationale for them, may be more inclined to adopt a tokenistic, box-ticking mentality, or simply to falsify data. As yet another saying has it, 'When numbers produce officials, why not take the risk [of falsifying the numbers]?',[6] though unreliability of official statistics is not a new phenomenon in China. One instance of this unreliability (though perhaps not of outright falsification) is cited by Murphy, who found that enrolment figures for compulsory education in a rural county in Jiangxi in the early 2000s took no account of attrition rates: a reported progression rate from primary to junior secondary school of 94 per cent actually turned out to apply to only 68 per cent of the relevant age cohort (the remaining 32 per cent having either dropped out or moved away between the first and fifth years of primary school) (2004, 8–9). Another indication of statistical confusion is cited by Lin, who observes that in 2003, three years after the central government announced successful achievement of the 'two basics' (see Chapter 3.3), 'only 12 of China's 31 provinces claimed to have universalised compulsory education "on the whole"' (2013, 1). As we saw in Chapter 3.4, by 2007, problems with the universal delivery of compulsory education were still apparent in some of the poorest provinces.

With victory declared (perhaps prematurely) in the struggle for the 'two basics', more discussion has centred on the need to improve, or level up, the 'quality' of schooling – but devising measurable targets for qualitative improvement has proven daunting. Critics object that central tinkering with performance criteria will not, on its own, create a governance system capable of effectively holding local officials to account, or of orienting their efforts towards locally appropriate objectives (Zhou and Lian 2011). This applies both to the governance of subordinate officials, and to the latter's methods for evaluating and controlling schools and teachers. In their Gansu study, Liu *et al.* (2009) found that both teacher perceptions of the transparency of their annual evaluations, and their students' performance, were highest in districts where seniority as well as examination results played a role in determining teacher remuneration. But they also found that in districts where teachers were under particular pressure from officials to maximise students' examination results, their tendency to 'game' the system (for example by preventing poor students from sitting exams) was enhanced (470) (see Chapter 7 on the teaching profession). For officials, as for teachers, 'gaming behaviour' is encouraged by the top-down, target-driven 'tournament model' of governance. Zhou (2007), on the basis of a case study of village elections in the 1990s and 2000s, argues that the solution can only lie in a greater element of bottom-up accountability.

Another outcome of the highly competitive, 'winner-takes-all' system for evaluating cadres and determining promotion was to weaken incentives for observing budgetary rigour or fiscal sustainability. From the early 1990s, as the drive to achieve the 'two basics' intensified, officials were increasingly incentivised to fulfil quantitative targets for expanding access to compulsory schooling even when they lacked the financial wherewithal to do this. Taking on large amounts of debt was one solution. The fact that this might prove unsustainable in the long run was of little concern to many officials, given that they would presumably have been promoted or moved on in the interim. The implications of this for levels of educational funding, and their distribution, are discussed further below.

Financing basic education

Two questions predominate in discussions of the financing of education in contemporary China: how high (or low) has total spending been, and how equally (or unequally) has it been distributed? We return to the first question below, after discussing the distribution of spending up to the early 2000s.

Given the highly decentralised nature of educational finance for most of the post-Mao period, inequalities in education spending might be expected to map onto broader patterns of inequality in Chinese society. Socio-economic inequality has grown rapidly since the 1970s, when the Gini coefficient was estimated at around 0.33 – relatively high for socialist countries at that time, though lower than in most industrialised societies. That national figure masked 'an unusually large gap between the incomes of urban and rural regions, and between prosperous and poor rural regions'; the Gini coefficient for urban China in this period was 'a remarkable 0.16' (Walder 2015, 331). The rural–urban gap arose from both the extractive nature of the command economy, suppressing farm prices in order to subsidise urban industry, and the strict controls on rural–urban migration imposed by the household registration system. As noted in Chapter 2, the liberalisation of the agricultural economy in the early Reform period, and the growth of township and village enterprises, gave a significant lift to many rural incomes. However, the more urban-focused policies of the early 1990s fuelled a renewed growth in inequality. The national Gini coefficient rose to between 0.35 and 0.40 during the 1990s, to 0.44 in 2006, and more recently to between 0.50 and 0.55 (Chen *et al.* 2010, 20; Yu and Xiang 2014). Meanwhile, in addition to urban–rural inequality, a new class divide emerged *within* urban China: in 2008, the *China Statistical Yearbook* reported that the richest quintile of the urban population had an average income of 43,614 yuan, while the average for the poorest was 4,754. The poorest quintile of the population accounted for only 4.7 per cent of national income and consumption, the wealthiest for over 50 per cent (NBS 2008).

As the economic fortunes of different regions have diverged, so have levels of expenditure per student. Tables 5.1 and 5.2 show inter-provincial divergences in levels of per-student spending. However, as Lin (2013) argues, at least as significant have been intra-provincial inequalities, which in turn have varied considerably between provinces. Comparisons of inequality levels *within* richer and poorer provinces also call into question the common argument that inequality in the distribution of educational resources is an unavoidable but temporary outcome of underdevelopment. Lin found that inequality in educational spending within Jiangsu, one of the richest provinces, actually grew between 1994 and 2001, even while in Henan and Ningxia (two poorer provinces) it significantly declined (to levels much lower than in Jiangsu) (2013, 14). He also found that in Shanghai, over the same period, 'the role of the municipal government in equalising education' was 'not significant'. This, he argued, gave the lie to claims that 'the richer the province, the more equalised the education', even though state legislation officially required provincial governments to correct imbalances, 'and rich provinces are fiscally able to do it'. His data suggested that equalising education spending was simply not a priority for provincial elites.

A key part of the explanation for this can be traced back to the extremely elitist focus of early post-Mao education policy – and spending – centred on key point schools. Deng Xiaoping's April 1978 speech to the National Education Work Conference made the new leadership's priorities very clear:

> In order to speed up the fostering of talented individuals, and raise the overall level of education, it is necessary to consider concentrating resources on the construction of key universities and key primary and secondary schools so as to improve the standard and quality of the instruction that they offer as fast as possible.
>
> (IED 1978, 1607)

Table 5.1 Average expenditure per primary student – selected regions, 1995–2011 (yuan)

Year	*1995*	*1999*	*2001*	*2003*	*2005*	*2007*	*2009*	*2011*
China (nat. average)	476.25	695.08	971.47	1,295.39	1,822.76	2,751.43	417,1.45	6,117.49
Beijing	1,040.05	2,253.39	3,683.93	5,245.24	7,100.98	10,684.09	16,061.18	24,920.45
Shanxi	483.31	635.54	871.92	1,029.64	1,564.09	2,388.74	3,954.29	5,836.91
Inner Mongolia	499.53	834.85	1,272.04	1,774.15	2,441.31	3,856.75	6,808.09	10,936.78
Liaoning	607.53	861.22	1,114.77	1,585.24	2,348.69	3,618.6	5,577.51	8,659.43
Shanghai	1,591.53	3,106.81	4,875.97	7,030.12	9,767.45	13,591.86	17,340.39	21,183.5
Jiangsu	621.53	926.33	1,256.1	1,801.89	2,845.84	4,726.26	7,073.34	10,573.86
Zhejiang	766.7	1,359.96	2,018.44	2,866.95	3,983.28	5,234.73	7,471.38	9,668.21
Anhui	355.4	524.89	645.27	865.35	1,268.94	2,054.25	3,165.87	5,684.98
Jiangxi	319.86	511.94	769.53	949.69	1,293.44	1,906.76	2,647.43	4,263.61
Shandong	405.48	618.01	1,001.45	1,266.19	1,791.1	2,724.59	3,576.59	5,706.54
Henan	306.16	408.82	536.64	677.43	972.74	1,628.08	2,271.1	3,316.26
Guangdong	857.33	1,208.81	1,489.62	1,928.62	2,200.07	2,850.92	3,946.07	6,067.42
Chongqing		594.73	838.16	1065.4	1,731.02	2,612.38	4,428.77	7,217.07
Guizhou	216.06	363.38	545.41	694.91	1,019.89	1,574.49	2,492.49	3,784.47
Yunnan	451.49	719.18	968.56	1,225.41	1,649.84	2,215.56	3,615.77	4,968.29
Tibet	597.63	1,077.63	1,764.61	2,577.95	3,095.76	4,982.78	7,753.5	11,623.62
Gansu	314.82	503.83	686.82	865.15	1,215.78	1,948.32	3,501.4	5,158.49
Xinjiang	582.39	855.11	1,363.76	1,741.17	2,418.05	3,631.16	5,526.37	8,477.3

Table 5.2 Average expenditure per junior secondary student – selected regions, 1995–2011 (yuan)

Year	*1995*	*1999*	*2001*	*2003*	*2005*	*2007*	*2009*	*2011*
China (nat. average)	1,059.68	1,432.37	1,740	2,163.31	2,896.71	4,070.31	6,019.71	8,749.89
Beijing	2,264.82	4,318.08	5,912.85	7,667.27	11,175.08	17,102.25	24,190.34	40,036.33
Shanxi	964.62	1,140.24	1,496.94	1,744.76	2,417.88	3,587.3	5,343.59	7,857.53
Inner Mongolia	807.11	1,244.53	1,632.5	2,108.51	2,953.97	4,324.77	7,647.15	11,871.23
Liaoning	1,127.57	1,757.2	1,945.76	2,466.83	3,447.3	4,875.59	7,163.37	11,781.52
Shanghai	2,592.12	5,228.74	6,340.72	9,281.98	13,972.99	17,760.96	24,004.46	30,250.11
Jiangsu	1,231.62	2,184.86	2,644.47	3,098.24	4,041.85	5,977.7	8,624.39	13,716.98
Zhejiang	1,413.3	2,642.01	3,619.89	5,051.47	6,827.17	8,428.38	10,752.38	14,398.32
Anhui	719.83	1,000.57	1,180.66	1,427.53	1,859.15	2,760.99	4,298.87	7,590.48
Jiangxi	623.16	902.27	1,177.28	1,392.29	1,920.6	2,876.7	4,212	6,150.15
Shandong	981.11	1,237.48	1,553.13	2,088.6	3,117.76	4,424.39	6,110.8	9,614.89
Henan	779.79	956.27	1,040.93	1,161.86	1,577.84	2,568.5	3,727.16	5,818.09
Guangdong	1,876.98	2,092.7	2,551.07	3,598.71	4,354.44	4,971.79	5,870.59	7,835.41
Chongqing		1,317.96	1,458.41	1,984.81	2,922.64	3,806.5	5,485.39	8,535.32
Guizhou	504.24	670.06	994.07	1,165.37	1,617.94	2,394.16	3,362	5,221
Yunnan	1,079.73	1,452.3	1,536.83	1,786.65	2,405.33	3,160.41	5,166.08	6,688.97
Tibet	2,173.58	3,978.25	4,448.34	4,542.15	5,268.13	7,068.87	9,007.04	11,263.49
Gansu	713.28	954.27	1,224.58	1,397.07	1,853.86	2,647.09	4,719.83	6,495.61
Xinjiang	1,240.07	1,366.05	2,045.83	2,478.86	3,194.35	4,903.67	8,178.72	12,297.18

While Deng appeared to suggest that the focus on 'talented individuals' would contribute to overall educational improvement, Education Minister Liu Xiyao, speaking at the final plenary session, openly acknowledged that a price would have to be paid for the prioritisation of 'key point' institutions:

> Financial and material resources must be even further concentrated on key point institutions, for the purpose of improving their quality, even if this means that [overall development of the education system] is slower, or is somewhat sacrificed (*xisheng yi dian*).
>
> (IED 1978, 1620)

What this 'sacrifice' would entail was further spelt out by the Politburo in May 1980:

> For a certain period of time, we must bravely take the decision to acknowledge imbalances. Those areas with favourable conditions must strive to achieve a high standard of education, but backward regions cannot aspire to such high standards. Large cities and small cities are different; cities and villages are different; coastal areas and inland regions are different; advanced areas and backward areas are different. It is imperative to concentrate on (*zhua hao* – 'grasp') key point [institutions]. Educational investment and teaching personnel must be concentrated in order to allow advanced areas to reach a high standard first of all. If equality is prioritised, then nothing will be achieved. As for how additional resources should be spent in future, this is a matter for further consideration. Wherever an area enjoys good educational conditions, with a good prospect of fostering talented individuals, extra resources should be made available there.
>
> (IED 1980, 1813)

Thøgersen (1991), reviewing the development of secondary schooling during the 1980s, noted that the bulk of state funding went to urban key point schools, and the salaries of their teachers. This bias was justified in official propaganda by emphasising that urban *danwei* workers paid more taxes to the state, and were therefore entitled to state benefits, such as education; since peasants did not pay the same taxes, they should fund education themselves (50). The fact that those key point schools then provided the benchmark for the rest of the system put rural areas under pressure to extend primary schooling from five to six years, and junior secondary schooling from two years to three. But this shift towards a 6-3-3 model, reflecting the urban focus on 'quality', meant rural areas having to 'pay for an education over which they have limited control', and which strained their limited resources even further (59).

As we have seen, Beijing appeared to change course from 1985, proclaiming the universalisation of basic education a priority, but this was not accompanied by any new diversion of central government resources towards schooling for the masses; indeed, contemporaneous fiscal reforms cut the centre's share of taxation revenue in favour of subordinate levels of government (Lin 2013, 84–5). Subsequently, provincial and county authorities were repeatedly urged to take the lead in balancing local inequalities in education spending. However, Lin argues that they routinely evaded this responsibility, focusing their funding on key point institutions, while leaving townships and villages to fund more ordinary schools (7–8). As noted above, this was largely a matter of personal self-interest, but it was also important for maintaining local competitiveness. No region would unilaterally disband its key point schools, or level down their funding. To do so would not only rob locals of access to 'top quality' schools, but also deprive officials of showcase institutions that could serve them well as they jousted for favour in the promotions 'tournament'. Indeed, Lin claims that so strong was the felt need for 'showcases to compete with other provinces' that even officials in poorer provinces, more dependent on the limited subsidies that the central government disbursed, were still 'likely to distribute education unevenly' (20).

Despite significant unevenness in the distribution of educational opportunities during the 1978–93 period, and a widening in the urban–rural divide in this respect, within particular districts, key point schools retained the reputation of being relatively meritocratic in the way in which they determined access (Thøgersen 1991). Admission was through selective examinations, and opportunities for entry were otherwise very limited (see Chapter 8). These schools were still seen as being largely beyond the realm of market forces. But this would change drastically with the marketising reforms of the early 1990s.

The state of the urban economy at that time is captured in contemporary aphorisms: 'those who design guided missiles are paid less than those who sell tea eggs' (*zao daodan de bu ru mai chayedan de*), and 'surgeons are worth less than hairdressers' (*na shoushudao de bu ru na titoudao de*).[7] Employees of SOEs or public institutions found themselves at a significant financial disadvantage *vis-à-vis* those able to trade on the open market. In one sign of the crisis in teachers' remuneration, in 1993, the year that the *dagang* ('framework') for education proclaimed the ambitious objective of 'on the whole popularising nine years of compulsory education before 2000', it was observed that 'only in two places, Beijing and Tibet, can teachers' salaries be paid on time' (Lin 2013, 7). Many public sector workers, including teachers, left to work in the private sector at about this time (Sun and Chen 1997). In the hope of raising salaries for those who remained, the central government licensed practices with a strong market flavour, permitting key point schools to 'transform' themselves into pseudo-private entities (see Chapter 9), and allowing schools and school districts increased leeway to supplement teacher income through various supplementary (often performance-related) payments and bonuses (see Chapter 7).

In 1994, the SEC specified six methods for funding primary and secondary education: surcharges (i.e. taxes) levied by local governments; contributions from industry and social organisations; donated funds from community organisations and individuals; tuition fees from students; income from school-run enterprises; and subsidies from the central authorities (cited in Hawkins 2000).

At the same time, the SEC estimated that around 40 per cent of funding for pre-collegiate education was coming from non-governmental sources. The central government continued to fund teachers' basic salaries (though the funds were collected at local level, remitted to the centre, and then allocated to teachers), but the basic salary as a proportion of teachers' total income was declining, particularly in more prosperous areas (see Chapter 7). Hawkins reports that concerns over equity, amongst other issues, led the government to begin recentralising certain tax powers shortly afterwards, arguing that this demonstrated how powers that have been 'granted to the localities can be quickly withdrawn' (2000, 447).

However, the recentralisation of the taxation system that took place in 1994, while it may have been partly justified with reference to equity concerns, was not in fact followed by any significant expansion of redistributive spending by the central state. Its primary aim was to secure a larger share of total taxation revenue for the central authorities, following a shrinkage in their slice of the fiscal cake from 40 per cent in 1985 to less than 25 per cent in 1993 (Lin 2013, 83). The effect was dramatic: the central government share of taxation revenue rocketed to around 55 per cent of the total for 1994, while that of local governments fell off a cliff (from almost 80 per cent to around 45 per cent) (84–5). But whereas the revenue and expenditure levels of different levels of government had risen and fallen in tandem through the 1980s and early 1990s, the reform of 1994 brought no rebalancing in the responsibilities of the central and subordinate tiers. Instead, the centre racked up huge budget surpluses, while localities went deep into the red. And even when money was disbursed downwards by Beijing, 'transfers for equalising purposes continued to be a minor part of the centre's overall transfers' (20). By the late 1990s, Hawkins was writing of the 'fiscal retreat of the state from public education', and noting that concerns were being voiced over the impact of funding cuts on educational quality even in Beijing (2000).

This retreat from responsibility for funding public goods was accompanied by consciousness-raising efforts aimed especially at the peasantry (already noted in Chapter 3.3). As Murphy puts it, 'by urging farmers to adopt a progressive mentality whereby they invested in education, an emphasis on individual and societal responsibility excused the state from much of the burden of educational investment' (2007, 89). Various initiatives (loans and grants, conditional transfers, coordination of charitable giving) were portrayed as demonstrating the state's commitment to fulfilling its socialist and humanist duties to provide schooling to the masses. But these, like the 'to the county' administrative shift discussed above, 'fell far short of fully redressing the inadequacies in the provisioning of affordable quality education that so disillusioned rural people' (90).

By the early 2000s, concerns over educational inequality in general, and the condition of rural schooling in particular, were mounting – not just amongst rural residents, but amongst the mainly urban writers and readers of highbrow journals and broadsheet newspapers. Surveying such materials, Hu (2014) found that the rather vague term 'educational equity' (*jiaoyu gongping*) scored a steadily increasing number of hits over the period from 1979 to 1994, but that the more specific issue of 'urban–rural educational inequality' (*cheng xiang jiaoyu chaju*) was seldom referenced in print until after 2002. In 2004, the publication of *Zhongguo Nongmin Diaocha* (literally 'investigation of Chinese farmers') drew attention to the plight of peasants in poorer parts of Anhui Province, and in particular to the abuses of corrupt officials whose extraction of illicit taxes and charges was fuelling a local protest movement (Chen and Wu 2007); it was almost immediately banned, but continued to be widely circulated. Signalling official concern over the politically destabilising implications of mounting rural unrest, the MOE's own pronouncements reflected and reinforced the shifts in public debate; textual analysis of MOE documents indicated a shift in emphasis from 'efficiency', prior to 2005, to 'equity' and 'equality' thereafter (Lin 2013, 10). Meanwhile, as noted in Chapters 3.3 and 3.4, much commentary focused on the persistent failure of the government to meet its own benchmark of spending 4 per cent of GDP on education. Standard estimates of total public expenditure on education showed it hovering between 2.74 per cent and 3.3 per cent of GDP between 1992 and 2004 (Painter and Mok 2008, 142), considerably below a global average of 5 per cent (Kipnis and Li 2010, 328).

But was Chinese education as underfunded as many supposed? On the basis of a Shandong case study, Kipnis and Li argued that overall levels of spending on education were almost certainly far higher than officials statistics indicated. Even those statistics showed that, if spending on private schooling, tuition fees and other non-state spending were added to the figure for the public budget, the total for 2006 would rise from around 3 per cent to 4.6 per cent (328). However, Kipnis and Li insisted that even this was an underestimate, since it failed to take account of funding sources that were ignored or not systematically costed by official statisticians.

The range and scale of such sources was considerable. Significant among them were 'unrepayable loans' to finance the construction of often impressive new schools and colleges; decisions on lending – from state banks to state entities – were typically political rather than commercial, premised on the assumption that higher levels of government would ultimately not allow lower levels to default. Another method involved the county government striking a deal with a private enterprise to pay for the building of a school in return for a tax rebate, thereby effectively 'disguis[ing] some of its tax revenue to shield it from the grasping hands of the prefectural and provincial governments' (334). 'Free land' also constituted a highly significant source of uncosted funding; Kipnis and Li write that 'in all the counties we visited, we never heard of a school paying rent on the land on which it was built' (335).[8] Further sources included payments from 'work units' for access to particular schools for children of their workers (an arrangement discussed in the previous chapter in relation to kindergartens); what amounted to 'free labour', either by unpaid or under-paid *minban* teachers, or by villagers dragooned into providing *corvee* labour for school construction (337); donations by wealthy individuals (often with invisible strings attached) (338); and various fees charged at senior high level (338–341).

But while overall levels of funding for education in the early 2000s may have been considerably higher than generally assumed, Kipnis and Li's analysis reaffirmed the picture of extreme distributional inequality (341). Rural households were subject to a number of direct impositions that did not apply to their urban counterparts, including education taxes, higher fees and unpaid labour; their land could also be requisitioned for schools for minimal compensation. The policy of 'concentrating' rural schooling from upper primary level onwards in county town boarding schools also imposed costs on rural families, both in terms of boarding fees and the 'opportunity cost' of children's lost labour. Since many of the additional sources of educational funding identified by Kipnis and Li disproportionately benefited 'elite schools or school districts with adequate levels of industrial development', their findings suggested a further skewing of investment to the detriment of families from poorer districts, or of those less likely to access elite schools (341).

The 2006–7 reforms to the financing of education in rural areas made a significant contribution to alleviating the burden on rural residents. The collection of an 'education tax' direct from rural households had been banned in 2002 (Kipnis and Li 2010, 329–30), but other forms of charging continued in many areas. From 2007, with fees and charges for textbooks outlawed for the duration of compulsory schooling, and their eradication made a key criterion in local cadre evaluations, the understanding of basic education as a universal entitlement was strengthened (Murphy 2007, 90). However, as costs incurred by rural households during the compulsory phase fell, the lure of the urban labour market and the spread of credentialism were fuelling spending on non-compulsory education – at preschool, senior high and tertiary levels (Kipnis and Li 2010, 341). The burden of fees charged at these levels, and the costs of 'shadow education' in the expanding after-school tutorial sector (increasingly perceived as crucial to exam-focused competition) have fallen especially heavily on the poorest groups in society (the urban poor, migrants and peasants), with consequences we discuss in Chapter 9.

The steady increase in public spending on education through the early 2000s culminated in 2012 with attainment of the long-heralded 4 per cent target. As the state's contribution to school funding increased, urban areas witnessed a renewed drive to clarify the distinction between 'private' and 'public' educational provision. Measures to curb abuses such as selection in primary and junior secondary school admissions, or the charging of exorbitant 'school choice fees' by senior high schools, were tightened (see Chapters 8 and 9). Increased public support brought requirements for more rigorous accounting by schools to local authorities, and a greater bureaucratisation of the relationship between teachers, school principals and government officials (Zhou and Lian 2012).

Nevertheless, it is difficult as yet to determine what impact these relatively recent changes have had, or will have, on educational inequality at sub-provincial level or across the urban–rural divide, let alone for migrant and 'left-behind' children. As we shall see in subsequent chapters, the selective impulse is a many-headed hydra that draws sustenance from the different ability of key point schools and their ordinary counterparts to secure funding, to attract and retain the most highly qualified teachers, to recruit the 'best' students, and thus to remain top of the examination league tables. The expansion of key point schools in a context of shrinking student cohorts offers one potential means of suppressing the intensity of competition for school places. For example, Kipnis and Li note that the expansion of a former key point school in one Shandong county meant that it became able to accommodate more than half of local senior high students (though 40 per cent of them were charged exorbitant 'school choice fees' related to their entrance exam results) (2010, 332); in other regions too, key point schools have recently been encouraged to expand. But the divide between key point institutions and the rest remains, as do socio-economic and residency-based differences in the quality of public schooling households are able to access.

Conclusion

The 'abyss', noted by the League of Nations delegation in the 1930s, between the schooling available to the 'masses' and 'luxurious' provision for an urban intelligentsia, having been purposely reinstated at the advent of the Reform era, has since become an entrenched feature of China's educational landscape. The determination to prioritise the establishment and maintenance of a network of elite key point institutions meant that, in the early post-Mao years, the funding of education for the masses, especially in the countryside, was largely left to the entrepreneurialism of local state actors and communities themselves. And when entrepreneurialism was unleashed on a larger scale from the 1990s, this allowed urban institutions already privileged by virtue of state largesse to capitalise on their prestige, even while taxation reform further exacerbated resourcing problems in many rural districts. Elderly graduates of Republican-era missionary schools (or the many newer converts to Christianity) might have recalled that disturbing verse from the Parable of the Sower: 'For whosoever hath, to him shall be given, and he shall have more abundance ...'.

Whatever the morality of this situation, by the early 2000s its political implications were increasingly troubling to Party leaders, prompting attempts to reduce the fiscal burden on rural residents, restrict the marketisation of public education, and subject schools and local school districts to more stringent regulation and bureaucratic supervision. Remarking on the early phases of this rebalancing attempt, Painter and Mok speculated that a concerted attempt to 'de-marketise' and 'de-privatise' education would 'exceed the capacities of the state', due to the strength of vested interests and the entrenchment of 'local bureaucratic empires'. While acknowledging that the central state was now 'handing over more money', they were sceptical regarding its ability to enforce 'tougher standards' and 'prevent resistance and evasion by local actors who benefit from the system through their use of local discretionary powers' (2008, 147). Since 2012, the 'left turn' in social policy (and ideological rhetoric) that we noted in Chapter 3.4 has been putting such assertions regarding state capacity to the test. A charitable interpretation of President Xi's anti-corruption campaign is to see it as part of a more determined drive to enforce compliance with a revivified ethos of public service. But even if this is so, whether it can be done through the imposition of top-down discipline alone remains moot.

Crucial to rebalancing the education system is closing the funding gap between rural and urban schools, and between key point schools and the rest. However, even with more money going from the centre to rural counties to offset the loss of income from locally levied taxes and fees, the gap remains huge; in some cases, a single urban secondary school may still have a budget larger than an entire county (Economist 2014). Incentivising local officials to prioritise the needs of the poorest citizens remains extremely hard, when the interests of the wealthier and more influential classes – including those of officials themselves – are heavily vested in the maintenance of lavishly resourced key point schools. For this reason, attempts to curb inequalities by tightening school 'zoning' rules and clamping down on selective entrance tests appear to have yielded mixed results, as we discuss in Chapter 8.

The tension or contradiction in official rhetoric between an emphasis on 'excellence' and 'world-class-ness' on the one hand, and nods in the direction of equality on the other, meanwhile legitimises the continuing prioritisation of the former over the latter. And as the resources and personnel available to different schools and different regions have diverged, so has the content of education itself. This has happened with the active encouragement of the central authorities, eager both to produce globally competitive Chinese champions in various fields, and to nurture and celebrate models of 'advanced' pedagogical practice that can be publicised for national emulation. The metaphor of the 'tournament', used by Zhou in his analysis of official behaviour, is at least as relevant to any account of life within the school gates, as the following chapter on curriculum makes plain.

Notes

1 Defined by Brown as meaning, 'in political reality', 'a rigidly hierarchical, severely disciplined party in which rights of discussion and debate were rigorously circumscribed' (107).
2 Prior to 1996, Chongqing municipality was part of Sichuan Province.
3 This was interpreted by some as a thinly veiled attack on the position of Jiang Zemin and Li Peng – senior leaders for whom most intellectuals had little respect.
4 In Chinese, this is a rather ingenious pun: *lao da nan, lao da nan, lao da chu mian jiu bu nan.*
5 The tendency to skimp on the cost of school buildings was scandalously revealed by the 2008 Sichuan earthquake, which saw a number of schools collapse while the nearby residences of local officials remained standing.
6 *Shuzi chu guanyuan, bu xi zao jia.*
7 Like many such aphorisms, both of these are puns in Chinese.
8 But the costs in such cases were often borne by the villagers whose land was confiscated for educational use. Compensation packages in such cases have often been less than reasonable.

6 The school curriculum

Ideology and control

The role of centrally mandated curricula and textbooks in transmitting state ideology is deeply entrenched in China. As Party ideology has evolved during the post-Mao era, so have curricula, textbooks and the pedagogical practices advocated (if not always adopted) for classroom use. Meanwhile, growing regional and class inequalities, and a desire to expedite learning for students with 'elite' potential, have prompted greater curricular diversification. Some implications of ideological and social change for pedagogy and curriculum have already been touched upon in earlier chapters. Here we examine the forces that have influenced key shifts in curriculum policy from primary through to senior high level, and discuss the implications for specific school subjects.

Examining what has changed, and why, also requires considering what has stayed the same. In this respect, there are striking continuities in curricular and pedagogical debate between the 'pre-Liberation' (pre-1949) and post-Mao eras. This is undoubtedly in part a factor of culture – understood as an evolving and porous tradition, rather than an ineffable, immutable civilisational 'essence'. In the case of China, this tradition involves expectations concerning the 'exemplary' or moralising role of schooling, the latter's relationship with a 'pedagogical' style of governance (Fitzgerald 1996), and the importance of educational qualifications to social status (Bakken 2000). Nevertheless, the school curriculum in the post-Mao period has not been simply a one-way conduit for state propaganda. There is 'intense debate' over both the literary and scientific content of schooling, which are 'manipulated endlessly by state elites, but [are] often at least partially reflective of popular demand' (Kipnis 2011, 9).

The ancient and profound influence on Japan of traditional Chinese conceptions of education's core functions helps explain the readiness of China's earliest educational modernisers to borrow from their island neighbour (Harrison 2001). In the face of the Western challenge, civilisational survival seemed to them, as to their Japanese counterparts during the Meiji era (1868–1912), to demand 'self-strengthening' above all else. This involved both prioritising acquisition of knowledge needed for technological and military modernisation, and moulding a cohesive citizenry. A resulting utilitarianism 'with Chinese characteristics' allied faith in Western science and progress (or their more tangible manifestations) to the longstanding conviction that schooling was primarily about the moral transformation of the individual (Curran 2005). Science and progress, after all, could not profit China unless imperial subjects could be transformed into modern citizens, and the ancient empire into a modern nation state. As a leading reformer, Cai Yuanpei, put it, 'to have utilitarianism one must have morality' (Curran 2005, 203).

Curran (2005) shows how the ideas of Herbart – mingling 'child-centred' pedagogy, concern for structure, clear ethical guidance and a central role for history in moral education – appealed to early Japanese and Chinese modernisers, as to Prussian nation-builders before them. This appeal owed much to traditional conceptions of education-as-moral transformation, and the moralising role of orthodox, state-centred Confucian historiography (see Moloughney and Zarrow 2011). Another constant, linking Republican-era modernisers to premodern tradition, was a persistent focus on *rencai* ('talented men'), and hence on schooling's role in the training and selection of a bureaucratic and technocratic elite.

Later foreign influences included those of American pragmatists from the 1920s onwards, and Soviet technocrats during the 1950s. However, from our twenty-first century vantage point, it is the Japanese influence that appears most enduring, with its emphasis on technological and industrial 'catch-up', alongside preservation of a national 'essence' seen as threatened by Western hegemony. Such aims dictated insistence on collective commitment to state-led national 'rejuvenation'. As noted in Chapter 3.1, the Reformist backlash against ultra-egalitarian Maoism featured explicit reference to the Meiji precedent – and, with it, a highly elitist vision of education's nation-building purposes. As in pre-war Japan, in post-Mao China uneven distribution of the fruits of development along with maintenance of an oligarchical political order has been justified by reference to the supremacy of national goals.

This chapter traces how school curricula have reflected and reinforced the ideological and social changes already noted in Chapter 3. It begins by considering the official curriculum development apparatus, and the important role within this of the People's Education Press (PEP). Trends in official curricular discourse are then examined, focusing on gradual moves towards pluralism and the debate over 'quality' (*suzhi*). We then consider changes to the structures and rituals of schooling and the ethos these embody, before discussing shifts in the curricula for particular subjects, especially those tasked with moulding political consciousness. Finally, the overall implications of curriculum development during the post-Mao period are assessed, focusing on the construction of citizenship in a context of increasing domestic social stratification and international tension.

The PEP and the official curriculum development process

The PEP was established in 1950 as a unit within the Ministry of Education tasked with supplying textbooks for schools throughout the new PRC (a role it was effectively performing by the mid-1950s). It thus traces its origins to the high water mark of Soviet influence (Adamson 2004; Jones 2005). Centralised decision-making, and reliance on experts from universities and colleges rather than on consultations with schoolteachers, reflected both Soviet models and the similarly controlling and hierarchical mindset of the preceding Kuomintang (KMT) regime (though the KMT had never managed to implement curricular standardisation). As Pepper notes, the CCP were more extreme centralisers than even their Stalinist mentors, instituting a national college entrance examination (the *gaokao*) that effectively reinstated the imperial *keju* abolished by the Qing regime in 1905 (Pepper 1996). To the PEP fell the task of developing the curriculum these examinations would test, and thus of defining the criteria for admission into 'New China's' technocratic elite.

From the beginning, this curriculum was heavily weighted towards disciplines deemed essential to nation-building and industrialisation: the national language (*Putonghua*), Politics, Maths, Science and Russian (as the vehicle for importing foreign expertise). A conventional subject-based curriculum and highly teacher-centred style of pedagogy characterised schooling at all levels. Within the PEP, subject-based units operated as discrete silos, with considerable power vested in respective Chief Editors (Adamson 2004). The Sino-Soviet split of 1960 saw English supplant Russian as the preferred foreign language, and prompted greater openness to Western pedagogical ideas. The PEP became less reliant on outside experts, and more responsive to teachers' needs and concerns. While curricula and textbooks became more coherent, political swings necessitated frequent revisions. Finding itself on the wrong side of the 'Red-Expert' divide at the outbreak of the Cultural Revolution, the PEP was closed down in 1967. Reconstituted in the following decade, it at first had to rely largely on 'commissioned assistance' to produce its textbooks, since many of its staff had been rusticated (Adamson 2004, 132). By 1980, it was once more fully operational, ensconced in new headquarters on Sha Tan Hou Street, just north of the Forbidden City.

At least until the early 2000s, the tasks of curriculum development and textbook production were effectively performed in tandem by the PEP, rather than being distinct, sequential processes. Official syllabuses sometimes provided *post hoc* rationalisation for the textbooks – a confusion somewhat obscured by the practice of initially designating new texts and syllabi as 'experimental' (*shiyan xing*). For example, in 2000 the PEP embarked on an extensive revision of its existing English Language textbooks, employing 'foreign experts' to assist in this.[1] However, no new curriculum for English was issued until the following year; the ongoing work on textbook revision thus proceeded alongside discussions of the draft curricular guidelines. This *modus operandi* persisted despite the existence since 1983 of a 'Curriculum and Teaching Materials Research Institute' (CTMRI) established by the Education Ministry, with its own committees responsible for specific school subjects; PEP editors served on these committees alongside advisors from tertiary institutions.[2] Although the curriculum reforms of 2001 heralded an ostensible separation of curriculum development and textbook production functions, PEP has in practice retained a foot in the former camp.[3] As the Education Ministry's textbook publishing arm, it retains a crucial voice in discussions of curriculum, while its texts remain the most widely used and a benchmark for competitors.

Curriculum development in the early post-Mao years – the return of academic elitism

The Cultural Revolution had witnessed chaotic curricular diversity, but in this, as in other respects, the late 1970s saw a rush to restore the *status quo ante*. This meant a reassertion of the principle of one national syllabus and one textbook (*yi gang yi ben*) for each school subject. In 1977, PEP editors were sequestered in a hotel in the Fragrant Hills west of Beijing, and given a few weeks to produce new texts; unsurprisingly, they drew heavily on the pre-Cultural Revolution editions. Although the politicisation of textual content was diluted, laudatory references to the senior leader, now Chairman Hua Guofeng, were retained. When Hua was supplanted by Deng Xiaoping shortly thereafter, another hasty round of revisions was required. During the 1980s, orthodox socialist messages still featured in textbooks, if less stridently than before. Emphasis was already starting to shift towards the inculcation of personal and civic morality, along with patriotism (Jones 2005; Adamson 2004).

While navigating the shifting shoals of political correctness, curriculum developers also faced the challenge of calibrating the difficulty of their texts. Those produced in the immediate post-Mao years were widely criticised by teachers for being *nan* (difficult/demanding), *jian* (hard to understand) and *fan* (overloaded [with content]). The curricular pendulum had swung wildly from Maoist 'redness' to a prioritisation of technical 'expertise', as editors and other leading educators sought to compensate for the 'lost decade' of the Cultural Revolution. The Education Ministry's 1980 teaching plans heavily emphasised Language, Science and Maths, while emphasis on Politics was correspondingly reduced (IED 1980, 1862) (a shift reflected in and reinforced by the new *gaokao* syllabus – see Chapter 8). As Zeng (co-author of this volume) remembers from her own schooldays, Science textbooks of this time were written by scientists as if for adult readers; they were essentially 'pedagogy-free'. Things subsequently improved once the restored system bedded in and revisions became less frequent and arbitrary, with new curricula generally piloted in 'draft' or 'experimental' form before being rolled out nationally (on the case of History, see Jones 2005).

If the new textbooks were meant to balance the elitist demands of the key point sector and the needs of the 'average' student or teacher, the balance was thus heavily weighted towards the former. Key school students were also encouraged to draw on a growing supply of supplementary learning materials, published in response to market demand. Meanwhile, others progressed as far as resource constraints and their more limited capacity – or that of their teachers – would allow. As noted in Chapter 3, numerous official pronouncements represented this widening of educational inequality as an inevitable concomitant of the race to produce 'talent'. 'The unfortunate consequence of this compromise', according to Thøgersen, 'was that education in non-key general schools became primarily aimed at preparing students for a higher education to which they had only minimal chances of ever getting access' (1991, 81).

PEP editors were far from oblivious to the challenges involved in delivering the new curriculum. Extensive and detailed teachers' guides (*jiaoshi yongshu*) were produced to accompany the textbooks, setting out in elaborate detail how they should be used in the classroom. These guides reflected awareness that many teachers, especially (but not only) at primary level, possessed shaky subject knowledge and little professional training (the proportion of *minban* teachers remained high throughout the 1980s – see Chapters 3 and 9). Editors also spent much time travelling around China addressing teachers and local officials, organising model lessons, and generally attempting to provide some sort of in-service training that, it was hoped, would percolate down to classroom level.

In practice, however, the curricula for urban and rural schools, and for 'key' schools and the rest, diverged markedly during the 1980s. Meanwhile, a rift opened up between advocates of streaming and selection, and defenders of egalitarian uniformity. Thøgersen juxtaposes two 1979 articles in the journal *Jiaoyu Yanjiu* ('Educational Research') encapsulating the opposing positions (1991, 84–5). Sun Zhen stressed the need to 'teach students according to their abilities' (*yin cai shi jiao*) in order to pick out the top students (*jianzi*) as early as possible and train them up in special classes. Reflecting an instrumental conception of education focused on generating 'human capital', he echoed Deng Xiaoping's exhortation to 'bring up talented people fast'. The egalitarian case was put by Ma Jixiong, who stressed the arbitrariness, and deleterious consequences, of selecting 'talented' students at a particular age. However, Ma offered no real answer to how divergent interests and abilities could be considered in a classroom of 60 students. 'The failure of egalitarians to show how the quality of education can be raised for all students, while simultaneously encouraging individual development, is' Thøgersen noted, 'an obvious weak point in their argumentation' (85). Egalitarians were uncomfortable not only with the trend towards streaming, but also with the vocationalisation drive, which some blamed for aggravating 'the phenomenon of students looking down upon labour and on the labouring people' (*Jiaoyu Yanjiu*, No. 2, 19–21, p. 19; cited in Thøgersen 1991, 114; see Chapter 10).

'Quality education', patriotism and curriculum development after 1989

Reinstatement of labour education, in the form of military training, was one element of the official response to the political unrest of 1989, though the association of labour with collective punishment did nothing to reform the prejudice against it (see Chapters 3 and 10). However, moral and patriotic education apart, the future direction of curriculum development remained a matter of some uncertainty for several years after Tiananmen. Would concerns over the detachment of urban students from the gritty realities of life on the farm or the factory floor lead to a radical rethink of post-Mao elitism? In the event, as noted in Chapter 3, no such rethink took place. Instead, the renewed and intensified pursuit of marketisation, now focused increasingly on the cities, exacerbated the social stratification to which education had already contributed. That stratification in turn constituted a huge obstacle to attempts to maintain curricular uniformity across the whole system. In apparent recognition of this, a list of 'key points for national education plans over the next ten years' issued in January 1992 called for publishers to produce (by 1995) different teaching materials 'to suit the demands of different systems of study and different levels' (IED 1992, 3258). As the 1993 '*Gangyao*' made plain, curricular diversification was to be embraced rather than resisted (IED 1993, 3467). Market principles were also invoked to challenge the PEP's monopolistic position, on the assumption that competition would automatically yield higher-quality teaching materials (Wang 2001, 36).

The mid-1990s thus witnessed the beginning of a gradual shift away from the principle of 'one syllabus, one textbook' towards a principle, ultimately enshrined in the 2001 curriculum reform, of 'one syllabus, multiple textbooks' (*yi gang duo ben*). Wealthier and more 'advanced' provinces or municipalities – such as Shanghai, Zhejiang and Guangdong – were among the earliest areas licensed to pilot their own texts for subjects including English and History (Adamson 2004; Jones 2005). Such tentative moves towards diluting curricular uniformity coincided with further watering-down of egalitarian messages, but implied no retreat from the principle of ideological conformity. Rather, as themes of class struggle and revolution faded from textbooks, the emphasis on personal morality, collective values and patriotism was strengthened.

Emphases on moral education and collectivism (without socialism) were among the features of East Asian school curricula that attracted Chinese officials during the 1990s. Countries such as Japan and Singapore were admired for their combination of rapid modernisation and industrialisation with strong social discipline (and one-party rule) (Rappleye 2007). Such models were ideologically and culturally congenial to a regime now cut adrift from its socialist moorings, but intensely suspicious of triumphalist Western 'hegemonism'. At the same time, as Chinese curriculum developers looked East, they also noted increasing criticism in Japan and elsewhere of rigid, uniform and content-heavy curricula; concerns over the intellectually deadening effect of rote-learning; and a desire to reform pedagogy so as to promote 'creativity' and 'critical thinking'. In China, such concerns were also crystallised in an earnest public debate over why the country had never won a Nobel Prize (Lovell 2006).

Thøgersen's observations of teaching in Beijing Normal University's Number 2 attached Middle School – 'a showcase of Chinese teaching at its very best'– illustrate the issues that increasingly preoccupied curriculum developers during the 1990s (1991, 112). He reported 'little variation in teaching method', as teachers religiously followed the textbooks, sources of the information students would need to pass the *gaokao*. Discussion of content was 'very rarely connected to the outside world'; in studying the natural sciences, students were required to memorise abstract principles, but not to reflect on how these 'were utilized in production' (112). In a Politics class, the teacher went through Mao's article 'On Practice' without once relating it to 'any phenomenon outside the realm of philosophy'. 'The students were asked to learn the definition of "social practice" by heart without any reflections over the glaring contrast between this teaching method and the content of the text' (112) (in Politics classes, this focus on abstruse Marxist philosophy, and the extremely dry approach to teaching it, has barely changed in forty years – see Vickers 2009a, b). Nationally, pedagogical experiments that attempted to relate lesson content to local conditions and production needs remained 'exceptions' (113). The science curriculum during the 1980s was 'characterized by subject specialization, emphasis on the physical sciences, infrequent practical activity by students, emphasis on content rather than process skills, and theoretical rather than applied approaches to the subject matter' (Lewin 1987, cited in Thøgersen 1991, 113).

Reducing the emphasis on rote learning and cultivating generic 'skills' were central objectives of the 'quality education' (*suzhi jiaoyu*) drive from the mid-1990s. In curricular terms, *suzhi* implied abandoning 'examination-oriented education' (*yingshi jiaoyu*) and promoting approaches better geared to fostering initiative and spontaneity – goals articulated by Zhu Kaixuan in a major 1997 speech (IED 1997, 4209). 'Using science and education to create a prosperous nation' – the key theme of President Jiang Zemin's 1998 Peking University speech – became a widely repeated slogan (IED 1998, 89). That autumn Jiang emphasised that 'the key to creativity lies with talent, and the growth of talent relies on education' (IED 1998, 190). The SEC issued directives stressing the 'important task of reducing excessive burdens on teachers and students' (e.g. IED 1994, 3667), something that Education Minister Chen Zhili proclaimed as essential in order to 'holistically implement *suzhi jiaoyu*' (IED 2000, 484). As we saw in Chapter 3.3, this was accompanied by concerns that excessive pressure was both cramping creativity and impairing youthful morals. 'We must not make young people spend the whole day inside poring over books', Jiang insisted in 2000, 'we must let them participate in social activities, broaden their horizons, and increase their experience of society.' Ensuring their 'overall healthy growth' was crucial (IED 2000, 513).

In many respects, including the atmosphere of moral crisis generated by sensationalised accounts of student violence, educational debate in China echoed that in contemporary Japan (Rappleye 2007). There, soul-searching over the horrors of 'examination hell', and the alienation and moral turpitude this was seen as fostering, contributed to calls for 'relaxed education' (*yutori kyouiku*). At the same time, pressures for greater flexibility and diversity, not only in curriculum but also in institutional arrangements (encompassing school choice and privatisation), drew on OECD discourse regarding the demands of the 'global knowledge economy'. However, subsequent Japanese attempts to make the curriculum more 'student-centred' had limited impact, either because they coincided with already established trends (at primary level), or because they clashed with the demands of unreformed college entrance examinations (at secondary level) (Bjork 2011). Meanwhile, attempts to push a wider agenda of diversity and choice were resisted, with some success, both by teachers' unions and by the Ministry of Education, who were concerned at the implications for equality of opportunity and social cohesion (Takayama 2011).

Japanese debates over *yutori kyouiku*, themselves heavily influenced by Western precedents, significantly influenced discussions surrounding China's curriculum reform of 2001. Academics based at East China Normal University in Shanghai played a prominent role in pushing for greater diversity and flexibility, for more 'integration' of subject content, and for more 'student-centred' methods. Prominent amongst them was the Japan-educated Zhong Qiquan, a principal consultant to the Education Ministry prior to the 2001 reforms. However, more conservative academics at Beijing Normal University (BNU), including the Soviet-educated Wang Cesan, were vocally sceptical. Wang, influenced by the Soviet thinker Zankoff, criticised what he saw as the excessively stark distinction drawn in the new curriculum guidelines between disciplinary knowledge on the one hand, and the fostering of individual development or generic 'skills' on the other (Wang 2004). He protested at what he called the new tendency to 'despise knowledge'. This prompted an acerbic response from Zhong, who branded Wang a 'mouldy old cheese' (*fa hui de nailao*) (Zhong and You 2004).

Among the aims of the 2001 reform were the promotion of integrated science curricula, increased provision of laboratories, and the introduction at primary level of practical scientific activities (such as making weather vanes or growing beans). However, the absence or inadequacy of corresponding reforms to assessment has caused confusion and resistance amongst teachers (see Chapter 8). Meanwhile, school textbooks have typically maintained the division between Biology, Physics and Chemistry, even if their covers proclaim integration. A persistent focus on test preparation is also evident in the style of instructional materials. Dealing with 'the structure of a cell', the most recent Beijing junior secondary textbook simply tells students what a cell is and describes its structure (Beijing Chubanshe 2013). By contrast, an American text aimed at students of the same age, having explained that the cell is 'the fundamental building block of life', goes on to discuss its applications in industry and the 'life sciences' – highlighting connections with the world beyond the classroom (McGraw Hill 2002). Such material is far more limited in the Beijing text, which also features fewer visual aids (e.g. diagrams and photographs). When it comes to 'practical' exercises related to the topic of 'the cell', the Beijing text requires students to take a mouth swab and make a microscope slide, while the American one envisages them finding leaves to put under the microscope. In the former case, the aim is seemingly to train students as laboratory technicians; in the latter, to encourage them to explore the environment for examples of 'cells'.[4]

Reformist calls for 'student-centred' and 'integrated' approaches thus did not in fact succeed in dissolving the longstanding boundaries between school subjects, or in converting established subject communities to the new gospel. The development of curricula and textbooks for specific subjects remained heavily influenced by academic specialists, not least BNU academics, from amongst whom key advisors to PEP and the MOE have long been drawn. In so far as new texts combined emphasis on key 'knowledge points' with exhortations to 'learn by doing', for example through experimentation and project work, they often prompted complaints from teachers struggling to find time to complete the lessons as expected (Du 2006). Textbooks produced since 2001 have tended to feature many 'optional' units, as well as supplementary materials. However, both timetable constraints and the need to prepare for high-stakes public examinations that still test formulaic knowledge have in practice constrained pedagogical innovation. So too have entrenched ideas concerning the role of the teacher and the nature of learning. Kipnis records witnessing a 'creativity' class in a Shandong primary school in 2000 which consisted of requiring students to memorise and recite Tang dynasty poetry (2011, 71–2).[5]

As in Japan, some have also pointed out that the introduction of more sophisticated and demanding pedagogical techniques, as well as the active promotion of curricular diversity, threaten further to undermine equality of educational opportunity. For example, Dai argues that these innovations pose particular challenges for rural schools – thus contributing to an exacerbation of the rural–urban divide (Dai 2006).[6] To the extent that lack of examination reform has stymied pedagogical change, such fears might appear overdone. However, besides the disadvantage they experience due to structural aspects of the public examination system (see Chapter 8), moves such as the increasing emphasis on English proficiency (and its increased weighting in public examinations) cannot but disadvantage students in more remote areas where the supply of qualified teachers is especially problematic (see the following chapter).

But besides practical obstacles to implementation of the curriculum reforms, there are also significant cultural, philosophical and political ones. Exhortations to be 'student-centred' and teach generic 'skills' imply a liberal, constructivist epistemology. This is radically at odds with deeply ingrained assumptions concerning the role of the teacher as exemplar and transmitter of authorised knowledge – a tension reflected in criticisms of the excessively 'passive' role envisaged for teachers under the reforms (Fan 2005). It is also in fundamental conflict with traditional conceptions of the curriculum as a corpus of officially mandated texts, and, by extension, with the role of government in prescribing epistemological 'correctness'. This contradiction is reflected in attempts to marry calls for the cultivation of 'high-quality' talent through liberalised pedagogical approaches with demands for enhanced moral and patriotic education[7] (or, in President Jiang's words, 'simultaneous progress in material and spiritual civilization', IED 1998, 201). It is hard to reconcile a vision of the student as autonomous generator of new knowledge with an emphasis on inculcating uncritical patriotism and deference to authority. This is a contradiction inherent to the definition of *suzhi* itself, with talk of 'intellectual' quality emphasising criticism, even while 'political' or 'moral' quality requires unquestioning acceptance of Party orthodoxy (see Kipnis 2011, 73–7) Meanwhile, as Murphy and Johnson observe, 'tension between central control and local initiative' has remained acute in the field of curriculum and pedagogy (2009, 449).

Notwithstanding such contradictions, the drive for *suzhi* has served to legitimise the increased stratification of schooling, not only through prioritising the cultivation of 'talent', but also through discourses associating academic success with the possession of 'socialist spiritual civilization' (Murphy 2004). Especially during the 1990s, official pronouncements tended to blame the problems of the rural poor on their fecklessness, disregard of population policy and generally low *suzhi* (see Chapter 3.3). Central government rhetoric and policy have subsequently evinced rather more concern for the predicament of rural students. However, by comparison with the societies of Japan, South Korea and Taiwan, in mainland China the promotion of pluralism and diversity has been less constrained by concerns to maintain uniformity and equality of opportunity.[8]

Routines, rituals and schools as institutions

In heavily text-oriented educational cultures such as that of China, textbooks can reveal much about what is taught and learnt, but it is important also to understand the context in which they are used. So before examining the content of particular subjects, we first consider aspects of schools as organisations. These include the buildings and classrooms themselves, the way in which the school day is structured, and other routines and rituals that together constitute what is often called the 'hidden curriculum'.

Throughout the Reform period, schools have ranged from rudimentary mud huts in remote rural villages, to glittering concrete-and-glass edifices in urban centres. The balance has shifted dramatically from the former to the latter, as rural primary schooling has been regularised, village schools closed and 'concentrated', and funding available for school construction increased, albeit more dramatically in some regions than others. Pressures from both below and above have encouraged investment in modern school buildings and facilities (Kipnis 2011). As discussed in Chapter 3.3 and the previous chapter, increased funding for education in rural and remote regions from the early 2000s has especially boosted spending on infrastructure (i.e. buildings). Meanwhile, both the key point system (from the late 1970s) and marketisation processes (from the 1990s) have enabled prestigious state-run schools to attract greater resources (see Chapter 9). The differential funding of schools within the same area is often starkly visible in their buildings and facilities. In contrast to Japan, where relative uniformity is reflected in quite standardised school architecture (Cave 2007), in China variations in size, construction quality and facilities often visibly testify to *de facto* official endorsement of an elite/mass divide.

The decoration of these buildings has meanwhile conveyed more explicit socialising messages. Slogans relating to official campaigns – including the perennial exhortations to follow population policy and 'raise population quality' – have been daubed in large characters on school walls and other public structures (Murphy 2004). The portraits of Marx, Engels, Lenin and Stalin that until the 1990s typically adorned school walls (especially at secondary level) were by the early twenty-first century increasingly crowded out by images of Chinese heroes from earlier periods, or of national symbols such as the Great Wall (though Chairman Mao and the Mao-era 'model worker', Lei Feng, have remained much in evidence). Schools have also organised activities and displays relating to events of special national significance – such as the achievement of sending China's first astronaut into space in 2004, or the Beijing Olympics of 2008. Decorative elements have thus reinforced the political and moral messages conveyed through the formal curriculum at any particular time.

While the ideological messages on classroom walls may have changed since the 1970s, the standard pattern of classroom organisation has remained largely constant. The typical classroom, from primary to senior high school, features desks arranged in serried rows, facing a teacher's desk and blackboard at the front – reflecting standard practice both in China's Asian neighbours and the former Soviet bloc (see Alexander 2000). And classes are large. Kipnis reports class sizes of 50–60 students at primary level, and as high as 70 in some secondary schools (2011, 107). Such large classes have remained the norm despite the demographic decline resulting from population planning. Far from complaining, parents tend to see large class size as 'evidence that other parents [have] manoeuvred to have their children put in that class and, thus, that the teacher of that class [is] excellent' (Kipnis 2011, 107). This reflects the assumption that 'teachers teach more by setting an example than by giving individual attention to students'. However, it is profoundly at odds with central elements of the *suzhi jiaoyu* reforms, which envisage more discussion and self-directed project or group work. Class sizes in excess of 50 require and assume clear patterns of authority and discipline and, by extension, clear rules of intellectual and behavioural 'correctness'.

The moral surveillance of students is a core role of teachers throughout primary and secondary schooling (see Woronov 2016, Chapter 3). Responsibility for this rests primarily with the 'homeroom teacher' or *banzhuren* for each class, who is assisted by appointed student monitors selected for their exemplary moral and academic performance. Discipline is additionally fostered through various routines and rituals that punctuate the school calendar. Whole-school calisthenics, regimented assemblies (often – especially from the 1990s – involving veneration of the national flag and singing of the national anthem), participation in the Young Pioneers (the Communist equivalent of the Scouting movement) and, for older students, military training (again, since the 1990s; see Chapter 3.3), all contribute to a strongly collectivist and patriotic ethos. But while the dominant ethos has remained collectivist, it is no longer egalitarian – tests, examinations, sports contests and competitions of various kinds all ram home the message that life chances are dependent on individual merit. As Hansen argues (2013), schools and teachers, certainly at secondary level, have come to see it as their duty to prepare students for the intensely individualistic competition that characterises twenty-first century Chinese society. Since success entails mastery of an authoritative canon of moral and academic correctness, education becomes an exercise in competing to conform.

The persistent divide between 'elite' schools and the rest, as well as the effects of the One Child Policy on familial aspirations, have intensified this competitiveness (Fong 2004). Deweyan progressivism attracted renewed interest from Chinese scholars and policymakers in the 1980s–90s, and was one influence on the curriculum reforms of 2001. However, as already noted, habit, culture and the backwash effect of unreformed public examinations have dampened the impact of those reforms. Despite calls for 'integration' and 'skills'-focused pedagogy, timetables for schools at all levels have continued to be organised around discrete subjects, with the most time dedicated to the subjects accorded greatest weighting in examination syllabi. Moreover, recent attempts – linked to the 'quality'-oriented reforms – to limit school hours and lighten the burden of studying have in practice given a huge boost to the private tutorial industry, as has happened elsewhere in East Asia (Kipnis 2011, 77–81; see Chapter 9).

Both competitive intensity and disciplinary objectives are reflected in the length of the typical school day, the organisation of school timetables, and the provision of homework. Primary schools may start classes at around 8 a.m. (with perhaps a half-hour 'reading period' before that), and end at 4 or 4:30 p.m. (Kipnis 2011, 113–17). Junior middle school classes may run from about 7:30 a.m. to 4:30 or 5 p.m. (41–2), and high schools start earlier and end later. However, the volume of homework that students do outside class effectively lengthens the typical school day. In this respect, Kipnis reports that Shandong's Zouping county has 'at least seen some limits enforced on competitive intensity' at primary level since the early 2000s, with homework curtailed especially for the most junior grades, and Saturday classes cancelled (69–70). However, he notes that such measures had not been enforced in other Shandong counties. Meanwhile, the shift since the 1990s towards concentrating upper primary and junior secondary schools in rural areas, in forcing more students to board, has also subjected them to a more regimented regime (Murphy 2004). For boarding students, barely a minute in the school day is reserved for unstructured recreation or free reading. When not actually in lessons, or having their midday nap, students are generally either engaged in some other form of teacher-led activity, or sat at their desks doing homework (Kipnis 2011, 41–2).

Despite years of official calls for a reduction of homework burdens and study intensity, the *China Daily* in 2015 reported the results of a survey finding that Chinese primary and secondary students spent an average of 3 hours per day on homework, 'twice the global average', and far more than students in Japan or Korea (Liu J. 2015). Sleeping hours for the children surveyed dropped 'below eight hours' from the age of 12 – in other words, from the end of primary school. Almost 90 per cent of high-school students surveyed claimed that they usually finished their homework after 11 p.m. And across all age groups, students spent most time (72 per cent) on homework for Maths, the subject they also generally considered to be the most difficult.[9] The prioritisation of Maths, along with Chinese language, Science and (more recently) English, is evident in officially stipulated time allocations for various subjects during the years of compulsory schooling (see Tables 6.1 to 6.4 in the Appendix).

The heavy curricular emphasis on Maths and Science – something the PRC shares both with its East Asian neighbours and its former Soviet mentor (see Chapter 2) – is also strongly associated with notions of patriotism. The entire school curriculum is pervaded by what Kipnis terms a 'scientistic ideology', preaching that scientific weakness was the prime cause of China's nineteenth century 'humiliation', and, by the same token, that in science lies the key to national 'modernisation and strength' (2011, 112). He notes the widespread perception that 'the smarter students gravitate toward the sciences' (something true across East Asia), and that the percentage of students enrolled in the science stream for college entry is far higher at more prestigious high schools. During the Reform era, English language skills have also increasingly come to be seen as important both to personal prospects and the national modernisation project, because of the importance of English in international trade and as the global *lingua franca* for scientific research. Following the curriculum reforms of 2001, English began to be taught from Grade 3 in many urban primary schools.

Those reforms also stipulated a broadening of the curriculum to include more instruction in Art and Music during the compulsory years. The fact that these subjects are not required for the *gaokao* has limited interest in teaching and learning them, although they can nonetheless play a role in the competition for high-school places (see Chapter 8). Kipnis reports that 'the expanded curriculum' was 'successfully implemented' in primary and junior secondary schools in Zouping (69), with the school consolidation movement enhancing the capacity to provide specialist instruction in these areas (something small village schools would struggle to do). But the pressure of examination preparation can nonetheless prompt teachers to encroach on time allocated to areas less important for this purpose. For example, while national curriculum guidelines currently allot four teaching periods a week to Maths during the compulsory years, a BNU scholar notes that 'most schools arrange more than five periods' (Wei 2014). And in so far as music and art lessons have been provided, their content has frequently been geared to promoting patriotic messages and 'traditional' values, rather than encouraging the sort of self-expression and free-flowing creativity which *suzhi jiaoyu* was supposed to entail.

A note on Physical Education (PE)

One area traditionally accorded a similarly low priority in the Chinese school curriculum is PE. While sports are popular as extra-curricular activities, time for playing them has typically been squeezed by examination pressure, which increases after entry to junior secondary school. In his ethnographic study, Kipnis recounts how one boy, a keen basketball player, found that, from the last year of junior secondary onwards, he was only able to play for around 'forty minutes on every third Sunday' (Kipnis 2011, 48–9). Even at primary level, 'activity periods' supposedly set aside for PE, music or free reading can be 'taken over for some other pedagogical purpose' (116–17). Although the pressure on students to forfeit sports for study may be less intense at non-'key' schools, it is nonetheless strong and widespread.

In this respect, the situation in China differs significantly from that in Japan, where participation in extra-curricular sporting clubs is almost universal in junior secondary schools. There, sports are widely seen as a means of 'cultivating the spirit', with the militarism of the pre-war period surviving in an emphasis on 'hard training', 'commander-style coaches' and 'strict hierarchy' (Miller 2011). While mass conscription was abolished in 1945, and 'peace' embraced as a national ideology, sports in Japan have thus largely maintained their pre-war function of regimenting the populace. In China, by contrast, militaristic messages are explicit in the content of schooling (and in the wider media), and since the 1990s, secondary-school students have had to attend PLA-run 'boot camps' (for many, a welcome break from the monotony of the classroom). However, except for the tiny proportion of athletically gifted students in specialised classes or academies, sports have occupied a relatively peripheral role in the daily or weekly routine of the typical Chinese student.

The low priority accorded to sports education has attracted criticism. In the run-up to the 2008 Olympics, sports were hailed as a potential remedy for a range of physical, social and moral maladies – including childhood obesity, asthma, short-sightedness, excessive individualism, and the various alleged moral failings of singleton children (Mao *et al.* 2007). Exercise has also been touted as a crucial means of raising 'physical quality' (*shenti suzhi*), reflecting a neo-eugenicist concern with national health and strength. Although they have been exhorted to devote more attention to physical education since the 1990s, only since 2010 have junior secondary schools been compelled to provide one hour of PE every day (including the traditional half hour of morning calisthenics). Crucially, PE is now evaluated, which means that students are strongly encouraged not to miss it, and parents instructed not to let them do so. In some cases, students are marked down for missing PE lessons even if they are ill (since students' 'performance' in PE is typically scored in terms of attendance). However, schools and kindergartens are also sensitive to parental concerns about the risks of excessive physical activity (see Tobin *et al.* 2009, Chapter 2).

The place of PE in the curriculum thus illustrates the tensions running through contemporary educational debate. Official policy has reflected concerns to promote population health, maximise national strength, inculcate a collectivist ethos and heighten patriotism. These goals (whatever their merits) would arguably be better served by an extensive network of sports clubs on the Japanese model than by half-hour sessions of relatively light exercise and annual one-week boot camps. However, intense competition for examination success – not just between individual students and their parents, but also between teachers and schools – tend to make PE seem a distraction from the serious business of schooling. Also at work here, according to Kipnis, are traditions of 'literary masculinity' that associate male prowess more with success in the examination hall than on the sports field. Deep-rooted cultural beliefs as well as the nature of public examinations thus combine to dictate an overwhelming focus on mastery of the written word as embodied in authorised texts. It is to the content of those texts that we now turn.

Curricular change in selected school subjects

In the following analysis of the content of particular school subjects, we focus on those of particular relevance to the shaping of values, identity and citizenship. This may disappoint readers hoping for a fuller exposition of the secrets of China's perceived success in Maths and Science education, discussed briefly above. In the conclusion to this volume, we discuss at some length the significance of Shanghai's recent performance in the OECD's PISA tests. As may be deduced from the foregoing sections, that performance is largely explained by timetable weighting, hard graft and continuous testing, rather than by pedagogical wizardry. Moreover, as we stressed in our opening chapters, it is education's political and socialising aspects – often neglected in studies of Chinese schooling – that we particularly aim to elucidate here.

'Thought and Values', 'Morals' and 'Politics'

It is often claimed that the teaching of morality, values and citizenship in Chinese schools during the reform era has become 'less politicised' by comparison with pre-1978 practice. During the Maoist era, and especially the Cultural Revolution, students of all ages were urged to exercise vigilance against 'class enemies', exhorted to follow the self-sacrificing example of revolutionary heroes, and initiated into the cult of the omniscient Chairman. After 1978, propaganda became less blatant, especially at primary level, with curricula and textbooks focusing more on issues of personal morality and social relationships. The post-1978 period as a whole has witnessed a shift from overtly revolutionary and socialist messages towards a focus on inculcating personal and civic values such as collectivism, discipline, patriotism and a 'scientific' outlook. However, the extent to which this constitutes 'depoliticisation' is debatable.

'The whole classroom rocks with laughter whenever communism and Marxism-Leninism are mentioned', recalled Thøgersen after visiting an elite Beijing high school during the late 1980s (1991, 130). Other contemporary reports likewise cast doubt on the effectiveness of political or ideological education 'due to the great disparity between the reality students experience in the society [*sic.*] and what is taught in the classroom' (Lin 1993, 9). But for the Communist Party itself, moral and political education have remained far from a laughing matter, as testified by the official response to the 1989 Student Movement (see Chapter 3.3). The subsequent move to commit the Party to more radical marketisation, while effectively discarding socialism, witnessed increasing appeals to patriotic themes.

Collectivist values have remained central to the ethical outlook that the curricula for Morals (*de yu*), 'Values and Society' (*pinde yu shehui*) 'Thought and Values' (*sixiang pinde*), 'Thought and Politics' (*sixiang zhengzhi*) – or equivalent subjects – seek to inculcate from primary to senior high level.[10] However, as the regime has increasingly sought to draw on the resources of 'traditional' Chinese ethical thought to buttress its legitimacy, its emphasis and choice of exemplary figures has shifted. Lin records a story from a 1980s junior secondary school citizenship textbook hailing the heroic dedication of a worker who insisted on completing the task in hand rather than stopping to resuscitate his son, whom he had found lying unconscious after receiving a high-voltage electric shock (1993, 5). The morality of sacrificing the life of one's son for the sake of workplace discipline is not something endorsed by early twenty-first century textbooks. For one thing, Chinese society is no longer structured around work units demanding utter loyalty from their members in return for cradle-to-grave welfare; for another, such callousness to a family member is incompatible with the Confucian teachings now celebrated as the epitome of civilised Chinese ethics (Confucius and other figures are nowadays quoted far more extensively in school texts than Chairman Mao – see Vickers 2009b, 69). Collective loyalty is instead directed elsewhere (depending on the age of the students) – at family, classmates, school, community and, ultimately, the nation, or 'Great Chinese National Family'.

Since 1989, 'Education in the National Situation' (*guoqing jiaoyu*) has remained a central theme of the secondary school Civics or Politics curriculum. Rather than identifying the regime with class interests or the pursuit of 'revolution', *guoqing* education instead emphasises the Party's pivotal role in achieving modernisation and making the country 'strong', while highlighting numerous threats to this project. Some of these are internal, such as China's large population, immense size, and diversity, all of which require a firm hand at the national tiller and avoidance of 'destabilising' political experiments. But students are also reminded that China's pursuit of national renewal faces deliberate obstruction by malevolent Westerners and Japanese. Under the cover of a professed concern for 'human rights', students are warned, these hypocritical ex-imperialists will use any trick or stratagem to frustrate China's resumption of her proper place in the world (see Vickers 2009a, 73–7). Texts not only for History (see below), but also for Morals, Civics and Politics, repeatedly allude to China's 'humiliating' victimisation by foreign 'bullies', exhorting students to ensure that this is never repeated (Vickers 2009a, b).

Whatever their direct significance in shaping students' worldview (arguably slight), texts for the most blatantly propagandistic school subjects serve as a weathervane for ideological shifts affecting the curriculum more generally. These shifts do not signify, as Law claims, the emergence of a significantly more depoliticised, liberal, 'multi-level, multi-dimensional' model of citizenship education for a 'global age' (Law 2011). Moreover, claims that recent experiments in 'school-based curriculum development' for moral education have furthered such liberalisation are misleading (Ye 2014), given the very limited scope of these initiatives, and their restriction to the most politically anodyne of themes. They leave inviolate the Party's core messages concerning the supreme value of patriotism, the inviolability of Chinese unity, various threats to the project of national renewal, and inveterate foreign hostility. These provide a deeply politicised, if no longer socialist, scaffolding for the worldview that the curriculum as a whole conveys.

History

Like all Chinese regimes before it, the Communist Party has always sought to 'use the past to control the present' (Jones 2005). School History texts during the Cultural Revolution relentlessly emphasised class loyalty and revolutionary heroism, while condemning 'feudalism', 'imperialism' and Soviet 'revisionism'. Textbooks during the 1980s returned to the more sober orthodoxies of a Marxist narrative 'with Chinese characteristics' – although this came to seem increasingly anachronistic as economic reform, media liberalisation, and increased openness to the outside world exposed students and their teachers to new and varied sources of information.[11] Chinese and world history was still told as a narrative of progress through the inevitable historical stages – from primitive communism through slave society, feudalism and bourgeois capitalism to communism. 'Peasant rebels' retained their status as proto-revolutionaries, and class struggle remained both iron historical law and moral imperative. Nonetheless, class hours for History at junior secondary level (History has not been taught as a discrete subject at primary level) were significantly increased after 1981, reflecting the importance attached to the subject as a 'vehicle for promoting moral-ideological conformity' in the politically unstable atmosphere that persisted through the 1980s (Jones 2005, 87). And especially from 1986, class struggle and historical materialism began to be downplayed in favour of a heightened emphasis on patriotism, reflected, for example, in acknowledgement of the KMT's contribution to the war against Japan (85). Fulminations against 'feudalism' and 'imperialism' lost some of their previous vehemence.

The 1989 unrest emboldened conservatives to demand a ratcheting up of anti-capitalist rhetoric. Shanghai's local authorities commissioned a textbook entitled *A Simplified History of Social Development* (*Shehui fazhan jianshi*) to be distributed to all secondary schools. In tones reminiscent of the Cultural Revolution, this fulminated against the 'capitalist states' blamed for fomenting unrest:

> The internal function of a capitalist state is to suppress the revolt by the proletarians [*sic.*] and the working class; the external function is to facilitate economic expansion and exploitation and to invade small and weak countries … [capitalist states] use all kinds of propaganda machines to praise the capitalist exploiting class, to promote capitalist selfishness, to spread their rotten lifestyles and to poison and numb the wills [*sic.*] of the working class.
>
> (Cited in Lin 1993, 10)

However, the collapse of the Soviet Union and China's renewed marketisation drive subsequently prompted a winding down of attempts to encourage mass identification with the global proletariat.

As noted above, the 1990s witnessed tentative steps away from curricular uniformity, as more 'advanced' regions were encouraged to raise 'quality' to the higher level their superior resources permitted (on Shanghai, see Vickers and Yang 2013). At the same time, some PEP editors and their academic advisors became interested in ideas – such as those associated with the *New History* movement in the UK and USA – that advocated using History to teach generic skills. Reference to using History to promote 'analytical skills' had already featured in the 1986 curricular guidelines, and in those drafted in 1988 which, thanks to the 1989 unrest, were not officially promulgated until 1992 (Jones 2005, 86, 90). But while for Western educators the use of History to foster skills of critical analysis was associated with promoting active democratic citizenship, in China it was the pursuit of success in the 'global knowledge economy' that rendered this approach attractive to officials.[12] The challenge for curriculum developers has been to square analysis of primary sources and debate of alternative viewpoints with the imperative of retailing a state-authorised, nationalistic narrative that delivers 'correct conclusions' (86).

The 2001 reforms saw these contradictory aims enshrined in the new guidelines, and heralded a further diversification of curricula and textbooks (see Rose 2013). At the same time, two overlapping controversies affected curriculum development and textbook production. On the one hand, tensions emerged over pedagogy, as attempts were made to 'integrate' History with Geography (in a new 'History and Society' subject) and, especially at senior secondary level, to adopt a thematic rather than chronological approach. On the other hand, political sensitivities implied risks for innovative authors or editors; opponents or rivals would be quick to point out lapses in ideological correctness. Thus Professor Su Zhiliang, having edited a radically thematic senior secondary textbook series for Shanghai, saw approval for this withdrawn by the local authorities after pressure from 'conservative historians' (Su 2011; Vickers and Yang 2013).

The case of History underlines the need to regard official curricular rhetoric with scepticism. Official guidelines after 2001 called both for greater international understanding and tolerance, and heightened patriotism, founded on pride in China's civilisational legacy and determination to resist external threats. The tensions inherent in efforts to make History education at once more 'global' and more 'national' are discussed by Li Fan of BNU, an advisor to PEP's History subject unit (Li 2011). Li notes that the urge to promote 'national unity' encompassing both the Han and the various 'minority nationalities' has given rise to a series of arcane disputes over which historical figures qualify as 'national heroes' – maintaining the approach of handing down 'correct' official verdicts of praise or blame. Meanwhile, the pursuit of greater global understanding is undermined, according to Li, by stereotypical accounts of 'traditional' Chinese and Western civilisations, depicting the former as essentially autocratic and the latter as essentially democratic.

Citing his own Shanghai textbook series, Su Zhiliang claims that recent years have seen a trend towards more balanced treatment of foreign countries in general, and Japan in particular (though others dispute this; see Rose 2013). He points to extensive and positive coverage of the Meiji Restoration; acknowledgement of modern Japan's achievements in education, science and technology; and the recognition of Japanese influence on Chinese modernisers. He also claims that treatment of Japan's invasion of China has become less strident. However, despite Su's relatively sympathetic treatment of Japan, his text tells students that:

> Japan … did not reflect [on] its own history seriously and did not criticise its guilt thoroughly, which resulted in many flawed ideas on imperialism being still current. That the Japanese right wing is more and more rampant day by day and that Japanese leaders glorify the war of invasion are all phenomena closely related to these flawed ideas. With growing economic power, Japan is now actively trying to gain a permanent seat in the United Nations Security Council. However, this meets resistance from the Asian neighbouring countries, which Japan invaded, and from all peace-loving people.
>
> (Su *et al.*, cited in Su 2011, 156)

What counts for a 'think-point' in even the most liberal of contemporary texts is illustrated by the subsequent discussion question: 'According to you, how can Japan become a "leading country, universally recognised by the international community", when displaying an attitude towards denying its own history?'.

Having discarded most of the baggage of revolutionary socialism, History as a school subject nowadays heavily emphasises: the glories of traditional Han culture and civilisation; national unity premised on the inviolability of borders bequeathed by the Qing Empire; and China's 'century of humiliation' by foreign imperialists, ended only by the triumph of the Communist Party in 1949. Meanwhile, textbooks maintain almost complete silence regarding such self-inflicted catastrophes as the Great Leap Forward and the Cultural Revolution. The lack of balance or proportion this entails has been criticised by some domestic scholars, both on grounds of historical accuracy and for threatening to destabilise relations with neighbouring states. The most notable instance of this was a 2006 article by Zhongshan University professor Yuan Weishi, published in the magazine *Freezing Point* (*Bing Dian*) (Hayford 2006). Yuan was subsequently barred from publication, and the magazine closed down.

Chinese Language and Literature (Yuwen)

'Thought and Values' and History make explicit the ideological assumptions and historical narrative underlying the official programme of political socialisation, but the main curricular vector for socialising messages is the subject of Chinese Language (at secondary level, 'Chinese Language and Literature'). Its large proportion of class hours, central importance in tests and examinations, and use of memorable stories rather than dry 'facts' all render it a supremely powerful tool for indoctrination. At the same time, the exalted status of the written language – deriving from its hallowed role as instrument of statecraft, bearer of ancient wisdom, and pre-eminent symbol of cultivation and refinement – have placed it at the centre of public debate over how China's cultural legacy should be defined and transmitted to the next generation.

Content aside, the Chinese script itself embodies certain messages concerning the nature and purposes of education. Throughout the primary years, especially early on, students spend much of the school day (and more time at home) copying out characters; there is no other way to learn them. Moreover, the status of calligraphy as an elevated art form reinforces an emphasis on handwriting. Chinese leaders throughout history, not least Chairman Mao and President Jiang Zemin, have sought to demonstrate their exemplary cultivation and fitness to rule by bestowing samples of their calligraphy on their subjects. A regular, measured and correct command of the written script is widely taken to reflect good character; by the same token, sloppiness in writing suggests low *suzhi* or 'quality'. The fact that answers to public examinations need to be written out by hand further underlines the importance of mastering this skill. The process of doing so requires long diligence in the faithful reproduction of exemplary forms; patience and obedience are essential to success (see Kipnis 2011, 96–103).

While changes to the 'canon' of core texts in the senior high curriculum spark heated debates among literary cognoscenti, it is the textbooks for younger students that have the widest and most profound impact. Analysing primary textbooks published in 1990, Lin noted relatively few references to class relationships or the construction of socialism (1993, 12) – themes that had predominated during the 1970s (the 1978 syllabus began with a quotation from Chairman Mao). Texts instead emphasised moral values relating to: studying (diligence, a sense of curiosity, an enquiring mind); proper social conduct (mutual respect, politeness, willingness to help others and to sacrifice oneself for the greater good); courage in the face of adversity; and steadfastness in confronting devious and malevolent enemies (12–14). Major Communist leaders (including some demonised during the Cultural Revolution) featured prominently as moral exemplars, joined by a broad pantheon of figures drawn from Chinese and Western mythology, literature and history. Scientists were celebrated as role models, with texts stressing their contribution to the development of the nation. Political leaders were 'depicted as intelligent, far-sighted and humorous; yet ... also close to the ordinary people, concerned with their sufferings and well-being' (15).

PEP's early twenty-first century primary language textbooks, now with glossy covers, full-colour illustrations and cute cartoon characters enlivening the text, still feature an essentially similar gallery of moral exemplars. Celebration of patriotism is pervasive. In a story in the first book, a mother tells her son about the flag-raising ceremony on Tiananmen Square – a martial display of loyalty to the Party-State. 'I really want to go and see it!' he enthuses (PEP 2006, 1A, 102–3). Thoroughly cleansed of its earlier associations with spontaneous mass demonstrations, the Square appears again at the opening of a Grade 6 unit on the theme of patriotism. This begins:

> Every time we see the five-star flag fluttering, and every time we sing our rousing national anthem, the spirit of patriotism swells in our breasts. We feel proud that we are Chinese, and take pride in the strength and prosperity of our motherland, as it increases day by day.
>
> (PEP 2006 6A, 17)

In the following passage, patriotic commitment is exemplified by Zhan Tianyou, 'our country's outstanding patriotic engineer', whose success in constructing the Beijing–Changsha railway 'two years ahead of schedule' delivered 'a telling riposte to imperialists who despise China' (20).

Such allusions to the record of national victimhood are frequent, and supply the context for numerous moral fables. A whole unit of the 2006 Grade 5 textbook is devoted to the 'Century of Humiliation', starting with an account of the Western destruction of the old Summer Palace (the *Yuanmingyuan*), and ending with a poem celebrating the recovery of Hong Kong (PEP 2006, 5A, 114–28). This is followed by a unit on Chairman Mao and the establishment of the PRC – Mao's only appearance in these texts – representing the founding of the PRC as the moment when the Chinese people 'stood up' (135–53). The most hateful foreign oppressors are identified early on in the course: the textbook for Grade 1 students features a story about Wang Er Xiao, a small boy killed by Japanese soldiers when he raises the alarm at their approach (thus exemplifying sacrifice for the greater good) (PEP 2006 1B, 99–100). A long story in the Grade 4 text tells how 'Little Hero Yulai' steadfastly refused to betray his family to the Japanese invaders, referred to throughout as *guizi* ('demons') (PEP 2006, 4B, 59–69). This is followed by an open letter to the United Nations from a Chinese child whose father has died on a UN mission, stressing how Chinese children yearn for peace. 'Save the children! We want peace not war!', he pleads (71).

Figures from the Communist pantheon who have retained their place in the primary language texts are depicted as kindly, grandfatherly types, with no substantive reference to their socialist ideals. Lenin himself appears in a story about robins in winter which seeks to inculcate the virtues of humility and honesty (PEP 2006, 3B, 18–19). Zhou Enlai's experiences as a young student in France form the subject of a passage entitled 'Studying for the sake of China's revival' (PEP 2006, 4A, 121–3). Deng Xiaoping, referred to as 'Grandfather Deng' (*Deng Yeye*), makes several appearances, for example in the Grade 2A text, where he exemplifies a pioneering interest in information technology (PEP 2006, 2A, 34–7). The treatment of deceased Communists as saintly moral exemplars renders them hardly less remote than Confucius, who is celebrated as a model of the virtue of humbly respecting one's teachers in the Grade 3 text 'Confucius reveres his teacher' (*Kongzi bai shi*) (PEP 2006, 3A, 67–8).

Confucius has become a prominent symbol of the drive in recent years to revive the teaching of classical literature, alongside other aspects of 'traditional' culture – something that has impinged on curriculum development at all levels. Although this trend has powerful official sponsorship, it has not gone unchallenged in intellectual circles. Chinese literature textbooks for secondary level have long featured texts highly critical of aspects of traditional culture. Prominent among these have been works by Lu Xun, an early twentieth-century writer who lambasted the injustice, inhumanity and 'slavish' behaviour he saw as endemic in Chinese society. Senior secondary textbooks during the post-Mao period have gradually incorporated more classical texts, and adopted a more nuanced and positive appraisal of aspects of pre-revolutionary society and culture. Lu Xun's writings have remained a mainstay of the curriculum, but selections and interpretations have significantly shifted. In 2007, PEP's new senior high texts drastically reduced extracts from Lu Xun, excluding the most 'revolutionary' examples. At the same time, they featured new extracts from swashbuckling martial arts epics by authors such as the popular Hong Kong-based writer Jin Yong (Louis Cha) – selected in the name of 'student-centredness'. This shift from earnest political engagement to populist escapism was not universally welcomed (Zhu 2012).

Yuwen has thus remained a vehicle for didactic moralising during the post-Mao decades, but its moral content has undergone significant change. This reflects the transformation in the regime's projected self-image – from revolutionary vanguard of the toiling masses to guarantor of socio-political stability, engineer of prosperity and champion of national revival. Searing critiques of social injustice and allusions to class struggle have largely given way to celebrations of Chinese culture and 'traditional' family values, and exhortations to enhance and defend national strength and status. Among the themes especially emphasised since the post-Tiananmen launch of the Patriotic Education Campaign (see Chapter 3.3) are the memory of 'national humiliation' (*guochi*) and the threat to China's rise posed by the 'hegemonising' aspirations of hostile foreign powers.

English Language

One barometer of China's relationship with this threatening outside world has been curricular policy on the teaching of foreign languages. As in other Soviet bloc countries, in China during the 1950s, Russian was the most widely taught foreign language, but the Sino-Soviet split of 1960 was followed by a sudden swing towards the teaching of English. Amidst the atmosphere of paranoid xenophobia that characterised the early phases of the Cultural Revolution, foreign language instruction briefly ceased altogether, but the Nixon visit of 1972 heralded a patchy revival of English language teaching.

The status of English as the primary foreign language has never since been seriously challenged. Its crucial importance in fostering international commercial and diplomatic links, and in facilitating technological transfer, has become so apparent as to transcend the periodic tensions between China and the world's main English-speaking power, the United States. Ever since the *gaokao* was reinstated, a foreign language (meaning English, for the overwhelming majority of students) has been one of three required subjects. Its weighting was initially much lower than Maths and Chinese (50:100:100), but by the mid-1980s it had already been raised to near-equivalence (100:120:120). The importance attached to English is reflected both in the distribution of class hours, and in moves since 2001 to extend instruction to primary level (see Tables 6.1–6.4 in the Appendix).

Unlike some of their counterparts elsewhere (e.g. in Hong Kong – see Sweeting and Vickers 2007), Chinese curriculum developers have not attempted to represent the English language as a culturally neutral communication tool. The 1980s witnessed a decline in 'overtly political' textbook content (though overt moralising continued), involving a 'defrosting in the portrayal of Western societies' (Adamson 2004, 168). The 1993 syllabus explicitly stated that 'political messages should be restricted to patriotism and socialism, but that foreign culture should be included for the sake of international understanding' (188).

However, the choice of foreign cultures to be covered, and their representation, is revealing of established views both of the outside world, and of China itself. References to the United States and Britain have predominated, with British and American protagonists conforming to entrenched stereotypes – generally white, often blond. When African Americans have featured, it has often been as victims of white oppression, or in other stereotypical roles.[13] Attempts to portray English as a means of communication with societies beyond the 'advanced' English-speaking nations met with mixed results, at least until the early 2000s. In 2001, a story written for *Junior English for China* (*JEFC*) featuring a fictional female Indian scientist, was altered so that the key protagonist became a male Briton surnamed 'White'. Editors also appeared uncomfortable with depictions of foreigners that subverted assumptions of the nation as ethno-culturally homogenous. A suggestion to revise a passage on 'fish and chips' in *JEFC* to explain that curry had become Britain's favourite dish was rejected on the grounds that curry did not seem sufficiently 'British'. Care has also been taken to ensure that English language textbooks uphold the orthodox narrative of Sino-Western relations. A tale of 'buried treasure' constructed around the true story of an early-nineteenth century British sailor who eloped with the daughter of a Pearl River pirate chief was rejected for inclusion in *JEFC*. Reference to Chinese piracy, at however remote a period, was off-limits. Implicit challenges to the worldview presented in more 'politicised' subjects (History, Chinese, Thought and Values) were thus studiously avoided.[14]

If the depiction of foreign cultures and peoples in English language textbooks has often been stereotyped and anodyne, this is in part because of editors' consciousness of the expectations and limitations of teachers. The supply of suitably qualified teachers has been a key constraint on efforts to expand the teaching and learning of English. This was especially so in the early post-Mao years, when the few English teachers were overwhelmingly concentrated in the 'key schools'. The earliest Reform-era textbooks reflected the general emphasis on 'quality', being generally pitched at a level just below that expected of key school students. However, a 1986 survey identified problems with English language competence – even amongst key school students – which were blamed on the persistence of the grammar-translation method (Adamson 2004, 170). This prompted PEP to solicit outside assistance for textbook development, eventually entering into collaboration with Longman. Far from subverting PEP control, under this arrangement Chinese editors retained the final say on textbook content. Neville Grant, sent by Longman to Beijing, was compelled repeatedly to redraft his material, but expressed admiration for the 'sensitivity' of his local colleagues 'to the views of teachers and what they felt would work' (177). The upshot was a compromise between the comfortable familiarity of the grammar-translation method, and the more communicative approach fashionable amongst international specialists in the teaching of English as a foreign language.

During the 1990s, the PEP's *JEFC* and *Senior English for China* (*SEFC*) texts remained by far the most widely used instructional materials in English language classrooms. However, as with History and other subjects, certain more 'advanced' regions were already permitted to develop their own materials, and the reforms of 2001 encouraged further diversification. Indeed, PEP itself began to diversify its output – revising the *JEFC* and *SEFC* texts while also developing new series targeted at different sectors of the textbook market. In 2000, it acquired the rights to *Go For It!*, a series published by Thomson Learning that adopted a highly communicative approach (it was originally aimed at teenage immigrants to North America), and adapted this for use in urban high schools. At the same time, the Education Ministry endorsed moves to begin foreign language instruction from primary Grade 3, and PEP and other publishers entered this new market.

This diversification reflected changes in Chinese society that were rendering insistence on curricular uniformity increasingly hard to sustain. By the 1990s, urban schoolchildren were increasingly able to access commercially published English learning materials, as well as private English language tuition, and the growing intensity of educational competition (fuelled by the expansion of higher education) was leading them to do so at younger and younger ages. However, since it was overwhelmingly urban rather than rural schools that were able to offer English instruction to a reasonable standard at secondary, let alone primary, level, this became one more factor exacerbating urban–rural inequality in educational opportunity. In the huge municipalities of Beijing and Shanghai, English instruction now begins in the first grade in many primary schools, while in many rural or township schools there is no English instruction at all. Just as English opens a window onto the wider world for urban youth, it thus also widens the chasm dividing them from their rural counterparts.

The nation in the curriculum – urban, Han, male

The widening of divisions between cities and countryside, East and West, has thus prompted abandonment of textbook uniformity – but to what extent has instructional content reflected China's social diversity? Textbooks for subjects like Geography, History and Morals/Civics/Politics feature numerous depictions of 'minorities' – usually young, attractive and female – attired in traditional dress, and often singing and dancing. However, discussion of the histories and cultures of non-Han groups is minimal; they figure principally as recipients of benefits bestowed by the 'advanced' Han (see Vickers 2009b). The 2006 edition of the primary Chinese language course, for example, features a unit on 'the West' (*Xibu*) celebrating the achievements of the PRC in bringing modernisation and development to these 'minority' regions, in particular through the construction of the Beijing–Lhasa railway (PEP 2006, Book 5, Unit 1, 1–16). As early as 1986, 'eradicating ethnic chauvinism and localism' were dropped as an objective of the History curriculum, on the grounds that 'ethnic contradictions' had been successfully eradicated. But ongoing ethnic tensions were tacitly acknowledged in the awarding to 'minority' figures (including Genghis Khan) of the title 'national hero' (*minzu yingxiong*), and in the increased prominence of references to 'the peaceful liberation of Tibet' (Jones 2005, 85). Meanwhile, the transition from socialism to an essentially Han-centric nationalism has complicated efforts to represent the nation in ways that encompass minority populations (Leibold 2011).

At primary level, instruction for many 'minority' groups has been provided in their own languages, but further advancement requires mastery of *Putonghua* and of the standardised national curriculum. Promotion of the use of *Putonghua* in schools across China as a whole – including Han regions where different spoken languages are used – has been crucial to the Party's nation-building strategy ever since 1949, and was repeatedly emphasised in official policy during the early Reform period. Quite apart from that political campaign, the distribution both of wealth and of 'cultural capital' in contemporary China mean that the life chances of Tibetans, Uighurs and other ethnic groups largely depend on acquiring Han knowledge and assimilating to Han norms (Chen Y. 2008). In the face of increasing Han migration, for example, 'Tibetans want schools to provide the skills needed to compete with the influx of outsiders' (Postiglione 2009, 13). More aspirational Tibetan and Uighur families have thus proved willing to send their offspring to boarding high schools in 'inland' (*neidi*) regions. Such practices help produce within 'minority' communities the kinds of divisions – between an increasingly cosmopolitan urban elite and the rest – that have come to characterise Chinese society as a whole (Chen 2014). The assimilative pressure of Chinese 'linguistic imperialism' is therefore extremely powerful, and may lead over time to the Tibetan and Uighur languages being 'pushed into the private sphere' across much of the far west (as Han 'dialects' – such as Wu in Shanghai – increasingly have been) (He B. 2014, 62). However, acceptance of Chinese rule does not inevitably follow. The increased learning of *Putonghua* has not brought about a lessening of tensions in China's far west, and the official response to such tensions – ramping up patriotic education, intensifying policies of sinification and further restricting religious expression – seems unlikely to improve matters.[15]

If the civilisational gold standard is Han, it is also urban. Like minorities, rural residents are implicitly or explicitly represented as deficient in 'quality' (*suzhi*) (Murphy 2004), and in need of transformation through education (*jiaohua*). Throughout the post-Mao period, the world depicted in textbooks has generally been an urban one. The equation of development and 'advanced' culture with urbanisation, with cities conceived as agents of modernisation dragging the 'backward' countryside behind them, is by no means peculiar to China. Perhaps in part thanks to the legacy of the Cultural Revolution, the romanticisation of village life seen in some other rapidly industrialising countries has been relatively absent (although admittedly the residue of Gandhian rural idealism in India, for example, has made little appreciable difference to the lot of villagers there; Kumar 2015). Furthermore, the physical removal of rural students to urban boarding schools, a trend that has grown since the 1990s, itself reflects assumptions about the normative quality of urban life (Murphy 2004).

The portrayal of gender roles in school texts has also remained highly stereotyped. We have already noted China's relatively impressive record on girls' enrolment (see Chapter 2); and especially for urban women, higher education participation rates have increased dramatically, even if female students are still disproportionately concentrated in lower status institutions and courses (see Chapter 12). However, those differences in status, and related assumptions concerning 'the gendered division of labour and role patterns' have been strongly reflected in instructional materials, especially those for young children (Ross 2006, 43).[16] In fieldwork related to a 'Spring Bud' project in Shaanxi, Ross found that 100 per cent 'of scientists, workers, peasants and soldiers' in social studies texts were male, whereas '100 per cent of teachers and 75 per cent of service personnel' were female. While total numbers of males and females in these texts were roughly equal, only 5 per cent of characters 'named or central to a storyline' were female. In a mathematics textbook, meanwhile, males appeared far more frequently than females, and 'in privileged settings and occupational roles that ... implicitly derogate female mathematical abilities' (43). When observing classroom dialogue at kindergarten and primary level, she found the same gendering of roles. She also noted that when these issues were raised with 'lead editors of publishing houses' in 2001, sceptics 'wondered whether the public desired the kinds of gender transformation called for by presenters'.[17]

Conclusion

In post-Mao China, Ross argues, 'narrowly utilitarian' developmentalism, 'strong China nationalism' and the 'naturalisation of gender' have been crucial to framing debates over the importance of women's education (2006, 29–30); but in fact her argument holds if the word 'women' is omitted. As we noted in the first two chapters, a profoundly instrumentalist vision of the relationship between state and citizen has characterised modernisation discourses and education policy in post-Mao China. In the case of women, this means that 'educated girls become valued as mothers of development and the means for reducing poverty, containing population growth, engendering public health, and strengthening the nation' – but that female lives are 'rarely considered as ends in themselves' (29–30). More generally, though, education in post-Mao China has been seen primarily as a means for maximising human capital or 'talent' (male or female), and building a stronger state. This perspective has continued to permeate instructional materials in schools, even as socialist messages have been superseded by emphases on patriotism, competition and the market.

The stark contrast between the egalitarian extremism of the Mao era and the competitiveness and elitism of today disguises certain fundamental continuities. Mitter argues that the mass mobilisation of Mao's campaigns, their weakening of traditional habits of self-abnegation (*vis-à-vis* the family and other sources of authority), and their emphasis on the transformative potential of the human will made them crucial to transmitting the 'dynamism' of 'the individuated self' to the Chinese population – a goal of Chinese reformers since the late nineteenth century. At the same time, the collectivist agenda of Maoism constituted a strong countervailing discourse, working to contain and channel the energy of the 'masses'. Nonetheless, Mitter insists, 'even the disastrous Great Leap Forward had been intended to stimulate the release of individual dynamism even if it was part of a collective enterprise' (2014, 115). In the post-Mao era, 'the transfer of that psychology to the sphere of economics was at least partly responsible for the enthusiasm for investment and enterprise' (116). This argument is supported by Hansen's recent ethnographic studies in a rural Zhejiang high school (2013), where she found the atmosphere and rhetoric of examination-preparatory 'pep rallies' reminiscent of Red Guard activism.

While arguably inheriting a certain democratisation of aspiration from the preceding era, however, post-Mao China's leaders have sought assiduously to dampen expectations of democratised social outcomes. The school curriculum has played a crucial role in efforts to stimulate individual dynamism and harness it to the project of modernisation, while legitimising the emergence of a highly stratified social as well as political order. Already from the 1980s, Han-centric patriotism was increasingly deployed alongside a diluted socialism to bolster regime legitimacy, but the balance tipped emphatically towards nationalism from the 1990s. At the same time, the discourse of *suzhi* or 'quality', identified with the attributes of an educated urban elite, was increasingly invoked. Allied to neo-Darwinian notions of a hyper-competitive international order, this has explained the inevitability of inequality, and the need to tolerate it in pursuit of the greater national good. The essentialisation of gender and ethnicity has served further to justify a hierarchical division of labour in pursuit of the overarching goal of modernisation and 'comprehensive national strength' (*zonghe guoli*).

Powerful state-centred patriotism and a naturalisation of ethnic and gendered attributes have been strongly evident in mainstream discourse both in China and its East Asian neighbours. Indeed, as we noted at the start of this chapter, early Chinese notions of modern nationhood itself, along with conceptions of education's role in national construction, were heavily influenced by Japanese precedents. Ironically, the enduring influence of those precedents has become all the more apparent since the 1990s, even as anti-Japan nationalism has increasingly infused the school curriculum. Looking for ways to tame the individualism that marketisation fostered, the authorities turned both to nationalism and to Confucian revivalism, in the process referencing contemporary Japanese practice (for example in moral education) (Rappleye 2007). As Kipnis argues (2011), the Communist Party was thus responding to and exploiting assumptions concerning the moralising or exemplary function of schooling that had deep cultural roots. No longer aiming at socialist transformation, it was working with the grain of popular belief in order to bolster its own authority. But the social ethos that Chinese schooling has thus come to reflect and reinforce contrasts significantly with that of Japan. While both exhibit extreme credentialism (see Chapter 8), this is balanced by quite different forms of collectivism: more vertically ordered and authoritarian in the Chinese case; more horizontal, consensual and group-oriented in the Japanese.

Despite the profoundly ideological nature of the school curriculum, much research on education in China, as elsewhere, has tended largely to ignore questions relating to the political or ethical content of schooling. This is especially true of the studies we labelled 'practice-oriented' in our introductory chapter. These have provided much invaluable data – often quantitative – on matters such as enrolment and progression rates for different populations (girls, minorities, etc.), and on some of the more measurable aspects of pupil performance. At the same time, they are typically premised on a vision of schooling as an exercise in the more or less efficient supply of a uniform product: essence of human capital, the elixir of economic growth. But not only are this elixir's economic effects arguably misunderstood and overrated (an issue to which we return in our concluding chapter); it can also produce some unpleasant side effects. To understand these, we must open the bottle and taste the contents.

Notes

1 These included one of the current authors – Vickers.
2 In 1986, a 'Teaching Materials Inspection Committee' was established by the Ministry, ostensibly to provide independent, objective evaluation of textbooks (Shanghai and Zhejiang were granted limited autonomy over curriculum development at this time). However, Jones comments that 'since committee members were to be MOE-appointed and supervised it is difficult to imagine how [the goals of independence and objectivity] could be attained' (2005, 83).
3 Jones notes that the drafting of the 2001 history curriculum featured 'little involvement' by PEP, for the first time in 'more than 40 years' (2005, 92) – though it is possible the degree of PEP involvement varied from subject to subject. To the extent that this was the case for history, she speculates that it may account for the 'innovative', 'lively' as well as controversial nature of some of the texts that were subsequently produced. But by the end of the decade, resistance from many teachers and criticism from conservatives seems to have caused the pendulum to swing back towards more conventional pedagogical approaches, more ideologically orthodox content, and more control from Beijing (Vickers and Yang 2013).
4 This example derives from the experience of Zeng, who used both sets of materials while home-schooling her teenage son prior to his move to a school in New Zealand.
5 Kipnis notes that by 2005 such 'creativity classes' had been abandoned throughout Zouping County (his fieldwork site).
6 Although Brock (2009) claims that rural teachers in Gansu proved well able to implement more 'child-centred' methods (albeit with training and support provided by a large DfID-MoE project) – doing so 'even better than their counterparts in Beijing and Shanghai'.
7 Patriotic Education was accorded a *Gangyao* all of its own in 1994 (IED 1994, 3680), and there was a conference in December that year on 'National Defence Education' for primary and secondary schools.
8 Though prominent Japanese scholars have severely criticised the ministerial push for 'diversity' and 'flexibility' there as, in part, a cover for a neoliberal pro-privatisation agenda that has contributed to a significant rise in inequality (see Kariya 2011).
9 In the early 2000s, students in key point schools were often required to do 100 sums for homework every day – work that mothers were expected to check. They would be expected to make no more than 2 errors in 100.
10 The title of the subject that teaches 'morals', 'ideology' or 'politics' at different levels of schooling has changed over time. Ye notes how the term 'ideology' was dropped from the title of the subject at primary level after 2001, while acknowledging that this does not really signify a slackening of the focus on political socialisation (2014, 40).

11 Academic historiography in 1980s China also increasingly diverged from the stale Marxist orthodoxy still retailed in school textbooks – see Dirlik (2011).
12 Though on the mainland, as in Hong Kong, some Chinese educators certainly were attracted by the underlying liberal-democratic ethos, and during the 1980s tended to be less coy on this score (on Hong Kong, see Vickers 2005).
13 PEP's *Junior English for China* (JEFC) textbooks of the early 2000s featured a black American family as well as a white one amongst its gallery of fictional international characters – with the black child depicted playing basketball in the illustrations at the front of the book. It would be interesting to know how Barack Obama's election as American president has influenced standard depictions of African Americans in Chinese textbooks, and in the media more generally.
14 This paragraph draws on the experience of Vickers, who worked for the PEP between 2000 and 2003 on a number of English language textbook projects.
15 Also likely to be counter-productive is the extremely didactic conventional approach to teaching morality, by reference to a set stock of exemplars. The school curriculum does not challenge Han students to understand alternative views on social, cultural (let alone political) issues of importance to 'minorities' – and it is difficult to see how it could, under current circumstances. However, He Baogang suggests that encouraging more Han students to learn minority languages, and requiring Han officials in 'minority' regions to attain proficiency in the local language, would help to promote mutual respect (2014, 63).
16 Similar messages also permeate propaganda – for example from the 'All China Federation of Women' – aimed at the adult population (see Fincher 2014).
17 Vickers, when working for PEP, experienced a similar reaction when he drafted a story for an English textbook about a team of girls beating boys at football. This was revised on the grounds that 'boys might be upset' on reading such a story, given the loss of face entailed. By contrast, as Ross notes, 'girls do not "lose face" when they lose out to boys' (44). Shi Jinghuan of Tsinghua University similarly testifies to the lack of attention to gender issues in the curriculum (2004).

Appendix

Table 6.1 Class hours for compulsory education (primary and junior secondary), 1992

	Grade 1	*Grade 2*	*Grade 3*	*Grade 4*	*Grade 5*	*Grade 6*	*Junior 1*	*Junior 2*	*Junior 3*	*Total for primary*	*Total for junior sec.*
'Thought and Values'	1	1	1	1	1	1				204	
Politics							2	2	2		200
Chinese	10	10	9	8	7	7	6	6	5	1,734	568
Maths	4	5	5	5	5	5	5	5	5	986	500
Foreign Language I							4	4			272
Foreign Language II							4	4	4		400
Society				2	2	2				204	
History							2	3	2		234
Geography							3	2			170
Nature	1	1	1	1	2	2				272	
Physics								2	3		164
Chemistry									3		96
Biology							3	2			170
PE							3	3	3		300
Music							1	1	1		100
Painting							1	1	1		100
Labour			1	1	1	1				136	
'Labour and Technology'							2	2	2		200
Weekly teaching hours	23	24	24	25	25	25	32	33	27	3,074	8,038

Source: MOE (1992).

Table 6.2 Class hours for compulsory education, 2001

Grade 1	*Grade 2*	*Grade 3*	*Grade 4*	*Grade 5*	*Grade 6*	*Junior 1*	*Junior 2*	*Junior 3*	*Ratio in teaching hours*
Morals and Life	Morals and Life	Morals and Society	Morals and Society	Morals and Society		Thought and Values	Thought and Values	Thought and Values	7–9%
							History and Society		3–4%
Chinese	Chinese	Chinese	Chinese	Chinese	Chinese	Chinese	Chinese	Chinese	20–22%
Maths	Maths	Maths	Maths	Maths	Maths	Maths	Maths	Maths	13–15%
		Foreign Language	Foreign Language	Foreign Language	Foreign Language	Foreign Language	Foreign Language	Foreign Language	6–8%
PE	PE	PE	PE	PE	PE	PE and Health	PE and Health	PE and Health	10–11%
Art (music, painting, etc.)									9–11%
Comprehensive practical activities[a]									16–20%
Local or school-based curricula[b]									16–20%
26	26	30	30	30	30	34	34	34	274/week
910	910	1,050	1,050	1,050	1,050	1,190	1,190	1,122	9,522/year

Source: MOE (2001).

Notes: [a] Comprehensive practical activities are supposed to include community service, project work, 'integrated studies' and so forth.
[b] In practice, these class hours have often been assigned to test preparation for other subjects (especially Maths, Chinese or English).

Table 6.3 Class hours for full time six-year secondary 'key point schools', 1981

	Junior			*Senior*			*Teaching hours*
	1	*2*	*3*	*1*	*2*	*3*	
Politics	2	2	2	2	2	2	384
Chinese	6	6	6	5	4	4	1,000
Maths	5	6	6	5	5	5	1,026
Foreign Language	5	5	5	5	5	4	932
Physics		2	3	4	3	4	500
Chemistry			3	3	3	3	372
History	3	2		3			266
Geography	3	2			2		234
Biology	2	2				2	192
Physiological Hygiene			2				64
PE	2	2	2	2	2	2	384
Music	1	1	1				100
Painting	1	1	1				100
Teaching hours/week	30	31	31	29	26	26	5,554
Elective curriculum					4	4	240
'Labour'[a]	2 weeks			4 weeks			432

Source: IED (1981, 1926).

Note: [a] Literally 'Labour and Technology' (*laodong jishu*).

Table 6.4 Credits/class hours for senior higher schools, 2003

Field	*Subject*	*Compulsory credits (Total 116 credits)*	*Elective I*	*Elective II*
Language and Literacy	Chinese	10	'Optional' courses extending the curricula for regular subjects, intended to cater to the 'diversity' of students' interests and aptitudes	Local/'school-based' curricula
	Foreign Language	10		
Maths	Maths	10		
Humanity and Society	'Thought and Politics'	8		
	History	6		
	Geography (human and physical)	6		
Science	Physics	6		
	Chemistry	6		
	Biology	6		
Technology	Technology (including IT and general technology)	8		
Arts	Art (music and painting)	6		
PE and Health	PE and Health	11		
Comprehensive practical activities	Research activities	15		
	Community service	2		
	'Social Practice'	6		

Source: MOE (2003).

Note: The credits listed here are the total for the whole three-year senior high-school period. One credit generally equates to 18 teaching hours. The curriculum is supposed to be delivered in 'modules' consisting of 36 teaching hours (i.e. two credits).

7 The teaching profession

Training, retention and professional development

Implementation of any officially prescribed curriculum hinges on the readiness of the teaching profession to perform as expected. Official rhetoric in post-Mao China has harped incessantly upon this truism, hailing teachers (in the Soviet idiom) as 'gardeners' and 'engineers of the people's souls'. As bearers of the 'expert' knowledge seen as crucial to facilitating modernisation, teachers saw their stock rise (rhetorically, if not materially) as the Maoist emphasis on 'redness' was downplayed. But rhetorical exaltation of teachers' social role did not necessarily imply improved status and living conditions. Those at the pinnacle of the profession – key point school teachers with degrees from top universities – experienced marked improvements from the outset of the Reform period. However, many of their less-qualified comrades, especially in the countryside, were consigned to continued penury, with aspersions cast on their fitness to teach at all. Engineering the souls of farmers was not a priority for the triumphant developmentalist wing of the Party; engineering engineers was, implying a focus on training a technocratic vanguard. For those not engaged in grooming top-level talent, or deemed unqualified for 'government teacher' (*gongban*) status at all, professional prospects from the late 1970s through the 1990s were frequently grim – as is attested by attrition rates (see below).

Despite the new emphasis on 'expertise' over 'redness', conceptions of the teacher's fundamentally exemplary role have persisted. In the previous chapter, we noted shifts in the ideological content of schooling towards a more catholic definition of 'patriotism'; in the same way, especially since the 1990s, public definitions of the role of the teacher have appealed less to 'socialism' and more to 'tradition'. The role of teachers in socialising youth has remained a key concern of policymakers and party leaders – one repeatedly invoked at times of heightened anxiety over political stability or social harmony (see Chapters 3.1–3.4). But among the qualities many teachers have at times been asked to exemplify is a selfless disregard for material reward – and this in a context of increasingly rampant materialism.

In analysing the development of the teaching profession since the late 1970s, our focus in this chapter is on the 'regular', or 'academic', system (issues specific to the vocational or technical sector are dealt with in Chapter 10). The chapter is divided into three sections: the first dealing with the evolution of pre-service teacher training; the second with provision for professional development and in-service training; and the last with issues relating to the recruitment and retention of teachers. The implications for the teaching profession, for teacher-training institutions and for policymaking of rapid social change constitute a recurring theme – bearing out Paine and Fang's observation that 'reforming professional development' in such circumstances 'is a bit like changing the tires on a car while the car is in motion' (2007, 187–8).

New demands on the profession – reflecting the rising expectations of government, parents and the wider public – have been reflected in changes to the structure and content of training programmes. This has resulted in several tensions: between conflicting pedagogical demands (e.g. to teach 'critical thinking' while exemplifying uncritical patriotism and moral conformity – see previous chapter); between higher entry requirements and subsequent prospects for promotion or remuneration; and involving the challenge of persuading more highly qualified teachers to work in poorer, less 'developed' areas. Another prominent theme, linking to Chapters 11 and 12, involves the relationship between changes to teacher education and the broader reforms to higher education since the 1990s – reforms in turn related to the regime's efforts to channel the aspirations of an emergent urban middle class.

It may be easy to derive the impression that – official rhetoric notwithstanding – teachers have been put-upon, marginalised and exploited during much of the Reform period. However, while that may have been so for many (especially in rural primary schools), it would be wrong to conclude that the reforms discussed here simply 'happened to' teachers. As Gordon White observed very early in the Reform period (1981), teachers formed an important element of the 'intelligentsia' constituency supporting efforts to reverse the experiments of the Maoist era. Pepper found that many professionally qualified teachers approved of reasserting the primacy of 'quality' – on the assumption that most of their colleagues had been delivering a sub-standard product (1996; see Chapter 2). The teaching profession has never been monolithic. As White put it,

> there is a great deal of social distance between the humble primary school teacher, "the king (or more likely queen) of the kids," and the exalted university professor [or key high school teacher], lauded by developmentalist leaders as a jewel in the diadem of socialist construction.
>
> (White 1981, 91)

The widening class divisions of post-Mao China, fuelled by the hierarchical and elitist bent of educational reform, have been as much a feature of the teaching profession itself as of the society it serves.

Pre-service teacher education

The fact that pre-service teacher-training arrangements are here discussed first does not imply that these have always or necessarily constituted the most important form of professional development for teachers. As detailed below, the widespread employment of *minban* teachers lacking officially recognised qualifications meant that, particularly in the 1980s and 1990s, the drive to raise 'quality' involved a massive programme of in-service training. However, that drive itself implied an ideal scenario in which, eventually, all teachers would receive appropriate training and certification prior to assuming regular classroom duties. For reasons discussed later, attainment of this ideal has proved elusive. Meanwhile, the definition of 'appropriate' training – in terms of content and mode of delivery – has provoked continuing debate amongst educators, policymakers and the broader public.

Institutional arrangements and teachers' qualifications

In June 1980, a national conference on teacher education was convened in Beijing. This set the seal on the reintroduction of the Soviet-inspired, hierarchical, tripartite system of teacher training that had existed before the Cultural Revolution:

> Higher teacher-training institutes (*gaodeng shifan yuanxiao*) train teachers for secondary schools; teacher training schools (*shifan zhuanke xuexiao*) train teachers for lower secondary schools; secondary teacher-training schools (*zhongdeng shifan xuexiao*), including schools for kindergarten teachers, enrol lower secondary school graduates and young people with the same level and train them to be primary school and kindergarten teachers.
>
> (*Jiaoyu Yanjiu*, No. 4, August 1980, 9, cited in Lo 1984, 170)

The higher teacher-training institutes – principally national and provincial-level normal universities – offered four-year, degree-level programmes for prospective senior high school teachers. In the early rush to meet teacher shortages, two-year programmes were also offered in some places, but these were mostly phased out during the 1990s, when new 'teacher qualification standards' made four-year courses mandatory at this level. The usually city-based normal colleges or schools (*shifan zhuanke xuexiao*) for training lower secondary school teachers at first offered a two-year post-secondary programme, increased to three years from the 1990s. Due to persistent teacher shortages at senior high level, until the 1990s graduates of these sub-degree courses often went on to teach there rather than at the junior level. The secondary-level normal schools, usually located in county towns, meanwhile provided vocational training for primary teachers.

The supply of qualified teachers for senior high schools – particularly key point schools – was of paramount concern in the early Reform period, since these institutions were tasked with providing a steady stream of elite candidates for higher education. Here the emphasis was on qualitative enhancement rather than quantitative expansion. By contrast, the enormous growth of junior secondary schooling during the Cultural Revolution had involved employing a large proportion of under-qualified teachers at that level. Official figures for 1980 showed that whereas around 50 per cent of primary and senior high school teachers held the relevant qualifications, the figure for junior secondary teachers was just 10 per cent (*Renmin Jiaoyu,* No. 1, January 1981, 41, cited in Lo 1984, 168). This data legitimised the drive to curtail provision of 'substandard' junior secondary schooling which, Pepper suggests (1996), was motivated as much by a desire to manage popular educational aspiration (curbing 'excessive' demand for higher education) as by strictly qualitative concerns.

The restoration of what were, at least on paper, neatly hierarchical institutional arrangements for teacher training was thus accompanied by attempts to impose a stricter line on teachers' qualifications. However, it also coincided with the decentralisation of the financing and administration of schooling, which confined the fiscal responsibilities of central government to the commanding heights of the education system (see Chapter 5). The only teacher training institutions directly funded by the Education Ministry in the early Reform years were the six regional normal universities – many of whose graduates were destined for key point senior high schools. Other institutions relied on resources provided by provincial or county authorities. The caveat 'if the local situation allows', which accompanied so many education policy pronouncements in the 1980s (see Chapter 3.2), effectively licensed local governments to economise, for example by using normal schools equipped to train prospective primary teachers to train staff for senior high level (Lo 1984, 174). The 1993 Teachers Law of the PRC sternly condemned such abuses, proclaiming clear legal standards for teaching qualifications (IED 1993, 3570). By continuing to avoid responsibility for financing most teacher training during the 1990s, the central authorities largely relied on exhortation and pressure brought to bear through the system of cadre evaluations (discussed in Chapter 5).

Nonetheless, by the early 2000s significant progress had been made in enhancing the qualifications of the teaching workforce. This was largely due to massive programmes of in-service training (see below), but also owed much to declining birth rates and a consequent fall in primary school enrolments. In the five years between 1999 and 2004, the school population at primary level dropped by almost 17 per cent, from 135 million to 112 million (Paine and Fang 2007, 177). Over the same period, the number of primary school teachers declined by about 230,000. Meanwhile, between 1999 and 2009 the percentage of teachers at this level possessing the required qualifications increased by 3 per cent (from 96 to 99 per cent) (Zeng 2012b, 105). More specifically, the percentage of the teaching force at primary level with *zhuanke* (professional diploma) qualifications or above climbed from around 25 per cent to 75 per cent over the 2000–9 period. Meanwhile, a modest increase of 12 per cent in the junior secondary population between 1999 and 2004 was accompanied by an increase of about 10 per cent in the teaching force at this level, with the proportion of 'fully-qualified' teachers – those with either *zhuanke* or *benke* (bachelor's degrees) – rising by 8 per cent to 94 per cent (Paine and Fang 2007, 177). The proportion of junior secondary teachers with an undergraduate education climbed from 17 per cent in 2001 to 59 per cent in 2009 (Zeng 2012b, 106). By 2012, even in rural schools, the proportion of teachers with lower than the minimum qualifications was 0.48 per cent (Zeng and Yu 2015, 166). (At senior high level, the minimum qualification is a bachelor's degree; at junior secondary level, it is a sub-degree level *zhuanke* diploma.) Figure 7.1 indicates the steady rise in teachers' qualification levels since 2000, in terms of the average number of years of education completed by teachers at each phase of schooling.

By contrast with the picture of declining or only modestly rising student numbers at primary and junior high levels, the rapid expansion of higher education from the late 1990s prompted a similarly rapid growth in the senior high school population (of 112 per cent between 1999 and 2004 – Paine and Fang 2007, 177). This trend is illustrated in Figure 7.2. The proportion of teachers at this level with the required qualifications (i.e. a bachelor's degree or above) nonetheless stood at over 90 per cent by 2009, up from 70 per cent in 2001, with a small proportion (about 3 per cent) by then boasting postgraduate degrees (up from about half a per cent a decade earlier) (Zeng 2012b, 107). At all levels of schooling, the current proportion of qualified teachers – according to official figures – is thus impressive when compared with the equivalent figures for 1980. However, as figures on recruitment and retention suggest (see below), amongst qualified teachers there has been considerable stratification. Official statistics may also significantly underestimate the number of unqualified and unregistered *daike* ('stand-in') teachers, employed on short-term contracts, working in schools of one sort or another around the country (*daike* teachers effectively, if not legally, occupy the same status as *minban* teachers up to the 1990s).[1]

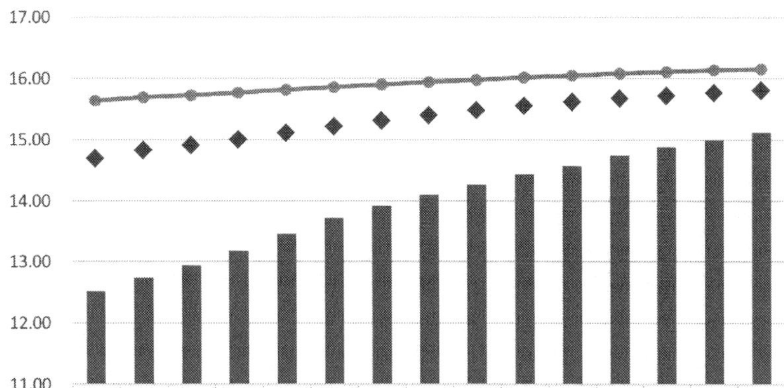

	2000	2001	2002	2003	2004	2005	2006	2007	2008	2009	2010	2011	2012	2013	2014
Primary	12.52	12.74	12.94	13.18	13.46	13.72	13.92	14.10	14.26	14.43	14.57	14.74	14.88	15.00	15.12
Junior	14.70	14.83	14.90	15.00	15.11	15.21	15.31	15.40	15.48	15.56	15.62	15.67	15.72	15.77	15.81
Senior	15.63	15.70	15.73	15.77	15.81	15.86	15.90	15.94	15.98	16.02	16.05	16.08	16.11	16.14	16.16

Figure 7.1 Teachers' qualifications (average years of education completed), 2000–14.
Source: NBS.

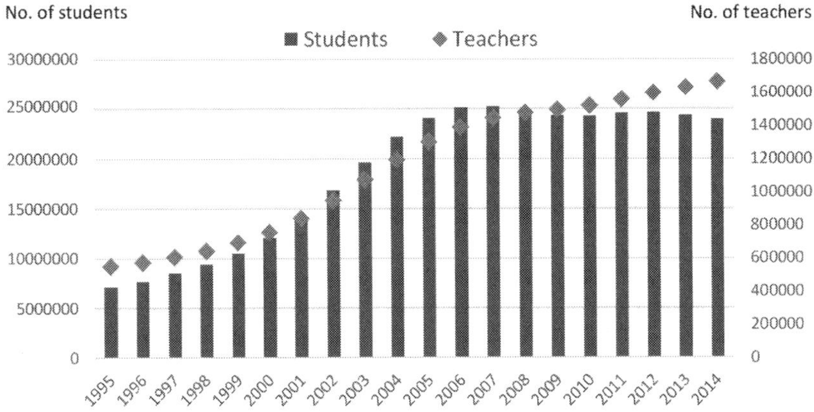

Figure 7.2 The rising population of senior high school students and teachers, 1995–2014.
Source: NBS.

Curriculum

The post-Mao reversal of the emphasis on 'redness' at the expense of expertise was reflected in the stipulations of a 1979 document entitled 'Manage teacher education well, and develop educational science' (*Banhao shifan jiaoyu, fazhan jiaoyu kexue*, Bejing, PEP, 1979, 11–12, cited in Lo 1984, 162). Four specific categories of knowledge or skills were identified:

- political and professional dedication;
- a sound knowledge of subject content;
- understanding of pedagogical principles;
- the ability to analyse and discuss educational problems.

However, Lo's 1979–81 fieldwork indicated that in practice instruction in subject knowledge was typically stressed to the virtual exclusion of everything else – as both officials and public demanded a pedagogical diet of solid, 'scientific' knowledge in place of 'red' propaganda. Over thirty years later, a report by Beijing Normal University (BNU) claimed that, of the three components of pre-service teacher education programmes, the 'subject-specific curriculum' still accounted on average for 72 per cent of instruction, the 'common core curriculum' 21 per cent, and 'the specialist curriculum in education' for about 7 per cent (BNU 2014).

An indication of the apparent shift from 'redness' to 'expertise' in the early Reform era is Lo's observation that there was 'little in the available literature to suggest that regular courses of political studies, in the form of Marxism, Leninism and Mao Zedong Thought, are offered in many teacher training institutions' (Lo 1984, 163). He claimed that political education for teachers consisted mainly of 'informal processes'. While such reports of the demise of political instruction may have been exaggerated, the 1980s (particularly the early 1980s) witnessed the dominance in educational debate of what Paine (1995) terms a 'modernisation discourse', stressing technical rationality and drawing heavily on Western precedent and scholarship. Tensions between the latter and a 'nationalisation discourse', stressing 'correct ideas', became more acute in the later 1980s. After 1989, 'nationalizers' such as Premier Li Peng responded to the student disturbances by calling for a strengthening of the 'thought and politics work' of teachers (IED 1990, 2919), while mandating special classes in 'socialist theory' for school cadres and teachers (IED 1990, 3059) (see Chapter 3.2).

If formal instruction in 'Thought and Politics' was relatively neglected during the 1980s, its status within the compulsory 'core curriculum' was thus re-emphasised after 1989 – for teacher trainees as for all tertiary-level students. The blurring of 'modernising' and 'nationalising' discourses that Paine detected in the mid-1990s has subsequently continued, particularly as ideological 'correctness' has come to be defined less in class-based or revolutionary terms, and more with reference to 'traditional Chinese values' (see Chapter 6).[2] There may nowadays be fewer explicit references to 'politics' or 'socialism' in documents stipulating teachers' roles and duties (for example in the criteria for appointing 'special rank teachers' – see below). However, the shift towards defining teachers' exemplary function more in 'moral' than 'political' terms does not necessarily signify any radical 'depoliticisation' of the profession, especially with 'patriotism' now enshrined as the chief moral virtue (Vickers 2009a, b). And as we noted in Chapter 3.4, there has been a return to more explicit political indoctrination since the leadership transition of 2012.

Just as instruction in 'Politics' is part of a 'common core curriculum' taken by all university and college students, so 'subject specific' content is essentially identical for those on teacher-training and standard degree courses. Specific preparation in pedagogy or classroom management is thus delivered through the curricular sliver – typically less than 10 per cent of instructional content – represented by the 'specialist curriculum in education'. This situation has long been lamented by educators and policymakers. A report by BNU in 2008 recorded that the 'teaching practice module usually takes the form of an intensive practicum, conducted over a period of 6–8 weeks', and condemned the 'obvious insufficiency' of this. It was noted that this was 'generally arranged in a "one-off" manner in the seventh or eighth semester (i.e. right at the end of the course)', and that some institutions had no regular arrangements with partner schools, leading them to scatter their trainees amongst many different venues, sometimes by sending them back to their home areas (IALEI 2008).

Those comments echo Lo's from the early 1980s: 'Even when teaching practice is organised, preparations are poor, primary and secondary schools do not cooperate, and standards of performance are not set' (Lo 1984, 166). In the mid-1990s, Paine observed that the one-semester course on pedagogy and teaching methods had become 'ossified', with teacher educators continuing to rely on an antiquated text by the Soviet educator, Kairov, which both they and their students found dull and irrelevant (Paine 1995). A newly qualified junior secondary Maths teacher in Shanghai, made the subject of an illustrative 'vignette' by Paine and Fang (2007), stated that her pre-service training had been 'mostly theoretical' (reflecting features of the school curriculum discussed in the previous chapter), leaving her 'unfamiliar' with her roles in 'teaching a class' (*shangke*) and 'preparing a lesson' (*beike*) (184). She admitted to relying heavily on the teachers' guides (handbooks accompanying school textbooks) when preparing lessons. More positively, she felt 'surrounded by help', both from her mentors and colleagues within the school (who convened regular meetings to discuss lesson preparation), and from district-organised induction programmes. However, as Paine and Fang observe, Shanghai constitutes a 'best case scenario' that many remote or rural communities are simply incapable of emulating (186).

Given the sustained criticism of pre-service programmes for their inattention to practical training, how can the apparent lack of change be explained? As early as June 1980, the Vice Minister of Education, Gao Yi, called for the restoration of pedagogical courses and teaching practice, and urged the six key normal universities to set an example (Lo 1984, 166). However, these very institutions were leading the charge in the opposite direction, seeking to burnish their reputations for research in fields other than pedagogy or teacher education. Such behaviour was encouraged by widespread public celebration of scientific, theoretical or disciplinary 'expertise', implying an academic hierarchy in which teacher education occupied a very lowly position. The prestige of teaching had not been boosted by the blatant politicisation of the Cultural Revolution years – but, in truth, schoolteachers had never enjoyed a particularly exalted status, notwithstanding the timeworn injunction to honour one's teacher as a father. Teaching was the traditional resort of the failed aspirant to official appointment. More concretely, as the monetisation of the economy progressed, and brought increasing differentiation in salaries, teachers found themselves near the back of the queue for the material rewards offered to workers seen as key to the modernisation drive. Students and their parents were keenly aware of this, and no amount of official exhortation could attract the best *gaokao* performers to enrol on teacher training courses. At the same time, the reinstatement of the *gaokao* itself strengthened demand for teachers with a solid factual grounding in the examined subjects, hence intensifying the pressure on institutions to produce subject specialists.

Reform since the 1990s

Significant changes to the institutional arrangements for pre-service teacher education occurred during the 1990s. However, these tended to exacerbate rather than curb the established emphasis on academic subject content over practical training. By the early 1990s, specialist teacher-training institutions were increasingly derided as poorly equipped and qualitatively defective; a common joke in educational circles was that 'third-rate students take teacher-training courses, and third-rate teacher-training students become teachers' (see Gu 2007). There was also dissatisfaction at the practice (referred to above) of hiring graduates of secondary-level training institutions to teach at secondary schools. This led to measures aimed at raising standard entry qualifications for the teaching profession – though, as ever, with due regard for 'local conditions'. Thus it was stipulated that from the late 1990s primary teachers in urban areas would be required to have at least junior college training, prompting a dramatic fall in the number of secondary-level normal schools – from 875 in 1998 to 317 in 2003 (MOE figures cited in Paine and Fang 2007, 181). In a drive to achieve economies of scale and improve facilities, a fashion for institutional mergers also took hold across the higher education sector (see Chapter 12). Former specialist institutions were merged so that, by the late 1990s, more or less every city could boast its own comprehensive four-year college. As a result, the overall number of four- and three-year universities and colleges offering pre-service teacher training declined between 1998 and 2003, from 229 to 188. By 2004, 54 per cent of tertiary-level institutions providing pre-service teacher education were comprehensive universities rather than specialist teacher-training colleges (181).

This restructuring coincided with the massive expansion, and further marketisation, of higher education from the 1990s (see Chapters 11 and 12). In addition to merger mania, competition within the sector – both for institutional prestige and what were by now fee-paying students – led to a further blurring of distinctions between 'normal' and 'comprehensive' institutions. Some of the most prestigious comprehensive universities began to offer teacher-training courses and establish faculties or departments of education. In the belief that the involvement of these institutions would raise 'quality', the government had long encouraged them to provide teacher education, but in the era of tightly restricted, highly elitist higher education, they had shown little interest in doing so. Meanwhile, normal universities and colleges (those that maintained their autonomy) were for the first time formally permitted to transform themselves into comprehensive institutions. Market forces were a key factor here: fee-paying students now forced to compete for jobs in an open labour market valued the prestige of a degree from a comprehensive university. Meanwhile, local government officials were incentivised to establish grand new comprehensive institutions by the workings of the cadre appraisal system (Zhou 2007) (see Figure 7.3 and Chapter 12). According to Paine and Fang, in some cases increased competition does appear to have forced specialist institutions to raise their game – Shanghai's two normal universities, they report, have 'worked hard in recent years to revise their curriculum and training materials to respond to the various market demands' (181).

Overall, however, it is unclear that the closure, merger or 'comprehensivisation' of teacher training institutions, along with the push to raise entry-level qualifications for the profession, achieved the desired effect. On the one hand, comprehensive universities with no tradition of teacher education were not necessarily better equipped to provide it than the old specialist institutions. On the other, allowing former specialist institutions to offer programmes in areas

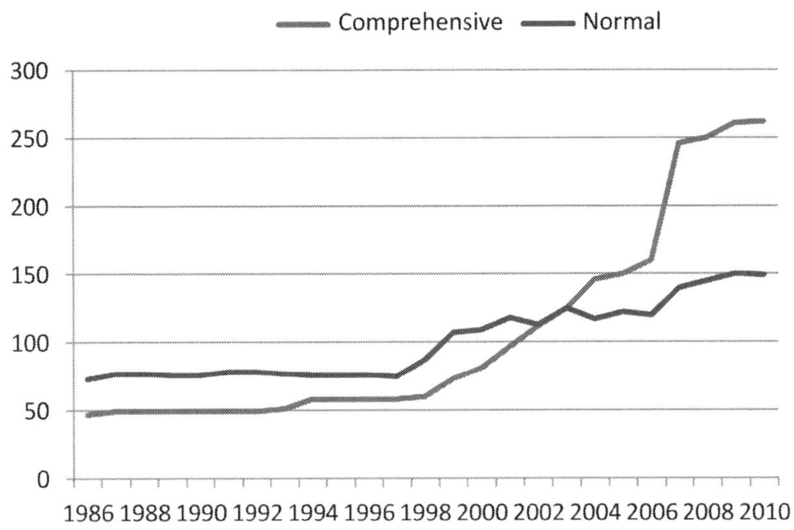

Figure 7.3 Comprehensive and normal (teacher training) institutions offering four-year bachelor's degrees, 1986–2010.

Source: NBS (2011).

unrelated to education was seen by some scholars and officials as encouraging them to neglect their historic strengths (Gu 2007). Upgrading primary teacher education programmes to four-year college degree level (at least in urban areas) has led to more subject-specific training of new teachers, and in turn to more teaching by subject in primary schools, despite the fact that primary teachers are generally still expected to teach the whole curriculum (Zhou *et al.* 2007).[3] The Department of Teacher Education within the Ministry of Education itself has been opposed to reducing the number of specialist teacher education institutions, but has been powerless to resist this trend (Guan 2009).

Shanghai Normal University, Beijing's Capital Normal University and colleges in other 'advanced' areas have led the way, since the early 2000s, in promoting degree-level, subject-specialist training of primary teachers. In urban areas, Maths, Science, Chinese and English are increasingly taught by specialists from primary grade one, as also are more 'minor' subjects like Art, Music, PE and IT (Wang 2012) (Moral Education or 'Thought and Values' is still generally taught by non-specialists). However, in rural primary schools, remoteness, scale and problems of teacher recruitment mean that it is still typical to find one teacher per grade teaching the entire curriculum. As noted in Chapter 3.4, this has been one rationale for 'concentrating' upper primary schooling in urban boarding schools, which many rural students attend after completing grade 4 (see also Murphy 2004). Until the early 2000s, it was still common to find multi-grade instruction (*fushiban*) in small schools in the most remote areas, but these have largely been closed down as even very young children have been enrolled in boarding programmes. The push for greater subject-specialisation amongst primary teachers is driven both by the equation of 'quality' with subject-specific expertise, and by competitive pressures related to the jockeying for access to key point junior secondary and senior high schools (see next chapter). Advocates of greater specialisation have also invoked international precedents for employing specialists to teach science or music at primary level (e.g. Hudson 2004; Holden and Button 2006). But one effect of this trend has been to maintain the gap in primary teachers' average qualification levels between provinces, and especially between urban and rural areas (see Zeng 2012a, Chapter B5 and p. 110).

Echoing the comments of Gao Yi almost thirty years earlier, in 2007 Premier Wen Jiabao visited BNU and publicly reprimanded leading normal universities for neglecting what he saw as their prime responsibility – to train teachers. In yet another attempt to compel these institutions to lead by example, Wen announced the introduction of a 'Plan for Free Tuition for Teacher Trainees' (State Council 2007). Under this scheme, the six normal universities under the Education Ministry were to allocate half of their total enrolment to 'fee-free' students (especially from Western regions), on condition that these students then returned to teach in their home areas for at least ten years.[4] This scheme did not prove popular with university staff – some at BNU, for example, complained that most 'fee-free' students lacked interest in teaching, and simply wanted admission to BNU with a lower *gaokao* score and free tuition (implying that these students were likely to discount or evade the obligation to devote ten years to the profession after graduation). Anecdotal evidence indicates similar dissatisfaction amongst staff at other major normal universities, with many complaining that the students on this scheme were not sufficiently qualified to cope with the demands of the curriculum.[5] At BNU, disgruntlement fuelled some talk of trying to abandon the 'Shifan' tag altogether and position the institution unambiguously as a comprehensive university by reclaiming the title 'Furen University' (BNU's pre-1949 predecessor institution). Far from persuading the normal universities to recommit to their original vocation, this scheme highlighted the low social and academic status of specialist teacher-training courses and institutions (and after Premier Wen stepped down in 2012, it effectively went into limbo).

In a further attempt to address the tendency for teacher-education-oriented degree courses to morph into regular academic programmes, experiments with various models of postgraduate teacher training have been promoted since the early 2000s. These have included 3+2, 4+1 and 4+2 patterns, whereby students first take a three- or four-year regular academic degree, before going on to complete a one- or two-year teacher training programme, often designated as an MA level qualification (IALEI 2008). Such initiatives have been inspired partly by the ambition (cherished by many normal university professors) to create a more level playing field between 'comprehensive' and 'normal' universities, as well as between faculties of education and other faculties within the same institution. While allowing equal competition in the provision of regular bachelor's degrees, the intention has been to use the new postgraduate programmes to strengthen and extend the practicum offered to teacher trainees. These moves have also been related to a desire to upgrade teachers' professional training and make it more 'practice-oriented', consistent with the requirements of the 2002 curriculum reform (with its expectation that teachers would adopt more 'integrated' and 'creative' approaches). American and British models of teacher training have been a significant influence in this area.

However, as with many ostensibly vocational programmes in China (see Chapter 10), standardisation or coordination of curricular planning, teaching practice or 'educational foundations' courses has tended to be weak or non-existent, and content has often drifted towards abstract or theoretical concerns. In 2011, in an attempt at standardisation, the Education Ministry for the first time issued a set of 'curriculum standards for teacher education courses' – distinguishing between 'subject knowledge', 'general (*tongshixing*) knowledge' (relating to '*suzhi*') and 'professional knowledge' (of teaching and learning) (MOE 2011a). It is, as yet, hard to determine what effect this has had on how universities or colleges actually run their teacher education programmes – although teaching practicums have been significantly lengthened. But one problem with requiring professors in education departments or faculties to deliver or organise more practice-oriented instruction is that, especially at the most prestigious institutions, professors of education in China (as in other East Asian societies) typically have little or no experience of teaching in schools, and have never received any practical teacher-training themselves.

The intensification, from the early 2000s, of attempts to steer pre-service teacher training in a more practical direction were related to the goals of the 2001–2 curricular reforms, with their greater emphasis on 'analytical skills', 'critical thinking' and 'quality' (*suzhi*). However, as noted in the previous chapter, ideological constraints (i.e. the imperative to inculcate 'correct thinking' and uncritical patriotism) limit the scope for pedagogical innovation in subjects such as History or Civics/Politics. The sciences perhaps offer more scope for introducing active, 'student-centred' teaching methods, but academic educationalists tend to be social scientists with an uncertain grasp of Physics, Chemistry and Biology. The work of the Japanese scholar Manabu Sato, much cited by the influential Shanghai-based reformer Zhong Qiquan (see previous chapter), tends to cite examples of pedagogical innovation at primary level – where the subject matter is less challenging – rather than at secondary level. And in China even more than in Japan, even when teachers embrace innovative goals and are trained in the appropriate methods, the pressures of test or examination preparation, especially (though not only) at secondary level, have tended to foster disillusionment regarding the practicability of implementing 'innovative' techniques (Sargent 2015 – see below on in-service training; on Japan, see Bjork 2011).

Meanwhile, 'graduate schools of education' at prestigious comprehensive institutions such as Peking University or Renmin University have preferred to focus on the pursuit of 'pure' academic research, rather than stoop to the mundane task of organising a teaching practicum. Peking University's School of

Education, for example, established in 2000, has specialised in research on public policy or the economics of education. The most prestigious normal universities such as BNU and East China Normal University (ECNU) have sought to get out of the business of providing undergraduate-level education courses altogether, to focus instead on postgraduate programmes and research (ECNU did actually discontinue its undergraduate programmes in the early 2000s). An experiment at BNU with a 4+2 programme was abandoned in 2011 after two years (the last students graduated in 2013) because of problems in recruiting students. Driven to compete with other faculties in the provision of four-year, subject-focused bachelor's-level courses, the Education Faculty found itself at an insurmountable disadvantage. Vested interests clearly play a big role here. For the Education Faculty to abandon its own four-year degree programmes and focus instead on the two-year pedagogical course (ostensibly the logical solution) would have seemed tantamount to institutional or professional suicide, in a context where academic prestige is so bound up with subject-specific expertise.

Competitive pressures operating at school level are also fundamental to the maintenance of the subject-focused, academic bent of pre-service teacher training. When recruiting new staff, school principals will almost invariably favour candidates with degrees from mainstream academic departments over those with degrees from departments or faculties of education; and the higher the degree, the better. Since the early 2000s, there has been a growing tendency for urban key point senior high schools to recruit teachers with postgraduate degrees, creating a widening qualifications gap *vis-à-vis* schools in county towns or rural areas (Zeng 2012a, 119). Even if these highly qualified recruits have little aptitude for teaching, and lack pedagogical training or experience, their presence on the staff roster is guaranteed to impress parents. Invited to give a speech to students at one of Beijing's top high schools in 2012, one of the present authors witnessed chaos descend on the hall for several minutes, while a young teacher attempted to distribute hand-outs to the assembled students. Apologising afterwards for the disruption, her exasperated senior colleague sighed, 'But she has a PhD in Chemistry…'.

In-service training and professional development

Even with Maoist 'permanent revolution' emphatically consigned to the past, in the sphere of teacher education the post-Mao period has thus witnessed almost continuous reform. This is as true of in-service as of pre-service provision. While this can be interpreted as an inevitable consequence of efforts to adapt to rapid social change ('changing the wheels while the car is in motion', as Paine and Fang put it), the teacher-training infrastructure, like the education system more broadly, has not just reflected but also helped to shape China's societal transformation. And perhaps its most profound contribution in this respect relates to underlying features of the system that have remained relatively constant: strong state oversight; a focus on epistemological and moral 'correctness'; and clear hierarchies of professional expertise.

The in-service training system operated on an enormous scale in the early post-Mao years, when – as of 1981 – one third of the roughly three million secondary school teachers, and 2.5 million primary teachers (out of a total of 5.5 million) were reported as being enrolled in 'some kind of in-service training' – compared with the 790,000 enrolled in pre-service programmes (Lo 1984, 172). These immense figures were related to the drive to 'upgrade' *minban* teachers lacking the officially required qualifications – and the numbers taking such courses declined by the 1990s as the proportion of *minban* teachers fell. However, in-service training of one kind or another has remained of crucial importance to many practising teachers, not least due to the persistent inadequacy of pre-service programmes in training participants to face a classroom or prepare a lesson.

The institutional infrastructure for in-service training, essentially modelled – like the pre-service system – on Soviet precedents, consisted of 'colleges of education' (*jiaoyu xueyuan*) at provincial and municipal level, and 'teacher refresher schools' (*jiaoshi jinxiu xuexiao*) at county and district level. These institutions, especially the 'colleges of education', have provided full-time as well as part-time training courses, but their main role has been to offer programmes for practising teachers, as well as conducting a certain amount of practice-oriented research. Amongst the rash of educational directives that ushered in the Reform era in 1977 was a Ministry 'opinion' on 'strengthening in-service training for primary and secondary teachers' (IED, 1977, 1588), a task that was primarily assigned to these colleges and refresher schools (though regular institutions of teacher education – the 'normal' universities, colleges and schools – also played a role). Over the following decade and more, they also became the primary vehicles for the drive to 'upgrade' the qualifications of *minban* teachers prior to their redesignation as *gongban*. The main thrust of these 'upgrading' programmes was to strengthen teachers' grasp of the subject-specific curriculum. Since inadequately qualified *minban* teachers were often holdovers from the excessive 'redness' of the Mao years, they were deemed to require a hefty dose of 'expertise'. The emphasis on subject knowledge was thus 'even more explicit' with in-service training courses than with their pre-service counterparts (Lo 1984, 168).

As more and more teachers reached the minimum qualification standards, the demand for such 'upgrading' programmes declined – albeit at different rates in different parts of the country. And during the 1990s, the colleges of education and refresher schools were also caught up in the wave of mergers sweeping the higher education system (for example, the Shanghai College of Education was merged with ECNU – Paine and Fang 2007, 182; see Chapter 12).[6] As with pre-service training institutions, the number of specialist providers of in-service teacher education declined.

Many that remained were reoriented towards offering short courses for practising teachers rather than formal qualifications, positioning them as intermediate institutions between the normal universities on the one hand, and on the other local 'pedagogical research units' (*jiaoyan shi*) and subject-based 'pedagogical research groups' (*jiaoyan zu*) in schools. *Jiaoyan shi*, located within each local Bureau of Education, are staffed by former teachers (*jiaoyan yuan*) tasked with coordinating in-service training in their subject area. As the system moved, at least in urban areas, from seeking to upgrade under-qualified teachers to focusing on improving the performance of qualified staff, the 2010 Education *Gangyao* ('Framework') announced as a 'target' the requirement that teachers undergo a minimum of 360 hours of in-service training in every five-year period (MOE 2011b). This move to compel teachers to engage in 'lifelong learning' (*zhongsheng jiaoyu*) reflected a combination of longstanding concerns with teaching quality, and the influence of Western discourses concerning the 'global knowledge economy' and concomitant demand for 'skills', 'innovation' and 'creativity'.

In 'advanced' areas that boast the full panoply of in-service and pre-service training institutions, as well as the best-equipped and best-staffed schools, support for professional development can be impressive. Thus the novice Shanghai secondary school teacher of the early 2000s who described herself as 'surrounded by help' cited the support of her senior teacher mentors, who both observed and commented on her classes, and allowed her to observe their teaching; the activities of the *jiaoyan zu* and the *beike zu*, groups of subject teachers who gather to exchange reflections on their practice and discuss lesson plans; and the local district's induction programme of lectures by expert teachers (Paine and Fang 2007, 184–5). The *jiaoyan shi* system – another 1950s Soviet import – links schoolteachers to a hierarchy of subject-specific units at local, provincial and national level dedicated to facilitating the dissemination of best practice (Guo 2003).[7]

This infrastructure has attracted considerable approbation from Western researchers for its systematic approach to the organisation of 'professional learning communities'. Sargent, for example, writes of 'interlocking teacher networks' – both 'homophilous' (involving horizontal peer interactions) and 'heterophilous' (hierarchical or vertically ordered) – that 'provide schools and teachers with access to a flow of rich and fresh flowing innovative ideas for the sustained improvement of teaching' (2015, 127). What such accounts perhaps overlook is the extent to which these networks are designed not just as instruments for pedagogical improvement, but also as tools for political control. After all, the sort of all-encompassing fusion of 'homophilous' and 'heterophilous' teacher networks that Sargent describes is archetypally Leninist.

'Expert teachers', 'backbone teachers' (*gugan jiaoshi*) or 'special rank teachers' (*teji jiaoshi*) play a crucial role in such networks, modelling and disseminating best practice. The bestowal on teachers of honorific titles had precedents in the period of Soviet influence during the 1950s. However, the formal title of 'special rank teacher' was an early innovation of the Reform period, announced by Deng Xiaoping at the National Education Conference of 1978 as a means of raising 'the political and social status of teachers' and promoting teaching excellence (Ko and Adamson 2011). Holders of this rank have been expected not just to model pedagogical technique, but also to exemplify desirable moral and political qualities.[8] Explicit reference to politics in the criteria for *teji jiaoshi* nomination was dropped in the 1990s, but Ko and Adamson found that all of the 14 special rank teachers in their sample were members of the Communist Party or affiliated parties (13).

While major urban centres may boast cohorts of 'special rank teachers' ready and willing to mentor junior colleagues, rural teachers have generally been far less well served. Paine and Fang contrast the case of their Shanghai novice with that of a *minban* teacher working in a one-room, multi-grade village school in Inner Mongolia (Paine and Fang 2007, 185–6). This teacher cycled to the county town every weekend to attend training courses and meet other teachers with whom she could share experiences and discuss problems. The training sessions involved watching video recordings of CCTV programmes featuring model lessons delivered by experienced teachers – on video equipment transported by donkey cart from a neighbouring township. Even these sessions constituted a 'rare opportunity' made possible through collaboration between UNICEF and the Chinese government. Since the early 2000s, the Internet has become an increasingly important vehicle for disseminating information to teachers and facilitating networking.[9]

As part of efforts to develop and extend support to practising teachers, over the past decade some areas have also seen the establishment, with financial assistance from the local government, of new 'studios' (*gongzuo shi*) of school principals or *teji jiaoshi*. These are intended to play a leading role in organising lectures, discussions and debates on teaching, school management and other matters relevant to teachers' professional development, enabling relatively inexperienced or poorly qualified teachers to benefit from the 'know-how' of their better-qualified peers (supplementing activities organised by local Education Bureau *jiaoyan yuan*, often long-exiled from the chalk-face). However, a study of one such initiative in Anshan city, Liaoning Province, found that *teji jiaoshi* were not particularly motivated to involve themselves in the activities of these studios, due to the extent of their existing commitments (Wu *et al.* 2012). Perhaps more to the point, their primary employers – usually key point schools – were anxious to limit the time and energy they devoted to 'outreach' activities. From the point of view of local governments, on the other hand, one function served by offering 'ordinary' teachers opportunities to sit at the feet of 'special rank' teachers is the legitimation of the institutional hierarchies consequent upon the preferential resourcing of key point schools.

Many teachers highly value opportunities for in-service training, in part (but not only) due to linkage between attendance at training sessions and the earning of performance-related salary increments (see below). Special training opportunities are sometimes also presented as 'rewards' to 'outstanding' teachers: the chance for an expenses-paid trip to the big city, to attend lectures by famous educators and academic experts, is a prize highly coveted by many staff in the provinces.[10] However, not all training is seen as useful or beneficial. In the lead-up to the central government's much-heralded leap in educational investment to 4 per cent of GDP, in the context of the 2010 *Gangyao* (see Chapter 3.4), a 'national training plan' (*Guopei jihua*) was introduced (MOE 2011b). This funnelled large amounts of money (over half a billion yuan annually) to local government-run training institutes (*jiaoshi jinxiu xuexiao* and *jiaoyu xueyuan*), which were tasked with providing the bulk of the training teachers had to undergo as a condition of promotion or contract renewal. Staffed by permanent state employees with little incentive to engage actively with schools, such institutions typically provide courses geared to pleasing officials further up the administrative hierarchy. Hence complaints from teachers in Beijing and other major cities in recent years of their transformation into 'training slaves' (*peixun nuli*) – echoing talk of a broader 'enslavement' of the profession, associated with insecure employment conditions and extreme competitive pressure (Zi 2016; see below).

On the one hand, therefore, the highly developed hierarchical networks of subject-based *jiaoyan shi* and *jiaoyan zu* and the infrastructure of state-run training institutes have helped disseminate best practice and supported a strong sense of 'subject community' amongst teachers. On the other hand, however, the very strength of these institutions has reinforced divisions between school subjects. Until the early 2000s, this presented no problems for ordinary teachers, who, at least at secondary level, faced little pressure to transcend subject boundaries. However, the curriculum reforms of 2001–2, with their calls for 'integrated learning' and the promotion of generic, cross-curricular 'skills' (e.g. 'critical thinking'), have imposed conflicting demands on teachers. Quite apart from the mismatch between examination requirements and curricular guidelines (discussed in the previous and following chapters), implementing innovative teaching methods requires extensive opportunities for appropriate in-service training. Sargent suggests that this is widely available, in particular through the networks of experienced *gugan* ('backbone') teachers. However, Zhao Mingren (2014) argues that pressure to conform to the expectations of local *jiaoyan yuan* (not to mention examination-obsessed principals, teachers and parents), who exercise considerable influence over opportunities for career progression, added to the conservatism of local training institutes,[11] has tended to strongly dis-incentivise innovation or experimentation on the part of junior teachers. Willingness to engage in pedagogical experimentation, in other words, depends largely on individual teachers' sense of professional autonomy – and in this respect, security of tenure and conditions of employment are highly significant. It is to those issues that we turn next.

Recruitment and retention – salaries, benefits and incentives

From the beginning of the Reform period, fiscal decentralisation, a widening urban–rural divide and (especially from the 1990s) the opening up of varied and lucrative new employment opportunities in the cities have posed problems for recruiting and retaining qualified teachers – particularly in poorer regions and rural areas (see Chapter 5). Whatever other factors may contribute to minimising attrition rates, paying teachers at a reasonable level is crucial to keeping them in the classroom. From 1949 until the advent of the Reform era in 1977, teachers were divided, for salary purposes, into two categories: *gongban* (state-certified or 'regular') and *minban* (non-certified and 'community-managed'). *Minban* teachers, employed by the communities whom they served, were generally paid whatever the village (it was usually a village) could afford, and since this was often insufficient to support their livelihood, many engaged in farming or other work on the side. Indeed, during the Cultural Revolution, when farm labour was an integral part of the curriculum, teachers and students would typically cultivate the school 'plot' together. *Gongban* teachers, by contrast, were paid different salaries according to their qualifications: those who had completed four-year programmes were paid more than the graduates of three-year courses. As with other state-sector employees, there were no increments for years of service. Socialism of the Maoist variety sought to level not just class divisions, but generational ones as well (see White 1981; Pepper 1996).

After 1977, the salary structure for all public employees, including *gongban* teachers, was reformed to permit some to benefit from salary increases once a year. However, these were neither automatic nor available to all. Often, the power to recommend employees for increases rested with the party committee, and the criteria for awarding them left vague. As a result, allocations were sometimes made on the basis of perceived 'need', or to those whose 'turn' had come around, or on the basis of political criteria or connections. Between the late 1970s and mid-1980s, average salaries for *gongban* teachers increased from about 40 to 50 yuan per month (IED 1981, 1980), while rates of pay also began to diverge somewhat.[12] *Minban* teachers were still paid by the village or work unit (at far lower rates), and as rural collectives were broken up, the funding for their salaries often evaporated. In the early Reform period, the contrast between official solicitude for regular teachers, and dismissiveness towards the plight of their rural *minban* counterparts, was striking. In October 1979, teachers in *minban* primary and secondary schools in rural areas were told that they would 'have to continue subsisting in the way they have up until now' (IED 1979, 1748), but the following month special subsidies and allowances were announced for 'class teachers' (*banzhuren*) in regular schools (IED 1979, 1756).

The resulting crisis in rural basic education began to cause official concern during the early 1980s (see Chapters 3.1 and 5). In February 1981, former Education Minister (by then Vice-Chair of the CPPCC), Yang Xiufeng, warned that 'if the teaching force is unstable and ill at ease (*dongdang bu an*), this will not just have a serious impact on the quality of education, but will also increase instability in our society in many other respects' (IED 1981, 1908). Later that year, the State Council announced that 'supplementary fees' could henceforth be used to supplement the income of *minban* teachers, and stipulated limits for such fees; but the text of the directive itself acknowledged that fee-charging was already widespread, and indicated that those provinces or regions that had already raised fees up to or beyond the recommended level should decide for themselves what to do (IED 1981, 1980). Typifying the *laissez-faire* approach to fiscal decentralisation during this period, local authorities were simply exhorted to take account of 'local conditions' and avoid placing an 'excessive burden' on local people. But from the mid-1980s onwards, the drive to 'upgrade' *minban* teachers to *gongban* status through provision of in-service training intensified (Lewin *et al.* 1994), and by the early 1990s many had already made the transition (IED 1992, 3365).

This had considerable implications for the increasingly strained finances of local governments, which thereby assumed responsibility for their salaries and pensions.

Amongst the Education Reforms of 1985 was the introduction of bonus payments for *gongban* teachers, theoretically based on their performance (a system introduced in all SOEs at this time). State workers, including teachers, were henceforth paid a notionally variable bonus in addition to their basic salary, but performance-related pay remained an alien concept in the context of what was still essentially a command economy.[13] This began to change from the early 1990s, as the marketisation of the urban economy took off. Under the *jiegou gongzi zhi* (or 'structured salary system') introduced nationally in 1994, basic salary levels were mandated by the state, but local authorities were licensed to award increments and bonuses as 'local conditions' allowed. Under this system, basic salary varied by teachers' grades, but seniority in itself brought no benefits. It was not until 2006 that seniority (length of service at a particular grade) became a new dimension to the nationally mandated 'professional ladder' (*zhi cheng*), but by this point the significance of basic pay (set nationally), as distinct from performance-related bonuses and other payments (awarded by local authorities), was already diminishing for many teachers (MHR 2006).

Ding and Lehrer (2007) look at the use of 'incentives' and their association with certain measures of 'teacher quality' in secondary schools in an urban county of Jiangsu Province in the early 2000s. On top of the basic salary of 6,000 yuan, teachers were awarded increments for seniority, and further rises according to 'grade'. They were ranked in four grades from 'superior teacher' through 'first' and 'second' to 'third class teacher', with interns and newly hired staff receiving only the basic salary. According to the local salary schedule for 1998, 'superior teachers' were paid from almost a third to over four-fifths more than 'third class teachers' (193) – with the most experienced earning about double the basic salary. 'Ranks' were based on the county Education Bureau's assessment of each teacher's qualifications, professional achievements and teaching skills.

As presented by Ding and Lehrer, the deployment of such criteria seems eminently objective and reasonable, but the devil lies in the details of measurement. A commonly used proxy for 'teaching skills' at senior high level is the *gaokao* performance of the students taught by a particular teacher, compared with those taught by other teachers (with student scores in the *zhongkao* or other tests used to assess the performance of junior secondary or primary teachers). Moreover, the responsibility of teaching a *gaokao* or *zhongkao* preparatory class (Years 12 or 9) is itself typically treated as a reward for high performance (Kipnis 2011, 153–4). Principals will generally only entrust such a crucial and onerous task to teachers in whom they have particular faith, and these staff then automatically receive an increment on top of their basic salary (typically at a ratio of 1.3 or 1.4 the standard rate), with additional bonuses if their class scores particularly well in the examinations (often calculated according to incredibly complex statistical formulae; Kipnis 2011, 153).

In assessing candidates for promotion, the county Education Bureau investigated by Ding and Lehrer also considered the reports of administrators and 'superior teachers' who randomly attended their lessons. Credit was given to teachers who introduced 'new and effective teaching methods'. Qualifications were assessed by reference to a national five-point system of college rankings, along with the years of education completed. 'Professional knowledge' was gauged according to the number of articles on instructional methods published by the candidate in professional journals. Ding and Lehrer also report that candidates were credited for their efficacy in evaluating and monitoring students' performance, general solicitousness for the welfare of their young charges, and 'work ethic' – but they do not reveal how these qualities were measured. Local education officials informed Ding and Lehrer that the ranking system had 'noticeably altered teacher behaviour' – encouraging teachers to be more solicitous of their students, to monitor them more closely and show more willingness to offer extra help to those who were falling behind (194).

It is scarcely surprising that officials, or indeed school principals, should endorse a system granting them such power over teachers, but Ding and Lehrer themselves also clearly need little persuading of the merits of performance-related pay – hence their rather superficial interrogation of the methods used to determine 'performance'. While declaring that the ranking system and performance-related increments reflect 'the willingness and ability of local leaders, and indirectly the community, to reward its teachers' (194), they have little to say about how patterns in the distribution of such rewards reflect or reinforce the hierarchisation of schooling and the teaching profession – or about the wider implications of these processes. They do note that 'national or provincial key schools have a higher percentage of instructors in the superior class' (23.9 per cent versus 12 per cent), although the average experience of key point school teachers is slightly shorter (10.27 years versus 12.01) 'because ranked schools can attract younger teachers with higher degrees' (199). Kipnis reports that key point schools prefer to employ teachers in their twenties or thirties because of the intense demands of the job – they doubt the capacity of middle-aged staff to stand the pace, particularly when it comes to teaching examination-preparatory classes (2011, 153–4; see above), while those in their forties are likely to be seen as 'worn out'. The key point schools in Ding and Lehrer's study also boasted a considerably higher proportion of teachers, especially at the 'first class' and 'superior' levels, who were teaching the subject they studied at college.

Meanwhile, the hierarchical differentiation of teachers' remuneration has seen fortunes for the profession diverge not just on the basis of perceived 'performance', but also according to level of school and location. The 2012 *Blue Book of Teachers* (Zeng 2012a), taking 1993 as 'Year Zero' (indexed at 100), shows salaries for primary and junior secondary teachers stagnating or declining between 1994 and 1998, and only catching up with the rise in the Consumer Price Index (CPI) by the end of the decade. These figures illustrate graphically the effects on teachers' income of the taxation reforms of the 1990s, to which many local governments responded by trimming their education budgets.

By 2008, the rise in teacher's salaries from the 1993 base point stood at more than double the rise in the CPI (185). However, a more relevant measure of the financial attractiveness of teaching as a profession is the comparison between salaries for teachers and those for other professions. Overall, the average rise in primary teachers' salaries has failed, by a substantial margin, to keep pace with increases for the working population (*zhigong*) as a whole, or with those for workers in commercial enterprises (*shiye danwei*) or the public sector (*jiguan danwei*) (186–199). Junior secondary teachers have fared better, with salary increases more or less matching those for the general working population, but the statistics do not compare their salaries with those of graduates of similar qualifications – a comparison that, as the *Blue Book* notes, the OECD typically uses when monitoring teachers' remuneration (204–5).

Between 2000 and 2008, average increases in salaries for teachers in rural areas apparently outstripped those for their urban counterparts – especially at primary school level (123 per cent versus 66 per cent) (200–1), reflecting the impact of measures taken to boost spending on rural public goods from around the early 2000s (see Chapters 3.4 and 5). However, given that primary teaching salaries overall were falling behind remuneration rates for the general workforce, this rate of increase could not compensate, on its own, for the perceived hardship of a rural teaching post. Moreover, the *Blue Book* indicates that salaries for rural teachers have remained markedly lower than those for urban ones, and observes that scholars have yet to supply a 'satisfactory explanation' for this (Zeng 2012a, 203). And while living costs are generally far lower in rural areas, so that teachers' salaries 'go further' there, overcoming graduates' aversion to rural employment would arguably require boosting pay at least to urban levels. Indeed, policy on salaries for teachers in 'minority' regions has long recognised the logic of offering extra rewards for a 'hardship posting', with Tibet and Qinghai (also predominantly ethnic Tibetan) coming near the top of the league for teachers' overall pay (Zeng and Yu 2015, 57; on the early Reform period, see Chapter 3.1).

This is one indication of how, when it comes to paying teachers, nation-building concerns still seem to trump those of equity. In its breakdown of pay levels on a province-by-province basis, the *Blue Book* shows the proportion of total pay accounted for by the state-mandated basic salary steadily declining in the early 2000s, and consistently lowest in prosperous eastern provinces, and in Western border regions largely populated by restive 'minorities'. In other words, it is these regions that have done most to 'top up' their teachers' pay with allocations from local budgets. As of 2014, this meant that in Beijing and Shanghai teachers' basic salary accounted, on average, for only a quarter of their total pay packet; in Tibet, one third; and in Xinjiang, one half. However, in a swathe of populous provinces including Hubei, Jiangxi, Henan, Hunan, Anhui, Guangxi, Sichuan, Jilin and Heilongjiang, the figure was closer to 70 per cent (Zeng and Yu 2015, 57). In the age of the Internet, awareness of such imbalances has become increasingly widespread. Recent years have witnessed a number of strikes by teachers in provinces at the bottom of the salary league.

Meanwhile, despite the higher salary level enjoyed by urban teachers, the *Blue Book* data shows that in cities the profession has increasingly struggled to attract qualified male recruits. Between 2000 and 2009, the proportion of female teachers in urban schools increased from 77 to 79 per cent at primary level, 61 to 64 per cent at junior high level and 46 to 53 per cent at senior high level (137–8). In rural schools meanwhile, the percentages rose from 42 to 46 per cent (at primary level), 37 to 42 per cent (junior high) and 29 to 42 per cent (senior high) – with the figures for 'county towns' bisecting those for city and rural areas, but displaying the same gradual upward trend. The report's authors interpret this feminisation of teaching, at least in the cities, as the product of the rising proportion of female students in higher education, the wider range of alternative employment options in urban areas, and a growing (and self-fulfilling) perception of teaching as a 'feminine' profession (139). To this list should perhaps be added factors such as the rising cost of urban living, and intensifying pressure on men as the primary 'breadwinners' to find employment in more lucrative sectors (Fincher 2014).[14] This phenomenon may also be related to the attractiveness of female teachers as marriage partners, in a society where it is overwhelmingly mothers who are expected to take responsibility for their children's education. Young female teachers in cities like Shanghai or Beijing may thus stand a good chance of finding wealthy or high-status husbands, while the marital prospects of their male colleagues may be rather less elevated. This is an area that warrants further research.

As Zeng and her contributors observe, a coincidence of economic growth, expansion of higher education and a decreasing proportion of men in the teaching profession is by no means exclusive to China – and, like their counterparts in many 'developed' countries, Chinese educators have also become concerned about the consequences for children's socialisation of a growing gender imbalance within the profession (2012, 138). But besides the lure of higher salary levels (tempered by the higher cost of living), a key attraction of state employment in Shanghai and Beijing (in particular), for teachers as for others, is the prospect of *hukou* transfer, conferring the right to put one's own children through the local schooling system. For many teachers, especially if they are also parents, the attraction of employment in city schools derives not just from salary levels, but also from the self-fulfilling belief that the overall 'quality' of the educational environment is superior.

Conclusion

That urban educators should have begun to worry about gender balance in the teaching profession, while for rural areas recruitment or retention of qualified personnel of whatever gender remains a challenge, is just one reflection of the broader social divides that have characterised China's post-Mao development. Since the early 2000s, a falling school-age population and expanded higher education system have eased teacher shortages. Especially since 2006, the financing of education in rural areas has also been put on a firmer footing, and new schemes introduced (such as the *tegang jiaoshi* programme) to bring graduates to teach in rural schools. Linked to such efforts, as we noted in Chapters 3.3 and 3.4, was a trend to 'concentrate' rural upper-primary and junior secondary schooling in large boarding establishments in county towns – effectively bringing rural children to where urban-trained teachers are more willing to go. However, such measures have brought problems of their own, including that of forcing young children to undertake sometime lengthy and hazardous journeys to school. Nor do they address educational inequalities at the crucial pre-school or early primary stages, when children are simply too young to leave their parents. And for all that central government subsidies have done, over the past decade, to improve rural education in absolute terms, in relative terms the gap with conditions in prosperous urban areas has remained gapingly large. As we noted in Chapter 5, forty years of differential development has created huge vested interests in maintaining the educational advantages that wealthier regions have accrued.

The weight of such vested interests helps explain why China has not adopted systems of the kind seen in Japan or France, whereby teachers are employed not by individual schools but by the state or local board of education – and are then rotated between schools within the same district (Alexander 2000; Cave 2007). This is a glaring paradox at the heart of a system that, as this chapter has shown, is otherwise characterised by strong state control of the teaching profession. Here the interests that count are particularly those vested in the maintenance of the key point schools. Since rotating teachers away from these would effectively destroy their key point status, such a move would, very literally, have revolutionary implications. The experience of other societies bears this out: pre-war Japan's highly elitist schooling system, central to which was a national network of 'key high schools' (*koutou gakkou*), was swept away and replaced with the more egalitarian post-war model as a result of crushing defeat and foreign occupation; England, meanwhile, having avoided such upheavals, has retained one of the most institutionally unequal schooling systems in the developed world, despite numerous attempts (variously half-hearted or ill-conceived) at reform.

Rather than tackle head-on the vested interests supporting the current dispensation, policymakers and administrators have preferred to resort to measuring 'performance' as a means of monitoring teachers, motivating them and legitimising professional and inter-school hierarchies. In one sense, this can be seen as representing a shift from an administrative system relying, like the Soviet one, mainly on control of 'inputs' – involving strong standardisation of curricula and textbooks, as well as of pre- and in-service training for teachers (Alexander 2000) – to control of 'outputs', principally in the form of students' test and examination results. In fact, as this chapter and the next one show, educational administrators in the post-Mao period have always relied heavily on both. However, growing marketisation since the 1990s (see Chapter 9) and the injection of greater competition into the mechanisms for rewarding teachers appear to have increased the pressures on the profession, even as material conditions have improved. In early 2016, the eminent historian Zi Zhongyun was moved to write of a 'triple enslavement' of teachers: to 'the system'; to school principals (endowed with increasingly autocratic 'executive' authority); and to students and their parents (Zi 2016). Arguing that their reduction to the status of 'tools' had debased the essential moral and aesthetic functions of teaching, the main object of her blistering critique was the pervasive use of students' examination results as the overriding benchmark for judging teachers. It is to the role of assessment in the education system that we turn next.

Notes

1 The use of the term *daike* rather than the old *minban* label is specifically designed to diminish expectations amongst these contract teachers of the kind of transfer to 'tenured' status that was granted to *minban* teachers in the 1990s.
2 The ideological tilt towards 'patriotism' since the early 1990s has been reflected in positions taken by some of China's most prominent educators. For example, Gu Mingyuan, cited by Paine in the mid-1990s as a 'moderniser', at a 2008 BNU conference on 'educational leadership' delivered a speech larded with nationalistic references to China's ancient and glorious pedagogical traditions.
3 Tang (2009, 42), discussing the proportion of the teacher education curriculum devoted to specifically 'pedagogical' concerns in former teachers' colleges (*shizhuan*) in Hunan, shows that this is far lower than in a selection of OECD countries.
4 Zeng (the present co-author) conducted a follow-up study to investigate what happened to these students after graduation, and found that most returned to their home province, but generally to key point schools rather than to ordinary schools in backward areas.
5 This is based on conversations in Shanghai with academics associated with East China Normal University.
6 In Beijing there are 'teacher training colleges' (*jiaoshi yanxiu xueyuan*) – offering compulsory in-service courses for teachers; every year (in the case of junior staff) teachers have to take so many hours of training in these institutions. In existence since the 1950s, and modelled on Soviet precedents, they used to be called 'teacher training schools' (*jiaoshi jinxiu xuexiao*).
7 Zeng (the present co-author) and collaborators have in recent years conducted research into the teaching, by 'class teachers' (*banzhuren*), of issues related to 'mental health' or the handling of deviant behaviour of one sort or another. They were struck by the almost identical approach used to teach such issues by teachers in different schools – and were told that they were using the model provided by the 'moral education pedagogical research unit' (*deyu jiaoyanshi*).
8 *Teji jiaoshi* are often invited to serve on official advisory committees of various kinds, such as those convened by PEP to solicit advice on textbook revision. As a young editor at PEP in late 2000, Vickers attended a meeting of such a committee at which the self-image of these teachers as moral exemplars became clear. The teachers asked that textbooks be rendered 'more interesting' for students, and that they also be 'permeated with moral education'. They bridled at Vickers' suggestion that there might be a contradiction between these two objectives.
9 The China Education and Research Network was established in 1994 as 'China's first and largest national academic internet backbone' (CERNET 2006). Satellite television was widely used in the late 1990s and early 2000s for delivering in-service training for schoolteachers in more remote regions. In the case of one Continuing Education Programme for K12 teachers that ran from 1999 to 2002, about 70 per cent of courses were delivered in this way (Paine and Fang 2007, 178).
10 This practice of offering training opportunities in the metropolis to 'excellent' teachers from the provinces has gone on throughout the Reform period. Organisations such as the People's Education Press (where Vickers worked in the early 2000s) and the major

normal universities have been instrumental in organising competitions for teachers and training events for the winners.

11 The growth of private or online vehicles for teacher training may increasingly break down the monopoly of the old teacher-training institutes – but how or whether this happens, and its implications, must be subjects for future research.

12 Shi Qing-ping, a teacher since 1982 at Beijing No. 11 High School (interviewed by the present authors in September 2010) corroborated these figures.

13 Benefits of 'key' workers, such as teachers in key point schools, at this time typically took non-monetary forms – for example, free accommodation and healthcare provided by the 'work unit'. (See Chapter 4 on ECEC.)

14 Appendix 3 of the 2012 *Blue Book* compares teacher salary increases to data on cost of living, GDP per head and average salary levels for selected regions.

8 Evaluation, assessment and the senior high school

If curriculum and pedagogy – dealt with in the preceding chapters – are the essential components of any education system, then assessment is the motor that drives the machine. In China, moreover, the sorting or ranking function of assessment is sanctified by ancient tradition; the imperial state organised public examinations for centuries before anything approaching an education system in the modern sense existed. In the twenty-first century, some analysts or advocates of a 'China model' of governance argue that this tradition has helped shape foundations for political legitimacy that are more meritocratic than democratic (Bell 2015). Certainly, as we saw in Chapter 3, the post-Mao leadership has attempted to tap such beliefs, imposing increasingly stringent educational requirements on its cadre force.

But in China, no less than elsewhere, meritocracy is at once a seductive ideal and a sociological myth. While in theory it distributes power and opportunity to the most deserving, in practice the wealthiest or most privileged almost always stand the best chance of winning the race to prove their 'merit'. As Michael Young illustrated in his famous satirical essay, to the extent that this encourages them to see their dominance as the result of justice rather than mere good fortune, it can breed arrogance and disdain for the less fortunate (Young 1961). The dangers of this are all the greater when the distribution of wealth, power and privilege is already radically skewed; and when the standard of educational facilities available to different social groups is extremely uneven. As we have already seen, this kind of unevenness was built into the fabric of the post-Mao education system.

In China, as elsewhere in East Asia, the senior high school occupies a pivotal position within the assessment regime. It is thus with the systems for determining admission to and progression from senior high school that this chapter is chiefly concerned. It begins by outlining the main tests to which students at different levels have been subjected. It then discusses the politics of assessment: its status as a tool of state policy, as a focus of public concern, and hence as a potential source of tension between government and populace. Of supreme importance is the 'college entrance examination' (*gaokao*), to which we turn next. The complex and highly controversial system of provincial 'quotas', recent reforms (notably the introduction of provincial *gaokao*), and the implications of China's system of household registration (the *hukou*) are central here, as they pertain to the fraught question of educational opportunities for the burgeoning migrant population. But since prospects for college entrance are heavily determined by the kind of senior high school one attends, this has become the key battleground in the struggle for educational opportunity. Following a brief analysis of recent innovations in the assessment system, the final section of the chapter thus deals briefly with the contentious issue of 'school choice' – highlighting how widening disparities of wealth and privilege have influenced access to the best schools. This is intimately related to the phenomenon of marketisation – the subject of the subsequent chapter.

Three closely interrelated sets of issues emerge. First, the intensely political nature of assessment is exemplified especially by the system of provincial quotas for college entry. Designed to ensure recruitment of a geographically diverse elite, these quotas mean that the level of examination performance required for access to top universities has varied widely according to residency. The sensitivity of attempts to recalibrate them was illustrated in 2016, when parents in the populous central and eastern provinces of Hubei and Jiangsu demonstrated against moves to grant increased quotas to more impoverished Western regions. Second (and closely related to the latter issue), the implications of class or social background for educational success, and the challenge of reconciling assessment practices with the demands of social equity, have attracted increasing attention in educational debate (see our discussion of college admission patterns in Chapter 12). Third, as we discussed in Chapter 6, assessment is a crucial factor in the 'quality'-oriented reforms pursued by officials since the 1990s. Assessment reform is thus also a pedagogical and professional issue. But attempts to promote critical thinking and creativity can clash with the imperative of political control; and in the absence of robust monitoring and legal oversight, diversification of assessment in the name of flexibility and 'innovation' can serve as a cover for nepotism and corruption.

Assessment in Chinese schooling from cradle to college – an overview

Testing begins early in the educational career of the Chinese child. In rural areas, where kindergarten provision is patchy at best, children may be spared the rigours of formal assessment until they reach primary school. However, for many urban children, examination pressure can begin far earlier – with intense competition for places in the best kindergartens involving informal selection (for example, 'interviews' to assess the aptitude of three- or four-year-olds). This has in turn fed a burgeoning demand for private tutoring, even of infants, with a view to securing the earliest possible head start in the race for places in elite schools (see Chapters 4 and 9). Marketisation of the education system in recent years has both tapped into and intensified a 'mania' for tests and exams observable since the advent of the Reform period (Thøgersen 1991, 73).

In the first two decades of the post-Mao era, the first formal public examination that students faced was typically the 'secondary school entrance examination for primary students' (*xiaoxue sheng chuzhongxue kaoshi* – or *xiao sheng chu*). Following the ostensible universalisation of junior secondary schooling, this test was gradually abolished between the late 1990s and early 2000s (Ako 2009, 158), and finally outlawed nationally in the 2006 revision of the Compulsory Education Law. Nonetheless, selective methods continued to be widely used to determine access to 'key' junior secondary schools (see below), and regular testing of primary students has remained standard practice. In primary schools during the 1980s, exams were 'normally held in all subjects two to three times each term, and weekly tests were common in most subjects' (Thøgersen 1991, 73) – a pattern that has persisted (Kipnis 2011). At secondary level, most schools set monthly tests (*yuekao*) in all subjects, in addition to termly examinations set at district level (*chuxian tongkao*), the results of which are used to rank and stream students.[1] Thøgersen cites a 1986 calculation that 'a Chinese student from the time he or she entered primary school to the senior secondary school final examination had gone through between ninety and one hundred screenings based on academic tests' (1991, 73). While the structure of public assessment has since changed, regular testing remains central to the educational experience of all Chinese students.

Ever since the late 1970s, some educators and officials have voiced concerns over the manner and frequency of tests and examinations, and their use in sorting and streaming. In a 1981 article in the prestigious journal *Jiaoyu Yanjiu* (*Educational Research*), Chen Yuanhuai wrote, 'When we analyse the direction and content of the university entrance examinations in certain subjects, we find to a large degree that they solely test memory and neither thinking ability nor intelligence' (cited in Thøgersen 1991, 74). If this was true of the *gaokao*, it was even more so of tests administered at lower levels. But despite continuing anxiety about the pedagogical implications of this approach, the subsequent thirty years have witnessed little fundamental change in the style and content of exams (see below).

Meanwhile, senior officials and experts have repeatedly bemoaned the pressures on students, teachers and parents caused by what Education Minister Jiang Nanxiang in 1979 termed 'the one-sided tendency to seek higher transition rates' (Thøgersen 1991, 75). But this tendency was hardwired into the system by the establishment of key point or feeder schools, and the stark hierarchisation of institutions at every level. Just as *gaokao* success determines the local status of key point senior high schools, so the success of primary and junior secondary schools in securing promotion to these is crucial to their reputation. This has incentivised schools to stream their students, grooming the most promising for the next selective hurdle. In the absence of radical steps to impose greater uniformity on the resource base and teaching workforce of different schools, the competitive urge has survived official efforts to tame it (see Chapters 3, 5 and 9).

Assessment reform at the primary-to-junior secondary and junior-to-senior secondary interfaces has thus proved largely ineffective in alleviating examination pressure. In junior secondary school, the pressure intensifies, as students prepare to sit the senior high entrance exam (*zhongkao*). In the 1980s and 1990s, this meant, for many, the difference between going to senior high school or not; senior high enrolment – regular plus vocational – stood at about one quarter of junior secondary enrolments during the 1980s, rising to just over a third by the late 1990s. Following the dramatic expansion of higher education in the late 1990s, senior high schooling expanded rapidly, as prospects of progressing to college greatly improved. While the *zhongkao* remained a crucial rite of passage, its significance changed. Whereas up to the 1990s it marked for most the termination of their educational career, today its primary function is to sort students into 'regular' and 'vocational' categories, with only the former permitted to take the *gaokao* (on the vocational 'track', see Chapter 10). It has become the main 'bottleneck' in the education system, assuming greater significance than the *gaokao* itself in determining who gets the opportunity for a college education (Lin 2006). As Wang *et al.* note, 'once disadvantaged students reach academic high school, the pathway to access college (though not necessarily elite colleges) is downhill' (2014). Less than 10 per cent of students nowadays drop out of academic high school – and 87 per cent of high school graduates access college.

The prospect of a regular tertiary education remains the holy grail for students and their parents. In the 1980s, when only a minority of graduates from regular senior high schools could hope to gain entry to college, being consigned to 'slow' or 'medium' streams drastically reduced one's chances of further progression; Thøgersen notes the 'intolerable' conditions in lower streams during this period, with students conscious of their status as 'failures' (1991, 85). Nowadays, given the expansion of tertiary education, the prospect of higher education of some sort awaits most senior high graduates, but the falling off in motivation that Thøgersen witnessed has remained evident amongst those consigned to the vocational track (see Chapter 10).

This, then, in broad outline, is the treadmill of tests that Chinese students have faced throughout the Reform era. Some implications for curriculum and pedagogy have already been discussed in Chapter 6; likewise, some of the unintended consequences of attempts to reduce homework burdens and curtail the focus on testing are noted in our discussion of 'shadow education' in the next chapter. In what follows, we examine the mechanics – and politics – of the testing regime, with particular reference to the *gaokao*.

The politics of assessment

As noted in earlier chapters, conceptualisations of the teaching and learning process in China (as elsewhere in East Asia) have traditionally featured emphasis on 'correctness': factual, interpretative, behavioural and political; the supremacy of the authorised text; and the exemplary role of the teacher. These ideas, broadly shared by policymakers, teachers and parents, underpin an assessment regime that aspires to evaluate both academic mastery and moral-political orthodoxy. In this sense, post-'Liberation' Soviet templates, emphasising ideological conformity as well as scientific knowledge, mapped neatly onto earlier efforts at combining technological modernity with moral didacticism; Communism required a shift in political content, but not in pedagogical principles. Chinese Communism thus marries traditional notions of the ruler as 'father' and 'teacher' with technocratic modernism of the Soviet stamp. The 'Mantle of Heaven' – or of Historical Materialism – in conferring political legitimacy also implies the prerogative, or duty, to offer moral guidance.

During the Reform era, the Party has increasingly emphasised the meritocratic credentials of its leading cadres. Whether in the case of the largely Tsinghua-educated technocrats of the Hu–Wen era, or the Arts, Social Science and Law graduates more predominant under Xi and Li from 2012, senior leaders' educational qualifications have been highlighted as betokening fitness to rule (Bell 2015). This principle has been extended ever further down the rungs of the administrative ladder: the confirmation in office of the new state leadership in March 2013 was accompanied by media reports trumpeting plans to recruit 600,000 'college graduates' to serve as village cadres: scholar-officials for the twenty-first century.[2] Meanwhile, systems for evaluating state functionaries – including teachers – draw upon a long indigenous tradition, spanning imperial, Republican and Maoist periods, of standardised, numerically based practices for assessing people (Kipnis 2011, 151).

The 1977 decision to reinstate the *gaokao* signified the abandonment of radical Maoist attempts to remodel society, and the embrace instead of a tried and tested mechanism for enforcing social stability and ideological conformity. The supplanting of 'class background' and 'political behaviour' (widely seen as synonymous with *guanxi* or connections) with academic performance as the central selection criterion was immensely popular with intellectuals 'whose support was essential to the "Four Modernizations"' (Thøgersen 1991, 71). Vogel hails the 1977 intake as the first since 1949 to be selected on an entirely 'meritocratic' basis (2011, 206). There was little time to prepare the first post-Mao *gaokao*, scheduled for the winter of 1977, which was followed within months by examinations for the 1978 college intake; 1978 thus saw two cohorts embark on their higher education – the first in the spring, and the second in the autumn. The scramble for college entry between 1977 and 1979, when many *gaokao* entrants were young people 'sent down' during the Cultural Revolution, supplied a focus for energies that might otherwise have fuelled political dissent (which did indeed surface in the form of the 1978 'Democracy Wall' movement). However, the chances of success were slim: only 5.8 per cent of applicants were eventually able to enrol in 1977–8 (Vogel 2011, 206). And from 1980 onwards it became extremely difficult for formerly rusticated youths to compete with newly minted graduates of the key point high schools.

As we note in Chapters 3 and 10, an early priority for the post-Mao leadership was to avoid the overproduction of regular senior high graduates, precisely with the aim of limiting and stabilising demand for higher education. Vocationalisation of senior high schooling was promoted not just with the aim of promoting job-ready 'skills', but also (or primarily) in order to constrain credentialism and keep aspiration within the bounds of what the labour market could satisfy. The dramatic

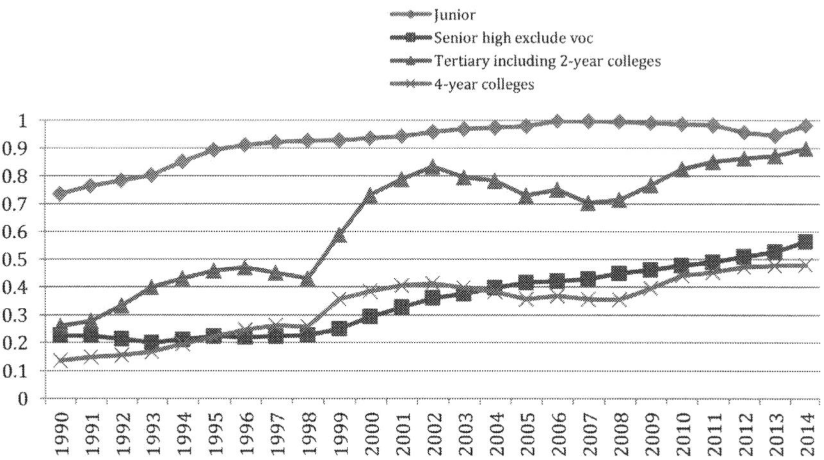

Figure 8.1 Enrolment rates for secondary (junior and senior) and tertiary education, 1990–2014.

Source: NBS (2015).

post-1998 expansion of the higher education system (see Figure 8.1) challenged this longstanding strategy; in Tsang's words, this was one of a number of 'heart-wrenching dislocations' caused by sudden, unheralded shifts in education policy (2000). It was followed by a significant growth of regular senior high schooling, and a rise in *gaokao* candidates' prospects of attending college. While the vocationalisation drive subsequently resumed (after a brief hiatus), early twenty-first century Chinese society thus acquired just that politically combustible cocktail of rampant credentialism and graduate under-employment that twentieth-century policymakers had long striven to avoid (see Chapter 10).

The *gaokao*

Assessment typically creates a 'backwash' effect on curriculum and pedagogy, but contemporary Chinese schools are subject to a veritable backwash tsunami, with the *gaokao* at its epicentre. Although the *gaokao*'s role within the education system as a whole has remained essentially unaltered, there have been significant changes both to its administration and to syllabus content. Until 2003, it was a truly national examination, in that students across the country took precisely the same question papers at precisely the same time. Exceptions to this rule were Shanghai and Guangdong, which from the late 1980s were allowed to set their own papers. For logistical, financial and political reasons, in the early 2000s more and more provinces followed this path. But before discussing such reforms, we first examine those features of the *gaokao* that have remained broadly constant throughout the post-Mao era.

The *gaokao* syllabus generally consists of a compulsory component taken by all students, and further papers to be taken by applicants for science and engineering or for arts and humanities courses. The compulsory element has always included tests of Chinese Language, Mathematics and a foreign language – generally English (though Japanese, Russian or French are sometimes offered as alternatives) (see Chapter 6). In the 1980s and 1990s, all applicants were also required to sit a Politics paper, but from 2002, when the *gaokao* syllabus was revised (following revisions to the senior high curriculum), some regions dropped this requirement for applicants in the science stream (though science students were still required to take Politics classes during the first two years of senior high school, preparatory to the *huikao* – see below). As various provinces began setting their own versions of the *gaokao*, minor variations emerged in the non-compulsory component of the examination, but the pattern remains broadly similar across the country. In 2013, it was announced that the foreign language paper would be formally dropped from the core syllabus, but the practical effect of this may prove negligible, since universities retain the power to require students to demonstrate foreign language competence through other tests such as TOEFL or IELTS.

Ever since 1977, question papers for all public examinations – the *zhongkao* as well as the *gaokao* – have been compiled through a system known as *fengbi mingti*, or 'closed question setting'. The use of a question bank system, whereby questions are selected randomly from a secure database, has never been attempted, perhaps because of concerns that any database might not remain secure. Instead, question papers are compiled annually by a group of teachers selected by the Examinations Centre (*kaoshi zhongxin*), whether at national or provincial level. Local 'offices for teaching and research' (*jiaoyan shi*) (see previous chapter) recommend teachers for this task. The fact that the *kaoshi zhongxin* is a bureaucratic body rather than an examination board run by educational professionals contributes to the difficulty of translating curricular change into assessment reform. Reflecting recognition of a need to shake up this system, the Education Ministry has increasingly called for a process of *mingti shehuihua* – literally, 'socialisation of question setting' – envisaging involvement of a more diverse range of institutions and organisations in the setting of examinations (changes to English testing are one example of this).[3] However, what this might mean in practice has yet to be spelt out.

The question-setting team, or *mingti xiaozu*, typically consists of teachers from key schools, subject representatives from local *jiaoyan shi*, and academics – the same groups routinely called upon to advise on curriculum or textbook development. Once appointed, they are incarcerated for over six months in the comfortable surroundings of a dedicated *kaoshi zhongxin* hostel, guarded by a detachment of the People's Armed Police (PAP). The fact that few are willing to undertake this ordeal more than once affects the consistency of question papers from year to year. The process of printing and transporting the papers is also overseen by the PAP; public transport is never used. The setting of public examinations is thus conducted with all the discipline and secrecy of a military campaign.

Its gatekeeping role in relation to higher education has rendered the *gaokao* an important tool for maintaining social and political stability – not least as regards the integration of 'ethnic minorities'. In the early post-Mao years, a drastic fall in the proportion of minority students entering university put pressure on officials to address an issue seen as threatening to inter-ethnic harmony and stability (Henze 1984, 151). Students from officially designated minority ethnicities (*shaosu minzu*) were entitled to take a special version of the examination in their own language. Those who take this 'ethnic' (*minkaomin*) track generally attend *minzu* colleges or universities that feature courses on ethnic cultures and languages, but do not offer a fully comprehensive range of disciplines. On the other hand, minority applicants who take the standard *gaokao* (*minkaohan*) in Chinese can enter regular universities with a lower score than Han students. As Leibold puts it, 'the current system propels minority communities in the direction of a dual form of alienation: forcing them to choose between ethnic segregation via the *minkaomin* pathway or impact integration via the *minkaohan* pathway' (2014, 317). The preferential terms on which minorities are entitled to enter college have meanwhile given rise to vehement complaints, particularly since the Tibet and Xinjiang protests of 2008–9, that they are being 'spoilt' by the government. Reactive nationalism amongst Han 'angry youth' (*fenqing*) has produced growing calls for college entrance procedures to be 'equalized', removing what some see as unfair minority 'privileges' (see Leibold 2014). Responding to such criticisms, Zhang defends the special admissions arrangements for minority students, citing the precedent of 'affirmative action' in the USA; but he argues for a broadening of the criteria on which assistance is offered to underprivileged groups, suggesting that factors such as family income be considered, as well as ethnicity (2011).

While the bar for college entry has thus been lowered (in some respects) for minorities, for another group – women – it has been selectively raised. Media reports have pointed to numerous instances of universities seeking to limit admissions of women, especially in fields where a preponderance of female students is seen as potentially detrimental to state interests (Fincher 2014). At police and military universities, for example, the practice of requiring much higher *gaokao* scores from female applicants appears 'particularly entrenched'. Meanwhile, at the Shanghai International Studies University, scores required in 2012 for admission to courses in Hebrew, Arabic, Ukrainian, Korean and Russian were lower for male students, allegedly because administrators believed that 'Arabic nations [and others] don't want to deal with women'. In 2012, the China University of Political Science and Law, in Beijing, required a score of 632 points from women applicants for science courses, but only 588 points from their male counterparts (Sharma 2013). Fincher (2014) depicts this as part of a much broader pattern of institutionalised discrimination against women in urban China. How long such differential entrance requirements have existed is unclear, but women have been consistently disadvantaged in access to higher education throughout the post-1949 era (Zhou *et al.* 1998).

Of broader significance for the *gaokao*'s role as an instrument of socio-political engineering is the system of provincial quotas with which it is associated. From the 1950s (and indeed before), national-level institutions were concentrated in certain regions: the Northeast (where much of China's heavy industry was located), Wuhan, Xi'an and (to a lesser extent) Guangdong – but above all in Shanghai and Beijing. By contrast, Shandong hosts only one national-level institution (the China Maritime University), as does Anhui (the Chinese University of Science and Technology, established in the 1980s). Amongst the more populous inland (*neidi*) provinces, Henan, Shanxi and Hunan have no top-level national universities, and Sichuan relatively few in relation to its huge population ('top-level' here denoting institutions in the '985 Project' – see Chapters 11 and 12). In some cases, cities were deliberately overlooked in the post-'Liberation' distribution of academic spoils: thus Nanjing and Chongqing, capitals of the defeated Kuomintang regime, were originally chosen to host no key national institutions (see Chapter 11).

In theory, this uneven geographic distribution of top universities could be counterbalanced simply by allocating places to the highest-scoring *gaokao* candidates nationally. However, in practice provinces or municipalities with the highest concentrations of prestigious universities have always been allowed to reserve places for local students (i.e. those holding the local *hukou*). Distributive inequality was thus a feature of the *gaokao* system from the beginning, but was further exacerbated by expansion and marketisation during the 1990s. Previously, student numbers – and hence entry quotas – were tightly regulated by the Ministry of Education's Planning Division (*jihua chu*).[4] After the system was reorganised and enrolments expanded in the late 1990s (see Chapter 12), more authority to determine quotas for provincial-level institutions was in practice ceded to provincial authorities. This effectively involved backroom negotiations amongst provincial governments and the Ministry; as Long Denggao of Tsinghua University put it, '[The quota] is usually a compromise provincial governments make among themselves' (quoted in Fu 2013).

Similarly opaque were the criteria used for setting quotas at those top universities under the direct authority of the Ministry, such as Peking, Tsinghua and Fudan. The higher quotas for local students at such institutions were sometimes explained by reference to the substantial support – in the form of money or land – that they receive from local governments, and hence local taxpayers. But they also receive very considerable funding from the central government – amounting, in the case of Fudan, to 44 per cent of its annual budget for 2011 (Fu 2013). In the early 2000s, officials and parents from Guangdong Province repeatedly voiced complaints over the small size of the quota allotted to Cantonese students for entry to the country's most prestigious universities, Peking and Tsinghua. In 2012, these universities took 84 students out of every 10,000 Beijingers sitting the *gaokao*, but only two from every 10,000 Cantonese (Fu 2013). It was pointed out that the number of successful applicants from Guangdong (population 105 million) was more or less the same as those from the three key point high schools affiliated to Beijing Normal University.[5]

Since 2008, the central government has nonetheless sought to rectify inter-provincial inequality in quotas for access to four-year university programmes.

The *People's Daily* claimed in 2016 that a 'cooperative project to increase college quotas in central and western regions' (*zhihuan zhongxibu diqu zhaosheng xiezuo jihua*) had closed the 'regional gap' in admissions chances from '17 per cent' in 2007 to '5 per cent' in 2015 – with an effect equivalent to building 'forty new universities' in these regions with the capacity to enrol 5,000 students per year (Zhang and Sun 2016). However, adjusting quotas for access to four-year college courses does not equate to equalising opportunities for admission to the top tier of elite universities (see Chapter 12). The shift away from blatant discrimination in the allocation of provincial quotas seems unlikely to detract from privileges of class, wealth and urban residency, underpinned by the concentration of key point senior high schools and other educational facilities in cities. In particular, the premium attaching to the right to attend senior high school and, by the same token, to sit the *gaokao* in metropolitan regions such as Beijing, Shanghai or Tianjin remains considerable.[6]

Reform of the **gaokao** *system*

As noted above, criticisms of the rigidity of public examinations have been voiced ever since their reinstatement in the late 1970s, intensifying with debates over 'quality education' (*suzhi jiaoyu*) from the 1990s. But despite the system's intensely competitive and intellectually stifling nature, the political risks attendant on any sweeping change have restricted the scope of reform. Adjustments have generally involved introducing parallel or additional forms of assessment designed to garner extra revenue for institutions, to capture varieties of 'talent' that slip through the conventional net, or do both at once. The former, revenue-raising, function was served by the introduction in the mid-1980s of a 'twin-track' system for college entrance, enabling institutions to recruit off-quota students for a fee agreed with their 'work unit' (see Chapter 11). Meanwhile, another group of applicants afforded a leg-up over the *gaokao* hurdle were those categorised as 'specially talented' in the sports or the arts (*tezhangsheng*) – recruited, in the manner of American football scholars, to represent universities in inter-collegial competitions. Originally a rather narrowly defined category, the definition of *tezhangsheng* would later be controversially expanded.

Undoubtedly the most important administrative reform to the *gaokao* system over the past thirty years involved the introduction of distinct forms of the examination set locally (at provincial or municipal level) rather than centrally in Beijing. The introduction of plural *gaokao* roughly tracked the diversification of the school curriculum; Shanghai and Guangdong were among the first regions granted limited autonomy over curricula and textbooks in the late 1980s (rights extended to other regions only after the national curriculum reform of 2001 – see Chapter 6); they were also the first to be granted authority to set their own question papers (*zizhumingti*). Beijing was granted *zizhumingti* authority in 2004, followed by 16 other provinces in subsequent years – though from 2014, all but the five regions with the highest concentrations of top universities reverted to the unified *gaokao*.[7] The stock justification advanced for this reform invoked the increasing diversity of Chinese society. It was claimed that the experience and outlook of city kids in tower blocks were just too different from those of their counterparts down on the farm or up in the mountains to make it practicable or 'fair' to test all students in the same way (Ako 2009, 151). And as with the pursuit of wealth, so with that of educational 'quality', it was regarded as axiomatic that those capable of advancing faster should be urged onward.

But the particular alacrity of Beijing and other 'advanced' regions in embracing the *zizhumingti* reform was also related to growing public criticism of differential *gaokao* quotas. In August 2001, three Qingdao students attempted to sue the Ministry of Education in the Supreme People's Court over 'discrimination', on the grounds that they had been denied admission to top Beijing universities that had admitted local students with lower *gaokao* scores (Zhang 2015).[8] The fact that *gaokao* scores could easily be compared across different provinces – something facilitated by growing Internet use – was becoming acutely embarrassing to officials in more privileged regions. In 2001, Beijing students could gain entry to undergraduate programmes in key point universities with a *gaokao* score of 488; Shandong students needed to score 607 (sina.com 2001; see also Zhang 2011). Following the shift to *zizhumingti*, officials could claim that scores across provinces were not strictly comparable, even if the fact that provinces continued to rank their students on the same points-based scale meant that inter-provincial comparisons of the difficulty of university entry continued to be widely circulated and discussed (see Ako 2009, 150).

Meanwhile, top universities were steadily granted the power to engage in 'autonomous' or 'independent' recruitment (*zizhu zhaosheng* or *duli zhaosheng*). The Higher Education Law of 1998 heralded this shift, though in practice little changed until, in 2003, 22 'pilot' universities were granted the freedom to allocate 5 per cent of their admissions quotas as they wished. By 2010, this right had been extended to 90 'elite' institutions (Economist 2016). The rationale advanced for this move related to a sense that the rigidity and narrowness of the *gaokao* was frustrating the implementation of 'quality'-oriented curricular reforms. As a professor from the Dalian Naval Academy put it, 'In an age of social transformation, a major concern in the educational field is the inconsistency between tertiary graduate supply and the diversified social requirements of specialized workers suited to particular lines of work' (Yu 2011, 707). The *duli zhaosheng* initiative was thus ostensibly designed to recruit, through a combination of school recommendations, written tests and interviews, 'specially talented' students (*tezhangsheng*) whose skills might be overlooked in the standard admissions process. In both form and rationale, this procedure closely paralleled Japan's 'Admissions Office' (AO) tests, introduced at around the same time. Applicants thus selected were subsequently required to pass only the most basic level of the *gaokao* (the *yi ben xian*) to qualify for admission.[9]

The task of independently determining their own admissions requirements, and setting their own tests, imposed a considerable burden on academics and administrators (as it does in Japan). From 2011 China's elite universities therefore decided to pool their resources and establish university 'alliances' that would collaborate in devising written tests for the *duli zhaosheng* route. In addition to any burden-sharing benefits, these alliances also bestowed a certain safety in numbers, enabling individual universities to deflect mounting popular criticism of their 'independent' recruitment practices. The growing controversy was documented by Li Xuelin (2011), who identified three 'stages' – from initial approval, to growing doubt and questioning, to outright criticism by 2011, the year the new 'alliances' were established. A *Beiyue* grouping of prominent comprehensive universities was led by Peking University, a *Huayue* association specialising in Maths and Science was fronted by Tsinghua,[10] while a third league, the *Zhuoyue Lianmeng*, featuring institutes of engineering, was led by the Harbin University of Military Engineering (Yu 2011). Universities within each association collaborated in setting their own standardised tests, which applicants would take before being invited to interview. At their interviews, they were asked to prepare a short presentation on a given topic, and then quizzed on this by a panel of academics.[11]

But the introduction of new admissions tracks for elite universities was plagued by problems of corruption and poor transparency. The *duli zhaosheng* arrangements typically involved agreements with certain key point high schools to admit a proportion of their top graduates. By 2010, institutions allowed to operate 'independent' admissions policies enrolled over 30 per cent of their intake in this way, and in the case of Fudan almost 60 per cent (Economist 2016). But dependence on political favour, added to the weakness of legal oversight, left institutions highly vulnerable to pressure from the well connected, and susceptible to corruption. In 2013, a scandal broke over allegations that Renmin University, in Beijing, was charging up to one million yuan for admission via the *duli zhaosheng* channel – with the Dean of the Education School and the Head of the University Admissions Office among those implicated. In 2015, the government capped quotas for universities using non-*gaokao* routes at 5 per cent of overall admissions (Economist 2016).

The fate of these reforms illustrates both the difficulties in establishing a trusted alternative to the standard *gaokao*, and the related challenge of implementing 'quality-oriented' curricular reforms that emphasise analytical skills over memorisation. Analytical skills, in contrast to memorised facts or formulae, are not readily susceptible to assessment through 'objective' tests with 'marker-proof' marking schemes detailing single correct answers to each question. Testing them relies on the qualitative judgement of assessors who themselves possess a capacity for independent reasoning, along with a professional ethos that mandates its exercise. However, the bureaucratic system of 'examination centres' (described above) prioritises secrecy and control over professional expertise and transparency; professional educators are co-opted to help set the papers, but never trusted to direct the entire process. Moreover, the *duli zhaosheng* experiment demonstrates the problems involved in handing academics such authority when their autonomy is politically compromised. Given the weakness of civil society and the rule of law, and a correspondingly weak sense of teaching or academia as a self-governing profession (see previous chapter), the established, rigid, bureaucratic assessment process remains more popularly trusted than any 'independent' alternative. Long Denggao's observation that the *gaokao* quota system is 'just a microcosm of the central government's attempt to control academia' applies to the system of public assessment as a whole (quoted in Fu 2013).

Other reforms to the public assessment system

The **huikao** *and 'high school academic proficiency test'*

In addition to efforts to alter the *gaokao* itself, or to open up alternative routes into higher education, there have also been attempts to introduce new forms of assessment at lower rungs of the educational ladder. Originally billed as a high school graduation certificate, the *huikao* was first piloted in Shanghai from 1985, and then implemented nationally from the early 1990s (SEC 1990). It was designed to mitigate what many officials and educational experts saw as the tendency of *gaokao* 'backwash' to lead to a narrowing of the senior high school curriculum. All students – whether intending to take the 'sciences' or 'humanities' version of the *gaokao* – were therefore to be tested in ten subject areas. In practice, however, the *huikao* was generally treated as one more hurdle on the route to the *gaokao*. Results were widely used to stream students for *gaokao* entry. In some schools it was taken at the end of the first senior high grade, thus leaving the final two years clear for an exclusive focus on *gaokao* preparation.

In the aftermath of the curriculum reforms of 2000–1 (implemented at senior high level from 2004), the non-selective function of the *huikao* was re-emphasised. As part of efforts to dampen *gaokao* competition (and thus promote 'quality education'), the *huikao*'s status as distinctive qualification was stressed, and it was announced that henceforth anyone – even those who had never attended high school – could take it, and that resits would be permitted. At the same time, the Ministry took steps to discourage the practice of resitting the *gaokao*, and sought to ban high schools from running (highly lucrative) *fu du ban* classes for students preparing to retake it. However, the value of the *huikao* as an independent qualification – always limited, except for those, mostly rural boys, aspiring to join the army (or certain state enterprises) – was further undercut by the rapid expansion of higher education from the late 1990s. By making college entry a realisable goal for more and more regular senior high students, this inevitably reinforced perceptions of the *huikao* as simply a way-marker on the road to the *gaokao*. In the early 2000s, a number of provinces either abolished the *huikao* entirely, or delegated its administration to city or county level (Li and Yan 2012, 542).

From 2005, anxieties that this was causing an erosion of 'quality' at senior high level in some regions were one factor prompting the Ministry to contemplate further reforms. Between 2007 and 2011, the *huikao* was supplanted in most regions by a new high school 'academic proficiency test' (*xueye shuiping ceshi*), loosely based on America's 'National Assessment of Educational

Progress' (Wang and Liao 2011). The aim of ensuring that students attained minimum proficiency in a broad range of subjects remained, but tests in specific subjects might be more or less demanding for students in 'science' and 'humanities' streams. The link between these proficiency tests and the *gaokao* also became more explicit. In 2014, the Ministry announced that the range of subjects tested would be expanded to fourteen, and that students would then be allowed to submit results for three of these in their applications to college – a move hailed as promoting curricular diversity and encouraging students to pursue their personal interests (Jing 2014).

Diversity was also a feature of the system for administering these tests, responsibility for which (as for the *gaokao* by the early 2000s) lay with the various provinces. Indeed, 'diversity' was increasingly invoked as a mantra: when Shanghai issued its own plans for implementing the new tests, it hailed them as providing a baseline for 'diversified university recruitment' (Cheng *et al.* 2009, 16).[12] In practice, the standards expected or required of students in particular subjects may vary considerably between, say, Shanghai and Henan. Whereas the diversification of the *gaokao* system in the early 2000s was linked to political sensitivities over the inter-provincial comparability of scores, the lack of comparability of *xueye shuiping ceshi* was ostensibly a more technical issue (related to the lack of question banks or a functioning system for standardising test papers). A shift to grading students by broad categories (A to E) rather than numerically was meanwhile explained as a means of reducing their 'stress' (Jing 2014), though how this would work in the absence of similar reforms to the *gaokao* remained unclear. Unlike the *gaokao*, the *xueye shuiping ceshi* adopts a less rigid testing format, with the aim of encouraging students to display 'innovation' and 'creativity'; by the same token, responsibility for setting these tests lies far more with professional educators than bureaucrats. It remains uncertain how much 'diversity' and 'flexibility' will increase as a result. However, to the extent that it does, the effects may be liberating for teachers and students in urban key point schools, but daunting for their counterparts elsewhere.

Experiments in **zhongkao** *reform – the case of Shenzhen*

Ever since the mid-1980s, various reforms, economic or educational, have been piloted in the several coastal 'Special Economic Zones' (SEZ). Shanghai has often been at the forefront of educational experimentation, but after the curriculum reforms of 2001, the authorities in Shenzhen sought to assume a vanguard role in the new drive for curricular 'integration'. This involved reforms to the local *zhongkao* syllabus, abolishing the old subject-based papers in History, Geography, Physics, Chemistry and so forth, and replacing them with just two 'integrated' papers in natural sciences and social sciences (in addition to the papers in Maths, Chinese and English that are compulsory for all students). But after ten years of this integrated approach, in 2011 it was abandoned, and conventional subject-based papers reinstated. The fate of this initiative illustrates the difficulties of implementing sweeping curricular reform in the absence of fundamental change to the capstone of the schooling system – the *gaokao* syllabus.

As a sub-provincial entity, Shenzhen did not attain the power to set its own version of the *gaokao* after 2002. It did, however, possess authority to reform arrangements for allocating senior high school places, so it was at this level that officials focused their efforts. But teachers complained that the 'integrated' format of the examination did not correspond to the school curriculum or to textbooks. For example, as we noted in Chapter 6, even when content on physics, chemistry and biology was contained within one set of textbook covers, it was still presented separately, rather than in a properly integrated fashion. Another source of complaint was that, since Shenzhen's espousal of curricular integration differed from practice elsewhere, teachers found it more difficult to compare notes or discuss best practice with counterparts from other provinces, or elsewhere in Guangdong (Yi 2012). More to the point, however, was the perceived mismatch between the new *zhongkao* syllabus and the curriculum at senior high level, where *gaokao* preparation remained the overwhelming focus. Hence the eventual 2011 decision to 'raise the white flag' to the *gaokao* and revert to a conventional subject-based syllabus. A Shenzhen University academic opined that what ultimately mattered was whether the syllabus addressed the needs and demands of local students: 'If 90 per cent of people are focused on the *gaokao*, then curriculum reform should focus on preparation for the *gaokao* exam, and satisfy the demands of the citizenry' (Yi 2012).

Local efforts to reform the system for allocating senior secondary places were not limited to changes to *zhongkao* syllabuses. Shenzhen's Education Bureau also experimented with a move to the sort of 'examination plus quota' system that Kipnis describes in Shandong's Zouping County. Introduced in Zouping during the 1990s, this aimed to promote educational 'quality', while ensuring that even students from the poorest junior secondary schools had a chance of entering elite senior high schools. While initially effective in reducing inter-school competition, the Zouping reform never reduced competition between students – since *zhongkao* results still determined 'which students at a given junior middle school received the quota-determined places to attend senior middle school' (Kipnis 2011, 67). And competition amongst schools re-emerged during the 2000s, following the expansion of senior high school places (itself a knock-on effect of the expansion of higher education). This rendered the quota system less significant – since all above-quota places were allocated on the basis of examination scores alone (i.e. in the old way). In Shenzhen, however, not just the nature of reform, but the sudden and arbitrary manner of its introduction, provoked resistance and protests. Given that parents begin planning (and investing) for examination competition years in advance, there is huge sensitivity to any shifting of the goalposts.

Admissions to junior secondary school – the experience of Beijing

As already noted, from 2006 public examinations were formally outlawed at the primary–junior secondary interface. The achievement of universal compulsory education had supposedly eliminated the need for selection at this stage, and already in 1996 the State Council had proclaimed strict limits on schools' ability to select students (either on the basis of 'special abilities' or 'school choice fees'). In 1998, Beijing's Education Bureau announced its move to a computerised system for allocating junior secondary places (*da pai ban*), and imposed its own stringent restrictions on the recruitment of *tezhangsheng* or 'three good' (*san hao*) students by public schools,[13] and on the charging of 'school choice fees' at this level (Ren and Yang 2013).

However, in practice selection in some form or other has remained widespread at this stage. Competition for admission to key point senior high schools still begins at primary level, as students compete for admission to the 'best' junior secondary schools that promise better prospects of testing into a top high school. One widespread ruse from the 1990s to early 2000s was to blur the distinction between 'public' and 'private' schooling by establishing *minban* 'branch' schools or 'schools within schools' (*xiao zhong xiao*) (Ren and Yang 2013; for more on this practice, see the following chapter). To the extent that a school could claim to be non-public, it could circumvent the restrictions on selective admissions. But more fundamentally, attempts to stamp out competition for junior secondary school places – by one means or another – have proven highly problematic in the context of wide variations in the quality or reputation of schools at this level.

Although the existence of 'key point' junior secondary schools is not formally acknowledged, their existence is universally known. Education bureaux prize them as models of teaching 'excellence' and as crucial to a district's competitiveness in the education 'market'; officials are not likely to give them up or level them down willingly. As Yang Dongping argues, the core problem is that, having long operated a system of key point schools from primary level upwards (barring the hiatus of the Cultural Revolution), China has institutionalised a system in which particular schools attract the best teachers, the best students, and higher levels of funding (as much as three times more than 'ordinary' schools in the same district) (quoted in Ren and Yang 2013, 44–5). In the Beijing districts with the highest concentrations of key point junior secondary schools (Haidian, Xicheng and Dongcheng), Ren and Yang's report for the *Caixin* magazine found that well under half of places were allocated through the official *da pai ban* system. Similar conditions were common in other major cities, and increasingly prevalent in smaller urban centres.

This left ample scope for continuing selection of students. A particularly widespread example involved the recruitment of 'outstanding' students through *zhan keng ban* – special classes originally established by some key junior secondary schools during the 1980s (often in collaboration with tutorial schools or other organisations) to select and train primary students for participation in 'Mathematical Olympiads'. Students were tested for admission to these classes, and subjected to regular further testing thereafter. Between 2003 and 2011, the Beijing authorities on no less than three occasions officially announced the banning of the use of 'Olympiad' scores as a criterion for selection into junior secondary schools. In 2012, primary schools in Haidian District were compelled to close their special Maths Olympiad preparatory classes. But pupils interviewed by Ren and Yang confided that the classes had reopened shortly afterwards under different names (such as 'hobby maths' – *quwei suxue*), teaching identical content (2013, 46). Some schools responded to a ban on testing final-year primary students by testing them one year earlier – in the fifth rather than the sixth grade. Further methods of bypassing the prohibition on selective testing included: informal recommendations from primary schools; special agreements with public 'work units' (*danwei*) to admit their employees' children; the recruitment of students demonstrating 'outstanding' ability in areas (e.g. music, sports) claimed as a school 'specialty'; informal recommendations from the local government (e.g. head of the Education Bureau or mayor); or automatic promotion from an affiliated primary school. The reporters wrote of 'tacit understandings' between officials and key point schools camouflaging the continuation of selective practices 'under the banner of "educational fairness"' (44).

In a development that ostensibly had little to do with selection into junior secondary school, from 2007, standardised testing of Grade 5 students (those in the penultimate year of primary schooling) (*wu nianji tongce*) was introduced in many regions (on the model of the OECD's PISA tests). This was billed as a means of assessing the performance of schools rather than students. The tests were introduced on top of, or in addition to, existing examinations, and their likely implications for teaching and learning were not widely canvassed; this was seen as exercise in bureaucratic monitoring. As such, the results were meant to be confidential, but competitive pressures intervened. Principals knew where their own schools ranked in the results, and those ranking highly were unlikely to maintain secrecy. The stakes involved for schools (and teachers, often awarded merit pay on the basis of these results) often led them to place considerable pressure on pupils, in some cases to the extent of 'gaming' the test by seeking to exclude certain groups.[14] Primary schools and some private tutorial centres also established informal arrangements with certain 'key' junior secondary schools to 'recommend' their highest-achieving students for admission.[15] It appears that the results of the *wu nianji tongce* were used for this kind of purpose: in 2011, a Beijing parents' website claimed that, in Haidian and other municipal districts, scores in this test were typically given a 60 per cent weighting in the allocation of places in key point junior secondary schools (Ran 2011).

Although parents may grumble about the competitive pressures to which their children are subjected, many will tolerate them if it seems that everyone is more or less in the same boat. For precisely this reason, some measures ostensibly aimed at dampening competition in order to promote educational 'quality' are especially unpopular with more underprivileged parents (see also the following chapter).[16] As we discuss below, a return to open selection would for many be preferable to a system that can be gamed by the wealthy or well-connected. As the *Caixin* reporters summed up the situation in 2013:

> Those who have power use connections, those who have money go abroad to pursue their education, those with no money study hard for the Maths Olympiads; those with no money, power or energy go to the back of the queue. The psychology of parents becomes warped, and so does that of their children.
>
> (47)

Power, privilege and 'school choice'

Much controversy in the early 2000s over the role of money, connections or other factors in subverting the standard mechanisms for allocating school places centred on the concept of 'school choice' (*ze xiao*) (a term borrowed from the North American education policy lexicon). While 'diversification' of assessment practices at all levels benefited some residents of major urban centres, others found it much more difficult to take advantage of new 'choices' created by reform. A similar pattern has been observed in the USA, where Witte argued that voucher schemes, if universally applied rather than specifically targeted, would tend to entrench social privilege, disproportionately benefiting those with higher 'social capital' (2001).[17] In China, some have noted the prevalence of 'reform phobia' *(gaige kongju zheng)* amongst rural residents and poorer families, many of whom see standardised examinations as their one and only opportunity for social mobility (see Zeng 2009; Yang 2014 and the following chapter).

Once educational inequality has taken root in a society, it tends to prove stubbornly tenacious – the British private schooling system being one notorious case in point (Perkin 1989, 450). China's most wealthy and powerful groups have proved similarly reluctant to surrender their established educational privileges. An emergent class divide was evident in the findings of a 2009 survey on 'school choice' (Zeng 2009). This compared the transitions from primary through to senior high school in 'tier one' cities (provincial capitals) and 'tier two' or 'regional' cities (*diquji chengshi*), as well as parental attitudes towards different arrangements for allocating school places. Those in major cities were more critical of the pressures attendant upon reliance on high-stakes public examinations in allocating junior secondary places. By contrast, their counterparts in smaller cities were somewhat more supportive of selective public examinations at every level: 42 per cent of parents in second-tier cities expressed a preference for open public testing as a means of allocating places in junior middle schools, compared with 36 per cent in provincial capitals. Conversely, support for 'market mechanisms' (i.e. payment of 'school choice fees') was higher in the larger cities. However, the policy promoted by the central government – of 'zoning' junior secondary schools and abolishing choice and selection – was opposed by all but a tiny minority of parents. In other words, despite different attitudes to the role of money or 'merit' in allocating school places, few seemed to trust the state to guarantee a uniformly high standard of public schooling for all.

The following chapter on 'marketisation' discusses the role of money in distributing educational opportunity, especially since the early 1990s; but other significant sources of educational privilege with earlier roots have persisted. Employees of large state work units (*danwei*) have traditionally been entitled to send their children to attached kindergartens, primary and junior secondary schools. Although such rights have been whittled down since the 1990s (see Chapters 3 and 4), 'institutional power' (*jigou de liliang*) remains a significant determinant of educational opportunity. For example, the child of a BNU professor is entitled to free attendance at the university's attached kindergarten, whereas access to this much-sought-after preschool facility cost around 300,000 yuan per year (as of 2013) for the few 'outsiders' granted admission. In another longstanding practice, some *danwei* or companies lacking their own educational facilities also contract particular schools to admit the children of their employees on a preferential basis – sometimes collaborating with local authorities to establish 'jointly constructed' (*gongjian*) schools (Kipnis 2011 cites examples of this practice in Zouping – e.g. p. 30). In Beijing, for example, such agreements grant preferential access for the children of ministry officials to BNU's kindergarten and affiliated schools. However, children from a particular *danwei* typically still have to compete with each other to secure a place and, if admitted, their parents must still pay substantial fees.[18]

It would be a mistake to see this institutionalised 'unfairness' as signifying a descent from some halcyon era of unsullied meritocracy – family ties, political connections and work unit privileges have always given some an advantage in the race for educational credentials. Commenting on Bo Xilai's entry into Peking University in 1977, Garnaut notes that while Bo 'relied in part on his father pulling strings,' he later 'made it known that he, unlike Xi Jinping,' had also sat for the *gaokao*; such a procedure was not then obligatory for the sons and daughters of party leaders (2012, 29). However, what distinguishes the exercise of 'school choice' in the early twentieth century from the operation of privilege in the early Reform period is the pervasive power of money. This is not only a matter of straightforward bribery and corruption. Those with money can move district, pay for private schooling, have their children tutored in 'special talents' (*tezhangsheng*), tap key social networks, or even purchase a new *hukou*.

Thus, while the multiplication of entrance routes has often been justified as a means of identifying 'quality' students overlooked by conventional assessment methods, its social implications are to widen access to the most prestigious schools for those with wealth and connections, while narrowing it for the rest. The erosion of the significance of conventional public examinations at the key transition points may disadvantage those least equipped to navigate newer, less familiar and less transparent paths to educational advancement. This is one reason why those who end up at the bottom of the educational heap, in the universally derided vocational sector, derive overwhelmingly from poor, non-professional, less-educated and generally under-privileged backgrounds (see Chapter 10).

Conclusion

The era of mass higher education has arrived in urban (if not rural) China, but what has this meant for the nature of college-preparatory schooling, the operation of the examinations system, and equity in educational access? The experience of Japan offers a useful comparative benchmark in this regard. As the education system there hit the limits of quantitative expansion by the 1990s, policymakers introduced measures aimed at qualitative improvement. *Yutori kyouiku* ('relaxed education') was promoted with the intention of ratcheting down examination pressure and affording students more time and space to think, explore and develop 'skills' of creativity and critical analysis (see Chapter 6). This was linked to 'quasi-privatisation policies such as "school choice"', promoted as rendering the system more flexible and responsive to diverse student aptitudes and parental aspirations (Kariya 2011, 263). However, elite universities essentially maintained their rigid and narrowly framed testing practices, even as less prestigious colleges admitted almost all who could pay the fees. Wealthier, more educated and 'aspirational' parents, perceiving that public schooling was becoming a less effective preparation for college-entrance examinations, therefore increasingly opted to send their children to private high schools. The resulting 'bright flight', along with the growth of shadow education, raised new barriers to social mobility for those from poorer backgrounds. 'Japanese education,' Kariya concludes, 'thus reveals the effects on social equality of expanding education opportunities through privatisation' (264).

The following chapter analyses processes of marketisation and privatisation in the Chinese context, and their effects on educational opportunity. The essential story here is one of growing disparities in economic, social and cultural capital contributing to, and feeding off, educational inequalities. A mid-1990s study of 'educational stratification' concluded that recent economic growth and social transformation had favoured the children of high-rank cadres and professionals, residents of large cities, and men more than women' (Zhou *et al.* 1998, 217). This pattern has persisted as wider inequality has worsened. Focusing on the role of exams in determining educational opportunity for the rural poor, Hannum *et al.* (2011) argue that these 'reinforce inequalities observed in other stages of educational transition', and reflect communal as well as family disadvantage. They also found that 'cultural capital', in the form of fathers' education, correlated strongly with students' prospects of examination success. A 2011 study of rural Anhui found children from poorer and less-educated families likely to be less ambitious and adventurous in their choice of college, and more prone to fall off the ladder of educational opportunity at an early stage. Changes to the admissions procedures of key point junior and senior secondary schools seemed to further disadvantage 'working class students' who were 'very unlikely to get into a key school since their parents lack [a] strong social network … even if they were willing to pay the additional fees' (Gao 2011, 188). A realistic assessment of their chances was leading many rural students to drop out of junior secondary school – as many as a third in some provinces (Yi *et al* 2012 – see next chapter).

As we noted in Chapter 3.4, the central government has in recent years sought to tighten controls on 'school choice' and selective assessment during the compulsory phase. In March 2015, the Ministry of Education announced a stricter enforcement of school 'zoning' rules, stipulating that from September all primary and 90 per cent of secondary students would have to attend the school nearest to their home. Although this repeated previous proclamations, there were signs that schools and parents were taking this announcement more seriously. One such sign was a sharp rise in house prices near key point schools, reaching as much as ten times the average per square metre in one Beijing district. This had the effect of 'reinforcing the schools' privileged intake by a different means' (Economist 2015).[19] Meanwhile, although tests for admission into primary and junior secondary schools have in theory been banned since 2006, they evidently continued in some form, in some areas, long after that date. The fundamental issue undermining measures to curb competition for school places is the 'self-reinforcing' status of key point institutions, and the government's continued sanctioning of glaring inequalities in the resourcing of different state schools.

The intensity of that competition, and its relationship with assessment practices, has also been in profound tension with calls since the 1990s for 'quality education', partly inspired by Japanese precedent. Lack of reform to examinations is attributable in part to inertia, but also reinforced by public suspicion of innovation. High-stakes, once-and-for-all public examinations assessing recall of facts or appliance of formulae are widely seen as 'fair' and 'objective'. Any move towards more subjective assessments of analytical skills or creativity would also conflict with the deep-rooted assumption that in matters moral as well as scientific there are 'correct answers'.

Perhaps most fundamentally, however, the existing system of assessment ultimately serves the imperative of social and political control. Replacing a bureaucratically operated system of public assessment with one answerable to autonomous educational professionals has been tried, to a limited extent, in some of the country's elite higher education institutions – only for the experiment to collapse amidst allegations of corruption and sleaze. But the weakness of trust in educators' professional ethos, or their capacity to govern themselves, is reinforced by weaknesses in civil society and the rule of law that are in turn largely attributable to political factors. It is hard for a Leninist party to credibly establish the concept of a self-regulating, autonomous profession. Then again, entrusting the operation of public examinations to autonomous professional bodies was never the practice of China's imperial rulers.

It is with that hallowed tradition that the regime has increasingly associated itself as it has sought to make meritocracy, more than Marxism, the basis of its legitimating ideology. The political importance that the meritocratic ideal has therefore assumed during the Reform era helps explain official anxiety to demonstrate commitment to promoting greater fairness in the allocation of school and college places. But China's experience also illustrates how a strong ideology of meritocracy can encourage an overweening sense of entitlement amongst those on whom educational success has bestowed power, wealth and status.

For this reason, Bell argues that the sustainability of a meritocratic system requires not only efforts to distribute educational opportunity more fairly, but also intensive moral instruction, particularly in the virtue of humility (2015). However, there is little sign of this amongst Chinese elites today. Instead, as we discussed in Chapter 6, the discourse of 'quality' or *suzhi* has if anything tended to naturalise and justify growing social stratification by class and residency. Meanwhile, the marketisation of education, and of society more broadly, has made it easier for the wealthy to purchase the appurtenances of meritocracy. It is to that process that we turn in the next chapter.

Notes

1 Some urban key point schools have been permitted to exempt themselves from these tests, but most schools are required to administer them.
2 This was a headline story in the *China Daily* on 15 March 2013. Such moves also served as make-work schemes for graduates facing increasingly uncertain employment prospects (see Chapter 12).
3 For example, Li and Yan (2012) suggest a possible role for private companies in 'professionalising' the assessment system.
4 One of the present authors (Zeng), seconded to the MoE's Planning Office (*jihua chu*) between 1996 and 2000, remembers a visit to Nanjing in 1998, during which a provincial education planning official complained bitterly about the Ministry's power to set quotas, and the 'unfair' constraints this placed on the capacity of universities in Nanjing to expand.
5 Henan students' chances of being admitted to Tsinghua or Peking were about the same as those from Guangdong, but the former were worse off, since Henan had just one '211 university' that would favour local applicants (see Chapters 11 and 12). According to Fu, the central government (as of 2013) was actually planning to invest less in higher education in Henan, and further raise the bar for local students hoping to attend top universities elsewhere.
6 One survival of the kind of manpower planning associated with the command economy is the priority accorded to different kinds or levels of universities in selecting students. 'Grade 1' universities take priority over Grades 2 and 3. But the top 'priority group' (*tiqianpi*) consists of 'professional' or specialist institutions (Normal Universities, universities of Forestry, Agriculture, etc.). BNU's best students tend to come through this route. The really confident senior high students who want to get into Peking or Tsinghua will not apply for the *tiqianpi* process. BNU is also a 'Grade 1' institution, but relatively few students will choose to list BNU or other specialist institutions in the standard category on their application form – where they can only list two 'Grade 1' universities.
7 Those five regions are Beijing, Shanghai, Tianjin, Zhejiang and Jiangsu. The reasons cited for the other 11 abandoning *zizhumingti* related to cost and the challenge of maintaining the quality of test papers (Yuan 2016).
8 The Supreme Court refused to take the case until it had been considered in lower courts – i.e. the local court in the area where the MOE is located; the students then decided (on 6 September) to withdraw their case.
9 The ultimate model for this approach is the entrance tests and interviews administered by elite Western universities such as Oxford or Cambridge.
10 *Beiyue* and *huayue* are puns on the Chinese terms for NATO and the Warsaw Pact – an allusion to the longstanding rivalry between Peking University (*Beida*) and Tsinghua. These alliances were also intended to assist their members in lobbying the government (as the UK's 'Russell Group' does).

11 In 2012, the first year in which these alliances operated, the standardised tests covered a range of subjects similar to those included in the *gaokao*. But in 2013, the range was drastically reduced: *Beiyue* only tested applicants for the sciences in Physics and Maths, and Arts and Humanities applicants in Maths and Languages; *Huayue* tested all students in 'Maths and Logic', and then either 'Exploring Physics' (*wuli tanjiu*) (for science students) or 'Reading and Expression' (*yuedu yu biaoda*) for the rest. By contrast, the *Zhuoyue Lianmeng*, which in 2012 set a test consisting of three components, retained this model relatively unaltered in 2013. However, having held their tests on different days in 2012, and found that this led to some students applying to all three, in 2013 the three 'alliances' all held their tests on the same day.

12 'Diversified recruitment' here referred to the *duli zhaosheng* practices becoming increasingly widespread around this time – see above.

13 'Three good' students were defined as those who combined moral, academic and sporting excellence.

14 One rumoured effect of this has been for some schools in Beijing to suggest to parents of migrant students that they take their children to a psychiatric clinic for assessment, in the hope that they will be certified as 'subnormal' or suffering from 'learning disabilities', and can then legitimately be excluded from the *'tongce'* test.

15 Since this practice is technically illegal, it is hard to find sources that discuss it.

16 For example, Gao (2011) notes that the increased practice of automatic promotion from the junior to senior sections of integrated key point secondary schools in Wuhu (Anhui Province) has tended to disadvantage 'working class' students (it is unclear how widespread this practice has become elsewhere).

17 Witte's study has been quite influential amongst Chinese scholars researching the issue of 'school choice'. See, for example, the 2009 report by one of the present authors (Zeng) for the Ministry of Education.

18 Pressure since around 2006 to curtail the role of money in securing access to key point schools (see the following chapter) has been greatest for those under district or county jurisdiction, but those attached to particular *danwei* tend to be less constrained. In Beijing, the famous Number 4 High School (*Beijing Si Zhong*, *alma mater* to many of China's top leaders), administered by *Xicheng Qu* (Western District – home to most ministry compounds), has in recent years seen its status as the 'Chinese Eton' somewhat eroded, while the BNU Number 2 Affiliated Middle School, obliged to offer free compulsory education only to children of BNU's own employees, has been much freer to market itself to wealthy Beijingers keen to exercise 'choice'.

19 According to this report, families have in some cases been buying one-room apartments not to live in, but simply in order to be able to register an address in the prized school district.

9 Marketisation, competition and schooling

As we discussed in Chapter 3, post-Mao China's embrace of the market was at first tentative, largely rural and small-scale; but from the early 1990s, as the focus shifted to the cities, both the pace and scale of change increased. In education, subsequent years witnessed the rapid emergence of a private schools sector, as well as increased collaboration between state and non-state actors. These phenomena were related, as noted in Chapter 5, to a wider marketisation of public service provision largely aimed at supplementing insufficient state expenditure. The emergence of a prosperous urban middle class, consisting predominantly of one-child households, meanwhile fuelled demand for educational services of all kinds.

However, the related, though distinct, phenomena of marketisation and privatisation have had an extremely uneven impact. During the 1990s, at the same time as thousands of 'schools for aristocrats' were opening to cater to *nouveuax riches* in coastal cities, rural schooling in many regions was experiencing an acute public funding crisis. Meanwhile, millions of rural dwellers began migrating to the growing cities to find work. The reluctance of local authorities to provide schooling for their children prompted the emergence of very different forms of private education. Non-state educational providers have thus emerged to cater for both the 'top' and 'bottom' ends of the socio-economic spectrum. Meanwhile, serving all points in between, a thriving 'shadow education' system has grown up, as the competitive pressures of public examinations have fuelled massive growth in the private tuition industry. This chapter analyses in turn these and other forms of provision – from 'people-managed' (*minban*) rural schools, private schools for urban elites, hybrid 'public–private' models and the 'shadow education' system, to 'black schools' for migrant children. Here the focus is on schooling; in Chapters 11–12 we discuss the marketisation of higher education, while the role of the private sector in providing childcare and pre-schooling has been discussed in Chapter 4.

Just as the school curriculum has reflected growing tensions between values of competition and solidarity, or individualism and collectivism (Chapter 6), the ethos of the market has also permeated educational institutions themselves, spurring the emergence of new forms of provision. But the increasing marketisation of education and other public services is a trend by no means confined to contemporary China. We therefore begin by asking to what extent the promotion of privatisation and marketisation has been influenced by external forces, or betokens an ideological convergence between Chinese state elites and their neoliberal counterparts in the West. That market mechanisms and private providers have made substantial inroads is undeniable. However, the reasons for this, and its implications for China's integration into a new global economic (and educational) order, are by no means so clear-cut.

Marketisation and Communism – pragmatism or ideology?

As Deng Xiaoping rose to dominance in the late 1970s, the world economy was being profoundly reshaped by the breakdown of the post-war Keynesian consensus. Indeed, Harvey argues that it was the collapse of Bretton Woods that 'opened up a space for China's tumultuous entry and incorporation into the world market' (2005, 121). China's 'spectacular emergence as a global economic power' was, he claims, 'in part an unintended consequence of the neoliberal turn in the advanced capitalist world'. The weakening or abandonment of capital and exchange controls, along with a renewal of free-trading zeal in key Western economies, were crucial both in enhancing China's attractiveness to overseas investors, and opening overseas markets to Chinese exports. But if the international triumph of neoliberalism facilitated this rapid growth, to what extent did it also convert Communist leaders to the creed of Friedman and Hayek?

China's record of substantial reform to the command economy, accession to the WTO, engagement with international financial markets, and moves to float the yuan suggests a smooth convergence with 'Washington consensus' orthodoxy. However, as Harvey observes, these and other 'neoliberal elements' have been 'interdigitated with authoritarian centralised control' (120). As South Korea, Taiwan and Singapore had already demonstrated by the 1970s, authoritarianism and the capitalist market were eminently compatible. For these regimes, as for Deng's China, market capitalism was a useful tool for maximising export-driven economic growth, and with it the fiscal surpluses that could boost state power and purchase performance legitimacy. But they did not subscribe to a neo-Cobdenite faith in the link between economic and political liberalism: the restriction of state authority was no part of their agenda. China's post-Mao leaders, like most of their East Asian counterparts, have remained convinced strong-state corporatists. 'China Inc.' did not operate in quite the same way as 'Japan Inc.', but both were animated by the conviction that collective goals – whether of nation or Party-State – trumped not only the short-term pursuit of profit and shareholder value, but also the promotion of individual autonomy.

China's adoption of elements of the 'new public management' has thus been highly selective. In the 1980s, CCP leaders consulted that apostle of free-market capitalism, Milton Friedman, who was then fresh from advising the right-wing Chilean dictatorship. Friedman hailed freewheeling Hong Kong as a potential model for the mainland – though Deng himself seems to have been more enamoured of authoritarian Singapore (Vogel 2011). In 1988, Premier Zhao Zhiyang told his American visitor that 'the state would regulate and control the market, while the market controls the economy' (Friedman and Friedman 1998, 543). 'That is impossible', was Friedman's blunt verdict. 'The state is organised from the top down; the market, from the bottom up. The state can control part of the economy, and the market part, but the combination Zhao described is not feasible'. The relationship between state authority and market forces was then, and has remained, controversial within the Party, and Zhao's own memoirs suggest that he was – or later became – a more convinced free-marketeer than this equivocal utterance suggested (Zhao 2009). However, in 1989 he was ejected from power by elements more unequivocally committed to maintaining authoritarian control over the economy, as over politics and society.

The intensification of marketising reforms from 1992 might appear to indicate that, on reflection, the CCP leadership had decided to follow Friedman's prescription after all. The abandonment of centralised manpower planning and creation of a freer market for labour; the cutting loose of unprofitable SOEs; restrictions on the commercial activities of state agencies (e.g. the People's Liberation Army); expanded scope for private enterprise in education as in other fields; and the fee-driven expansion of higher education – all would have met with the approval of the Sage of Chicago.

Nonetheless, as we noted in Chapter 2, the distinction between state and non-state spheres has remained blurred. China has studiously avoided the precedent of the former Soviet Union where, thanks largely to the ministrations of Friedman's disciples, 'shock therapy' led to mass impoverishment and the state's near-collapse (Harvey 2005, 122). Instead, there has been a sweeping marketisation of the public sector alongside retention of state provision or ownership of key institutions such as banks and schools. As Whitty *et al.* note in their comparative analysis of school reform policies (1998), marketisation and privatisation are in fact distinct processes that can and have been pursued separately; marketisation can happen without relinquishing state control to the private sector. In the case of China, though, a further problem in clearly delineating spheres of state and market control is the fact that the Party has continued to permeate many ostensibly private institutions as well as public ones (Huang 2008).

The advance of public service marketisation in America and Britain reflected, according to Perkin, the triumph of 'managerial' professionals over their 'public service' counterparts. In the 'new society', he writes,

> the dominant professions … are, surprisingly perhaps, not the high priests of the new technology but those who employ and set them to work, the corporate managers and state bureaucrats. They are the elites who will make or break modern post-industrial society, who will lead it to its full potential of service to the community or pitch it down into the abyss of corruption, violent conflict, and self-destruction.
>
> (1996, 7)

For Perkin, broadly speaking, corporate managers represent the values of the free market, and bureaucrats those of public service. Attempting to categorise societies according to the degree of dominance of one group over the other, he notes that in post-war Japan the bureaucratisation of the large corporations and their intimate links with each other and with the government resulted in a 'managed capitalism' that placed 'individualism in the arms of collectivism'; the competitive impulse was sublimated in the service of the company and, ultimately, the nation (Perkin 1996, Chapter 7). Meanwhile, the Soviet Union, seemingly the archetypal bureaucratic command economy, was in fact far more dependent 'for its food and consumer goods on peasants' private plots and the so-called "mafia" ... than communist theory allowed' (7).

Marketisation Chinese-style has differed significantly from all these models. Mindful of the cautionary example of Soviet collapse, the CCP has pursued *Perestroika* without *Glasnost*. It has had to grapple with the rampant corruption that results from placing relatively untrammelled power in the hands of party cadres. But marketisation has also brought rapid economic growth and improvements in living standards that have lent the Party a degree of performance legitimacy. Meanwhile, compared with Japan, Chinese bureaucratisation has been more flexible and informal – at once less clearly rule-governed and more hierarchical. Japan's painstaking consensus-building – preventing the arbitrary exercise of authority, but also frustrating decision-making (Murphy 2014) – is something with which Chinese cadres have been more readily able to dispense. In China, state and market inter-penetrate above all through the institution of the Party itself, which has come to function less as a rigid ideological sect, and more as a broad church encompassing social, political and economic elites. As we noted in Chapter 3.3, this transformation was formalised in 2002, when the Party changed its rules to admit businessmen as full members, while enshrining Jiang Zemin's 'Three Represents' in its Constitution. Distinguishing between Perkin's 'public service' and 'managerial' professionals is therefore extremely hard in China. The Party-State incorporates and claims the loyalty of both – and they are often the same people.

Still, neither the Party itself, nor still less the society over which it presides, are monolithic. State-market interpenetration has provoked criticism from at least two directions. On the so-called 'New Left', figures such as Kong Qingdong of Peking University or Wang Hui of Tsinghua have advocated reining in the market, proposed more state intervention to tackle social inequality, and expressed hostility to neoliberal globalisation. At the same time, on the 'Right', suspicion of the overweening power of the Party-State and frustration at controls on civil society have inclined many liberal thinkers to echo Friedman's call for a clearer separation of state and market. Zhang Weiying (an economist and former Peking University Vice-President) and Mao Yushi (Director of the Unirule Institute of Economics – partnered, amongst others, with America's Cato Institute[1]) are among those who have called for an expansion of the sphere of the market, partly on the grounds that this will help entrench civil liberties.

Neoliberal ideas have enjoyed a generous airing in China, especially since the 1990s, and boast more or less doctrinaire adherents in academia, business and even within the Party itself. Chinese officials have become fluent in the language of global finance, and polished performers in international economic forums from APEC to Davos. This has led many foreign observers to conclude that China's rulers have converted lock, stock and barrel to the gospel of the market. 'Is Milton Friedman's *Free to Choose* replacing Chairman Mao's *Little Red Book* as the bible of the People's Republic?' asked Bloomberg's 'Management Blog' in 2013, thrilled at official hints that a reduction in subsidies to state-owned enterprises might be imminent (Sirkin 2013).[2]

However, the mainstream Party view of the market has in fact remained consistently pragmatic. As we noted in Chapter 5, the Party has not resiled from the principles of democratic centralism or its own political monopoly, notwithstanding its abandonment of other communist precepts. Media coverage of events in Iraq, Afghanistan, Syria and even India ceaselessly reminds China's citizenry of the dangers of state weakness or collapse. Looking for ways to promote growth, placate the masses and fill state coffers, the regime has keenly experimented with market-based policies, in education as in other fields. But it has also been quick to restrict or regulate private enterprise whenever its activities seem to threaten social stability or political control. This abiding tension between marketisation and the imperative of state control is nowhere better exemplified than in the evolution of the phenomenon of *minban* education.

Green shoots of educational entrepreneurialism – *minban* schools in the countryside

Just as broader economic marketisation began in the countryside, so did the emergence of pseudo-private or non-state schooling. But while both derived impetus from the liberalisation of the commune-brigade structure during the 1980s, in the case of education this was unplanned. As village communities, especially in poorer areas, sought to compensate for an accelerating erosion of state provision, 'community-run' or *minban* schools proliferated. These had roots traceable to the 1950s, and even earlier. From the early twentieth century into the Communist period, modern, 'regular' schools had been located mostly in cities and major towns, as the development of urban schooling was prioritised. Keen to impose greater control over education in the countryside, but unwilling to devote significant resources to it, the post-1949 regime initially allowed the creation of *minban* schools 'to fill the gap between public and private as regular private schools were taken over by the state [see below] and *sishu* [traditional local tutorial schools] were … closed or reorganized' (Pepper 1996, 194). *Minban* schools, many of them converted from old *sishu*, subsisted in villages and on the margins of the urban, regular system. They charged low fees and were run on a cooperative basis by and for the local community.

But many within the Party and the educational profession were uncomfortable with this situation. As we discussed in Chapters 2 and 3, some objected on 'quality' grounds to an over-hasty expansion of mass schooling. Soviet-inspired state planners meanwhile worried of a mismatch between the supply of 'talent' and the development of an industrial base capable of utilising it. The spectre of an unruly mass of over-educated, under-employed youth also haunted the authorities. And to the extent that community-run-and-financed schools were capable of operating independently of the Party-State, they also represented a potential challenge to the regime's Leninist logic. It was for such reasons that officials 'vacillated' over the question of *minban* schooling, first licensing a massive expansion, then clamping down after 1952, with an insistence on the need to 'overcome egalitarianism' and coordinate with 'industrial production', as the *People's Daily* put it in 1953 (cited in Pepper 1996, 196). By the early 1960s regular, publicly run key schools catered to a selected academic elite; *minban* experiments – for example, in junior secondary vocational education – were occasionally allowed, but faced peremptory closure or co-optation.

The result was a system of public schools that were intensely selective, highly elitist and urban-centred, reproducing existing patterns of social inequality by recruiting disproportionately from cadre families or those with 'bad class background' (Unger 1982). Meanwhile, rural schooling by the 1960s was organised through communes and production 'brigades', having been drawn within the ambit of a 'collectivised' state constructed at horrendous human cost (Dikotter 2013). But if schools were technically no longer *minban*, the teachers working in them often were. A focus on 'quality' in secondary and tertiary education (including teacher training), and reluctance to devote substantial public resources to village schools, meant that the supply of qualified teachers officially assigned to rural areas was extremely low. Schools were largely staffed by unqualified (or under-qualified), locally recruited *minban* teachers paid, in cash or kind, by the local collective. In an era when almost every aspect of life was ordered by the collective 'work unit', and goods acquired through 'work points', the *gongban/minban* distinction was in any case largely moot (see Wang X. 2002).

This tension between the regime's radically egalitarian rhetoric, and its highly inegalitarian education policies, was crucial in the build-up to the Cultural Revolution. Now, suddenly, 'quantity' was emphasised over 'quality', while key schools and colleges were closed, sometimes later to reopen in new guise. As Pepper observes, 'the only way there could be schools in every village and commune was by forcing every locality to assume responsibility for its own' (428); in effect, the entire system adopted the *minban* model under the *gongban* banner. Absent a mechanism for redistributing funding for education within, let alone between, provinces, the standard of provision from locality to locality differed wildly (Pepper 1996, Chapter 16). For those in poorer, more remote rural areas, the old, one-room *sishu* model was often all that the community could afford. But even there, schools might enjoy a not-so-hidden subsidy, as 'sent-down youth' or rusticated intellectuals were assigned to teaching roles (see Chapter 3.1). Numbers of the latter were highest during the Cultural Revolution, but earlier too (e.g. during the 'Anti-Rightist Movement' of the late 1950s), so-called 'rightists' or those with 'bad class background' constituted the main supply of qualified *minban* teachers (Bonnin 2005).

As discussed in Chapters 2 and 3, the oppressive political foundations of this experiment contributed to its ultimate unsustainability. After 1978, the capacity of localities to expand provision on their own initiative was drastically curtailed; 'quality' was once again the watchword. While the 'work points' system had allowed rural communes to retain the costs of welfare provision, this arrangement broke down when the communes were dissolved in the early 1980s. The availability of basic schooling consequently declined in many regions. From 1985, the government reversed course and committed to universalising nine years of basic education – but fiscal decentralisation led to growing divergence in funding levels and standards of provision (see Chapter 5). Resort to fully *minban* schools and teachers became, for many poorer rural communities, the only means of maintaining, let alone expanding, basic schooling. Although now stripped of the rhetoric of revolution from below, it was once again a case of 'education for the people, managed by the people' (*renmin jiaoyu renmin ban*).

Just as the fiscal crisis behind this resurgence in rural *minban* provision was coming to a head in the mid-1990s, Deng Xiaoping relaunched the national drive towards economic marketisation. Despite some moves during the 1980s towards market-oriented reforms, particularly at the lower end of the tertiary sector and in adult education (Mok 1997; see also Chapter 11), in urban areas at least, marketisation had made very limited inroads at the level of schooling. But the post-1993 reforms unleashed a wave of commercialisation that swept across many sectors of Chinese society – state and non-state, public and private. It was in this context that very different kinds of private or pseudo-private educational provision rapidly emerged – this time catering overwhelmingly to urbanites.

Sensitive to public reaction against a rash of advertisements for 'schools for aristocrats' (see below), in 1993 the central government rechristened all private schooling as *minban* – a practice that continues to this day (the complexity and confusion surrounding this redefinition are illustrated by the inconsistencies in official statistics for *minban* education displayed in Table 9.1). While this euphemism is on one level blatantly disingenuous – given the history of the *minban* term – on another level its use betrays a fundamental truth about official attitudes towards education. Whether for rich or poor, in the countryside or in the city, private initiative in education has been licensed or tolerated as a matter of expediency rather than principle. The state hovers over the private sphere, ever watchful, always ready to step in. As public finances have steadily improved from the mid-1990s into the 2000s, 'de-marketisation' and 'de-privatisation' of public services have been pursued (Painter and Mok 2008). But in a society now characterised by burgeoning inequality and entrenched networks of vested interests, this has been a complex, contested process.

Minban moves upmarket: 'schools for aristocrats' (*guizu xuexiao*)

In early 1994, tourists visiting the mausoleum of Qin Shihuang near Xi'an were treated to a telling symbol of 'socialism with Chinese characteristics'.[3] Near the sepulchre of the ancient autocrat stood a large billboard advertising a 'school for aristocrats' (as an additional mark of exclusivity, the phrase was printed

Table 9.1 Minban education in numbers, 1994–2013[a]

Year	*Early childhood*			*Primary*			*Secondary*			*Tertiary*		
	Schools	*Students*	*Staff*	*Schools*	*Students*	*Staff*	*Schools*	*Students*	*Staff*	*Colleges*	*Students*	*Staff*
1994	18,284	1,036,234	56,273	1,078	203,621	14,970	888	164,711	10,893	–	–	–
1995	20,780	1,099,866	60,710	1,465	284,513	21,040	1,202	271,726	17,383	–	–	–
1996	24,466	1,303,902	72,594	1,453	463,220	29,383	1,467	384,539	26,013	–	–	–
1997	24,643	1,348,830	85,853	1,806	522,284	38,713	1,702	545,526	3,639[b]	–	–	–
1998	30,824	1,707,810	109,306	2,504	727,645	40,588	2,146	526,996	49,238	–	–	–
1999	37,020	2,224,282	145,458	3,264	976,862	519,420	2,593	1,071,772	69,950	–	–	–
2000	–[c]	–	–	–	–	292,340	–	–	41,352	–	–	–
2001	–	–	–	–	–	107,441	–	–	–	–	–	–
2002	–	–	–	–	–	132,869	–	–	231,819	131	317,453	44,356
2003	55,536	4,802,297	383,942	5,676	2,749,341	162,825	6,330	3,979,427	291,604	175	812,076	86,996
2004	62,167	5,841,073	466,024	6,047	3,283,213	192,704	7,172	5,004,152	345,419	228	710,856	81,891
2005	68,835	6,680,925	535,984	6,242	3,889,404	225,715	7,783	5,991,935	404,212	252	1,051,663	103,712
2006	75,426	7,756,871	636,914	6,161	4,120,907	246,898	7,796	6,417,771	434,801	278	1,337,942	123,230
2007	77,616	8,687,481	714,152	5,798	4,487,915	268,842	7,583	6,585,046	450,494	297	1,630,661	144,022
2008	83,119	9,820,338	808,666	5,760	4,804,015	286,070	7,321	6,686,763	456,873	640[d]	4,012,486	304,200
2009	89,304	11,341,694	932,783	5,496	5,028,766	300,532	7,001	6,640,151	458,837	658	4,461,395	330,377
2010	102,289	13,994,694	1,168,429	5,351	5376,255	313,927	6,758	6,721,835	463,647	676	4,766,845	348,857
2011	115,404	16,942,090	1,436,575	5,186	5,678,255	186,026	6,676	6,775,449	606,071	698	5,050,687	371,554
2012	124,638	18,527,444	1,633,779	5,213	5,978,535	196,875	6,704	6,863,666	636,434	707	5,331,770	387,458
2013	133,451	19,902,536	1,848,754	5,407	6,286,015	204,861	6,910	6,939,927	665,808	718	5,575,218	398,400

Source: NBS.

Notes: [a] Official statistics also provide figures for *minban* teachers at primary and secondary level prior to 1994, but these are far greater than those for the years from 1994 onwards, indicating a shift in the definition of '*minban* teacher' from 1993.

[b] The figure for 'staff' for 1997 looks anomalous, but this is the figure provided in the official statistics. It is likely that the last digit is missing.

[c] It is unclear why figures for 2000–2 are incomplete, though this may be connected to confusion over the status of *zhuanzhi xuexiao*. (See the section below on 'public–private hybridisation'.)

[d] From 2008, the figure for *minban* tertiary institutions includes *duli xueyuan* ('independent colleges') (see Chapter 12).

in English). The poster featured beaming children in neatly pressed uniforms, gleaming facilities with neo-Gothic flourishes, and a mock-feudal school crest. In the city of the First Emperor, parents of China's new 'little emperors' were being invited to purchase a future of privilege for their offspring.

The 1993 Education *Gangyao* ('Framework') had mandated government at all levels to encourage the establishment of schools by 'social institutions and citizens' (see Chapter 3.3). Already, in 1987, a directive on 'managing the operation of schools by social forces' had allowed for the establishment of *minban* schools, while emphasising that they were supplementary to, rather than a substitute for, public provision (MOE 2004). The new policy seemed to go further, and was reinforced by the 1995 Education Law with its calls for *minban* schooling to receive 'active encouragement, strong support, correct guidance, and sound management'. And in December 2002, a 'Minban Education Promotion Law', passed just as 'capitalists' were formally admitted to the Party (see above), set the seal on the emergence of a significant private schooling sector.

The most significant growth of 'pure' private enterprise in education occurred at the preschool level (see Chapter 4), and in the private tutoring industry (see below). Like the old rural *minban* schools, many newer private schools emerged to cater for under-served populations (e.g. migrant children – see below) or under-resourced rural areas. But the 1990s also saw the establishment of numerous elite institutions, often boarding establishments, serving wealthier urban families either unable to access elite state schools through the customary ordeal-by-testing, or simply eager to gild their child's formative years.[4]

Non-profit schools had been established in Guangdong and Zhejiang as early as 1984 (Zhang 2009) – though on a strictly 'experimental' (and non-elitist) basis. Fee-paying schools catering to a privileged elite had a long history in China, notably in the form of the dozens of missionary-run institutions (by no means all elitist) that had sprung up in treaty ports from the late nineteenth century onwards. But precisely because of this association with the 'semi-feudal, semi-colonial' pre-'Liberation' past, their revival was greeted with considerable ambivalence. From 1992, however, there was an explosion of the private schooling sector which, while most spectacular in the prosperous east, was by no means confined there. In relatively impoverished Guangxi, 1993 reportedly saw the opening of 400 private schools (Lin 2007, 45).

Such schools were obliged to follow the state-mandated curriculum and use officially approved textbooks,[5] but the more expensive institutions – charging multiples of average annual salary levels – have been able to supplement these in spectacular fashion. They typically start intensive instruction in English far earlier than public schools, employing native-speaking teachers for this purpose. Computer science classes are usually also a staple of the curriculum. Olympic-size swimming pools, professional running tracks, state-of-the-art gymnasia, huge theatres and landscaped grounds provide the setting for a lavish array of extra-curricular activities.

The first widely publicised 'school for aristocrats' was Guangya Primary School in Chengdu, founded in 1992 (Lin 2007, 45), though the greatest clusters were to be found in prosperous coastal regions. By 1997, Guangdong had 70 such schools, while Beijing and Shanghai had 40 each (50). Given the unwillingness of state banks to lend to purely private enterprises, many faced challenges in raising their initial capital.[6] In 1993, the Ying Hao School was established in Guangdong, on the basis of an ingenious but dubious credit-raising method. The school demanded large initial 'deposits' (*jiaoyu chubei jin*) from parents, in return for reductions in school fees; the deposit was to be returned when the student graduated. Other private school consortia swiftly copied this ruse. Within a year, the funds thus raised in Guangdong alone amounted to 1.5 billion yuan – equivalent to almost one sixth of the province's annual public expenditure on education. By 1998, this had risen to 10 billion yuan (Zhang 2009).

It was at this point that the government – at both provincial and national levels – stepped in. A number of widely publicised scandals involving the embezzlement of school funds sparked fears about the inherent instability of this funding model.[7] But the sheer size of the sector was itself sufficient to arouse official unease; allowing such broad scope for wholly private initiative, particularly in the sphere of education, was inconsistent with the regime's instinct for control, as well as representing a challenge to its limited regulatory capacity (see Painter and Mok 2008). In 1998, schools were banned from raising funds through *jiaoyu chubei jin*; henceforth, they could only charge tuition and boarding fees. In 2000, a further directive ordered the return of deposits already taken from parents. A number of schools or school chains were forced into bankruptcy, and many that survived the transition to an entirely fee-funded model experienced 'serious problems' (Zhang 2009).[8]

At the national level, the rapid inflation, and sudden bursting, of this elite schooling bubble is illustrated by the case of the Nanyang Education Group. Established in 1993, its first school – Shanxi Nanyang International School – opened in Taiyuan in 1994, followed in 1995 by another school in Datong (in northern Shanxi). At this point total investment in the company amounted to 150 million yuan. From 1996, the consortium began expanding to other provinces, and by the end of the century had established a *minban* tertiary college, Beijing Xinghua University. In 2002, the Group consisted of ten institutions with a total capital of over 1 billion yuan, and over 20,000 students and staff. But having derived most of its capital from a variant of the *jiaoyu chubei jin*, it now found itself starved of credit, though its early foundation, size and extensive connections enabled it to survive longer than most. Much like a pyramid scheme, without a constant supply of new depositors, the deposit-based funding model was liable to collapse. Anticipating such an outcome, in 2004 the Group's founder and former chief executive, Ren Jingxi, suddenly fled (allegedly to New Zealand). In 2005, Nanyang's schools closed or were taken over by the local authorities (*Zhongguo Xinwen Zhoukan* 2006a, b).

Among the *guizu xuexiao* established in the 1990s, those that survived this regulatory squeeze, including the Ying Hao Group (now listed on the stock market) and the Hujia Group in Beijing, tended to be older, larger and better capitalised. The size of a school network also gave it a stronger negotiating position *vis-à-vis* local authorities, given the disruption to provision of schooling that its sudden dissolution was likely to cause. But many of the early 'schools for aristocrats' succumbed. This was due only in part to the outlawing of their original funding model. A more fundamental challenge came from the entry of prestigious public 'key point schools' into the educational marketplace.

Public–private hybridisation

As the renewed marketisation drive of the 1990s gathered impetus, all sorts of public institutions were allowed or encouraged to monetise their assets or services. The taxation reforms of 1994, coinciding with an extensive restructuring of SOEs, meanwhile disrupted the funding of many key point schools tied to public institutions (see Chapters 3.3 and 5). Both fiscal insecurity and growing pressure to compete with the upstart *guizu xuexiao* spurred many into entrepreneurial action (Painter and Mok 2008). The prestige of public key point schools, along with their public status itself, gave them decisive advantages over purely private entities not only in attracting students, but also in securing credit from state-owned banks.

Regular public schools traded on their prestige in several ways. The most widespread involved the levying of 'school choice fees' (*ze xiao fei*) on parents desperate to enrol their offspring in key point junior secondary schools. In 2005, a survey of 600 parents in major cities published in the online edition of the *People's Daily* found more than two-thirds determined to exercise school choice if necessary (46 per cent), or actively considering it (23 per cent) (Ako 2009, 159). A survey the following year found that the proportion of parents actually paying such fees varied from over a quarter (amongst private entrepreneurs) to around 6 per cent (amongst migrant workers) (160); proportions correlating closely, though not exactly, with levels of family income.[9] This phenomenon fuelled expanded enrolments and larger class sizes at the most 'successful' schools (Wu 2013). Senior high schools, for their part, could charge additional 'top-up fees' to parents whose children achieved marginally below the cut-off score in the *zhongkao*; often calculated on a sliding scale linked to examination scores, these fees could be very high.[10] In 2001, the State Council imposed 'Three Limits' on school choice fees, relating to their level, the margin within which they could be levied, and the proportion of students admissible on this basis. But these limits were widely breached, and the early 2000s witnessed a significant increase in this practice (Ako 2009, 159–61). Media reports drew attention to how the cost of this competition for school places added to pressures on children. In one much-publicised case in 2005, a 13-year-old girl in Ningxia committed suicide and left a note apologising to her parents for the expense she had caused them (161).

Meanwhile, the income to be derived from school choice fees further enhanced the advantages of key point schools in funding and facilities, especially since they continued to benefit from special support from the government, nationally and locally. Indeed, such support was ramped up by a 1995 SEC decision to construct over 1,000 national-level 'model high schools' (*shifanxing gaoji zhongxue*) with 'world-class' facilities and the 'best teachers'. By 2009, Shanghai alone boasted over 30 such schools, which local officials treated as prestige projects. Official largesse, very high fee income, and the competition to attract such fees, led many key point schools to acquire ever more elaborate facilities, from heated indoor pools and observatories to two-to-a-room student dormitories (Ako 2009, 162–3).

As key point junior and senior secondary schools increasingly operated like businesses, many also set up fee-charging 'branch' entities, either in separate locations or within the precincts of the original institution. Discussing this phenomenon of 'franchising', Ako reports one principal claiming that his successful model could be replicated 'like KFC' (164). Conflicts of interest abounded, with some head teachers established their own consulting companies to advise on the establishment of private schools (165). Franchised 'branches' often charged fees ten times or more higher than those of the 'mother school' (166). Meanwhile, amongst the various forms of 'schools within schools' (*xiao zhong xiao*), one that became increasingly common from the mid-2000s was the 'international section', preparing students for entry to overseas universities.[11]

The marketisation of public schooling proceeded in ways that were often complex and confusing. From the early 1990s, local governments could establish 'people-run, publicly subsidised' (*minban gongzhu*) schools as a means of expanding educational provision on the cheap. Otherwise operating on the same basis as fully private (*minban*) schools (e.g. with regard to staffing and administration), these received varying levels of financial assistance from the local authorities (on Shanghai, see Ding 2011). A sub-category of the *minban gongzhu* model, first codified by Shanghai's municipal government in 1996, was the 'converted' (*zhuanzhi*) school.[12] Clearly inspired in part by America's 'Charter Schools', this involved transferring schools from public to private management. One variant involved over-subscribed key point schools opting out of the state system to gain more freedom to expand; another, often related, involved transferring the management of a 'failing' school to a more 'successful' one (Wu 2013). As Ding notes, government officials themselves often seemed confused over whether these 'converted' schools were to be classed as 'public' or *minban*: the MOE in Beijing generally taking the former line, the Shanghai authorities the latter. In practice, however, 'converted' schools were administered in the same way as the bureau-sponsored *minban* schools (Ding 2011, Chapter 6). By 2003, at the peak of Shanghai's 'conversion' movement, they accounted for about 40 per cent of *minban* schools in the city (146).

However, the wholesale privatisation of public schooling was not something that the Party was ultimately prepared to countenance. As public concern mounted during the early 2000s over levels of inequality and the cost of basic public goods, the central government moved to rein in marketisation, at least during the compulsory phase. In 2006, the same year the abolition of school fees for rural residents was announced (see Chapter 3.4), the central government decreed that 'converted' schools would have to choose between becoming wholly private or public. Thereafter, with public funding for education also increasing, many formerly 'converted' junior secondary schools returned to the public fold; by 2013 they had entirely disappeared from the educational landscape in Beijing. However, as discussed in the previous chapter, this did not necessarily betoken total elimination of selection at junior secondary level. There has also remained a considerable and expanding market for elite private schooling,[13] and for schools catering to groups whose needs are particularly ill-served by the state system (see below and Chapter 10). Meanwhile, the entrenchment of market-oriented behaviour within the state system has further manifested itself in the rapid growth of a 'shadow education' sector.

Out of the shadows – the market for supplementary education

Both the emergence of fully private schools, and growing marketisation of the public sector, have been fuelled by intense credentialism. Many of the first urban ventures in private educational provision in the early 1980s took the form of evening classes and weekend schools for students preparing to retake the *gaokao* (Lin 2007, 44). But from the 1990s, this expanded rapidly, as a vast tutoring industry emerged to 'shadow' the regular schooling system. Estimates of its scale vary: a 2007 national survey reported an overall participation rate of just under 50 per cent, while an earlier (2004) investigation of urban households gave figures of 74 per cent for primary, 66 per cent for junior secondary and 54 per cent for senior secondary students (cited in Zhang and Bray, 2016). Use of tutorial schooling has subsequently continued to rise. When tutoring in non-academic activities (more common among primary students) is excluded, participation seems to peak around the final year of junior secondary school – i.e. just before students take the *zhongkao* examination for entry to senior secondary school.

China is, of course, far from alone in witnessing an enormous recent growth in 'shadow education'. The practice of paying for after-school tutoring has recently spread elsewhere too: to former Soviet bloc states, for example, and parts of North and South America (Bray and Lykins 2012). But it is especially endemic across East Asia. Why has this happened? What factors make the use of private tutoring particularly widespread in these societies? And to what extent do the factors operating in China differ from those at work in neighbouring countries?

Culture has been widely cited as key to explanations of the intensity of this educational competition. Thus Zhang and Bray tell us that 'Chinese cultural traditions emphasize diligence and respect for education' (2). In discussing the cultural and historical roots of 'educational desire', Kipnis notes how a concept of 'literary masculinity', prizing academic diligence, has long been central to ideals of male success in China (2011, 117–121). This rings true, and applies more or less to other 'Confucian heritage' societies.

But culture cannot wholly explain the recent and rapid growth of private tutoring in East Asia as a whole, or in China in particular. Social and systemic factors are also crucial. It is often remarked that East Asian education systems are 'examination-oriented', but high-stakes public examinations are not unique to the region. However, for reasons discussed in Chapter 2 (including the 'situational nationalism of the late industrialisers' and a strong discourse of catch-up modernisation), curricula and examinations in these countries heavily emphasise the testing of a fairly narrow range of subjects – especially Maths, the 'national language', Science and, more recently, English. Tuition in these subjects, especially Maths and English, is most in demand. Moreover, assessment methods are highly standardised and rigid: answers, typically elicited by multiple-choice questions, are either 'correct' or 'incorrect'. There is little or no scope for markers to make professional judgements about the quality of a candidate's reasoning or argumentative flair. Rather, as discussed in the previous chapter, the application of set formulae or the recall of factual knowledge are prioritised. Cramming can prove a particularly effective route to success under such a testing regime. And a special premium will attach to the guidance of teachers with supposedly privileged insight into the mysteries of question setting.

Expansion of college education has also boosted demand. When both college and college-preparatory senior high schooling were confined to an elite, the market for supplementary education remained relatively small. But as higher education systems across East Asia have expanded, credentialism has exploded. In China, the rate of promotion from senior high school to university rose from 27.3 per cent in 1990 to 86.5 per cent in 2011 (Zhang and Bray 2016). Competition for college entry has thus become a mass obsession. Although tertiary education is more widely available than ever, the supply of places in prestigious public 'key' high schools or top universities remains highly restricted, so jockeying for access has intensified. In addition, despite attempts to introduce a greater element of flexibility, in practice the *gaokao* represents a once-in-a-lifetime opportunity for the vast majority of students (see the previous chapter). And since attendance at an elite high school is seen as crucial to *gaokao* success, it is at the junior–senior secondary interface (around age 15–16) that competition has become fiercest (Woronov 2016).

The nature of the labour market also heightens the stakes attached to examination success. In Japan, rigid seniority-based promotion systems deter most young people from stepping off the examinations-to-employment conveyor belt. In China, the labour market is in many ways more dynamic and flexible, but, since the 1990s, the fee-based expansion of higher education has gone hand-in-hand with the abandonment of state job assignments and the advent of a free market for graduate employment, intensifying competitive pressure.

As the stakes of examination success have risen, so has the capacity and willingness of urban families to invest in their children's prospects. China's One Child Policy has played a role in concentrating familial investment on a smaller number of offspring (Fong 2004; Zhang and Bray 2016). But the costs associated with intensifying educational competition have themselves become a major factor in limiting family size across contemporary East Asia (on Japan see Murphy 2014). Meanwhile, in China as elsewhere, the relative weakness of public welfare provision, as well as cultural expectations concerning filial care for elderly parents, reinforces an inclination to see spending on children's education as an investment in the future of the whole family. These factors help explain why demand for supplementary education has ballooned since the 1990s, developing into a mass craze that feeds off itself.[14] Kipnis notes how even some relatively poor families have managed to garner the resources to meet the necessary costs (2011, 77–81).

However, rather than serving a remedial function, helping students who have fallen behind in regular classes, supplementary education in China is overwhelmingly competitive. As Zhang and Bray show, 'students were more likely to receive tutoring in urban than in rural areas, in elite schools, and during the period of compulsory education' (2016, 97). And on the basis of fieldwork in Chongqing, Zhang reports that 'shadow education was alien for the students interviewed in village schools' (2014, 443). In Chongqing, only 11 per cent of rural students received tutoring, compared with 74 per cent of their urban counterparts. A survey of adolescents in Beijing similarly found that richer students received significantly more tutoring than poorer ones (Zeng 2012b). The differential availability of tutoring reflects and helps to reinforce existing disparities in wealth and social opportunity.

So much for demand – what of supply? Provision of supplementary education takes a huge variety of forms, from informal one-on-one meetings to online courses. Likewise, providers range from commercial enterprises, such as the huge Xin Dongfang chain, employing numerous full-time tutors teaching a range of subjects, to individual college students looking to earn some pocket money.

However, the most sought-after tutors are 'famous teachers' (*mingshi*) working in elite state schools. Zhang's Chongqing study shows that it is common there for senior teachers in leading schools to establish commercial tutoring centres. The introduction, in 2009, of a 'merit-pay' system within the city's state-run schools may have further boosted such practices. This has tended to exacerbate inequality within the profession, not least since seniority is one criterion on which 'merit' is judged. The incentives for junior teachers to moonlight for extra income are therefore little affected and, in any case, small increments in regular pay can be dwarfed by fees earned from tutoring. Zhang reports the case of a Physics teacher who earned 1,000 yuan for a single two-hour session – equivalent to one-sixth of his official monthly salary (2014, 447). Moreover, since students' examination results are a key measure of a teacher's 'merit', tutoring one's own students and thereby enhancing their final grades can bring a double reward.

The trend for key point school teachers to use the private tutoring market to monetise their prestige amounts, in Zhang's words, to a 'public–private conspiracy'. The provision by teachers of paid supplementary tuition to their own students is just one instance of the resulting conflicts of interest. Junior teachers employed in private tutoring centres run by senior colleagues from the same school could also find themselves subject to implicit or explicit pressure. Many teachers accepted commissions from tutorial schools in return for 'introducing' their services to students or their parents. Teachers and principals in key schools often claimed special knowledge of examination question-setting policy as a way of marketing their commercial, after-school services. All this tended to create 'a distorted education system where the shadow and the mainstream were intertwined' (Zhang 2014, 449).

Governments – central and local – have not been oblivious to the potentially corrupting effects on public schooling. The Minban Education Law of 2002 sought to outline a basic regulatory framework for private supplementary tutoring. In 2008, the Education Ministry issued a set of 'Rules of Professional Ethics of Teachers', stipulating that staff 'should reject paid tutoring with consciousness, and should not gain personal profit from their positions as teachers' (cited in Bray and Lykins 2012, 74). But responsibility for enforcement lies at provincial level, where the official response has varied. Chongqing is unusually relaxed about schoolteachers tutoring their own students (forbidding it only on weekdays); many other provinces ban it outright. In practice, though, such restrictions have been widely ignored. In Guangdong, despite the threat of severe penalties, 60 per cent of public school teachers were found to be providing paid tutoring to their regular students (Kwok 2010, 55).

If attempts to restrict supply (at least involving public school teachers) have proven largely ineffective, an alternative approach might be to restrict demand. As we noted in the chapter on curriculum (Chapter 6), East Asian governments have in recent years sought to lighten the burden of testing and homework. China's *suzhi jiaoyu* reforms have stipulated reductions in class hours, with the aim of providing students with a more fully rounded education. However, rather than frolicking in the fresh air or curling up with an improving novel, most students have headed straight for the tutorial centre. In the absence of significant reform to testing methods, or alteration to the stakes involved in examination success, students, parents and teachers alike have felt driven to make up for lost classroom time. All connive in the practice of private tutoring because it seems in their interests to do so – especially when everyone else is doing the same (Kipnis 2011, 77–81; Zhang 2014, 450).

Commercial tutoring thus 'seems set to become a standard component in the lives of young people at all levels of education', especially in urban areas (Zhang and Bray 2016, 11). At the individual level, it may bestow advantages in examination competition, while enabling some students from ordinary schools to sit at the feet of 'famous teachers' (5). But this is merely to acknowledge shadow education's status as a 'positional good' with overwhelmingly deleterious consequences for society as a whole (Bray and Lykins 2012, 68). Estimates of the direct cost to households vary, from 3.4 per cent of average annual income in Shenzhen to upwards of 10 per cent for a third of the families in Zhang's Chongqing sample (2013). The effects of this are naturally felt most keenly by those on lower incomes.

Nonetheless, as a way of occupying teenagers' time, tutorial schooling serves other purposes. Activities crowded out of students' lives by shadow education may include worthy cultural or sporting pursuits. But they might equally involve behaviour disturbing to adult or official sensibilities. History shows (and human nature suggests) that sexual experimentation and gang violence, for example, are by no means intrinsically alien to Chinese youth culture; neither is political agitation. Many Chinese adults retain vivid memories of the Red Guard era, not to mention the 1989 Student Movement. Better, perhaps, to have youngsters bored but safe in a tutorial school than roaming the streets outside. As a form of childcare for potentially obstreperous adolescents, intensive supplementary education is a force for social and political stability, or one more instrument of parental and political control.

In so far as it corrupts ordinary schooling, however, shadow education is a potentially destabilising cause of public discontent. When a teacher tutors her own daytime students, she may refrain from teaching crucial elements of the curriculum in regular lessons, retaining these for the favoured recipients of after-school guidance. More generally, time and energy spent moonlighting in the commercial tutoring sector can only detract from the energy and commitment a teacher devotes to the 'day job'. Participation in intensive, after-school, examination-focused tutoring may also sap students' interest in their regular classes – especially when the private tutor, but not the regular teacher, is a *mingshi*. The teacher may then feel compelled to compete for her students' attention by focusing more narrowly on examination preparation. As Bray and Lykins comment, 'from the perspective of the mainstream', supplementary education 'may subtract as well as add' (2012, 74).

But perhaps the most fundamental challenge posed by supplementary education is to social equality, and hence to societal cohesion and 'harmony'. When tutoring serves a remedial function, helping students who have fallen behind their peers for whatever reason, it can benefit both the individual and society as a whole. Some have also argued that tutoring helps to contain discontent on the part of elites frustrated with the egalitarian strictures of public schooling systems (on Japan, see Dawson 2010). Those able to 'supplement' their schooling may at least remain within the state sector, rather than going private. However, in practice the uptake of supplementary education has been at least as prevalent amongst students in the private or pseudo-private sectors as in the state sector, while wealthier urban families on average spend the most on tutoring (in absolute terms, if not as a proportion of their income). In China, as in other societies from East Asia to Eastern Europe where commercial tutoring has become a collective mania, it overshadows the entire education system, tending greatly to exacerbate social stratification (on Hong Kong, see Bray and Kwok 2003).

Minban schools for the children of migrants

Nowhere has the stratification of educational opportunity been more in evidence in post-1990s China than in the case of the children of rural-to-urban migrants. Notwithstanding haphazardly enforced regulations, the tutoring 'industry' has been formally recognised as a legitimate commercial activity at least since the *Minban* Education Law of 2002. However, the often genuinely 'people-managed' schools for migrant children that proliferated in the 1990s and early 2000s enjoyed no such protection under that law. This is despite the fact that, unlike commercial tutorial centres, they performed a genuinely remedial function, compensating for glaring failings in the formal schooling sector.

Writing on private schools for the poor has become a thriving sub-genre of educational research literature in recent years. The academic James Tooley, winner, in 2007, of the *Financial Times'* first annual essay prize,[15] has been prominent in advocating private educational provision as an equitable and efficient alternative to reliance on the state. In *The Global Education Industry* (2001), he relates how, at an International Conference on Private Schools held in Beijing in 1999, the Deputy Director of the local Education Bureau told him that 'the government's hold on education has been broken' (2001, 24). But Tooley makes no mention of private schools for children of China's urban poor; his examples instead relate mainly to elite private schools of the kind discussed above. These, he was told by the same official, would help 'close the gap between rich and poor', because 'if richer groups buy private education, then state resources will be available for the poor' (25).

However, at the time Tooley was writing, children of migrant workers, far from being offered special state largesse, were effectively excluded from Beijing's education system altogether, as a consequence of the *hukou* (household residency) system. From the 1980s, as communes were disbanded, agriculture effectively privatised, and the apparatus of state planning reformed, more and more under-employed rural labourers moved to the cities in search of work – a flow that greatly increased from the 1990s, as a result of the economic shifts discussed in Chapters 3.3 and 3.4. Initially, the state formally retained a system of 'custody and repatriation' for returning 'non-resident' labourers to the countryside whenever this was deemed desirable. That practice was abandoned in 2003, but most rural migrants remained unable to transfer their *hukou* to the urban areas where they lived, and were thus denied access to state education, healthcare and housing (Goodburn 2009, 496).

The increasing flow of rural migrants to the cities coincided with, and was spurred on by, administrative and fiscal decentralisation (see Chapter 5).[16] As the collective economy was dismantled, sub-provincial (county, township or district) governments were increasingly left to foot the bill for basic public services. But there were no reliable, judicially enforceable procedures for securing transfers to poorer areas, or making subventions to cities facing an influx of migrants. Local governments thus sought to limit their responsibilities, and the *hukou* system gave them a powerful means of doing so (Zhu J. 2004). Meanwhile, as possessors of local *hukou* in major cities have become an increasingly privileged social stratum, they have also constituted a powerful vested interest blocking meaningful reform to the system. Exhortation, negotiation and gradualism have marked efforts to widen access for migrants to urban public services, even while coercive state authority has been used to clamp down on grassroots initiatives by migrants themselves.

On his 1999 Beijing visit, had Tooley visited areas with high concentrations of migrant residents, he would have found community-run schools reminiscent of those in the slum quarters of urban India. Discussing this situation in 2006,

Kwong asserted that 'the Chinese government has not intentionally discriminated against migrant children' (175). Indeed, at national level, the ban on rural migrant children attending city schools was lifted in 1996. By 2003, the State Council was urging local governments to accommodate all children within the public education system – expounding the principle of the 'two mains' (*liang ge wei zhu*): 'according the main [responsibility] for management to the government of the host region, and placing the main [burden] on public primary and secondary schooling' (State Council 2003). However, local responses were widely divergent: while Xiamen was already moving to regularise *minban* migrant schools by 2003, they were still being closed down in central Shanghai. Policy on integrating migrants was, and has remained, far more restrictive in the major metropolitan centres, such as Beijing, Shanghai and Guangzhou.

Most restrictive of all was Beijing, site of a 2004–5 survey by Goodburn (2009). Since the 1990s, schools in the capital as elsewhere had been allowed to require special payments from parents of 'non-resident' children – rendering public schooling prohibitively expensive for most. Regulatory reforms in 2004 theoretically allowed migrant children to study in local schools without the payment of 'donations' (*zanzhu fei*). However, obtaining the necessary 'approval permit for temporary schooling' was so complex as to be all-but-impossible for most parents. In practice, migrant parents with children in local state-provided compulsory education paid five to six times the fees charged to local students (498). Moreover, widespread discrimination against those few migrant children who made it into the state system reinforced parents' preference for unlicensed, migrant-run 'black' schools.

Some of these operated in space rented from government schools, but conditions in others were squalid. The 'Hope School' in Haidian District was built by students, teachers and parents, and 'situated on a rubbish tip which was still in use by the migrant community'. It consisted of a small walled area with four 'dark classrooms' and an additional room where the four teachers lived. Bitterly cold in winter, the school lacked both water and electricity. Children sat at simple desks on wooden stools, 'two to a seat'. So overcrowded was the classroom Goodburn observed that she had to stand outside the doorway to observe lessons, which were periodically 'interrupted by gusts of wind, which swept large amounts of dust and sand through the open door and tiny glassless windows (2009, 499).

Such schools charged the kind of fees that migrant families could actually afford, but their teachers were typically under-qualified and overstretched, the curriculum rudimentary, and organised sports or exercise minimal. Moreover, the constant threat of arbitrary closure precluded investment in better facilities, while compelling funds to be set aside for pay-offs to local police. In Fengtai District in 2001, fifty migrant schools were closed just three days before the new school year was about to begin (500). And in the run-up to the 2008 Beijing Olympics, such 'black' schools were closed *en masse*.

Considering the reasons for continuing restrictions on migrants' access to public education, Goodburn dismisses official concerns over a 'lack of school spaces'; municipal statistics showed that, in 2002, Beijing schools had as many as 300,000 spare places (501). Both officials and media have also often cast aspersions on the 'quality' of migrant families, portraying migrant children on the one hand as 'threatening' to drag down local educational performance, and on the other as victims of inattentiveness from 'low-quality' parents. The latter accusation was, according to Goodburn, 'unjustified' (502). Many of her informants claimed that the education provided in unlicensed 'black schools' was better than that available in their home villages – a reflection of the under-funding of education in many rural areas during this period, and also a symptom of parental rebellion against attempts to make rural schooling more vocationally oriented (502) (see Chapter 10).

Indeed, an earlier survey of Beijing's migrant schools (Han 2001) – which estimated the size of the 'market' at 200 schools attended by 40,000 students – found that the school enrolment rate amongst children of migrant families was higher than the average for rural areas. Han reported per-semester fees for migrant students at public schools as 600 yuan per semester for primary level, and 1000 yuan at junior secondary level – almost certainly an under-estimate of the total cost (since this ignores various additional fees that schools might also charge migrant families – see Goodburn 2009, 498). By contrast, *minban* migrant schools charged a basic tuition fee of 300 yuan (including provision of textbooks), with miscellaneous fees (e.g. for lunch and snacks) also considerably lower than at state schools. A 2005 investigation of migrant schooling in Shanghai's Pudong District reported fee levels of around 500 yuan per semester (Huang 2005). Here it seems that closures of *minban* schools for migrant children had the effect of raising student numbers in the remaining institutions, allowing these to achieve significant economies of scale (though the authors do not tell us whether this had anything to do with the intentions of the local authorities).

The persistence, through the first decade of the new century, of attempts to limit migrant access to urban schooling stemmed, fundamentally, from a desire to control migration's potentially destabilising social consequences, and to protect the privileges of urban residents. This did not, as some have claimed (e.g. Kwong 2006, 175), simply involve a failure by local governments to implement benevolent instructions from the national capital. Notwithstanding Beijing's exhortations, as of 2008 national law still did not hold local governments responsible for the schooling of all local children regardless of residency status. And crucially, the central state provided no extra funding to help cover the costs of schooling migrant children. Goodburn's analysis of official attitudes highlights the salience of concerns relating to social control: 'When migrant communities come together to provide such basic goods as schooling, their actions may seem less like acts of entrepreneurship within the state framework, and more like attempts to create an alternative system altogether' (2009, 504). In other words, grass-roots initiatives that bypass the state are seen as a potential threat to Party legitimacy.

Since the great clearance prior to Beijing's Olympics, educational access for migrant children in the capital has improved. The 'black schools' have generally not reappeared, as changes in national and local regulations now allow most migrant children free access to urban schools during the compulsory education phase. The state has thus largely reclaimed responsibility for the schooling of migrant children from an unlicensed private sector. The turning point (delayed in Beijing by the Olympics) seems to have come around 2005–6, when Premier Wen Jiabao stepped up central government efforts to cajole or persuade cities to grant migrant children greater access to public schooling. By this point, several factors were already softening the stance of authorities in many regions: healthier local revenues; falling numbers of locally registered students; and, perhaps crucially, a tightening labour market.

However, the liberalisation of educational access has been less radical than it might appear. The right to sit for the *gaokao* (college entrance examination) in a certain province or municipality is still tied to possession of the relevant *hukou*. Therefore, migrant students attending schools in Beijing or Shanghai typically leave half-way through junior secondary school (Grade 2) so as to spend a year in their home province preparing to take the *zhongkao* (senior high school entrance examination). Often, only those willing to enter vocational higher education, rather than the academic variety, may continue within the local education system (see Chapters 8 and 10). *Hukou* conversion has become easier in many cities, but the Twelfth Five Year Plan (2011–15) explicitly endorsed more stringent requirements for Beijing, Shanghai and Guangzhou, as a means of shifting the focus of urban growth elsewhere (Miller 2012, 39). Since these cities boast the majority of China's most prestigious universities, their *hukou* is far more valuable than others. Points systems recently piloted in Guangzhou and Beijing's Tongzhou District, similar to those some countries operate for granting residence visas, theoretically bring *hukou* transfer within reach of many – but extremely limited quotas in practice continue to exclude all but a privileged, or lucky, few (Economist 2015). Short of *hukou* transfer, even certifying a migrant child's eligibility for public schooling, though somewhat easier than in the early 2000s, continues to be obstructed by 'bureaucratic barricades' in many cities (Lan 2014, 253).

Meanwhile, those 'migrant' children (often in fact city-born and bred) who are now admitted to public schools in major cities frequently experience serious discrimination. In one extreme but not exceptional example, a Shanghai school forced migrant children and 'locals' to use different entrances, study in different school buildings (migrants taught by lower-paid, less qualified teachers), and play in different playgrounds (Lan 2014). Lan represents this as a response conditioned by the marketised pressures to which urban schools are exposed; 'local' parents demand the segregation of migrant children, and may otherwise withdraw their offspring. With teachers' bonuses dependent on students' examination scores, and schools' ability to charge 'school selection fees' and secure other donations dependent on academic reputation, schools feel compelled to pander to prejudiced perceptions of migrant children as academically inferior (252).

Minban rural boarding schools and 'left-behind children'

The continuing link between *hukou* and *gaokao* eligibility has limited the attractiveness of urban secondary schooling to migrant parents (at least in the largest, most restrictive, cities). Moreover, as we have seen, the craze for supplementary tutoring imposes a special burden on poorer parents. Even when they can scrape together the necessary funds, the long and frequently unsocial hours worked by many migrant labourers also make it especially difficult for them to supervise their children outside school hours; and their often limited education renders them unable to assist with homework. Leaving children in the care of grandparents in the home village remains a default option, but since most of the rural elderly have little or no schooling, this course is seen as liable to undermine a child's educational prospects (Hansen 2012). A market has thus arisen for institutions providing round-the-clock supervision, preparing students for their provincial *gaokao* while combining the normal school curriculum with supplementary education – all at a price that many migrants can afford.

Since the 1990s, local governments in many regions have established 'concentrated' junior secondary schools – and in some cases elementary schools too – with large boarding facilities to cater to students from far-flung villages (simultaneously closing thousands of small village schools) (see Chapter 3.4). The intention behind this movement to 'concentrate' schooling in county towns was to enable children from 'backward' rural areas to receive an 'advanced' urban education, thus improving their overall 'quality' (*suzhi*) (Murphy 2004). Conditions in many of these schools have been described as 'Dickensian', and the effects of boarding on young children's health and educational performance severely criticised (Roberts 2015). However, despite this, there is significant demand from rural parents for boarding establishments; and in more densely populated provinces, where the state has not undertaken any extensive construction of boarding schools, many have looked to the market instead to provide these. These schools are particularly popular with migrant workers who want their children supervised during weekends and holidays, and would rather have teachers do this than poorly educated grandparents.

A 2011 study of a poor rural county (Lankao) in Henan Province found boarding schools especially popular amongst migrant parents, but also with other peasant families, whose children were unlikely to test into the better county-town state junior secondary schools due to the poor educational resources of rural areas (Huang *et al.* 2013, 15). An earlier (2007) investigation of *minban* junior secondary boarding schools in Lu Yi County showed that these catered to around 15 per cent of the relevant age group, and that 'left-behind children' of migrant workers (*liushou ertong*) generally accounted for over half of students – in some cases over 90 per cent (Jia *et al.* 2007). The cost of such schools – around 900 yuan per term (including tuition and boarding, but excluding food) – is 'affordable' for most rural families (Huang *et al.* 2013, 14). Indeed, in the 1990s and early 2000s, when poorly funded state schools in many rural areas charged substantial fees, private schools were often the cheaper option for rural parents (Lin 2007, 54).

Many state-run boarding junior high schools have been described as providing a 'boot-camp' style of education (e.g. Murphy 2004; Kipnis 2011),[17] but conditions in *minban* boarding establishments are typically even more regimented.

In many state schools, reforms associated with the 'quality education' (*suzhi jiaoyu*) drive have seen timetables trimmed and holidays extended – even if this has not always had the desired effect (see above, and Chapter 6). By contrast, in many 'ordinary' private schools (distinct from, and far more numerous than, the elite establishments discussed above), activities unrelated to examination preparation are typically sacrificed (Lin 2007, 53–4). This is especially so in *minban* boarding schools. In those of Lankao, not only was the average school day much longer than in local state schools, but so also was the school year – by around 80 days (Huang *et al.* 2013, 15). Moreover, for those students who fail the *zhongkao* (high school entrance examination) at the first attempt, such schools will sometimes also offer an additional year's study to prepare them for a second try (a service also taken up by some graduates of public junior secondary schools) (Hansen and Woronov 2013, 244).

As Table 9.2 illustrates, the daily grind in private junior secondary schools generally features no regular sport, music or extra-curricular activities. Lack of resources constrains the capacity of schools to offer instruction in these areas. However, in relentlessly focusing on examination preparation, these schools are meeting the demands of their 'consumers' (i.e. parents); only 19 per cent of rural parents questioned in a 2009 survey identified 'reducing the burden on primary and secondary students' as a priority for education policy – half the figure for their counterparts in major cities (38 per cent), for whom this ranked as the most significant concern. Top of the list of rural parents' concerns (chosen by 60 per cent) was 'improving the quality of teachers' (Yuan and Zhang 2010, 194). 'Young and capable teachers' will seldom opt to work in rural schools or in non-elite private schools (Lin 2007, 53). This poses particular problems for English language teaching; in many ordinary private schools, including rural *minban* boarding schools, 'English learning relies on textbooks and a tape recorder' (54).

Unlike the urban 'black schools', rural *minban* boarding schools have generally not had to cope with active hostility from local officials. Indeed, the Lankao county government actively encouraged their establishment from around 2000 (when rural educational budgets were especially squeezed).[18] However, such schools have sometimes struggled to deal with the unforeseen consequences

Table 9.2 Daily schedule at a private rural boarding school in Lankao, Henan Province

Activity	*Time*
Wake-up call	5:40
Morning exercise, early study, breakfast	6:00–8:00
Lessons (four periods)	8:10–12:00
Lunch, midday study, midday rest	12:00–14:40
Lessons (four periods)	14:50–18:20
Dinner	18:20–19:10
Lessons (two periods) (for Years 7–8)	19:10–20:50
Lessons (three periods) (for Year 9)	19:10–21:40

Source: Huang *et al.* (2013, 14).

of policies emanating from the central government, or of their implementation at provincial level. In Henan, the 2006 policy of 'two frees and one subsidy' (*liang mian yi bu*) (abolishing school fees and textbook charges, and subsidising boarding costs) was initially applied only to state schools. The result was a significant widening of the differential between the costs of state and non-state schooling. A mass exodus from *minban* schools into the state sector ensued, causing many school closures, and ultimately adding to the fiscal burden of the government, which had to pay the full cost of educating all affected students (Jia *et al.* 2007).

In this instance, after intense lobbying, the Henan authorities soon compromised, agreeing that *minban* schools would also benefit from the new subsidies – though as a 'reward' for their contribution to basic education, rather than as a matter of legal entitlement. Wu Hua, the head of Zhejiang University's Centre for Minban Education, argued that since the *liang mian yi bu* initiative was related to the state's commitment to provide free and universal schooling, funding should follow students wherever they were studying; in effect calling for a form of voucher scheme (Jia *et al.* 2007, 13).

While *minban* boarding schools contribute to providing more equitable access to education for the children of rural or migrant parents, they cannot compensate entirely for the inadequacies of state provision. Huang *et al.* point out that many do not honour their obligation to provide education to all students through to Year 9 (the end of compulsory education). In 'School Y', attrition rates were high: classes in Year 7 (the first year of junior secondary schooling) had around 60–70 students, falling to just over 40 two years later (2013, 14). *Minban* rural boarding schools catering for the 'left-behind' children of migrants operate precariously at the margins of the education system, serving China's most marginalised social groups. Typically subsisting on a financial shoestring, it takes little to push them out of business. Parental expectations and poverty dictate a Spartan regime of relentless test preparation, while large class sizes and over-worked, under-qualified teachers mean that special assistance can seldom be given to struggling students. The result is often what two Nanjing-based researchers have called an 'alienation' (*yihua*) of the 'essence of education' (*jiaoyu de benzhi*) (Wang and Wang 2013, 44).

There are exceptions, including the impressively well-equipped schools featured in commercials for charities active in rural education.[19] Some charitable donations sponsor students at regular state schools, while others fund schools run directly by the charity in question. The most famous (or notorious) of these ventures, 'Project Hope', founded in the 1990s, raised millions of dollars from donors within China and abroad, much of it from Hong Kong and overseas Chinese communities, before becoming mired in successive corruption scandals. It epitomised the complex entanglement of state and market, public and private, illustrating how the mirage of civil society activism often dissolves, on closer inspection, into another manifestation of the Party-State. Project Hope was established by the China Youth Development Fund (CYDF), which in turn is operated by the Chinese Communist Youth League (Bandurski 2011).

As Murphy observes, during the 1990s and early 2000s, the 'well-publicised activities' of such state-sponsored charities 'enabled the Party-State to demonstrate to rural people that, despite withdrawing from public goods provisioning, it nevertheless fulfils its caring responsibilities, helping to create the conditions under which citizens could claim basic social entitlements' (2007, 87). (As we noted in Chapter 3.3, the 'Great Western Development Strategy' also featured a form of enforced philanthropy, involving assistance from wealthier coastal provinces to poorer inland regions.)

Thus the commercialisation of Chinese education extends to the practice of philanthropy, affording the chief beneficiaries of the country's rapid growth the opportunity to 'give something back' (or purchase legitimacy for their wealth) in much the same way as comfortable Westerners may quieten their consciences by sponsoring a Somali child, or paying for a school roof in Mali. In 2011, the head of another CYDF-sponsored venture – 'China-Africa Project Hope' – the 24-year-old, California-educated daughter of one of China's wealthiest businessmen, spoke of the 'second-generation rich' becoming the 'second-generation benevolent' (*ren er dai*) (Bandurski 2011). But of course, the fact that rural education still provides a substantial market for the charitable sector, as for shoestring *minban* schools, points up the continuing weakness of state provision in many poorer regions. And the portrayal of rural or 'left-behind' children as objects of charity for their affluent urban compatriots highlights the salience of 'First World'/'Third World' divisions within the borders of a single country.

Conclusion

Advocates of privatisation and competition in public service provision, in China as elsewhere, have tended to invoke the role of the market in promoting efficiency, catering to 'diversity' and accommodating 'choice' (Lin 2007; Wu 2013). These are arguments that cannot lightly be dismissed in the Chinese context, where the hand of the state has for so long lain so heavy on everyday life. In the absence of other methods of holding the regime to account (e.g. electorally), market mechanisms have seemed, to many liberally minded Chinese, the most ready means of injecting accountability and flexibility into the system. Moreover, the huge diversity of contemporary Chinese society undeniably strains the capacity of the state to provide education in a manner that is both uniform and equitable.

In the context of urban China, however, 'diversity' serves largely as a euphemism for 'class'. Educational marketisation has been intimately connected to the rapid re-emergence of class-based social stratification, given a peculiar twist by residency-based rights to public service access. In the early post-Mao years, the reintroduction of competitive public examinations and a stratified education system, topped by urban key point schools, ensured that credentials, power and privilege accrued primarily to relatively privileged city-dwellers. As money flowed into the urban economy from the 1990s, and schooling was simultaneously commercialised, wealthier urbanites were free to purchase preferential educational access for their children. With wealth increasing and competition for credentials intensifying, the expense of commercialised educational 'choice' rose dramatically. In the cities, pressure from residents to curb costs has typically been coupled with a determination to restrict competition from migrants. For their part, rural residents and migrants have sought to both to widen and level the playing field for educational competition.

From around 2005–6, fears over discontent at spiralling costs, rampant marketisation and inequality in educational access prompted the government to modify the 'neoliberalism' of the preceding period, in the process reasserting a measure of central control (Murphy 2007, 89–90). This reflects Hawkins' observation regarding the entire post-1949 period, that 'there is a history of experimentation with different levels and degrees of decentralisation, always against the background of a highly centralised political economy, and often followed by a re-centralisation as authorities retrench fearing loss of control' (2006, 27).

In the countryside, the post-2005 shift took the form of the 'two frees and one subsidy'; in the cities, a clampdown on the commercial activities of state schools, and clarification of their 'public' status. More recently, controversy has centred on the issue of 'school choice', seen by critics such as Yang Dongping (see Chapter 3.4) as emblematic of the inequality of public education and its corruption by money. As we saw in the previous chapter, the administration of Xi Jinping is currently attempting to restrict 'choice' by imposing a zoning system on public schools.

However, with marketisation so entrenched, and the distribution of wealth so stratified, the likely consequence of restricting outlets for fee-based 'choice' within the public sector will be a renewed boom in elite private and overseas schooling. A measure ostensibly aimed at breaking the link between wealth and educational access could lead to more of the wealthiest exiting public schools altogether – widening the social divide between the 'choice-rich' and 'choice-deprived'. Meanwhile, as with earlier measures to restrict school hours and holiday exam preparation classes, blocking the competitive impulse within the state system could divert it towards the supplementary private tutoring industry.

All of which brings us back to the complex sources of that competitive impulse itself – cultural, economic, political and institutional. As we have seen, the vision of education as a ranking and sorting system, governed by tests and examinations, has exceptionally deep roots in China. But meritocracy as a state ideology has also been deliberately elaborated, sustained and adapted over centuries as a tool of political control. In post-Mao China, even while curriculum developers and academics have increasingly lamented the examination-focused narrowness of schooling, the constant quantitative evaluation of students, teachers, schools – and the officials responsible for administering the system (see Chapter 5) – has been institutionalised and reinforced. Schooling has become an exercise in the competitive acquisition of 'numeric capital' (Woronov 2016).

And the stakes in the race to amass it have been raised by labour market liberalisation and higher education expansion, combined with restrictions on family size and suppression of welfare entitlements.

In these circumstances, few can afford not to view education primarily as an investment good – a matter of maximising the family stock of 'human capital'. This phenomenon, and the factors causing it, is of course far from unique to China. But it manifests itself there in a particularly stark and extreme form. We return to the implications of this – social, ethical and political – in the concluding chapter of this volume. First, however, we investigate how the Party's agenda for human capital formation and labour market management, reflecting its enduring *dirigiste* instincts, has clashed with the competitive credentialism that educational marketisation has helped to stoke. Nowhere is this contradiction more apparent than in the field of vocational education and training.

Notes

1 Funded by the Koch brothers, libertarian backers of the Republican Party.
2 The author was seemingly unaware that, by this point, almost forty years had passed since Mao's *Little Red Book* had actually enjoyed 'biblical' status in China.
3 One of the present authors (Vickers) saw this billboard on a visit to Xi'an in early 1994.
4 Lin notes that rising divorce rates were also one significant factor in the popularity of boarding schools (2007, 48).
5 The only exceptions to this rule are international schools, open only to those holding foreign passports.
6 This is one instance of a much wider problem in China's 'market economy' – i.e. the reluctance of state-owned banks to lend to small, independent investors. Most will lend to SOEs or to whomever the Party tells them to lend to, meaning that credit for ordinary businessmen is extremely scarce. In Zhejiang and elsewhere, this has led to the establishment of informal credit networks – *minjian chouzi* – that are technically illegal. In 2012, Wu Ying, a Zhejiang businesswoman, was sentenced to life imprisonment for her role in running one such network.
7 In Wuhan, for example, the founder of a school who had secured the services of Prof. Liu Daoyu, a prominent academic, as school 'sponsor', disappeared with the school's funds, leaving Liu in a highly embarrassing position (see Huang and Chen 2001).
8 Zhang Tieming himself (the source for this paragraph) was involved in the provincial committee in Guangdong that reformed the law on private schools in 2006–7.
9 The 'outlier' in these statistics was that a higher proportion of manual labourers than clerical workers or bureaucrats reported paying choice fees, even though the latter on average earned considerably more than the former. This may be explained by the fact that some bureaucrats (especially) still enjoyed free access to educational facilities run by, or on behalf of, their 'work unit'. See previous chapter.
10 Hansen and Woronov (2013, 250) report parents of students below the cut-off for free entry to one regular senior high in rural Zhejiang paying fees of up to 20,000 yuan (US$3330).
11 Beijing's Number Four Middle School, *alma mater* of many senior Party officials, was amongst those establishing such a section.
12 In Beijing, the No. 2 Affiliated Junior Middle School of Beijing Normal University became a *zhuanzhi* school, changing its name to *San Fan Zhongxue*.
13 Including for single-sex girls schools – see Lin (2007).
14 Evidence regarding students' attitudes towards private tutoring is mixed. Research in Hong Kong (with a very similar culture of tutoring to mainland cities) indicates that

students are more ‘satisfied’ with life if they are receiving tutoring than if they are not (perhaps unsurprisingly, in a context in which most of their peers are being privately tutored after school) (Shek and Li 2014). However, somewhat confusingly, Shek and Li also report a correlation between time spent in tutorial classes, and students’ feelings of ‘hopelessness’ (113).

15 The *Financial Times* was at that time owned by Pearson, a major publisher of school textbooks with a significant interest in expanding the market for private provision of educational services.

16 Zhang (2009) claims that the first *minban* school for migrants was established in Shenzhen in 1990.

17 Kipnis (2011, 41) provides a detailed timetable for a boarding public junior middle school in Zouping, Shandong. Here, formal classes began at 7:40 but ended at 16:40, and – in contrast to the situation at ‘School Y’ – there were scheduled between-class exercises, as well as supervised extra-curricular activities. Students’ daily routine was nonetheless highly regimented, with almost three hours of ‘study hall’ in the evening when they were required to do homework quietly at their desks. Murphy (2004, 11) provides a timetable for a boarding primary school in Jiangxi, which is considerably less intense, with more rest and less homework scheduled – but there, too, the daily routine is highly disciplined; ‘free time’ does not feature.

18 According to Huang *et al.*, the investors in such schools were generally ‘local boys made good’ – in part motivated by a desire to give something back to their home region.

19 Murphy (2007, 89) cites one example of such a commercial for the Jiangxi Charity Foundation, aired by the provincial television station in 2004. On a visit to Beijing in December 2013, I saw a similar commercial being shown repeatedly on CNN.

10 Vocational and technical education

It is only forty years since China was hailed as offering a possible cure for 'the diploma disease'. Ronald Dore was far from alone in expressing qualified admiration for the attempt, during the Cultural Revolution, to 'create schools without the goal of the bread-and-butter, certificate-seeking, lifelessly instrumental motive for learning' (Dore 1980). UNESCO, along with many Western development agencies, recommended a similar approach (Thøgersen 1991, 28). This was envisaged as drastically altering or abolishing secondary-level selection into segregated 'regular' (i.e. academic) and 'vocational' tracks, and the invidious jostling for status that went with it. Access to higher education and further training would become more flexible and in-service, rather than a once-for-all rite of passage into a rigidly bureaucratised workforce. Thus liberated, teachers could pursue a 'new, workable pedagogy which might get children learning either from interest or from a conviction of the substantive worth of what they are learning' (Dore 1980). This, at least, was the vision that enthralled many who observed China from afar (see Pepper 1996, Chapter 1).

It proved to be a mirage. For one thing, the selective function of schooling was not absent during the 1970s; it was strongly present under a different guise. Class background and political connections rather than examination success determined access to further education and employment (Unger 1982). Despite slogans hailing the integration of labour and academic learning (such as 'intellectuals shall be proletarianised, and the working people shall be intellectualised') training remained overwhelmingly pre-service, and manual labour unconnected to any pedagogical purpose. Cultivating a facility for political rhetoric superseded command of technical know-how as the primary objective of all education, whatever the putative focus of learning.

The unquestionable neglect of technical and vocational training during the Cultural Revolution lent legitimacy to post-Mao efforts to move educational debate 'from the political to the technical sphere' (Thøgersen 1991, 40). China, it was argued, urgently needed more technically and vocationally skilled labour to modernise its economy and bring prosperity to its people – and for this, the reinstitution of a vocational secondary track was essential. But along with the rejection of Maoism in education went a virtual refusal to acknowledge the 'social distributive' function of schooling, and a focus instead on its 'qualifying' functions (14–16). Students were exhorted to consider not what their education might do for their careers, but what their labour might do for their country.

For the 'broad masses', however, the selective role of education never ceased to be paramount. It was hugely boosted from 1977, when the national college entrance examination (the *gaokao*) was reinstated, fuelling the 'testing mania' that Thøgersen observed during the 1980s (73). Thirty years on, it has yet to subside, having been further exacerbated by the 'One Child Policy' introduced in 1978. Enforced especially strictly in China's cities, and justified by reference to a neo-eugenicist discourse of 'population quality' (*renkou suzhi*), this compelled urban families to invest their hopes for the future in a single, 'high quality' offspring (Fong 2004).

In the educational sphere, 'quality' has been consistently associated with the acquisition of academic credentials rather than the mastery of technical skills. In this chapter, we discuss why this has been so, analysing repeated official attempts to curb demand for academic higher education and divert a major portion of the nation's youth into vocational training. Repetition, indeed, is a major theme of this story. Reading the literature on technical and vocational education in China, it is striking how, from the 1980s to the present day, officials and academics constantly return to the same refrains. Administrators, educators and students themselves have been exhorted to prioritise vocational education; perceptions of its 'low status' have been lamented; and its importance to national development has been emphasised. But such calls appear largely to have fallen on deaf ears. Why?

Popular disparagement of vocational education: 'Culture' or contingency?

Culturalist explanations have often been officially advanced for the widespread Chinese aversion to vocational education (Woronov 2016, 6–8).[1] But many scholars also emphasise the significance of culture as an explanatory factor. Schmidtke and Chen (2012) stress the influence of Confucian conservatism in prescribing a social hierarchy whose uppermost rungs were reserved for educated *literati* distinguished precisely by their exemption from manual labour. There was no place for vocational studies in the training of the 'superior man'. Kipnis (2011), for his part, notes the persistence in contemporary Chinese culture of traditional images of masculinity that celebrate scholarly success rather than, say, martial exploits.

The importance of culture cannot be discounted, but it is hard to name a single society in which productive manual labour has been esteemed more highly than martial, political or priestly pursuits. Writing in the midst of America's 'Gilded Age', Thorstein Veblen observed that the status of the 'leisured class' is associated not just with the 'conspicuous consumption' of expensive luxuries, but with other markers of a lifestyle removed from graft and toil (Veblen 2007). In imperial Britain, meanwhile, the centrality of the City of London to the institutions of Empire was intimately linked to perceptions of finance as a 'gentlemanly' occupation (Cain and Hopkins 2016). Unlike the grubby business of managing a factory or engaging in 'trade', a financial career was seen as compatible with aristocratic gentility. In prizing sporting and athletic prowess, Britain's elites may otherwise have been more 'martial' than China's 'sagely' *literati*, and less 'mercantile' than America's 'robber barons'. Nonetheless, whether governed by 'merchants', 'soldiers' or 'sages' (Priestland 2012), in practice no society – even when professing the Gospel of the Carpenter of Nazareth – has placed craftsmen, farmers or manual labourers atop its occupational hierarchy.

But if craftsmen were relatively 'humble' in pre-modern societies, the advent of industrialism often rendered them more so. The labourer's impoverishment, the erosion of his dignity and his 'alienation' from the products of his toil were lamented by Marx, Ruskin, Tolstoy, Gandhi and innumerable romantic *litterateurs*. The enforced obsolescence of many skilled crafts, along with their distinctive traditions of learning, was high on the list of charges levelled at capitalist modernity. John Dewey too, in emphasising 'learning through doing' and the need to reconnect education with communal life, shared a concern to counter modernity's 'alienating' tendencies – if tempered by American optimism regarding its possibilities.

Dewey's ideas were one inspiration for the foundation, in 1917, of the Chinese Society for Vocational Education (Curran 2005). In 1922, the Republican Government sought to make vocational training, for the first time, an integral part of the 'New School System'. Huang Yanpei, a leading advocate of vocational education, adumbrated its aims: 'to give work to the unemployed and to give joy to those working', but Schulte observes that this 'joy' was 'less about individual fulfilment than about the joy to serve society' (2013, 230, cited in Woronov 2016, 29). It was seen primarily as something for 'rural and poor citizens' (Schmidtke and Chen 2012, 437). Elites considered vocational training important in equipping the lower orders to assist in the creation of a strong and prosperous state with a disciplined, well-trained and well-equipped army – a project both inspired by, and directed against, imperial Japan. Developing a vocational track was also 'a way to tackle the social problem of the working classes by managing their aspirations for additional education and upward mobility' (Woronov 2016, 30). For the higher orders in China as elsewhere, the consequences of failure in this regard were crystallised in the threat of Bolshevism.

It was Soviet Russia during the 1920s that witnessed what were, up to that point, the most radical state-sponsored experiments in integrating academic study and manual labour – but this radicalism was short-lived. The 'cultural revolutionaries' of Narkompros, championed by Lenin's widow Krupskaya, and again inspired by Deweyan ideas, advocated the integration of academic learning and productive toil, dispensing with conventional textbooks and examinations (Fitzpatrick 1979). The results were chaotic, not least because the idealists in Moscow were incapable of translating their vision into practicable guidelines comprehensible to existing teachers. By the 1950s, when it was sending advisors to newly Communist China, the USSR had consigned such experiments to history's dustbin, reinstating the conventional divide between academic and vocational tracks. Nonetheless, in pre-Cultural Revolution China, when overall educational levels were low, 'vocational education graduates were considered intellectuals who were respected for their skills and contributions to the Party, their work units and the nation' (Hansen and Woronov 2013, 245).

This status derived from the scarcity value then appertaining to secondary education of whatever kind, access to which was mediated by competitive public examinations. But this mechanism was seen as favouring those with 'bad class backgrounds'. As already noted, the Cultural Revolution thus sought to abolish selection by examination, while removing the stigma attached to manual labour.

Thøgersen distinguishes between the (often contradictory) 'economic, moral/political, pedagogical and job-preparatory purposes of combining theory with practice' (1991, 97). Before 1978, the economic purposes (i.e. supplementing school funds) and the moral/political mode predominated, and afterwards, the job-preparatory argument. However, 'during both periods, the pedagogical argument, which calls for adapting productive activities to the learning process rather than the other way around, has had a very limited influence' (97). In other words, pedagogical didacticism, rooted in a vision of the teacher as authoritarian exemplar, persisted, even if the moral/political content of schooling had changed. The Deweyan conception of 'doing' as a means of 'learning', an important component of 1920s Russian theory, still struggled to thrive in Chinese soil (as indeed it had in Russia, too).

The Reform leadership's reimposition, from the late 1970s, of the division between vocational and 'regular' tracks in secondary education was related to a renewed desire to limit access to academic further education, and to 'cultivate comprehensive developed personnel in line with social requirements' (Wu and Ye 2010, 72, cited in Schmidtke and Chen 2012, 433). In other words, vocational education was once again tasked with providing footsoldiers for industrialisation and underpinning social stability, while abjuring any commitment to elevate the status of manual labour.

One symptom of the post-Mao embrace of developmentalism and 'catch-up modernisation' is that the models invoked by advocates of vocational education have almost invariably derived from 'advanced' industrialised countries (see Chapter 3.2). By the end of the 1980s, Germany alone was involved in more than forty cooperative projects in vocational education (Yang 2008). Seldom considered, on the other hand, has been the very mixed experience with vocational education of developing, largely agricultural economies more comparable with China (Thøgersen 1991, 110–11).

However, attempts to gear vocational education to the satisfaction of 'social requirements' are constantly frustrated by shifts in the nature of those requirements (see Wolf 2002). In China since the 1970s, the vastness and rapidity of the economic transformation has rendered this problem especially acute. Changes in the labour market make the widespread popular aversion to vocational education entirely rational, rather than simply a product of irrational 'cultural' prejudice (Hansen and Woronov 2013, 246). Whether for urban or rural students, vocational secondary education has generally led – especially since the labour market reforms of the 1990s – to relatively low-paid, insecure work, while precluding access to the more lucrative and prestigious careers open to college graduates. Even following improvements to welfare provision since the mid-2000s, many urban and most rural parents can expect little state support in the event of sickness or retirement. Securing a college education for at least one child is thus a matter not only of 'face' or family pride – though these are important considerations – but also of pressing economic necessity.

The technical and vocational education system in the early Reform period

Policy

Whether or not the restitution of a vocational 'track' in secondary schooling was the appropriate solution, the problem it was supposed to address was very real in the late 1970s: the shortage of skilled workers and middle-level technicians. This was widely blamed on the irresponsible destruction of vocational training during the Cultural Revolution. The 1980s consequently witnessed a major expansion in technical and vocational education at the senior high level. Looking back in 1991, Li Tieying (State Councillor with responsibility for Education) noted with satisfaction that the proportion of senior high students enrolled in vocational as opposed to 'regular' schools had risen from 21 per cent in 1980 to 48 per cent ten years later (IED 1991, 3101) – thus (almost) fulfilling a 1983 pledge that, by 1990, half of all students at this level should be in vocational schools (Thøgersen 1991, 100).

At the 1978 National Conference on Education, Deng Xiaoping made expansion of agricultural and technical/vocational education (TVE) central to plans for secondary schooling reform. Reasons cited included not only the need for skilled workers essential to pursuing the 'four modernisations', but also limited college places, the consequent 'wastefulness' of keeping so many students in regular secondary schools, and serious youth unemployment. Although some criticised the 'capitalist' precedents for the two-track system, reformers argued that a society's education system 'reflects its level of economic growth and is therefore to a large degree independent of the subjective will of individuals'. Indeed, current practice in developed societies was widely cited to buttress the impression that vocationalisation of secondary education was 'a manifestation of objective "laws" rather than a political choice' (Thøgersen 1991, 98). Throughout the 1980s, state and Party organs reiterated this message. In 1985, the CCP Central Committee issued a 'Decision' stipulating that 'socialist modernisation' urgently required 'millions of intermediate and junior engineers, managerial personnel and technicians':

> Without a huge contingent of such workers …, advanced sciences and technologies and sophisticated equipment cannot be translated into productive forces … [V]ocational and technical education constitute the weakest link in the whole of China's education. Therefore, it is imperative that we take effective measures to change this situation …
>
> (Quoted in Lewin *et al.* 1996, 4)

This 'Decision' formalised policy shifts already well underway. In 1980, the Central Committee had declared that 'some general secondary schools' must be changed 'into vocational schools in an active and gradual way', and called for the establishment of a 'network' of different kinds of TVE institutions (Lewin *et al.* 1996, 2). At the same time, it was determined that 'educational development below the county level should "face the countryside"'. However, according to Thøgersen (1991, 99), there was evidence of initial foot-dragging, with the move to vocationalisation swiftest in the most industrialised areas: Jilin, Liaoning, Heilongjiang and Jiangsu. It was here that the demand for vocationally trained graduates was most clear and present; elsewhere, it was often more a question of hoping that demand would arise to absorb supply.

Structure and administration

There was in fact nothing 'gradual' about the shift to a two-track system of secondary education after 1978, as Table 10.1 indicates. The precipitous fall in the number of general or 'regular' senior secondary schools after 1979, and sudden appearance of several thousand vocational and technical schools, was intimately related to the equally sudden reintroduction of competitive college entrance examinations (the *gaokao*). Attendance at 'regular' senior high schools entitled students to sit for these examinations, whereas vocational or technical high school graduates were excluded. The 1986 commitment to universalising nine years of compulsory education lent added urgency to the task of diverting junior secondary graduates away from the college-entry senior high track. As Woronov observes (2016, 4–6), as access to secondary schooling expanded, the *zhongkao*, or high school entrance exam – rather than the more widely discussed *gaokao* – increasingly became the crucial determinant of life chances (see Chapter 8). Rural–urban inequality in educational access was meanwhile further entrenched, since the concentration in urban areas of the best regular schools has meant that the percentage of students entering regular senior high schools has tended to be lower in poorer, rural areas. In addition, holders of rural *hukou* have typically been required to attain significantly higher senior high school entrance

Table 10.1 Number of senior high schools by type, 1979–94

			SMS		
Year	*General*	*AMS + VMS*	*Technical*	*Normal*	*WTS*
1979	40,289	–	1,980	1,053	–
1981	24,447	2,655	2,170	962	–
1983	18,876	5,487	2,229	861	3,443
1989	16,050	9,173	2,940	1,044	4,102
1992	14,850	9,860	2,984	919	4,392
1994	14,242	10,217	3,093	894	N/A

Note: Data from Lewin *et al.* (1996, 3).

exam scores than their urban counterparts in order to gain admission to academically oriented 'key schools'.[2]

In the early post-Reform years, a crucial distinction existed between 'specialised schools', whether technical or 'normal' (i.e. teacher training-focused), on the one hand, and 'agricultural and vocational' or 'skilled worker' schools on the other. Under the Soviet-style system of job assignments in place up to the mid-1990s, students at the former, but not the latter, were virtually guaranteed employment on graduation. The main types of vocational schools during this period were as follows:

- *Vocational middle schools (VMS)* (*zhiye zhongxue*): Occupying the lowest, and cheapest, tier of the urban senior high school hierarchy, during the 1980s most of these were converted former general secondary schools. Most were run by the local Education Bureau, and a few by SOEs. These schools were only open to students with urban residency (*hukou*). Their popularity depended, according to Thøgersen, 'mainly ... on job prospects: a more lively economy with a ... more flexible job structure creates a greater demand for VMS graduates' (1991, 103).
- *Agricultural middle schools (AMS)* (*nongye zhongxue*): These were the equivalent of VMS for rural areas. In official policy, they were often linked to plans for 'diversification' of the rural economy. Like VMS, during the 1980s most AMS were converted former regular secondary schools (generally the shabbiest and most poorly equipped). As more rural students realised that they had 'very few chances of entering university', applications for AMS picked up somewhat, but the relatively slow progress of the vocationalisation reform in rural areas was attributed to their persistent unpopularity (Thøgersen 1991, 105). In the 1980s, most graduates went back to working the family land. Some AMS were officially classified as junior rather than senior secondary schools, or as 'combined' junior–senior secondary schools – though this practice was rapidly phased out from around 2000 (according to statistics in the official NBS yearbooks).
- *Workers training schools (WTS)* (*gongren jishu xuexiao*) *– or technical schools:* Supervised by the Ministry of Labour, but mostly accountable to the organisations that funded them (local commerce bureaux or SOEs), these schools were often partially staffed by SOE technicians. Entry to WTS was through entrance examinations (taken either at the end of junior or senior secondary school). In the 1980s, many students were children of workers in the SOE responsible for the school, and destined for jobs in the same enterprise through the 'replacement' (*dingti*) system, which the Central Government was trying to abolish. WTS combined classroom instruction with practical training in a school factory or in the 'hosting enterprise' (107).
- *Specialised middle schools (SMS)* (*zhongdeng zhuanye xuexiao*): These institutions were tasked with training primary-level teachers, health sector workers (nurses and laboratory technicians), accountants (often under

> the rubric of 'finance and economics'), and middle-level technicians for industry. Based on Soviet models, they stood at the top of the secondary TVE hierarchy. But, as with other vocational schools in the 1980s, many were encouraged to shift their recruitment focus from senior to junior secondary graduates – with the aim of diverting more students, earlier, from competition for entry to regular higher education. Meanwhile, other SMS were 'upgraded' to the status of 'specialised colleges' (*zhuanke xuexiao*), a process that was to accelerate during the late 1990s and 2000s (see below). One type of state-managed 'specialised' vocational education that has survived down to the present is that operated by the People's Liberation Army, which continues to provide one route off the farm for many rural youth.[3]

From early on in the vocationalisation drive, the government sought, as a 1985 Central Committee directive put it, to 'bring into full play the initiative of enterprises and establishments as well as the departments concerned' (cited in Lewin and *et al.* 1996, 5).[4] The Education Reform Law of 1986 stipulated the goal of requiring vocational students to rely on 'market mechanisms' to secure jobs after graduation (Woronov 2016, 34). In practice, however, such calls for public–private collaboration and labour market liberalisation initially met with a mixed and lacklustre response. Until the early 1990s, the vocational training system, like the still unreformed state-run economic sector, remained largely 'pillarised', with different SOEs or government agencies responsible for their own training arrangements. For example, the Beijing Transport School (*Beijing Jiaotong Xuexiao*), responsible for training bus and train drivers, answered to the Beijing City Transport Bureau (*Jiaotong Ju*). Many other WTS were controlled by local commerce bureaux (*Shangye Ju*), and were often referred to as 'Commercial Schools' (*Shangye Xuexiao*). Others fell under the auspices of 'Bureaux of Light Industry' (*Qing Gongye Ju*) or 'Resources Bureaux' (*Wuzi Ju*).

As marketisation gathered pace from the early 1990s, and the system of state job assignments was rapidly dismantled, these bureaux were to find their authority rapidly eroded. Surveying the vocational education landscape in the mid-1990s, Lewin *et al.* observed a growing diversity of managerial or administrative arrangements. Especially in some larger cities, many technical and vocational schools were jointly run by the municipal Education Bureau (providing teachers, facilities and funds for 'academic subjects') and by 'production units' or SOEs (providing the same for specialised or vocational subjects). They reported that 'about 50 per cent' of vocational schools in Beijing, and 'the majority' in Shanghai, were administered in this fashion (1996, 5). Outside large cities, schools run directly by production units were more common.

Following the gradual breakdown of the 'closed' or 'pillarised' model of technical training associated with the planned economy, development of a system of accredited apprenticeships involving private enterprise has proved difficult. Assuming a regulatory rather than controlling role has proven problematic for the Communist authorities in many spheres, and vocational education is no exception. In 1991, the State Education Commission announced a '100 key point vocational high schools' project (IED 1991, 3101). The precise outcome of this is unclear, but such initiatives have not been notably successful in addressing the needs of small business or much of the private sector (Guan and Shi 2013; Molnar and Koen 2015). On the other hand, the lack of a culture of business involvement in apprenticeship provision; a prevalence of low-skilled, labour-intensive manufacturing jobs; and more recently of insecure, low-skilled service sector employment have made it hard to persuade entrepreneurs of the need to invest much in training their employees (Woronov 2016, 25).[5] Hand-wringing on this score has been a running refrain of much Chinese scholarship (Zhang and Xu 2010; He 2013).

Finance

In terms of resources as well as status, vocational and technical schools were the 'poor cousins' of regular senior high schools. In theory, they received the same *per capitum* as regular high schools, but mid-1990s data showed average funding per student lower than in regular high schools, and on a downward trajectory (Lewin *et al.* 1996, 10). Even parity would have meant the relative under-funding of vocational institutions, given the higher equipment costs they would be expected to incur. As it was, far more regular than vocational high schools met minimum standards for laboratory facilities (44 per cent versus 22.6 per cent) or experimental equipment (42.6 per cent versus 18.7 per cent) (9). Many computing courses offered by vocational schools taught 'largely redundant programming skills' using 'dated software' (13).

The funding squeeze on vocational institutions was exacerbated by increasing reliance on user fees to fund all forms of post-compulsory education – a problem that was even more acute by the mid-1990s (see below). Until then, WTS generally enjoyed relative financial security by virtue of their connection with an SOE, though most VMS and, especially, AMS were less fortunate. Where possible, schools commonly supplemented their funds by leasing out land, buildings or facilities, or by earning income on their students' labour (a common expedient for hospitality and catering schools that ran training hotels or restaurants) (9). During the 1980s, many AMS were still following a 'half-work, half-study' model, with students engaged part-time in productive labour. This led to accusations that they were perpetuating 'Cultural Revolution ideas' (Thøgersen 1991, 105), but it owed more to financial necessity than political ideology.

Curriculum and assessment

However TVE was administered, curricular oversight and the professional training of teachers was – as it still remains – the responsibility of local education bureaux, and ultimately of the Ministry in Beijing. The Party's enduring instinct for control means that curricula for many subjects in vocational schools 'still tend to be written by bureaucrats at the national level, who follow official precepts, maintain a focus on cognitive learning, and do not take local conditions into account' (Schmidtke and Chen 2012, 441). Training is often 'decoupled from skills needed on the job', equipment is inadequate, and course content 'outdated'. The focus is 'on theory, cognitive skills, and rote learning rather than applied skills and critical thinking', while linkages with industry are 'few and far between' (442–3). These observations, made in 2012, closely echo those of Lewin *et al.* in 1996, to the effect that 'much teaching tends towards the theoretical rather than the practical' (12) – and Thøgersen's comments on classes he observed in Beijing during the late 1980s (1991, 111–12; see also Chapter 6). Criticisms of vocational curricula and pedagogy have been remarkably consistent throughout the post-Mao period.

Vocational schooling – especially in VMS and AMS – has thus often offered little more than a debased variant of the regular high school curriculum, along with vocationally oriented courses of dubious pedagogical value. In VMS during the 1980s, there was supposed to be a 1:1 split between vocational and general subjects, but up to two-thirds of time for the former was spent on 'basic theory related to the speciality' which left 'little time for practical training' (Thøgersen 1991, 104). Lewin *et al.* (1996) blamed a 're-academicisation' of vocational training on a lack of appropriate equipment or learning materials.

Reinforcing the 'academic' or 'theoretical' bent of much TVE has been the persistent reliance on written examinations for assessing students. Although practical experience or job placements have featured in many programmes, developing a system for assessing and accrediting these has proved problematic (see below). The notion that the knowledge that 'counts' is what can be tested through a timed, written examination dies hard in China. While boosting Chinese performance in international 'league tables' based on written tests, this handicaps efforts to devise ways of assessing practical, 'on-the-job' competencies.

Ironically, given this relative neglect of practical skills, vocational programmes have typically been 'mono-valant', narrowly focusing on a single occupation (Lewin *et al.* 1996, 10). Many graduates thus lack the generic skills needed to adapt to shifts in the labour market, or qualifications seen as reliably certifying their possession of such skills. In the freewheeling 1990s, when secondary schools of all kinds were being encouraged to marketise, Lewin *et al.* also wrote of the 'fallacy of competition' for fees leading to boom-and-bust cycles in attractive specialisms. An oversupply of trainees would suddenly flood the market, leaving many unable to find relevant employment. Courses in accountancy, public relations, finance and textile manufacturing proliferated in AMS, where they were preferred to agriculturally related ones since, by the mid-1990s, everyone in the countryside was looking for a route off the farm.

Teachers

The nature of the implemented TVE curriculum was of course highly dependent on the teaching force. Recruitment and retention of qualified teachers tended to be far easier for WTS and SMS, which could often borrow staff from their affiliated SOE, than for VMS or AMS, which enjoyed no such connections. As of 1995, 65 per cent of teachers in technical schools were graduates of appropriate college-level courses, whereas this was true of only 30 per cent of their VMS counterparts (Lewin *et al.* 1996, 7). The problem of recruiting specialised teachers was especially acute in VMS converted from regular senior high schools, though finding teachers for academic subjects was less problematic. AMS experienced the worst difficulties, and during the 1980s employed many teachers on a part-time basis (Thøgersen 1991, 104). This period witnessed an expansion of training colleges for TVE teachers and of 'short-term vocational universities', often private (Mok 1997). However, recruiting good staff to teach vocational subjects proved difficult because of both the low social prestige attached to such jobs, and the fact that 'those with high levels of skill may be able to earn considerably more income by practising their profession than by teaching it' (Lewin *et al.* 1996, 7).

Taking stock in the early 1990s

By the beginning of the 1990s, the vocational track accounted for about half of all senior high school enrolments. But only 20 per cent of the relevant age group was then receiving any schooling at this level, only half having actually completed junior secondary school (IED 1991, 3101). As Li Tieying noted in a key speech in January 1991, annually, 5.5 million primary graduates and 7 million junior secondary graduates were therefore entering the labour market without any vocational training. To underline the dire implications, he cited a 1989 survey showing that farmers graduating from vocational senior high schools earned significantly more not only than those who were merely primary or junior secondary graduates, but also more than the few who had attended regular senior high schools. The failure to raise enrolments in vocational schools was thus, he argued, hampering efforts to upgrade the nation's 'human capital' and boost individual earning power.

Irrespective of the reliability of these figures, Li's decision to focus on the situation of rural students reflected the fundamental purpose of vocationalisation: keeping the labouring population, especially its agricultural component, in its place. The government was battling strong countervailing pressure resulting from the reintroduction of the *gaokao* and *zhongkao*, which oriented regular secondary schooling decisively towards test preparation and college entry. As Thøgersen observed, this was the fundamental reason why vocationalisation was so rushed and so little debated in the early Reform years, contributing to a failure to 'design a curriculum capable of transmitting useful general and specific skills to the large majority of students' (1991, 115). This issue would remain unresolved during the 1990s, even as a host of marketising reforms to the urban economy, to the labour market, and to education itself transformed both demand for, and supply of vocational schooling – and brought more and more rural youth into China's cities.

Growth and reform in the vocational sector during the 1990s

The low prestige of vocational education, though far from unique to post-Mao China, was reinforced by memories of the manual labour performed by 'sent-down youth' during the Cultural Revolution, and by the continuing use of labour as a form of punishment. 'Re-education through labour' (*laodong jiaoyang*) has remained a pillar of the Chinese correctional system, often used to punish religious or political dissidents as well as petty criminals.[6] In the aftermath of the student protests in 1989, Thøgersen speculated about a likely extension of the use of labour education as a form of punishment. Were this to happen, he wrote, 'its prestige will drop even lower, and it will become even more difficult to bring into play the pedagogical aspect of the concept' (1991, 117).

In the event, a form of 'reeducation through labour' was applied to new entrants to postgraduate programmes in 1989–90, who were sent to rural areas or to factories to teach and work for one year in order to expose them to 'the real China'. This scheme was quickly abandoned, but for undergraduate and high school students, military training was instituted to instil discipline and dispel unhealthy liberal-democratic proclivities (see Chapter 3.3). Though reduced in length, these programmes have been retained, and even extended (with appropriate adaptations) to primary school level. Despite occasioning many complaints, labour and military education have not simply been tools of state repression; in recent years some urban parents have even seen a spell in military boot camp as an ideal corrective for unruly 'little emperors' (although others prefer a less disciplinarian approach with a greater emphasis on children's 'rights') (He N. 2014). But the association of labour with governmental or patriarchal discipline has not enhanced general perceptions of the status of manual graft.

In illustrating the political threat posed by under-occupied and over-educated youth, the 1989 Student Movement prompted a renewed, if short-lived, official emphasis on restricting college access (see Chapters 11 and 12). The vocationalisation drive also acquired new momentum, manifested in a flurry of pronouncements between 1991 and 1993. In his 1991 speech, Li Tieying announced that henceforth 70 per cent of senior high schools should be 'vocational', and only 30 per cent 'regular', justifying this in relation to the challenges posed by the universalisation of 9 years of compulsory education (IED 1991, 3101). With more and more candidates eligible to apply for senior high school, it was important to divert as many as possible into economically useful but politically anodyne fields. When the State Council formally adopted the 70:30 target, it called for a 'concentration of efforts' to ensure that, at the very least, a majority of senior high students were enrolled in vocational schools (IED 1991, 3221–2). Results were mixed; a 1993 progress report found that the proportion of the cohort in vocational schools was 61 per cent in Beijing, 54 per cent in Liaoning and 50 per cent in Sichuan (IED 1993, 3495). In 1996, a new 'Vocational Education Law' stipulated a half-half divide between 'regular' and TVE senior high enrolments (Woronov 2016, 35). Ministry of Education statistics showed that this was achieved by 2000, implying little change from ten years earlier (though absolute numbers of students in each sector had almost doubled) (MOE 2013).

The intervening decade had witnessed considerable upheaval in the administration of TVE, as marketisation undermined or fundamentally altered many structures of the planned economy (see Chapter 3.3). The centralised system of job allocation (the *fenpei zhidu*) was gradually abandoned, breaking the link between specialised technical schools and a state sector 'iron rice bowl' (Woronov 2016). Many local bureaux at the pinnacle of the old pillarised state planning system, encompassing much of the TVE sector, lost their functions, as taxation reforms from 1994 forced more and more SOEs to operate in the marketplace. Transport bureaux, for example, lost control over local bus services, and the ability to allocate jobs in this sector. Having seen their functions steadily eroded, in 1998 commerce bureaux were abolished, and their functions subsumed under those of various other bureaux. Their TVE responsibilities were transferred to local bureaux of education. Other schools remained within the old state-planning system – Woronov discusses one example in Nanjing (2016, 37–9) – but their status *vis-à-vis* the educational bureaucracy was confused and ambiguous, and their future increasingly uncertain.

The same marketising and taxation reforms fraying the links between technical schools and state entities were also associated with 'increased direct costs of post-compulsory education' across the board (Lewin *et al.* 1996, 6). By the middle of the decade, many public senior high schools were charging increasingly inflated fees to students with marginally below-par test scores. Since vocational and technical schools were relatively cheap, they became a more attractive option for students from poorer backgrounds whose families could afford neither top-up 'school choice' payments for public senior high schools, nor high fees for academically oriented private schools. Moreover, the wages obtainable in certain fields – computing, foreign language-related occupations, the hospitality and catering sector, and repair and maintenance – were attractive compared with those that fresh graduates of regular, academic high schools could command. In a context of continuing restrictions on the expansion of college places available to regular senior high graduates, this also enhanced the draw of vocational schooling.

The dismantling of the job allocation system, by placing a greater premium on acquiring marketable 'skills', might also be assumed to have rendered the vocational track more alluring (Lewin *et al.* 1994, 219). However, as we have seen, the extent to which such skills were actually taught in vocational schools was highly variable. The 1990s witnessed new efforts to revise and improve curricula, and to strengthen links between the vocational education sector and industry. The SEC and Ministries for Trade and Labour called in 1998 for a 'holding fast to the principle of linking education and production' (IED 1998, 50), but how this link would be realised in practice remained unclear. In the late 1990s, many SOEs were struggling to survive, while the economy remained mired in a period of relatively low growth (especially following the 1997 Asian Financial Crisis).

Developing outreach programmes to vocational schools was therefore something few enterprises were motivated to engage in. Under the command economy, providing apprenticeships and vocational education was a function of the SOEs, and has remained relatively strong where SOEs remain locally significant, as in Northeast China.

China's government – like those of America, Britain, France and Korea, amongst others – has sought to import elements of the German vocational training system (Brunstermann 2001), but has had limited success in doing so. German apprenticeships are locally organised, communally rooted, involve close collaboration between enterprises and 'company unions', and are highly expensive – thus making the system very hard to replicate (Wolf 2002, 141–45). Moreover, as Wolf suggests, the key benefits of the German system are perhaps social rather than economic, and consist of providing young people with a sense of identity and dignity (145); the Chinese system tends to do the opposite, as evidenced by Woronov's ethnographic study (2016).

Consistent with Premier Zhu Rongji's attempted repositioning of the state as a market regulator rather than direct provider, efforts to systematise a national TVE qualifications framework were stepped up from the mid-1990s. Lewin *et al.* reported that, in 1995, the National Examinations Authority was working on plans 'to develop a national system of certificates and diplomas' for vocational and technical education (1996, 8). The qualifications models most frequently referenced have been German – for example, the 'KOMET' system for assessing students in higher vocational education (Xiao and Li 2014); but the assessment of vocational competencies still tends to rely on written tests (see below). From the mid-1990s, the number of vocational qualifications officially accredited at national level has steadily increased, but creating a national framework for systematically comparing qualifications awarded by various institutions in different provinces has become ever more complicated as the sector has diversified.[7]

Since the 1990s, there have been efforts to assess and rank the 'quality' of provincial TVE systems. One such attempt, by Chen and Ma (2005), placed Zhejiang, Beijing, Shanghai, Tianjin and Jiangsu in a 'top' group, reflecting the longstanding CCP penchant for identifying local 'models' in various fields that are then promoted for emulation across the nation (see Chapters 3.2 and 3.3). But the predictable outcome of this exercise – with the usual suspects featuring in the 'high-quality' tier – suggests that measures of quality may reflect the influence of economic prosperity on vocational education systems, rather than *vice versa*. Factors alluded to in previous chapters apply here: for example, the advantages that wealthier provinces have in recruiting the most qualified teachers (see Chapter 7), and the greater ease with which graduates in economically booming regions find employment. In inter-provincial as well as international comparative studies of educational 'performance', it is easy to confuse cause and consequence in the relationship between schooling and economic growth. Ambitious recent proposals for a national qualifications framework are potentially vulnerable to this confusion – if and when they are actually implemented (see Zhao Z. 2014).[8]

The expansion of higher education and its implications for TVE (since 1998)

Despite the many problems discussed above, the early- to mid-1990s in retrospect came to be seen as a 'golden age' for TVE. As the Eighth Five Year Plan concluded in 1996, officials celebrated that 57 per cent of senior high students were now in vocational schooling, and set a target of 60 per cent for 2010 (IED 1996, 3936; 3970). A key reason for the increase in vocational enrolments was the relatively measured pace of higher education expansion, which restricted the growth of the regular high school sector. Greater labour market openness also created opportunities for those with certain vocational skills, and the TVE sector was given a pioneering role in reforming the 'iron rice bowl' system of state employment: 'from the early 1990s on, most vocational graduates were not allocated jobs in the state sector' (Woronov 2016, 34). However, the dismantling of the job allocation system and spread of competitive recruitment practices also fuelled credentialism. Mid-level managerial, technical and other skilled jobs previously reserved for vocational school graduates increasingly went to those with college degrees (Hansen and Woronov 2013, 246). Demand for academic qualifications thus intensified, even as the capped growth of regular college places limited supply.

The post-1998 expansion of higher education, by dramatically raising that cap, triggered an immediate decline in TVE enrolments – both proportionally and in absolute terms. By 2005, vocational enrolments were down to just below 40 per cent of the total (MOE 2013). The authorities seem at first to have been taken by surprise, but in 2002 the State Council announced a renewed push to expand vocational education, and the state has since 'poured resources into developing vocational training at all levels' (Hansen and Woronov 2013, 242). Total enrolments in vocational high schools appeared to pick up from around 2002–3, and from 2006 also increased relative to those in regular senior high schools (MOE 2013). By 2013, the Ministry's figures showed a 55:45 split between enrolments in the academic and vocational tracks at this level (with total student numbers by this point almost double those of 2000). Woronov states that this was achieved by holding down the national *zhongkao* pass rate to 50 per cent (while allowing for regional variations), thus restricting the number of students able to access regular high schools. Her interpretation of the Ministry statistics may somewhat exaggerate the proportion of junior secondary graduates going on to vocational senior high schools.[9] In Zouping County, Shandong, Kipnis reported that, by the early 2000s, 'roughly 80 percent of junior [secondary] school graduates go to academic senior [high] school' (2011, 82), though it is hard to say how representative this may be of the national picture.[10] The attractiveness of the vocational track has meanwhile been further eroded by urban de-industrialisation, causing more and more TVE graduates to gravitate towards low-paid and relatively insecure service sector jobs (Hansen and Woronov 2013, 246).

The overall growth of TVE in the 2000s was accompanied by increasing diversification of provision. Alongside the various remaining state- or SOE-run schools, many more private vocational schools arose to occupy the bottom rung of the TVE hierarchy. At the other end of the spectrum, Hansen and Woronov report an experimental vocational 'track' within a regular public senior high school in rural Zhejiang (2013, 247). The result of this diversity has been to confront junior secondary students with a 'bewildering array of choices' (247); even researchers are confused, with Woronov writing that 'because so many different kinds of schools are called vocational or technical schools, it is difficult to conceptualise a vocational education system that holds together with any overall coherency' (2016, 35). Wang condemns this proliferation of forms of provision as 'wasteful', and calls for stronger official coordination and regulation (Wang D. 2010).

Increasing institutional diversity has been accompanied by continuing variability in instructional quality. Some schools combine secondary and post-secondary vocational training in a five-year *dazhuan* programme, but most vocational schools offer a three-year *zhongzhuan* (secondary vocational) programme. This typically involves two years of classroom study – general and 'technical' – and a final year of apprenticeship (*shixi*), often 'extremely informal' (Hansen and Woronov 2013, 247). Physical conditions in the Nanjing schools Woronov visited in 2007–8 were very poor indeed, suggesting that the relative under-investment in TVE noted by Lewin *et al.* in the 1990s had persisted. Also little changed was the typical curriculum, still consisting of a diluted version of that for regular senior high schools, supplemented by supposedly vocational lessons with dry or irrelevant content. Hansen and Woronov witnessed tourism students memorising tour guides,[11] bookkeeping students practising the abacus, computer science students playing computer games during class, and abysmally low motivation all round (2013, 253). Many classes were taught by unqualified staff: in the regular rural high school in Zhejiang, regular subject teachers took vocational lessons, and in Nanjing many classes were taken by staff on part-time (effectively zero-hours) contracts, including retired elementary school teachers and local postgraduate students (the latter with no teacher training and generally 'no pedagogical skills') (255).

Meanwhile, the hands-on training or internship (*shixi*) component of vocational courses has often been both irrelevant and exploitative. Woronov's Nanjing bookkeeping students spent a month performing data entry for a private company that paid the school for this work, but not the students (2016, 124). The businesses most willing to collaborate with vocational schools have often been small private firms looking to reduce their costs. Such firms also tend to expose their employees to greater risks. One survey found that 40 per cent of vocational students suffered some sort of injury during their internship period (Jia 2008). Many firms have been reluctant to offer better terms to interns for fear that other companies will reap the rewards of this investment by 'poaching' the best of them; high mobility amongst skilled and semi-skilled workers, reflecting low commitment to their employers, is the flip side of minimal welfare provision and weak protection of workers' rights. Woronov argues that this also applies to teachers, and contrasts the behaviour of contractual and permanent staff in one of the Nanjing schools in her study. She argues that the casual attitude and relatively lax work ethic of many (though not all) contract teachers reflects the reality of life as an insecure employee in the modern service economy (2016, Chapter 3).

Demand for vocational education has nonetheless been far from uniformly low. For urban students, the advent of mass college education appears to have exacerbated the stigma of vocational schooling, since TVE graduates' prospects of entering a regular college are extremely slight. Students in the Nanjing schools surveyed by Woronov were typically described by their teachers as 'stupid and lazy', and many accepted their designation as failures (Hansen and Woronov 2013, 249).[12] In rural Zhejiang, by contrast, diversification of provision led to a more gradated form of stratification, with TVE by no means seen as a dead end. The vocational stream within the local regular senior high school was perceived as relatively prestigious, not because of the content of the training on offer, but due to 'the mere fact that these vocational students were physically integrated into a regular high school' (250). Moreover, this strategy paid off for some, since the top 20 per cent of vocational students were eventually allowed to transfer to the regular track – making them eligible to sit the *gaokao*. After just three years, though, this experiment was abandoned, to the relief both of the school authorities, and of parents of children in the regular track, who feared that their offspring were being contaminated by the 'low *suzhi*' vocational students (assumed to have 'bad study habits'). From 2012, most students in the township who failed to test into regular senior high schools were to go to a large, new, better-equipped vocational school offering a wide range of specialisms. Given the chance, however, most parents would still have opted for a vocational track within a regular high school, because of the possibility (albeit slim) that this offered their children of transferring to the regular, *gaokao*-preparatory stream.

While noting the strength of popular resistance to vocational education in their Jiangsu and Zhejiang field sites, Hansen and Woronov cite rapid growth in the sector as evidence that, especially in rural areas, parents are 'both demanding and resisting' TVE. For many rural students vocational education at least offers a route into urban employment. However, as the economy slows down, the labour market tightens, and prospects of access to regular college improve (while the population of high school graduates shrinks), resistance to vocational education may increasingly triumph over demand for it.

Tertiary TVE and routes into urban employment

A key plank in the post-1998 strategy for buttressing the attractiveness of secondary-level TVE involved expanding tertiary-level vocational provision. Until the 1990s, vocational high schools were generally either two- or three-year institutions, but from 1999 onwards many were upgraded or merged to form four-year technical and vocational colleges (*zhiye jishu xueyuan*) (IED 1999, 215). This rash of institutional mergers was part of a wider trend across the tertiary education field in the post-1998 period, discussed further in Chapter 12. Vocationalisation at tertiary and secondary levels was largely governed by the same logic: the need to divert students away from 'regular', academic studies. Official statistics show a marked increase from 2000 in the number of vocational colleges, offsetting a decline in the number of 'higher technical schools' (*gaodeng zhuanke xuexiao*). The total number of institutions offering tertiary-level vocational programmes climbed from around 200 in the year 2000 to over 1,100 in 2010 (NBS 1999–2010, cited in Sun 2015, 23).

What, though, is the qualitative difference between vocational instruction at 'high school' and 'college' level? Graduates from two- or three-year courses receive a *dazhuan* diploma, while those from four-year *benke* (undergraduate-level) programmes earn a bachelor's degree. However, the extent to which *benke* programmes offer qualitatively superior training to sub-degree college or high school courses is variable. Where institutions have been able to forge particularly strong links with local industry, the quality of 'hands-on' as well as academic instruction may be relatively high.[13] Generally, though, tertiary vocational colleges face similar challenges to their secondary counterparts, prompting persistent calls for greater 'professionalisation' of instruction at both levels.

Since the mid-2000s, the concept of 'teachers with dual certification' (*shuangshi xing jiaoshi*) has been promoted, envisaging staff with mastery of both academic subjects and technical competencies, capable of teaching conventional and practical classes (Zheng and Zhou 2010; Cao 2007). Indeed, dual certification has been used as a benchmark for determining the ranking of schools and allocation of public funding (Johnston *et al.* 2016, 134–5). But recruiting and retaining teachers with hands-on technical experience continues to present formidable challenges, as does standardising and measuring the relevant competencies within a system where the written exam rules supreme. Teachers usually obtain professional certificates by 'enrolling in a short-term training course and passing a written examination'. Enterprise employment experience is 'not always a requirement' (134). In a sample of Zhejiang computing students, those taught by teachers with 'direct occupational experience' displayed significant improvements in their technical skills, whereas 'professional certification' had 'no positive impact' (131).

For many students, however, the attractiveness of vocational higher (or secondary) education, such as it is, lies not so much in the skills it imparts as in the route into urban employment or further study it may afford. This is particularly so for those from the rural or 'backward' regions from which China's legions of migrant workers mostly originate. In measures related to the 'Great Development of the West' (*Xibu da kaifa*) (see Chapter 3.3), localities in the prosperous coastal regions have been 'paired' with their counterparts in relatively impoverished inland or Western areas for a variety of purposes, including the recruitment and training of labourers. In an arrangement known as *ding dan shi,* cities such as Shanghai or Shenzhen, or provinces like Zhejiang or Guangdong, have sponsored vocational schools or colleges in 'backward' areas. The latter sign agreements with the authorities or with particular companies in the sponsoring region, who undertake to find employment for some or all of their graduates.[14] Such schemes are one way in which 'developed' areas have sought to deal with growing labour shortages, while the prospect of eventual employment in the prosperous East is attractive to students from poorer regions. But this illustrates how some programmes touted as contributing to 'Western development' have in practice involved a form of internal colonialism, tapping the resources of the West – human or mineral – to further enhance the prosperity of the East.[15]

Indeed, participation in vocational education at all levels tends to reflect and reinforce established social divisions – of regional origin (or residency), class and gender. Students are disproportionately drawn from relatively impoverished Western or rural regions and from backgrounds with 'low cultural capital'. Highlighting the significance of social class, Hansen and Woronov note that vocational students tend to come overwhelmingly from the bottom of the social heap – none in their sample was from a wealthy or 'new middle class' background, or had '"intellectual" parents working in the educational field'. Tellingly, they report that 'all of the vocational teachers we met were adamant that they would be horrified if their own children were to attend the same vocational schools where they themselves worked' (2013, 251). In rural communities, demand for vocational education is stronger, and the tendency to see vocational students as 'failures' less pronounced, since any form of non-agricultural training is seen as at least enhancing opportunities for urban employment. However, both rural and urban students have remained quite starkly segregated by gender, with boys 'the major beneficiaries of technical training courses' – even in agriculture, where male out-migration has led to a 'feminisation' of the sector (Postiglione 2006, 7). Meanwhile, girls typically take courses in low-skilled service-oriented fields; the bookkeeping students interviewed by Woronov testified that their families considered this 'a good career for girls' (2016, 52). This pattern of highly gendered fields of study, reflecting the gender stereotyping noted in Chapter 6, holds at tertiary level, too (see Chapter 12).[16]

The use of *ding dan shi* and similar arrangements represents a significant shift since the 1980s and early 1990s, when rural vocationalisation efforts were directed far more at restricting migration to the cities (Lewin *et al.* 1994, 20). Wang reflects the new economic thinking, when he writes of vocational education's role in 'accelerating' the transfer of millions of labourers from the agricultural to the industrial sector, as well as imparting 'scientific knowledge' to farmers (Wang D. 2010, 107). However, recruiting more rural labour for the urban economy has not meant flinging open the city gates to 'peasants'. Belying talk of integration, the new welfare system still divides inter-provincial migrants from *bona fide* residents. In 2012, the central government required all provinces and municipalities to submit plans to open their schools to migrant children. Shandong, where college entrance is most competitive, was among the quickest to comply (see Chapter 3.4). Beijing and Shanghai were the last, and committed only to opening vocational senior high schools and two-year colleges; 'managing' or 'reducing' migrant inflow remained the watchwords (Liu R. 2015, 164).

Elsewhere, the welfare guarantee represented by rural land use rights may outweigh the lure of formal urban residency; in her Suzhou survey, Sun found virtually no migrant vocational students aspiring to transfer their *hukou* (2015).[17] The provincial contributory insurance scheme (*wu xian yi jin*) introduced under Xi Jinping represents an advance for many workers, but for most migrants their land-use rights remain a far more significant, though still precarious, guarantor of their welfare.

Conclusion

In his *Critique of the Gotha Programme*, Marx argued that while inequalities would still characterise an initial, 'lower' phase of 'communism', these would eventually evaporate as proletarian dictatorship guided the infant system through its 'prolonged birth pangs from capitalist society' (Brown 2009, 21). As Brown paraphrases, 'the division of labour would be overcome, the distinction between mental and physical work would vanish, ... and the communist principle would be established: "From each according to his ability, to each according to his needs"' (21). In Reform-era China, however, the abandonment of Maoism has meant the triumphant reinstatement of the invidious social distinctions so abhorrent to Marx. Skilled or semi-skilled 'physical' workers have become cannon fodder for the national charge to Great Power status. And vocational education has served primarily as a means of modulating the flow of adolescents into academic further education, while reconciling the 'failures' to their future as a new *lumpenproletariat*.

Much of the debate surrounding the merits of vocational education, in China as elsewhere, has turned on the need to produce a 'skills mix' appropriate to shifting economic demands. Wang Dewen (2010), for example, invokes comparison with the East Asian 'Tigers' and Japan, which he sees as having successfully used vocational training to 'upskill' their economies in the post-war period. For him, vocational education is the silver bullet that will make Chinese workers more 'productive' and the economy more 'innovative'. But how did the relationship between vocationalisation and economic growth actually work in post-war East Asia (or elsewhere)?

TVE in post-war Japan, Korea and Taiwan was part of systems providing relatively equal access to primary and junior secondary education. The strong grounding in basic skills that these systems provided, more than their TVE training, is generally seen as having been crucial in supporting their rapid and relatively equal economic growth (Wolf 2002; Lewin 1993). Once students entered the workforce, income differentials between TVE graduates and those of academic high schools or colleges were relatively moderate, and job security generally high. Much the same was true of most Western economies until the 1970s; in emphasising the 'higher returns' to vocational secondary education, it is significant that Wang cites research on the US economy published in 1971 (Wang D. 2010, 107). In 1970s America or Japan, as in pre-1990s urban China, vocational training could plausibly offer a route into secure lifetime employment. Moreover, this was a consequence less of the type or quality of the training itself than of the relationship between the labour market and systems of social welfare and taxation. Societies such as the Nordic countries and Germany that have managed most successfully to suppress the social stigma attached to TVE have tended to combine well-funded TVE and job retraining programmes with relatively generous social welfare policies. By contrast, in post-industrial contemporary Japan, with its minimalist approach to social welfare provision (especially for young adults), the function of TVE in the 'systematic sorting and socialising ... to fill the shifting bottom of its economic miracle has [already] unravelled' (Slater 2010, cited in Woronov 2016, 89).

This is not to say that the quality of vocational education is unimportant. Here, as we have seen, post-Mao Chinese TVE has been afflicted by persistent problems. These include widespread underfunding; a shortage of qualified teachers; poor quality teaching materials; and a pedagogic approach ill-suited to fostering 'hands-on' technical competence. However, the specific skills that TVE imparts are always difficult to match with labour market requirements, and are subject to rapid obsolescence as those requirements change – a process recently accelerated by globalisation, advances in information technology and increasing automation. Official figures cite a high employment rate for vocational graduates (96.56 per cent in 2010), but it is hard to tell whether this reflects growing demand for 'skilled labour', or the proliferation of large numbers of low-paid, low-status jobs that vocational graduates are willing to perform, but college graduates are not (Hansen and Woronov 2013, 256).

Fundamentally, difficulties in adapting TVE to the demands of employers, and in 'selling' it to parents and students, arise not just from problems with instructional quality, but also from the perception of vocational education as a dead end. Nor is this an irrational prejudice: entering vocational education effectively kills one's prospects of ever aspiring to a managerial or bureaucratic career. Any mobility that vocational graduates experience during their careers is far more likely to be horizontal than vertical – in other words, from one insecure, low-paid job to another. Like increasing numbers of young people in post-industrial Europe or Japan, most vocational students in twenty-first century urban China are destined for a future as members of a new 'precariat' (Woronov 2016, 20).

And they know it, as Woronov's research amongst students in Nanjing shows. Behaviour that educated, middle-class Chinese observers regard simply as evidence of 'low *suzhi*' (e.g. sleeping or misbehaving in lessons) she interprets as a rational response to the meaninglessness of vocational schooling:

> Between lack of training in any real vocational skills, actual curricular content, or exams that matter, the Nanjing vocational schools have lost their coherent centre. There are no grounds for disciplinary control and no meaning for students. Why not sleep all day?
>
> (Woronov 2016, 89)

Tracking students through the process of job-seeking and into the labour market, Woronov observes how many confounded expectations that they should behave as 'rational economic actors', developing career 'strategies' and 'investing' in their own futures (129). A neo-Victorian faith in self-help and improvement made little sense to them. Their consequent rejection of mainstream middle-class norms could in some respects be liberating. However, the 'atomisation and individuation' caused by endemic insecurity seemed likely, in Woronov's view, to hamper their development of any cohesive class consciousness (149).

As the labour supply tightens, and costs in China's urban economy mount, economists are increasingly questioning the sustainability of the labour-exploitative model of growth hitherto pursued, dependent on large flows of foreign direct investment and technology transfers. A 2015 OECD report called for greater investment in welfare as well as training, as a means of shifting the model from 'made in China' to 'created in China' (Molnar and Koen 2015). However, even if such investment were forthcoming, the challenge of shifting attitudes towards vocational education would remain formidable. The legacy of China's 'Confucian' heritage certainly does not help in this respect, but even without it there are plenty of factors supporting a quite rational aversion to the vocational track. Fundamentally overcoming these would require far more than well-rehearsed calls for attitudinal change or 'thought reform'. It would involve a revolution in the social contract – radically reducing the huge differentials in income, power, status and opportunity between the college- and non-college-educated populations. However, having witnessed such an experiment once within living memory, and now with far more to lose, urban elites have little appetite for a repeat performance. It is not just Confucianism that is today a major cause of opposition to, or suspicion of, vocational education; it is the legacy of Maoism itself.

Notes

1 Woronov further notes that 'culturalist' explanations for the unpopularity of vocational education were more popular amongst 'middle-class informants' than working-class ones (as were perceptions of vocational students as 'lazy and immoral'). It is easy to see why arguments focusing on moral or cultural failings should be more palatable to established elites than institutional or political critique.

2 Yang Dongping, in his 2010 Education 'Blue Book', reprints a 2009 article from the *China Youth Daily* (*Zhongguo Qingnian Bao*) entitled 'The only reason why I cannot go to a key-point school is because I was born in a rural village' (Yang 2010, 310–12).

3 However, some issues with the vocational training offered by the army appear similar to those affecting the civilian system. On the one hand, McGregor (2010) emphasises the increasing 'professionalisation' of the PLA in recent years. But a report for the Rand Corporation (Chase *et al.* 2015) notes

> a culture of engaging in insufficient training, of training in insufficiently challenging or realistic circumstances, and of striving to avoid failure in training by ensuring that success is prearranged through scripted exercises rather than embracing failure as an opportunity to learn.
>
> (48)

The report also suggests persistent problems with recruitment of highly qualified personnel due to the attractiveness of wages in the urban economy, and a widespread unwillingness to work in remote regions. It claims that attrition rates among mid-career soldiers are high due to 'the limited range of opportunities the PLA provides for professional development, continuing education, and acquisition of skills that will serve the soldier after he or she returns to civilian life' (54).

4 This directive reiterated a policy adumbrated as early as 1980 – see Thøgersen (1991, 99).

5 A problem far from unique to China – see Wolf (2002).

6 In November 2013, the government announced that it intended to abolish the reeducation through labour system, but it remains unclear what this will in fact entail.

7 Such problems are not unique to China: the European Union, with its similarly huge 'Single Market', has also experienced difficulties in creating a workable common qualifications framework (Lester 2015), resorting to rather vague bureaucratic definitions of 'competences' and 'knowledge' that render benchmarking problematic.

8 Zhao advocates a regular system for monitoring various measures of 'quality' – from policy formation, through investment and infrastructure, institutional performance, to students' 'competencies' (assessed through PISA-style tests). Johnston *et al.* (2016, 137) report the issuing (by 2012) of standardised certificates in computing by the Ministry of Human Resources, but do not discuss when this started, or the extent to which the certification system extends to other fields. The exams seem to be based entirely on written tests rather than on assessment of any practicum.

9 The MOE statistics used by Woronov combine different forms of vocational secondary education – some of which recruit mature students or graduates from regular senior high schools who fail to test into regular college. It is therefore hard to know the exact proportion of junior secondary school leavers entering vocational senior high schools, but it is likely to be significantly lower than the figure provided for total enrolments at this level.

10 Kipnis represents Zouping as rather more educationally 'advanced' than the national average, but not by a huge margin.

11 This is something Vickers encountered in 2004, when visiting Huaqing Pool (*huaqing chi*), the site of the 1936 'Xi'an Incident'. He was shown around the site by a very young guide who turned out to be a student from the local 'tourism school' doing her work experience. She said that she was busy revising for her final exam, which involved memorizing one particular Xi'an guidebook.

12 The low level of motivation and self-esteem of many vocational students is also reflected by the findings of a recent survey conducted amongst students in two vocational colleges in Suzhou, about a third of whom confessed that they had ended up in their particular college 'because they had no choice' (*mei you banfa*) (Sun 2015).

13 One example of such a case being Zhejiang University's Institute of Silk Textile Technology in Hangzhou – formerly an independent college.

14 Examples involving rural areas in Hunan and Chongqing are discussed respectively by Song *et al.* (2009) and Zhu Dequan (2004). Another case involving Shenzhen and the authorities in southwestern Xinjiang, brought to Shenzhen the Uyghur workers whose dormitory was subject to a fatal mob attack in June 2009, in turn sparking riots in Urumqi several days later (Hess 2009).

15 This was a view widely shared by participants in a seminar convened by Vickers in Chongqing in 2005 (see Vickers 2007a).

16 It is also borne out by a recent case study of vocational colleges in Suzhou (Sun 2015).

17 This is especially the case for holders of rural *hukou* in the environs of cities such as Suzhou, where migrants can nowadays access education and other public goods relatively easily, and where land for development is also in very short supply – creating a high possibility that the local government will seek to buy up farmers' land for urban expansion.

11 Higher education from 1977 to the mid-1990s

In an age of mass schooling and, increasingly, of mass higher education, what is the significance of the hackneyed observation that 'knowledge is power'? Marxist ideologues attribute shifting epistemological trends to tectonic movements in the socio-economic 'substructure', as 'hegemonic' classes seek to legitimate their dominance of the 'means of production'. For Lenin, 'scientific' insight bestowed on a revolutionary vanguard the capacity to guide or hasten history, if not to divert its inevitable course. Chairman Mao's declaration that 'power grows out of the barrel of a gun' pointed unashamedly to organised violence as the ultimate source of political authority. But underlying Maoist violence was the assumption that power always tends to accrue to a self-perpetuating elite possessed of what sociologists have come to term 'cultural capital'. Asserting the claims of 'redness' over 'expertise' involved attacking the links between academic attainment, qualifications and elite status. During the Cultural Revolution, only those deemed sufficiently 'red' were granted access to the training that conferred 'expertise'. However, even Maoists did not completely abandon the concept of specialised professional knowledge, focusing instead on whom to recruit into the professional class, and by what criteria.[1]

In *The Rise of Professional Society* (1989), Perkin posits three phases of social development, each characterised by different ideals. Pre-industrial societies are permeated by an 'aristocratic ideal' based on 'passive' property in land, enabling 'the ideal citizen, the leisured gentleman, to offer his unique contribution of political rule, moral leadership and encouragement of art, literature and sport' (3). In 'industrial societies', an 'entrepreneurial ideal' by contrast celebrates 'the self-made man who rose to wealth and influence by his own intrinsic worth and won out in open competition' (3–4). Here Perkin also notes the existence of a rival 'working class' ideal of collectivism and co-operation, 'never achieved in practice'. Finally, the 'professional ideal' of post-industrial society differs from the others 'in emphasising human capital rather than passive or active property, highly skilled and differentiated labour rather than the simple labour theory of value, and selection by merit defined as trained and certified expertise' (4).

This scheme clearly draws on, and extends, the class-based Marxist vision of phases of social development. But unlike what he calls 'the vulgar Marxists', Perkin refuses to see historical transitions simply as economically determined.

Rather, these different ideals 'compete in the societal market for income, power and status' across the three dimensions of economics, politics and ideology – none of which is necessarily pre-eminent in any particular place or time. For example, industrial society is based on capital ownership, but this in turn depends on 'the concept of absolute property' and its legal and political underpinnings. What is often forgotten, Perkin argues, is that those with the capacity to shape 'socio-ideological, cultural, intellectual or spiritual power' in any society have often transformed this 'into wealth and political authority' (5). Particularly 'long-lived political success' has tended to accrue 'to priests and bureaucrats', imperial China being a classic case in point. In elaborating a framework for 'the history of power' that echoes Perkin's,[2] Priestland observes that 'the selection of Chinese elites by exam … inevitably gave them a more sagely and less militaristic attitude to the world than their counterparts elsewhere' (2012, 31). He relates Mao's hostility to traditional *literati* values to his Social Darwinist sense that China's neglected 'military spirit' needed strengthening.

Following Mao's demise, 'sagely' ideals appeared re-ascendant. The reconstruction of higher education was prioritised, while the reinstatement of the *gaokao* restored the meritocratic principle, and with it the significance of social and cultural capital.[3] Expertise had triumphed over 'redness'. Or had it? Until June 1989 it certainly seemed so, but even then state control over higher education remained strong: after all, universities, along with much else, still adhered to 1950s Soviet blueprints. Soviet-trained technocrats proliferated within the leadership, just below the top rung of revolutionary elders – amongst whom advocates of state planning remained influential (Zhao 2009).[4] And until the late 1980s, the Soviet Union itself seemed far from a busted flush. Even as China used Western and Japanese money and expertise to rebuild higher education, the Soviet-inspired infrastructure and its underlying ethos were retained. Liberalisation was undertaken not out of conviction of the intrinsic value of academic autonomy, but for the fundamentally instrumentalist purpose of nurturing technocrats to spearhead the drive for economic growth and state aggrandisement. Even before 1989, there was pressure to subordinate sagely pursuits to mercantile or military ends; indeed, such tensions underlay the intellectual ferment of this period.

By the late 1980s, Gorbachev's Soviet Union constituted a very different sort of model – exciting for some, deeply unsettling for others – but thereafter China and Russia took diametrically opposite paths. While abandonment of state repression opened the way to the USSR's dissolution, in China the Party-State doubled down on a combination of political authoritarianism and free-market reform. As the economy grew, the professionalisation of many fields advanced, to be further boosted by the rapid expansion of higher education after 1998 (discussed in the next chapter). However, as in the former Soviet Union, a widening gulf appeared between the values of an emergent professional class, stressing adherence to rules and 'just reward' for merit (Perkin 1989, 8) – and the ethos governing political and economic life, where bonds of loyalty associated with the 'warrior band' or mafia gang remained more salient. Especially since the late 1990s, the Party has assiduously sought to co-opt educated, urban, middle-class professionals, as well as entrepreneurs (see Chapter 3.3), but it remains to be seen how sustainable the resulting social compact will prove. Much may depend, as Perkin argues, on whether a public service or managerialist form of professionalism wins out; or, in other words, on whether professionals act as a self-serving clique, or put their expertise at the service of the public (see Chapter 9).

Such issues re-emerge in the following chapter, where we examine the expansion and stratification of higher education since the late 1990s. Here we analyse the restoration of the system from the end of the Cultural Revolution to the mid-1990s, a period during which tertiary education remained the preserve of a small elite. Following a brief overview of earlier developments, we discuss the structure of higher education during the 1980s, focusing on debates over reform. We review changes in curriculum and the conduct of research, and analyse shifts in the broader intellectual climate – leading up to, and following, the Student Movement of the late 1980s. Among the emergent sources of tension within academia was the challenge of marketisation to established ideas of the intellectual's social and political role. Market-oriented reforms, by contributing to labour mobility and affording opportunities for some institutions to tap new funding, also contributed to the growing systemic inequalities dealt with in the chapter's final section. By the end of this period, the injection of the logic of supply and demand into tertiary education, as into other areas of society, was beginning to put 'sagely', elitist conceptions of higher learning under new strain.

Modern higher education in China

The ancient tradition of the Chinese scholar-bureaucrat is associated with strongly statist conceptions of the purpose of higher learning, and of the proper role of the educated man. The ideal of governance *by* sages, celebrated in the canonical 'Confucian' classics, was in practice allied to strict governance *of* sages. In the late imperial period, the commanding heights of the education system were closely supervised through officially sponsored academies and, in particular, the civil service examinations. At the opposite 'pole' of the traditional system were numerous local private academies (*shuyuan*) – often viewed with official suspicion, and subject to arbitrary closure (Hayhoe 1999, 116). But examination success, and the chance of an official career that it conferred, remained the ultimate objective for most members of the *literati* class. Speaking truth to power was, in theory, incumbent upon an honourable official, but so was obedience to an emperor embodying pseudo-religious as well as political authority.

As priest-bureaucrats to the emperor's pope-king, officials were charged not just with administrative responsibility but also with moral leadership. The academies of the imperial era were secular seminaries, teaching a curriculum to which moral concerns were central. The classics paraded before pupils a gallery of historical or mythical figures – models of the wise ruler, the upright official and the subtle counsellor – all exemplifying the creed of filial piety. 'Once a teacher, a father for life', went the traditional saying, and the prevalence of paternal and pedagogic metaphors reflected both assumptions concerning the nature of authority, and the hierarchical realities of the patronage networks into which young scholars were socialised. The abolition of the imperial examinations in 1905, and of the imperial throne itself in 1911, shattered the capstone of these networks and orphaned an entire generation of scholarly aspirants (Curran 2005). But traditions of 'pedagogical politics' survived into the post-imperial era (Fitzgerald 1996), along with expectations regarding the public role of the intellectual, and the teacher's relationship with his students.

Before the 1911 collapse, a late burst of modernising reforms saw the wholesale import of many features of modern Japanese education (Harrison 2001, see also Chapter 6). This influence was more apparent at school than university level, but hundreds of Chinese scholars studied at colleges and universities in Japan – geography, language and culture rendering it a more congenial destination than Europe or America. Strongly patriarchal and statist elements in traditional educational thought (shared with China), as well as their preoccupation with technological and military self-strengthening, had earlier drawn Japan's modernising elites to German precedents: 'Tokugawa traditions, reinforced by German influence, produced an autocratic government slow to sanction autonomy or forthright politicking by scientists and professors' (Bartholemew 1989, 269). Prussia and the German states had pioneered the adoption of civil service examinations in Europe, and the prestige of Germany's bureaucracy and her universities was mutually reinforcing (as in France, so in Germany, academics themselves were civil servants).[5] The combination of sagely and military values that characterised the imperial German state and its universities was profoundly attractive to East Asia's nationalist modernisers.

As efforts to construct a modern system of higher education have continued down to the present, three elements of China's pre-modern intellectual inheritance have arguably remained especially influential: first, a scholarly tradition (*guan xue*) strongly associated with service of the state; second, a pedagogical emphasis on memorisation and mastery of authorised texts, along with a tendency to seek solutions to social and political problems in officially mandated ethical transformation (echoed in numerous official statements regarding 'thought reform' – see Chapter 3); and third, a relative lack of interest in scientific epistemology. This last feature, involving a conception of science as a source of technical 'fixes' rather than an approach to understanding the world, was remarked on by Joseph Needham, who saw its roots in pre-modern religion and philosophy (Needham and Wang 1954). However, authoritarian politics and the pervasive ideology of 'catch-up modernisation' are crucial to explaining the persistence of this narrowly technical orientation, along with other aspects of intellectual conservatism. It was the dissident physicist Fang Lizhi who observed in 1989:

> Our common people – and actually our political leaders too – don't realize that science is a kind of culture. They think of it as just something that … lets you repair electric lights. They don't understand the system of thought that lies behind.
>
> (Quoted in Link 1992, 200)

Higher education in the Republican era: Liberalism by default?

For almost two decades after the fall of the Qing dynasty in 1911, China essentially had no functioning central state, and it was in this context that most of the country's first modern universities were established. Returnees from Japan played crucial roles in intellectual life during this period, but a particularly influential figure was Cai Yuanpei, whose experiences in Europe left him convinced of the importance of faculty autonomy in university governance (Hayhoe 1999, 51). Christian missionary involvement in higher education was important, but American influence was pre-eminent, as the United States overtook Japan as the primary destination for overseas study (Ng *et al.* 2002). The prevalence of American models and American-trained personnel helped foster a liberal academic atmosphere, significantly boosted by the prolonged visit from 1919 to 1921 of the apostle of progressivism, John Dewey. Hayhoe sees this as a time when 'Western' ideals of 'academic freedom and autonomy were transformed into forms of intellectual freedom and social responsibility suited to the Chinese context' (1999, 63), although the binary juxtaposition of 'Western' and 'Chinese' this implies is rejected by others (e.g. Dikotter 2009). As the earlier references to imperial Germany illustrate, not all aspects of 'Western' intellectual tradition have been conducive to academic autonomy.

As Hayhoe emphasises, 'cultural conflict' has been a perennial feature of the search for a Chinese model of modern higher education, and liberal dominance during the Republican period was hotly contested. Kuomintang attempts to extend Leninist forms of control over universities, for example by establishing a national student organisation affiliated with the party, were successfully resisted. Nonetheless, with the pursuit of national strength widely seen as 'the primary intellectual aim', even many who rejected much of the moral content of classical learning remained strongly animated by an ethos of state service (Luo 2011, 60–1). Cai Yuanpei, staunch advocate of academic self-governance, took this further with his abortive 1927 proposal for a national 'university council' (*daxue yuan*), which would have placed the entire education system under the authority of an independent board of scholarly guardians (Hayhoe 1999, 51). The oasis of academic freedom that Peking University under Cai became 'laid the foundation for all that has followed' in the development of 'western-style' academic institutions in China (Yang 2006, 212). At the other extreme stood the Communists, who in Yan'an established colleges as extensions of the state or army, with most faculty and administrators 'concurrently members of the border-region bureaucracy'. In this sense, Hayhoe observes, 'Yan'an institutions represented a kind of continuity with classical Chinese bureaucratic patterns of higher education as preparation for public office' (1999, 62).

Communism and higher education: The statist tradition resurgent

In Communist higher education policy, Soviet influence was paramount. Even Yan'an radicalism and the 'worker-peasant-soldier' colleges of the Cultural

Revolution were inspired, at least in part, by the Soviet Union's own 'Cultural Revolution', that had coincided with Stalin's First Five Year Plan (1928–32) (Fitzpatrick 1979). The chief outcome of that episode had been unprecedented 'social mobility' for an entire generation of peasant-worker cadres and technocrats, who formed the backbone of the Soviet *nomenklatura* into the 1970s. However, once installed as the new elite, these individuals behaved like their pre-revolutionary predecessors, restoring conventional 'meritocratic' routes into higher education, and thus enhancing the prospects of their own privileged children. No longer revolutionary in social terms, by the 1950s the Soviet system was effectively a Franco-German hybrid. Germanic disciplinary traditions, pedagogic practices and a culture of intense respect for academic expertise were combined with a Napoleonic institutional hierarchy firmly subordinated to the Party-State – the entire structure serving the requirements of the command economy and the military (Taylor 2013, 10). This Stalinist formula was what Soviet experts prescribed for the 'New China' after 1949.

The 'adjustment of faculties and departments' (*yuanxi tiaozheng*) undertaken from 1952 represented a sweeping shift from American and Japanese models towards Soviet ones. The relatively liberal form of academic governance characteristic of the Republican period was swept away, and replaced by absolute state control premised on a narrowly instrumentalist vision of higher education's purposes. In place of comprehensive universities combining teaching and research across a range of disciplines, specialist institutes and academies were established, chief among them the Chinese Academy of Sciences. Existing universities refocused on particular fields. In Beijing, Peking and Yenching Universities had previously boasted their own schools of engineering, but after 1952 the latter were merged with Tsinghua University. While Tsinghua henceforth focused on the sciences and engineering, its arts, humanities and law faculties, along with Yenching's remaining faculties, were transferred to Peking University. Private, mostly religious, institutions (such as Yenching) were abolished, merged with or transformed into public, secular colleges focusing on particular disciplines; the new Beijing Normal University, for example, absorbed much of Furen University, a Catholic foundation. Meanwhile, central to the remodelled higher education system of the 1950s was the new People's University (*Renmin Daxue*) in Beijing, which, in Hayhoe's words, combined 'authoritarian, Soviet-derived patterns with state Confucianist values' (1999, 118).

In 1957, the rationalisation of the university system was codified, specifying eleven categories of institution: in addition to comprehensive universities (one per province), the other categories comprised engineering; education and teacher training (entrusted to 'normal' colleges and universities); agriculture and forestry; medicine and health; finance and economics; politics and law; fine and performing arts; language and culture; sports; and studies of – and for – 'minority nationalities' (*shaosu minzu*). Each category of institution was responsible to a different national ministry (*bu*): thus the Agricultural University (*Nongye Daxue*) fell under the authority of the Agriculture Ministry. Teacher training colleges other than the top normal universities were administered by provincial Education

Departments (*jiaoyu ting*): Shenyang Normal College, for example, answered to the Education Department of Liaoning Province. Comprehensive universities, apart from 'key point' institutions responsible to the central Education Ministry in Beijing, also came under the direction of provincial Education Departments. The resulting 'compartmentalisation' (*tiaokuai fenge*) produced a pseudo-feudalistic network of states within the state. Central government departments, with their affiliated higher education institutions, formed regimented *danwei* with their own welfare, judicial and security functions. The system was intimately related to the centralised work assignment system, in which various ministries and departments played a central role – a system that survived into the 1990s (see below, and Chapter 3.3). In the early Reform years, comprehensive universities accounted for only about 5 per cent of all higher education institutions (Henze 1984, 121).

This arrangement also allowed for strong government control over curriculum, teaching, finance, administration and personnel, whether exercised through national ministries or provincial departments. A key tool of curricular command and control was the Higher Education Press (*Gaodeng jiaoyu chubanshe*), sister organisation to PEP (see Chapter 6). During the 1980s, university textbooks were still generally based on highly didactic Soviet models. Although curricula and textbooks have subsequently become considerably more diverse, the 1953 State Council ruling underpinning central control over curricula has not been repealed by subsequent reforms (e.g. the *Higher Education Law* of 1998).[6] Curriculum standards are still monitored by the central authorities, at least for the particularly sensitive 'core' subjects of politics, military training, Chinese literacy and foreign language (together accounting for a quarter of course credits). At some times, central supervision has been looser, at others (as under President Xi Jinping from 2014) it has been significantly tightened.

The period from 1966 to 1976 represented a hiatus in the development of conventional higher education, as China experienced what Hayhoe calls 'the dark days of the Cultural Revolution' (2006). But there was method in the Maoists' madness, and the notion of 'cultural revolution' itself was not unprecedented, as we have seen, having originated in the Soviet Union during the 1920s. It is therefore worth briefly comparing the nature of the Leninist[7] and Maoist campaigns, and their implications for the subsequent development of their respective societies.

In both societies, 'cultural revolution' was associated with a concerted drive to redistribute opportunity, and ultimately power. However, there were profound differences in how Lenin and Mao viewed both culture and the revolutionary role of the intelligentsia. For Lenin, revolution required redefining culture itself and redistributing opportunities to enjoy it, but the *avant-garde* role of the intelligentsia remained crucial. The priority was to put knowledge and science at the service of the Soviet state by drafting the proletariat into the intelligentsia, and focusing all energies on industrialisation and modernisation. For Mao, by contrast, the remaking of culture was a precondition for the transformation of society. Glorying in the notion of the Chinese masses as a 'blank slate', he insisted that – as Meisner puts it – 'the cultural hegemony of the masses was not so much the product of, as the prerequisite for, [socialist] modern economic development' (1989, 287). Hence China's Cultural Revolution involved not just class-based criteria for entry to colleges and universities, but also sweeping attempts to redefine what qualified as 'knowledge'. And while Soviet professors had largely remained in place while the make-up of the student body changed, in China this was not the case. Many professors were 'sent down' to the countryside and instructed to 'learn from the masses', their place at the lectern taken by instructors with more impressive political than academic credentials.

The difference between the 'dictatorial party-state' of Lenin and Stalin and the 'mass-mobilising party-state' envisaged by Mao largely explains the contrasting social and political consequences of the two cultural revolutions (Skocpol 1979). A crucial outcome of the educational innovations of the First Five Year Plan, according to Fitzpatrick (1979), was a quite dramatic burst of 'social mobility'. When the dust settled, an entire new elite of educated worker-peasant cadres had emerged, who went on, following the purges of the 1930s, to become the leading stratum within the Party-State and the professions for the next forty years. It was thus the beneficiaries of Cultural Revolution who acceded to power, even if the 'Great Retreat' under Stalin, when many Tsarist cultural and educational norms re-emerged, subsequently contributed to an *embourgeoisement* that locked in elite privilege. In China, by contrast, there was a triumphant resumption of authority by the very elites Mao had sought to crush, and a rush by rusticated 'intellectual' youth to resume their interrupted education. It was thus, by and large, the victims of Maoist radicalism, rather than its beneficiaries, who acquired power in the following years. This helps account for the unabashedly elitist nature of post-Mao educational development, and the relative neglect of egalitarian concerns in public policy more generally.

In place of egalitarianism, 'quality' in higher education was defined, from the late 1970s, primarily in terms derived from the Western societies and Japan with whom it was deemed imperative to 'catch up'. In this sense, the underlying premise of higher education policy was not so very different from what it had been in the era of Soviet influence during the 1950s; only the object of the 'catching up' enterprise had changed. Cynicism regarding egalitarianism was also reinforced by the record of Maoist radicalism at tertiary level: 'politically defined "quality" resulted in an "equality" that was expressed more in revolutionary rhetoric than in the concrete provision of higher education on a more equal basis in terms of class, sex or ethnic origin' (Henze 1984, 152; see also Unger 1982). Hence the readiness with which Chinese traditions of *guanxue*, and an overwhelmingly statist and instrumentalist conception of the purposes of higher learning, were reasserted following the Maoists' defeat.

The higher education system in the early Reform period

Universities and colleges were absolutely central to early post-Mao efforts to refocus China's developmental strategy. Deng Xiaoping consciously aligned himself with the scientists and intellectuals marginalised during the Cultural

Revolution.[8] As Vogel notes, the latter in turn came to form an important political constituency for Deng,[9] who, unlike Mao (but like Zhou Enlai, Zhao Ziyang and Hu Yaobang), was 'instinctively comfortable with intellectuals' (2011, 142). But apart from concerns to shore up his political base, Deng appeared to harbour an 'almost magical faith in the role that science would play in China's renewal' (Vogel 2011, 201). On resuming office in 1977, he immediately sought to 'micromanage' science, technology and education policy, focusing 'on the high end'. Downplaying class struggle and 'thought reform', he insisted that science and technology be viewed as a 'force of production' (209). Science, for Deng, had no 'class' character, and he never denigrated intellectuals as 'bourgeois'.[10] 'The erroneous attitude of not respecting intellectuals must be opposed', he declared. 'All work, be it mental or manual, is labour' (cited in Vogel 2011, 202). Intent on improving working conditions for scientists, he also strongly promoted overseas study (see Chapter 13). For Deng, as for the leaders of Meiji-era Japan, the overriding objective was to 'catch up with the most advanced countries in the world' (201).

With hindsight, an aura of inevitability may appear to surround the gradual ditching of state planning, but Vogel stresses the extent of initial 'conservative' (i.e. leftist or Maoist) resistance within the Party and the Education Ministry to 'meritocratic' reforms to higher education. Nevertheless, the striking speed with which this resistance crumbled suggests that it was prompted more by caution than conviction; once senior officials were convinced that a Maoist comeback was unlikely, most clambered aboard Deng's bandwagon. For Deng, reform to tertiary education was certainly an urgent priority, but politically it was also an easy place to begin the reformist drive. With 'political' criteria for college entrance licensing unbridled corruption, instructional quality notoriously poor, and a serious skills shortage hampering the push for the 'four modernisations', the Maoist model had few enthusiastic defenders.

Reform to higher education involved significant expansion of enrolment, but an even more dramatic increase in investment, in an effort to raise 'quality' and make up for lost time. As at school level, resources were concentrated in 'key point' institutions (accounting, in 1981–2, for around 10 per cent of the national student population) (Henze 1984, 124). There was massive pent-up demand for higher education amongst 'intellectual' youth 'sent down' to the countryside during the Cultural Revolution; in 1977, 'at least 10 million' people applied for the first round of reintroduced college entrance examinations, of whom 278,000 eventually secured a college place (115). Transition rates from senior high school to college were around 5 per cent from 1976 to 1981 (116), rising thereafter primarily due to the closure or vocationalisation of senior high schools (see Chapter 10). Such was the demand for tertiary education and training amongst adults during the early 1980s – stoked by mandatory training requirements for cadres – that by 1985 enrolment in adult higher education institutions (many originating in the non-formal sector key to Cultural Revolutionary higher education) had reached over 1.7 million (Hayhoe 1999, 118). But perhaps the most noteworthy statistics relate to state investment in higher education as a proportion of the total education budget. Here China signalled not only an about-turn from the Maoist emphasis on the 'masses', but a significant departure from the then standard educational prescription for 'developing' countries – as endorsed by the World Bank and other international agencies.

Planning and its discontents

Return to pre-Cultural Revolution normalcy meant reinstatement of the apparatus of Soviet-style state planning. The first post-Reform Five Year Plan, published in 1982, prioritised the recruitment of sufficient graduates for positions in industry, the bureaucracy and the professions essential to the task of modernisation. Higher education itself was redefined as a 'productive force'. In 1979, tertiary education received a higher percentage of the state budget (at central and local levels combined) than primary education (though a lower percentage than secondary education) (World Bank 1983, cited in Henze 1984, 138). It was only private – i.e. family – spending on primary education that pushed overall expenditure at that level above the tertiary figure. The 30 per cent of educational spending that tertiary education received that year compared with averages of 23 per cent for 'late-developing' economies and 24 per cent for OECD countries (the contrast with Japan, Korea and Taiwan was particularly marked – see Green *et al.* 2007). This challenged World Bank orthodoxy on 'rates of return' to investment in primary, secondary and tertiary education, but was justified by the professed need to make up for years of Maoist neglect (Henze 1984, 140). Even so, higher education received a large slice of a relatively small pie: 'with around 3% of the Gross National Product spent on education; 2.1% if we take central government expenditure only', China in the early 1980s was 'where the average developing country stood at the beginning of the 1960s' (140).

The World Bank was directly involved from an early stage in Chinese debates over higher education reform, as officials sought both Western advice and legitimacy for their political choices (see also Chapter 13). The Shanghai authorities released to a visiting World Bank delegation figures for 1979 suggesting a drastic gulf between the 'requirement' for and supply of 'new scientific and technical manpower' (cited in Henze 1984, 134). The basis for such calculations, as for others produced by the state planning apparatus, was unclear. The same delegation was shown 1977–82 statistics for college graduates by field of specialisation that revealed huge year-on-year fluctuations in the percentage assigned to different fields; in 1981, a massive 74 per cent of the total graduated from teacher training programmes. Even when – as with teaching – the supply of graduates appeared to answer a real social need, matching individuals to jobs through the centralised system of work assignments often proved difficult. In 1982, the *People's Daily* lamented:

> A relatively large number of college graduates are assigned to large cities, the interior, large units, and state-operated enterprises, where they become 'superfluous' personnel, but small cities, outlying districts, small units, and

> collectives ... have been assigned a small number of college graduates, which has made the phenomenon of a shortage of qualified personnel even more serious.
>
> (Cited in Henze 1984, 135)

A 1983 attempt to reassign many graduates to 'backward regions' prompted open rebellion. The Ministry of Education responded by appealing to parents to let their children 'go wherever the motherland needs them most to put their abilities to good use' (cited in Henze 1984, 137). But with memories of enforced rustic exile during the Cultural Revolution painfully fresh, and leading cadres manoeuvring to ensure favourable postings for their offspring, calls for patriotic self-sacrifice were predictably ineffective.

Related to problems in matching graduates' skills to changing labour market demands, some argued, was the structure of the university system itself. In a 1986 World Bank report (cited in Min *et al.* 1995), Min Weifang of Peking University and the American scholar Henry Levin criticised the small size of China's Soviet-style universities, and the often narrowly specialised focus of their curriculum. They recommended expanding universities both in scale and curricular breadth, through introducing general education (*tongshi jiaoyu*) courses to foster creativity, critical thinking and greater adaptability amongst students. They were effectively pressing for an Americanisation of Chinese universities, involving a move back to the kind of comprehensive, multi-disciplinary institutions that had dominated the sector in the Republican period. Although Min and Levin's recommendations were not immediately acted upon, their report played a significant role in framing debate over the future direction of reform, in a context of burgeoning contact and exchange between Chinese and North American universities.

Among the issues highlighted in the 1986 World Bank report were imbalances in the assignment of personnel amongst and within universities themselves – a problem already preoccupying Chinese policymakers. Although national statistics suggested a relatively healthy teacher–student ratio of 1:4.5, as of 1980 (Henze 1984, 129), this masked wide variations between institutions. It also ignored the fact that many of those designated as 'teaching staff' did not actually teach. Some were unwilling (preferring to focus on research), some too poorly qualified (especially those trained during the Cultural Revolution), and others simply incapable (often due to old age); as Deng himself had complained in a key 1977 speech on education, 'those who are fit for work are really very few' (IED 1977, 1573). At Peking University in 1983, the average age of full professors was 70; of associate professors, 54 (Henze 1984, 131). In an attempt to resolve such imbalances, many academics were rapidly promoted during the early 1980s, but the cultural prestige attached to seniority, and old professors' tendency to linger on campus rather than depart for the teahouse or golf course, delayed any fundamental redistribution of status and power.

Another phenomenon singled out for criticism by Min and Levin was the high ratio of ancillary staff to scholars and students in most universities. The job assignment system made universities, along with all urban work units (*shiye danwei*), responsible for providing employment for 'non-intellectual' youth, especially those completing military service. The student population appeared low relative not only to the number of academic staff, but also to the number of administrators, drivers, caretakers, security guards, gardeners, sweepers and other staff. The use of universities as a source of 'outdoor relief' for retired soldiers and 'returned youth', alongside tight restrictions on student recruitment, was seen by Min and Levin as symptomatic of 'low efficiency' in the higher education sector. Others shared their view of the 'wastefulness' of the current system. One of the present authors (Zeng), herself a university student during the mid-1980s, remembers her tutor telling her then that her costs were being supported by the taxes of 60 farmers.

University governance – scholars take command?

Assignment of personnel was just one area in which the lack of institutional autonomy increasingly grated; another involved the continuing division of the system into Soviet-era disciplinary silos, impatience with which was fuelled by greater exposure to American models. Elite institutions such as Tsinghua University were among the first to try to assume a more 'comprehensive' identity, as they sought to establish or re-establish humanities and social science faculties.[11] Efforts by academics to determine their own institutional priorities were related to their authority over other matters, including curriculum design, textbook adoption, and the setting of research agendas. And central to debates over institutional autonomy were questions of whether, and how, to separate Party and administrative work, and the power of academics *vis-à-vis* administrators.

The Central Committee's 1985 'Decision on the Reform of the Education System' promised greater autonomy to universities (IED 1985, 2285), but this reflected the state of a debate long underway. Ever since the 1950s, higher education institutions had had a double-headed leadership, with a president heading the formal administration, but a 'party secretary' leading a parallel hierarchy of party committees. During the 1980s, power tended to shift from the latter to the former, as part of the general post-Mao reaction against the overt politicisation of all aspects of Chinese life. Henze cites the example of Shanghai Jiaotong University, where already by the early 1980s power had ostensibly migrated from party committees to a 'university affairs committee' or 'university council' (*xiao-wu weiyuanhui*), membership of which was not restricted to party members (1984, 129–30). Such bodies had existed in the 1960s (before being abolished during the Cultural Revolution), but whereas then they had been appointed, now they were sometimes elected by the faculty.

Where they existed, these committees represented a clear advance in the 'academic governance of universities' (*jiaoshou zhixiao*) for which Cai Yuanpei had called half a century earlier. However, the political upheaval of 1989 prompted a sharp retreat on this front, with the push for greater autonomy not to resume until the early 2000s (see below and the following chapter). Even during the 1980s, the power of the party committee to ratify all academic appointments meant that it retained a crucial gatekeeping function. And although the principle of scholarly autonomy was important for some academics, for many the more immediate objective was to trim the excessive power of administrators over housing and other benefits (use of cars, permission to travel and so forth). Liu Da, President of Tsinghua University during the early 1980s, complained of the disproportionate share of his time and energy occupied with social services rather than academic affairs: 'it is not society which manages the universities but rather the universities which manage society' (quoted in Henze 1984, 132). In the Chinese context, greater academic autonomy actually correlated with greater centralisation of the non-academic functions of the university-as-'work unit', allowing the 'educational establishment', as Pepper put it, to '[retreat] into its own sphere and [reassert] control over itself, cutting off outside political and non-academic interference' (quoted in Henze 1984, 132).

But just as scholars experienced a loosening of their Stalinist shackles, they found themselves increasingly subject to 'non-academic interference' of other kinds. Especially during the later 1980s, tinkering with the central planning model of university finance increased, with institutions offered more freedom to raise funds through selling their services on the market. The extent to which this represented a gain in terms of academic autonomy was already a focus of controversy within Chinese academia by the end of the decade.

Reforms to curriculum and research: 'American branches' grafted onto a 'Soviet tree planted in a Chinese garden'

Market forces would later come to play a growing role in shaping institutional priorities, but in the early 1980s, policymakers relied on administrative levers to steer institutions into servicing the technical demands of the modernisation drive. Ideological indoctrination continued, but no longer permeated instructional content as it had before 1977, when 'worker propaganda teams' were tasked with criticising 'bourgeois intellectuals'. In place of ideology came a utilitarian emphasis on Science, Technology, Engineering and Medicine (STEM). At undergraduate level, enrolments in STEM, Forestry, Agriculture, Finance and Economics accounted for 50–60 per cent of the total throughout the 1980s (NCEDR 2009, 75). The applied social sciences (Finance, Economics and Law) and Engineering witnessed significant growth over the decade (from 3 to 13 per cent in the case of finance and economics), while other sciences saw slight declines (Hayhoe 1999, 123). But only around 5–7 per cent of enrolments were in social sciences. Apart from STEM, the only other major curricular focus was Education, accounting for between a quarter and a third of regular tertiary enrolments.[12] Consistent with the overall focus on fostering technical expertise was the rapid expansion of postgraduate education from 1981, with the emphasis again heavily tilted towards STEM. In 1980, STEM, Finance, Economics and other fields of direct relevance to economic production, accounted for over 60 per cent of postgraduate enrolments, rising to over two-thirds by 1982 (Henze 1984, 117).

The research infrastructure initially remained very much within the Soviet mould, with most research conducted in specialised institutes rather than in universities, which focused on teaching. In 1977 came the re-establishment of the State Science and Technology Commission, and funding for research in STEM fields was subsequently ramped up. Although social sciences were accorded only secondary importance, in 1977 Deng Xiaoping backed the establishment of a new 'Chinese Academy of Social Sciences' (CASS) to join the 'Chinese Academy of Sciences' (Vogel 2011, 209). CASS and CAS enjoyed ministry status, and therefore did not fall under the purview of the Ministry of Education. Institutional autonomy did not necessarily entail academic freedom; the first head of the newly established CASS was Hu Qiaomu, Mao Zedong's former secretary and a staunch ideological conservative (Zhao 2009, 104). Nevertheless, as the decade wore on, university-based academics were also encouraged to undertake research, graduate schools (with MA and PhD programmes) were established along American lines, and new funding sources were made available. First for natural sciences (from 1986), and then for social sciences (from 1987), competitive, peer-reviewed research funding schemes were introduced (Hayhoe 1999, 125).

New funding procedures did not, however, necessarily denote a fundamental shift in the process whereby research priorities were determined. This was particularly true in the public policy field, including research into education policy (Yang 2006). As Yang puts it, 'research on public policy was non-critical and concerned with how to better reflect the CCP's and the Government's existing goals' (209). It generally did not probe how those goals were defined, whose interests shaped or were served by them, or their fundamental desirability. Research tended to be overwhelmingly normative, focused on generating 'how-to' prescriptions for planning and implementation. Even while a more open, less centralised and ostensibly more academically driven funding infrastructure was being established, much public policy research was still conducted within government departments (often by researchers seconded from universities), or in government-affiliated institutes. Strong government influence over the 'research imagination' was thus ensured (Yang 2006, 210). To a large extent, this situation has endured down to the present – although, as we noted in Chapter 3.4, the early 2000s witnessed often lively debate over education policy, within the officially prescribed parameters.

Meanwhile, in terms of colleges' educational functions, the early Reform years witnessed considerable variation in the type and length of courses, as institutions attempted to cater for a mixture of adolescent school-leavers, 'returned youth' and adults requiring retraining. In additional to the conventional four-year undergraduate degree (*benke*), three-year vocationally oriented programmes (*zhuanke*) were also widely offered (see Chapter 10), mainly via less prestigious institutions (see below). Within institutions, too, there was a clear hierarchy of courses and disciplines, with the STEM subjects generally enjoying greatest prestige. Any subjects likely to lead to a rural work assignment were widely shunned by students. These included Forestry and Agriculture, but also teaching (Hayhoe 1995)[13] – despite the fact that teacher training was accorded such a high priority in official enrolment quotas.

While 'imbalances' in the supply of graduates in different fields aroused anxiety, so did the quality of the instruction they received. As at school level, there was a major drive to revise textbooks in the years after 1977, spearheaded by the Higher Education Press. But in the 1980s, Soviet-style textbooks – aimed at a hot-housed elite rather than a mass market – remained in widespread use, generally featuring an almost total neglect of pedagogical considerations. The typical teaching style was seen as 'dry, dull and stereotyped', characterised by teacher-centred instruction, widespread copying from textbooks, and a general failure to 'cultivate the ability to do independent work' (Henze 1984, 128). It was this that prompted Pepper's question: 'Can American branches be grafted onto a Soviet tree planted in a Chinese garden?' (cited in Henze 1984, 128). Scepticism on this score was heightened by the continuing presence in university curricula of compulsory courses in Party history, Politics and Marxist theory.

However, during the late 1980s, even these politics courses were by no means immune from the broader ideological ferment affecting university campuses. In the early Reform years, political education continued to disseminate the socialist boilerplate of revolution and class struggle, barely engaging with increasingly divergent social reality. But following a shift in official policy from about 1986, this began to change. Politics instructors attempted – as Hayhoe puts it – to 'keep pace with' shifts in student values, while also trying to 'pre-empt some of these changes through such classroom practices as teaching through dialogue, encouraging student initiative and inculcating in students a sense of historical mission and destiny' (1993, 35). New or revised texts maintained a 'general framework of Marxist philosophy', but 'embellished and rationalised' this with references to a wide range of classical Chinese and Western sources (32). Hayhoe reminds us that the compilers of these texts, mostly quite young, were themselves 'products of the more open academic and cultural environment of recent years' (32): it is difficult, she argues, to know to what extent shifts in political education during the late 1980s encouraged this greater openness or reflected it. The greater self-governance exercised by academics during the late 1980s appears to have rubbed off on student associations. The relative openness of intellectual debate, and assertiveness of the scholarly community, encouraged many students to explore, question, criticise and see themselves as active, participatory citizens (see also Link 1992).

But behind the scenes, the apparatus of centralised bureaucratic control over universities, far from being weakened, had actually been strengthened during the post-Mao reforms. In place of Maoist 'mass movements', a 'three-pronged bureaucracy, comprising the Communist Party, the Communist Youth League and the student work system' provided the authorities with the tools to facilitate 'top-down supervision by the Party-state and bottom-up collaboration from loyal activists and the student body at large' (Yan 2014, 498). And at the centre of this apparatus stood the university's Party Secretary, commanding a hierarchy of regular cadres, assisted in turn by hand-picked 'student cadres'. The whole structure extended (as it still does) 'beyond the university walls', constituting 'part of the larger control framework headed by the CCP's central or provincial committee on higher education work (*gaojiao gongwei*)' (498). During the 1980s, lively intra-party debates over the direction or continuation of the reforming drive meant that this bureaucracy was itself divided between 'liberals' and 'conservatives'. But the apparatus of control remained, to be powerfully reanimated after 1989.

The intellectual climate

After years of disparagement, under Deng intellectuals were encouraged once again to see themselves as pivotal to the strengthening and transformation of the nation. Little encouragement was needed. An elevated conception of their public role went hand in hand with the strong sense of political and social responsibility traditionally integral to *literati* caste identity (Yang 2006). Modern Chinese intellectuals of whatever ideological hue inherited the tradition of scholar-as-moral-exemplar; figures as varied as Liang Shuming, Hu Shi and Cai Yuanpei had all sought to assume the exemplary mantle, or had had it thrust upon them. With dedication to the 'quest for national strength' prominent amongst the qualities demanding scholarly exemplification (Luo 2011, 60–1), social science research tended to focus more on idealistic prescription than analysis. Whatever they thought of his other ideas, many would have concurred with Marx's famous dictum (from the *Theses on Feuerbach*): 'philosophers have hitherto interpreted the world …; the point is to change it'.

But if the parameters of intellectual inquiry remained circumscribed, for China's universities the 1980s were nonetheless a period of optimism and idealism unparalleled since the 1930s. A new spirit of openness animated the old Soviet-style institutions, and interest in Western – especially American – ideas was widespread. Regular classes may have provided only limited intellectual stimulation (for reasons alluded to above), but this was often available elsewhere. Zeng (the present co-author), a student during the late 1980s, attended talks on Western music and philosophy organised by her Physics Department. Elderly professors toured the country giving free lectures on various topics. Works popularising liberal messages, such as the book series *Towards the Future* (*Zou xiang weilai*) and the television documentary *River Elegy* (*He Shang*) (see Jones 2005, 86), attracted mass audiences. And interest in the West and Japan was fuelled by exchanges with overseas institutions and frequent visits by foreign scholars (Hayhoe 1999; see Chapter 13).

An atmosphere of relative liberalism thus prevailed, but the intellectual climate was far from settled. Sporadic 'campaigns', notably that against 'bourgeois liberalisation', were launched to combat the supposed ill effects of excessive 'Westernisation'. Not only were individuals or factions pitted against each other, but the minds of some top leaders, not least Deng himself, were seemingly divided between liberal and conservative impulses (Zhao 2009). For Deng, the hope that economic and intellectual liberalisation would release energies that could be harnessed to the 'modernisation' drive was balanced by the fear that those same energies might threaten the 'cardinal principle' of Party control (Zhao 2009, xxii) – fears exacerbated by the Student Movement of the late 1980s (see Zhang *et al.* 2002). As we noted in Chapter 3.2, discontent was fuelled not just by liberal idealism but by various concrete grievances relating to day-to-day student life: the allocation of dormitory places, the management of dining halls and the power of administrators more generally. But for students these were tangible symptoms of a wider malaise, arising from increasingly rampant corruption and the distortions inherent in the semi-planned, semi-market economy.

The crackdown of the summer of 1989 was accompanied by a drastic regimentation of campus life. Work in politically sensitive areas was subjected to tight supervision; in September, the SEC introduced new regulations governing invitations for foreign social scientists (natural scientists and language experts were exempted). Universities were henceforth required to undertake background checks to establish foreign scholars' 'attitudes towards China' (*dui hua taidu*) (IED 1989, 2881). These were later extended to inspections of teaching materials used by social scientists from overseas, and stipulations that they be teamed with local counterparts of high 'political quality' (*zhengzhi suzhi*), to prevent the 'spread in class' of 'any decadent capitalist notions or capitalist talk over issues such as "rights", "freedom" or "democracy"' (IED 1990, 3080). Meanwhile, new 'rules for student behaviour' ordered:

> Protect the interests of the Motherland. Do not engage in any activity that harms the honour or glory of the Motherland, breaches the four cardinal principles, or endangers social order. Oppose any activity that destroys social peace and unity.
>
> (IED 1989, 2902)

The flow of draconian new regulations continued through 1990, with students at elite universities central to the 1989 protests (such as Peking University or Fudan University in Shanghai) sent for especially prolonged periods of military training (IED 1990, 3024).

With failings in 'Thought and Politics' education officially identified as a crucial cause of the 1989 disturbances, the relevant teaching materials were thoroughly revised. As noted in Chapter 3.2, anxiety to shore up Party control was accentuated by the dramatic crumbling of the Soviet bloc. New politics texts invoked the concept of the 'national situation' (*guoqing*), emphasising the crucial role of the Party in guiding China towards 'modernisation' while preventing the kind of chaos and collapse experienced by the USSR. In a 1993 analysis of changes to political education in Chinese universities, Hayhoe lamented the narrow materialism implicit in the *guoqing* narrative. The attempt to 'carry through an authoritarian, top-down process of social change that allows for economic progress yet permits no challenge to the political system', was likely, she argued, to 'encourage the "all-out Westernisation" it pretends to decry'. This was because it was premised on the 'instrumental-technical reason' that Hayhoe (following Habermas) took to be characteristic of 'Western modernization', involving 'ossification of the moral and aesthetic knowledge of the cultural life-world' (1993, 43). In other words, debate over the direction China's 'modernisation' could or should take was being stifled, with higher education instead assigned a purely instrumental role in furthering material prosperity and technological progress. 'The only recourse from this cultural aridity', Hayhoe concluded, 'is likely to be various kinds of material satisfaction' (43).

Rampant materialism has indeed been an increasingly salient feature of Chinese society since the 1990s, but refuge from 'cultural aridity' has also been sought in nationalism and various forms of neo-traditionalism. Hayhoe intriguingly remarks on increased student interest in Mao and his writings during the early 1990s, seeing this as a manifestation of 'resistance' to the messages of official *guoqing* education (it was perhaps also a harbinger of trends later associated with the work of 'New Left' scholars). But she also notes echoes in *guoqing* discourse of the pseudo-fascist concept of *guocui* ('national essence'), much discussed in the Republican era (and, like many other terms in the nationalist lexicon, borrowed from Japanese) (1993, 38). More salient in 1990s public discourse than stereotypically oriental notions of moral and aesthetic harmony were strident assertions of nationalist grievance, premised on racialist concepts of identity and a neo-Darwinian worldview. With the rise of 'totalitarian nostalgia' and populist anti-Americanism (Barmé 2000; Gries 2005), a xenophobic and essentialist strain of nationalism came to dominate popular and academic debate.

However, the kind of essentialism Hayhoe decries in *guoqing* or *guocui* discourse is ironically echoed in the dichotomy she posits between indigenous 'Chinese' and 'Western' scholarly values, as when she writes:

> It is unlikely, if not impossible, that Chinese scholars will fully embrace the notion of academic freedom. ... The tradition of an integrated view of knowledge that emphasizes practical social and political action, and also of intellectual authority and scholarly participation in government, precludes a commitment to academic freedom with the connotations of the neutrality of theoretical knowledge and a detachment from direct political and social involvement that characterised the concept in European history.
>
> (1999, 142)

In calling for an indigenisation of Chinese social science scholarship, Yang similarly invokes a contrast between Chinese academics, traditionally 'dependent' on political authority and 'taking responsibility for all under heaven', and their Western counterparts, 'speaking truth to power' (2006, 212). Like Hayhoe, and exemplifying the 'anti-globalist' position we outlined in our introductory chapter, he criticises the entrenched acceptance of 'western' modernisation theory and the 'scientific' paradigm for social science research, while identifying the continuing influence of Marxism, 'rationalist epistemology' and other 'western' theories as symptomatic of a 'colonisation' (or 'self-colonisation') of Chinese academia. Chinese policy researchers, he argues, need to 'develop their unique perspectives and values based on rich local experience and an awareness of their local society and culture' (218).

Yang nonetheless departs from this 'Western'–'Chinese' dichotomy when he notes that scholars from both traditions have historically shared a 'social commitment' – albeit manifested in different ways – that is now threatened by 'market forces' (212). He sees this as narrowing the caste identity of 'intellectuals', downgrading them from 'social trustees' to 'expert professionals':

> In a society where serious writers are now prepared to kowtow to the vulgar (*meisu*) for the sake of fame and gain, Chinese intellectuals move from a 'priestly' ideal to a 'professional' contract, not only giving up their priestly vocation, as has happened to their Eastern European colleagues, but also becoming as irrelevant as western intellectuals in their nation's 'politics'.
>
> (Yang 2006, 213, citing Cheek 1992, pp. 125, 140)

If marketisation or 'globalisation' are intrinsically 'Western' phenomena, then this could be taken to reinforce Yang's claims regarding the 'self-colonisation' of Chinese academia – and his calls for a recovery of 'indigenous' wisdom.

However, the attempt to distinguish 'indigenous' from 'alien' can involve a whole new level of 'hegemonic subordination', whereby different perspectives rooted in local experience are dismissed or subsumed within an abstract notion of 'Chineseness' (Dirlik 2011, 28). As Dirlik notes, Chineseness itself is a 'historical construct', so that 'making anything Chinese is an unstable idea and may depend above all on practices that differ from one location to another' (29). Moreover, Chinese social scientists have always been part of scholarly communities that are 'international in scope', and increasingly so since the 1980s. 'Differences between Chinese and Euro/American social science' are therefore, Dirlik continues, 'not just differences between an inside and an outside', but are 'increasingly internal to Chinese academia itself' (29). The Taiwan-based scholar, Allen Chun, attacks the whole notion of 'indigenous discourse', arguing that it is 'predicated on the misleading illusion that theory is culturally Western' (2012, 277). Since all theory springs from efforts to understand and critique societal conditions, he argues,

> knowledge does not have to be societally complicit, especially in the way it conforms to societal sensibilities and political correctness; this complicity inhibits its critical function and affects our ability to define the nature and relevance of theory in practice.
>
> (278)

Complicity in the maintenance of political authority or societal norms, as we noted above, has been a strong feature of the Chinese tradition of *guan xue*. However, it is not a 'given' or immutable feature of scholarship 'with Chinese characteristics', but an aspect of the intellectual scene both actively constructed and hotly contested by generations of scholars before and since the advent of Communism. During the Reform era, new ways have been found to politically discipline intellectual activity, increasingly involving the use of market mechanisms. Heightened calls for an 'indigenisation' of scholarship have been both a feature of official strategies of control, and a reaction to the growing intrusion of market forces associated with 'globalisation'. But as we saw in Chapter 9, marketisation, although a 'global' phenomenon, has been pursued in distinctive ways, and for particular reasons, in the Chinese context.

Marketisation, reform and control from the late 1980s to mid-1990s

Marketisation of higher education in post-Mao China arose both from a need to make up for shortfalls in public funding, and from an official desire to direct scholarly energies towards areas likely to promote economic growth and away from more speculative (and potentially subversive) terrain. From the 1980s until the mid-1990s, funding was severely constrained. Nor was this a problem for higher education alone: as state socialism was gradually dismantled, the Communist authorities struggled to find new ways of raising revenue from the growing commercial sector (Huang 2008). With tax revenues evaporating, one official response was to encourage public institutions to engage in commercial operations – every work unit for itself in the era of market socialism (see Chapter 5). Institutions of all descriptions, not least the hallowed People's Liberation Army, rapidly established business empires of dubious relevance to their purported public functions (McGregor 2010).

It was in this context that the marketisation of tertiary education gathered momentum. There had been significant moves to 'reactivate' private schools and colleges from as early as 1979 (Henze 1985, 122), gathering pace during the 1980s, particularly in areas such as secondary-level vocational training and adult education, seen as peripheral to the state-led drive to nurture elite 'talent' (see Mok 1997). But a combination of factors – the gradual dismantling of the job assignment system from 1986, the failure of academic salaries to keep pace with accelerating inflation, and the mounting crisis in public finances – intensified pressure on universities to 'create an income' (*chuangshou*) from the mid-1980s onwards (Hayhoe 1999, 120–22). This led to increasingly divergent fortunes for different faculties, departments and institutions: those well placed (by virtue of geographical location, field of expertise, connections or institutional prestige) to profit commercially might prosper, but others were brutally cut adrift. One result was a severe 'brain drain', as scholars from inland areas gravitated to universities in the wealthier east, while some already ensconced in famous institutions cashed in their prestige and left for the world of business (129).

This 'brain drain' was just one symptom of the problems that 'market socialism' posed for the state-managed deployment of skilled labour. In the early 1980s, the centralised system of job assignments was restored in its classic 1950s form, but as market forces increasingly strained the planners' limited powers of foresight, universities and colleges were granted more scope to reach agreements with particular employers, subject to official ratification. Finally, in 1988–89, the task of assigning graduates to work units was completely devolved to higher education institutions. But this decentralisation was widely associated with 'rampant nepotism', especially as an economic slowdown accentuated the challenge of placing graduates in suitable jobs. Job-related anxiety was a significant factor in the student discontent of the late 1980s. After Tiananmen, the job assignment system was temporarily recentralised, while student numbers were significantly curtailed, with the aim of reducing graduate under-employment. In 1989, total enrolments were down by over 70,000 from their 1988 peak of 669,000, and by 1992 had risen only marginally to 625,000 (Hayhoe 1995, 91). Reporting on a survey of universities conducted in early 1992, Hayhoe detected 'wide concurrence with the view that conditions are simply not yet ripe for competition on equal terms among young professionals' (84).

Nonetheless, even while the future direction of reform hung in the balance, earlier marketising measures were not reversed. Central to these was the introduction of a 'twin-track system' (*shuangguizhi*) for enrolments. The standard route into graduate employment was via the *gaokao* and the state-directed work placement system. But the State Council's 1985 'Decision on the Reform of the Education System' created an alternative track for 'work unit-sponsored students' (*wei pei sheng*). This allowed universities to register a limited number of applicants with below-par *gaokao* scores, provided their fees were paid by the sponsoring work unit (*danwei*) (see Figure 11.1). These students were then obliged to return to their *danwei* on graduation. Sponsoring organisations – including local governments, the judiciary and other public bodies as well as SOEs – thereby gained a steady supply of skilled workers. For universities and

Figure 11.1 Numbers of contract (*daipei*) and self-funded (*zifei*) students, 1986–99.
Source: NBS.

colleges, such arrangements became an important source of additional funding. Universities were incentivised to develop new programmes with a view to securing contracts with sponsoring *danwei*. The reform was officially billed as advancing the 'autonomy' of higher education institutions, but was an exercise in commercialisation rather than academic liberalisation.

In addition to *daipei* or 'contracted' students, from the mid-1980s universities were also empowered to enrol a limited number of 'self-funding' (*zifei*) students. These were charged tuition fees and had no job assignment on graduation. By 1992, according to Zhou (1994), *zifei* and *daipei* students together accounted for 25 per cent of total higher education enrolments. This figure was seemingly at odds with Hayhoe's report (based on 1991 data from the national statistical agency and the *China Daily*) of a post-1989 squeeze on self-funding and *daipei* applicants. But as it happened, that squeeze, especially as applied to *daipei* students, was very short-lived. 1991 and 1992 saw steep increases in the numbers recruited through these tracks, even while quotas for publicly funded enrolments remained static. Expansion of *daipei* enrolments had the advantage, from the official point of view, both of keeping down the government's financial commitments, and ensuring that more students would study in vocationally relevant rather than 'speculative' fields (since the *daipei* category was supposed to help work units address shortages of qualified staff). In the early- to mid-1990s, government funding for universities covered no more than a third of total overheads, prompting fierce competition to recruit fee-paying students 'outside the plan' (see Yin and White 1994). This led institutions to offer substantial 'discounts' on their required *gaokao* scores – of up to 100 points, depending upon the course.

Following the 1992 relaunch of the marketisation drive, the principle of user fees began to be far more widely applied, as we saw in Chapter 9. The State Council's 1993 *Gangyao* ('Framework'; see Chapter 3.3) stated that tertiary students should henceforth be charged fees 'on principle'. Channelling the new official viewpoint, Zhou depicted a wide-ranging 'crisis' in higher education funding and access (1994). A widening of the differential in *gaokao* scores between regular and self-funding applicants was creating 'unfairness' that demanded urgent action. The growth in higher education spending since 1978 (from 1.5 to 9.5 billion yuan) was meanwhile far outstripping that of taxation revenue (up by a factor of 2.7). Rising spending could not keep pace with increasing student numbers and the effects of inflation. The only solution, the SEC decreed, was to levy a charge on the principal beneficiaries of higher education: the students themselves. This was both necessary and right, given that the latter remained a tiny elite (2.7 per cent of the 18–21 age group) who stood to reap substantial financial rewards in the newly liberalised employment market. (Massification of the higher education system would later increasingly undermine this logic by devaluing qualifications – see next chapter – but while enrolments remained curtailed it retained a certain force.) Finally, Zhou asserted that charging fees for higher education was the 'international norm', perhaps reflecting the

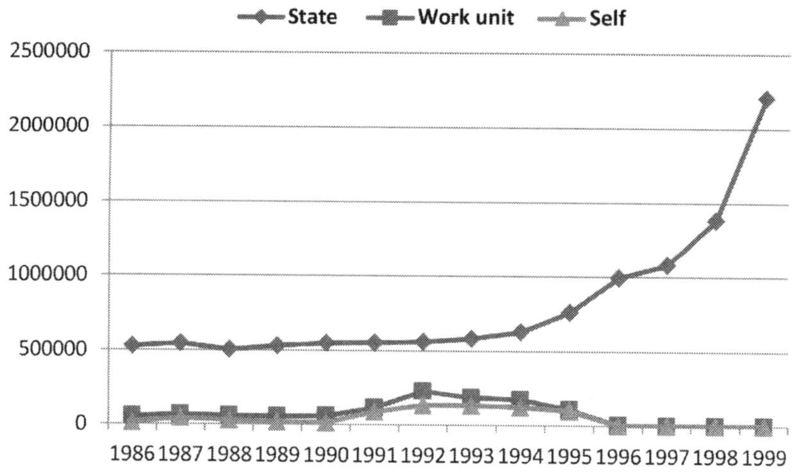

Figure 11.2 Distribution of students by funding model, 1986–99: state-supported;[a] sponsored by a work unit (*daipei*); self-funded (*zifei*).

Source: NBS.

Note: [a] Denotes students recruited according to officially determined quotas. From the mid-1990s, most of these students were also required to pay fees.

fashion for invoking neoliberal America as the benchmark for 'normalcy' (no major European country levied substantial university tuition fees in the 1990s, though China's East Asian neighbours did).

For all these reasons, abolishing the 'twin tracks' (*shuanggui*) and merging them (*bingui*) was represented as an urgent imperative: fees would be introduced for all students from the autumn of 1994, with certain exceptions (e.g. for teacher trainees); by 1996, the *zifei* and *daipei* tracks would be effectively closed (Figures 11.1 and 11.2). Acknowledging that annual fees of 1,000–1,500 yuan would be burdensome for the estimated '8 per cent' of 'poor students', Zhou nonetheless insisted that, at 10–15 per cent of total tuition costs, these were low by 'international standards'. With a little thrift, he argued, most families would somehow cope. A former mayor of Shenyang had wisely admonished his citizens for wasting money on New Year firecrackers: prudence dictated that investment in education be prioritised. For the genuinely indigent, charity was the answer – during a visit to the provincial university, Hunan's Party Secretary had given 200 yuan 'out of his own salary' to a 'poor student'. Donations from companies, entrepreneurs, alumni and so forth would boost support for the needy and deserving, calibrated according to their *gaokao* scores. A transformation in popular attitudes would usher in an American-style culture of philanthropy. Students would 'come to realize their duty to parents and country' as they were liberated from the psychological shackles of state dependence. 'Every emancipation', Marx himself had written, 'is a restoration of the human world and of human relationships to man' (20).[14] In an impressive feat of ideological acrobatics, the Communist sage was thus invoked in support of a Friedman-esque attack on statist welfarism.

Although the 'merging of the tracks' was heralded as advancing 'fairness' by removing the link between wealth and higher educational access, in practice it had no such effect. Instead, with fees laxly regulated, universities continued to charge applicants differentially on the basis of their *gaokao* scores; the difference being that now fee payment was the rule, rather than the exception. Meanwhile, in a parallel reform, the structure of academic salaries was altered: henceforth, 70 per cent would be paid out of regular budgets, but the remainder on a basis of 'matching funds', with the university paying another 15 per cent only if the 'cost centre' (department, faculty, research centre, etc.) managed to bring in the same amount. The aim was to compel senior management to focus on 'earning' money from sources (including student fees) besides regular public funding. By 2000, at one university investigated by Yan (2010, S112), just under a third of academic salaries were funded by government, with the remainder funded by the university from other sources. As late as 1996, the government was still providing over 80 per cent of higher education funding, with tuition and other fees accounting for about 14 per cent; but the contribution of fees rapidly climbed thereafter (to 21 per cent in 2000 and 31 per cent in 2005 – of much higher totals) (S108; see next chapter).

As market fervour gripped society following Deng's 1992 'Southern Tour', universities flexed their entrepreneurial muscles. In March 1993, the south wall of Peking University's campus was torn down and the land rented to private stores and restaurants. Min Weifang of Peking University extolled universities' role in 'community development' (Min *et al.* 1995) – a euphemism for wide-ranging commercialisation. University enterprises (*xiaoban qiye*), first established during the 1980s, now proliferated. (Lenovo *(lianxiang)*, founded in 1984 by a group of professors at the Chinese Academy of Sciences, was an early example.) Science parks such as that at Zhongguancun in Beijing's Haidian District, loosely modelled on Taiwan's Hsinchu Science and Industrial Park (see Chapter 2), also expanded and multiplied. But the invisible hand of the market was firmly held by the guiding hand of the Party-State, which continued to 'aggressively support favoured firms and industries' (Naughton 2004). Just as Taiwan's Hsinchu Park was 'narrated as a nation-building project' (Sum 2004), so its mainland cousins were presented as integral to state-led development. The novelty was that now the role of material incentives in stimulating scholarly dedication to the national cause was unabashedly acknowledged.

Students, meanwhile, exhorted to pay their fees out of a sense of 'duty to country', were to have their patriotism tested as universities rapidly ramped up fee levels from the mid-1990s onwards (from around 400 to 1,000 yuan by the end of the decade).[15] The same period saw the establishment of many new courses in humanities, arts and social sciences, relatively cheap to run and thus a ready source of income. From 1979 to 1993, the students enrolled in these fields had amounted to no more than a fifth of total enrolments, but from 1994 a sudden upsurge saw them account for between a quarter and a third of the total (NCEDR 2009, 75).

The rapid expansion of such courses also reflected the breakdown of the work placement system that accompanied the extension of tuition fees. If fee-paying arts and humanities graduates had trouble finding suitable employment, this was no longer the responsibility of the university. And as universities sought to compete for fee income, more and more diversified beyond their specialist fields. Soviet-style institutional specialisation supporting state-directed manpower planning no longer made any sense. Between 1995 and 1996, the entire higher education system was therefore reorganised along geographical lines. Formal ties between specialist universities (in Agriculture, Aeronautical Science and so forth) and particular ministries were broken or loosened, with almost all elite institutions henceforth placed under the supervision of the SEC (see the next chapter). Second-tier institutions came under the authority of provincial departments of education.

The reforms of the mid-1990s thus pushed in two directions at once: funding was further decentralised, with universities encouraged (or effectively compelled) to market their services; but administrative control was centralised and rationalised, with the Soviet-style patchwork of ministerial jurisdictions supplanted by a more symmetrical hierarchy. Meanwhile, despite these sweeping changes, the Party remained wedded to an elitist vision of the scope and purposes of higher education. Just as in the 1950s, the primary purpose of China's universities was still seen as nurturing 'talent' to spearhead industrial and technological modernisation and economic development. Official justifications for the introduction of fees assumed that graduates would remain a tiny elite whose scarcity value would ensure large returns on their educational investment. But the rapid rise of an aspirational urban middle class on the one hand, and pressures on universities to generate income on the other, rendered strict restrictions on student numbers increasingly untenable. Although the post-Tiananmen leadership remained wary of moving towards a mass higher education system, pressure was building for more rapid expansion.

Conclusion

The restructuring of higher education from the mid-1990s onwards was part and parcel of the broader reforms to China's socio-economic structure spearheaded by Zhu Rongji, first as the Politburo's economic policy supremo, then as Prime Minister from 1998. For a time, Zhu was hailed in the Western media as a great liberaliser – 'China's Gorbachev' (McGregor 2010, 43–4). But foreign observers mistook the 'chaos' that initially resulted from Deng Xiaoping's 'rebooted reforms' for liberal intent. In fact, just as the aim of the SOE reforms was to create 'worldly enterprises that were both capitalist and commercial at the same time' (37), so in higher education, the Party-State moved to secure its control over the commanding heights of the system, while cutting loose the lower echelons to fend for themselves in a profoundly skewed marketplace (a pattern we have already observed lower down the educational ladder – see Chapter 9). The resulting combination of radical stratification and market-driven expansion, along with its implications, is explored in the following chapter.

By the late 1990s, as the dust settled on the initial 'chaotic' phase of the post-1992 reforms, it was clear that extensive restructuring of the Soviet-inspired system had left its Leninist core intact. The Soviet legacy endured not only in the massive privileging of STEM subjects; this, after all, is common to East Asian societies of both a 'socialist' and 'capitalist' stamp (see Chapter 2). More fundamentally, the principle of Party leadership, permeating the institutions of an ostensibly marketised society, was forcefully reasserted. Party supremacy had never been abandoned, even during the liberal high tide of the 1980s. What changed after 1989 was that its instruments of control, particularly over appointments and promotions, were deployed with renewed purpose and vigour. The double shock of their own Party's near-death experience and the subsequent collapse of the Soviet bloc convinced leaders both to suppress liberal tendencies within their own ranks, and enforce ideological consistency beyond them.

Meanwhile, the content of this ideology was itself undergoing significant change – reflected both in discourse on the social role of scholarship, and in official rhetoric on patriotism and citizenship. In bemoaning the 'professionalisation' of Chinese intellectuals since the 1990s (by which he means a proletarianisation of their conditions of employment),[16] Yang emphasises the erosion of their 'priestly' status and socio-political mission (2006, 213). Other observers (e.g. Hansen and Woronov 2013) have similarly noted the fading since the 1990s of a sense of intellectuals as an elite collectively responsible for the fate of the nation – vividly evoked in Perry Link's paean to the liberal elites of the 1980s, *Evening Chats in Beijing* (1992). But in ultimately blaming the corruption and degradation of Chinese academia on 'colonisation' (Soviet Marxist as well as Western neoliberal), and urging solutions rooted in China's 'unique cultural heritages' and 'rich civilisation' (2006, 218), Yang himself echoes the dominant ideological theme of post-Tiananmen China: nationalism.

The nationalist turn in official ideology not only invites comparisons with the former Soviet bloc (and many societies beyond it), but also suggests parallels with a much earlier sequence of revolution and reaction, in mid-nineteenth century Europe. Lewis Namier dubbed the risings of 1848 *The Revolution of the Intellectuals* (1992), and the same could be said of China's 1989 unrest. Showing how the revolutionaries of 1848 were animated by romantic nationalism as well as liberal idealism, Namier suggested that the subsequent history of Germany was largely the story of how they were seduced and cajoled into abandoning the latter in favour of the former. The result was the highly volatile combination of 'sagely' and 'militaristic' values that characterised both Imperial Germany and her most avid East Asian disciple, Meiji Japan (Priestland 2012, 77).

China's developmental strategy, the nationalist ideology that animates it and the purposes assigned to higher education all echo earlier German and Japanese experience – unsurprisingly, given Meiji Japan's profound influence on modern Chinese thought (Moloughney and Zarrow 2011). But Chinese intellectuals well-versed in the Marxist canon might also be reminded of the sage's observation, in *The Eighteenth Brumaire of Louis Bonaparte*, that 'the bourgeoisie … is bound to fear the stupidity of the masses as long as they remain conservative, and the insight of the masses as soon as they become revolutionary' (Marx 1983). Hence Napoleon III's success, until his defeat at the hands of Bismarck, in combining traditionalist mystique, romantic nationalism, straightforward repression and divide-and-rule to reinforce his control. A similar tactical combination has been central to the Chinese regime's post-Tiananmen legitimating strategy (Wright 2010) – with the crucial difference that the focus of patriotic loyalty is a Leninist Party, not an imperial pseudo-divinity.

The first two post-Mao decades witnessed the rapid expansion and contraction of the space for free enquiry and debate within Chinese universities. By the 1990s, the regime was subordinating intellectuals to the state in the name of patriotism and catch-up modernisation, while selectively utilising for this purpose the competitive apparatus of US-style New Public Management. Meanwhile, both the Party-State itself, and urban society more broadly, were rapidly professionalising, as certified 'merit' formally replaced class background or political correctness as the accepted route to career advancement. But as the professional ethos gained ground amongst the urban middle classes, so corruption and cronyism came to seem less tolerable and more threatening to party legitimacy. By the late 1990s, finding a politically safe method of channelling the intense aspirations of urban parents for their singleton children had also become a looming imperative for policymakers (Fong 2004). Expanding access to higher education, by tapping into and fostering competitive credentialism, offered one way of disciplining middle-class energies.

But in terms of the immediate aims assigned to the post-1978 higher education system – of generating 'talent' to support the 'four modernisations' – policymakers and educators were conscious of fundamental contradictions. These involved the tensions between political imperatives and official ideology on the one hand, and intellectual, or more specifically technological, ambition on the other. As Perkin observed of the defunct Soviet Union:

> Not only was an inordinate part of the investment in economically irrelevant Marxist-Leninist theology; the politically correct, rote-learning, unquestioning approach of the rest of the pedagogy stultified free thought and discouraged the kind of innovation, except perhaps in space research and military hardware, that ever-changing postindustrial society required.
>
> (1998, 212)

In Chapter 6, we discussed how reforms to the school curriculum from the late 1990s onwards sought to square this circle: seeking to promote educational 'quality' – encompassing critical thinking and innovative drive – while maintaining ideological uniformity and unquestioning loyalty. In the following chapter, we examine contemporaneous developments within higher education, where such contradictions have if anything been even more complex and acute.

Notes

1 Hence Walder's observation that 'Mao was not much of an anti-bureaucratic thinker' (2015, 34).
2 Though he does not cite Perkin.
3 As Perkin puts it (1989, 4), 'some acquire merit more easily than others'.
4 Led by Chen Yun (architect of China's First Five Year Plan).
5 Hayhoe (1995, Chapter 1) provides a very useful overview of the main characteristics of various Western traditions of higher education – although she goes on to characterise Chinese tradition as lacking a conception of academic freedom (a claim with which we take issue below).
6 The ruling was entitled *Dui gaodeng yuanxiao de jiaoxue anpai shixing tongyi jizhong lingdao* ('Arranging unified and concentrated leadership for teaching in higher education colleges'). On political oversight of higher education during the early 1950s, see Luo (2010).
7 The concept is perhaps more accurately described as 'Leninist' rather than 'Stalinist': the former had far more to say than the latter about the role of culture in the revolutionary project, and although the First Five Year Plan took place under Stalin's leadership, the leadership of Narkompros (the educational commissariat) remained dominated by Lenin's appointees, with the former leader's wife, Krupskaya, prominent among them (see Fitzpatrick 1979 and Meisner 1989).
8 An abortive 1975 attempt to reform higher education under Zhou Rongxin (a Deng appointee) ended with Deng's fall (again) and Minister Zhou's death as result of a 'struggle session' in April 1976 (Vogel 2011, 140). Deng's various initiatives in the field of 'technology, science, culture' then went into 'cold storage' for another two years (155).
9 This represented something of a turnaround, since Deng's role as leader of the 'Anti-Rightist Movement' of 1957 had resulted in his being previously regarded with widespread suspicion among Chinese intellectuals.
10 A viewpoint possibly influenced by, and reflected in, the fact that Deng's wife and three of his five children studied Physics at Peking University. (Again, this observation is Vogel's.)
11 Such moves by Tsinghua, Shanghai Jiaotong University and the Central China University of Science and Technology (*Huazhong Keji Daxue*) in the late 1980s and early 1990s were often a reflection less of idealistic commitment to liberal education than of a desire to broaden the education of scientists and engineers in the hope of making them more 'creative'. See our discussion of general education courses (*tongshi jiaoyu*) in the following chapter.
12 Enrolments in teacher training grew very rapidly during 1980, far outpacing growth in other fields; in 1981, they accounted for fully 74 per cent of higher education enrolments, falling back tó 28 per cent the following year as other fields 'caught up' (Henze 1984, 136).
13 Hayhoe notes that agricultural universities faced 'the most desperate situation in terms of the appropriate employment of their graduates', citing the startling statistic that, as of 1991, 'only 150,000 of the 1.2 million students trained [in agriculture] since 1949 are actually working directly in agricultural fields' (1995, 89).
14 The quotation is from *On the Jewish Question.*
15 We provide figures for fee levels in the early 2000s in the following chapter. We could not find statistics for the 1990s – these estimates are based on Zeng's memory of that period. (In the late 1990s, 1,000 yuan was about one month's salary for a junior academic.)
16 The term 'proletarianisation' is used by Perkin to describe the condition of professionals in the societies of late modernity (1989, 3).

12 Higher education since 1998

Expansion, stratification and control

To what extent is higher education a 'public good' or a 'private good'? This question is central to contemporary debates worldwide over the scale, purpose and funding of post-secondary education. In many societies, the past thirty years have witnessed a shift towards treating college studies as a standard rite of passage for a plurality, if not a majority, of school-leavers. Once publicly funded hothouses for meritocratic elites, today universities are increasingly perceived as market-led suppliers of essential credentials. But the transition to mass higher education has not followed a uniform path; in East Asia, more than in other 'developed' societies, the typical pattern has been to weight public expenditure heavily towards compulsory schooling, leaving universities to raise much of their funding from user fees or other sources (see Chapter 2). While successful test-takers enjoy subsidised tuition at favoured institutions, others have paid a high price for rising credentialism. Universal basic education has been acknowledged as a fundamental public good; less so higher education for the masses.

China's higher education system prior to 1998 was tasked with producing a technocratic elite to serve the state's developmental goals. Even when the system was rapidly marketised during the mid-1990s, this orientation remained basically unchanged, and Party control over the system's commanding heights was maintained. However, as noted in the previous chapter, both the general logic of marketisation, and the advent of student fees, by then pointed towards at least a partial redefinition of higher education as a consumption good. After 1989, Party leaders were initially disinclined to sanction increasing student numbers, instead constraining enrolments and disciplining unruly youth. However, as the 1990s wore on, a desire to harness and tame the aspirations of a burgeoning urban middle class featured more prominently in official calculations. As a self-important elite-in-waiting, students could be politically troublesome; but as paying investors in their own economic prospects, they could perhaps be relied upon to remain more intently focused on private gain.

The reasons for the 1998 decision to rapidly expand enrolments are discussed further below, but its consequences were dramatic. Li *et al.* (2015) note that China's gross college enrolment rate in 1990 was 3.4 per cent – below that for Brazil (11 per cent) or India (6 per cent). By 1998, this had risen to 6 per cent, but by 2007 it had rocketed to 22 per cent of the age cohort (18–22-year-olds) (188).

By 2015, enrolments had already reached a target set for 2020 of 40 per cent of 18–22 year olds in higher education (MOE 2016), prompting Minister Yang Guiren to declare a new 2020 target of 50 per cent.

But the bulk of this expansion has been concentrated at the lower levels of a very steep institutional pyramid. In 2003, 25 per cent of 18–year-olds took the *gaokao*, and 17 per cent were able to access a tertiary college of some kind. However, only 5 per cent of this cohort entered four-year colleges, with a further 2 per cent entering elite 211 colleges, and 1 per cent the even more prestigious 985 institutions. The proportion entering Peking or Tsinghua universities – the pinnacle of China's higher education hierarchy – was 0.03 per cent (Li *et al.* 2015, 190). By 2012, total enrolments nationwide had reached almost 6.889 million, a multiple of 6.36 times the 1998 figure, among which four-year undergraduate students had increased 5.73-fold, and those on two-year programmes 7.31-fold (see Figure 12.1). As noted in Chapter 8, this expansion, combined with shrinkage of the age cohort, meant that the prospects for senior high school graduates of entering higher education of some kind rose from around 60 per cent to 80 per cent – making senior high school more than ever the crucial 'bottleneck' of the education system.

Rapidly expanding enrolments and increased institutional stratification were to place new strains on the implicit bargain between the state, colleges and youth. If students (or their parents) were now paying customers, growing graduate under-employment suggested that some were not getting what they had paid for.

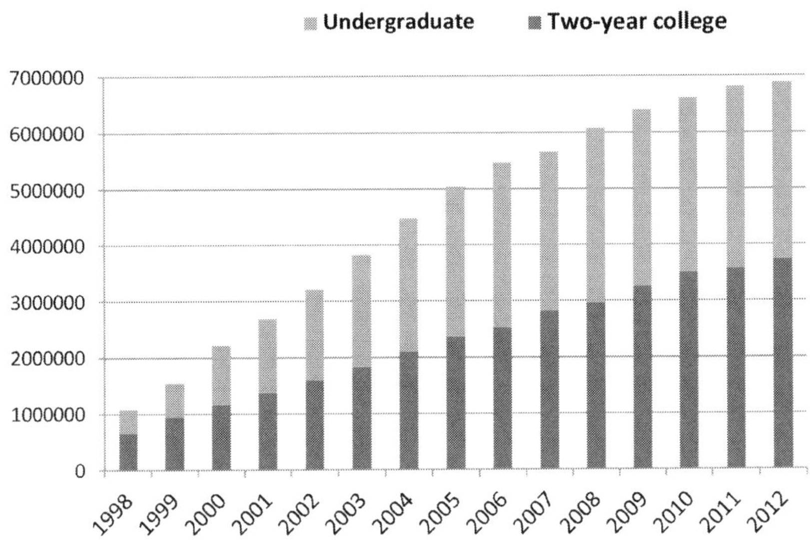

Figure 12.1 Enrolments in regular undergraduate programmes and two-year college programmes, 1998–2012.

Source: NBS (2013).

Meanwhile, elite universities charged with competing to nurture innovative and creative talent were also exhorted to reinforce and police ideological 'correctness'. Could they do both?

In this chapter, we trace post-1998 developments in higher education, analysing the reasons for massification, and its subsequent implications. These include a wave of institutional mergers, debt-fuelled expansion, and official efforts to manage the unforeseen consequences of rampant commercialisation. At the same time, there have been significant continuities in policy towards the system's 'commanding heights'. Persistent inequalities in access to colleges and courses have been a feature of the expanded system, with less-privileged students concentrated in less-prestigious institutions, while family background seemingly continues to influence not only enrolment patterns, but also post-graduation employment prospects. Finally, we focus on issues of governance – of universities as institutions, of faculty, and of their students – discussing control over both curricula and personnel. Discussion of the increasingly important international dimension of higher education is deferred to the following chapter. Here we conclude by considering briefly how the development of universities has reflected, and contributed to, the 'professionalisation' of society – and what that has meant in the Chinese context.

Reasons for the expansion

That motives for expanding college enrolments were primarily economic was reflected in the fact that the decision to sanction rapid expansion originated not in the SEC (which in 1998 reverted to Ministry status), but in the State Council. In 1997, China was hit by the consequences of the East Asian financial crisis. By 1998, the country had an unemployment rate of 9 per cent, largely as a result of lay-offs associated with the restructuring of SOEs. Tertiary places were meanwhile available for only around 6 per cent of the relevant cohort. Tang Ming, chief economist of the Asian Development Bank, advised Premier Zhu Rongji to expand enrolments on a fee-paying basis, as a means of unlocking family savings, boosting consumer spending and domestic demand (Kipnis 2011, 86 – citing Bai 2006). It would also ease unemployment by delaying the entry of millions of school-leavers into the labour market. At the Third National Conference on Education in 1999, President Jiang Zemin emphasised that the aspirations of both urban and rural residents underlined the potential for expanding 'consumption' of and 'investment' in higher education (Jiang 1999). Rather than a planned strategy for upgrading 'human capital', the 1998 reform was thus primarily an exercise in social pacification and economic stimulus, at minimal cost to the state. Its effectiveness in this respect was illustrated by the subsequent rapid rise in the share of higher education costs derived from fees rather than the government (Yan 2010; see previous chapter).

In fact, enrolments had already been rising since 1992–3 (see above and previous chapter). In 1993, the SEC adopted a goal of 7 per cent enrolment of school-leavers by 2000 (Hayhoe 1999, 252). Meanwhile, in Guangdong, Shanghai and other economically 'advanced' regions on the eastern seaboard, local officials were already clamouring for a more rapid expansion (Hayhoe 1995). There, a desire to increase the supply of skilled manpower appears to have been a more significant factor. This might have been expected to dictate a focus on vocationally oriented tertiary institutions (*da zhuan*), which did indeed expand. But from 1998, it was in regular university places that the most significant growth occurred.

This shift occurred in the context of economic, fiscal and administrative reforms that encouraged public institutions, including local governments and universities, to behave in an increasingly 'entrepreneurial' fashion (Chapters 3.3, 5 and 9; Huang 2008). The 1998 reforms further encouraged both local officials and university managers to view higher education as an industry. They thus came to see it as desirable to expand the local tertiary education sector as fast and as far as possible, in competition with other cities and provinces. Spurring them on was the cadre evaluation (*zhengji*) system, which attached prime importance to officials' record in promoting economic development (Shue and Wong 2007).

In the race to generate fee income, state universities not only hiked regular tuition fees, but also introduced variable charges for new modes of provision. Whereas dormitory residence had previously been part and parcel of the college experience, now 'day students' living at home were allowed to enrol at a discounted rate. In Shandong, as of 2005, many courses awarded bonus *gaokao* points to applicants with a local urban *hukou*, who were often the only ones allowed to register as day students (Kipnis 2011, 87). Meanwhile, many institutions rented out their facilities for the teaching of non-accredited courses. By 2011, Shandong's universities were accommodating more than 50 per cent of local school-leavers (up from 6 per cent in 1998). This came at a hefty price: in Zouping County, by 2005, parents with a child in college were often paying 13,000 yuan per year in fees and living expenses (87). Families were often willing to save for decades to send a child to college. But it was often those who could afford it least who ended up paying the most, for inferior returns (88). Expansion of enrolments was concentrated at the lower tiers of the system, where state subsidies were lowest and fees consequently highest.

Reflecting the fact that initiative in this instance lay elsewhere, the Ministry of Education was clearly unprepared for the sudden expansion. As late as January 1998, Zhu Kaixuan (NPC Education Committee Chairman), addressing an 'Education Work Conference', stressed that higher education would continue to 'follow the path of stability and development', while focusing on reforms to management and improvement of 'quality' (IED 1998, 3). Along with most professional educators, Ministry officials on the whole remained wedded to a highly elitist vision of higher education. By contrast, a group of Peking University scholars under Min Weifang were urging a fee-driven expansion of the sector (see previous chapter). Indeed, World Bank advisors, including Min, had been advocating this since at least 1986, when they recommended an enrolments target of 15 per cent of school-leavers by 2000 – though by the time the millennium arrived, even Min was expressing some concern over the impact of fee inflation on equitable access (quoted in Li and Wei 2000). But while the World Bank connection has led some to blame foreign influence for the growing marketisation of higher education, the crucial impetus for such policies was domestic rather than external (see Chapters 9 and 13).

Whatever its causes, the hasty growth in enrolments was widely seen as detrimental to quality – supposedly still the priority of educational priorities. Among its consequences, according to Yao (2005), was an exponential rise in the student–teacher ratio, which doubled between 1997 and 2002 in regular higher education institutions. Min and his colleagues had pinpointed relatively low ratios as evidence of spare capacity in the sector (see previous chapter), but Yao emphasised that this teaching workforce was ageing and under-qualified; of 53,000 full professors, over 20,000 were above the age of 56. Professors educated before the Cultural Revolution were on the cusp of retirement, and that 'lost decade' meant a dearth of suitably qualified senior faculty to replace them. According to Yao, only 30 per cent of faculty had postgraduate qualifications, and only 7 per cent doctorates (2005, 32). The promotion of overseas study was already important to schemes for 'upgrading' faculty (see next chapter), while the graduate schools established from the 1980s were producing more scholars with postgraduate credentials. But as of 2012, the proportion of academic staff with doctoral degrees remained low, at under 20 per cent (Zhao Y. 2014, 98).

The post-1998 expansion of college enrolments thus appears to have been a classic attempt at what Kipnis terms the 'governing' of 'educational desire' (2011). The authorities faced demand 'from below' for credentials, attributable partly to deep-rooted cultural beliefs, but greatly accentuated by the prevalence of singleton children in urban households (Fong 2004). This encouraged Party leaders to view the rapid expansion of college access as a safety valve at a time of potential social and political instability.[1] But in sanctioning expansion, they radically challenged the strongly statist and elitist vision of higher education to which most officials and professional educators still adhered. As discussed below, lavishly funded new schemes were consequently introduced to buttress the elitism of the sector's upper echelons. Meanwhile, however, lower levels were left financially far more reliant on market forces.

Stratification and inequality in an expanded system

As it has expanded hugely in scale, the tertiary education system has also become increasingly stratified. The relationship between competitive public entrance examinations and social inequality has already been discussed in Chapter 8. Such inequalities result not simply from the assessment system itself, but from multiple and cumulative forms of disadvantage experienced from early childhood onwards. Girls, rural residents (including children of migrant workers), minorities and those from poor communities have continued to face substantial disadvantages in accessing tertiary education, despite the massification of the sector. As Wang *et al.* conclude (2013), college 'is a rich, Han, urban, male club'.

Writing two decades earlier, Hayhoe (1999) had reached a similar conclusion. On the one hand, women's participation in formal higher education had risen from 24 per cent in 1978 to almost 34 per cent by 1990, while their representation amongst junior faculty had also grown. But the proportion at senior levels remained low, with labour market discrimination against female graduates if anything worsening since 1978 – and continuing into the twenty-first century, according to Fincher (2014). Meanwhile, though nationwide statistics were unavailable, a 1992 case study of universities in the Northwestern region revealed that rural and 'minority' status, as well as gender, was associated negatively with access to higher education (Hayhoe 1999, 219). There and elsewhere (165), inequalities in access, across all dimensions – gender, ethnic and residential – were greater at centrally funded elite institutions than at less prestigious provincial colleges.

The task of tracking changes over time in access to higher education is complicated by the unreliability of official statistics, the difficulty of sampling the relevant populations, and rapid, wrenching demographic shifts. Hayhoe's 1992 data (see Hayhoe 1999) is not directly comparable with that used by Wang *et al.* (2013), though both draw on fieldwork conducted in the Northwest. The latters' findings have been challenged by Hu (2014), who argues that a focus on high school graduates (i.e. the population of potential applicants for higher education) reveals that residency is the only factor that significantly affects access. Indeed, official statistics show that the proportion of female students at regular higher education institutions rose from around a third in 1990 to almost precisely half of a much larger total in 2007 (NCEDR 2009, 74).

However, sampling only high school graduates neglects the complex and cumulative nature of disadvantage – from preschool level onwards. Hu also overlooks the importance of stratification within the higher education system. As Wang *et al.* point out, evidence from other societies suggests that 'decreases in disparities in access to *any* college are sometimes accompanied by increases in disparities in access to *elite* colleges' (2014, 1132). Their 2013 study clearly suggests that the 'urban, Han, male and rich' profile of the student body is especially pronounced at elite, centrally funded institutions, and in the more prestigious disciplines (Liu 2010 reports similar findings from a case study in Anhui).

This pattern emerges all the more clearly from a related study by Li *et al.* (2015) based on a 2003 national dataset of *gaokao* candidates. This finds that the main dimension of inequality is overwhelmingly urban–rural; urban youth were five times more likely to take the *gaokao*, and seven times more likely to access any college. Furthermore, they were 11 times more likely than their rural counterparts to access relatively prestigious 211 institutions, and 43 times more likely to enter Tsinghua or Peking Universities (191–2). By contrast, inequalities between those holding urban *hukou* from poor and non-poor counties in different regions were relatively minor – perhaps due to the greater proportion of more highly educated *ganbu* (official) families in poorer urban counties (Li *et al.* 2015, 200). Especially disadvantaged were those from rural areas of central and western China (196), particularly if they were also female or from an 'ethnic minority' (201–3). But Li *et al.* do not consider the politics of provincial *gaokao* quotas, and their implications for equitable access (discussed in Chapter 8). Nor do they discuss the trend towards overseas study, particularly among wealthier urban youth (see next chapter). This may help account for the relative equality between urban youth from poor and non-poor regions, since it takes a number of 'non-poor' youth out of the reckoning.

The expansion of higher education has thus not significantly enhanced social mobility for holders of rural *hukou*, though it may have done so for those with urban residency. Rural residents, minorities and women have tended to gravitate disproportionately to lower status institutions offering foundational diplomas or vocational courses (see below). To be sure, as the economy has grown rapidly, and as rural migrants have flocked to the cities, many have experienced significant social mobility. However, the contribution of higher education to this phenomenon is moot. For the exceptionally gifted, or the exceptionally fortunate, it can provide an escape route from social disadvantage. In general, though, the most significant consequence of market-driven expansion has been an explosion of credentialism that has exacerbated financial burdens on the poorest.

The state's strategic priorities for higher education: The '211' and '985' projects

The disbursement of the government's own financial resources meanwhile revealed where official priorities lay. In 1993, as much of the public sector was being impelled towards the market, the SEC announced a programme to select, by the twenty-first century, one hundred of the country's best universities for special financial support (IED 1993, 3447). What became known as the '211 Project' fuelled a rash of college mergers from the mid-1990s (see below), as institutions sought to enhance their claims to elite status. But despite an ostensibly open, competitive applications process, the 211 Project continued the established strategy of identifying and nurturing 'key point' institutions, selected partly on the basis of political considerations. One aim of the new scheme was to establish leading comprehensive universities for each region of the country. Thus Tibet University in Lhasa, along with institutions in Ningxia and Qinghai, was selected as a '211' institution, despite poor performance according to standard measures of research or teaching quality.

The '985 Project', announced in May 1998 by President Jiang Zemin in a speech marking the centenary of Peking University, similarly coincided with an extension of the marketisation of higher education. Both '985' and '211' projects sought to inoculate the commanding heights of the tertiary sector against the quality-diluting effects of expansion, while maintaining close state supervision of key institutions. The '211' institutions were generally at the front of the queue for '985' funding, but those with outstanding reputations in particular disciplines were specifically targeted. For this reason, '985' status was seen as especially prestigious. Funding involved contributions from both provincial and central governments, but in their desperation to secure the '985' imprimatur, some wealthier provincial or municipal governments lobbied for permission to declare an institution part of the programme entirely on the basis of 'local' funding (one example of this being East China Normal University; ECNU 2016). The vast majority of the institutions included in the 985 project were in Beijing, (which eventually boasted 9 of a total of 39) Shanghai (4), Guangzhou (2) and other cities in the East and Northeast (24); only ten were in 'inland' cities (Zhang *et al.* 2013).

Taken together, the 211 and 985 schemes have pumped huge amounts of money into the upper echelons of China's higher education system (in the first 'phase' of the 985 Project, from 1998 to 2003, the central government allocated 14 billion yuan to 34 universities; and in the second phase 18.9 billion went to 39 institutions) (Zhang *et al.* 2013). Elite universities have acquired truly 'world-class' facilities, their faculty and students have gained opportunities to engage in international exchange, and compensation packages for top scholars and scientists have become increasingly competitive globally.[2] These institutions have meanwhile largely been spared pressure to increase enrolments or maximise fee income. This influx of public funds has undoubtedly helped boost research output, especially in the sciences (see below and next chapter).

However, both schemes have attracted intense domestic criticism. Their statist premises were at odds not just with the thrust of wider reforms to higher education, but also with the increasingly cosmopolitan and liberal ethos of many academics. Improved facilities, salaries and opportunities for international exchange came with an increased dependency on the state that, many complained, threatened the quality of research. This was a matter not only of political interference, but also of bureaucratic demands for immediate results. Vast funds have been funnelled willy-nilly to 'key' universities, typically with the requirement that the money be spent within the fiscal year. Chen Xuefei of Peking University warned that a rushed, ill-considered and unrealistic drive for 'world-class' status could cause misallocation of resources, exaggerated expectations, and damage to staff confidence and performance (2006, 156). (See our discussion of rankings in the next chapter.) Objecting to 'statism', Li and Zhang point out that Harvard, MIT and Oxford stress the cultivation of autonomous individuals capable of exercising independent critical judgement (2012). By contrast, they argued, the 985 Project saw universities solely in terms of national developmental goals, neglecting their role in socialising citizens or fostering attitudes conducive to the pursuit of original research.

Despite (or perhaps because of) the huge amounts of money involved, the effectiveness of these projects in spurring reform of university governance has also been questioned. Wang (2008, 36) argued that they did nothing to reward or incentivise improved performance, since, once 211 or 985 status had been obtained, in practice no institution risked losing it. Moreover, he complained, political criteria rather than academic excellence were often crucial in determining the distribution of funding. Lamenting the problems of excessive bureaucracy and short-termism, Meng pointed to how the channeling of 985 and 211 funding through university administrators had enhanced their authority over academic faculty (2010). Academics have had to apply for such funding – for example to attend overseas conferences or conduct a new research project – to the university personnel department, whose officials have little or no relevant academic expertise (a complaint that may strike a chord amongst academics working in other systems).

The prestige and the funding that come with '211' and '985' status, combined with the rapid expansion of higher education enrolments, have meanwhile contributed to policies at provincial level that exacerbate strains within the sector. The cadre evaluation system and the desire to impress visiting dignitaries from Beijing prompted many officials in the early 2000s to focus public investment on 'key' institutions – often in the hope of securing the coveted '985' or '211' imprimatur. In 2012, Liaoning Province spent the same amount on financial support for 'key' institutions within its remit as on subsidies for students across the province, and in Shanghai the skew towards investment in flagship universities was even greater. In an attempt to rebalance provincial spending, in 2012 the Education Ministry set a benchmark of 12,000 yuan per year for provincial government subsidies to the costs of each student (Zeng 2013).

To the surprise of many, given the criticism directed at them, the 985 and 211 Projects were renewed in 2010, when the State Council issued its new 10-year 'framework' (*Gangyao*) for educational development.[3] This may have been due partly to a desire rapidly to fulfil the longstanding pledge to raise public education spending to 4 per cent of GDP (see Chapter 3.4). Where possible, the Finance Ministry has generally preferred to direct spending towards projects more susceptible to monitoring by the central government. The new windfall for '985' and '211' institutions enabled them further to enhance their facilities and offer competitive salaries and benefits to internationally renowned scientists (see below).

The financial basis for the transition to mass higher education

The financial advantages of 'key' institutions enabled them to keep fee levels down, to the benefit of their disproportionately wealthy, urban intake. This sort of outcome is, of course, far from unique to China. In Britain, for example, the hugely expensive, state-subsidised Oxbridge tuition system caters to a student body disproportionately drawn from the 'independent schools' sector. And in Japan, Tokyo and Kyoto Universities, nurseries of the country's elite, not only recruit disproportionately amongst male private high school graduates, but also – as 'national universities' – charge substantially lower fees than many lower-status private colleges (Kariya 2013, 85).

What distinguishes China's experience of higher education massification – besides its relationship with the radical stratification of schooling and the peculiarities of the college entrance examination system (discussed in earlier chapters) – are its rapidity and the accompanying transformation of university funding. Following the 1985 CCP Central Committee resolution on reforming higher education (introducing the *shuangguizhi*, or 'twin-track system'), a grand total of 2,030 self-funding students were recruited in 1986 (0.18 per cent of the total) (Bai 2008, 70). Only three years later, in early 1989, the State Council endorsed the principle of charging fees to all students, announcing that henceforth all would have to pay a small fee (from 100 to 300 yuan), but implementation was suspended following Tiananmen. When fees were finally introduced across the board, from 1993, limits on charges to students outside the state-determined 'quota' were abandoned, leaving universities free to set their own fee levels. This led to a rapid expansion of out-of-quota enrolments (see previous chapter).

According to Bai, such brazenly market-oriented behaviour undermined universities' reputation in the eyes of the public. From 1994, the central government attempted to regulate out-of-quota fees, but its efforts essentially amounted to exhorting universities not to overcharge. In 1999, a new State Council directive once again announced curbs on 'twin-track' recruitment. In June that year, new measures, including a student loans scheme, were announced, aimed at assisting those in financial difficulties (Bai 2008, 73). But this had the effect of further fuelling fee inflation. In just one year (1999–2000), average annual tuition fees jumped from around 3,000 to 4,500 yuan, at a time when the monthly salary of a middle-ranking university professor was 800 yuan.

It was not until 2004–5 that the State Council intervened decisively to cap the level of university tuition fees, this time imposing limits rather than just issuing recommendations (Bai 2008). Fees remained more or less static between 2005 and 2010 (*Zhongguo Jiaoyu Wang* 2013); figures supplied by Zeng Yaqing (2006) indicate a median level of around 5,000 yuan, with 'normal' universities typically charging a lower rate, and courses with a technical component charging significantly more. However, universities increasingly complained that the constraints on fee increases were causing them financial difficulties, and in 2013 the Ministry relented – allowing applications for permission to increase fees on a case-by-case basis. The following year, universities submitted proposals to provincial education bureaux for fee increases averaging 62.2 per cent (Han 2014).

The imposition of limits on student fees had not been accompanied by a broader overhaul of the funding system. Universities were left to make up any fiscal shortfall through other means, which many did by taking out large loans from state-owned banks (as did many senior high schools; see Chapter 5). Both borrowers and lenders assumed that the government would not allow state-owned educational institutions to default. This assumption was particularly strong in relation to local 'flagship' institutions, whose efforts to secure '211' and '985' status were often accompanied by debt-fuelled spending sprees. The result was to load universities with a colossal debt burden. By 2008, the 72 centrally funded universities owed a total of around 36 billion yuan, and by 2010 the total debt of all universities was estimated at around 500 billion yuan (Chen and Zhang 2010, 53). However, those who had gambled on a government bail-out were vindicated in 2012, when, following the decision to increase government education spending to 4 per cent of GDP, much of the extra money was used to pay down the debts of universities and local education bureaux. For example, Jilin University, which by 2003 was already sinking under 4.5 billion yuan of debt, was thrown a financial lifeline. By contrast, Beijing Normal University, whose President had boasted of his fiscal rectitude, was left to rue its misplaced prudence. What consequences this precedent may have for the future fiscal management of higher education institutions remains to be seen.

Expansion and institutional reorganisation

What – besides megalomania or cupidity – drove this insatiable thirst for cash? Although fee caps exacerbated university indebtedness, both prior fee inflation and growing reliance on loans were closely associated with the marketisation drive that was already underway. They were also related to pressures faced by institutions newly cut adrift after the mid-1990s break-up of the old ministerial fiefdoms (see previous chapter). While the 211 and 985 projects sparked intense competition at elite level for state favour along with concomitant prestige and financial security, institutions lower down the evolving collegiate hierarchy also strove to attract students, boost reputations and maximise income.

These factors help explain institutional responses to the rapid post-1998 expansion of enrolments. Besides the straightforward scaling-up of existing institutions, mergers, 'upgrades', new 'branch campuses' and various forms of pseudo-privatisation were amongst the most characteristic strategies adopted. Here we deal with each in turn.

Mergers

Writing in 1996, Hayhoe noted how the 211 Project sparked a rush of institutional mergers, as local authorities sought to form new comprehensive universities to attract the new funding (1999, 259). She foresaw a possible reversal of the post-1949 're-ordering of colleges and departments' (*yuanxi tiaozheng*), and a partial return to the institutional order of the halcyon, pre-'Liberation' era. In the event, 1996 marked only the initial phase of a sustained merger boom, as structural reforms (discussed in the previous chapter) sent many more institutions dashing for the matrimonial altar. The launch of the 985 Project prompted the establishment of more flagship local universities, while the accelerated expansion of enrolments intensified competition for students in a market where size, and prestige, mattered. Selection criteria for the 211 Project strongly incentivised the acquisition of 'comprehensive' status, but so too did those for the 985 Project, since this strongly encouraged interdisciplinary work. Ranking schemes, such as that launched by Shanghai Jiaotong University in 2003, as well as the criteria for allowing institutions to open postgraduate programmes, or for allocating prestigious 'academician' (*yuanshi*) or *Changjiang* scholar positions, also took account of an institution's 'comprehensiveness'. In a 2010 article entitled 'Reflections after the dust has settled', Zhou and Luo claim that, between 1990 and 2006, there were a total of 431 mergers involving 1,082 institutions, with the number peaking in the year 2000 (2010, 21). The merger mania was epitomised by Zhejiang University, which became one of China's largest (and highest-ranking) universities by the early 2000s as it swallowed up a number of smaller colleges around the province.

Zhou and Luo represent the restructuring of the higher education system through mergers as a carefully planned, phased process. In their scheme, a 'gestation phase' (*yun niang qi*) (1985–91) was followed by an 'exploratory phase' (*tan suo qi*) (1992–7), then 'across-the-board implementation' (*quanmian tuijin*) (1998–2005), and finally 'adjustment and stabilisation' (*tiaozheng luowen*) from 2006. Describing the 1985–91 period as one of 'gestation' overstates the extent to which there was then a settled consensus amongst policymakers over the promotion of institutional mergers, or anything else. Of embryonic schemes 'gestated' during those years, many were aborted or frozen during the post-Tiananmen hiatus. Nevertheless, by 1991 Min Weifang was among those once again pressing for mergers on the grounds that they would facilitate 'improved managerial effectiveness' and economies of scale (Min 1991).

The relaunch of market-oriented reforms in the early 1990s prompted a steady stream of merger activity. Focusing on the area of medical education, Zhou and Luo describe how, before restructuring, every level of government (provincial/municipal and county) as well as every major SOE had its own medical college. Since many were relatively small and poorly equipped, creating larger, better-resourced institutions seemed sensible. The incorporation of medical colleges into comprehensive universities was also proclaimed to be consonant with 'studies of international medical education' (Zhou and Luo 2010, 22). Conforming to the general pattern, the incorporation of medical institutions into comprehensive universities peaked in 2000–1, when, for example, Beijing Medical University became a college of Peking University. Similar mergers occurred in Shanghai, Wuhan and elsewhere.

With the SOE reforms of the mid-1990s, and the related restructuring of the higher education system (see previous chapter), responsibility for medical education was transferred from the Health to the Education bureaucracy. The educational arm of the medical establishment thus became the medical arm of the educational establishment, so that henceforth health education would be financed out of the education rather than the health budget. According to Zhou and Luo, this promised more consistent funding levels per student, on at least the same basis as for other disciplines – freeing medical educators from the necessity of negotiating for funding with SOE managers or bureaucrats whose main responsibilities and interests lay elsewhere.

However, the benefits of mergers were often more apparent to institutional managers and reputation-conscious local officials than to faculty and students. From the perspective of the latter, disadvantages might include escalating administrative costs (as larger institutions required additional layers of administration); difficulties of transport between multiple campuses; and friction between the institutional cultures of specialist colleges and the larger universities into which they were now subsumed. For example, medical colleges all operated affiliated hospitals that were essential for training purposes, but running these posed an entirely novel challenge for regular university administrators. Meanwhile, a number of famous medical colleges lost their identities as they were subsumed within larger comprehensive institutions. With this, some feared, would come the loss of a distinctive medical mission.

A case study of Fudan University's merger with Shanghai Medical College (SMC) found that teacher–student ratios increased – seen as a welcome correction of the under-utilisation of 'teaching resources' long lamented by observers such as Min Weifang (see previous chapter); the 'quality' of new students (as measured by *gaokao* scores) rose; postgraduate enrolments climbed; and the output of 'international publications' grew significantly (Xu 2003). But the same study also highlighted an increase in the proportion of non-teaching staff – including drivers for the fleet of shuttle buses required for transport between the SMC and the main Fudan campus. It also cited the 'transaction costs' of marrying two such different institutions, the administrative complexity that resulted and the 'emotional costs' experienced by senior faculty who effectively lost status. Moreover, basing promotion decisions on publications seemed inappropriate, or at least inequitable, when applied to medical professors who were expected to spend significant time in practice. Some of these problems echo those noted by critics of the contemporaneous drive to merge or 'upgrade' teacher-training institutions (see Chapter 7).

In short, Xu saw 'economies of scale' as a crude justification for institutional mergers; the advisability of merging needed to be carefully considered on a case-by-case basis (Ding 2004 echoed the same criticism). The clear implication was that this had not happened in the case of the Fudan–SMC union and others rushed through at the height of the 'merger boom' in 2000–1. Moreover, even when statistics showed apparently irrefutable improvements in 'quality' – as measured by entrants' *gaokao* scores or faculty members' citation indices – Xu cautioned that causation was often more difficult to ascribe than might at first appear. After all, from the late 1990s onwards many prestigious universities were in receipt of considerable public largesse. To the extent that 'quality' indicators were ticking up, in many cases this may have been due more to increased funding and other reforms than to institutional mergers *per se*.

Institutional upgrades

Another way in which colleges catered for expanding demand for regular higher education was through upgrading – a strategy we discuss in relation to teacher training in Chapter 7. This phenomenon is far from unique to China. In 1992, England redesignated as 'universities' all polytechnics – institutions that had previously focused on vocational and technical education (at both sub-degree and degree-level), and on teaching rather than research. This reform was closely related to the massification of English higher education. As the former head of Kingston University (an ex-polytechnic) wrote in 2012, it was the new universities that had done 'the heavy lifting in terms of overall student expansion – and in widening participation for students from … working-class homes and ethnic minorities' (Scott 2012). In 1994, Hong Kong followed the British lead, upgrading its own polytechnics to full university status. In a related move, in the same year various colleges of teacher education were merged into a new Hong Kong Institute of Education, offering degree-level and postgraduate courses.[4]

On the Chinese mainland, most of the institutions that sought to upgrade were former two-year teacher-training colleges (*shi zhuan*). Until the 1990s, every area (*diqu*) had had its own *shi zhuan*, dedicated to training teachers for local primary and secondary schools. As discussed in Chapter 7, pre-service teacher training in China had always focused more on 'subject knowledge' than on pedagogical methods or mentored teaching practice. *Shi zhuan* thus already offered a range of academic courses – from History and foreign languages to the sciences and Maths. Upgrading these to degree level was, in practice, largely a matter of extending course length. Former *shi zhuan* rushed to rebrand themselves, often dropping the 'normal' (*shifan*) or 'teacher training' tag (Tang 2009, 39), while cutting back on teacher education programmes and focusing those that remained even more intently on academic subject content (40). In impelling institutions to cater to demand for regular academic courses, marketisation thus undermined the distinctive missions of many former specialist colleges – a criticism also made of the 1992 British decision to 'upgrade' polytechnics (Havergal 2015). However, in the case of China, while some older vocational or technical colleges became 'comprehensive' regular institutions, the vocational higher education sector as a whole underwent renewed expansion – for reasons discussed in Chapter 10.

Branch colleges ('independent colleges') and joint ventures

One consequence of the 1990s reforms to the state sector was to further blur the line between the 'public' and 'private' spheres in China (Huang 2008). At secondary level, numerous key point institutions established pseudo-private 'branches' (see Chapter 9). At tertiary level, from 2000, 'independent colleges' (*duli xueyuan*) were introduced as part of post-1998 measures to rapidly increase the supply of higher education places at minimum public cost. Existing public universities were granted opportunities to trade on their institutional 'brand', while cadres encouraged the establishment of such colleges as a way of both boosting the local economy and satisfying educational demand. As explained by two of the Ministry of Education's own researchers, the proliferation of these 'independent colleges' reflected the shift towards a 'market economy', helping to meet the need for 'rapid expansion of the scale of higher education' and to further the 'healthy development of "people-managed" [*minban*] higher education' (Ma and Fan 2005).[5]

The expansion was certainly rapid; by 2006 there were already 318 independent colleges (Yu and Ertl 2010, 40). They took various forms: some were straight subsidiaries; others previously autonomous institutions 'merged' or taken over (see above); but their defining feature was that they were joint ventures, with the private (or non-university) partner usually providing most of the initial investment (Yu and Ertl 2010). Ownership was typically shared between the mother institution – which contributed its name, awarded course credits, and seconded staff – and the local government, which contributed land. Further funding came from bank loans and student fees, with any operating surplus shared between the mother institution and investors. Ma and Fan, the men from the ministry, drew attention to difficulties in squaring the role of 'investors' with China's legal prohibition on running educational institutions for profit – a provision, as we have seen (Chapter 9), honoured more in the breach than the observance. Despite being branches of public institutions, 'independent colleges' typically operated as if they were private ventures, charging fees two or three times higher than those of their 'parent' (Yu and Ertl 2010, 40). But if they were indeed private, any support from the parent institution ought, according to Chinese law, to have been costed and paid for. In short, the emergence of numerous branch colleges further highlighted the tensions between the traditional vision of higher education as a public service, and its growing marketisation as a consumer good.[6]

Taking China's most entrepreneurial province as their focus, Chen and Chen (2009) examined how central government regulations regarding the operation of 'independent colleges' (*duli xueyuan*) were applied in Zhejiang. They stressed the particularly 'active role' of the provincial authorities, illustrated by Zhejiang's hosting of China's first transnational branch campus: the University of Nottingham, Ningbo (established in 2004). This activism involved some creative interpretation of ministry regulations. For example, national regulations stipulated that 'independent colleges' must have a separate campus from the parent institution. However, Zhejiang's Education Bureau ruled that separation could be achieved by planting trees to demarcate the boundary between the two, 'or other similar measures' (19). At the same time, the provincial authorities also sought to emphasise the responsibilities of parent institutions for supporting teaching at their branch colleges. Among the practices recommended, as a means of encouraging student diligence, was the provision of opportunities for some of the better students at branch colleges to transfer to the parent university.

The ministerial view stressed the importance of ensuring that 'independent colleges' occupied a clearly defined, and relatively lowly, position in the institutional hierarchy. In order to maintain 'quality', and to benefit from capacity-building support from the 'mother institution', they should not be allowed to grow too large – a benchmark of 4,000–6,000 students, or one quarter of the size of the parent university, was recommended (Ma and Fan 2005, 32). Their role should be to cater to 'market demand', which entailed teaching basic undergraduate degree courses in fields best calculated to enhance graduate employability.

Chen and Chen's research on Zhejiang identifies a large gap between the intention of the original Ministry regulations, and their local interpretation. However, while many central officials and scholars have criticised persistent local flouting of national decrees, the two Chens were more sanguine – arguing that it was sensible for the regulatory framework to leave some scope for regional variation and 'innovation'. In the case of Zhejiang, the need for flexibility in management of the higher education 'market' was dictated by particular constraints on local students' access to prestigious public universities. China's richest province, Zhejiang's comparatively well-resourced schooling system performed very highly on standardised measures of student performance, but it boasted only one top-ranking public university (Zhejiang University). The system of provincial *gaokao* quotas meant that Zhejiang students had to perform exceptionally well to gain access to prestigious universities in Beijing or Shanghai (see Chapter 8). The provincial authorities therefore faced particular challenges in squaring huge demand for tertiary education with limited supply at the 'high end'.

A phenomenon related to the spread of branch campuses is the establishment of vast 'university cities' (*daxue cheng*) on the outskirts of many Chinese cities. This was similarly spurred by the congruence of universities' expansionary ambitions with those of local officials to boost economic growth. The relative ease with which officials could requisition land from farmers meant that universities could acquire out-of-town sites at minimal cost. Indeed, districts have often competed to attract major universities: Shunyi and Changping counties (on the outskirts of Beijing) engaged in a bidding war for the right to host Beijing Normal University's new campus (Changping won). In some cases, old campuses are sold off, but in others they have found new educational uses, sometimes serving as the sites of new 'independent colleges' (Yu and Ertl 2010, 43). At the same time, the establishment of 'university cities', by moving more students to the peripheries of major cities, makes them easier to control and monitor, minimising the risk of any recurrence of 1989-style disturbances.

*Private (*minban*) colleges*

In China, as in other East Asian societies, the state has sought to preserve the elitism of selected national universities, while channelling new demand elsewhere. However, in the Chinese case this has been achieved mainly through forms of provision, such as 'independent colleges', that maintain a strong element of public oversight. In Japan and Korea too, the state exercises considerable control over private universities, but China has been much more reluctant to accommodate autonomous providers. And as yet, there are no Chinese equivalents of elite private institutions such as Japan's Keio or Waseda.

The relatively small number of private colleges (distinct from the 'quasi-private' independent colleges), which offer only undergraduate degrees, are the bottom feeders of the regular higher education sector. They do not qualify for formal 'university' status although, confusingly, many claim the title (e.g. Zhejiang Shuren University).[7] As of 2010, China boasted 300 universities, more than 400 public colleges, over 300 independent colleges, but only 44 private colleges. Moreover, most of these were established during the mid-1990s; subsequent expansion has generally been associated more with commercialisation of the public sector (paralleling practice at high school level – see Chapter 9) (39). While 'independent colleges', sponsored by prestigious 'mother institutions', have tended rapidly to acquire full degree-awarding powers, private colleges have often struggled for similar recognition, and have suffered in the competition to attract the best-qualified students. Many began life as two-year 'junior colleges' (*chuji xueyuan*),[8] and even five years after the 1998 expansion (in 2003), only nine had attained full degree-awarding status.

In their study of English and Engineering courses in four south-eastern institutions, Yu and Ertl (2010) found that fees in both private and independent colleges were around double those in public institutions. Students of these colleges had also achieved similar *gaokao* scores – significantly lower than their counterparts in the public sector. In other words, these colleges' took in students who, before 1998, would not have accessed any form of regular higher education.

However, in other respects those enrolling in 'independent' and 'private' colleges were found to diverge markedly; rural students accounted for almost 40 per cent of the latter, but less than 20 per cent of the former (49). Half of those at the independent college had made it their first choice, suggesting a preponderance of 'wealthy but lower achieving students who decided to enroll in expensive independent colleges in the first place' (50). By contrast, only 15 per cent of private college students had done the same, indicating that most had initially aimed higher, only to be relegated to the private sector during the 'clearing' process. Yu and Ertl attribute this to 'an imbalance of knowledge between urban and rural applicants' (50). Private college students were far more likely to have parents with no more than primary education; only 3.8 per cent had fathers who had attended university. Parents of independent college students 'held more prestigious occupational positions' and tended to be richer than those associated with any other institutions (51). Fathers of private college students, by contrast, were much more likely to be construction workers or farmers with relatively low incomes (54).

Independent colleges thus cater largely to the children of wealthier urban households, while private colleges, offering a less marketable product for the same high price, serve a less privileged clientele. Meanwhile, rural or working-class families who cannot afford fees for regular private colleges are the main 'consumers' of vocational further education (see Chapter 10). Nor do youngsters from such backgrounds fare any better in accessing public institutions, whose state-subsidised fees thus have a socially regressive effect. Moreover, being female as well as rural accentuates the disparity in access, particularly at private institutions, since rural parents tend to be less willing to pay high fees on behalf of their daughters (Xie *et al.* 2010). 'Women's access to higher education opportunities', conclude Xie *et al.*, 'is steadily increasing, but new increases in educational opportunities for women will primarily benefit urban women' (40).

The concentration of poor and female students in lower-status, and often more expensive, private colleges, is a phenomenon also observable in Japan, where demographic decline has recently begun to threaten some colleges with closure (Nippon.com 2015). In China, an even more rapid expansion of higher education looks set to be followed by a dramatic drop in the college-age population – posing particular challenges for private colleges and newer local four-year colleges. This trend also presents an acute dilemma for policymakers, who may be forced to countenance either mass college closures or further expansion in access to regular higher education – both options with potentially destabilising social implications.[9]

Higher education and employability – onto the 'ant-heap'

That potential for instability relates in particular to the problem of graduate unemployment or under-employment. Until the early 1990s, the command economy afforded elite status and its perquisites to most college graduates. But by the late 1990s SOE reform and higher education expansion left far more graduates exposed to the vagaries of the market. When the East Asian Financial Crisis hit China, the graduate employment rate fell from 97 per cent in 1997 to 76.8 per cent the following year; by 2001, it had recovered to 90 per cent, but thereafter slid to 70 per cent by 2008 (Lai *et al.* 2011). Meanwhile, the number of university graduates was expanding exponentially, more than doubling between 2004 and 2009 – from 2.8 to 6.1 million (Phoenix New Media 2013). In terms of employment rates and, more especially, job quality, those from rural families fared worse than their urban counterparts. Surveying graduates from 14 provinces, Lai *et al.* found that starting salaries for rural students were 16.4 per cent lower in 2002, and 12.2 per cent lower in 2009;[10] in other words, even college entry did not erase rural disadvantage.

The term *yi zu* (literally 'ant tribe') has been used to describe graduates aged 22 to 29 whose monthly income is lower than 2,000 yuan (Lian 2011). Typically low-paid white-collar urban workers loaded down with unserviceable student loans, many live in over-crowded boarding houses in squalid 'urban villages'. Their plight has caused considerable moral panic. Some local governments have tried to curb collective renting on grounds not just of fire risk, but also of the potential for violent arguments amongst unrelated young people new to living in unsupervised groups (almost all college students live in campus dormitories). An additional concern for officials, older residents and parents is 'immorality', or extra-marital sex amongst cohabiting youngsters (migrant workers as well as *yi zu*). But the erosion of traditional moral strictures is hardly surprising, given that few *yi zu* can afford to save for a formal wedding, or set up an independent household (for more on this issue see Woronov 2016).

Most *yi zu* are from relatively poor rural or small-town backgrounds; graduates with urban *hukou* can generally live with their parents, and have better prospects of finding employment through family connections. A study of *yi zu* in Nanjing found that around a third were graduates of supposedly 'elite' 211 universities (though seldom of 985 institutions) (Lian 2011). Having often left home to the acclamation of their communities, with the expectation of a glorious career ahead, an ignominious return from the big city can constitute serious loss of face for this group. For this reason, Lian concludes, 'the idea that "ants" can go home and become local elites is a "fairy tale" (*tong hua*)'.

However, most *yi zu* have studied at regular institutions of higher education below elite level. A comparison of the employment prospects of graduates from more vocationally oriented two-year colleges and newly 'upgraded' four-year colleges in Hunan Province shows how the latter can fall between two stools (Peng 2010).[11] Unable to compete with their counterparts from four-year comprehensive universities, they also lack even the limited practical training that two-year programmes typically provide. Nonetheless, in contrast to sub-degree level vocational training, an undergraduate degree even from a less prestigious institution theoretically qualifies its holder for a wide range of positions (see Chapter 10). Peng's findings suggest that the career aspirations of four-year college students have 'diversified', with the overwhelming majority in his (admittedly limited) sample (about 75 per cent) seeking jobs in the civil service or public sector – in stark contrast to the situation a decade earlier, when private sector employment (especially with foreign firms) was far more sought after.[12] Moreover, while around half of the students expressed a willingness to participate in government schemes to employ graduates as cadres in Western regions or rural areas, over a third showed no interest, preferring to take their chances in the metropolis.

The failure of conventional academic higher education to confer directly 'job-related skills' is often cited as a key cause of graduate unemployment (Lian 2011), but this does not explain the particular disadvantages of graduates with rural backgrounds. Lai *et al.* (2011) blame the insufficiently 'modern' attitudes of the latter, whose upbringing and peculiarly intense examination-oriented education have left them ill-equipped to cope in a rapidly changing, increasingly cosmopolitan employment market. This disadvantage may be further heightened by Chinese employers' increasing use of elaborate Japanese-style testing and interviewing of job applicants, often aimed at measuring candidates' problem-solving skills, 'creativity', 'leadership' and aptitude for 'teamwork' – qualities unlikely to be fostered by the especially rigid, high-pressure testing culture of rural or small-town high schools (see Chapter 9). But this looks like an attempt to rationalise patterns of disadvantage based largely on ingrained perceptions of rural students' low 'quality' (*suzhi*).

Expanding vocational higher education has been seen as one way of dealing with the problem of graduate unemployment, though government efforts in this direction have signally failed to enhance the attractiveness of the vocational track, for reasons discussed in Chapter 10. However, the extension of the vocationalisation drive to tertiary level has been just one aspect of the official strategy for managing and directing higher education provision. Though parents and students have become fee-paying consumers of college education, the laws of supply and demand have not been allowed free rein. And just as the Party has sought to regulate the broader higher education market, so it has reinforced its authority over individual institutions.

Higher education governance

Subscribing to the neoliberal axiom of state inefficiency, many governments since the 1980s have preached 'autonomy' in public service provision. In this view, all that is needed for efficiency to triumph is 'accountability', secured through regulation of competing providers. In the Anglo-Saxon world, the whittling away of block grants for research, 'diversification' of funding sources, and increasing reliance on user fees and loans have profoundly marketised higher education, in the process shifting the basis on which academic 'value' is judged (Collini 2012). At the same time, new measures to ensure 'accountability' for the expenditure of public funding have brought increased bureaucratisation and enhanced government control. In Japan, the 'corporatisation' of national universities from 2002, far from granting greater autonomy, if anything led to increased subservience to central diktat (Kaneko 2013). The security traditionally afforded by state patronage has been eroded, while discretionary funding fuels ever more intense competition for ministerial favour.

The case of China in some respects reflects these international trends. As discussed above, the expansion of enrolments and broader state sector reforms during the 1990s left institutions themselves – especially newer or 'upgraded' second-tier colleges – responsible for raising far more of their own funding. By 2001, the Central Government's contribution to higher education spending stood at 53 per cent, down from 83 per cent in 1993, though rising student numbers meant that overall expenditure had vastly increased (Yang *et al.* 2007, 580). Meanwhile, growing fiscal decentralisation has ostensibly been accompanied by enhanced institutional autonomy. The *Higher Education Law* of 1998 mandated a 'Presidential Responsibility' system, granting presidents the authority to determine their own institutional priorities. 'Based on their own teaching needs', proclaimed Article 34, 'higher education institutions take the initiative in designing their own teaching plans, selecting textbooks and organising teaching activities' (cited in Yang *et al.* 2007, 580).

But the concepts of 'autonomy' and 'accountability' undergo a peculiar transmutation in the Chinese context. In particular, the role of the Party itself within higher education institutions remains crucial, in ways often overlooked in the English-language literature (e.g. Watson 2007; Yang *et al.* 2007). As we saw in the previous chapter, Party control over college administration (and curricula) was significantly tightened after 1989, putting a stop to most talk of liberalising academic governance. And the same *Higher Education Law* that in 1998 called for the empowerment of university presidents also re-emphasised the ultimate authority of the Party Secretary.

From the mid-2000s, however, demands for greater faculty autonomy once again became more frequent and vocal. One contribution to this debate came from Li Yanbao, Party Secretary of Zhongshan University in Guangzhou (2008). Li criticised the prevailing confusion over the roles of University President and Party Secretary, who is typically the senior institutional leader. Official documents, including the *Higher Education Law* and directives from the *Zhong Zu Bu* (Central Organisation Department of the CCP), had, he claimed, only exacerbated this confusion (9). But Li himself underlines the Party Committee's responsibility for setting the institution's 'political line', for organising 'Thought and Politics' education and, in particular, its ultimate authority over organisational and personnel matters (appointments and promotions). The President, he pointed out, would almost always negotiate with the Party Secretary before recommending anyone for appointment. The 'confusion' to which he alludes thus ends up seeming more terminological than actual. (In an attempt to 'normalise' their status in foreign eyes, some Party secretaries have recently taken to using the English title 'Chancellor' on their namecards.)

Impatience with constraints on faculty autonomy has been most openly expressed at prestigious 985 institutions, expected to conduct teaching and research to the highest 'global' standards. In 2012, an article in the *Tsinghua*

Journal of Education cited a 'basic consensus' (*jiben gongshi*) concerning the need for reform to university administration (Peng 2012). Its author related the weakness of professors' committees in university governance to low institutional autonomy *vis-à-vis* the Education Ministry. As a result, he argued, amongst three 'types' of authority within universities – political, academic and administrative – the 'political' had become overmighty. While refraining from direct attacks on the authority of the Party Committee, critics have called for it to be more clearly defined and circumscribed by 'law', with some suggesting that it should function more like the governing councils of many Western universities.

But scholars at prestigious universities often enjoy levels of autonomy far beyond those of their counterparts at lower-level colleges (Yang *et al.* 2007) Paradoxically, their very closeness to government affords them special license. As Yang and Welch write of Tsinghua University, 'the political affiliation between … senior administrators, government officials and national leaders have [*sic.*] been an important factor in helping Tsinghua attain some measure of university autonomy' (2012, 663).[13] The same applies within the vast network of 'party schools' charged with training CCP cadres; the Central Party School in Beijing, run prior to his elevation to the state presidency by Xi Jinping, has become a hothouse of open intellectual debate by comparison with the far more regimented local party schools, or with most university social science faculties (McGregor, 2010). China's Communist Party, inspired in part by the example of Lee Kuan Yew's Singapore (see Vogel 2011), has sought to foster creativity and 'innovation' amongst the elite, while maintaining regimentation for the masses.[14] This has been accompanied by rapid growth in salaries and emoluments for top scholars working in STEM fields. In 2010, Chinese scientists on average earned around US$40,000 per year, but by 2016 those returning from overseas to prestigious Chinese institutions could command starting salaries of more than US$120,000 (Chen 2016). Stratification in income and status has increased both between institutions and within them (Yan 2010).

Even at elite institutions, Party organs retain crucial authority over appointments and promotions (Zhang and Cheng 2008), but as a cataract of cash has flowed into top universities, the carrot of financial incentives, as well as the stick of political sanctions, has become a potent instrument of control. Gradated bonus payments for publications – especially in ranked 'international' journals – help keep scholarly noses to the grindstone. Meanwhile, government organs and SOEs remain overwhelmingly the most significant sources of funding for research projects. Provincial universities often maintain offices in the capital to enable them better to lobby for such funding.[15] Seconding faculty to central ministries also helps establish relationships useful in securing government-financed projects. As in many Western institutions, securing substantial research funding – from whatever source – can enable scholars to establish sizeable fiefdoms within their institutions, while negotiating 'buy-outs' from their regular teaching responsibilities.[16] But Party-supervised personnel departments, operating in consultation with deans and department heads, typically vet applications before these are sent to ministries or funding councils. Ability to influence the flow of project funding has thus become a key source of institutional power, encouraging scholars to aspire to managerial roles.

If the 1980s were a decade of 'idealism' in higher education, and the 1990s of 'commercialism', the 2000s have been widely seen by those within the sector as marked by the dominance of 'bureaucratic privilege' (Zhang and Cheng 2008). Bureaucratic influence has been additionally reinforced by elaborate ranking systems (alluded to above) rewarding institutions for the number of faculty appointed as 'academicians' by China's Academies of Science, Social Sciences and Engineering, or enrolled as *Changjiang* scholars (the state's highest academic accolade).[17] In 2010, the government's Education *Gangyao* ('Framework') hinted at administrative reform, but vague references to a 'modern university system' (*xiandai daxue zhidu*) left it unclear what if any changes to university governance were envisaged. In practice, changes since then have consisted primarily of massively increased investment, especially in STEM, along with more draconian political supervision over teaching and research in other areas.

Curriculum reform – squaring creativity with conformity

As noted in the previous chapter, Chinese higher education has been heavily biased towards STEM fields throughout the Communist era. In addition, the demands of the Soviet-style command economy encouraged extremely narrow specialisation; as of 1987, there were 1,343 officially recognised disciplines. As manpower planning was subsequently reformed, then abandoned, so disciplines were combined or merged, and by 1998, the official count had fallen to 249 (Zhang 2012, 394). Some faculty and department structures, and disciplinary categories, have been remodelled along American lines. However, the Soviet legacy endures in the large proportion of specialised colleges and universities; of 2,305 regular higher education institutions (as of 2013), less than a quarter are 'comprehensive', and the vast majority of the remainder are focused on STEM fields plus finance and economics (Rhoads *et al.* 2014, 27–8). Overall, the balance has if anything shifted even further away from humanities and social sciences towards vocational higher education, science and engineering (Yan 2014, 505). In 2007, engineering courses alone accounted for over one-third of all enrolments in regular higher education institutions (NCEDR 2009, 75).

The drive for 'world class' status for Chinese universities has spawned a veritable deluge of scientific papers, boosting institutions' international rankings. Yang and Welch note that, in 2006, China overtook Japan and the UK 'to become the world's second largest producer of research papers' (2012, 661) – begging the questions of what qualifies as a 'research paper', and how individual papers are evaluated (see next chapter). But the push for 'world class-ness' has had implications for curriculum too, with the debate over learning at tertiary level echoing calls for 'quality education' in China's schools (see Chapter 6). Senior academics and policymakers have increasingly seen excessive specialisation as disadvantaging Chinese universities *vis-à-vis* their international 'competitors'. They have noted that major American research universities, those hotbeds of innovation and generators of Nobel Prizes, are mostly comprehensive institutions that encourage interdisciplinary work and provide students with some general grounding in the liberal arts. One response has been to encourage or compel the 'comprehensivisation' of previously specialised universities. Thus Tsinghua University, often described as China's 'MIT', has sought (like MIT itself) to expand teaching and research in the social sciences and humanities (Yang and Welch 2012). And as we have seen, from 1993 'comprehensivisation' was incentivised by the 211 Project, helping to trigger a wave of institutional mergers.

Since the early 2000s, elite universities such as Tsinghua and Peking have also pioneered attempts to broaden the undergraduate curriculum, at least for a select few, through interdisciplinary programmes based in new 'colleges' (such as Peking's 'Yuanpei College', established in 2007) (Shi 2016) – though attempts to extend *suzhi jiaoyu* to universities date back at least to a 'Cultural Quality Education' campaign launched by the SEC in 1995 (Zhang 2012, 397). The ostensible model has been the foundational courses taken by many first- and second-year American college students. The term '*tongshi jiaoyu*' ('general education') was borrowed from the Chinese University of Hong Kong, where scholars in the mid-1980s had sought to devise an 'international' (i.e. American-style) programme combining the broad humanistic learning and moral exemplarity of a traditional Chinese *literatus* (*junzi*) with 'Western' conceptions of a liberal education (396). However, as Zhang notes, the rationales cited for promoting *tongshi jiaoyu* were consistently instrumentalist: 'to make China stronger as a nation and to catch up with the international standards' (398).

Surveying *tongshi* education courses in several Chinese universities since the 1990s, Shi (2016) notes that all of them partly involved repackaging the 'common courses' long compulsory at all institutions, consisting largely of classes in 'Politics'. From the late 1990s, Ministry directives have stipulated 315 hours of political education for arts and social sciences students, and 210 hours for their science and engineering counterparts (Yan 2014, 501). At Renmin University in Beijing, the old 'common courses' – Politics and foreign languages – became the 'Basic Quality' component of the *tongshi* curriculum, and were given increased weighting. There the reform actually increased constraints on course choice, precisely in order to compel students to study outside their disciplinary comfort zone (Zhang 2012, 409).

Investigating *tongshi* education at Renmin University from 2007 to 2011, Zhang found that most faculty and students endorsed the principle of curricular broadening, but saw career preparation as the main purpose of college education. Confusion over the meaning of *tongshi* education was rife, the whole reform having been introduced from the top down. Few faculty understood the pedagogical innovations expected of them, and those who did were frustrated by logistical constraints (for example, extremely large class sizes). Students enrolled on less 'marketable' courses, such as History, seemed to welcome the chance to broaden their disciplinary portfolio, but others found the interdisciplinary courses superficial, or objected to the political indoctrination conducted under the *tongshi* banner. Departmental identity remains key for faculty, and especially students, since the Ministry still maintains strict enrolment quotas for particular departments; the *gaokao* score required of entrants to a prestigious engineering faculty is likely to be far higher than that demanded by a literature faculty within the same university. Students on more competitive programmes thus have little incentive to dilute their disciplinary specialisation (Zhang 2012, 414). Meanwhile, the extreme emphasis on publications in faculty evaluations at top 'research-oriented universities' also encourages increasingly narrow specialisation, which feeds into teaching.

Both Zhang and Shi conclude that *tongshi* education reforms have therefore had a rather superficial impact on students' learning. The utilitarian and nation-building values informing these reforms contradict the more liberal philosophy of the American universities that are their ostensible model. Epitomising this contradiction is the heavy weighting given to courses in 'Politics' that aim to vaccinate students against any free-thinking contagion to which their other classes may expose them. At institutions below the elite level, space for students to exercise choice or develop autonomous study habits typically remains very limited; a study of upgraded former teacher training colleges in Hunan found that 60 per cent of courses were compulsory, and 35 per cent taken up by 'general education' (including Politics and foreign language classes) (Tang 2009). But even at elite institutions, uncertainty over the parameters for open or critical discussion of social and political issues persists. Indeed, the situation has significantly worsened since 2014, with official attempts to restrict the teaching of 'Western thought' (State Council 2015), and students encouraged to 'report' on lecturers who express unorthodox ideas.

Disciplining and controlling university students

Politics courses constitute one important, if relatively crude, means of inculcating patriotism, discipline and loyalty to the Party. Beyond this, the ordering of student life at college around class meetings, gatherings of the Communist Youth League, various patriotic ceremonies and, for members, Party meetings, also aims to reinforce political conformity. The official political discourse has been described as 'fatiguing, depoliticising and cynicism-inducing' (Wedeen, cited in Yan 2014, 503) – though such effects, in so far as they promote docility, may not be entirely unwelcome to the authorities. However, in a move reminiscent of the Soviet conflation of political dissent with psychological abnormality, programmes of compulsory counselling and mental health monitoring have also been introduced in recent years, enabling the Party 'to monitor students' thoughts and detect irregularities' (Yan 2014, 503).

More broadly, 'bureaucratic surveillance and hierarchical intervention have supplanted political indoctrination and mobilisation' in the post-Deng period (Yan 2014, 500). The apparatus of surveillance, consisting of Party and Communist Youth League committees (all ultimately answerable to the Party Secretary), has remained. At the same time, all students are organised into a 'quasi-military structure' from classroom (*ban ji*) to year cohort (*nian ji*) to college level, with the student Party Branch constituting 'the most powerful self-regulating agency' (500). Yan observes that 'the most important pillar of the structure is the revived post of political counsellor (*zhengzhi fudao yuan*) [PC]' (previously abandoned during the later Maoist years) who, according to a Ministry instruction of 2006, 'should be present in all college and university classrooms' (499).[18] A ratio of one PC to every 200 students is officially stipulated, and in some universities PCs are required to reside in student dormitories. In general, the apparatus of control tends to be more rigid and intrusive at normal colleges than at other types of higher education institutions (Chang 2015). Ensuring the ideological conformity of those destined to instruct future generations is a particular priority for the Party.

Meanwhile, the tools for 'engineering stability' through higher education not only consist of systems for disciplining and regimenting students, but also encompass material incentives for those exhibiting superior ideological 'correctness'. China's colleges are the prime recruiting grounds for new Party members. As Yan puts it, 'with traditional control measures such as compulsory job assignments waning …, the material benefits from CCP membership are becoming the most important incentives for political loyalty' (506). In 2010, 11 per cent of university students were CCP members, enjoying benefits including 'direct admission to graduate school' for some, as well as enhanced prospects of recruitment into Party-State agencies or SOEs. A 2009 survey showed that less than 13 per cent of student applicants for Party membership claim actually to 'believe in Communism', the rest citing 'materialistic purposes' (cited in Yan 2014, 506). But in this respect, they simply reflect a post-revolutionary re-envisioning of Chinese Communism as a self-perpetuating, pseudo-meritocratic oligarchy.

Conclusion

In the mid-1990s, reviewing a century of giddying switchbacks in the history of China's universities, Hayhoe (1999) sought to draw comparisons with the North American experience. China's Soviet-era system was undergoing radical reform, and the rampant commercialisation of America's colleges was only just beginning. From that vantage point, it seemed plausible to suggest that expanded provision, combined with a rebirth of comprehensive universities, might offer the prospect of enhanced social mobility for millions of Chinese. Alluding to Clark Kerr's 1960s vision of the 'multiversity' – serving 'diverse populations' and driving economic growth in addition to pursuing traditional enlightenment goals – Hayhoe outlined a similar vision for Chinese higher education (307). At the same time, she cautioned that in China, as in Japan and Korea, the 'enlightenment process' might well be 'stifled' by the emergence of new hierarchies and the reinforcement of rigid bureaucratic control.

Taking the economic aspect of this vision first, it is clear that massive public investment in elite institutions has been closely allied to the government's pursuit of growth and technological advancement; but it is far less clear that the expanded scale of tertiary education has had anything to do with this. Indeed, had China's leaders believed otherwise, they might well have been deluded. Peng (2011) argues that the expansion of higher education since 1998 has led to greatly expanded public debt and increasing graduate unemployment or underemployment, while contending that any contribution to GDP growth has been minimal. With respect to Western societies and Japan, Alison Wolf insists that the post-1960s shift towards mass higher education not only had 'little directly to do with the demands of the economy', but 'may actually be doing more harm than good, to the economy as well as to other of … universities' fundamental concerns' (2002, 199). She argues that growing credentialism has not only siphoned an increasing proportion of public and private resources into higher education, but has also been accompanied by a widening gulf in access to prestigious institutions for those from the most and least privileged backgrounds.

The emergence of a similar pattern in China was therefore entirely predictable, even if it has been even more rapid and dramatic. As recently as the 1980s, the complaint that 'nuclear scientists were worse off than street peddlers' was commonly heard in China's cities (Xiang and Shen 2009, 513). In the peculiar mix of market and command economy that characterised that era, social or cultural capital did not necessarily entail material wealth – or vice versa. However, since the 1990s, as marketisation has swept the public sector, including universities, wealth has become far more readily 'convertible' into other forms of capital, concentrating privilege and facilitating its transfer down the generations.

In fact, the frantic post-1998 expansion of higher education was not conceived primarily as a means either of retooling China's labour force for the knowledge economy or of promoting social mobility, but as a ploy for boosting consumer spending. The mass of students would support growth less through their skills than through their fees. Meanwhile, elite institutions seen as crucial to national development were cordoned off and accorded enormous public largesse. Rising concerns at the capacity of the labour market to absorb millions of new graduates soon prompted attempts to reinvigorate secondary and tertiary vocational education. But the problem in China, as elsewhere, has been that widespread use of graduate qualifications to screen job applicants (something the Party itself has mandated for official positions since the 1980s) makes it virtually impossible to tame the genie of credentialism. In 2011, former Premier Zhu Rongji, who had sanctioned the shift to massification, emerged from retirement to dismiss the 2010 Education *Gangyao* ('Framework') as 'empty talk', expressing particular concern at the six-fold increase in university enrolments since 1998. Originally intended to stimulate the economy, Zhu complained that the expansion 'had instead led to rampant academic plagiarism, declining academic morality, and rising unemployment of university graduates'. He also criticised the continuing insufficiency of state support for rural schooling (Bevis 2014, 167).[19]

Zhu's comments reflect divisions and uncertainty amongst policymakers over strategy for the further development of higher education, but also concerns about the ramifications that expansion is already having for social and political stability. Reflecting on the collapse of Communism in Eastern Europe, which still haunts

Chinese leaders, Perkin observed that the 'explosion' of higher education that 'accompanies the transition to the professional society' means that it is 'no longer possible for controlling elites to rely on the ignorance of their people to accept their propaganda' (1996, 17–18).[20] 'The politics of the new society' had to be 'directed to the rational self-interest of a more intelligent population'. In China, the rapid post-1998 expansion of higher education was conceived largely as a means of channelling the 'rational self-interest' of a burgeoning middle class towards the pursuit of credentials. And since China, unlike the USSR of the 1980s, subsequently witnessed staggering economic growth, the labour market proved far more capable of offering graduates the realistic prospect of personal advancement – even if many still found themselves underemployed.

This has led some observers to use 'professional' in a rather different sense from Perkin. For example, Hansen and Woronov argue that the fee-based expansion of higher education has transformed graduates from 'intellectuals' conscious of a collective responsibility for the fate of the nation into a mass of 'professionals', 'depoliticised' and focused on personal success (2013). No longer a 'presumptive elite', students today, according to Yan (2014), are better characterised as 'professionals-in-waiting', or a 'professional working class' (506). 'Professional' here denotes a salaried functionary, rather than a member of an autonomous, self-regulating community of skilled practitioners. As for university professors, Yang concludes that 'being an academic' is nowadays 'little different from any other civil service job', so that 'the professionalisation of intellectual life has shaded into careerism' (2006, 213). Ironically, marketisation therefore seems to have made a reality of that Cultural Revolutionary slogan, 'the intellectuals shall be proletarianised' (*zhishi fenzi yao laodonghua*).

Like other symptoms of higher education massification, this is not a uniquely Chinese phenomenon. But nor is professionalisation-as-proletarianisation a guarantee of political docility amongst students and young college graduates – as recent events in Hong Kong and Taiwan have demonstrated (Vickers 2017). The combination of xenophobic resentment, political frustration and economic anxiety that fuelled student protests there in 2014 constitutes a troubling precedent for the regime in Beijing. As the economy slows and market conditions worsen, in what directions will the 'rational self-interest' of mainland graduates point?

This question is key to explaining efforts by the current leadership to frame narratives of China's destiny around themes of nationalism and anti-corruption, while tightening limits on open debate – within universities and beyond. Hayhoe's fears of a 'stifling' of the 'enlightenment process' appear to have been amply realised. Though no longer tethered to a self-consciously Marxian epistemology, narrowly scientistic and instrumentalist notions of the purposes of higher education have continued to pervade official rhetoric, while universities have been subjected since 2012 to increasingly strict ideological control. In short, policy has once again defaulted to tactics of 'thought reform', seeking to persuade individuals to view their self-interest through the prism of nationalism and a 'muscular objectivism' premised on classic modernisation theory (Appadurai 2001, 5, cited in Yang 2006, 214).

The purchase of this narrative on the consciousness of the educated middle classes is hard to assess, and depends on a number of factors. Amongst these, however, is the extent and nature of their exposure to the world of ideas beyond China's borders; hence the recent strictures on 'Western thought'. For most of the post-Mao period, the engagement of Chinese scholars, students and policy-makers with that wider world has been far more extensive and profound than that of their Soviet counterparts in the pre-perestroika era. It is to that phenomenon that we turn next.

Notes

1 In 1995, Hayhoe noted a 'tremendous surge of support' for expansion 'in both the economically dynamic South-Central region and the more impoverished Northwest', concluding that officials might struggle to rein in the growth in enrolments (1995, 252).
2 In 2000, Zeng's monthly salary was 800 yuan; in 2005 it was 2,000 yuan; and in 2013, 10,000 yuan.
3 New applications for the 985 or 211 projects were closed from 2011; 39 institutions have 985 status, and about 100 are enrolled in the 211 scheme.
4 Ma and Fan refer to the British and Hong Kong precedents, though it is unclear what, if any, direct influence these had on policy on the mainland (2005, 29).
5 The authors were both vice-directors of the Development Research Section of the Ministry of Education.
6 Official concerns to ensure 'quality' led, in 2003, to a new directive preventing independent colleges from issuing degrees under the name of their parent institution, sparking protests from outraged parents and students. Perceptions of the value of independent college degrees subsequently suffered, but demand persisted (see Yu and Ertl 2010, 40–1).
7 According to Yu and Ertl (2010), the Chinese branch campuses of Nottingham and Liverpool universities are strictly speaking 'the only private or independent universities in China' (39), though even these are joint ventures with (public) Chinese institutions. Under Chinese law, *bona fide* 'universities' must admit undergraduate (*benke*) students through the national college admissions process (*tongzhao*), and offer postgraduate programmes.
8 These were essentially adult education colleges issuing diplomas rather than awarding their own degrees.
9 In recent years, a new variety of private college has emerged in the form of several institutions established by wealthy individuals (the head of *Xin Dongfang*, a chain of tutorial schools, has established one such institution, as has the automobile manufacturing entrepreneur Li Shufu, who established 'Jili University'). But in a context of demographic decline and graduate under-employment, this is not a trend the government appears keen to encourage. It is still very difficult for such institutions to get official certification from the Education Ministry.
10 A problematic feature of this research is that the samples for the 2002 and 2009 surveys conducted by the team were not entirely comparable – with each investigating a slightly different range of provinces and institutions.
11 This study focused especially on Hunan College of Engineering (Hunan Gongxue Yuan), sampling 800 students from the Department of Material and Chemical Engineering.
12 These findings require updating, since is quite possible that the post-2012 anti-corruption campaign has significantly dented the attractiveness of public sector employment amongst graduates. Peng also found that most students expected the university to help them find a job, but that 70 per cent found its career advice service 'useless'.

13 Indeed, the lack of institutional appetite for asserting greater autonomy was illustrated in 2015, when six elite universities (including Peking and Tsinghua) were invited by the Ministry to submit proposals for their own 'charters', setting out distinctive academic 'missions'. However, the universities immediately sought safety in numbers, and submitted draft charters that were identical in their commitment to following the guidance of the Communist Party. Anxieties related to the political climate meant that the process did not lead to any strengthening of autonomous faculty governance.

14 Thus those being groomed for senior roles in government have in recent years been sent for training to Harvard's Kennedy School of Government, while middle-ranking cadres are packed off to Singapore.

15 These include East China Normal University, Jiangnan University, Sichuan University, South-West University and Zhejiang University. But some of the most prestigious institutions, such as Fudan in Shanghai, have not done this – apparently considering that their fame renders such lobbying unnecessary.

16 At the same time, substantial opportunities exist for corruptly siphoning off such funds for personal use, though reliable data on this – as on the scale of corruption in China generally – is hard to come by.

17 The nearest British equivalent might be a fellowship of the Royal Society – except that Changjiang scholars are appointed through a bureaucratic process rather than elected by existing 'fellows'.

18 It would appear, however, that the strictness with which this directive is enforced varies considerably from university to university. It does not seem to be rigorously enforced at elite institutions.

19 This speech was not reported in the official media, though Zhu's comments were circulated on social media (Sina Weibo) (Bevis 2014, 167).

20 For essentially similar reasons, McGregor argues that the professionalisation of the People's Liberation Army poses challenges for Party authority over the military (2010).

13 The international dimension

The migration of people and of ideas is central to the story of education in post-Mao China. We have already discussed some of the educational ramifications of the movement of rural dwellers to the cities, which has been described as 'the biggest migration in human history' (Miller 2012). However, the significance of that phenomenon is closely linked to China's burgeoning traffic, educational as well as commercial, with other societies. Whereas an explicit aim of the Cultural Revolution was to close the gap between the cities and the countryside, erasing the urban advantage in 'cultural capital', that superiority has subsequently been reinstated and radically enhanced. This has much to do with the vast expansion of contacts between urban China and the outside world. For many young urbanites in Beijing, Shanghai or Guangzhou today, villages two hours away by bus are far more alien than the societies of Hong Kong, Tokyo, or even London.

One way of interpreting this is to argue that, in essence, Mao was right. 'Opening up' has exposed China to Western hegemony or cultural imperialism. As a 'developing' country positioned on the 'periphery' of a 'World System', it has found its policies and practices shaped by the international ascendancy of financial capitalism. And as in economics, so in education and other fields, the prevalence of overseas study and exposure to 'global' discourse has increasingly determined 'what counts as scholarship' (Yang 2006, 216–17). The result, according to this view, is a deracination of Chinese elites and their co-optation by the forces of transnational global capitalism.

China's complicity in the emergence of a neoliberal global order is unquestionable – but does this imply a passive or peripheral role for its elites? In previous chapters (e.g. Chapter 9), we noted how the Party's adoption of many elements of neoliberal ideology has been selective and provisional. Here we look at the role of overseas study in official strategies for 'modernisation', as well as in popular competition for status and credentials. Our main focus is on the implications for China itself, but we also indicate ways in which Chinese educational internationalisation has affected other societies. These extend well beyond the effects of transnational study (whether outbound or, increasingly, inbound), to China's participation in international programmes of educational testing and ranking, and the recent pursuit of 'educational diplomacy'. One ironic consequence of this cross-border educational traffic is that, during the very period when the Party has been abandoning socialist internationalism for nationalism, many urban Chinese have become profoundly transnational in their outlook and interests. While official strategies for internationalisation remain permeated by the imperative of maintaining loyalty to the Party, this cultural transformation may profoundly challenge that project.

Historical context

The internationalisation of Chinese education is not a new phenomenon. The popular classic *Journey to the West* (*Xi You Ji*) stands as a literary monument to a pre-modern era of scholarly exchange with India, then the centre of a vast Buddhist civilisational sphere. Chinese scholars studied alongside their counterparts from elsewhere in Asia at the Indian university of Nalanda (Sen 2005). China's own academies meanwhile attracted scholars from Korea, Vietnam and Japan. In short, not only did the intellectual universe of the pre-modern 'Sinosphere' extend well beyond China itself; the sources of its scholarly traditions were never purely 'indigenous'.

To be sure, periods of relative intellectual openness alternated with attempts to quarantine the Celestial Realm from barbarian contamination. One period of relative closure extended from the early eighteenth century to almost the end of the nineteenth. However, this was succeeded by a half-century 'Age of Openness' (Dikotter 2009). The foreign communities then in China were often associated with the subjugation or exploitation of local populations, but they also left a considerable legacy in the field of education. Christian missionaries, in particular, established many educational institutions and pioneered schooling for girls and women (48–50). Hong Kong's Chinese elites meanwhile founded some of the earliest modern schools on the mainland (36–9). By the 1930s, Chinese constituted the largest cohort of foreign students in American universities (63), and a cosmopolitan English- or Japanese-speaking elite – educated overseas or at universities such as St John's (in Shanghai) or Tsinghua or Yenching (in Beijing) – was prominent in public affairs.[1] In the 1930s, the Nationalist government also invited the international 'Becker Commission' to advise on the reorganisation and centralisation of tertiary education (Dikotter 2009, 58).

'Liberation' in 1949 spelt the end for Western involvement (the Japanese having been expelled in 1945), but definitely not for all international educational exchange. The 1950s influx of Soviet advisors was matched by an exodus of students; study in the USSR became a formative experience for a generation of young Communists, including Li Peng and Jiang Zemin, who would later guide China through a crucial phase of its post-Mao 'opening'. But after the Sino-Soviet split of 1961, opportunities for international educational exchange ceased, at least in an outbound direction (Bevis 2014). Select parties of foreign sympathisers (of the variety dubbed 'useful idiots' by Lenin) were invited to marvel at the achievements of revolutionary Maoism; and in the wake of the 1972 Nixon visit, small groups of language students began to arrive (Wood 2000). The Japanese were among the quickest to revive bilateral cultural and educational ties. But it was not until the end of the decade that a fuller resumption of Sino-Western educational exchanges became possible.

Foreign aid and consultancy in post-Mao educational policymaking

The sensitivity surrounding this recalibration of 'relations with foreigners' is reflected in the title of the relevant chapter of Zhao Ziyang's memoirs, 'Opening Painfully to the World' (2009, 101–10). As noted in our Chapter 3, greater international openness during the 1980s (and subsequently) was accompanied by sporadic campaigns – against 'spiritual pollution' or 'bourgeois liberalisation' – aimed at countering or containing the ideological challenge of 'foreign' ideas. Advice on modernisation was initially sought from reformist East European socialists: the Czech economist Ota Sik, and the exiled Pole, Wlodomierz Brus. In late 1979 and early 1980, they held seminars in China advocating 'market socialism', and although refraining from questioning the 'framework of state ownership and the planned economy', had an 'eye-opening' effect on many Chinese scholars (Bevis 2014, 136). Exposure to alternative visions of socialism helped to legitimate a new, home-grown heterodoxy: 'socialism with Chinese characteristics'.

However, it was to the 'developed world' of the USA, UK, Japan and Europe that China's leaders looked for the expertise and technology crucial to the 'four modernisations'. Both the evidence of economic performance and the logic of strategic calculation pointed in this direction. More than anything else, it was Cold War geopolitics that had driven China and America together, and as the 1979 invasion of Afghanistan brought a renewed freeze to US–Soviet relations, the Americans proved especially keen to extend bilateral aid to the People's Republic, in education as in other fields (Bevis 2014). American goodwill also smoothed China's path when it came to re-engaging with multi-lateral institutions such as the World Bank.

China's engagement with the Bank coincided with the gathering ascendency of what became the 'Washington Consensus', characterised by belief in the superiority of market mechanisms in the provision of public goods as in the economy more broadly, and a corresponding suspicion of the interventionist state. Such 'neoliberal' or, perhaps more accurately, 'neo-libertarian' ideas (Morris 2016), have undoubtedly enjoyed considerable influence in China since the 1980s. Yang Rui sees the World Bank and WTO as threatening China's 'educational sovereignty' by peddling a vision calculated to buttress the Western-dominated global order (2010), while Kajanus argues that these institutions (amongst others) 'sanction and mobilise the internationalisation of education' (2015, 48). However, as we stressed in Chapter 9, post-Mao China has by no means presented a passive 'blank slate' onto which hegemonic foreign forces have been free to carve their agenda.

The re-engagement with multi-lateral institutions around 1980 was sudden and sweeping (Yang R. 2010, 421). According to Yang, relations with the UN agencies, especially UNICEF, were relatively 'equal', but those with the Bank and the WTO far more problematic. World Bank involvement in China has certainly been extensive: between 1981 and 2007, there were 284 projects involving education with a total expenditure of over US$42 billion. The first of these, in the field of higher education, aimed to increase undergraduate and postgraduate enrolments, and improve 'teaching quality' and 'research capacity' following the devastation of the sector during the Cultural Revolution. By June 1985, '2,471 people … had been sent overseas for training', and in that year a follow-on project extended funding for overseas training to many more Chinese scholars (422). Those trained through these schemes went on to become 'the policy makers and implementers of China's fast higher education development' (Yang R. 2010, 424). Meanwhile, the Bank flew in famous economists and other experts to lend their authority to its agenda. By the mid-1980s, it was organising seminars for Chinese officials that fed into discussions over drafting of the government's 'five-year plans' (Bevis 2014, 137).

With respect to tertiary education, the Bank was by this point already urging a fee-driven expansion of enrolments; we discussed its 1986 report in Chapter 11. Reports in 1995 and 1999 recommended further 'diversification' of funding sources (higher fees and student loans), greater institutional 'autonomy' in student admissions, as well as mergers and consolidation. Yang Rui observes that the Higher Education Law of 1998, many aspects of which faced opposition from university leaders, was 'in line with World Bank suggestions' (2010, 423). He argues that WTO entry in 2001 set the seal on the triumph in China of market-oriented neoliberalism, pointing out that a key advocate of user-fees, Lao Kaisheng, 'frequently cites the World Bank and WTO to justify this view' (428). Contemporaneous shifts in higher education management towards marketisation, greater public–private collaboration and reduced per-capita public funding paralleled developments overseas.

However, invoking international precedents or recommendations to legitimate particular policies is not the same as blindly following them, nor does correlation necessarily imply causation. Indeed, Yang acknowledges that while China's accession to the WTO theoretically covered trade in 'educational services', the country's negotiators were able to secure very significant restrictions in this area. These rendered threats to 'educational sovereignty' essentially nugatory. Compulsory education and military education remained entirely off-limits to foreign providers, who could otherwise operate only through joint ventures with local entities. The agreement placed no limits on transnational flows of students (though in practice these had already been abandoned – see below). It allowed the employment of foreign teachers, provided they could demonstrate relevant qualifications and a specified level of experience. But since almost all the entities employing foreign instructors were public institutions or joint ventures (ultimately subject to Party oversight), this involved no real compromise of state control.[2]

The avoidance of any such compromise has been the bottom line for the Party. The initial agreements allowing UN organisations to operate in China stipulated that they conduct all their work through state agencies, with in-country appointments approved by the Foreign Experts Bureau. China's rising international clout, and its increasing contributions to the UN budget, have since stifled efforts to change this, with the result that UN agents have struggled to articulate positions independent of the Chinese government. Organisations that have attempted a more interventionist approach – the Ford Foundation in the late 1990s sought to promote 'action-oriented' educational research with assistance from 'radical' scholars – have tended to provoke official suspicion and defensiveness.[3] A 'middle way' was followed by the UK's Department for International Development (DfID), which through its Gansu Basic Education Project (1999–2006) offered Chinese and foreign scholars opportunities to conduct research and freely access project-related data, while itself refraining from sanctioning any specific set of findings (Brock 2009). Meanwhile, Japan's JICA aid agency, a large donor from the 1970s to early 2000s, disbursed considerable funds for small-scale projects with relatively light-touch monitoring (see Ako 2009).

No longer a recipient of bilateral aid, China today is itself a significant donor – in Africa and elsewhere. But even when the country remained relatively poor, its sheer size, strategic importance and commercial potential prompted many international actors to accept restrictions on their freedom of operation. This was true also of education-related businesses such as textbook publishers – often seen as powerful players *vis-à-vis* 'developing country' governments. To the present co-author (Vickers), who was involved in Sino-foreign collaboration over textbook development from 2000 to 2003, it was quite evident that the Chinese side ultimately called the tune (see also Adamson 2004).[4]

As earlier chapters have evidenced, that tune was largely composed of variations on the theme of 'catching up' with the 'developed world' – a world that, by the 1980s, was increasingly subscribing to the neoliberal postulates of the Washington Consensus. In her ethnographic study of transnational Chinese students, Fong remarks on how such ideas, pervasive in school textbooks and state-controlled media, had come to permeate popular discourse by the late 1990s. China was seen as 'backward', and thus in need of 'development' and 'modernisation', in order to catch up with 'advanced countries' characterised by the 'high quality' (*gao suzhi*) of their citizenry (2011, 11–12). The same orientation towards the 'developed world' has been evident in educational scholarship and policymaking, with references to the USA, UK, France, Germany, Japan and Singapore predominating. Nonetheless, even this relatively limited menu has allowed experts and decision-makers to mix and match to suit their own tastes: for example, invoking Japan and Singapore rather than America or Britain as models in the field of moral and civic education (Rappleye 2007). As Fong writes, 'although their motivations, experiences and trajectories were shaped by the global neoliberal system, they were also the ones who helped to build it' (2011, 216).

Overseas study at tertiary level

Fong is referring above to transnational students rather than to policymakers or educational experts, but the two categories have increasingly overlapped as overseas study has become more common (by 2003, the Education Minister,

Zhou Ji, boasted a PhD from SUNY Buffalo). Beginning with targeted and relatively small-scale schemes in the early post-Mao years, the stream of students travelling abroad has since become a torrent. Between 1978 and 2011, an estimated 2.25 million studied overseas (Dervin 2015, 2), over 90 per cent of them after the year 2000 (Kajanus 2015, 46). In 2012, 400,000 students were overseas, and Chinese accounted for 14 per cent of all international students worldwide (Dervin 2015, 2–3). From 1999–2000 to 2010–11, the number of Chinese students in the USA alone tripled to around 150,000 (Bevis 2014, 173).

Alongside quantitative expansion have come changes in students' demographic profile and aims, as well as in the social implications for China and receiving countries. In the early phase, from around 1980, participants were state-funded and selected by examination. In 1979, the MOE set an annual quota of 3,000 exchange scholars for the next five years, subsequently redefining 'scholars' to include graduate students (Kajanus 2015, 54); initially, most participants were relatively mature, some in their forties (Bevis 2015, 135). Overseas study became, and would continue to be, a key element of professional development for Chinese faculty (Hayhoe 1999, 259). The need for qualified personnel remained acute not only through the 1980s, but also when tertiary education underwent increasingly rapid expansion during the 1990s; overseas training was seen as an important means of 'upgrading' faculty to make up the shortfall. However, especially in the early years, the selection of students reflected the state's prioritisation of fields seen as likely to contribute most directly to economic growth and technology transfer (especially military-related) (Bevis 2014, 136).[5] The privileging of STEM subjects over the humanities and social sciences also meant that the vast majority of scholarship recipients were men,[6] usually from relatively elite backgrounds (Kajanus 2015, 55).

Self-funded overseas study became theoretically possible from 1981, but permits were initially highly restricted. From 1984, however, restrictions were steadily eased, perhaps partly because bureaucratic elites were anxious to secure for their own offspring the attendant benefits in status and earning potential (58). Growing awareness of the qualitative distinctiveness of overseas tertiary education, and increased wealth, meant that market forces increasingly drove student flows, with implications for social stratification. The Tiananmen Incident of 1989 led to a hiatus, while also prompting many students to prolong their foreign sojourn. But in 1992, Deng Xiaoping appealed to them to return, promising that past political attitudes would be forgotten (Bevis 2014, 149).[7] In 1993, the Party Congress declared a new era of openness, with the slogan 'Support overseas study, encourage people to return, give freedom to come and go!' (*Zhichi liuxue, guli hui guo, lai qu ziyou*) (Xiang and Shen 2009, 515). The 1990s cohort went mostly for postgraduate study, usually straight after completing their undergraduate degree, and were therefore younger, on average, than their predecessors. A substantial number were also, in reality, economic migrants. In some cases, subversion of host country visa restrictions was aided and abetted by agents in China and by substandard, profiteering diploma factories or language schools overseas. In others, such as Japan, where labour shortages in certain sectors were intensifying, the relative ease of securing employment while studying and subsequently was a significant attraction for many (Xiang and Shen 2009).

The transformation of overseas study into a mass phenomenon from around 2000, though proportionally still involving only a tiny percentage of tertiary students, is attributable to several factors. Crucially, China's first cohort of single children was reaching college age in a context of rapidly rising urban incomes, creating a 'generation of urban singletons' living 'as First World children in a Third World country' (Fong 2004). They were both objects of heightened parental expectations and vehicles for concentrated familial investment. As competition for college access within China has become more intense, more have gone overseas at younger ages, for undergraduate programmes or language courses (Xiang and Shen 2009, 516). The economic returns to overseas study have meanwhile become less clear, but this has hardly dented urban parents' keenness to send their children to American institutions – particularly when inability to test into a prestigious local high school presages failure to enter a 'good' Chinese university (Yang, D. 2016). Yang emphasises that this is not solely a matter of securing economic returns, but also involves the social status or 'face' (*mianzi*) of the family as a whole. In other words, study abroad, especially in America or the UK, has become an important means of acquiring 'cultural capital'.

With numbers of students travelling overseas rising, a growing proportion have been female, reflecting willingness of parents to invest in 'singleton' offspring of whatever gender. Figures for the UK cited by Kajanus show that of a total of 145 Chinese students (undergraduate and postgraduate) in 1980, 88 per cent were male; in 1990, 75 per cent of 2,200; in 2000, 51 per cent of 10,500; and in 2010, 45 per cent of 51,000 (2015, Table 3.1). The balance of subjects studied has also shifted, with increasing numbers studying business, management, economics and more stereotypically 'feminine' fields such as languages or the 'applied' social sciences (including education) (46). Xiang and Shen suggest a difference between young men and women from the perspective of the 'marriage market' (2009, 517). Invoking Bourdieu's distinction between 'economic' and 'cultural' ladders of social stratification, they argue that direct economic returns to overseas credentials may be more important for men, but 'cultural capital' and heightened social status more so for women. In so far as these attributes render women more 'marriageable', they may of course yield economic returns as well. For more mature, highly qualified single women, meanwhile, overseas study may also offer the prospect, through marriage to a foreigner and/or settlement abroad, of escape from the strictures of a society that still expects women to marry by 25 and subordinate themselves to their husband's family (Fincher 2014; Kajanus 2015). For many men as well as women, however, such plans often fall flat, as they lose 'opportunities to build the careers and families necessary for respectable adult identities in China', instead devoting their youth 'to low-skilled work and an expensive but low-prestige education in developed countries' (Fong 2011, 218).

While the attractions of tertiary education overseas have remained high due to perceptions of its relative 'quality' (however defined), an increasingly competitive graduate labour market since the 1990s has prompted more discrimination in the choice of institutions (Kajanus 2015, 70–71). Like the government and employers, Chinese parents and students have increasingly referred to global university rankings or 'league tables'. Indeed, the generation of these rankings is one instance of China's active – indeed leading – role in shaping the global higher education market (see below). The reliance of Chinese 'consumers' on these measures has influenced how institutions in many countries assess their own performance. Kajanus notes how, at the international higher education recruitment fairs regularly held since the late 1990s, institutional rankings have been an overwhelming concern for students and their parents (2015, 48–50).[8] Meanwhile, as Chinese have fuelled the growth of the international student market, many governments, especially in the 'Anglosphere', have cut public subsidies to higher education. By driving universities into greater dependence on their overseas 'marketability', this has dictated ever-closer institutional attentiveness to rankings.

Seeking to expand its own programmes for nurturing 'high-level talent' at minimal cost, the Chinese government has adroitly capitalised on the eagerness of foreign universities to raise their profile on the mainland. In 1996, the China Scholarships Council (CSC) was established as a central source of funding for overseas study, especially at doctoral level, soliciting applications from the country's top-ranked universities; its resources have been massively expanded since around 2010. Since overseas host universities are required to offer fee waivers to recipients of these scholarships, cash-hungry British institutions have mostly demurred; with few scholarships of their own to offer, they have gained a reputation within China for admitting the 'rich and stupid'. For their part, leading American universities, reluctant to allow Chinese officials a role in selecting doctoral applicants, and with ample scholarship funding of their own, have taken relatively few CSC students. By contrast, European and Australian universities, many of them especially eager to establish an international reputation or to foster ties with China (and, at least in Europe, often amply funded by the state), have been much keener (on Australia, see Trounson 2015).[9]

As patterns of overseas study have altered, so have its effects – on the individuals involved, and on Chinese society as a whole. Studying overseas might be expected to cultivate a more cosmopolitan outlook, but the experience of those living and learning abroad has been complex and varied. In the 1980s, those travelling overseas tended to be relatively mature, and many had direct experience of the hardships of the Cultural Revolution. For them, the contrast between living standards in urban China and developed countries was enormous (Bevis 2014, 142–4). Often isolated from their compatriots, they were compelled to mix and integrate. However, for their younger successors from the 1990s onwards, greater exposure to Western popular culture and the growing prosperity of China's cities have reduced the sense of distance and strangeness (144). As Fong observes, enjoyment of the capabilities and lifestyle associated with the 'imagined developed world community' to which many aspire is increasingly possible for urban elites within China itself (2011). And once overseas, twenty-first century Chinese students often cluster on foreign campuses in large numbers, obviating the necessity to integrate.

More selective in their choice of destination, many students also become distinctly ambivalent in their embrace of local society and culture. Often attracted by the prospect of studying with 'an ethnically, racially and intellectually diverse group of students and faculty' (Yang, D. 2016, 145), many develop an appreciation for the religious and political freedoms they observe once abroad (Fong 2011, 160). However, primed in part by the patriotic content of the school curriculum – a core theme of which is the 'filial nationalism' that Fong observes among many of her informants[10] – many also react angrily and defensively to the criticisms of China they frequently hear from non-mainland Chinese, foreigners and the media. Rowena He has documented some of the online and face-to-face conflicts that have occurred amongst Chinese students in North America over issues such as China's human rights record, the Tiananmen Incident and Tibet (He 2015). To some extent, political conformity has been orchestrated through embassy supervision of Chinese student associations, but social media (itself closely monitored and sometimes guided by state agents) has also played a crucial role. The Internet has served as a potent vehicle for Chinese nationalism as for other forms of radicalism, often functioning as an 'echo chamber' that reinforces extremism and prejudice rather than challenging it.

China's rapid economic rise since the 1990s has also narrowed the gap between wage levels for overseas graduates who remain abroad and those who return; earlier concerns of a 'brain drain' have largely dissipated. After 1989, political factors kept some individuals in exile, but for most, economic or personal considerations have predominated. State programmes designed to entice returnees 'provide the new elite with symbolic and political capital, and ... incorporate them into the establishment' (Xiang and Shen 2009, 514). The keenness of senior officials to affirm the superior 'quality' of returnees, and treat them as a 'special social category', is perhaps not unrelated to the fact that many are their own offspring (520). However, by no means all have returned to find China's streets paved with gold. Unemployment or under-employment has awaited many; in 2003, an estimated 7,000 returnees were unemployed in Shanghai alone. At this time, concerns that Chinese universities and corporations could not absorb a sudden influx of scientists prompted the government to call on people to 'serve the country overseas' (*wei guo fu wu*) rather than 'return to China' (*hui guo fu wu*) (Zweig *et al.* 2004). Continued economic growth and new funding for top universities have since expanded opportunities (see below) – but not at a rate sufficient to keep pace with the numbers of budding scientists and scholars graduating from overseas institutions. Meanwhile, the transformative effects of returnees on urban culture and 'human capital' have been concentrated in the major metropolitan centres of the eastern seaboard, from which most overseas students came in the first place (Bevis 2014, 149).

Student migration has thus both reflected and intensified China's broader social stratification. Xiang and Shen suggest that mainland elites since around 2000 have followed a strategy pioneered earlier by their Hong Kong counterparts: as access to domestic higher education has expanded (with more 'working class' students admitted), they have increasingly sought comparative advantage by sending their offspring to universities abroad (2009, 514). The increasing prevalence of self-funded overseas study has reflected the growing ability of many urban Chinese to pay, but has also reinforced the role of family wealth in determining social opportunity. As of 2010, the typical cost of studying abroad was 5–13 times the average annual income of urban households (Kajanus 2015, 46). In the case of the UK, second only to the USA as a 'prestigious' destination, costs in 2007 were equivalent to 23 times the average *per capita* income of urban residents, and 70 times average rural incomes (Xiang and Shen 2009, 516).

Internationalised secondary schooling

In the twenty-first century, the popularity of the UK as an educational destination has also extended to secondary level (assisted perhaps by the international appeal of the *Harry Potter* franchise). By 2015, figures from Britain's Independent Schools Council showed that 21 per cent of non-British pupils whose parents lived overseas came from China (Espinoza 2015). Private schools in Britain and elsewhere have cast their spell over Chinese parents chiefly through the promise of advantage in the competition for university places (Xiang and Shen 2009, 514). Meanwhile, elite schools – both public and private – within China itself have competed for the same pool of students, offering internationalised curricula 'on-shore' (518; see Chapter 9). These range from the international sections of prestigious public schools such as Beijing's Number 4 Middle School (twinned with Eton), to private high schools such as Wen Lai College in the Shanghai suburbs, which operates both English-language and Japanese-language streams, and sends students for their final year or two of high school to either Canada or Japan, prior to college application.[11]

Parental motives for sending children abroad for secondary schooling can be complex and diverse. For many, extricating their child from the extreme intensity of China's educational competition is a significant consideration. The overseas option has also had a special attraction for wealthier parents who contravened the family planning regulations by having more than the stipulated one or two children. And for those concerned about possible political instability, or intent on securing a foreign bolthole for more cynical reasons (e.g. placing corruptly acquired wealth beyond the reach of the Chinese state), foreign residency for a child can serve as a familial insurance policy (on the Bo Xilai case, see Garnaut 2012). But a common denominator is the desire for prestigious college-level credentials, and the access to elite global circles that this confers. In this respect, the ability of 'little overseas students' to acquire not just qualifications, but also the manners, accents and social networks of Anglosphere elites, contributes to their status as a 'new' but 'real aristocracy' (in the words of a journalist quoted by Xiang and Shen 2009, 517).

However, the transformative impact of this educational exodus is not one-way. The influx of Chinese money into English private schools has inflated fee levels and intensified competition for places, contributing to a decline in the proportion of local private pupils (Espinoza 2015); this in turn has fuelled support amongst some of the 'priced-out' middle classes for government schemes to remodel public schooling on the model of their 'independent' counterparts (see Wiborg 2015). Perhaps even more significantly, the urge to tailor their appeal to the expectations of Chinese parents has prompted shifts in the hallowed ethos of English 'public' (i.e. private) schools. Traditionally priding themselves on their capacity to mould 'character' on the sports field as well as in the classroom, schools have increasingly sought to emphasise their university admissions records and examination results (Cain and Hopkins 2016, 724).

Sino-foreign educational collaboration

Notwithstanding the recent growth of high school international programmes, for most students in China the experience of learning from, or with, foreigners comes at college level, if at all. From the 1980s, as it began to send scholars overseas for training, the government also brought in 'foreign experts' as university teachers or researchers. After 1989, regulations governing foreigners' activities on Chinese campuses were drastically tightened (see Chapter 3.3), but more were recruited from the mid-1990s. In the early twenty-first century, as money has poured into higher education, schemes for attracting academic 'talent' have become more ambitious: 2008 witnessed the launch of a 'Thousand Talent Initiative', followed in 2011 by a 'Thousand Foreign Experts Programme' (Bevis 2014, 164). The financial terms have become increasingly enticing; top scientists willing to relocate from the West can nowadays expect to earn far more in China than in Japan (Rappleye and Vickers 2015). But it is telling that most making the move work in 'politically neutral' STEM fields, or as language teachers, rather than in the humanities or social sciences (Bevis 2014, 165). Political considerations also dictate a preference for recruiting foreigners on an individual basis, leaving administrative control firmly in Chinese hands.

However, inter-institutional collaborative ventures, offering more extensive access to foreign expertise and facilities, have also been selectively approved. At the most ambitious level, this has involved establishing joint-venture satellite campuses, of which Nottingham University Ningbo (2004) was the first, and New York University's Shanghai branch (2013) one of the latest. More specialist partnerships have included the Johns Hopkins–Nanjing University Center for Chinese and American Studies (from 1986) and Harvard University's 'Senior Executive Program' in Shanghai (Bevis 2014, 162–3).[12] Very recently, some Chinese universities have been permitted to contract overseas partners to provide accredited courses (sometimes online) for their students. More limited forms of partnership, from simple exchange agreements upwards, have meanwhile proliferated. Universities of the Anglosphere and the more developed East Asian societies (especially Singapore and Hong Kong) have been particularly active in forming partnerships, though European universities, many now also operating in English, have become increasingly involved. But Japanese institutions have been less engaged than those of many other countries; only in 2015 did Tokyo University became the first Japanese university to form a 'strategic partnership' in China – with Peking University (Japan Times 2015).[13]

Rapid growth in the number and variety of Sino-foreign programmes has sparked concerns over both 'quality control' and the related issue of 'educational sovereignty' (Yang R. 2010). Anxieties over quality prompted a moratorium on new initiatives in 2008, when 64 joint programmes were closed down in Shanghai alone (426). However, the lack of administrative mechanisms for on-going quality assurance remains unresolved (427); in their absence, the authorities tend to lurch between total neglect and arbitrary, draconian sanctions. Indeed, an attraction of contracting prestigious foreign universities to offer courses in China is that the latter are backed by the quality assurance infrastructure of the home institution. In so far as this implies an abdication of Chinese control, it can conjure up the spectre of foreign 'colonialism' (Rhoads *et al.* 2014, 176–7). But since such courses have been overwhelmingly in the fields of business, management or the hard sciences (Yang R. 2010, 426), they present little ideological or political threat.

At the same time, awareness of international education's potential as an agent of 'soft power' has contributed to ambitions to transform China into a provider as well as a consumer. Enhancing competitiveness in the international student 'market' was one factor behind the 2012 decision to channel a large portion of the increase in central government education spending to universities (Bevis 2014, 158; see Chapter 3.4). As of 2010, 240,000 overseas students were enrolled in China's higher education institutions (154), mostly language students on exchanges of up to a year (159). In 2002, 77 per cent of international enrolments in Chinese universities were from Asia, mainly Japan and South Korea (Welch and Cai 2011, 17), but by 2010–11 the Japanese had been overtaken by the Americans, the US contingent rising to 15,000 from under 3,000 in 1999–2000 (Bevis 2014, 173; Rappleye and Vickers 2015). However, only a small proportion of foreign students work towards Chinese degrees (Bevis 2014, 159), mostly Asians in receipt of Chinese government scholarships, joined more recently by a growing number of self-funding degree students from countries such as Vietnam and South Korea (Welch and Cai 2011, 18). Partly with the aim of attracting more foreign degree students, attempts have been made to develop English-medium programmes in a number of disciplines, though with mixed results. The integration of overseas students into campus life has been constrained by the requirement, introduced since 1989, that they occupy separate dormitories from their Chinese counterparts; arranging homestays for foreigners is also fraught with complexity.

Indeed, the same political factors that determine the sphere within which overseas institutions can operate in China also limit the international attractiveness of Chinese higher education itself. Chinese universities' popularity with foreign partners, scholars and students owes less to their inherent quality as centres for research and teaching than to the economic and strategic importance of China itself. Learning *about* China, rather than learning *from* China, generally remains the primary motivation for foreign engagement. In some fields, especially the hard sciences, this may be changing as money is pumped into state of the art research facilities, but in the humanities and social sciences change is harder to accomplish. Even while more individual scholars evince an open, critical outlook, teaching and research activities remain significantly limited by institutional and ideological constraints.

The research environment and the striving for 'world-class' status

'A new era of global ambition' is trumpeted in the title of a volume co-authored by professors of several of 'China's rising research universities' (Rhoads *et al.* 2014). But even here, while hailing official commitment to 'developing world-class universities', the authors note the difficulty of defining 'world-class'. They broadly endorse ranking systems based on 'quantifiable outcomes' (21–30), but nonetheless acknowledge a less quantifiable aspect of 'world-class-ness': 'high levels of academic freedom and institutional autonomy'. On this score, they report that 'among those faculty members willing to speak out about the issue, there was general consensus that much room for improvement exists' (21).

Many basic limitations on academic freedom relate to the administrative factors discussed in Chapters 11 and 12, and to the politics of censorship more broadly. As the Internet has become increasingly crucial to accessing information, China's 'Great Firewall' has significantly hampered academic research. Meanwhile, to the extent that foreign universities seek to operate in the Chinese market, the political reach of the Chinese state can extend overseas too. As one US-based China scholar put it, foreign entities 'realize that respecting Chinese laws also means respecting limitations on their academic and intellectual freedom' (cited in Bevis 2014, 166). Foreign scholars who criticise the regime can risk being blacklisted, incurring damage to their own careers and deleterious consequences for their institutions (see our discussion below of 'cultural diplomacy').[14]

In China itself, control over universities and academics is also exercised through managerialist strategies related to the drive for 'world-class' status. For example, incentives relating to pay, promotion or contract renewal have been introduced to boost publications in leading international journals (those included in the SCI and SSCI rankings) (on the case of Fudan University, see Xu 2003). This strategy is of course far from unique to mainland China; similar policies in Taiwan have turned scholars there into 'paper producing machines' (Chou and Ching 2012, 200). Asian researchers often tailor publications to appeal to Western editors or reviewers, rather than focusing on research that is locally relevant or useful. Chou and Ching observe how Taiwanese scholars have become relatively successful in publishing articles in SCI/SSCI journals, but 'score' rather low on the key citation indices. In other words, they publish many papers that hardly anyone reads. This lends some credence to arguments stressing the baleful effects of Anglo-centric 'cultural imperialism', but there is another side to the story. Especially in social science and humanities fields, Anglo-American journals deluged with China-related manuscripts often struggle to find suitable reviewers to assess submissions. This, combined with the growing international fascination for things Chinese, can lead to relatively light-touch refereeing – contributing to a corruption of academic standards all round. [15]

Corruption, in fact, has become a major theme in contemporary debates about the research culture in Chinese universities. In Chapter 8, we discussed controversies over entrance examination reform, but concerns over corrupt practice extend much further. Zhao documents various scandals involving plagiarism and falsification of research results (for example, fraudulent crystallography papers, or the notorious case of the fake 'Hanxin chip'), as well as a deluge of 'low-quality patents' for essentially worthless or banal 'innovations' (Zhao Y. 2014, 109–10). He attributes the generally low quality of scientific research in part to an exponential growth in doctoral programmes from 2004 onwards (2014, 98). More fundamentally, though, he argues that these phenomena are driven by 'wishful thinking' and 'intense competition' within universities, conditioned by 'upward accountability' to rigid and unchallengeable 'authorities' who seek to govern the system through resort to 'a uniform and quantifiable standard' (112–16). Highlighting similar problems, Yang Rui (2016) sees academic corruption as endemic to 'East Asia' as a whole, exacerbated by deep-seated 'cultural' factors, including an emphasis on *guanxi* or 'relationships', an extremely hierarchical distribution of power within institutions, and weak links between 'merit' and career advancement.

As we have observed in earlier chapters, cultural explanations only take us so far. Yang argues that Japan's cultural distinctiveness from its neighbours is reflected in its 21 Nobel Prizes for science and technology. However, to the extent that universities there are relatively 'uncorrupted', this is attributable to a combination of political, institutional and cultural factors: relative media openness; job security for academics; largely seniority-based (rather than meritocratic) promotion; and the post-war entrenchment of traditions of faculty governance informed by an intensely collectivist ethos. Collectivism and rigid seniority-based promotion, in themselves far from conducive to academic freedom or productivity, help shield Japanese academics from the intense competitiveness to which their Chinese counterparts are exposed, reducing the temptation to plagiarise or falsify findings. Incidentally, these are precisely the features of the country's universities that Japan's government is intent on reforming, deploying for this purpose the same neoliberal language of 'competition', 'performance' and 'accountability' that nowadays permeates Chinese policy discourse (Rappleye and Vickers 2015). Of course, these are not uniquely 'Asian' trends. But Chinese and East Asian academia is perhaps particularly vulnerable to the corrupting effects of a managerialist, ultra-competitive vision of tertiary education. This is owing to the overwhelming prevalence of narrowly instrumentalist understandings of universities' social purposes, a phenomenon ultimately rooted in the historical orientation of these societies towards catch-up modernisation (Vickers 2016; Yang R. 2016).

International league tables

The desire to measure and demonstrate catch-up helps explain the decision to enter Shanghai in the OECD's PISA tests from 2009. Another factor may have been the city's rivalry with Hong Kong, which participated in PISA from the outset in 2000. Officials sought affirmation of the 'quality' and 'equity' of their education system, as well as 'lessons' to be derived through international comparisons (Kong 2012). The OECD itself, meanwhile, assiduously solicited the involvement of the world's largest education system. But Chinese officials needed little persuasion of the value and legitimacy of 'uniform, quantifiable standards' for measuring academic performance. After all, it was Shanghai Jiaotong University that in 2003 pioneered the first global university rankings, designed as a means of establishing the international standing of China's universities as they were pushed to attain 'world-class' status (Luxbacher 2013). The actual significance of Shanghai's PISA performance is discussed in our final chapter.

As Zhao Yong (2014) emphasises, beyond the pursuit of status and prestige, the value of such exercises from an official standpoint lies fundamentally in their utility as tools of control. Far from exaggerating the international standing of Chinese universities, the Shanghai Jiaotong indicators have actually tended to accord them a lower ranking than, for example, those employed by *Times Higher Education* (Rhoads *et al.* 2014, 23). The Chinese authorities hope thereby to goad institutions into overtaking foreign rivals as centres for scientific and technological innovation;[16] fostering complacency would undermine that purpose. Hence apparently waning enthusiasm for PISA participation: in mid-2014, Shanghai began to signal its possible withdrawal, even as discussions proceeded about additionally involving Beijing, Jiangsu and Guangdong (Vaughan 2014; Dervin 2015, 2). Fearful that a Shanghainese withdrawal might undermine the credibility of the PISA enterprise, OECD figures scrambled to secure continued Chinese participation. Meanwhile, the organisation's testing supremo, Andreas Schleicher, had begun promoting a new 'Assessment of Higher Education Learning Outcomes' (AHELO) – similarly quantitative and standardised – portraying this as a means for East Asian universities, in particular, to 'show their worth' and achieve a more 'level playing field' *vis-à-vis* their established Western 'competitors' (Morgan 2015).

Education and cultural diplomacy

However, even without such proffered assistance, Chinese universities have increasingly made their presence felt internationally, not only through exchanges and partnerships, but also as agents of cultural diplomacy. In 2015, Xiamen University became the first major Chinese higher education institution to open an overseas branch campus, in Malaysia (with English the main language of instruction); a non-profit venture represented as reciprocating the contribution of the university's original founder, an ethnic Chinese Malayan (Xiamen University Malaysia 2014). While that case perhaps signals a new departure, a more typical pattern has involved establishing not entire branch campuses, but 'Confucius Institutes'. Since 2003, Hanban (the 'Chinese Language Council International') has been dispatching overseas thousands of language teaching 'angels from China' aiming, in the words of its 2013 annual report, to build a 'spiritual high-speed rail' with the rest of the world (Dervin 2015, 5). Hanban is sometimes compared with organisations like the UK's British Council or Germany's Goethe Institute. But the fact that Confucius Institutes operate within established colleges, while maintaining their own funding, staffing and curricular materials, represents a significant difference.

Once again, issues of control are paramount, with the government intent that Confucius Institutes should give the world a 'correct' understanding of China (Bevis 2014, 169). Many foreign universities – almost 500 as of early 2015 – have concluded that the opportunity to boost their capacity in Chinese language instruction is too good to miss, and especially for institutions under pressure to attract external funding, Hanban's offer can seem 'a godsend' (170). However, the money seldom comes without strings attached. At Stanford, Hanban initially tried to insist that the appointee to a professorial chair it was proposing to fund would 'never discuss Tibet'. The kudos within China of the Stanford 'brand',[17] and its perceived value in lending worldwide legitimacy to Hanban's operations, in this instance prompted the Chinese side to compromise. But fears of handing Chinese state authorities significant influence over the content and focus of China-related teaching and research have deterred many institutions. Japan's flagship national universities will not host Confucius Institutes on their campuses, though several private universities have done so. And in 2015, the University of Stockholm, site of Europe's very first Confucius Institute, announced that it had declined to renew its contract, the vice-chancellor characterising the Hanban model as 'questionable' (Zhou 2015).

Conclusion

In his biography of Deng Xiaoping, Vogel compares China's post-Mao drive to learn from the West with Meiji Japan's 'Iwakura Mission' of 1871–73, when prominent Japanese officials and scholars toured Western nations *en masse* to garner inspiration for their country's modernisation (2011, 217). The comparison doubtless occurred to Deng himself (see Chapter 3). An attraction of the Meiji model for many contemporary Chinese reformers has been the promise of combining Western technical know-how with a version of 'indigenous' values supportive of the political *status quo*. Whether attributed to Japanese inspiration or not, this is essentially the strategy that Mao's successors have pursued. Moreover, as the state's educational activities have increasingly transcended China's borders, attempts to legitimate that strategy have also extended overseas.

A key premise of the narrative underpinning this is that contemporary China, like Meiji Japan, faces a world order dominated by 'hegemonic' Western powers that fundamentally threaten the country's autonomy or very existence (Vickers 2009b). Assumptions of a coercive relationship between neo-imperialist agents of 'neoliberal globalisation' on the one hand, and 'dependent' developing countries on the other, also enjoy some credence amongst critics of China's recent higher education internationalisation. Both Yang Rui (2010) and Rhoads *et al.* (2014), who subscribe to versions of this this view, nonetheless paradoxically urge closer engagement with international organisations, since only by mastering 'the rules of engagement' can China shape their agenda (Yang R. 2010, 420).

Profound inequalities undoubtedly permeate the global higher education 'market', but it is questionable whether their most important dimensions are national or international. Rather than pitting monolithic nation-states against 'hegemonic' international forces, educational politics increasingly cut across national boundaries. At the national level, there has certainly been significant convergence between Chinese policy and the agendas of international organisations such as the World Bank and OECD. Indeed, World Bank advisors in the 1980s were astonished at the alacrity with which many of their prescriptions were adopted by China's supposedly anti-Western, socialist regime, in contrast to the situation in India, where they felt frustrated by the 'quarrelsome, fractious' and 'short-term' political culture (Drake 2001, 227). But rather than implying subordination, China's engagement arguably reflects the considerable success its elites have already enjoyed in shaping the agendas of such international bodies to their domestic purposes.

More fundamentally, though, the growing transnational mobility of people and ideas implies a problematisation of the national/international dichotomy itself. For many Chinese, the experience of studying and living overseas has contributed additional layers of complexity to their identity or citizenship (Fong 2011). The same applies to the smaller number of foreigners who have spent years studying or teaching in China. Citing Appadurai, Carney observes:

> Never have static frameworks of nation-state/society, center/local, developed/underdeveloped, and so forth been more inadequate: "The apparent stabilities that we see are … usually our devices for handling objects characterized by motion. The greatest of these apparently stable objects is the nation-state, which is today frequently characterized by floating populations, transnational politics within national borders, and mobile configurations of technology and expertise" (Appadurai 2000, 5).
>
> (Carney 2009, 64)

To the extent that many middle-class urbanites have become increasingly 'transnational' in their orientation and experiences, the 'core'–'periphery' paradigm associated with World Systems theory is hard to sustain. Chinese elites today are both increasingly mobile and internationally influential, occupying positions in many overseas universities, multi-national agencies, corporations and financial institutions. The concept of 'Chineseness' is hardly adequate to capturing the complex identities such individuals may acquire, even if few may go as far as the Indian author, Arundhati Roy, who once declared herself a 'mobile republic' (see Vickers and Kumar 2015, 24). And the experiences of the internationally mobile are themselves diverse, as many transnational students become profoundly ambivalent towards both China and the 'developed world', and find that they are 'not used to anywhere any more' (Fong 2011, 220) – even while others retreat into the laager of chauvinistic nationalism (He 2015).

In so far as they come to slough off that nationalism and adopt a more cosmopolitan outlook, those who benefit most from transnational mobility may become more alienated from the majority of their compatriots for whom the nation-state remains inescapable and necessary. That alienation, and the global rise in socio-economic inequality of which it is one facet, has been associated with what Rodgers terms America's *Age of Fracture* (2011). The hollowing out of ethical discourse, the collapse of consensus over collectively guaranteed public goods, and the resort to a reductionist faith in the market as the arbiter of value have characterised contemporary China as well as much of the 'developed' world. In China, the linked phenomena of corruption and intense academic competition are among the consequences. But the Chinese strain of this condition has been especially virulent not simply due to the action of malevolent global forces, but because the combination of neoliberalism and neo-traditional authoritarianism has offered elites enormous opportunities to entrench and legitimate vested interests.

The interests, values and identities to whose emergence or transformation educational internationalisation has contributed are therefore complex and contradictory. For example, the narrow class interests of transnationally mobile elites are in acute tension with the interest that many also perceive in sustaining authoritarian Communist rule. This tension has been heightened, or thrown into sharp relief, by measures since 2012 to clamp down both on official corruption and on discussion, in university classrooms or the media, of 'Western thought'. In an attempt to dampen popular outrage at official corruption, and thus preserve Party legitimacy, the authorities risk weakening their capacity to secure the loyalty of the 'talented' individuals they believe China needs. At the same time, by tightening censorship and ramping up official propaganda, they unintentionally heighten the unfavourable contrast between China and a West with which more and more such individuals are intimately familiar.

But increasingly 'fractured' Western societies are today also subject to wrenching change and uncertainty. In the 1980s, 'the West posed a problem for Communist systems simply by being there' (Brown 2009, 459), but with social cohesion eroding and political extremism ascendant in post-2008 America and Europe, that challenge is not what it was. In education, meanwhile, market discourse, quantitative 'outcomes-based' performance indicators and league tables have filled the ethical vacuum, with China now supplying precedents for Western emulation – a phenomenon we discuss in our final chapter. It may be going too far to conclude that China today poses a problem for liberal democracy simply by being there, but the impoverishment of debate over education's social role that it arguably exemplifies has become truly international in scope.

Notes

1 Alongside an enormously influential Japanese-speaking elite, including Chiang Kai-shek (and, earlier, Sun Yat-sen) – products of the earliest 'wave' of overseas study at the very start of the twentieth century.
2 Meanwhile, in some respects, China seems to have taken marketisation of HE beyond even what would be conscionable in the West – e.g. experiments with the introduction of 'education shares' (Yang R. 2010, 429).
3 Zeng (the present co-author) worked in the Planning Dept of Education Ministry from 1996 to 2000, where she was involved in projects run in collaboration with UNICEF, the Ford Foundation and other international organisations. These observations are based on her experience.
4 The eagerness of large multi-national publishing conglomerates to curry favour with the Chinese authorities was epitomised by Thomson Learning's 2005 move to publish, in English, a promotional volume by China's Education Minister, Zhou Ji, on *Higher Education in China*.
5 Bevis reports cases of spying by Chinese students in America, particularly in relation to the gathering of military technology; as well as attempts by the Chinese secret services to recruit American students studying in China (146); though no doubt the CIA has been attempting the same with Chinese students in America.
6 Reflecting the low proportion of women studying these disciplines in Chinese universities.
7 Memories of the fate of the thousands of intellectuals who returned to China from overseas in the early years of the PRC may have inspired a certain caution amongst many exiled scholars during the 1990s.
8 The UCL Institute of Education (IOE), formerly an independent institution within London University, experienced a huge and sudden increase in overseas applications, especially from China, after its merger with UCL in 2014 led to it featuring on all the major international university league tables.
9 The expansion of CSC-funded studentships is a relatively recent phenomenon, and research on the receptiveness of universities in different countries to students on this scheme remains scarce. Our observations in this paragraph are therefore based largely on personal experience of working in universities in the UK and Japan, and of communications with colleagues in America, Australia and continental Europe.
10 Fong describes this as involving the identification of China with 'a long-suffering parent who deserved the filial devotion of her children, despite her flaws' (2011, 52).
11 Vickers visited the Shanghai school in early March 2016, with a delegation from Kyushu University in Japan. He has visited the international section of Beijing No. 4 Middle School several times to speak to students there.
12 It is notable that Harvard courses are largely reserved for high-flying cadres – those deemed worthy of what Bertrand Russell termed a 'license to think' (1932, 11–12). The 'licensing' of relatively open debate is a feature of the Communist Party's own major cadre training institutions. Meanwhile, Shanghai's municipal authorities send lesser (or less-trusted) minds to Singapore for instruction in discipline and probity.
13 Japanese institutions have numerous ties with their Chinese counterparts, and in the early Reform years were considerably more engaged with China than most Western universities. However, since the 1990s, while some leading Western universities have established branch campuses, country offices and collaborative research centres, Japanese universities have been distinctly restrained in their enthusiasm for broadening and deepening their Chinese links. Politics has clearly played a role here – on both sides.

14 Bevis cites the case of the 'Xinjiang 13' – America-based scholars who were banned from travelling to China after publishing a book critical of Chinese policies in Xinjiang.
15 For similar reasons, possibly supplemented by a desire to keep the student fee income flowing, Chinese postgraduate students in the social sciences and humanities can also experience relatively light-touch examining at some overseas institutions. (We are not aware of research on this issue, but base this observation on Vickers' experience working at a major UK research institute.)
16 The Shanghai Jiaotong rankings grant additional points specifically for the award of Nobel Prizes and Fields Medals.
17 Yang Rui (2011) notes that Min Weifang of Peking University and many other leading advocates of higher education reform in China 'cite almost exclusively Harvard and Stanford Universities to legitimize their policy moves' (42).

Conclusion

How should we evaluate post-Mao China's educational development? Besides occasioning intense, if circumscribed, public debate within China itself, the country's rapid 'rise' has meant that this question has increasingly preoccupied commentators elsewhere. From media froth about 'tiger mothers', to documentaries asking whether 'our kids' are 'tough enough' for Chinese-style schooling,[1] to cross-national comparisons of pupil performance, much English-language commentary converges on the same message: the Chinese are coming! By out-educating an effete West, they threaten to overtake their rivals economically, outfox them technologically, and outmanoeuvre them strategically.

In some respects, we have been here before. 'Education,' writes Archie Brown, 'was one area in which Communist states … did not have to fear comparison with the rest of the world' (2009, 577). And compared they were, during the Cold War, by both Eastern bloc regimes eager to trumpet their achievements and Westerners alarmed at the strategic menace these seemed to pose. There was indeed much to admire, since not only were high levels of literacy and numeracy the norm for these societies, but the Soviet Union itself 'shone', especially in 'mathematics, the hard sciences and engineering' (far less so in the social sciences and humanities). China appears to have gone one step further, harnessing educational success to the pursuit of rapid economic growth and improved livelihoods. No wonder that its achievements are alternately feted and feared – in terms sometimes evocative of that 'insidious' villain of Yellow Peril fiction, Dr Fu Manchu (holder of doctorates from four Western universities).

To what extent, though, has post-Mao China earned its widespread reputation for educational brilliance? In this closing chapter, while offering a tentative answer, we challenge assumptions that typically frame such questions. As we argued in Chapter 2, success is relative – how successful a country looks depends very much on our comparative perspective. But more fundamentally, what counts as success depends on what one thinks education is ultimately for.

Here it will be useful to return to the four perspectives outlined in our introductory chapter, and ask how China's educational performance appears from these different, if not entirely discrete, vantage points. To recap, we distinguished between orthodox, anti-globalist, practice-oriented and critical perspectives.

Orthodoxy denotes basic acceptance of mainstream official views of China's educational development, endorsing its goals, stressing its achievements and lauding the government's consistent 'pragmatism'. Anti-globalism involves greater emphasis on problems inherent in the country's developmental strategy, but tends to lay these at the door of global processes or 'hegemonic discourses' rather than Chinese agency. Practice-oriented approaches, largely agnostic on ethical or ideological matters, treat education as an essentially technical endeavour, seeking to identify and ameliorate instances of 'ineffectiveness'. By contrast, critical analyses encompass critique of the frameworks with reference to which 'effectiveness' is defined, probing how these are related to the political, socio-economic and cultural context.

We begin this chapter by alternately reviewing the educational record of post-Mao China through the prism of these four perspectives. Following this broad-brush overview, we undertake a more extended analysis of the PISA paradigm for evaluating educational success, for which Shanghai has become a poster-child. Shanghai is where orthodox attempts to burnish the educational achievements of post-Mao China have met the ostensibly practice-oriented agenda of Westerners anxious to identify 'what works'. As we show, this has involved serious distortions of Shanghai's educational performance, and that of China more broadly. But more fundamentally, attempts to frame Shanghainese or Chinese schooling as a shining success story reveal an impoverishment of conceptions of education's purposes. The implications of that impoverishment are the focus of our concluding section.

The four perspectives revisited

The educational achievements of the 'Reform and Opening' era, touted by upholders of regime-sanctioned orthodoxy, are real enough. As we noted in Chapter 2, China has comprehensively outperformed that other Asian giant, India, on virtually every conceivable educational measure – from the near-universalisation of basic schooling (for girls as well as boys) to, more recently, participation rates in higher education. Notwithstanding some exaggeration in government statistics, by the standards of many 'developing' countries, China's performance is impressive. Nor has the existence of problems been denied. Educational 'quality', rural provision of basic education, issues with vocationalisation, the challenge of inequality and the menace of corruption have all, at various times, attracted vocal official concern. This has typically been framed in ways that underline the essential wisdom of the Party's developmental strategy – drawing attention to problems with local delivery rather than broader systemic dysfunction. However, for defenders of orthodoxy, the capacity of an increasingly educated governing bureaucracy to acknowledge problems and adapt is itself testament to the strength of the 'China model'. With 'meritocracy' at the top, 'experimentation' in the middle and 'democracy' at the bottom, this 'model' itself reflects the legitimating function of educational accomplishment in a society now reconciled to its Confucian roots (Bell 2015).

If the orthodox perspective emphasises the pragmatism of official policy, anti-globalists are alive to the ideological premises that have shaped and informed it. Prominent among these are discourses of competition, economism and scientism that have come to dominate educational debate not only in China, but globally. In this view, the extreme marketisation of Chinese education since the 1990s is largely attributable to the global dominance of 'Washington Consensus' neoliberalism. As an impoverished China emerged from isolation, these discourses both profoundly influenced elites' understanding of the outside world, and dictated the terms of their re-engagement with it. At the same time, other external factors – particularly the 1989 global crisis of the Communist order and the subsequent Soviet collapse – reinforced their perception of the overriding need for political stability and national strength in the face of Western hostility. While official emphasis on the risks of instability may be self-serving, Chinese with memories of mid-twentieth-century conflict have good reasons to fear foreign malevolence and domestic chaos. While recognising that there may be a heavy cost attached to post-Mao China's focus on nurturing 'talent' at the expense of other goals, anti-globalists are inclined to see this as a price imposed ultimately by the 'World System' on 'semiperipheral' societies. China must join that 'System' to beat it.

While ideology permeates orthodox and anti-globalist arguments, practice-oriented scholarship generally cleaves to matter-of-fact objectivity. Exemplified by aid agency-funded research or programmes such as Stanford's 'Rural Education Action Project', this approach has yielded a wealth of invaluable quantitative data, to which we have referred at several points in this volume. Issues of educational access for under-privileged groups – rural children, migrants, girls, ethnic minorities – have been subjected to sophisticated statistical analysis, providing a much-needed corrective to often unreliable or partial official data. Econometrics (a common feature of this paradigm) has been widely applied, sometimes in areas (e.g. 'diffusion of educational innovation' – Sargent 2015) whose susceptibility to this treatment is far from obvious. Abstention from ideological or political critique may signify tacit endorsement or passive acceptance of the *status quo*; the assumption that philosophical, cultural or political considerations are largely irrelevant to the pursuit of educational improvement; or a meliorist conviction that intervention in educational practice is one way to promote progress in other spheres, including politics.

Political or ethical critique may thus be implicit in practice-oriented research, but in what we term critical scholarship, it is explicit and central to the analysis. This approach recognises that educational issues can seldom be reduced to technical considerations, but involve politics, cultural norms and entrenched privilege. In contemporary China, this is emphatically so with respect to the *hukou* system, college entrance quotas, educational funding arrangements, and pervasive marketisation. Fundamental reform in these areas would require tackling the enormous privileges of urban elites, including those of the ruling bureaucracy itself. But as Daniel Bell, advocate of 'the China model', has himself observed, 'central authorities lack sufficient power and motivation to overcome vested interests' (2015, 191).

History is crucial to such analysis, not least because it helps us understand how vested interests came to be 'vested' in the first place. In China, it is hard to sustain an argument that impersonal global forces were more important in this respect than domestic agency. Decisions such as those to prioritise the nurturing of elite 'talent' following the Cultural Revolution; to 'vocationalise' much of the high school sector from the 1980s; to expand fee-based higher education in a late 1990s 'big bang'; or to tie post-Tiananmen regime legitimacy to a virulent strain of nationalism were not simply technocratic answers to objective historical problems. Many were hotly contested within Chinese society and the Communist Party, but none were forced on the country from outside. Although neoliberal discourses originating in the West have certainly been influential, their reception has been selective and partial (see Chapter 9). And to the extent that such discourses have come to frame global debate, China itself has also exercised significant influence – whether by pioneering university league tables, participating in PISA, or contributing massively to the creation of an international higher education market (see Chapter 13).

In post-Mao China, policy on education, as on the provision of other public goods, has been governed by two overriding goals: the maintenance of socio-political 'stability', and the pursuit of prosperity. Stability means determination to preserve Party control, and prosperity supports this by offering various constituencies an enhanced stake in the *status quo* (China's Communists having learnt from the Soviet failure in this respect). Prosperity also enhances the resources at the command of the Party-State, boosting its capacity to project power abroad and to appeal convincingly to nationalist sentiment at home – even while some dominant elites become more transnational in their outlook and interests. The role of the educational ingredient in this formula has been essentially fourfold: generating 'human capital'; promoting loyalty to the Party-State and faith in its developmental model; channelling popular aspiration into politically innocuous, socially atomising competitive impulses; and, related to the latter, supplying the established social and political order with meritocratic legitimacy. Meanwhile, underlying both the developmental strategy itself, and conceptions of education's contribution to it, has been a fundamentally instrumentalist vision of the role of the citizen in relation to the state.

The PISA paradigm – education and national competitiveness

In their overwhelmingly economistic premises, the OECD's PISA tests reflect a similarly instrumentalist conception of education's social function. Since the 1980s, the language of entrepreneurship, human capital, the 'skills agenda' and the 'knowledge economy' has come to pervade the educational vision of the OECD and many developed societies, especially in the 'Anglosphere' and East Asia (Holborow 2015, 106; Park 2013).[2] In *Surpassing Shanghai: An Agenda for American Education Built on the World's Leading Systems* (Tucker 2011) – prepared in close collaboration with the OECD – 'high performance' is defined in terms of students' 'mastery of the kinds of complex knowledge and skills needed in advanced economies as well as their ability to apply that knowledge and those skills to problems with which they are not familiar' (15). A nod to the importance of 'equity' comes with an insistence that it complements and reinforces 'efficiency'. The authors thus assert that 'the most successful education systems ... uniformly invest the most money on the students who have the steepest climb up to reach high standards' (11). As will be clear from our earlier chapters, at no point has post-Mao China remotely fulfilled this condition, yet it is accorded exemplary status. Western observers appear to have found their faculties occluded by Oriental mystique. After visiting one elite Beijing school, former UK Education Secretary (and PISA aficionado) Michael Gove, enthusing over the 'high level' of the students' work, called for Britain 'to implement a cultural revolution just like the one they've had in China' (quoted in Zhao Y. 2014, 22).[3]

The capacity of PISA's methods to accurately assess even the narrow range of competencies they test has been severely questioned, without denting their popularity amongst Anglophone policymakers and commentators, who have found the OECD data – selectively cited – invaluable for whipping up moral panic (Morris 2016, 18). This penchant owes much to an idea of education as the tonic of equitable neoliberalism. If education on its own levels the playing field, offering equal opportunities to all, then prosperity becomes the outcome of individual merit, and poverty the just deserts of individual delinquency. Or, to reverse the equation, if economic productivity is a function of educational achievement, then 'there is no such thing as the "undeserving" rich' (14). An ideology of rugged meritocracy recommends itself to those committed, for whatever reasons, to the virtues of the small state and minimal welfare provision. And by generating a welter of ostensibly objective data on educational effectiveness, PISA offers them the tools to implement this vision; in the words of McKinsey's in-house motto, 'everything can be measured, and what gets measured gets managed' (9).

Even some fierce critics of PISA seemingly choose to fight on this relatively narrow terrain of national competitiveness and economic efficiency. Zhao Yong, author of *Who's Afraid of the Big Bad Dragon: Why China has the best (and worst) education system in the world* (2014), contrasts Chinese 'authoritarianism' with American 'liberal-democratic' values. He compares the current Western panic over Chinese educational 'success' to the equally histrionic responses to the 'Sputnik Shock' of the late 1950s, or to talk in the 1980s of 'Japan as Number 1'. However, his central criticism of the Chinese system is that its 'authoritarian education', essentially unchanged since imperial times, 'failed to cultivate talents to defend against Western aggressions backed by modern technology and the sciences in the 1800s' (4). For Zhao, it is apparently not so much liberal values in themselves, but their proven effectiveness in stimulating skills crucial to economic growth and national strength, that demonstrates their superiority over China's 'authoritarian' model. Even while critiquing Chinese statism, he thus implicitly endorses an essentially statist metric for educational performance.

Demystifying Shanghai

Shanghai's performance in terms of the skills tested by PISA – in reading, Science and Maths – is certainly strong. On almost every measure, the city's students outperform those in the other education systems surveyed, not just scoring more highly overall, but also exhibiting a more equal distribution of scores across the cohort. Moreover, evidence suggests that other prosperous Chinese regions may not be far behind; in 2012, students in Zhejiang Province, who participated unofficially in the PISA tests, scored almost as well as those from Shanghai (Zhao Y. 2014, 119). What, then, do these results signify?

For Zhang Minxuan, China's PISA director and former President of Shanghai Normal University, success results from 'high expectations', 'a prevailing culture [of] rigorous effort', the government's 'zeal and determination to make education a priority' and 'the commitment to eradicate inequality in education' (Cruz 2014; see also Zhao Y. 2014, 187). Cheng Kai-ming credits reforms to curriculum, pedagogy, examinations and educational administration with improving instructional quality, student engagement, homework loads and access (2011).[4] Abolition of 'key schools' and implementation of 'neighbourhood attendence' have, he claims, released 'teachers, parents and students from examination pressure' (37). Shanghai has also shown 'reason and compassion' in integrating migrant children into public schooling (38). Acknowledging the vast shadow education industry, he describes this as 'remedial', while also noting that parents are 'prepared to invest' in various expensive supplementary programmes (34). He pauses briefly to acknowledge 'challenges': 'students are still not given much autonomy, outstanding schools are still rare, and examination pressure still prevails' (40). However, this perfunctory caveat seems designed to buttress the credibility of his otherwise ringing endorsement.[5] He concludes by asserting that 'the spectacular reforms in Shanghai's education system have made possible a no less spectacular economic success' (45).

But what exactly is the relationship between education and economic growth? China's success in imparting basic literacy and numeracy skills to the bulk of its vast population, begun during the Mao era, has been widely credited with laying the foundations for its post-Mao industrial success (see Chapter 2). More recently, the vast expansion of secondary and tertiary education has certainly boosted the range and sophistication of the country's 'human capital'. However, how much of this translates into workplace productivity and economic growth is extremely hard to measure. In the sector where that link is supposedly most direct, vocational education, attempts to create a viable alternative to the academic track have proven highly problematic (see Chapter 10). Meanwhile, labour market liberalisation and higher education expansion since the 1990s have extended and intensified the competition for positional advantage (see Chapters 8, 9 and 12). Crucial for individual display and one-upmanship, but otherwise of little intrinsic value, the stellar test scores of Shanghai's students are therefore like the extravagant plumage of a peacock, if rather less appealing aesthetically and in other respects.

Amongst the consequences of the intensely competitive testing culture, reflected in and accentuated by marketisation (see Chapter 9), has been a significant cramping of the lives of young learners, and of the concept of learning itself. Study for purposes other than exam success is actively discouraged by many teachers and parents; in China as in test-obsessed Korea and Japan, research has indicated comparatively low intrinsic motivation amongst young learners (Park 2013; Kipnis 2011). Where activities extraneous to the examination curriculum are encouraged, for example in music or sport, the main purpose is often still to secure advantage in the competition for places on the next rung up the educational ladder. Hence the growing tendency for China's most privileged parents to send their offspring overseas for a more rounded, less regimented, less intense schooling – thereby, ironically, taking educational competition to a whole new level (see Chapter 13).

From the Party's perspective, the combination of regimentation and competition boosts human capital while simultaneously fostering discipline and political quiescence. Families compelled to invest massive energy and resources in the education of a (usually) singleton child are likely to have little to spare for the distractions of political or social activism. Harnessing a deeply entrenched ideology of meritocracy to the project of catch-up modernisation, the regime has followed a trail blazed by its East Asian neighbours, starting with Meiji Japan. This has involved an overwhelming focus on science and technology alongside a moralising diet of patriotism, 'political education' and (since 1989) military boot camp (see Chapter 6). Tapping deep reservoirs of nationalist sentiment, the Party has appealed to folk memories of 'humiliation' at the hands of assorted imperialists. Meanwhile, like other authoritarian East Asian regimes (such as Singapore's), it has sponsored a selective revival of Confucian learning, positing a hierarchically ordered polity modeled on the patriarchal family.

This rehabilitation of Confucian familism is related to other features of post-Mao (or, more accurately, post-1992) China: labour market reform, SOE restructuring, and the erosion or dismantling of cradle-to-grave welfare for many urban workers. Despite efforts since the Hu–Wen administration (2002–12) to construct a minimal safety net, publicly financed welfare provision remains very weak. A consequently very high dependence on employment for access to key goods such as healthcare and pensions is something China today shares with its East Asian neighbours. The weakness of public support compels reliance on the family for security. Entrenched expectations of filial commitment to the care of elderly relatives legitimise state parsimony, making a Confucian virtue of a necessity. The ranking or sorting function of schooling thus assumes heightened importance not just for students themselves, but also for their entire families. This is especially so when the system affords few second chances, and the college entrance examination is treated as a once-for-all rite of passage, branding one for life as a success or a failure. The resulting backwash effect, extending right down the educational ladder to early childhood, fuels intense competitiveness and disdain for a vocational track that disbars students from careers conferring real social status and material security (see Chapter 10).

Confucian tradition, as well as economic necessity, accentuates the meritocratic mystique surrounding competitive public examinations in ways that shape or constrain official action. As Kipnis observes (2011), the relationship between 'educational desire' and 'governance' is not all one-way: the importance popularly attached to education (for examination preparation) as well as the top-down cadre evaluation system to some extent compels officials to display commitment to expanding access and improving quality. However, official responsiveness to the aspirations of different social constituencies has varied widely. On the one hand, a consistent emphasis on the role of urban 'key point' institutions in supplying the state with elite 'talent' has primed the system for intense competition. Meanwhile, the pattern of economic growth, especially since the 1990s, has fuelled the rapid rise of an educationally demanding urban middle class whose disenchantment would pose a particular threat to regime stability.

China's *hukou* system of household registrations has enabled the Party to cater separately to the interests of different social segments – rural peasants, public sector workers, educated urbanites, 'minority' ethnic groups – thus minimising the risk that they will coalesce to challenge the *status quo* (see Wright 2010). Ironically, given the pervasive rhetoric of 'one China' patriotism, this has institutionalised a fragmented citizenship affording radically differentiated access to education. Cheng's assertion that Shanghai has shown 'reason and compassion' in integrating the children of rural migrants into its schooling system is grossly false; schools there and in other major cities often operate 'apartheid' models, segregating migrant children from 'locals' (Lan 2014; see Chapter 9). The central government has acknowledged the resulting tensions and called for more inclusive approaches, but its actions have so far not matched its rhetoric. The fact that thousands of migrant children are still excluded from local secondary schools, or leave them to prepare for high school entrance exams in their 'home' provinces, also significantly skews Shanghai's PISA performance.

Meanwhile, quite apart from issues of equity, policymakers and academics have been concerned that the education system is not effectively nurturing the innovative and creative talent deemed essential for economic and strategic purposes. As we noted in Chapter 6, *suzhi jiaoyu* (quality education) discourse has echoed concerns in neighbouring East Asian countries that highly standardised education systems cannot deliver the 'skills' required by 'knowledge economies'.[6] Such anxieties informed China's 2001 curriculum reforms, as well as the 2020 educational 'framework' document (*Gangyao*) promulgated in 2010. Attempts have been made to reduce the burden of homework and ratchet down competitiveness, with the aim of giving students the space to explore, reflect and pursue broader interests. Whatever distant observers may think of it, many Chinese officials, educationalists and parents are thus far from satisfied with a system in which success depends on the competitive investment of 'time plus sweat' (Yang Dongping, quoted in Zhao Y. 2014, 128).

Cheng suggests that such dissatisfaction betokens a healthy commitment to further improvement – but in China, as in Korea and Japan, attempts to reduce educational intensity run up against the reality of largely unreformed examination systems (as well as labour markets and welfare arrangements). Reductions to the length of the school day or to homework burdens thus drive educational demand into the private or 'shadow' sector (see Chapter 9). Zhao Yong explains this with reference to crowd psychology, writing of the 'prisoners' dilemma' (2014, 154–7), but it also reflects contradictions arising from an authoritarian political agenda. Combined with state-mandated curricula, state-centred patriotism and a culture of the teacher-as-omniscient-autocrat, ranking and sorting through public examinations is a crucial tool of social control. For political purposes, the regime expects students to compete to conform, but for economic purposes it hopes they will innovate and question. These objectives are rather hard to reconcile, as Bertrand Russell argued when he wrote, 'there can be no agreement between those who regard education as a means of instilling certain definite beliefs, and those who think that it should produce the power of independent judgement' (1932, viii).

Shanghai, then, is by no means the educational Shangri-La of PISA propaganda. The city's schooling system, like that of China more widely, remains riddled with institutionalised inequalities. Contrary to Cheng's claims, key point schools have not been abolished (except in name), examination pressure is as intense as ever, and a vast 'shadow education' industry distorts the learning process and drains family resources (see Chapters 8 and 9). The link between wealth and access to the best publicly funded schools persists, while many children of migrants remain effectively excluded from urban schools, or confined to segregated, second-class 'concessions' within them (Lan 2014). To the extent that there is a connection between Shanghai's prosperity and its students' test performance, it is more accurate to argue that the former causes the latter than the reverse. There are certainly far worse places in the world to go to school, but this is not a model that others need rush to replicate. Indeed, it exemplifies problems endemic to China's education system that many Chinese themselves have come to see as demanding urgent attention.

Rethinking educational 'success': Ends and means

How, then, should we judge educational 'success', in China or elsewhere? The criteria will depend largely on who is judging, their interests and ethical assumptions. This precludes any comprehensive, universal prescription for educational 'effectiveness', but it does not imply relativistic abstention from cross-cultural comparison or critique. Educational traditions, like 'culture' more broadly, are in any case never entirely homogenous, self-contained and discrete. As Amartya Sen points out, arguments between those prioritising discipline and order and others emphasising personal freedom have been a running feature of Western tradition – think of Plato versus Aristotle. As for East Asia, not only do interpretations differ regarding the 'authoritarianism' of Confucian philosophy, but Buddhist thought has always attached 'great importance' to freedom (Sen 1999, 234–5). And cultures can and do change over time; culture is history in the making, not immutable destiny.

Sen's own 'capabilities theory' offers as good a starting point as any for an attempt to conceptualise evaluative criteria. In expounding the importance of various freedoms to 'human flourishing', he distinguishes between their 'intrinsic' and 'instrumental' qualities. This distinction applies very well to education. For example, education's role as a 'positional good' – its role in labelling you as a '"top" or "near the top" sort of person' (Wolf 2002, 251) – is crucial instrumentally in distributing access to jobs and other social opportunities. But the intrinsic value of education lies elsewhere: in the knowledge, skills (social and technical) and values it imparts; and in its capacity to broaden our horizons and expand our humanity. Both intrinsic and instrumental functions are important, but how to balance the two? How can we reward 'merit' without penalising misfortune? And how can we stop credentialism from suffocating the intellectually liberating potential that is intrinsic to education in its fullest sense?

This brings us to a more fundamental dimension of the intrinsic-instrumental distinction, involving the status of students themselves. Are they primarily to be thought of instrumentally, as 'human capital' for national development? Or are they in fact intrinsic to that development, and the enhancement of their capabilities hence the ultimate measure of its success? In other words, are students – or indeed citizens – means to an end, or ends in themselves?[7] The most prominent dissident of early Reform-era China articulated this distinction in 1978, when he wrote: 'We want to be the masters of our own destiny. We do not want to serve as mere tools of dictators with personal ambitions for carrying out modernisation' (quoted in Pantsov 2015, 340).

An instrumentalist vision of population-as-human-capital is by no means unique to Communist China (though only there has it been manifested in a 'One Child Policy'). The Polish philosopher Leszek Kolakowski argued that totalitarianism (and concomitant instrumentalism) is implicit in Marxist idealism, since 'all-embracing "systems" of thought … lead inexorably to all-embracing "systems" of rule' (Judt 2008, 143). However, neoliberal market fundamentalism is similarly 'all-embracing'. Marxists and neoliberals share a linear conception of progress and a tendency to accord their own beliefs the status of revealed truth. Both typically assume the aims of development to be fixed and self-evident, rendering political or ethical critique largely superfluous. The role of education systems is to provide skilled personnel to maximise the efficiency of the established economic order, rather than individuals disposed to question its founding premises. Societies organised on this basis tend towards a technocratic or managerialist ethos, whereby the pursuit of 'efficiency' is secured by monitoring adherence to 'uniform and quantifiable standards' imposed by 'rigid and unchallengeable authorities' (Zhao Y. 2014, 112, 116). In post-Mao China, neoliberalism has thus proved compatible, up to a point, with the instrumentalism already inherent in the Communist system. The resulting hybrid has had profound implications for education.

To take economics first, we have already noted the weak evidential basis for a direct or necessary link between educational expansion and labour productivity; as Alison Wolf writes, 'it is extraordinary how many studies find no relationship between increases in schooling levels and growth' (cited in Morris 2016, 15). But this does not diminish the vital role of education in distributing opportunity within a given socio-economic context. Here the entire drift of post-Mao educational development has been to promote a radical hierarchisation of society: heavy public investment in elite universities alongside prolonged underinvestment in rural basic schooling; the huge and persistent funding gap between key point high schools and their ordinary counterparts; the monetisation of access to the best schools (most blatant in the 1990s and early 2000s); dead-end vocationalisation for the underprivileged; and an examination system hugely favouring formal residents of major cities have all helped make early twenty-first-century China one of the world's most unequal and class-ridden societies.

There was no inevitability about this. Writing on education and state formation in East Asia, Green argues that 'countries struggling to get on the developmental ladder can hardly afford to ignore the lesson that strong states get there first' (2013, 385). But the experience of Japan, South Korea and Taiwan suggests that 'strong states' can pursue equity without impairing their growth prospects (see Chapter 2). Although they shared a fairly instrumental preoccupation with 'human capital' generation, their relatively high and uniform levels of investment in schooling, along with measures to promote standardisation, helped ensure that the benefits of growth were relatively broadly shared. By the late 1980s, senior secondary education was almost universal in South Korea; in China today, urban students on average receive three more years of schooling than their rural counterparts (Economist 2014). Even judged from within the human capital paradigm, China's performance *vis-à-vis* both OECD and BRICS countries (excluding India) was recently rated 'shockingly poor' (Chang *et al.* 2016).

The fact that post-Mao China followed a different path is attributable in the last analysis to historically contingent political choices, rather than to cool 'pragmatic' calculation. As if intent on demonstrating Newton's Third Law, Beijing's scientific socialists reacted against the pseudo-egalitarian extremism of the Mao years by swinging to the opposite extreme of elitist pseudo-meritocracy (see Chapters 2 and 3). The traditional emphasis on supplying a 'quality product' for state service re-emerged triumphant – and has remained so, despite huge quantitative expansion since the 1980s. A shared rhetoric of 'collectivism', 'harmony' and 'stability' thus masks significant differences in China's educational ethos and those of post-war Japan, Korea or Taiwan. Put very simply, the primary bonds of social solidarity in China have been vertical rather than horizontal, and politics has helped to keep them that way. Broad-based growth and educational standardisation in Taiwan and South Korea helped create homogenous, educated and largely middle-class citizenries who ultimately challenged one-party rule. By contrast, the complex compartmentalisation of educational (and other) entitlements in China has kept citizens deeply divided from each other, but united in dependence on the state. Patriotic education has meanwhile served as an ideological adhesive: promoting loyalty to the Party, legitimating its developmental strategy and exhorting selfless devotion to the cause of national rejuvenation.

That emphasis on patriotism and ideological 'correctness' has important implications for capabilities of significance beyond the realm of economics – involving access to information and the freedom to participate actively in shaping communal life. As Sen argues, these capabilities are both instrumentally and intrinsically valuable. In an instrumental sense, societies that allow for an essentially free flow of information, and a significant element of bottom-up political accountability, are likely over the long run to make better collective decisions – or, at least, avoid the kinds of disastrous choices that lead to famines or other man-made catastrophes. But these freedoms are also constitutive of (or intrinsic to) our humanity and dignity. In this respect, as argued in Chapter 6, we need to be attentive not just to the amount or level of education provided, but also to its content. Education is not always intrinsically beneficial and life-enhancing; if it promotes chauvinism, intolerance and a warped worldview, it can corrode social bonds and freedoms that we have reason to value.

However, in calibrating both freedom of information and the ideological content of education, Party leaders have been mindful both of episodes of domestic tumult under Mao and subsequently, and of the experience of Communist regimes elsewhere. Brown argues that educational advance in the USSR proved 'a double-edged sword as far as the longer-term viability of the system was concerned'. So long as Soviet citizens made comparisons over time, and could take satisfaction from rising living standards, the regime was relatively secure. However, once they began to make comparisons 'across space rather than time, a great deal depended on their reference group'. By the 1970s, inhabitants of Soviet Central Asia, looking to Cultural Revolutionary China or impoverished Afghanistan, could be thankful for their own relative comfort and tranquillity. But educated Russians were 'ever more conscious of the freedoms enjoyed by West Europeans and North Americans that were denied to them' (2009, 417). In this context, Gorbachev's dramatic liberalisation, combined as it was with chronic economic stagnation, triggered an uncontrollable collapse of 'democratic centralism'.

The cautionary precedent of Soviet Russia has reinforced the strenuous focus of China's post-Tiananmen leadership on improving the livelihoods of educated urbanites, while keeping a firm lid on political dissent.[8] As noted in Chapter 13, the project of conditioning students – even those who venture overseas – to view the world through a nationalistic lens appears to have been strikingly successful. Rapid economic growth has meant that, for many young city-dwellers, comparisons over time have supported the sense of a relentless Chinese 'rise' towards the 'advanced' and 'developed' status represented by the West and Japan. But how sustainable is this strategy, or the worldview that underpins it?

Notwithstanding widespread pride in China's more elevated global standing, the early twenty-first century has witnessed a growing sense of dissatisfaction, even crisis, regarding the state of the education system. In Chapter 3.4, we discussed Yang Dongping's role in drawing attention to glaring inequalities in the distribution of educational opportunity. We also saw (in Chapter 3.3) how perceptions that the intensity of educational competition was stifling or warping the development of youth extended to the very top of the Party, prompting calls for 'all-round healthy growth' and intensified moral education. Political concern for students' moral fibre and psychological wellbeing has usually been intertwined with anxiety over potential threats to social order and 'stability'. As the current campaign against 'Western ideas' on university campuses illustrates, 'thought reform' remains a stock official response to rumblings of popular discontent. At the same time, official calls for less competitive intensity and more critical thinking and creativity have generally reflected instrumental economic goals (enhancing competitiveness in the 'global knowledge economy') rather than any embrace of the intrinsic virtues of freedom of speech or thought (see Chapter 6).

However, ethical concerns have also prompted broader and more searching critiques. Scholars have increasingly looked for inspiration to pre-modern Chinese thinkers,[9] for many of whom education's role in 'moral transformation', or character formation, was paramount. For example, Zhang (2013) laments how relentless testing fosters 'extreme individualism', while stultifying ideological conformity renders students profoundly atomised and alienated – not only from a sense of community, but also from a consciousness of their own 'unique' inner selves. By way of remedy, she proposes a fusion of Liang Shuming's vision of education as an inward-directed search for enlightenment with a Deweyan emphasis on the cultivation of a 'social self'. She calls for a greater recognition of the 'aesthetic' dimension of learning, and more space for creative use of 'narrative' in the classroom, in order to enable students to 'cultivate a continued sense of self in the radically changing Chinese society' (2). Peng Zhengmei similarly stresses the importance of 'aesthetics', attempting a similar fusion of 'Eastern' and 'Western' ideas, this time involving Wang Fuzhi and Heidegger.[10]

Meanwhile, the quest for concrete manifestations of these or similar ideals has led other commentators (from both the mainland and Taiwan) to Finland, whose education system they present as a mirror image of China's: low intensity; egalitarian; intellectually liberating and student-centred, but nonetheless 'high-achieving' (Chinese fascination with Finnish education, like that of the West with Chinese, having been fuelled by the PISA rankings) (see Chen 2011; Liu 2011). Just as a focus on economic competitiveness has prompted some Western policymakers and commentators to idealise Chinese practice, so concerns over the social and moral ramifications of competitive intensity have led some Chinese to view aspects of the West through a similarly rose-tinted lens. In China as in the West, remoteness and strangeness facilitates the process of constructing exotic educational utopias that can be invoked to criticise domestic systems.

Despite inevitable distortions and over-simplifications, such interest in foreign ideas and systems (and in those of China's own past) reflects a striving by at least some within China to move beyond the hoary paradigm of 'Chinese learning for fundamentals; Western learning for practical use' (*zhong xue wei ti, xi xue wei yong*). Explicitly separating discussion of 'useful' means from that of predetermined ends, that paradigm has framed much debate over education's role in modernisation ever since the late nineteenth century (see Chapters 1 and 2). Ironically, many Western policymakers today seem intent on reversing the formula – importing the authoritarian tools of Chinese (or East Asian) education, while somehow retaining their societies' liberal-democratic 'essence'. This focus on means to the virtual exclusion of ends reflects the widespread dominance of a narrowly 'functionalist epistemology' in educational scholarship (Carney 2009, 66), epitomised by what we have here termed the 'practice-oriented' approach.

Both China's post-Mao educational development, and much Western commentary on it, bears out the observation of a former President of the University of Chicago: 'industrialisation seems to charm people into thinking that the prime aim of life and hence of education is the development of industrial power' (quoted in Wolf 2002, 256). But industrial power is of value only in so far as it serves to enhance what Sen calls our 'capabilities' or 'freedoms'. From the vantage point of Japan – the prism through which Chinese visions of modernity have so often been refracted – the mid-twentieth century philosopher Watsuji Tetsuro wrote, 'economic organization is an inter-human ethical organization (*jinrin soshiki*) mediated by goods,' aiming not at 'the sating of desires in itself, but rather inter-human ethical unity through the sating of desires' (quoted in Sevilla 2016, 16). Education's role in creating a sense of identity, values and citizenship was crucial to that 'ethical unity', but for Watsuji its ultimate goal was not the moulding of blindly obedient footsoldiers, but the promotion of 'our self-awareness as individuals and human beings' (Sevilla 2016, 18). The 'skills' of critical thinking or creativity were thus important not solely or primarily for their 'problem-solving' economic utility, but for equipping us to critique the very frameworks within which 'problems' are defined.

The political agenda of education

Philosophical talk of 'enlightenment', 'aesthetics', or 'self-awareness' is all very well for urban intellectuals, but can it realistically form the basis for the educational agenda of a still semi-industrialised and 'developing' society? Do the toiling masses have time or leisure for such luxuries? As we saw in Chapter 9, many migrant workers and rural residents striving to secure an off-the-farm future for their children have tended to favour schooling that is especially relentless in its test-preparatory focus. Attempts to reduce the pressure of selective testing have if anything been least popular amongst such groups, since other means of allocating school places – through more strictly enforced 'zoning' rules, for example – threaten to close off opportunities for those too poor to move within the appropriate 'zone'. And reductions in class hours or restrictions on homework setting, to the extent that they are observed, tend to divert the competitive impulse into the private sector, fuelling an explosion in 'shadow education' that further disadvantages those least able to pay.

However, these observations do not warrant dismissing ethical critiques of the extreme forms that credentialism and competition have taken in contemporary

China, or seeing their implications as unrealistic or unaffordable. To quote Wolf again, 'our recent forebears, living in significantly poorer times, were occupied above all with the cultural, moral and intellectual purposes of education', to ignore which is to 'impoverish ourselves' (2002, 254). Lack of resources is hardly a problem for a state that, today, can finance the establishment of the Asian Infrastructure Investment Bank or ambitious reclamation projects in the South China Sea. But even when China was indubitably poor, in the early post-Mao years, it was not poverty that dictated the espousal of an elitist and instrumentalist vision of education.

The chief obstacles to reconceptualising and remodelling educational provision have been institutional and political. Inequality and credentialism were hardwired into the education system from the very beginning of the Reform era, with the prioritisation of investment in urban key point schools and key universities, the reinstatement of competitive entrance examinations to determine access to them, and radical decentralisation of responsibility for funding and administering other institutions. The chief beneficiaries of these policies were urbanites, particularly the residents of major metropolitan centres, who included all the most powerful and well-connected members of the Communist elite. With liberalisation of the urban labour market in the 1990s, expansion of higher education, and the substantial marketisation of schooling, these groups were then able rapidly to monetise their educational privileges, transforming themselves into a new middle class. By the early twenty-first century, the relatively classless society of the late 1970s had thus become highly stratified, with socio-economic and political elites deeply invested in an unequal and fragmented system of educational provision.

As Andrew Walder has observed, one advantage that Chinese reformers of the late 1970s held over their Soviet counterparts of the time was the relative weakness, thanks to the Cultural Revolution, of an entrenched *nomenklatura* with a vested interest in preserving the status quo.[11] There was thus a relatively broad constituency for radical reform, or at least a relatively weak constituency opposing it. The entrepreneurial dynamism that reform unleashed, first in the countryside, and later in the cities, brought improvements in living standards for millions that buttressed the regime's performance legitimacy. But the distribution of the resulting benefits today presents challenges for advocates of redistributive economic, social or educational reform, of a kind that their predecessors forty years ago did not face. The 'ossification' of the post-Mao socio-economic order means that the interests not just of a *nomenklatura*, but of a 250-million strong middle class, stand in their way (Xiang and Shen 2009, 513).

The patent challenge of inequality combined with the political difficulty of tackling it help explain the rise in contemporary China of an ideology akin to what historians of modern Germany have termed 'social imperialism',[12] involving the diversion of frustrations related to the domestic social and political situation into externally directed projects of national aggrandisement (see Vickers 2009a). Since the early 2000s, central policymakers have certainly sought to mandate a greater standardisation of educational provision, and have devoted increased resources to this end – but they have fought shy of confronting the extreme inequalities already embedded in the system. Meanwhile, the pervasive rhetoric of nationalism and an increasingly confrontational foreign policy encourage Chinese of all classes to rally to the flag, and to locate the ultimate source of their frustrations in an unequal or unjust international order. Translated to the international arena, the ethos of meritocratic competition pervading domestic society shades into a Darwinist vision of a global order in which a resurgent China must compete for recognition and influence.

But while it takes a particularly extreme form there, the combination of rising domestic inequality and nationalist populism is far from unique to the contemporary People's Republic. Education alone – *pace* the neoliberal missionaries of the OECD – cannot provide the technical fix for such societal ills. Meritocracy is a noble ideal but a deeply flawed one, whose flaws are exacerbated when linked to discourses of 'quality' (again with Darwinist undertones) that denigrate the less educated or less fortunate. At several points in this volume, we have indicated links between the intensity of educational competition, the structuring of the labour market, and the extent of public welfare provision. Investigating the precise nature of those connections is a crucial task for further research. It nonetheless seems safe to say that tempering the extremes of 'meritocratic' competition requires a system for delivering basic entitlements that can ensure reasonable dignity and security for all citizens. In this respect, there is as much to be learnt from post-Mao China's failures as from its successes. Explaining those failures and addressing them is, in the final analysis, more a matter of politics than of technocratic adjustment.

Notes

1 The allusion here is to the title of a 2016 BBC documentary: *Chinese School: Are our kids tough enough?*
2 By contrast, Morris notes that 'German policymakers view schooling in East Asia as an educational dystopia', seeing high test scores as the result of cramming, intense pressure on pupils, excessive testing and so forth (2016, 11).
3 Intriguingly, Gove's boss, Prime Minister David Cameron, allegedly described him as 'a bit of a Maoist' – with reference to his belief in the efficacy of 'creative destruction' (according to the memoirs of David Laws, a former cabinet colleague).
4 In the Tucker volume, Cheng does not acknowledge his personal relationship with Zhang Minxuan (he was his doctoral supervisor).
5 A strategy that Auld and Morris have identified as characteristic of the 'cluster' of think-tanks, consultants and global agencies that have made a business out of trawling cross-national tests of pupil performance for examples of 'best practice' that can be marketed to 'poor-performing' nations or systems (Auld and Morris 2016).
6 Concerns rejected by Park (2013), who argues that evidence for weak 'creativity' amongst Korean or Japanese students is lacking.
7 To the extent that they are conceived as tools to be valued in terms of their usefulness to the state or the market, the ranking and sorting function of education may assume greater paramountcy.

8 Pantsov tells us that, to the end of his life, Deng Xiaoping 'characterised Gorbachev with just two words: "very stupid" (*hen chun*)' (2015, 431).
9 Tobin et al (2009) also discuss this Chinese turn towards traditional educational thought in the concluding chapter of their book.
10 The reference here is to a paper presented by Peng Zhengmei of East China Normal University at a symposium hosted by Kyushu University's Department of Education in June 2016.
11 This refers to a paper delivered by Walder at Kyushu University in December 2015. See also his 2015 book, *China under Mao*.
12 The classic, though much-disputed, exposition of this thesis being Hans-Ulrich Wehler's *Bismarck und der Imperialismus* (1969).

Bibliography

NBS (National Bureau of Statistics)

Several references are made in the text (especially when providing sources for graphs or tables) to the *China Educational Statistics Yearbook* (*Zhongguo Jiaoyu Tongji Nianjian*) published by the *National Bureau of Statistics* (*Guojia Tongji Ju*) in Beijing. In recent years, these have been provided as an interactive digital database, accessible through Chinese university libraries (a different, less user-friendly version is openly accessible online).

IED (Important Educational Documents)

Official Chinese government documents from the collection *Zhonghua Renmin Gongheguo Zhongyao Jiaoyu Wenxian* (*Important Educational Documents of the People's Republic of China*), referred to in the text as IED:

IED 144: Education Ministry (1952). *You'er yuan zhanxing guicheng cao'an* (Temporary regulations for kindergartens). 18 March.

IED 578: Education Ministry, Health Ministry and Interior Ministry (1956). *Guanyu tuoer-suo you'eryuan ji ge wenti de lianhe tongzhi* (Joint notice on several problems relating to nurseries and kindergartens). 23 February.

IED 1573: Deng Xiaoping (1977). *zunzhong rencai, zunzhong zhishi* ('Respect talented personnel, respect knowledge'). 24 May.

IED 1588: MOE (1977). *Jiaoyubu guanyu jiaqiang zhongxiaoxue zaizhi jiaoshi peixun gongzuo de yijian* (Opinion of the MOE on strengthening the in-service training of primary and secondary teachers). 10 December.

IED 1607: Deng Xiaoping (1978). *Deng Xiaoping tongzhi zai quanguo jiaoyu gongzuo huiyi shang de jianghua* (Speech of Comrade Deng Xiaoping at the National Education Work Conference). 22 April.

IED 1620: Liu Xiyao (1978). *Liu Xiyao tongzhi zai quanguo jiaoyu gongzuo huiyi shang de zongjie* (Plenary address of Comrade Liu Xiyao to the National Education Work Conference). 16 May.

IED 1739: Politburo, State Council (1979). *Zhuan fa 'Quan Guo tuo you gongzuo huiyi jiyao' de tongzhi* (Notice of the release of a summary of the meeting of the National Work Conference on Early Childhood Education and Care). 11 October.

IED 1748: Education Ministry etc. (1979). *Guanyu bianjingxian (qi) shi zhongxiaoxue minban jioashi zhuan gongban jiaoshi de tongzhi* (Notice on the transfer from *minban*

to *gongban* status of primary and secondary teachers working in counties (banners) and cities in border regions). 31 October.
IED 1756: Education Ministry (1979). *Jiaoyu bu, Caizheng bu, Guojia laodong zongju guanyu zai quanguo putong zhongxue he xiaoxue gongban jiaoshi zhong shixing banzhuren jinzhan de tongzhi* (Notice from the Education Ministry, Finance Ministry and Central Labour Bureau regarding supplementary allowances for regular (*gongban*) class teachers in ordinary junior secondary and primary schools across the country). 27 November.
IED 1757: Education Ministry (1979). *Guanyu gaodeng xuexiao jiaoshi zhize ji kaohe de zanxing guiding* (Provisional regulations regarding the duties and evaluation of teachers in tertiary colleges). 27 November.
IED 1813: Education Ministry (1980). *Guanyu zhongyang shujichu dui jiaoyu gongzuo zhishi jingsheng de chuanda yaodian* (Key points of the Politburo Notice on the Guiding Spirit of Education Work). 27 May.
IED 1862: Education Ministry (1980). *Guanyu yin fa zhongdeng shifan xuexiao jaoxue jihua shixing cao'an he you'er shifan xuexiao jiaoxue jihua shixing cao'an tongzhi* (Notice on the issuance of trial proposals on the planning of secondary-level normal schools and training schools for kindergarten teachers). 14 October.
IED 1907: MOE (1981). *Quanrizhi liunianzhi zhongdian zhongxue jiaoxue jihua shixing cao'an* (Trial proposals regarding the teaching plan for full-time, six-year key point secondary schools), 18 January.
IED 1908: Yang Xiufeng (1981). *Zengjia jiaoyu jingfei zai guomin jingji zhong de bizhong, gaibian woguo jiaoyu de luohuo zhuangkuang* ('Increase education spending as a proportion of our GDP, change the situation of our national educational backwardness'). 26 February.
IED 1915: Education Ministry (1981). *Jiaoyu bu guanyu zai chengshi shixing liu nian zhi xiaoxue wenti de yijian* (Opinion on implementing the six-year system of primary schooling in cities). 13 March.
IED 1921: Education Ministry (1981). *Jiaoyu bu guanyu nida jiaoyu shiye 'liu wu' jihua he shinian shexiang xuyao yanjiu de wenti de tongzhi* (Notice on the planning of education work for the sixth five-year plan and on research into the requirements for the 10-year tentative plan). 7 April.
IED 1926: Education Ministry (1981). *Jiaoyu bu banfa quanrizhi liu nian zhi zhongxian zhongxue jiaoxue jihua shixing cao'an, quanrizhi wu nian zhi zhongxue jiaoxue jihua shixing cao'an de xiuding yijian de tongzhi* (Education Ministry Notice regarding the promulgation of the experimental draft of the teaching plan for full-time, six-year, key-point junior secondary schools, and of the experimental draft of the teaching plan for full-time, five-year junior secondary schools). 17 April.
IED 1935: State Council (1981). *Caizheng bu, jiaoyu bu, waijiao bu guanyu songqing shenpi shijie yinhang jiaoyu xiangmu daikuan xieding de baogao* (Report from the Ministries of Finance, Education and Foreign Affairs on the agreement regarding approval of a loan from the World Bank Education Programme). 14 May.
IED 1941: Central Committee of the Communist Party of China (1981). *Guanyu jiandang yilai dang de ruogan lishi wenti'de jueyi* (Decision on certain matters in the history of our Party since the establishment of the state). 27 June.
IED 1980: State Council (1981). *Zhuanfa jiaoyubu 'guanyu zengjia zhongxiaoxue minban jiaoshi buzhufei de banfa'* (Circulating the notice of the MOE: 'Methods for increasing supplementary payments to *minban* primary and secondary teachers'). 7 October.

IED 2021: Chen Yun (1982). *Guanyu gaishan zhongnian zhishifenzi daiyu wenti de yijian* (Opinion on resolving [improving] problems with the livelihood [remuneration] of middle-aged intellectuals). 1 July.

IED 2051: Zhao Ziyang (1982). *Guanyu di liu ge wu nian jihua de baogao* (Report [to the 5th meeting of the 5th National People's Congress] on the 6th Five Year Plan). 30 November.

IED 2055: People's Daily (1982). *Zhonghua Renmin Gongheguo guomin jingji he shehui fazhan di liu ge wu nian jihua (1981–1985)* (Sixth five-year plan for the development of the people's economy and society of the People's Republic of China). 13 December.

IED 2087: Central Committee of the Communist Party of China & State Council (1983). *Guanyu jiaqiang he gaige nongcun xuexiao jiaoyu ruogan wenti de tongzhi* (Notice on problems relating to the strengthening and improvement of rural education). 6 May.

IED 2134: Deng Xiaoping (1983). *Sixiang zhanxian bu neng gao jingshen wuran* ('There must be no spiritual pollution in the ideological field'). 12 October.

IED 2274: Deng Xiaoping (1985). *Gao zichan jieji ziyouhua jiu shi zou ziben zhuyi daolu* ('Pursuing bourgeois liberalization means following the capitalist road'). 6 May.

IED 2285: Central Committee of the Communist Party of China (1985). *Guanyu jaoyu tizhi gaige de jueding* (Decision on the reform of the education system). 27 May.

IED 2496: Central Committee of the Communist Party of China (1986). *Guanyu shishi 'yiwu jiaoyu fa' ruogan wenti yijian de tongzhi* (Notice of opinions on problems relating to the implemention of the 'Compulsory Education Law'). 11 September.

IED 2526: *Renmin Jiaoyu* (*People's Education*) (1986). *Xiang pingdu xuexi shenme* (What we can learn from Pingdu). October issue.

IED 2561: Deng Xiaoping (1986). *Qizhi xianming de fandui zichanjieji ziyouhua* ('Raising the banner of opposition to bourgeois liberalisation'). 30 December.

IED 2606: SEC, etc. (1987). *'Hebeisheng nongcun jiaoyu gaige shiyanqu gongzuo huiyi jiyao' de tongzhi* (Notice regarding the work conference on the Hebei Province experimental district for rural educational reform). 24 May.

IED 2656: He Dongchang (1987). *Nongcun jiaoyu fangxiang yao zhuangbian* (The direction of rural education must change). 4 September.

IED 2735: Li Peng (1988). *Zhengfu gongzuo baogao* (Government Work Report). 25 March.

IED 2789: He Dongchang (1988). *Zai guojia jiaowei shishi 'liaoyuanjihua' gongzuo huiyi shang de jianghua* (Speech at the SEC work conference on the implementation of the 'Prairie Fire Plan'). 29 August.

IED 2796: Deng Xiaoping (1988). *Cong zhanlue gaodu kaolu jiaoyu wenti* (Considering the education problem from the perspective of grand strategy). 12 September.

IED 2851: Deng Xiaoping (1989). *Shinian zuida shiwu shi zai jiaoyu fangmian* (The greatest mistake of the decade is in the area of education). 23 March.

IED 2869: *Zhongguojiaoyubao* [*Chinese Education* (newspaper)] (1989). *Fansi zuida shiwu jiaqiang sixiang jiaoyu* (Reflecting on the 'greatest mistake' and strengthening thought education). 24 June.

IED 2872: SEC (1989). *Guanyu yinfa Jiang Zemin shuji qi yue yi ri zhongyao pishi de tongzhi* (Notice on the important instructions issued by General Secretary Jiang Zemin on 1 July). 8 July.

IED 2873: SEC (1989). *Guanyu zai xiaoxuesheng zhong kaizhan 'reai zhongguo gongchandang reai shehuizhuyiguojia reai zhongguorenminjiefangjun' jiaoyu huodong de tongzhi* (Notice on the educational campaign amongst primary and secondary students to 'Love the Chinese Communist Party, Love the Socialist Motherland, Love the Chinese People's Liberation Army'). 20 July.

IED 2881: SEC (1989). *Guanyu jiaqiang dui shehui xueke waiguo xuezhe laihuajiangxue guanli de tongzhi* (Notice on strengthening the management of foreign scholars in the social sciences who come to China to lecture). 4 September.
IED 2902: Li Peng (1989). *Zhonguo jiaoyu qingkuang he jiaoyu guandian* (China's educational situation and educational outlook). 30 November.
IED 2919: Li Tieying (1990). *Zai guojiajiaowei 1990 nian gongzuo huiyi de jianghua* (Speech at the 1990 work conference of the SEC). 16 January.
IED 2952: SEC (1990). *Guanyu zhuanfa leifeng xiaoxue 'jianchi yong leifeng jingshen peiyu "siyou" xinren jingyan cailiao' de tongzhi* (Notice on promulgating the trial programme of the Lei Feng Primary School to develop the programme: 'Firmly grasp the Lei Feng spirit to nurture new people with the "four properties"'. 12 March.
IED 2956: SEC (1990). *Guanyu yi yapian zhanzheng 150 zhounian weiti dui zhongxiaoxuesheng jinxing aiguozhuyi jiaoyu de tonghzi* (Notice on using the 150th anniversary of the Opium War to promote patriotic education amongst primary and secondary students). 20 March.
IED 2972: Jang Zemin (1990). *Aiguo zhuyi he woguo zhishifenzi de shiming* (Patriotism and the mission of our nation's intellectuals). 3 May.
IED 2998: National People's Congress (1990). *Zhonghua renmin gongheguo guoqi fa* (National Flag Law of the People's Republic of China). 28 June.
IED 3024: SEC, etc. (1990). *Guanyu jieshou anpai Beijing daxue fudan daxue 90ji xinsheng dao jundui yuanxiao jinxing junzheng xunlian de tonghzi* (Notice on arranging for the 1990 cohort of new students at Peking and Fudan Universities to undertake military training at army colleges). 25 August.
IED 3029: SEC (1990). *Gaodeng xuexaio xiaoyuan zhixu guanli ruogan guiding* (Rules on maintaining order on campus in the tertiary education sector). 18 September.
IED 3059: SEC, etc. (1990). *Guanyu zuzhi zhongdeng xuexiao gangbu he jiaoshi xuexi shehuizhuyi lilun de tongzhi* (Notice on organising the study of socialist theory amongst cadres and teachers in secondary schools). 30 November.
IED 3080: Foreign Experts Bureau and Education Ministry (1990). *Guanyu gaijin he jiaqiang pinyong waiguo shehui kexue zhuanjia gongzuo de tongzhi* (Notice on improving and strengthening the work of employing foreign experts in the social sciences). 30 December.
IED 3101: SEC (1991). *Guanyu yinfa lingdao tongzhi zai quanguo zhiye jishu jiaoyu gongzuo huiyi shang jianghua de tongzhi* (Notice on the speeches of leading comrades at the national work conference on vocational and technical education). 25 January.
IED 3126: Jiang Zemin (1991). *Jiu jianchi dui qingshaonian jinxing jinxiandaishi he guoqing jaiyu wenti zhi Li Tieying He Dongchang de xin* (Letter to Li Tieying and He Dongchang on determinedly promoting education in modern history and the national situation amongst young people). 9 March.
IED 3138: People's Daily (1991). *Zhonghua Renmin Gongheguo: guomin jingji he shehui fazhan shi nian guihua he di ba ge wu nian jihua gangyao* (PRC: Framework for the ten-year programme for national economic and social development and for the 8th Five-Year Plan) [approved at the 4th session of the 7th National People's Congress]. 16 April.
IED 3221: State Council (1991). *Guanyu dali fazhan zhiye jishu jiaoyu de jueding* (Decision on strongly developing vocational and technical education). 17 October.
IED 3258: SEC (1992). *Quanguo jiaoyu hangye 10 nian guihua he 'bawu' jihua yaodian* (Main points of the ten-year plan to develop educational enterprise and the 8th Five Year Plan). 16 January.

IED 3266: Deng Xiaoping (1992). *Zai Wuchang Shenzhen Zhuhai Shanghai dengdi de tanhua yaodian* (Main points of conversations in Wuchang, Shenzhen, Zhuhai, Shanghai and other places). 18 January.

IED 3365: SEC, etc. (1992). *Guanyu jinyibu gaishan he jiaqiang minban jiaoshi gongzuo ruogan wenti de yijian* (Opinion on further strengthening and improving various problems relating to the work of *minban* teachers). 6 August.

IED 3447: Zhu Kaixuan (1993). *Zai guojia jiaowei 1993 nian gongzuo huiyi shang de baogao* (Report at the 1993 work conference of the SEC). 11 January.

IED 3467: Central Committee of the Communist Party of China & State Council (1993). *Zhongguo jiaoyu gaige he fazhan gangyao* (Framework for the reform and development of Chinese education). 13 February.

IED 3495: SEC (1993). *Guanyu zhuanfa quanguo zhengxie jiaoyu wenhua weiyuanhui 'guanyu Beijingshi Liaoningsheng Sichuansheng zhiye jishu jiaoyu'de diaocha baogao de tongzhi* (Notice on promulgating the CPPCC Education and Culture Committee's report on an investigation of vocational and technical education in Beijing, Liaoning and Sichuan). 1 April.

IED 3548: SEC (1993). *Minban gaodeng xuexiao shezhi zanxing guiding* (Temporary rules on the establishment of *minban* tertiary colleges). 17 August.

IED 3570: National People's Congress (1993). *Zhonghua renmin gongheguo jiaoshifa* (Teachers' Law of the People's Republic of China). 31 October.

IED 3574: State Council (1993). *Guanyu caiqu youli cuoshi xunsu jiejue tuoqian jiaoshi gongzi wenyi de tongzhi* (Notice on effective measures to rapidly solve the problem of arrears in the payment of teachers' salaries). 16 November.

IED 3575: SEC (1994). *Guanyu quxiao zhongxiaoxue luanshoufei xiangmu de tongzhi* (Notice on eliminating the untrammelled charging of fees in primary and secondary education). 21 November.

IED 3642: SEC (1994). *Zhongguo jiaoyu guoji jiaoliu xiehui zhangcheng* (Constitution of the Chinese Association for International Educational Exchange). May.

IED 3654: Li Lanqing (1994). *Zai quanguo jiaoyu gongzuo huiyi shang de zongjie jianghua* (Plenary speech at the National Education Work Conference). 6 June.

IED 3661: State Council (1994). *Guanyu 'zhongguo jiaoyu gaige he fazhan gangyao' de shishi yijian* (Opinions on the implementation of the 'Framework for the reform and development of Chinese education'). 3 July.

IED 3667: SEC (1994). *Guanyu yinfa 'shixing xin gongshi dui quanrizhi xiaoxue, chujizhongxue kecheng (jiaoxue) jihua jinxing tiaozheng de yijian' he 'shishi xin gongshizhi dui gaozhong jiaoxue jihua jinxing tiaozheng de yijian' de tongzhi* (Opinions on promulgating the 'new working hours and adjusted teaching plans for the all-day primary and junior secondary curriculum' and 'implementing the new working hours and adjusted teaching plans for the senior high school curriculum'). 5 July.

IED 3680: Central Committee of the Communist Party of China (1994). *Aiguo zhuyi jiaoyu shishi gangyao* (Framework for implementing patriotic education). 23 August.

IED 3724: Zhu Kaixuan (1994). *Jiji tuijin gaodeng jaoyu tizhi gaige* (Actively promoting reform of the higher education system). 16 December.

IED 3774: Zhu Kaixuan (1995). *Zai bufen sheng saomang gongzuo zuotanhui shang de jianghua* (Speech at the inter-provincial work conference on eradicating illiteracy). 24 February.

IED 3796: SEC (1995). *Guanyu yi kangri zhanzheng he shijie fanfaxisi zhanzheng shengli 50 zhounian wei ti shenru jinxing aiguo zhuyi jiaoyu de tongzhi* (Notice on using the occasion of the 50th anniversary of the War of Resistance against Japan and the World Anti-Fascist War to deepen patriotic education). 27 March.

IED 3905: SEC (1995). *Guanyu shishi 'liaoyuan jihua bai qian wan' gongcheng de yijian* (Opinion on implementing the 'Prairie Fire one hundred, one thousand, ten thousand' plan). 7 December.
IED 3929: SEC (1996). *Guanyu yi 1996 nian woguo zhengfu huifu dui xianggang xingshi zhuquan weiti dui zhongxiaoxue shenru jinxing aiguo zhuyi jiaoyu de tongzhi* (Notice on using the occasion of the 1997 resumption of the exercise of national sovereignty over Hong Kong to deepen patriotic education amongst primary and secondary students). 11 January.
IED 3936: Liu Bin (1996). *Zai guojia jiaowei 1996 nian jiaoyu gongzuo huiyi shang de jianghua* (Speech at the 1996 work conference of the SEC). 6 February.
IED 3965: SEC (1996). *Guanyu yinfa 'chengzhen liudong renkou zhong shiling ertong shaonian jiuxue banfa (shixing)' de han* (Letter on [trial] methods for coping with the education of school-age children of migrant workers in urban areas). 2 April.
IED 3970: SEC (1996). *Guanyu yinfa 'quanguo jiaoyu shiye "jiuwu" jihua he 2010 nian fazhan guihua' de tongzhi* (On promulgating the 9th Five Year Plan and 2010 developmental strategy for educational enterprise). 10 April.
IED 4049: SEC, etc. (1996). *Guanyu zai bufen shenghshi zhongxiaoxue kaizhan minzu changshi jiaoyu huodong shidian de shishi yijian* (Opinion on implementing pilot projects for developing national general knowledge at primary and secondary level in some provinces and cities). 18 September.
IED 4050: Li Peng (1997). *Jiaqiang fupin gongjian lidu jinkuai jiejue qunzhong wenbao wenti* (Intensifying the assault on poverty and rapidly solving problems with feeding and clothing the masses). 23 September.
IED 4204: SEC, etc. (1997). *Quanguo dianhua jiaoyu 'jiuwu' jihua* (National plan for digital education in the context of the Ninth Five Year Plan). 24 April.
IED 4209: Zhu Kaixuan (1997). *Dui dangqian ruogan jiaoyu redian wenti de zhishi* (Recognising several hot topics in education today). 28 April.
IED 3: Zhu Kaixuan (1998). *Zai guojia jiaowei 1998 nian jiaoyu gongzuo huiyi shang de jianghua* (Speech at the 1998 National Education Work Conference). 16 January.
IED 48: SEC (1998). *Zhongxiaoxue deyu gongzuo guicheng* (Guidelines for primary and secondary moral education). 16 March.
IED 50: SEC (1998). *Guojia Jiaowei, Guojia Jingmaowei, Laodong bu guanyu shixing "Zhiye jiaoyu fa" jiakuai fazhan zhiye jiaoyu de ruogan yijian* (Several opinions from the SEC, State Trade Commission and Labour Ministry on how to implement the [stipulations of the] 'Vocational Education Law' on the rapid development of vocational education). 16 March.
IED 89: Jiang Zemin (in *Renmin Ribao* (*People's Daily*)) (1998). *Jiang Zemin zai qingzhu Beijing daxue jianxiao yi bai zhou nian da hui shang de jianghua* (Speech by Jiang Zemin to commemorate the 100th anniversary of the establishment of Peking University). 4 May.
IED 90: SEC (1998). *Guanyu shenru xuexi Jiang Zemin tongzhi zai qingzhu Beijing daxue jianxiao yibaizhounian dahui shang de zhongyao jianghua jingshen* (Notice on deeply studying the spirit of Comrade Jiang Zemin's address at the meeting to commemorate the 10th anniversary of the establishment of Peking University). 4 May.
IED 119: SEC (1998). *Guanyu jiaqiang putong zhongxue laodong jishu jaoyu guanli de ruogan yijian* (Several opinions on strengthening the management of labour and technical education in regular secondary schools). 10 June.
IED 141: Chen Zhili (1998). *Gaoju Deng Xiaoping lilun weida qizhi, jinyibu jiaqiang gaoxiao dang de jianshe, ba you zhongguo tese shehui zhuyi de gaodeng jiaoyu shiye quanmian tuixiang 21 shiji* (Raise high the great banner of Deng Xiaoping Theory, further strengthen party construction in the higher education sector, comprehensively

take higher education enterprise [in the spirit of] socialism with Chinese characteristics into the 21st century). 4 July.

IED 190: Jiang Zemin (1998). *Chuangxin de guanjian zai rencai, rencai de chengzhang kao jiaoyu* (The key to innovation is talented personnel, and the nurturing of talented personnel depends on education). 24 November.

IED 201: Education Ministry (1998). *Guanyu guowuyuan ge bumen fenliu renyuan ben zhuanke jiaoyu de shishi yijian* (Opinion of the State Council and several departments on the distribution of manpower and the implementation of specialist education). 28 December.

IED 215: Education Ministry, State Planning Commission (1999). *Shixing anxin de guanli moshi he yunxing jizhi juban gaodeng zhiye jishu jiaoyu de shishi yijian* (Opinion on implementing the trial of the new management style and operating mechanism for provision of tertiary vocational and technical education). 11 January.

IED 224: Education Ministry etc. (1999). *Guanyu erpian diqu 'guojia pinkun diqu yiwu jiaoyu gongcheng' xiangmu wancheng qingkuang de huibao* (Notice on the situation regarding completion of the compulsory education plan for second-tier regions and poorer regions). 22 January.

IED 292: Jiang Zemin (1999). *Jiaoyu bixu yi tigao guomin suzhi wei genben zongzhi* (Education must take raising citizens' quality as its fundamental purpose). 15 June.

IED 321: Education Ministry (1999). *Guanyu xuexiao nei youguan qigong wenti de tongzhi* (Notice on problems with *qigong* in schools). 5 July.

IED 395: Central Committee of the Communist Party of China (1999). *Guanyu jiaqiang he gaijin sixiang zhengzhi gongzuo de ruogan yijian* (Several opinions on strengthening and improving work in Thought and Politics). 29 September.

IED 413: Jiang Zemin (in *Renmin Ribao* (*People's Daily*)) (1999). *Jiang Zemin zai Yingguo Jianchao daxue de yanjiang* ('Speech by Jiang Zemin at Britain's Cambridge University'). 22 October.

IED 472: Zhang Baoqing (1999). *Guanyu zhongguo jiaoyu jingfei wenti de huigu yu sikao* (Reflections and thoughts on problems with the funding of education in China).

IED 484: Chen Zhili (2000). *Qieshi jianqing xuesheng guozhong fudan, quanmian tuijin suzhi jiaoyu* (Practical [measures to] relieve students' excessive burdens and comprehensively promoting *suzhi* education). 7 January.

IED 491: State Council (2000). *Guanyu chengli guowuyuan xibu diqu kaifa lingdao xiaozu de jueding* (Decision on establishing the State Council leading group for the *Xibu Da Kaifa* [campaign to 'Open up the West']). 16 January.

IED 513: Jiang Zemin (2000). *Guanyu jiaoyu wenti de tanhua* (Conversations about educational problems). 1 February.

IED 534: Jiang Zemin (2000). *Zai xin de lishi tiaojian xia, women dang ruhe zuodao 'sange dianbiao'* (Faced with new historical conditions, how our Party should achieve the 'Three Represents'). 25 February.

IED 676: Education Ministry (2000). *Guanyu yinfa 'guanyu jiaqiang zhongxiaoxue jiaoshi zhiye daode jianshe de ruogan yijian' de tongzhi* (Several opinions on strengthening the moral construction of the teaching profession at primary and secondary level). 15 August.

Published sources

Adamson, Bob (2004). *China's English: A History of English in Chinese Education.* Hong Kong University Press.

Ako, Tomoko (2009). *Hinsha wo kurau kuni: Chuugoku kakusa shakai kara no keikoku* (The country that devours its poor: A warning from China's divided society). Tokyo: Shinchosha.

Alexander, R. (2000). *Culture and Pedagogy*. Oxford: Blackwell.

Alitto, G. (1979). *The Last Confucian: Liang Shu-ming and the Dilemma of Chinese Modernity*. Berkeley: University of California Press.

Ashton, D., Green, F., James, D. and Sung, J. (1999). *Education and Training for Development: The Political Economy of Skills Formation in East Asian Newly Industrialised Economies*. London: Routledge.

Auld, Euan and Morris, Paul (2016). 'PISA, policy and persuasion: strategies for translating complex conditions into education "best practices"', *Comparative Education* (forthcoming).

Avenell, Simon (2013). 'Beyond mimesis: Japan and the uses of political ideology in Singapore', in Morris, P., Shimazu, N. and Vickers, E. (eds), *Imagining Japan in Post-war East Asia*. Abingdon, Oxon: Routledge.

Bai, H. Q. (2008). '*Gaodeng jiaoyu xuefei zhidu bianqian yanjiu*' ('Changes in higher education tuition policy in China'), *Qinghua Daxue Jiaoyu Yanjiu* (*Tsinghua Journal of Education*), 29(2), 70–76.

Bakken, B. (2000). *The Exemplary Society*. Oxford: Oxford University Press.

Bandurski, David (2011). 'Another charity mess brews in China', *China Media Project*. Hong Kong: Journalism and Media Studies Centre, University of Hong Kong. http://cmp.hku.hk/2011/08/18/15011/ (accessed 4 November 2015).

Bardhan, Pranab (2010). *Awakening Giants: Feet of Clay – Assessing the Economic Rise of China and India*. Princeton, NJ and Oxford: Princeton University Press.

Barmé, Geremie (2000). *In the Red: On Contemporary Chinese Culture*. New York: Columbia University Press.

Bartholemew, James (1989). *The Formation of Science in Japan*. New Haven, CT: Yale University Press.

Baum, Richard (1996). *Burying Mao: Chinese Politics in the Age of Deng Xiaoping*. Princeton, NJ and Oxford: Princeton University Press.

Beijing Chubanshe (2013). *Sheng wu xue* (*Biology*). [Secondary school textbooks, Grades 1–3]. Beijing: *Beijing Chubanshe* (Beijing Publishing Company).

Bell, Daniel A. (2015). *The China Model: Political Meritocracy and the Limits of Democracy*. Princeton, NJ: Princeton University Press.

Bevis, Teresa Brawner (2014). *A History of Higher Education Exchange: China and America*. New York: Routledge.

Bian, Yanjie; Shu, Xiaoling and Logan, John (2001). 'Communist Party membership and regime dynamics in China', *Social Forces*, 79(3), 805–841.

Bjork, Christopher (2011). 'Imagining Japan's "Relaxed Education" curriculum: continuity or change?', in Willis, D. and Rappleye, J. (eds), *Reimagining Japanese Education*. Oxford: Symposium Books, 147–169.

BNU (Beijing Normal University) (2014). *Benke Jiaoyu Shouce* (*Handbook of Undergraduate Education*). Beijing: BNU.

Bo, Yang (1992). *The Ugly Chinaman and the Crisis of Chinese Culture*. Allen and Unwin, translation by Don Cohn and Jing Qing.

Bonnin, Michel (2005). 'A historical assessment of the "Up to the Mountains, Down to the Villages" movement' – Chinese version (*Shang shan xia xiang yundong zai pingjia*), *Shehui xue Yanjiu*, 2005(5), 154–181.

Bray, Mark and Kwok, Percy (2003). 'Demand for private supplementary tutoring: conceptual considerations and socio-economic patterns in Hong Kong', *Economics of Education Review*, 22, 611–620.

Bray, Mark and Lykins, Chad (2012). *Shadow Education: Private Supplementary Tutoring and its Implications for policymakers in Asia.* Hong Kong: Comparative Education Research Centre.

Bray, M., Ding, X. and Huang, P. (2004). *Reducing the Burden on the Poor: Household Costs of Basic Education in Gansu, China.* Hong Kong: Comparative Education Research Centre.

Brock, A. (2009). 'Moving mountains stone by stone: Reforming rural education in China', *International Journal of Educational Development*, 29(5), 454–462.

Brown, Archie (2009). T*he Rise and Fall of Communism.* London: The Bodley Head.

Brown, Kerry (2014). *The New Emperors: Power and the Princelings in China.* New York: Palgrave Macmillan.

Brunstermann, Birgit (2001). 'Sino-German co-operation in the field of vocational training', *China Perspectives*, No. 36, 47–56.

Cain, Peter and Hopkins, Anthony (2016). *British Imperialism.* London: Longman. Third edition.

Cao Ye (2007). '*Woguo zhiye jiaoyu "shuangshi xing" shizide neihan ji fazhan qushi*' ('The meaning of "double-qualified teachers" and their emergence in our national vocational education [system]'), *Jiaoyu Fazhan Yanjiu* (*Educational Development Research*), 10A, 22–26.

Carney, Stephen (2008). 'Learner-centred pedagogy in Tibet: International education reform in a local context', *Comparative Education*, 44(1), 39–55.

Carney, Stephen (2009). 'Negotiating policy in an age of globalization: Exploring educational 'policyscapes' in Denmark, Nepal and China', *Comparative Education Review*, 53(1), 63–88.

Carney, S., Rappleye, J. and Silova, I. (2012). 'Between faith and science: World culture theory and comparative education', *Comparative Education Review*, 56(3), 366–393.

Carnoy, D. (1993). 'Multinationals in a changing world economy: Whither the nation state?' in Castells, S., Carnoy, D., Cohen, S. and Cardoso, F.H., *The New Global Economy in the Information Age.* Pittsburg: Penn State University.

Cave, Peter (2007). *Primary School in Japan.* Abingdon, Oxon: Routledge.

CERNET (2006). 'About CERNET'. http://www.edu.cn/20060111/3170163.shtml (accessed 3 July 2016).

Chamberlain, Basil Hall (1890). *Things Japanese.* London: Trubner and Co.

Chang, Fang *et al.* (2016). 'China's looming human capital crisis: Upper secondary educational attainment rates and the middle income trap', *Stanford Center for International Development*, Working Paper No. 546.

Chase, Michael *et al.* (2015). *China's Incomplete Military Transformation: Assessing the Weaknesses of the People's Liberation Army.* Santa Monica, CA: Rand Corporation.

Chang Wan-ting (2015). *Chuugoku no daigaku gakuseikai ni okeru seijiteki shakaika ni kan suru kenkyuu* (*Research into political socialization through student associations in Chinese universities*). Kyushu University Education Department: MA dissertation.

Chen Daxing and Zhang Yuanyuan (2010). '*Woguo gaoxiao zhaiwuhua jiefanglue tanjiu: jiyu waibu xiangdu de fenxi*' ('An investigation into strategies for liberating China's colleges from growing indebtedness: an analysis of externalities'), *Guojia jiaoyu xingzheng xueyuan xuebao* (*Journal of National Academy of Education Administration*), 2010(5), 53–56.

Chen Guidi and Wu Chuntao (2007). *Will the Boat Sink the Water? The Life of China's Peasants.* New York: PublicAffairs.

Chen, H-C. and Chen X.-F. (2009). '*Guifan yu Biantong: Guojia duli xueyuan zhengce zai Zhejiang Sheng de shishi anlie yanjiu*' ('Policy regulation and policy accommodation: Implementation of the National Independent College Policy in Zhejiang Province'), *Gaoxiao Jiaoyu Guanli* (*Higher Education Management*), May, 14–20.

Chen Jiandong *et al.* (2010). 'The trend of the Gini coefficient of China', Brooks World Poverty Institute Working Paper 109.

Chen Song and Ma Shuchao (2005). '*Woguo bu tong diqu zhiye jiaoyu fazhan shuiping bijiao yanjiu*' ('A study on comparing provincial vocational education development'), *Jiaoyu Fazhan Yanjiu* (*Journal of Educational Development*), 2005(06), 8–13.

Chen, Stephen (2016). 'The rise of China's millionaire research scientists', *South China Morning Post*, 27 April 2016.

Chen Xuefei (2006). '*Lixiang daoxiang xing de zhengce zhiding: "985 gongcheng" zhengce guocheng fenxi*' ('Ideal orientation policy-making: Analysis on "985 Project" policy process'), *Beijing Daxue Jiaoyu Pinglun* (*Peking University Education Review*), 145–157.

Chen Yangbin (2008). *Muslim Uyghur Students in a Chinese Boarding School: Social Recapitalization as a Response to Ethnic Integration.* Lanham, MD: Lexington Books.

Chen Yangbin (2014). 'Towards another minority educational elite group in Xinjiang?', in Leibold, J. and Chen, Y. (eds), *Minority Education in China.* Hong Kong: Hong Kong University Press, 201–219.

Chen Yiu Por and Liang Zai (2007). 'Educational attainment of migrant children: the Forgotten story of China's urbanization', in Hannum, E. and Park, A. (eds), *Education and Reform in China*. Abingdon, Oxon: Routledge, 117–132.

Chen Zhihua (2011). *Fenlan jiaoyu: quanqiu di yi de mimi* (*Finnish education: the secret of being top in the world*). Beijing: China Youth Press.

Chen Zhili (2008). 'Preface', *The Rising of a Country through Education (jiaoyu daguo de jueqi)*. Beijing: Educational Science Press (*Jiaoyu Kexue Chubanshe*), I–V.

Cheng Fanping, Liu Yiguo and Wu Hua (2009). '2009 Blue Book of Education: China on the eve of tremendous changes', in Yang Dongping (ed.), *The China Educational Development Yearbook*. Leiden: Brill, 1–36.

Cheng Kai-ming (2011). 'Shanghai: How a big city in a developing country leaped to the head of the class', in Tucker, M. S. (ed.), *Surpassing Shanghai*. Cambridge, MA: Harvard Education Press, 21–48.

Chou, Chuing Prudence and Ching, Gregory (2012). *Taiwan Education at the Crossroad: Where Globalization meets Localization.* New York: Palgrave Macmillan.

Chun, Allen (2012). 'From sinicization to indigenization in the social sciences: Is that all there is?' in Dirlik, A. (ed.), *Sociology and Anthropology in Twentieth-century China: Between Universalism and Indigenism*. Hong Kong: Chinese University of Hong Kong Press, 255–282.

Collini, Stephan (2012). *What Are Universities for?* London: Allen Lane.

Connelly, Rachel and Zhang Zhenzhen (2007a). 'Educational access for China's post-Cultural Revolution generation', in Hannum, E. and Park, A. (eds), *Education and Reform in China*. Abingdon, Oxon: Routledge, 64–80.

Connelly, Rachel and Zhang Zhenzhen (2007b). 'Enrollment and graduation patterns as China's reforms deepen, 1990–2000', in Hannum, E. and Park, A. (eds), *Education and Reform in China*. Abingdon, Oxon: Routledge, 80–92.

Cruz, Neni (2014). 'No secret to Shanghai's success in education', *Philippine Daily Inquirer*, 7 February 2014.

Curran, Thomas (2005). *Education Reform in Republican China: the failure of educators to create a modern nation.* Ceredigion: Edwin Mellen Press.

Dai, J. (2006). '*Xin kecheng gaige beijing xia nongcun xuexiao jiaoyu de kunjing yu chulu*' ('The difficulties of rural education in the context of the new curriculum reforms, and some solutions'), in *Jiaoyu Kexue Yanjiu* (*Educational Science Research*), 2006(6), 17–19.

Dawson, Walter (2010). 'Private tutoring and mass schooling in East Asia: Reflections of inequality in Japan, South Korea, and Cambodia', *Asia Pacific Education Review* 11(1), 14–24.

Deng Xiaoping (1990). *Deng Xiaoping lun jiaoyu* [Deng Xiaoping on Education]. Beijing: People's Education Press.

Dervin, Fred (2015). *Chinese Educational Migration and Student-Teacher Mobilities.* Basingstoke: Palgrave Macmillan.

Dikotter, Frank (2009). *The Age of Openness: China Before Mao.* Berkeley: University of California Press.

Dikotter, Frank (2013). *The Tragedy of Liberation.* London: Bloomsbury.

Ding Weili and Lehrer, Steven (2007). 'Incentives and the quality of teachers and schools,' in Hannum, E. and Park, A. (eds), *Education and Reform in China.* Abingdon, Oxon: Routledge, 191–204.

Ding Xiaohao (2004). *Dui Zhongguo gaodeng yuanxiao guimo jingji yanjiu de huigu yu fansi* (Reflections on economic research into the scale of Chinese higher education institutions). Peking University School of Education: Research Centre for the Economics of Education.

Ding Xiaojiong (2011). *Policy Metamorphosis in China: A Case Study of Minban Education in Shanghai.* Lanham, MD: Rowman and Littlefield.

Directorate-General of Budget, Accounting and Statistics (2000). *The 2000 Survey Report on Family Income and Expenditures in the Taiwan Area, Republic of China* (in Chinese). Taipei: Directorate-General of Budget, Accounting and Statistics, Executive Yuan, Republic of China.

Dirlik, Arif (ed.) (2011). *Sociology and Anthropology in Twentieth-Century China: Between Universalism and Indigenism.* Hong Kong: Chinese University of Hong Kong Press.

Dong Hong-liang, Zhang Li and Ding Ya-song (2016). '*2015 nian quanguo gaodeng jiaoyu maoru xuelu dadao 40%*' ('National higher education enrolment rates for 2015 reach 40%'), *Renmin Ribao*, 16 January.

Dore, Ronald (1980). 'The diploma disease revisited', *IDS Bulletin* 11.2, University of Sussex: Institute of Development Studies.

Dower, John (1975). *Origins of the Modern Japanese State: Selected Writings of E.H. Norman.* New York: Random House.

Drake, E. (2001). 'World Bank transfer of technology and ideas to India and China', in Hayhoe, R. and Pan, J. (eds), *Knowledge Across Cultures: A Contribution to Dialogue Among Civilisations*, CERC Research Studies in Comparative Education 11, Hong Kong: University of Hong Kong, Comparative Education Research Centre.

Drèze, Jean and Sen, Amartya (2013). *An Uncertain Glory: India and its Contradictions.* London: Penguin.

Du, W. (2006). '*Guanyu kecheng gaige zhong jiaoshi gongzuo liang de diaocha he fenxi*' ('An analysis of teacher workloads following the curriculum reforms'), *Zhongxiaoxue guanli* (*School Management*), 3, 30–32.

Duara, Prasenjit (2009). *The Global and Regional in China's Nation-formation.* Abingdon, Oxon: Routledge.

ECNU (East China Normal University) (2016). *Xiao qing jian jie* (Introduction to the university). ECNU homepage, www.ecnu.edu.cn (accessed 3 July 2016).

Economist (2005). 'India and China: The tiger in front', *The Economist* (London), 3 March 2005.

Economist (2006). 'Planning the new socialist countryside', *The Economist* (London), 9 March 2006.

Economist (2010). 'The Beijing consensus is to keep quiet', *The Economist* (London), 6 May 2010.

Economist (2014). 'Down and out in rural China', *The Economist* (London), 23 August 2014.

Economist (2015). 'Managing migration: No riff-raff', *The Economist* (London), 26 September 2015.

Economist (2016). 'Grey zone: Coping with senility in Japan', *The Economist* (London), 9 April 2016.

Espinoza, Javier (2015). 'Record numbers of foreign pupils at UK schools', *The Telegraph*, 16 May.

Fairbrother, Greg (2003). *Toward Critical Patriotism: Student Resistance to Political Education in Hong Kong and China.* Hong Kong University Press.

Fan, J. (2005). '*Kecheng gaige zhong de jiaoshi xiaoji xingwei*' ('Teacher's passive behaviour in the context of the curriculum reforms'), in *Jiaoyu kexue luntan* (*Educational Science Review*) 2005(12), 13–15.

Fan Ping (2012). '*2011 nian nongmin fazhan baogao*' ('Report on rural development, 2011'), in Ru *et al.* (eds), *Shehui lan pi shu: 2012 nian Zhongguo shehui xingshi fenxi yu yuce* (*Society Blue Book, 2012*). Beijing: Social Sciences Academic Press, 284–296.

Fei, John, Ranis, Gustav and Kuo, Shirley (1979). *Growth with Equity: The Taiwan Case.* New York: Oxford University Press.

Feng Xiuxia (2015). 'Coming or going, migrants alter dynamics of labor', *China Daily*, 13 April. http://english.gov.cn/policies/infographics/2015/04/13/content_281475088090112.htm (accessed 24 September 2015).

Fewsmith, Joseph (2008). *China Since Tiananmen.* Cambridge University Press.

Fincher, Leta Hong (2014). *Leftover Women.* New York: Zed Books.

Fitzgerald, John (1996). *Awakening China: Politics, Culture and Class in the Nationalist Revolution.* Stanford, CA: Stanford University Press.

Fitzpatrick, Sheila (1979). *Education and social mobility in the Soviet Union, 1921–1934.* Cambridge University Press.

Fogel, Joshua (2004). *The Role of Japan in Liang Qichao's Introduction of Modern Western Civilization to China.* University of California, Berkeley: Institute of East Asian Studies.

Fogel, Joshua (2009). *Articulating the Sinosphere: Place and Time in Sino-Japanese Relations.* Cambridge, MA: Harvard University Press.

Fong, Vanessa (2004). *Only Hope.* Stanford, CA: Stanford University Press.

Fong, Vanessa (2011). *Paradise Redefined: Transnational Chinese Students and the Quest for Flexible Citizenship in the Developed World.* Stanford, CA: Stanford University Press.

Friedman, Milton and Friedman, Rose (1998). *Two Lucky People.* Chicago University Press.

Fu Yiqin (2013). 'China's unfair college admissions system', *The Atlantic*, 19 June.

Gao Lan (2011). *Impacts of Cultural Capital on Student College Choice Process in China.* Lanham, MD: Lexington Books.

Garnaut, John (2012). *The Rise and Fall of the House of Bo.* Penguin Specials.

Goodburn, Charlotte (2009). 'Learning from migrant education: A case study of the schooling of rural migrant children in Beijing', *International Journal of Educational Development*, 29, 495–504.

Gray, John (2006). 'Mao in perspective', *China Quarterly*, 187, 659–679.

Green, Andy (1990). *Education and State Formation.* Basingstoke: Palgrave Macmillan.

Green, Andy (2007). 'Education, globalisation and development: Changing the terms of engagement', in Green, A. *et al.* (eds), *Education and Development in a Global Era: Strategies for 'Successful' Globalisation.* London: Department for International Development, 7–47.

Green, Andy (2013). *Education and State Formation: Europe, East Asia and the USA.* Basingstoke: Palgrave Macmillan (second edition).

Green, A. and Steedman, H. (1993). *Educational Provision, Educational Attainment and the Needs of Industry: A Review of the Research for Germany, France, Japan, the USA and Britain.* Report Series 5. London: National Institute of Economic and Social Research.

Green, A., Preston, J. and Janmaat, J. G. (2006). *Education, Equality and Social Cohesion.* Basingstoke: Palgrave.

Green, A., Little, A., Kamat, S., Oketch, M. and Vickers, E. (2007). *Education and Development in a Global Era: Strategies for 'Successful' Globalisation.* London: Department for International Development.

Greene, J. M. (2008). *The Origins of the Developmental State in Taiwan: Science Policy and the Quest for Modernization.* Cambridge, MA: Harvard University Press.

Gries, Peter Hayes (2005). *China's New Nationalism: Pride, Policy and Diplomacy.* Berkeley: UC Press.

Gries, Peter Hayes and Rosen, Stanley (eds) (2010). *Chinese Politics: State, Society and the Market.* Abingdon, Oxon: Routledge.

Gu Qing (2007). *Teacher Development: Knowledge and Context.* London: Continuum.

Guan Peijun (2009). '*Yi kexue fazhan guan zhidao jiaoshi duiwu jianshe de renzhi lun he fangfa lun wenti*' ('Taking the principle of scientific development as the guide for dealing with epistemological and methodological problems in the construction of the teaching force'), *Jiaoyu Yanjiu* 2009(1), 47–52.

Guan Ping and Shi Weiping (2013). '*Xiandai xuetu zhi yu nongmingong peixun*' ('A modern apprenticeship system and migrant worker training'), *Jiaoyu fazhan yanjiu*, 2013(11), 37–40.

Guo Hua (2003). *Zai xin kecheng zhong shenfa de yi xiao wei ben jiaoyan zhidu* 'School-based pedagogical research units in the context of the new curriculum', *Renmin Jiaoyu*, 2003(5), 26–27.

Han Che (2014). '*Ningxia daxue xuefei baozhang re zhengyi*' ('Heated controversy over explosion in tuition fees at Ningxia University'), *51sxue*, news.51sxue.com/detail/id_40388.html (accessed 3 July 2016).

Han Dongping (2008). *The Unknown Cultural Revolution: Life and Change in a Chinese Village.* New York: Monthly Press Review.

Han Jialing (2001). '*Beijing shi liudong ertong yiwu jiaoyu zhuankuang diaocha baogao*' ('Report on an investigation into compulsory education for migrant children in Beijing'), *Qingnian Yanjiu* (*Youth Research*) – in two parts: 2001(8), 1–7 and 2001(9), 10–18.

Han Jin, Zhao Qingxia and Zhang Mengnan (2016). 'China's income inequality in the global context', *Perspectives in Science*, 7, 24–29.

Hannum, Emily, Park, Albert and Cheng Kai-Ming (2007). 'Introduction: market reforms and educational opportunity in China', in Hannum, E. and Park, A. (eds), *Education and Reform in China.* Abingdon, Oxon: Routledge, 1–23.

Hannum, E., Kong, P. and Zhang Y. (2009). 'Family sources of educational gender inequality in rural China: a critical assessment', *International Journal of Educational Development*, 29, 474–486.

Hannum, E., An, Xuehui and Hua-Yu Sebastian Cherng (2011). 'Examinations and educational opportunity in China: mobility and bottlenecks for the rural poor', *Oxford Review of Education*, 37(2), Expansion and equity in secondary education (April), 267–305.

Hansen, Mette Halskov (2012). 'Learning to organize and be organized: Student cadres in a rural boarding school', in Bislev, A. and Thøgersen, S. (eds), *Organizing Rural China, Rural China Organizing.* Lanham, MD: Lexington Books.

Hansen, Mette Halskov (2013). 'Learning individualism: Confucius, Hesse and pep rallies in a Chinese rural high school', *China Quarterly*, 213, 60–77.

Hansen, M.H. and Woronov, T.E. (2013). 'Demanding and resisting vocational education: A comparative study of schools in rural and urban China', *Comparative Education*, 49(2), 242–259.

Harrison, Henrietta (2001). *China: Inventing the Nation*. London: Arnold.

Harvey, David (2005). *A Brief History of Neoliberalism*. Oxford: Oxford University Press.

Havergal, C. (2015). 'Vince Cable: Loss of polytechnics was a mistake', *THE*, 5 March 2015.

Hawkins, John (2000). 'Centralisation, decentralisation, recentralisation – educational reform in China', *Journal of Educational Administration*, 38(5), 442–454.

Hayford, C. (2006). 'The history textbook debate in China', AsiaMedia, UCLA Asia Institute, 22 March. http://www.international.ucla.edu/cnes/article/41421 (accessed 22 January 2008).

Hayhoe, Ruth (1993). 'Political texts in Chinese universities before and after Tiananmen', *Pacific Affairs* 66(1), 21–43.

Hayhoe, Ruth (1995). 'Student enrolment and job assignment issues in China', in Postiglione, G. and Lee, W.-O. (eds), *Social Change and Educational Development: Mainland China, Taiwan and Hong Kong*. Centre of Asian Studies: University of Hong Kong, 82–93.

Hayhoe, Ruth (1999). *China's Universities 1895–1995: A Century of Cultural Conflict*. Hong Kong: Comparative Education Research Centre, University of Hong Kong.

Hayhoe, R. (2006). *Portraits of Influential Chinese Educators*. Hong Kong: Comparative Education Research Centre.

He Baogang (2014). 'The power of Chinese linguistic imperialism and its challenge to multicultural education', in Leibold, J. and Chen, Y. (eds), *Minority Education in China*. Hong Kong: Hong Kong University Press, 45–64.

He Ning (2014). '*Fumu: xiwang duo yixie chi ku jiaoyu – xuexiao: jia xiao xiezuo fang you chang qi xiaoguo*' ('Parents: We hope education will toughen up [our children]; schools: home-school collaboration is crucial for long-term effectiveness'), *Xin Kuai Bao* 26 August. http: www/epaper.xkb.com.cn/view/950108.

He, Rowena Xiaoqing (2015). 'Identifying with a "rising China": overseas Chinese student nationalism', in Vickers, E. and Kumar, K. (eds), *Constructing Modern Asian Citizenship*. Abingdon, Oxon: Routledge, 314–339.

He Zhen (2013). 'Vocational school-enterprise cooperation: Problems and policy analysis' ('*Zhiye jiaoyu xiao zhi hezuo zhong de wenti yu zujin zhengce fenxi*'), *Journal of Chinese Higher Education Research* (*Zhongguo gaojiao yanjiu*), 2013(1), 90–93.

Henze, Jurgen (1984). 'Higher education: The tension between equality and quality', in Hayhoe, R. (ed.) *Contemporary Chinese Education*. Armonk, NY: M.E. Sharpe, 93–153.

Hess, Steve (2009). 'Dividing and conquering the shop floor: Uyghur labour export and labour segmentation in China's industrial east', *Central Asian Survey*, 28(4), 403–416.

Holborow, Marnie (2015). *Language and Neoliberalism*. Abingdon, Oxon: Routledge.

Holden, H. and Button, S. W. (2006). 'The teaching of music in the primary school by the non-music specialist', *The British journal of Music Education*, 23(1), 23–38.

Hong Xiumin *et al.* (2015). 'The way to early childhood education equity – policies to tackle the urban-rural disparities in China', *International Journal of Child Care and Education Policy*, 9(5). http://ijccep.springeropen.com/articles/10.1186/s40723-015-0008-9 (accessed 17 July 2016).

Hu Hong-bin (2014). '*Woguo jiaoyu gongping yanjiu de huigu yu zhanwang – jiyu 2002-2012 nian CNKI qikan ju de fenxi*' ('Retrospect and prospects for research on educational equity in China – based on an analysis of the CNKI database from 2002–2012'), *Jiaoyu Yanjiu* (*Educational Research*), 2014(1), 54–59.

Huang Fei, Sun Yu-xuan and Diao Cai-xiao (2013). '*Minban chuzhong zai pinkun diqu xiangdui gongban chuzhong fanrong fazhan de xianxiang zhi tantao – jiyu Henan Sheng Lankao xian de diaoyan*' ('*Minban* junior secondary schools in poor areas compared to public junior secondary schools – a study of Lankao County in Henan'), *Qinghua Daxue Xuesheng Xuebao* (*Tsinghua University Students Journal*, 2013(3), 10–19.

Huang Guangming and Chen Qin (2001). '*Ban xue hai shi quan qian; Wuhan minban xuexiao yi wofeng dao bi*' ('Running a school or embezzling money? The collapse of a Wuhan *minban* school "bee's nest"'), *Nan Fang Zhou Mo* (*Southern Weekend*), 12 October. http://news.sohu.com/60/06/news146890660.shtml (accessed 23 October 2015).

Huang Jianpo (2005). '*Chenggong, shichang, shehui: guojia yu liudong renkou zinu de jiaoyu – yi Pudong xiqu de mingong zidi xuexiao wei lie*' ('Success, the market and society: The state and the education of migrant children – taking Pudong District migrant workers' schools as an example'), *Qingnian Yanjiu* (*Youth Research*), 2005(8), 1–10.

Huang, Yasheng (2008). *Capitalism with Chinese Characteristics: Entrepreneurship and the State.* Cambridge University Press.

Hudson, Peter (2004). 'Specific mentoring: A theory and model for developing primary science teaching practices', *European Journal of Teacher Education*, 27(2), 139–146.

IALEI (International Alliance of Leading Educational Institutes) (2008). *Transforming Teacher Education: redefining professionals for the 21st century.* Available from: www.nie.edu.sg

Ienaga, Saburō (2001). *Japan's Past, Japan's Future: one historian's odyssey.* Lanham, MD: Rowman and Littlefield.

Jacques, Martin (2009). *When China Rules the World: The rise of the Middle Kingdom and the end of the Western World.* London: Allen Lane.

Japan Times (2015). 'University of Tokyo, top school in China to form strategic partnership', *The Japan Times,* 9 February.

Jeffery, R., Jeffery, P. and Jeffery, C. (2007). 'The privatisation of secondary schooling in Bijnor: a crumbling welfare state?', in Kumar, K. and Oesterheld, J. (eds), *Education and Social Change in South Asia.* Orient Longman, 442–474.

Jia *et al.* (2007). '*Nongcun minban xuexiao xianru 'liang mian yi bu' kunjing*' (Difficulties with rural *minban* schools in the context of the 'two frees and one subsidy'), *Zhongguo Qingnian Bao* (*China Youth Daily*), 18 July.

Jia Dongyan (2008). '*Gao zhi xuesheng shixi qijian quanyi qinhai zeren rending xianzhuang yanjiu*' ('Research into assigning responsibility for infringements of the rights of vocational senior high students during their internships'), *Zhiye jiaoyu yanjiu* (*Vocational Education Research*), 10.

Jiang Ruili (2014). '*Cong xiaoche shigu pin fa kan che dian bing xiao zhi tong*' ('Observing the pain of [the policy of] abolishing points [small schools] and merging schools from the frequency of school bus accidents'), *Zhongguo Shandong Wang*, 11 December. http://news.sdchina.com/show/3150886.html (accessed 30 September 2015).

Jiang Zemin (1999). '*Zai di san ci quan guo jiaoyu gongzuo huiyi shang de jianghua*' (Speech at the Third National Education Work Conference), 15 June. fagui.eol.cn/html/201008/4636.shtml (accessed 3 July 2016).

Jing An (2014). 'China releases new guideline on academic proficiency test', *China Radio International*, 16 December. http://english.cri.cn/12394/2014/12/16/3861s856845.htm (accessed 22 June 2016).

Johnson, Chalmers (1995). *Japan: Who Governs? The Rise of the Developmental State*. New York: W. W. Norton.

Johnston, Jamie; Loyalka, Prashant; Chu, James; Song Yingquan; Yi Hongmei and Huang Xiaoting (2016). 'The Impact of vocational teachers on student learning in developing countries: Does enterprise experience matter?', *Comparative Education Review*, 60(1), 131–150.

Jones, Alisa (2005). 'Changing the past to serve the present: History education in mainland China', in Vickers, E. and Jones, A. (eds), *History Education and National Identity in East Asia*. New York: Routledge, 65–100.

Judt, Tony (2008). 'Goodbye to all that? Leszek Kolakowski and the Marxist Legacy', in *Reappraisals: Reflections on the Forgotten Twentieth Century*. London: Vintage, 129–146.

Kajanus, Anni (2015). *Chinese Student Migration, Gender and Family*. Basingstoke: Palgrave Macmillan.

Kamat, S. (2007). 'Walking the tightrope: Equality and growth in liberalising India', in Green, A. *et al.* (eds), *Education and Development in a Global Era: Strategies for 'Successful' Globalisation*. London: Department for International Development, 89–129.

Kaneko, Motohisa (2013). 'Japanese higher education and the state in transition', in Goodman, R., Kariya, T. and Taylor, J. (eds), *Higher Education and the State*. Oxford: Symposium Books, 171–197.

Kariya, Takehiko (2011). 'Japanese solutions to the equity and efficiency dilemma? Secondary schools, inequity and the arrival of "universal" higher education', *Oxford Review of Education*, 37(2), 241–266.

Kariya, Takehiko (2013). *Education Reform and Social Class in Japan*. London and New York: Routledge.

Kariya, Takehiko and Rappleye, Jeremy (2010). 'The twisted, unintended impacts of globalization on Japanese education', in Fuller, B. and Hannum, E. (eds), *Globalization, Changing Demographics, and Educational Challenges in East Asia (Research in the Sociology of Education, Volume 17)*, Bingley: Emerald Group Publishing, 17–63.

Kipnis, Andrew (2011). *Governing Educational Desire: Culture, Politics and Schooling in China*. Chicago and London: University of Chicago Press.

Kipnis, Andrew and Li Shanfeng (2010). 'Is Chinese education underfunded?', *China Quarterly* (202), 327–343.

Ko Po Yuk and Adamson, Bob (2011). 'Pedagogy and human dignity – the special rank teacher in China since 1978', *History of Education* 40(3), 371–389.

Kong Lingshuai (2012). *Reflection on Shanghai's Result in PISA 2009*. Lecture delivered at Teachers' College, Columbia University, 12 November 2012.

Kumar, Krishna (2007). 'Education and culture: India's quest for a secular policy', in Kumar, K. and Oesterheld, J. (eds), *Education and Social Change in South Asia*. Orient Longman, 196–217.

Kumar, Krishna (2010). 'India's children have a precarious right', *The Hindu*, 2 April. http://beta.thehindu.com/opinion/lead/article381710.ece (accessed 2 July 2011).

Kumar, Krishna (2015). 'Education and modernity in rural India', in Vickers, E. and Kumar, K. (eds), *Constructing Modern Asian Citizenship*. Abingdon, Oxon: Routledge, 31–49.

Kwok, Percy (2010). 'Demand intensity, market parameters and policy responses towards demand and supply of private supplementary tutoring in [the People's Republic of] China', *Asia Pacific Education Review* 11(1), 49–58.

Kwong, J. (2006). 'The integration of migrant children in Beijing Schools', in Postiglione, G. (ed.), *Education and Social Change in China: Inequality in a Market Economy*. Armonk, NY: M.E. Sharpe, 163–178.

Lai Desheng, Meng Dahu and Tian Yongpo (2011). 'Differences between the employment of higher education students from the cities and the countryside and the fairness of higher education: From the perspective of employment capability', *Chinese Education and Society*, 2011(1).

Lam, Willy Wo-lap (2006). *Chinese Politics in the Hu Jintao Era.* Armonk, NY: M.E. Sharpe.

Lan Pei-chia (2014). 'Segmented incorporation: The second generation of migrants in Shanghai', *The China Quarterly*, 217, March, 243–265.

Lau Siu-Kai (1981). 'Chinese familism in an urban-industrial setting: The case of Hong Kong', *Journal of Marriage and the Family*, 43(4), 977–992.

Law Wing-wah (2011). *Citizenship and citizenship education in a global age: Politics, Policies and Practices in China.* New York: Peter Lang.

Lee Kuan Yew (2000). *From Third World to First.* Singapore: Times Editions.

Leibold, James (2011). 'Filling in the nation: The spatial trajectory of prehistoric archaeology in twentieth-century China', in Moloughney, B. and Zarrow, P. (eds), *Transforming History.* Hong Kong: Chinese University Press, 333–371.

Leibold, James (2014). 'Han Chinese reactions to preferential minority education in the PRC', in Leibold, J. and Chen, Y. (eds), *Minority Education in China: Balancing Unity and Diversity in an Era of Critical Pluralism.* Hong Kong University Press, 299–319.

Leibold, James and Chen Yangbin (2014). 'Introduction', in Leibold, J. and Chen, Y. (eds), *Minority Education in China: Balancing Unity and Diversity in an Era of Critical Pluralism.* Hong Kong University Press, 1–26.

Lester, Stan (2015). 'The European qualifications framework: a technical critique', *Research in Post-compulsory Education,* 20(2), 159–172.

Levin, R. (2010). 'The rise of Asia's universities', *New York Times*, 20 April.

Lewin, Keith (1993). 'Investing in technical and vocational education: A review of the evidence', *The Vocational Aspect of Education*, 45(3), 217–227.

Lewin, Keith; Little, Angela; Xu Hui and Zheng Jiwei (1994). *Educational Innovation in China: Tracing the Impact of the 1985 Reforms.* London: Longman.

Lewin, Keith; Little, Angela; Xu, Hui and Li, Jiayong (1996). 'Quality and quantity in technical and vocational schooling in China', *China Research Monograph 7*. Beijing: British Embassy, Cultural and Education Section.

Li Fan (2011). 'New curriculum reform and history textbook compilation in contemporary China', in Muller, G. (ed.), *Designing History in East Asian Textbooks*, Abingdon, Oxon: Routledge, 137–146.

Li, H.-B. *et al.* (2015). 'Unequal access to college in China: How far have poor, rural students been left behind?', *China Quarterly*, 221(March), 185–207.

Li, S.-H. and Zhang, X.-Y. (2012). *'Woguo "985 gongcheng" daxue benke jiaoyu peiyang mubiao de queshi yu fansi'* ('The drawbacks and reflection of the training objective of the undergraduate education in China's universities of "985 Project"' [sic.]), *Gaodeng Jiaoyu Yanjiu Xuebao (Journal of Higher Education Research)*, December, 7–10.

Li She-yun and Li Qing (1999). '*Cong "fa zhi" dao "fa zhi" ershi nian gai yi zi – jianguo yilai faxuejie zhongda shijian yanjiu'* ('From "rule by law" to "rule of law": Changing one word in twenty years – research into a crucial issue in the legal field since the establishment of our state'), *Fa Xue* (*Legal Studies*), 1999(7), 2–5.

Li Wen; Park, Albert and Wang Sangui (2007). 'School equity in rural China', in Hannum, E. and Park, A. (eds), *Education and Reform in China.* Abingdon, Oxon: Routledge, 27–43.

Li Wen-li and Wei Xin (2000). '*Gaodeng jiaoyu guimo de kuoda yu heli de xuefei shuiping'* ('The expanding scale of higher education and reasonable fee levels'), *Jiaoyu fazhan yanjiu*, 2000(3), 35–39.

Li Xin and Yan Wenfan (2012). 'A comparative study on China-U.S. APTHS: Past, present and future', *US-China Education Review,* B5, 534–543.

Li Xuelin (2011). *'Gaokao fudao: Zhaosheng xinwen baodao xu pingheng san ge guanxi'* ('*Gaokao* counselling: News reports about student recruitment should balance the three relationships'), *Qingnian Jizhe,* 20 November. http://edu.qq.com/a/20111121/000186.htm (accessed 21 June 2016).

Li Yanbao (2008). '*Cong wenhua jianshe jiaodu sikao daxue jiaoyu jiaoxue de gaige'* ('Considering university reform from the perspective of cultural construction') *Zhongguo Gaodeng Jiaoyu*, 2008(23), 6–8.

Lian Si (2011). '*Yizu shenfen rentong yanjiu'* ('Research on the sense of identity amongst *yizu*'), *Shehui kexuejia,* 2011(12), 55–59.

Lin Jing (1993). *Education in Post-Mao China.* Westport, CT: Praeger.

Lin Jing (2006). 'Educational stratification and the new middle class', in Postiglione, G. (ed.), *Education and Social Change in China: Inequality in a Market Economy.* Armonk, NY: M.E. Sharpe, 179–198.

Lin Jing (2007). 'Emergence of private schools in China', in Hannum, E. and Park, A. (eds), *Education and Reform in China.* Abingdon, Oxon: Routledge, 44–63.

Lin Tingjin (2013). *The Politics of Financing Education in China.* New York: Palgrave Macmillan.

Link, Perry (1992). *Evening Chats in Beijing.* New York: W.W. Norton.

Liu Jing (2015). 'Study shows Chinese students spend three hours on homework per day', *China Daily,* 26 November. http://www.chinadaily.com.cn/china/2015-11/26/content_22520832.htm (accessed 2 February 2017).

Liu Mingxing; Murphy, Rachel; Tao Ran and An Xuehui (2009). 'Education management and performance after rural education finance reform – evidence from Western China', *International Journal of Educational Development*, 29, 463–473.

Liu Ran (2015). *Spatial Mobility of Migrant Workers in Beijing, China.* Heidelberg: Springer.

Liu Ye (2010). *A meritocratic project: A study of the expansion of higher education in contemporary China.* Doctoral thesis. London: Institute of Education.

Liu Ying (2011). *Fenlan: qiang guo qiang min* (Finland: strong country, strong people). Guangzhou: Nanfang Daily Press.

Liu, Y. and Feng, X. (2005). 'Kindergarten educational reform during the past two decades in mainland China: Achievements and problems', *International Journal of Early Years Education,* 13(2), 93–99.

Lo, Billie L. C. (1984). 'Teacher education in the eighties', in Hayhoe, R. (ed.), *Contemporary Chinese Education.* Armonk, NY: M.E. Sharpe, 154–177.

Lovell, Julia (2006). *The Politics of Cultural Capital: China's Quest for a Nobel Prize in Literature.* Honolulu: University of Hawai'i Press.

Luo, R., Zhang, L., Liu, C. *et al.* (2012). 'Behind before they begin: The challenge of early childhood education in rural China', *Australasian Journal of Early Childhood,* 37, 55–64.

Luo Yun (2010). *'"Renmin de daxue": 1949 nian xin zhengquan xia zhongguo daxue shenfen zhi jiangou – yi Beijing daxue wei ge'an'* ('"The University of the People": The construction of university identities under the new regime after 1949 – taking Peking University as an example'), Chinese University of Hong Kong, *Jiaoyu Xuebao* (*Journal of Educational Studies*), 38(1), 71–94.

Luo Zhitian (2011). 'The marginalization of classical studies and the rising prominence of historical studies during the late Qing and early Republic: A reappraisal', in Moloughney, B. and Zarrow, P. (eds), *Transforming History: The Making of a Modern*

Academic Discipline in Twentieth-Century China. Hong Kong: Chinese University Press, 47–74.

Luxbacher, Grete (2013). 'World university rankings: how much influence do they really have?' *The Guardian*, 10 September 2013.

Ma, L.-T. and Fan, W.-Y. (2005). *'Fazhan duli xueyuan de xianshi jichu ji zhengce tanxi'* ('A discussion of policies and practical foundations for the development of independent colleges'), *Zhongguo Gaodeng Jiaoyu* (*Chinese Higher Education*), 2005(8), 28–32.

Mao, Z., Lai, T., Chen, Y.and Ma, L. (2007). *'Guanyu wanshan "tiyu (yu jiankang) kecheng biaojun" de jian yi (shang): tiyu kecheng xingzhi de biaoshu he mubiao tixi de taolun'* ('Several suggestions for perfecting the Physical Education (and Health) Curriculum Standard (Part One): Expression of the nature of physical education curriculum and discussion about target system'), *Tiyu Xuekan* (*Journal of Physical Education*), 14(3), 1–4.

Marquand, David (2015). *Mammon's Kingdom: An Essay on Britain, Now*. London: Penguin.

Marx, Karl (1983). *The Portable Karl Marx*. London: Penguin.

McGraw Hill (2002). *Glencoe Science: An Introduction to the Life, Earth and Physical Sciences, Student Edition*. Glencoe/McGraw Hill.

McGregor, Richard (2010). *The Party: The Secret World of China's Communist Rulers*. London: Allen Lane.

McMahon, W. (1999). *Education and Development*, Oxford: OUP.

MDET (Ministry of Domestic Economy and Trade) (2002). *Document No. 267*. Beijing: MDET.

Meisner, Maurice (1989). *Marxism and the Chinese Experience*. Armonk, NY: M.E. Sharpe.

Meng, F. (2010). *'Cong "985 gongcheng", "211 gongcheng" kan woguo shijie yiliu daxue jianshe de ji dui maodun'* ('Various contradictions in our country's construction of world-class universities, as revealed in the "985" and "211" projects'), *Heilongjiang gao jiao yanjiu (Heilongjiang Research on Higher Education)*, 2010(1), 29–32.

MHR (Ministry of Human Resources) (2006). *'Guanyu yinfa "shiye danwei gongzuo renyuan shouru fenpei zhidu gaige fang'an" de tongzhi' he 'guanyu yiwu jiaoyu xuexiao shishi jixiao gongzi de zhidao yijian'* ('Notice of the promulgation of the bill to reform the remuneration system for workers in SOEs' and 'Guidelines on the implementation of performance-related pay for teachers in the compulsory phase'). Beijing: MHR, Doc. No. 56.

Miller, Aaron (2011). 'Beyond the four walls of the classroom: "Real" and "imagined" change in Japanese sports and education', in Willis, D. and Rappleye, J. (eds), *Reimagining Japanese Education*. Oxford: Symposium Books, Chapter 7.

Miller, Tom (2012). *China's Urban Billion*. New York: Zed Books.

Min Weifang (1991). *Improving Managerial Effectiveness of Higher Education Institutions: A Case Study of an Institutional Merger in Hubei Province, P.R. China*. Beijing: UNESCO.

Min Weifang, Ding Xiaohao and Guo Sure (1995). *'Gaodeng yuanxiao xi he zhuanye de guimo xiaoyi yanjiu'* ('Research into the effectiveness and appropriate scale of departments and disciplines in higher education institutions'), *Jiaoyu Yanjiu*, 1995(7), 7–12.

Mitter, Rana (2014). 'Mao Zedong and charismatic Maoism', in Guha, R. (ed.), *Makers of Modern Asia*. Cambridge, MA: Harvard University Press, 93–116.

Mitter, Rana and Major, Patrick (2004). *Across the Blocs: Exploring Comparative Cold War Cultural and Social History*. London: Frank Cass.

MOE (Ministry of Education, People's Republic of China) (1979). *Chengshi you'eryuan gongzuo tiaoli* (*Ordinance regarding the work of urban kindergartens*). Beijing: MOE.

MOE (1983). *Guanyu fazhan nongcun you'eryuan de ji dian yi jian* (Several opinions on the development of rural kindergartens). Beijing: MOE.

MOE (1992). *'Jiunian yiwujiaoyu quanrizhi xiaoxue chujizhongxue kecheng jihua'.* ('Curriculum for Primary and Junior High schools (pilot)'). *Renmin Jiaoyu* [*People's Education*], 1992(09): 2–8.

MOE (2001). *Jiaoyubu guanyu yinfa 'yiwu jiaoyu kecheng shezhi shiyan fang'an' de tongzhi* (Notice of the issuing of the 'Experimental programme for establishing the curriculum for compulsory education'). http://www.moe.edu.cn/publicfiles/business/htmlfiles/moe/moe_711/201006/xxgk_88602.html (accessed 26 October 2015).

MOE (2003). *Jiaoyubu guanyu yinfa 'putong gaozhong kecheng fang'an (shiyan)' he yuwen deng 15 ge xueke kecheng biaozhun (shiyan) de tongzhi* (Notice of the issuing of 'Experimental curriculum for senior high schools' and of the experimental curriculum standards for 15 subjects, including Chinese language and literature [*Yuwen*]). http://www.moe.gov.cn/publicfiles/business/htmlfiles/moe/s8001/201404/xxgk_167349.html (accessed 26 October 2015).

MOE (2004). *Ziliao: Zhongguo minban jiaoyu fazhan gaikuang he lifa jincheng* (Sources: an outline of the situation and the legislative process relating to the development of *minban* education in China). http://www.moe.gov.cn/jyb_xwfb/xw_zllssj/moe_183/tnull_2309.html (accessed 26 October 2015).

MOE (2011a). *Jiaoyu bu guanyu dali tuijin jiaoshi jiaoyu kecheng gaige de yijian* (Education Ministry opinion on the forceful promotion of reform to the teacher education curriculum). Document No. 6, 8 October.

MOE (2011b). *Guojia zhongchangqi jiaoyu gaige he fazhan guihua gangyao (2010–2020)* (Framework plan for the mid- to long-term reform and development of the national education system (2010–2020)). Beijing: Ministry of Education.

MOE (2013). *Composition of Students in Senior Secondary Schools.* http://www.moe.gov.cn/publicfiles/business/htmlfiles/moe/s8493/201412/181722.html (accessed 10 May 2016).

MOE (2016). 'Chinese education minister discusses education reforms and development at press conference'. http://en.moe.gov.cn/Specials/Specials_Spotlight/Spotlight_News/201603/t20160315_233577.html (accessed 26 July 2016).

MOF (Ministry of Finance (*Cai Zheng Bu*), People's Republic of China) (1973). *Guoying gongye, jiaotong qiye ruogan feiyong kaizhi banfa* (Methods for the disbursement of funds by SOEs and transport utilities). 15 May. http://www.chinalawedu.com/news/1200/22016/22019/22075/22085/2006/3/zh0183025302936002l960-0.htm (accessed 19 July 2016).

MOF (2012). 'The gradual improvement of the mechanism for ensuring the stable increase in the Central Ministry of Finance's investment in the "Three Rural Issues"' (*Zhongyang caizheng 'san nong' touru wending zengzhang baozhang jizhi jubu wanshan*). 25 October 2012. http://www.gov.cn/gzdt/2012-10/25/content_2250846.htm (accessed 29 September 2015).

Mok Ka-ho (1997). 'Privatization or marketization: Educational development in post-Mao China', *International Review of Education*, 43(5), 547–567.

Molnar, M. and Koen, V. (2015). 'Providing the right skills to all in China: From "made in China" to "created in China"'. *OECD Economics Department Working Papers*, No. 1219. Paris: OECD Publishing.

Moloughney, B. and Zarrow, P. (eds) (2011). *Transforming History.* Hong Kong: Chinese University Press.

Morgan, John (2015). 'Andreas Schleicher: "we will live through a time" when universities are judged on graduate learning', *Times Higher Education*, 13 December.

Morris, Paul (1998). 'Comparative education and educational reform: Beware of prophets returning from the Far East', *Education 3 to 13,* 26(2), 3–7.

Morris, Paul (2016). 'Education policy, cross-national tests of pupil achievement, and the pursuit of world-class schooling: a critical analysis'. London: IOE, inaugural professorial lecture.

Morris, Paul and Vickers, Edward (2015). 'Schooling, politics and the construction of identity in Hong Kong: The 2012 "Moral and National Education" crisis in historical context', *Comparative Education,* 51(3), 305–326.

Morris, P., Shimazu, N. and Vickers, E. (2013). 'Introduction', in Morris, P., Shimazu, N. and Vickers, E. (eds), *Imagining Japan in Post-war East Asia: Identity Politics, Schooling and Popular Culture.* Abingdon, Oxon: Routledge, 1–28.

Mundy, Karen (2002). 'Retrospect and prospect: Education in a reforming World Bank', *International Journal of Educational Development,* 22, 483–508.

Murphy, R. (2004). 'Turning peasants into modern Chinese citizens: "Population quality" discourse, demographic transition and primary education', *The China Quarterly*, March, 1–20.

Murphy, R. (2007). 'Paying for education in rural China' in Shue, V. and Wong, C. (eds), *Paying For Progress in China: Public Finance, Human Welfare and Changing Patterns of Inequality.* Abingdon, Oxon: Routledge, 69–95.

Murphy, R. and Johnson, D. (2009). 'Education and development in China: Institutions, curriculum and society', *International Journal of Educational Development*, 29, 447–453.

Murphy, R. Taggart (2014). *Japan and the Shackles of the Past.* Oxford University Press.

Myrdal, Gunnar (1968). *Asian Drama: An Inquiry into the Poverty of Nations.* New York: Pantheon.

Namier, Lewis (1992). *1848: The Revolution of the Intellectuals* (British Academy – The Raleigh Lecture on History 1944). Oxford University Press.

Naughton, Barry (2004). 'The information technology industry and economic interactions between China and Taiwan,' in Mengin, F. (ed.), *Cyber China: Reshaping National Identities in the Age of Information.* New York: Palgrave Macmillan, 155–184.

NCEDR (National Center for Education Development Research) (2009). *Educational Atlas of China.* Beijing: Sinomaps Press (*Zhongguo Ditu Chubanshe*).

Needham, Joseph and Wang Ling (1954). *Science and Civilisation in China Vol. 1: Introductory Orientations*. Cambridge University Press.

Ng, Peter Tze Ming *et al.* (2002). *Changing Paradigms of Christian Higher Education in China, 1888–1950.* Lewiston, NY: Edwin Mellen Press.

Nippon.com (2015). 'Universities struggle to cope with shrinking population and globalisation', *Nippon.com,* 16 March. http://www.nippon.com/en/features/h00095/ (accessed 28 May 2016).

Oakeshott, I. (2009). 'Minister turns to Confucius to raise school standards', *The Times*, London, 22 February.

OECD (2001). *Starting Strong: Early Childhood Education and Care.* Paris: OECD.

Oi, Jean (1995). 'The role of the local state in China's transitional economy', *The China Quarterly*, 1132–1149.

Overholt, W. H. (2012). 'Reassessing China: Awaiting Xi Jinping', *The Washington Quarterly*, 35(2), 121–137.

Paine, Lynn (1995). 'Teacher education in search of a metaphor: Defining the relationship between teachers, teaching and the state in China', in Ginsberg, M. and Lindsay, B. (eds), *The Political Dimension in Teacher Education.* London: Falmer Press, Chapter 5.

Paine, L. and Fang, Y. (2007). 'Supporting China's teachers: Challenges in reforming professional development', in Hannum, E. and Park, A. (eds), *Education and Reform in China.* Abingdon, Oxon: Routledge, 173–190.

Painter, Murray and Mok Ka-ho (2008). 'Reasserting the public in public service delivery: the de-privatisation and de-marketisation of education in China', *Policy and Society,* 27, 137–150.

Pantsov, Ivan (with Levine, Steven) (2015). *Deng Xiaoping: A Revolutionary Life.* Oxford University Press.

Park, Hyunjoon (2013). *Education in Japan and South Korea: Demystifying Stereotypes.* Abingdon, Oxon: Routledge.

Pascal, C. and Bertram, A. D. (1998). 'Accounting early for life long learning', in Abbott, L. and Moylett, H. (eds), *Early Education in the New Millennium,* London: Falmer Press.

Pei Minxin (2006). *China's Trapped Transition.* Cambridge, MA: Harvard University Press.

Peking University (2013). *'Beijing daxue zhangcheng' zhiding da shiji* (*Milestones in the development of 'the Charter of Peking University'*). Committee for the Drafting of the Charter, Peking University, 28 April. www.pkunews.pku.edu.cn/xwzh/2015-04/28/content_288463.htm (accessed 4 July 2016).

Peng Guozhu (2010). *Xinsheng ge benke yuanxiao xuesheng jiuyeguan diaocha yu duice yanjiu* (Research into students' attitudes towards job-seeking at newly upgraded four-year colleges, and related policies). MA dissertation, Zhongnan University.

Peng Qinghua (2011). *Gao xiao kuo zhao de jingji shehui gongxian yanjiu* (Research on the contribution of higher education expansion to the economy and society). PhD dissertation, Zhongnan University.

Peng Yanghong (2012). *'"Jiaoshou zhi xiao" yu "jiaoshou zhi xue" zhi ban – lun Zhongguo daxue neibu zhili jiegou biange de lujing xuanze'* ('Distinguishing between "administration by professors" and "academic governance by professors" – path choice of internal governance structure reform in Chinese universities'), *Qinghua Daxue Jiaoyu Yanjiu* (*Tsinghua Journal of Education*), 33(6), 106–110.

PEP (People's Education Press) (2006). *Xiaoxue Yuwen* (Primary School [Chinese] Language), *Grades 1–6.* Beijing: PEP.

Pepper, S. (1996). *Radicalism and Education Reform in Twentieth-Century China: The Search for an Ideal Developmental Model.* Cambridge University Press.

Perkin, Harold (1989). *The Rise of Professional Society: England Since 1880.* Abingdon, Oxon: Routledge.

Perkin, Harold (1996). *The Third Revolution: Professional Elites in the Modern World.* Abingdon, Oxon: Routledge.

Perkin, Harold (1998). 'Higher education and social progress: A comparative perspective', *History of Education* 27(3), 207–217.

Phoenix New Media (2013). '*Yi zu: zai xianshi zhong xun chulu*' ('Ant tribe: seeking a realistic way out'), *Feng Huang Cai Jing* (*Phoenix Financial*). http://finance.ifeng.com/money/special/yizufd/ (accessed 28 May 2016).

Postiglione, Gerard (2006). 'Schooling and inequality in China', in Postiglione, G. (ed.), *Education and Social Change in China: Inequality in a Market Economy.* Armonk, NY: M.E. Sharpe, 1–24.

Postiglione, Gerard (2007). 'School access in rural Tibet', in Hannum, E. and Park, A. (eds) *Education and Reform in China.* Abingdon, Oxon: Routledge, 93–116.

Postiglione, Gerard (2009). 'Dislocated education: The case of Tibet', *Comparative Education Review*, November, 483–512.

Postiglione, Gerard; Ben Jiao, Li Xiaoliang and Tsamla (2014). 'Popularising basic education in Tibet's nomadic regions', in Leibold, J. and Chen, Y. (eds), *Minority Education in China*. Hong Kong: Hong Kong University Press, 107–129.

Priestland, David (2012). *Merchant, Soldier, Sage: A New History of Power*. London: Penguin.

Qin Ke-zhu (2007). *'"Shifan sheng mian fei jiaoyu" zhengce huigui: xin shiqi jiaoshi jiaoyu zhengce de zhongda tiaozheng'* ('Reorienting policy on "free teacher education": a big adjustment in teacher education policy for the new era'), *Dangdai Jiaoyu Kexue*, 2007(8), 25–28.

Ran Hongmei (2011). 'Discussing the importance of the fifth grade standardized tests' (*tantan wunianji tongce zhongyaoxing*), *Beijing xiaoshengchu wang* (Beijing primary-to-junior secondary network), 1 November. http://www.xschu.com/xiaoshengchu/01/5009.html (accessed 1 August 2014).

Rao, N., Narain, K. and Cheng, K. M. (2003). 'Primary schooling in China and India: Understanding how sociocontextual factors moderate the role of the state', *International Review of Education*, 49, 151–174.

Rappleye, Jeremy (2007). *Exploring Cross-National Attraction in Education*. Oxford: Symposium Books.

Rappleye, Jeremy (2015). Review of Morris, Shimazu and Vickers (eds), *Imagining Japan in Postwar East Asia*. In *Comparative Education Review*, 59(2), 373–376.

Rappleye, Jeremy and Vickers, Edward (2015). 'Can Japanese universities really become "super-global"', *University World News*, 6 November. http://www.universityworldnews.com/article.php?story=20151103154757426 (accessed 2 February 2017).

Reilly, James (2012). *Strong State, Smart Society: The Rise of Public Opinion in China's Japan Policy*. New York: Columbia University Press.

Ren Bo and Yang Jiachou (2013). '"Xiao sheng chu" de mimi' ('The secret of promotion from primary to junior secondary'), *Caixin: shin shijie zhoukan* (*Caixin Century Weekly*), 39–48.

Reynolds, D. and Farrell, S. (1996). *Worlds Apart? A Review of International Surveys of Educational Achievement Involving England*. London: OFSTED.

Rhoads, Robert A.; Wang, Xiaoyang; Shi, Xiaoguang and Chang, Yongcai (2014). *China's Rising Research Universities: A New Era of Global Ambition*. Baltimore: Johns Hopkins University Press.

Roberts, Dexter (2015). 'China's Dickensian boarding schools', *Bloomberg Business*, 6 April. http://www.bloomberg.com/news/articles/2015-04-06/china-s-dickensian-boarding-schools (accessed 4 November 2015).

Rodgers, Daniel T. (2011). *Age of Fracture*. Cambridge MA: Harvard University Press.

Rong Jing-ben *et al.* (1998). *Cong yalixing tizhi xiang minzhu hezuo zhi de zhuanbian: xian xiang liang ji zhengzhi tizhi gaige* (The Shift from a Pressure-Type System to a Democratic-Cooperative System: Reform of the County and Township Levels of the Political System). Beijing: *Zhongyang Bianyi Chubanshe*.

Rose, Caroline (2013). 'Changing views of the Anti-Japanese War in Chinese high school history textbooks', in Morris, P., Shimazu, N. and Vickers, E. (eds), *Imagining Japan in Post-war East Asia*. Abingdon, Oxon: Routledge, Chapter 7.

Ross, Heidi (2006). 'Challenging the gendered dimensions of schooling', in Postiglione, G. (ed.), *Education and Social Change in China: Inequality in a Market Economy*. Armonk, NY: M.E. Sharpe, 25–50.

Ru Xin, Lu Xueli and Li Peilin (eds) (2012). *Shehui lan pi shu: 2012 nian Zhongguo shehui xingshi fenxi yu yuce* (*Society Blue Book, 2012*). Beijing: Social Sciences Academic Press.

Russell, Bertrand (1926). *On Education*. Abingdon, Oxon: Routledge (2010 reprint).

Russell, Bertrand (1932). *Education and the Social Order*. Abingdon, Oxon: Routledge (2010 reprint).

Sargent, Tania (2015). 'Professional learning communities and the diffusion of pedagogical innovation in the Chinese education system', *Comparative Education Review*, 59(1), 102–132.

Schmidtke, Carsten and Chen Peng (2012). 'Philosophy of vocational education in China: A historical overview', *Journal of Philosophy of Education*, 46(3), 432–448.

Scott, P. (2012). 'It's 20 years since polytechnics became universities – and there's no going back', *The Guardian*, 3 September 2012.

SEC (State Education Commission) (1990). *Guojia jiaowei guanyu zai putong gaozhong shixing biye huikao zhidu de yijian* (Opinion of the SEC on implementing a high school graduation examination [*huikao*] for senior high schools). Beijing: SEC, 20 August.

Sen, Amartya (1999). *Development as Freedom*. Oxford: Oxford University Press.

Sen, Amartya (2005). *The Argumentative Indian*. London: Allen Lane.

Sevilla, Anton (2016). 'Akutibu ra-ningu to mushin no kea: Daigaku kyōiku no genba kara' ('No-mind and care in the university'), in Nishihira (ed.), *Hontō ni kea suru no wa dare nano ka* (*Who Are the Ones Who Really Care?*) (forthcoming).

Shanghai Municipality (2016). *Shimin jiage xinxi zhinan* (*Citizens' guide to charges and fees*). Summarised online: http://www.tgtg365.com/article.php?id=2016 (accessed 17 July 2016).

Sharma, Yojana (2013). 'Top universities break rules on gender discrimination', *University World News*, 24 August. http://www.universityworldnews.com/article.php?story=20130823114249619 (accessed 21 July 2016).

Shek, Daniel T. L. and Li Xiong (2014). 'Subjective well-being of early adolescents in Hong Kong', in Shek, D., Sun, R. and Ma, C. (eds), *Chinese Adolescents in Hong Kong: Family Life, Psychological Well-being and Risk Behaviour*. Heidelberg: Springer, 93–110.

Shepherd, J. (2007). 'A very Chinese revolution', *The Guardian*, London, 7 December.

Shi Jinghuan (2004). *Zoujin jiaocai yu jiaoxue de xingbie shijie* (*Investigating the sexually discriminatory perspective of instructional materials and pedagogy*). Beijing: *Jiaoyu Kexue Chubanshe* (Educational Sciences Press).

Shi Yuanyuan (2016). *Chuugoku ni okeru shuuten daigaku no sendouteki jirei ni miru kyouyou kyouiku kaikaku ni kansuru kenkyuu* (Research into leading exemplars of reform to general/liberal arts education [*tongshi jiaoyu*] among China's key-point universities). Kyushu University Department of Education: doctoral thesis.

Shue, Vivienne and Wong, Christine (2007). 'Introduction: Is China moving towards a more equitable development strategy?', in Shue, V. and Wong, C. (eds), *Paying For Progress in China: Public Finance, Human Welfare and Changing Patterns of Inequality*. Abingdon, Oxon: Routledge, 1–11.

Sina.com (2001). *2001 nian gaokao quanguo ge sheng shi lu qu fensu xian yi lan biao* (2001 table of gaokao scores [required for entry to different higher education institutions] by province and city across the nation). http://edu.sina.com.cn/l/2001-08-02/13140.html (accessed 20 June 2016).

Sirkin, Harold L. (2013). 'China's economic policy: Is Milton Friedman replacing Chairman Mao?', *Bloomberg: The Management Blog*. 9 December. http://www.bloomberg.com/bw/articles/2013-12-09/china-s-economic-policy-is-milton-friedman-replacing-chairman-mao (accessed 8 October 2015).

Skocpol, Theda (1979). *States and Social Revolutions*. Cambridge University Press.

Song Qinghua, Yang Yun and Zhang Mingxing (2009). '"9 + 2" *Jiaoyu fupin moshi de tansuo yu shijian'* ('Research and practice into educational approaches to poverty alleviation'), *Zhiye Shikong*, 2009(3), 157–158.

State Council (1984). *Guoying Qiye di er bu li gai shui shixing banfa* (Experimental plan for the second stage of [moving to a system of] taxes on profits for SOEs). Beijing: State Council.

State Council (2003). *Guowuyuan guanyu jin yi bu jiaqiang nongcun jiaoyu gongzuo de jueding* (State Council decision on a further step towards strengthening rural education work). Beijing: State Council, 17 September.

State Council (2004). *Document No. 9.* (Notice on properly solving the pay and benefits of retired teachers of primary and secondary schools run by SOEs.) Beijing: State Council.

State Council (2007). *Guowuyuan bangongting zhuanfa jiaoyubu deng bumen guanyu jiaoyubu zhishu shifan daxue shifansheng mianfei jiaoyu shishi banfa (shixing) de tongzhi* (Notice of the State Council Secretariat transmission to the Education Ministry and other departments regarding (experimental) methods of implementing free instruction for teacher training students at normal universities directly under the Education Ministry), *State Council Secretariat*, 2007(34). http://www.gov.cn/zwgk/2007-05/14/content_614039.htm (accessed 28 June 2016).

State Council (2010). *Jiaoyu bu, caizheng bu guanyu shishi 'zhongxiaoxue jiaoshi guojiaji peixun jihua' de tongzhi* (Notice from the Education and Finance Ministries regarding the implementation of the 'national-level training plan for primary and secondary teachers). http://www.gov.cn/zwgk/2010-06/30/content_1642031.htm (accessed 16 June 2016).

State Council (Guo Wu Yuan) (2012). *Guo Wu Yuan bangongting guanyu guifan nongcun yiwu jiaoyu xuexiao buju tiaozheng de yijian* (Opinion of the State Council Office on the standardization of rural compulsory education: adjustment of the distribution of schools). Beijing: State Council, No. 48. http://www.gov.cn/zwgk/2012-09/07/content_2218779.htm (accessed 30 September 2015).

State Council (2015). *The Opinions on Further Strengthening and Improving Propaganda and Ideological Work in Higher Education Under the New Circumstances.* Beijing: State Council, 18 January. Online at chinacopyrightandmedia.wordpress.com (accessed 26 July 2016).

Stiglitz, Joseph (1996). 'Some lessons from the East Asian miracle', *World Bank Research Observer,* 11(2), 151–177.

Strauss, Julia (2006). 'Morality, coercion and state building by campaign in the early PRC: Regime consolidation and after, 1949–1956', *The China Quarterly*, 188(December), 891–912.

Su Zhiliang (2011). 'The "others" in Chinese history textbooks: a focus on the relationship between China and Japan', in Muller, G. (ed.), *Designing History in East Asian Textbooks*, Abingdon, Oxon: Routledge, 147–161.

Sudworth, John (2016). 'Counting the cost of China's left-behind children', *BBC News*, 12 April. http://www.bbc.com/news/world-asia-china-35994481 (accessed 14 April 2016).

Sum Ngai-Ling (2004). 'Informational capitalism and the remaking of "greater China": Strategies of siliconization', in Mengin, F. (ed.), *Cyber China: Reshaping National Identities in the Age of Information.* New York: Palgrave Macmillan, 205–236.

Sun Wenting (2015). *Chuugoku ni okeru koutou shokugyou kyouiku no 'shakaiteki chiiki' ni kansuru kenkyuu – Chuugoku no Suzhou shi wo rei toshite* (Research on the 'social status' of vocational higher education in China – the case of Suzhou). Kyushu University: MA dissertation.

Sun Ying and Chen Shuhua (1997). '*Bu rong hushi de gaoxiao shizi duanceng xianxiang*' ('Faults with college faculty that cannot be ignored'), *Keji, rencai, shichang* (*Technology, Talent and the Market*), No. B12, 39–40.
Sweeting, Anthony and Vickers, Edward (2007). 'Language and the history of colonial education: the case of Hong Kong', *Modern Asian Studies,* 41(1), 1–40.
Takayama, Keita (2011). 'Reconceptualising the politics of Japanese education, Reimagining studies of Japanese education', in Willis, D. and Rappleye, J. (eds), *Reimagining Japanese Education.* Oxford: Symposium Books, 247–279.
Tang, R. Q. (2009). '*Shizhuan shengge de difang yuanxiao jiaoshi jiaoyu xianzhuang diaocha yanjiu: yi Hunan Sheng shizhuan shengge de difang benke yuanxiao wei lie*' ('An investigation into the current situation of teacher education in local colleges upgraded from vocational teacher training schools [*shizhuan*]: taking the example of *shizhuan* in Hunan Province that have been upgraded to local undergraduate colleges'), *Jiaoyu yanjiu yu shixian* (*Educational Research and Practice*), 2009(3), 39–42.
Tang, S. and Zhong, Z. H. (1993). *Zhongguo xueqian jiaoyu shi* (*History of preschool education in China*). Beijing: The People's Education Press.
Tang, S. and Zhong, Z. H. (2000). *Zhongguo xueqian jiaoyu shi* (*History of preschool education in China*). Beijing: People's Education Press (second edition).
Taylor, John (2013). 'The state and higher education institutions: new pressures, new relationships and new tensions', in Goodman, R., Kariya, T. and Taylor, J. (eds), *Higher Education and the State: Changing Relationships in Europe and Asia.* Oxford: Symposium Books, Chapter 1.
Thøgersen, Stig (1991). *Secondary Education in China after Mao: Reform and Social Conflict.* Aarhus: University of Aarhus Press.
Thøgersen, Stig (2002). *A County of Culture: Twentieth-Century China Seen from the Village Schools of Zouping, Shandong.* Ann Arbor: The University of Michigan Press.
Tilak, J. (2002). *Building Human Capital in East Asia: What Others Can Learn.* New Delhi: National Institute of Educational Planning and Administration.
Tobin, Joseph; Wu, David and Davidson, Dana (1991). *Preschool in Three Cultures.* New Haven, CT: Yale University Press.
Tobin, Joseph; Karasawa, Mayumi and Hsueh, Yeh (2009). *Preschool in Three Cultures Revisited.* Chicago University Press.
Tooley, James (2001). *The Global Education Industry.* London: Institute for Economic Affairs.
Trounson, Andrew (2015). 'China deal to increase two-way scholarship student flow', *The Australian,* 15 April.
Tsang Mun C. (2000). 'Education and national development in China since 1949: Oscillating policies and enduring dilemmas', *China Review*, 579–618.
Tucker, Marc S. (2011). *Surpassing Shanghai: An Agenda for American Education Built on the World's Leading Systems.* Cambridge, MA: Harvard Education Press.
Unger, Jonathan (1982). *Education Under Mao: Class and Competition in Canton Schools, 1960–1980.* New York: Columbia University Press.
VanderVen, E. (2005). 'Village-state cooperation: Modern community schools and their funding, Haicheng County, Fengtian, 1905–1931', *Modern China,* 31(2), 204–235.
Vaughan, Richard (2014). 'Pisa prodigy Shanghai may pull out of tests', *Times Higher Education,* 30 May.
Veblen, Thorstein (2007). *The Theory of the Leisured Class.* Oxford University Press.
Vickers, Edward (2005). *In Search of an Identity: the Politics of History as a School Subject in Hong Kong, 1960s–2005.* Hong Kong: Comparative Education Research Centre.

Vickers, Edward (2007a). 'China's uneven development: Nationalism and inequality on the mainland', in Green, A., Little, A., Kamat, S., Oketch, M. and Vickers, Edward, *Education and Development in a Global Era: Strategies for 'Successful' Globalisation*. London: Department for International Development, 49–88.

Vickers, Edward (2007b). 'Frontiers of memory: Conflict, imperialism and official histories in the formation of the post-Cold War Taiwan identity', in Mitter, R. and Miyoshi Jager, S. (eds), *Ruptured Histories: War, Memory and the Post-Cold War in Asia*. Cambridge, MA: Harvard University Press, 209–232.

Vickers, Edward (2009a). 'The opportunity of China? Education, patriotic values and the Chinese state', in Lall, M. and Vickers, E. (eds), *Education as a Political Tool in Asia*. Abingdon, Oxon: Routledge, 53–82.

Vickers, Edward (2009b). 'Selling socialism with Chinese characteristics: *Thought and Politics* and the legitimisation of China's developmental strategy', *International Journal of Educational Development*, 29(5), 523–531.

Vickers, Edward (2015). 'A Civilizing mission with Chinese characteristics? Education, colonialism and Chinese state formation in comparative perspective', in Vickers, E. and Kumar, K. (eds), *Constructing Modern Asian Citizenship*. Abingdon, Oxon: Routledge, 50–80.

Vickers, Edward (2016). '*Sekai-teki sūzei toshite no jinbun shakai kagaku kiki*' ('The crisis of social sciences and humanities as a global trend'), *Chuo Koron*, February.

Vickers, Edward (2017). 'Altered states of consciousness: Identity politics and prospects for Taiwan-Hong Kong-mainland reconciliation', in Frieberg, A. and Chung C. K. M. (eds), *Reconciling with the Past: Resources and Obstacles in a Global Perspective*. Abingdon, Oxon: Routledge.

Vickers, Edward and Kumar, Krishna (2015). 'Introduction', in Vickers, E. and Kumar, K. (eds), *Constructing Modern Asian Citizenship*. Abingdon, Oxon: Routledge, 1–27.

Vickers, Edward and Yang Biao (2013). 'Shanghai's history curriculum reforms and shifting textbook portrayals of Japan', *China Perspectives*, 2013(4), 29–37.

Vogel, Ezra (2011). *Deng Xiaoping and the Transformation of China*. Cambridge, MA: Harvard University Press.

Walder, Andrew (2015). *China under Mao*. Cambridge, MA: Harvard University Press.

Wang Chengzhi (2002). 'Minban education: the planned elimination of the "people-managed" teachers in reforming China', *International Journal of Educational Development*, 22, 109–129.

Wang, C. (2004). *'Renzhen duidai "qingshi zhishi" de jiaoyu sichao: zai ping you "yingshi jiaoyu" xiang suzhi jiaoyu zhuangui tifa de taolun'* ('A critical reflection on the thought of "despising knowledge" in Chinese basic education'), *Beijing Daxue Jiaoyu Pinglun (Peking University Education Review)*, 2(3), 5–23.

Wang Dewen (2010). 'Reform and development of vocational education', in Cai Fang (ed.), *The China Population and Labor Yearbook, Volume Two: The Sustainability of Economic Growth from the Perspective of Human Resources*. Leiden: Brill, 93–116.

Wang Huan-xia and Liao Bo-qin (2011). '*Wo guo gao zhong xueye shuiping kaoshi de shijian kunjing yu zhidu shensi*' ('A reflection on the system of senior high school academic achievement test and dilemmas in its implementation'), *Jiaoyu Xuebao (Journal of Education Studies)*, 7(6), 77–83.

Wang Hui (2009). *The End of the Revolution: China and the Limits of Modernity*. London: Verso.

Wang Jianguo and Wang Xingping (2015). 'New urbanization: A new vision of China's urban–rural development and planning', *Frontiers of Architectural Research*, 4(2), 166–168.

Wang Junxiu (2011). '*Xiaoche shigu pinfa yuanyu 'chedian bingxiao' hou xiaoche zhidu bu wanshan*' ('The frequency of school bus accidents is a result of the imperfections of the school bus system after [the introduction of the] "abolish the points [small local schools] and merge schools" [policy]'), *Zhongguo Qingnian Bao*, 15 December.
Wang, L.-H. (2008). '*Woguo gaodeng jiaoyu de jixiao zhuanxiang jingfei gaige ji wanshan silu – yi "211 gongcheng" he "985 gongcheng" wei lie*' ('Reforms to special funding programmes and approaches to the improvement of Chinese higher education: the examples of the "211" and "985" Projects'), *Zhongguo Gaojiao Yanjiu (Chinese Higher Education Research)*, 2008(9), 35–38.
Wang, N. (2001). '*Woguo jiaokeshu xuanyong wenti yanjiu*' ('Research into the issue of textbook choice in China'), *Jiaoyu Kexue Yanjiu* (*Educational Science Research*), 2001(4), 34–37.
Wang Xiaobing, Liu Chengfang, Zhang Linxiu, Shi Yaojiang, Rozelle, Scott and Loyalka, Prasant (2013). 'College is a rich, Han, urban, male club: Research notes from a census survey of four tier one colleges in China', *China Quarterly*, 214(June), 456–470.
Wang Xiaobing, Liu Chengfang, Zhang Linxiu, Shi Yaojiang, Rozelle, Scott and Loyalka, Prasant (2014). 'Response to the commentary "Reassessing disparity in access to higher education in contemporary China"', *The China Quarterly*, 220, 1131–1135.
Wang Xiaojun (Grace) (2010). 'Girls' access to education in China: Actors, cultures and the windmill of development management', *CREATE Pathways to Access: Research Monograph No. 39*. CREATE: University of Sussex.
Wang Xiaoying (2002). 'The post-Communist personality: The spectre of China's capitalist market reforms', *The China Journal*, 47, 1–17.
Wang Yijie and Wang Yi (2013). '*Shengcun yali xia nongcun minban xuexiao de zuzhi yunzuo – xiang ji yu Y xiao de gean yanjiu*' ('Organizational operation of rural private schools under survival pressure: A case study of Y School'), *Hohai Daxue Xuebao (Zhexue shehui kexue ban)* (*Hohai University Journal – Philosophy and Social Sciences edition)*, June, 44–48.
Wang Yuanshen (2009). '*Jiguan hou qin gaige 30 nian lishi huigu*' ('Looking back on 30 years of the history of reform of [state] organs'), *Guojia jiguan shiwu guanli ju* (*National Government Offices Administration*). Beijing: State Council. http://www.ggj.gov.cn/hqzzs/zgjghq/2009/200901/200901/t20090114_265776.htm (accessed 20 July 2016).
Wang Zhiqiu (2012). '*Jiyu jiaoshi zhuanye biaozhun de xiaoxue jiaoshi zhiqian peiyang*' ('On the professional standards of pre-service training for primary teachers'), *Zhongguo Jiaoyu Xuekan*, No. 12, 72–76.
Watson, David (2007). 'Chinese universities in the service of society: A report on the China-England study of national policy on higher education management, second phase, 22–26 May 2006', *Research Update*, 6(291), 10 August. Beijing: Ministry of Education, National Centre for Education Development and Research.
Wehler, Hans-Ulrich (1969). *Bismarck und der Imperialismus*. Cologne: Kiepenheuer & Witsch.
Wei Kan (2014). 'Explainer: What makes Chinese maths lessons so good?' *The Conversation*, 25 March. http://theconversation.com/explainer-what-makes-chinese-maths-lessons-so-good-24380 (accessed 7 May 2016).
Welch, A. and Cai, H. X. (2011). 'Enter the dragon: the internationalisation of Chinese higher education', in Ryan, J. (ed.), *China's Higher Education and Internationalisation*. Abingdon, Oxon: Routledge.
White, G. (1981). *Party and Professionals: The Political Role of Teachers in Contemporary China*. Armonk, NY: M.E. Sharpe.

Whitty, Geoff, Power, Sally and Halpin, David (1998). *Devolution and Choice in Education: The School, the State and the Market.* Open University Press.

Wiborg, Susanne (2015). 'Privatising education: Free school policy in Sweden and England', *Comparative Education Review,* 59(3), 473–497.

Witte, John F. (2001). *The Market Approach to Education: An Analysis of America's First Voucher Program.* Princeton, NJ: Princeton University Press.

Wolf, Alison (2002). *Does Education Matter?* London: Penguin.

Wolf, Martin (2004). *Why Globalisation Works.* Boston: Yale University Press.

Wood, Frances (2000). *Hand Grenade Practice in Peking: My Part in the Cultural Revolution.* London: John Murray.

World Bank (1993). *East Asian Economic Miracle: Economic Growth and Public Policy.* New York: OUP.

World Bank (2002). *Globalisation, Growth and Poverty: Building an Inclusive World Economy.* Washington, DC: World Bank.

World Bank (2006). *Where is the Wealth of Nations? Measuring Capital for the 21st Century.* Washington, DC: World Bank.

World Bank (2009). *From Poor Areas to Poor People: China's Evolving Poverty Reduction Agenda: An Assessment of Poverty and Inequality in China.* Poverty Reduction and Economic Management Department, East Asia and Pacific Region, World Bank.

Woronov, T. E. (2016). *Class Work: Vocational Schools and China's Urban Youth.* Stanford, CA: Stanford University Press.

Wright, Teresa (2010). *Accepting Authoritarianism: State-Society Relations in China's Reform Era.* Stanford, CA: Stanford University Press.

Wu Xiaoxin (2013). *School Choice in China: A Different Tale?* Abingdon, Oxon: Routledge.

Wu, X. and Ye, Y. (2010). *Technical and Vocational Education in China.* Zhejiang and Paramus, NJ: Zhejiang University Press and Homa & Sekey Books.

Wu Yurong (2015). '*Zhongyang minda fuzhong quanguo qiajian gaokaosheng yin Beijing jiazhang zhiyi*' ('The Central Minzu University Affiliated Middle School becomes a 'pinch point' for college entrance examination students, raising questions among Beijing parents'), *Teng Xun Xinwen,* 11 September. http://news.qq.com/a/20150911/058381.htm (accessed 30 September 2015).

Wu Zhi-hui, Qian Jun-hua and Ou-yang Hai-yan (2012). '*Xuexiao changyu zhong jiaoshi zizhu fazhan de jizhi bianqian yu wenhua shengcheng – yi Anshan shi gangdu xiaoxue wei lie*' ('The systemic and cultural evolution of organisations for supporting teachers' professional development in the school context – the example of Gangdu Primary School in Angang City'), *Dongbei Shida Xuebao: Zhexue shehuike xueban,* 2012(3), 147–152.

Xiamen University Malaysia (2014). 'Key words for the establishment of the campus'. http://www.xmu.edu.my/a/5.html (accessed 4 April 2016).

Xiang Biao and Shen Wei (2009). 'International student migration and social stratification in China', *International Journal of Educational Development,* 29(5), 513–522.

Xiao Hua-yi and Li Zhong-ling (2014). 'KOMET – *gaozhi xuesheng zhiye nengli ceping de xianshi xuanze*' ('KOMET – the practical choice for assessing the capabilities of tertiary vocational students'), *Zhi jiao lun tan,* 2014(4), 47–49.

Xie Yu and Zhou Xiang (2014). 'Income inequality in today's China', *Proceedings of the National Academy of Sciences of the USA,* 111(19), 6928–6933.

Xie Zuozu, Wang Weihong and Chen Xiaowei (2010). 'A study of women's access to higher education in rural and urban China: an analysis across different types of higher education institutions', *Chinese Education and Society,* 43(4), 32–40.

Xiong Yihan (2015). 'The broken ladder: Why education provides no upward mobility for migrant children in China', *The China Quarterly,* 221, 161–184.

Xu Lan (2003). '*Wo guo gaodeng yuanxiao hebing de jingji fenxi*' ('An analysis of the economics of mergers in our national higher education sector'), *Zhongguo Gaodeng Jiaoyu Pinggu* (*Assessing Chinese Higher Education* (journal)) 2003(1), 18–22.

Xu Shufang and Li Shixia (1995). '*Qingdao shi zhiye you'er yuan guanli tizhi gaige de ji dian zuofa*' ('Several methods for reforming the administrative system for enterprise kindergartens in Qingdao'), *Xue qian jiaoyu yanjiu* (*Preschool Education Research*), 50(2), 48–49.

Xu Yan, Ai Feifei and Zhang Jue (2012). '*Quan guo ge dichu 'shi er wu' jiaoyu fazhan yanjiu – jiyu gesheng fen jiaoyu gaige fazhan mubiao ji renwu de fenxi*' ('"12th Five-Year [Plan]" education development research in all regions of the country: Empirical analysis based on each province's education reform development objectives and tasks'), *Jiaoyu fazhan yanjiu* (*Journal of Education Development*), 2012(9), 20–26.

Yan Fengqiao (2010). 'The academic profession in China in the context of social transition: An institutional perspective', *European Review*, 18, Supplement S1, S99–S116.

Yan Xiaojun (2014). 'Engineering stability: Authoritarian political control over university students in Post-Deng China', *The China Quarterly,* 218, 493–513.

Yang, Dennis T. (2016). *The Pursuit of the Chinese Dream in America: Chinese Undergraduate Students at American Universities.* Lanham, MD: Lexington Books.

Yang Dongping (2006). *Equity and Education in China: Ideal and Reality (zhongguo jiaoyu gongping de lixiang yu xianshi).* Beijing: Peking University Press.

Yang Dongping (2010). *Zhongguo Jiaoyu Fazhan Baogao (Annual Report on China's Education) 2010.* Beijing: *Shehui Kexue Wenxian Chubanshe* (Social Sciences Academic Press).

Yang Dongping (2011). *Pan dian 2011: Jiaoyu de shiwang he xiwang* (Reviewing 2011: Disappointment and hope in education). http://blog.sina.com.cn/s/blog_492471c80102dtwa.html (accessed 19 July 2016).

Yang Dongping (2014). '*Bu neng yinwei haipa fubai er jujue gaokao gaige*' ('We cannot refuse *gaokao* reform just out of a fear of corruption'), *Zhongguo Qingnian Bao* (*China Youth Daily*), 18 September.

Yang Jintu (2008). '*zhiye jiaoyu 30 nian – bolan zhuangkuo de zhongda biange*' ('Thirty years of reform in vocational education'), *Zhiye jishu*, 98, 4–6.

Yang Rui (2010). 'International organizations, changing governance and China's policy making in higher education: an analysis of the World Bank and the World Trade Organization', *Asia Pacific Journal of Education*, 30(4), 419–431.

Yang Rui (2011). 'Chinese ways of thinking in the transformation of China's higher education system', in Ryan, J. (ed.), *China's Higher Education Reform and Internationalisation.* Abingdon, Oxon: Routledge, 34–47.

Yang Rui (2016). 'Corruption undermines the rise of East Asian universities', *University World News*, 29 January. http://www.universityworldnews.com/article.php?story=20160126130528586 (accessed 4 April 2016).

Yang Rui and Welch, Anthony (2012). 'A world-class university in China? The case of Tsinghua', *Higher Education*, 63, 645–666.

Yang Rui, Lesley Vidovich and Currie, Jan (2007). '"Dancing in a cage": Changing autonomy in Chinese higher education', *Higher Education*, 54, 575–592.

Yao Lin (2005). 'The grim situation in China with regard to building a teacher base and rejuvenating the higher education system', *Chinese Education and Society,* 38(5), 31–37.

Yao, Y. (2010). 'The end of the Beijing consensus', *Foreign Affairs*, 2 February.

Ye Wangbei (2014). *Power and Moral Education in China: Three Examples of School-Based Curriculum Development*. Lanham, MD: Lexington Books.

Yi Hongmei, Zhang Linxiu, Luo Renfu, Shi Yaojiang, Mo Di, Chen Xinxin, Brinton, Carl and Rozelle, Scott (2012). 'Dropping out: Why are students leaving junior high in China's poor rural areas?', *International Journal of Educational Development* 32, 555–563.

Yi Yunwen (2012). '*Shenzhen chuzhong zonghe kecheng huifu wei fenke jiaoxue bei zhi kegai shibai*' ('Shenzhen's abandonment of an integrated junior secondary curriculum and return to a subject-based curriculum signals the failure of curriculum reform'), *Guangming Ribao*, 5 September.

Yin Qiping and White, Gordon (1994). 'The "marketisation" of Chinese higher education: a critical assessment', *Comparative Education*, 30(3), 217–221.

Young, Michael (1961). *The Rise of the Meritocracy*. London: Penguin.

Yu Chuan-Hai (2011). 'An ecological perspective on the cultivation of specialists with diversified capabilities', in Zhang, L. and Zhang, C. (eds), *Engineering Education and Management*. Heidelberg: Springer, 707–714.

Yu Jian (2010). *'Wu "xin" de jiaoyu'* ('Education with no "heart"'), *Nan Fang Zhoumo* (*Southern Weekend*), 6 May.

Yu Kai and Ertl, Hubert (2010). 'Equity in access to higher education in China: The role of public and nonpublic institutions', *Chinese Education and Society*, 43(6), 36–58.

Yu S. and Hannum, E. (2006). 'Poverty, health and schooling in rural China', in Postiglione, G. (ed.), *Education and Social Change in China: Inequality in a Market Economy*. Armonk, NY: M.E. Sharpe, 53–74.

Yu Xie and Xiang Zhou (2014). 'Income inequality in today's China', *Proceedings of the National Academy of Sciences of the United States of America*, 111(19), 6928–6933.

Yu Xiulan (2004). *Zhongguo jiaoyu de chengxiang chiayi: yi zhong wenhua zaishengchan xianxiang de fenxi* (The Urban-Rural Divide in Chinese Education: An Analysis of a Phenomenon in Cultural Reproduction). Beijing: *Jiaoyu Kexue Chubanshe*.

Yuan Guiren (Education Minister) (2016). *Yuan Guiren buzhang jiu "Gaokao mingti yi zhang juan" da rendahuiyi jizhe wen* (Minister Yuan Guiren's response to a journalist at the National People's Congress regarding 'unification of the *gaokao* test'). http://learning.sohu.com/20160310/n440064674.shtml

Yuan Yue and Zhang Hui (2010). *'Lingdian diaocha: cheng xiang zhumin yanzhong de jichu jiaoyu fuwu'* ('Horizon research: Basic education in the eyes of urban and rural residents'), in Yang Dongping (ed.), *Jiaoyu Lanpi Shu: Zhongguo Jiaoyu Fazhan Baogao* (Blue Book of Education: Annual Report on China's Education). Beijing: Social Sciences Academic Press, 184–196.

Zeng Xiaodong (2006). 'Early childhood education and care in China', in Peterson, P., Baker, E. and McGaw, B. (eds), *International Encyclopedia of Education* (third edition). Oxford: Elsevier Science.

Zeng Xiaodong (2009). *Jingzheng yu junheng: yiwu jiaoyu jieduan zexiao yanjiu baogao* (Competition and fairness: A report on research into school choice during the compulsory phase of education), report commissioned by the Beijing Academy of Educational Sciences.

Zeng Xiaodong (ed.) (2012a). *Zhongguo zhong xiao xue jiaoshi fazhan baogao (2012)* (Report on the development of teachers in Chinese primary and secondary schools (2012)). (*Blue Book of Teachers*). Beijing: *Shehui Kexue Wenxian Chubanshe*.

Zeng Xiaodong (2012b). '*Beijing shi 4, 8 nianji xuesheng ke hou buxi de daijia yu shouyi*' ('Costs and benefits of after-school tutoring for Beijing students in years 4 and 8'), *Jiaoyu Xuebao*, 2012(6), 103–109.

Zeng Xiaodong (2013). '*Hou 4% shidai: lu gai zenme zou?*' ('In the post-4% era, what route should we take?'), *Guangming Ribao,* 20 March.

Zeng Xiaodong and Sude Yuejie (2013). 'School choice: inflaming tension between government's efforts in education equity and traditional meritocracy oriented education in China?' Paper presented at the annual conference of the American Educational Research Association.

Zeng Xiaodong and Yu Xia (eds) (2015). *Zhongguo zhong xiao xue jiaoshi fazhan baogao (2014)* (Report on the development of teachers in Chinese primary and secondary schools (2014)). (*Blue Book of Teachers*). Beijing: *Shehui Kexue Wenxian Chubanshe.*

Zeng Yaqing (2006). *Dui woguo gaodeng jiaoyu shoufei jinxing zhengfu guanzhi de yanjiu* (A study of the regulation of college tuition fees in China). BNU: unpublished MA dissertation.

Zhang Donghui (2012). 'Education reform in a Chinese university: Knowledge, values and organizational changes', *Comparative Education Review*, 56(3), 394–420.

Zhang Han; Patton, Donald and Kenney, Martin (2013). 'Building global-class universities: Assessing the impact of the 985 Project', *Research Policy* 42(3), 765–775.

Zhang Huajun (2013). *John Dewey, Liang Shuming and China's Education Reform.* Lanham, MD: Lexington Books.

Zhang Liang with Andrew Nathan and Perry Link (2002). *The Tiananmen Papers.* New York: PublicAffairs.

Zhang Linxiu, Luo Renfu, Liu Chengfang and Rozelle, Scott (2007). 'Investing in rural China: Tracking China's commitment to modernization', in Shue, V. and Wong, C. (eds), *Paying For Progress in China: Public Finance, Human Welfare and Changing Patterns of Inequality.* Abingdon, Oxon: Routledge.

Zhang Nanxing and Sun Jihong (2016). '*Zhong xi bu diqu zhaosheng xiezuo jihua shishi de chengxiao ji yiyi*' (The efficacy and implications of the cooperative plan for student recruitment in central and western regions). http://opinion.people.com.cn/n1/2016/0517/c1003-28358048.html (accessed 10 June 2016).

Zhang Qianfan (2011). '*Zhongguo daxue zhaosheng zhibiao zhidu de hexian fenxi', Zhongwai Faxue'* ('A cross-regional analysis of the standards for college entry in China'), *Peking University Law Journal*, 23(2), 248–269.

Zhang Qianfan (2015). 'Legalising central-local relations in China', in Harding, A. and Sidel, M. (eds), *Central-Local Relations in Asian Constitutional Systems.* London: Bloomsbury.

Zhang Tieming (2009). '*Jiefang sixiang: wo guo minban jiaoyu fazhan de jieduan tezheng ji weilai fazhan de tupo dian – yi Guangdong sheng wei lie*' ('Emancipating mind: Stage characteristic of non-governmental education development in China and breakthrough of future development'), *Jiaoyu fazhan yanjiu* (Educational Development Research), 2009(15–16), 23–29.

Zhang Wei (2014). 'The demand for shadow education in China: Mainstream teachers and power relations', *Asia-Pacific Journal of Education,* 34(4), 436–454.

Zhang Wei and Bray, Mark (2016). 'Shadow education: The rise and implications of private supplementary tutoring', in Shibao Guo and Yan Guo (eds), *Changes in Education under China's Market Economy*. Rotterdam: Sense Publishers, 85–101.

Zhang Yingjie and Xu Han (2010). 'Exploring school-enterprise partnership from the perspective of historical evolution' ('*Xiao zhi hezuo shanbian lichen shijiao xia woguo xiao zhi hezuo guanxi de tansuo*'), *Zhijiao Tongxun* 2010(10), 24–27.

Zhang Yingqiang and Cheng Ying (2008). *Gaoxiao neibu guanli tizhi gaige: 30 nian de huigu yu zhanwang* ('Reform on internal management mechanism of HEIs: 30-year retrospect and prospect'), *Gaodeng Gongcheng Jiaoyu Yanjiu* (*Tertiary Engineering Education Research*), 2008(6), 32–38.

Zhao Mingren (2014). '*Xibei diqu xianji jiaoshi peixun jigou jianshe de wenti ji duice*' ('Problems and policy responses in the construction of the county-level teacher training infrastructure in the North-western region'), *Zhong xiao xue jiaoshi peixun* (*Primary and Secondary Schoolteacher Training*), 2014(11), 27–30.

Zhao Yong (2014). *Who's Afraid of the Big Bad Dragon?* San Francisco: Jossey-Bass.

Zhao Zhiqun (2014). '*Xiandai zhiye jiaoyu zhiliang baozhang tixi yanjiu*' ('Research on the quality assurance system of modern vocational education: Status and prospects') *Xinan Daxue Xuebao (shehui kexue ban)* (*Journal of Southwest University (Social Science Edition)*), 40(4), 64–70.

Zhao Ziyang (2009). *Prisoner of the State.* New York: Simon and Schuster.

Zheng Xiuying and Zhou Zhigang (2010). '*"Shuangshi xing" jiaoshi: zhi jiao jiaoshi zhuanyehua de fazhan mubiao*' ('"Double-qualified" teachers: standards for the professionalization of vocational teachers'), *Zhongguo zhiye jishu jiaoyu* (*Chinese Vocational and Technical Education*), 27, 75–78.

Zhong, Q. and You, B. (2004). '*Fahui de nailao: "Renzhen duidai 'qingshi zhishi' de jiaoyu sichao' duhou gan"*' ('Rotten cheese: Feelings after reading "A Critical Reflection on the Thought of 'Despising Knowledge' in Chinese Basic Education"'), *Quanqiu Jiaoyu Zhanwang* (*Global Education*), 33(10), 3–7.

Zhongguo Jiaoyu Wang (China Education Network) (2013). *Chuan guo ge di gaoxiao shoufei biaozhun dachuan.* www.gkcx.eol.cn/z/sfbz.html (accessed 17 March 2013).

Zhongguo Xinwen Zhoukan (China News Weekly) (2006a). '*Zhongguo zui da minban jiaoyu jituan pengkui shi mo*' ('The rise and fall of China's largest "minban" education group'). 15 June. http://news.sina.com.cn/c/2006-06-15/150610163888.shtml (accessed 15 October 2015).

Zhongguo Xinwen Zhoukan (China News Weekly) (2006b). '*Zhongguo zuida minban jiaoyu jituan "Nanyang" bengkui shimo*' ('The whole story of the collapse of China's largest private education group, Nanyang'), 29 June. http://news.people.com.cn/GB/37454/37459/4543913.html (accessed 20 July 2016).

Zhou Da-ping (1994). '*Gaoxiao wei shenme yao shixing xin de shou fei zhi?*' ('Why do universities have to implement the new fee system?'), *Liaowang Xinwen Zhoukan,* No. 36, 18–20.

Zhou De-yi *et al.* (2007). '*Wu nian zhi quan ke xing xiaoxue jiaoshi peiyang jiaoyu kecheng tixi yanjiu*' ('Research on the Curriculum system of five-year training of all-subject teachers of primary schools'), *Hunan Shifan Daxue Jiaoyu Kexue Xuebao,* 6(6), 91–96.

Zhou Jianjun and Luo Ping (2010). '*Chenai luoding hou de shenshi yu xingsi: guanyu woguo yixue yuanxiao yu zonghexing (duokexing) daxue hebing wenti de yanjiu*' ('Reflections after the dust has settled: research on the issue of mergers between medical colleges and comprehensive (multi-disciplinary) universities in China'), *Heilongjiang Gaojiao Yanjiu* (*Heilongjiang Research on Higher Education*), 2010(9), 21–24.

Zhou Jinyan, Yuan Liansheng and Zou Xue (2016). 'A review and evaluation of China's financial investment in education over the past two decades', in *Chinese Research Perspectives on Education,* Volume 3. Leiden: Brill, 111–130.

Zhou, Laura (2015). 'Swedish university severs ties with Confucius Institute', *South China Morning Post,* 9 January.

Zhou Li-an (2007). '*Zhongguo difang guanyuan de jinsheng jinbiaocai moshi yanjiu*' ('Governing China's local officials: An analysis of the promotion tournament model'), *Jingji Yanjiu (Economic Research)*, 2007(7), 36–50.

Zhou Xin (2011). 'Early childhood education policy development in China', *International Journal of Child Care and Education Policy,* 5(1), 29–39.

Zhou Xueguang and Lian Hong (2011). '*Zhengfu neibu shangxia ji bumen jian tanpan de yi ge fenxi moxing – yi huanjing zhengce shishi wei lie*' ('A model for analyzing negotiations between higher and lower levels within government – taking environmental policy as an example'), *Zhongguo shehui kexue* (*Chinese Social Science*), No. 5, 80–97.

Zhou Xueguang and Lian Hong (2012). '*Zhongguo zhengfu de zhili moshi – yige "kongzhi quan" lilun*' ('Modes of governance in the Chinese bureaucracy: A "control rights" theory'), *Shehuike Yanjiu* (*Sociological Research*), No. 5, 68–93.

Zhou Xueguang, Moen, Phyllis and Brandon Tuma, Nancy (1998). 'Educational stratification in urban China: 1949–94', *Sociology of Education*, 71(3), 199–222.

Zhu Dequan (2004). '*Xibu pinkun diqu nongcun "shuangzhengshi" jiaoyu fupin moshi tansuo*' ('Resarch into the 'dual qualification mode' of poverty alleviation through education in impoverished rural Western regions'), *Jiaoyu Yanjiu*, 289(2), 80–84.

Zhu Jieming (2004). 'Local developmental state and order in China's urban development during transition', *International Journal of Urban and Regional Research*, 28(2), 424–447.

Zhu Wencheng (2012). *Confucian themes and China's high school language and literature textbooks in the Reform Era*, University of London, Institute of Education, unpublished PhD thesis.

Zi Zhongyun (2016). '*Zhongguo jingshen de duoluo shiyu jiaoshi duiwu de nulihua*' ('The collapse of the Chinese spirit begins with the enslavement of the teaching profession'), *Dou ban.* https://www.douban.com/note/539970432/ (accessed 5 July 2016).

Zweig, David, Chen Changgui and Rosen, Stanley (2004). 'Globalization and transnational human capital: overseas and returnee scholars to China', *The China Quarterly*, 179, 735–757.

Index

Printed in Great Britain
by Amazon

66137760R00233